CLEMSON
Where the Tigers Play

**Sam Blackman, Bob Bradley,
Chuck Kriese, and Will Vandervort**

SPORTS
PUBLISHING

─ᏪᏉ─

Sam Blackman

To my loving parents, the late Sam (Clemson class of '33) and Beth Blackman, who introduced me to this special place of Clemson University and taught me that anything was possible through hard work; and to my sister Karen. Also to Tim Bourret and the late Bob Bradley, who have been and always will be an inspiration to me in my sports information career.

Will Vandervort

Thanks to my mom and my stepfather, the late Shirley and Carl Buck, for they were always encouraging me to pursue my dreams. And to Cindy Nelson, who has always believed in me and pushed me every day for many years to be the best I could be.

Chuck Kriese

Dedicated to my late parents, Maurice and Thelma Kriese, and to the Kriese family—you never know when you touch a life! I would like to thank those coaches who touched mine.

Tennis: Roland Leverenz, Paul Ditzenberger, Brother Rowland Driscoll, Larry Ware, Alan Cornelious, Harry Hopman, and Bill Branch; Basketball: Vic Sahm, Mike McGinley, John McLeod, Bill Green, Tom O'Brien, Ron Bargatze, Mr. Wilder, and Tony Corsaro; Track and Cross Country: Mr. Edwards, Bill Green, Ron Volpatti, and Bob Knoyce; Football: Art Phelan, Dutch Roembke, and Tom Snyder; Baseball: Maurice "Pop" Kriese and Vic Sahm.

─ᏪᏉ─

Sports Publishing books may be purchased in bulk at special discounts for sales promotion, corporate gifts, fund-raising, or educational purposes. Special editions can also be created to specifications. For details, contact the Special Sales Department, Sports Publishing, 307 West 36th Street, 11th Floor, New York, NY 10018 or sportspubbooks@skyhorsepublishing.com.

Sports Publishing® is a registered trademark of Skyhorse Publishing, Inc.®, a Delaware corporation.

Visit our website at www.sportspubbooks.com.

10 9 8 7 6 5 4 3 2 1

Library of Congress Cataloging-in-Publication Data is available on file.

Cover design by Tom Lau
Cover photo credit Dawson Towers and Clemson Athletics

ISBN: 978-1-68358-031-7
Ebook ISBN: 978-1-68358-040-9

Printed in China

Contents

Acknowledgments

Special thanks to Karen Blackman, Hannah Burleson, and Stephanie Withey for help in the production of this book. Also the authors would like to thank the Clemson Sports Information Office, Tim Bourret, Director; and assistants Phil Sikes, Jeff Kallin, Libby Kehn, and Brian Hennessy. We'd also like to thank the photographers who work so hard doing their jobs. Interior photos courtesy of Rob Biggerstaff, Rex Brown, Kerry Capps, Mark Crammer, Cayce McAlister, Bob Waldrop, Pat Wright, and our longtime friend Earle "Pepper" Martin.

Foreword

I had never seen Clemson before when I arrived in the fall of 1947. I had heard about Clemson from a couple of my friends in my hometown of Pineapple, AL, and also they had a good football team. My small rural town, Pineapple, didn't have a high school football team, but my buddies and I still enjoyed playing sandlot football on our own. I worked in a lumberyard for my father, and I guess that helped me build my body to get ready for football, and the military, as well. World War II was on, and all of the guys were being drafted to go fight in Europe or in the Pacific. I did my training in Fort Jackson and Fort Benning to be a paratrooper. I guess they thought that I was athletic, so they put me into that department. We were zigzagging with a group of ships toward the Philippines when they announced the war was over. We were all pretty happy that most of our eight months there and two more months in Japan were spent guarding prisoners instead of having to fight.

President Harry Truman initiated the GI Bill. I used it on flying lessons that I always wanted to take, and I didn't give much thought to attending college. Only by chance, I took my first train ride ever to Biloxi, MS, to see my sister. Her next-door neighbor just happened to be Clemson Head Football Coach Frank Howard's sister. Most folks have heard the story that Coach Howard had not seen me play football before going to Clemson. Of course, there were no videos, computers, or YouTube back then. Coach Howard's sister saw me swimming and said that she would like to tell her brother about my athleticism. Coach Howard sent me a letter and said to come up to Clemson as a walk-on football player. I planned to use the GI Bill to pay for school. It sounded better to me than doing the lumber mill job again.

Arriving after the long bus ride to Clemson, I didn't know where to go. I asked the first person I passed on the street, "Where is Coach Howard?" The fellow scratched his head and said, "Go up the street to the athletic office at the college." I then at last found Coach Howard. After having me do some exercises in the gym, he told me that I would have to try out, and he sent me to the barracks.

They had a scrimmage in the fall to start things out, and after I made a couple of long runs, Coach Howard told me that he was going to put me on a scholarship right away. It's a good thing, since I wasn't aware that all of my GI Bill money had already been used up on flying lessons that I had taken the summer before. [Coach Howard would in his later years say that Fred Cone was the best pure athlete and football player that he had ever coached.]

Coach Covington (Goat) McMillan was a great coach, as he worked with me endlessly in the gym as I learned how to play the "Spinner-back" position. You see, in those days, we ran a single-wing offense, and I would handle the ball first and then either hand it off or run with it. We did pretty well with those teams. We beat Missouri in the 1949 Gator-Bowl 24-23 and beat Miami in the 1950 Orange Bowl 14-13. What a wonderful group of guys that I had as my teammates!

I remember so many special people, such as Coach McMillan, Coach McFadden, and Coach Howard. The relationships and the life-long bonds are what really made Clemson so special. Maybe it was the time after the war and what we had been through that made such a unique group of men. We were ex-soldiers, and Clemson was the right place at the right time to get us going in the right direction after so much pain and uncertainty. Don Wade was one of my best friends on those teams. I can remember that he wanted me to teach him how to fly. I did teach him how to fly, and Don and I would hunt and fish together as friends for life.

Another good friend was Billy Preacher. Billy was from Richland, SC. He was one of the best guys that I knew. Billy was in the Reserves and I was not. When the Korean War started, Billy got called up into the regular army. Unfortunately, he was killed two weeks after he got there. I still think about Billy on many occasions. I also think of Don and guys like Ray Mathews, Dick Henley, Jack Brunson, Coach Howard, Coach McFadden, Coach McMillan, and so many more. The readers are going to get to read about all of them in this book.

Clemson was small, but it was mighty special. Our activities on the drill field, the practice fields, and our time in the barracks fill my memories. The faces of the young men who were my friends in my youth are clear today. Most of them are gone now, but I will never forget them. I am so happy that I can talk about some of them now. I am also grateful that now some of their stories will be told. God's providence in my own life was shown again and again during my time at Clemson. It was that special place for hundreds of young men, and it is today for young men and women, as well. Its influence has impacted our nation and will for many years to come.

When my wife Judy and our family visit the Clemson campus today, we see so many new things, but the feelings that we had many years ago are still the same. The folks who have done the planning for the university have done a great job.

Man-oh-man, is it pretty! They have used great insight in their planning of buildings, landscaping, and the sports facilities. They have kept the heritage intact, as they have kept it a place of great pride and class while building the facilities needed for the future.

When we walk the campus, the memories all come back to me. Those grounds that so many young men and women walk day after day are hallowed. Students have the best place ever to try to get their education, learn about themselves, and find out what God intends for them to do with their lives. I still see the faces, as well as hear the voices of those that I walked the grounds with so many years ago. I can still hear Coach Howard's whistle, Coach McMillan's voice, the sound of the fans cheering for us in the stadium and the voices of my dear friends who are no longer here. I am very proud and humbled by it all.

My wish is that Clemson will always stay a place of integrity, goodness, and honor. It is a good and noble place for men and women to prepare them for life. To me, it is a sacred place; for I know that God has had his hand in my life and all of the work that has been done here. Providence has allowed many simple turning points at Clemson that became strong foundations for my life and that of thousands of others.

The color of the sunset in the mountains at Clemson is something that we all know about. It has been described in paintings, by words, and in our school's alma mater. The purple and the orange are branded solidly in our minds and in our hearts. The sunset described in those pictures represents a peace of mind and of heart that will surely brighten the sunsets of our own lives. I hope that you will read every word of this book and learn about the heritage that we all have lived in our Clemson family. I hope it will resonate throughout your own family's lives as much as it has mine.

—**Fred Cone, '51**

Preface

What makes Clemson so special?

If you live in or around Clemson or you went to its great university, you understand why Clemson is such a special place.

It's a combination of things. From the history and traditions that surround the university, to Memorial Stadium, to Howard's Rock, to the Tiger Paw, to Littlejohn Coliseum, to Doug Kingsmore Stadium, to Lake Hartwell, and to the great people who live and work there.

Clemson has that "It" factor. It is really indescribable. A lot of people like to say Clemson is "Auburn with a lake." When I hear that, it tells me they have never been to Clemson. Clemson is unique. There is nothing else like it.

Someone will always ask, "What makes Clemson so special?" The answer is several things. But the best answer is to tell them, "There isn't just one thing. You have to come up here and experience it for yourself and then you will understand what makes it special."

Clemson is not just Where the Tigers Play, but it is home. That hometown feel generally allows Clemson to land some of the best students and athletes in the country. From eating a meat-and-three lunch at the world famous ESSO Club, to laying a blanket out on Bowman Field and studying on a beautiful spring day, Clemson has a little bit of everything to help students feel they are always at home.

"If you get them on campus, you have a chance," Clemson head football coach Dabo Swinney said.

Since coming to Clemson as the wide receivers coach in 2003, Swinney has been able to get a lot of big-time football players to attend Clemson University, including perhaps the biggest of them all.

In the fall of 2005, C.J. Spiller was one of the more highly thought-of recruits in the country. Everybody wanted him, including Clemson, but a native of Lake Butler, FL, Spiller was a shoe-in to attend his home state university.

"C.J. is a reminder to me that you don't listen to people when they tell you that you can't do something because you can," Swinney said.

For over a year, Swinney personally pursued Spiller. At Union County High School in Lake Butler, Spiller was a *Parade* and *USA Today* first-team All-America honoree after rushing for 5,511 yards and scoring 93 touchdowns. He was being courted by all the big-name schools, including Florida, Florida State, Miami, and Southern Cal.

"We recruited him, recruited him, and recruited him, and he would take the call every week and we would have fun talking," Swinney recalls. "Then he cut his list of schools from 50 to 30 to 20 to 15 and we kept hanging in there and he would laugh when I called him. We had a good relationship."

But back at Clemson few people, if any at all, believed the Tigers had a shot to sign Spiller. When the coaches got together during recruiting meetings and the talk of running backs would come up, Swinney would throw Spiller's name into the conversation.

"That's when Burton Burns would say, 'We aren't getting him. Let's talk about who we really have a shot at,'" Swinney recalled. "I would say, 'I'm telling you he is coming to visit, he told me he was.'"

Swinney finally got Spiller on campus by making up a fake contract while Spiller was deciding on what five schools he was going to visit. Outside of Union County High School during a recruiting visit, with a few of Spiller's friends present, Swinney pulled out his business card and proceeded to write a so-called contract on the back of it, which basically said Spiller would promise to visit Clemson as one of his five official visits.

He then had Spiller sign it and his three friends sign it as witnesses.

"I told him right there on the spot, I said, 'If there is one thing I have come to know is that you are a man of your word and I'm telling you right now, you've promised me you are coming,'" Swinney said.

Spiller first came to Clemson that following January during Martin Luther King Weekend, and a few weeks later he decided to become a Clemson Tiger.

"When I came for my visit and I was sitting in my room here and we were about to go get something to eat, it hit me," Spiller recalls. "It was telling me 'This was the spot for you.' I knew right then, even though Florida was at the top of the list, that this was the right place for me.

"Something came over me and said this is the spot for me to become a man, to learn and play for a great university. There is no better place to do that."

Spiller went on to set countless Clemson records, become a serious Heisman Trophy candidate, a unanimous All-America player, 2009 ACC Player of the Year, and is one of only three Clemson football players to have his jersey retired. But more important, Spiller is now a Clemson graduate.

"I am proud to be a Clemson graduate," he said. "This is my school and I am very appreciative of the positive effect Clemson has had on my life. I want to give back and say thanks."

Spiller, who plays for the NFL's Buffalo Bills, calls Clemson home during the off-season. He has a residence nearby and conducts his annual C.J. Spiller Instructional Football camp there, as well.

"I still think to this day, 'How did Coach Swinney pull this off to get me out of the state of Florida?'" Spiller said with a big smile. "But you know what? I'm glad he did because it taught me a whole lot. I learned a whole lot while I was here my four years."

He learned that Clemson is a special place.

"There is nothing like running down the Hill, and there is no place like Clemson," Spiller said. "When you talk about Clemson, you can't compare it to anything else. It is something you miss when you leave.

"Even though I'm in the NFL and I'm doing some things, I still miss it. You don't get to do Tiger Walk or run down the Hill or anything like that. At home games, we drive ourselves to the stadium. I like to tell the current players now to enjoy this because once it is gone, they are truly going to miss it."

—**Will Vandervort**

Introduction

The Poetry of Clemson Football

(Reprinted with permission and edited from the late Ken Burger's Baptized in Sweet Tea, *a Collection of Columns Celebrating the South)*

I know you're out there, clutching your season tickets, counting the days, deciding what to wear, wondering if it'll be hot or cold, if it will rain, waiting, somewhat impatiently, for the college football season to finally begin.

From big towns and small, all at once, you emerge from the back roads onto the interstates, like migrating herds, dogged, determined, flying the colors, caravans of cars and vans and pickup trucks, stocked to the gills with potato salad and fried chicken, sweet tea by the gallon, soft drinks, hard drinks, and just enough deviled eggs to go around twice.

It's an ageless procession of frat boys and pretty girls, sorority sisters, old and young, near and dear, distinguished alums, loud mouth louts, children in cheerleader uniforms, drunks in T-shirts and ties, tossing footballs and talking trash.

Then with folding chairs, tightly circled, in dusty lots and grassy fields, perfectly parked, acre upon endless acre, color coordinated, anxious and antsy, fiddling with satellite dishes and scraping paper plates while waiting for the shadows to fall and stadium lights to illuminate the dark sky, officially turning game day into night.

Once inside, stacked to the stars, elbow to elbow, buying programs and popcorn, stepping over each other, excuse me, excuse me, please and thank you, what a night, what a sight, sure hope the home team wins. And they might, or not, depending on the truth, and rumors, about sophomore tackles and redshirt quarterbacks and what the coach had to say about so-and-so last week.

A few boos for the visiting varmints, jumping jacks and leg lifts, practice punts that hang high in the lights, falling softly onto the cool wet grass, chewed up by the cleats of cutting cornerbacks, double checking coverages, assignments, and girlfriends gabbing in the grandstands.

Then down The Hill they come, smoke and cannon fire, combined to thrill and quicken pulses, gladiators in the arena, trotting, taunting, to the beat of a drum major, high-stepping, bringing the band and its audience to a chilling crescendo.

Awash in the ebb and flow, a touchdown here, a field goal there, the game unfolds, the good, the bad, for better or worse, damn the luck, and the referees, not to mention the tailback who fumbled on the one. Screaming helps, but you've got to pee, too much sweet tea, maybe later, in the second half, when the lines aren't so long, when only true believers are left, holding hands, singing alma maters in the rain.

Win or lose the traffic's tough, sitting still, inching nowhere, as the coach comes on the radio, explaining himself, finding victory in defeat, looking ahead to next week, next year, when things will be better, or worse, he really doesn't know.

But it's all brought to you by somebody's hot dog chili, perfect for tailgating, and the local bank that loves the home team, and you, the faithful fan, whose family's needs are always met by a former field goal kicker-turned-insurance salesman.

In the aftermath comes analysis, talk of change, pain, promise, and passion, for the game, the team, the common cause.

Back home the flags are stowed and pretty pennants put away, for another day, of hope and heartbreak, in those precious hours of fun and fashion called Clemson football.

PART I

STORIES AND HISTORIES

CLEMSON
Baseball

NCAA Tournament Appearances:

1947, 1950, 1958, 1959, 1967, 1975, 1976, 1977, 1978, 1979, 1980, 1981, 1987, 1988, 1989, 1990, 1991, 1992, 1993, 1994, 1995, 1996, 1997, 1998, 1999, 2000, 2001, 2002, 2003, 2004, 2005, 2006, 2007, 2009, 2010, 2011, 2012, 2013, 2014, 2015, 2016

College World Series:

1958, 1959, 1976, 1977, 1980, 1991, 1995, 1996, 2000, 2002, 2006, 2010

Southern Conference Champions:

1947

ACC Champions:

1954, 1958, 1959, 1967, 1976, 1978, 1979, 1980, 1981, 1989, 1991, 1993, 1994, 2006, 2016

Atlantic Division Champions:

2006, T-2010

ACC Regular Season Champions:

1954, 1958, 1959, 1967, 1973, 1974, 1975, 1976, 1977. 1978, 1979, 1981, 1982, 1984, 1985, 1988, 1991, 1992, 1994, 1995.

Top–25 Seasons:

1967 (7th), 1970 (18th), 1971 (22nd), 1975 (25th), 1976 (5th), 1977 (5th), 1978 (25th), 1979 (9th), 1980 (4th), 1987 (10th), 1988 (15th), 1989 (14th), 1991 (4th), 1992 (7th), 1993 (16), 1994 (4th), 1995 (8th), 1996 (4th), 1997 (24th), 1998 (19th), 1999 (13th), 2000 (5th), 2001 (13th), 2002 (3rd), 2005 (13th), 2006 (5th), 2007 (12th), 2009 (14th), 2010 (4th), 2011 (16th), 2013 (25th), 2016 (15th)

Clemson played on Bowman Field in 1896-1915.

When people think about Clemson Athletics, the first thing that comes to mind is Clemson football, and understandably so. However, baseball is not only the oldest, but perhaps the most successful program at Clemson.

Baseball was the first sport fielded by Clemson and was started in the spring of 1896. The first coach was Randolph Bowman, who coached the 1896, 1897, and 1899 Tigers. He could only coach part of the 1899 team due to an illness that ultimately took his life. Because of his dedication and love for Clemson and the cadets, the field in front of Tillman Hall was named Bowman field in 1899. He also helped clear the field and made it suitable to play baseball and other sports.

FAMOUS COACHES LEAD THE TIGERS

Clemson people know John Heisman was the head coach of the football program from 1900-'03, but few probably know he coached the baseball team, as well. The Hall of Fame coach coached the Tiger baseball team from 1901-'03. One of his pitching aces was John McMakin, who was a left-hander in 1900 and 1901. He went on to play for the Brooklyn Dodgers in 1902 and later became the head coach of Clemson from 1904-'06.

Carl "Vet" Sitton pitched for the Tigers during this era in 1903 and 1904. Sitton worked his way to the major leagues and pitched one year for the Cleveland Indians. Another

Head Coach John Heisman is pictured with his team before a game. Heisman is shown seated fourth from left.

early star at Clemson was John Maxwell. He was a catcher for the Tigers under Heisman and also played football.

Frank Dobson coached Clemson to three winning seasons from 1911-'13. Dobson was a pro baseball player before coming to Clemson, having played for the Pittsburgh Nationals organization. Walter Riggs, president of the Clemson Athletic Association at the time, thought it was unfair to keep shuffling coaches year after year. He offered Dobson a three-year contract, which was the first long-term contract offered and signed by a Clemson coach.

At Clemson he coached football, basketball, and baseball and was Clemson's first basketball coach, leading it to its only undefeated season (4-0) in history in the inaugural year (1911-12).

In 1914, Thomas Robertson led the Tigers to a 16-6 record and the most victories for the Tigers until the 1935 season.

Clemson was crowned state champion in 1929 under Head Coach Joe Guyon. The famous football player, who was a teammate of Jim Thorpe at the Carlisle Indian School and later played for John Heisman, helped lead Georgia Tech to a football National Championship in 1917. Guyon is a member of both the College and Pro Football Halls of Fame.

Football coach Jess Neely took over the baseball team in 1932 and led the Tigers to the State Championship. He again led Clemson to the state championship in 1935 with a 16-7-1 record.

The legendary Frank Howard coached the baseball squad in 1943 and led the Tigers to a 12-3 record during the war era.

Randy Hinson, who coached the Tigers in 1939 and 1940 before World War II, coached the Tigers in 1947. That season, Clemson won the Southern Conference Championship and was an NCAA Tournament participant. The Tigers defeated Auburn and Alabama to advance to the East Regional finals.

In the finals, Yale defeated Clemson 7-3. This game is interesting to note because former United States President George W. Bush played for Yale as its first baseman.

The 1947 team finished the year with a 24-5 record, including a 13-2 mark in the Southern Conference. It was the first Clemson team to win 20 or more games in a season.

Dean Walter Cox led the Tigers from 1948-'51, and his 1950 team advanced to the NCAA Tournament. During his career, Cox was 47-18-1 in the Southern Conference.

Assistant Football Coach and former Furman star Bob Smith led the Tigers in baseball from 1952-'57. In 1954, the first year of the Atlantic Coast Conference in spring sports, Smith led the Tigers to the school's first-ever ACC Championship. Clemson advanced to the NCAA Tournament, as well.

LONG-TIME SPORTS ADMINISTRATOR FRANK SHAUGHNESSY COACHED AT CLEMSON

Frank Shaughnessy, who coached the Tigers in 1907, was known for his ability as a sports administrator. He served many positions, from a pro hockey coach to the International Baseball League Commissioner (1936-1960).

A graduate in pharmacy at Notre Dame, he was captain of the baseball and football teams during his senior season. After his graduation in 1905, he coached baseball at Notre Dame. The summer before coming to Clemson, he played left field for Ottawa of the Eastern League. He ended the season with a .352 batting average. He also played with Washington and the Philadelphia Athletics.

At Clemson he coached the baseball teams during the 1907 and 1908 seasons, and he was head football mentor in 1907 as well, where he posted a 4-4 record. Shaughnessy made his name in baseball, but he took part in many other sports. Besides being a sports legend at Notre Dame, he managed the NHL's Ottawa Senators to the Stanley Cup Finals in 1915, and he coached football teams at Clemson, Washington & Lee, and McGill University. He retired as the president of the International Baseball League.

FLINT RHEM

Flint Rhem, probably one of the most famous Clemson athletes during this era, starred for the Tigers in 1922 and 1923 and later became a pitcher for the St. Louis Cardinals.

Rhem, who left Clemson after his junior year to sign with the Cardinals, had a very impressive junior season at Clemson that caught the eye of famous baseball scout Branch Rickey. In 1923, Rhem had a 7-2-1 record and completed all nine games. He had a total of 136 strikeouts for a 15.1 per game average. He also had two one-hit games that season and gave up only 40 hits all year, or 4.4 hits per game.

In a game against Furman on April 30, 1923, Rhem had 21 strikeouts and gave up only five hits in 13 innings with the game ending in a 3-3 tie. He gave up only six

Four Clemson Players in the early 1920s are pictured on Bowman Field. Flint Rhem is pictured second from left.

runs the entire year and had a 0.57 ERA. He pitched four shutouts that season. Both his ERA and his strikeouts per game average are still school records. Rhem's 136 strikeouts are still one of the best in school history.

Rhem played for St. Louis from 1924-'28, then again from 1930-'32 and in 1934 and 1936. He also played for the Philadelphia Phillies in 1932 and 1933 and the Boston Braves from 1934-'35. He helped the Cardinals win the 1926, 1931, and 1934 World Series and the 1928 and 1930 National League Pennants.

In 1926, Rhem had a 20-7 record for the Cardinals. In 12 seasons in the big leagues, he had a 105–97 record.

BILLY O'DELL: CLEMSON'S FIRST ALL-STAR

The Tigers won the first ACC Championship in 1954 thanks to a southpaw from Newberry, SC, who won 19 games in three years when there were only a total of 63 games played in those three seasons.

Bobby Morris, who caught more O'Dell pitches than anyone else because he was his battery mate in high school, American Legion, service, college, and textile ball, recalls that O'Dell's bread and butter pitch was his fastball.

Flint Rhem played at Clemson in 1922 and 1923. He played for the St. Louis Cardinals, Philadelphia Phillies, and Boston Braves.

"He had a good curve," Morris remembers. "His changeup wasn't all that great, but his fastball would come in and rise, and batters would swing under the ball. He threw a good hard ball. He was hard to catch."

Morris was behind the plate on May 8, 1953, when O'Dell had his only collegiate no-hitter against arch-rival South Carolina. He only struck out nine in this game and allowed four base runners, three by walks and one on his own error.

Morris threw out three runners attempting to steal, and one runner was left stranded. Only two balls were hit to the outfield.

O'Dell had a one-hitter against The Citadel just before no-hitting South Carolina and followed that gem with a two-hitter versus Furman. He had at least 15 games in which he struck out 10 or more batters, but his best night came in his freshman season (1952).

The Tigers squared off against South Carolina in Orangeburg in a night game. O'Dell started out by fanning the first five Gamecocks he faced. He also struck out the last quintet as well as 11 in between for a total of 21 strikeouts. He struck out the side in the first, third, seventh, and ninth innings. It was one of three games in his career where he allowed only four hits.

"From the standpoint of athletic ability, I always classified him like a cat out there on the mound," said Dick Swetenburg, who played with O'Dell from 1953-'54. "He could really move, and he was very versatile. He was a great fielding pitcher.

"Nobody bunted on Billy and got on base. He had a great move to first and not many people stole bases on him. And his battery mate from Newberry, Bobby Morris, complemented that."

After three seasons at Clemson, O'Dell signed with the Baltimore Orioles and also played with Milwaukee, San Francisco, Atlanta, and Pittsburgh in his major league career. He played in the big leagues for 13 years, registering 105 victories.

One of Billy's major league highlights came in 1958, four years out of Clemson, when the major league all-star game was in his own ballpark, the only one who ever played in Memorial Stadium.

O'Dell pitched three perfect innings and was named the game's MVP that night.

The former Tiger All-American said Ted Williams was the toughest player he ever faced.

"You talk about Ted Williams and then you talk about everybody else," O'Dell said. "He's the best hitter I've ever seen. He just hit the ball hard all the time. I've seen some great ones, but Williams was just a cut above everybody."

In his career at Clemson, O'Dell averaged 12.29 strikeouts per nine innings and had a 1.51 career ERA (0.79 his junior season). He recorded 19 complete games and 300 strikeouts.

"When he was on, he was tough," Swetenburg said.

WILHELM TOOK CLEMSON, COLLEGE BASEBALL TO ANOTHER LEVEL

Following a modest 9-4 start to ACC play in 1954, Clemson had posted a 10-30-2 mark in conference play from 1955-'57.

Bill Wilhelm had a 1,161-536-10 record at Clemson. He took the Tigers to six College World Series.

Frank Howard, who was also the athletic director at Clemson at the time, had talked to North Carolina legendary coach Walter Rabb in the spring of '57 when the Tar Heels were in town for a game. Howard was seeking Rabb's advice on hiring a full-time baseball coach to run the program.

Bob Smith was the head coach at the time, but Howard wanted to free Smith up where he could be a full-time assistant football coach, which was what he was originally hired for in 1950.

Rabb's recommendation was to hire his assistant coach, Bill Wilhelm. That's all Howard needed to hear, and Wilhelm agreed to take on the challenge of turning the Tigers' baseball fortunes around. What he did became legendary.

From 1958-'93, Wilhelm won 1,161 games at Clemson, while winning six NCAA District Championships, six trips to the College World Series, seven ACC Tournament titles, 11 ACC Championships overall, and 18 regular-season ACC Championships.

"Baseball got serious once Coach Wilhelm got here," said Bob Mahony, who played for Wilhelm from 1975-'76.

Wilhelm came on board as Clemson's baseball coach in September of 1957 and inherited a team that was 6-12 the spring before. The Tigers won the first ACC baseball title in 1954 but fell on hard times the next three seasons.

Wilhelm knew there was work ahead, but that didn't bother him. He had taken on tough challenges before and always came out on top.

Before coming to Clemson, Wilhelm served as Rabb's assistant at North Carolina, while at the same time working on his master's degree. He was also the starting catcher for the local Greensboro team of the Carolina League at night.

Bill Wilhelm never had a losing season in his 36 years at Clemson.

"Coach Wilhelm not only built baseball at Clemson, but he began to build it in the ACC and then the Southeast," Mahoney said. "He wanted people to be good. He demanded other schools build their baseball programs.

"I think he was one of the instigators of making people good and looking for good players and getting young people involved in the game, whether it was at the high school level or whatever. He wanted the ACC to be good.

As much as he wanted to dominate it and as much as he wanted to win it, it was because of him the other teams started to get good."

1958: "WE ACCOMPLISHED SOMETHING MEMORABLE"

Wilhelm was a winner at Clemson right out of the gate. His first game as a head coach in 1958 was against the touring Michigan State Spartans of the Big 10. Clemson not only defeated the Spartans, 7-5, that day, but it also handed pitcher Ron Perranoski his only loss of the season. Perranoski later enjoyed a sparkling major league career and was the Los Angeles pitching coach for many years after that.

The Spartans came back nine days later and handed Wilhelm his first collegiate loss on their way back to East Lansing, MI. Prior to the 3-2 loss, the Tigers had won their first four games under Wilhelm.

"He was a young man, himself, but he taught us so much at the time," said Howard Stowe, who pitched on Wilhelm's first Clemson team.

Wilhelm taught his players how to win by teaching them first how to work and to prepare for it.

"If you are going to be good, you better prepare to get better," he said.

Wilhelm prepared them to get better by first making them feel better about themselves. No one thought the appearance and organization of a team meant more to a team's success than the Clemson coach.

First he bought new uniforms, new equipment, and new Louisville Slugger bats. Then he required his players to dress nicely when out on the town and to look sharp at all times.

"I made them feel better about themselves," Wilhelm told theACC.com in 2008. "I had them wear a coat and tie on the road. I told them not to argue with the umpires, to respect the game. They were able to perceive that things were going to be different and they bought into it."

It did not take long for the 1958 team to buy in.

"We were a bunch of country boys. Wilhelm put us in new uniforms, something you could go to town in," Stowe said. "His attitude was to get after it. Have fun, be assertive, and don't beat yourself. He gave us confidence and confidence can take you a long way."

The Tigers' confidence won them 22 games that year, five more victories than the previous three seasons combined.

"He was tough," right fielder Bailey Hendley said. "He emphasized fundamentals. He was demanding, but fair. If you didn't do your job, you didn't play. He was big on not talking back to the umpires or the opposition.

"His attitude was 'Never talk to the other team. Let 'em sleep. We'll beat their brains out before they wake up.'"

Clemson beat a lot of teams' brains out that first year. After getting off to an 8-0 start, the Tigers finished with an 11-3 record in ACC play as Wilhelm found himself in a tie with his old team and mentor, Walter Rabb, for first place.

The two teams had split a pair of regular season games, each winning by scores of 2-1. Clemson won at Tiger Field, while UNC won in Chapel Hill. Back then only one team was selected from each conference for what was called the NCAA District Playoffs.

In the ACC playoff game, subsequently a championship game, Clemson put up three runs in the top of the first inning, thanks to an RBI single by shortstop Bud Spiers and two Tar Heel errors. Another UNC error in the ninth gave the Tigers another unearned run.

Clemson's 4-1 win gave Wilhelm the first of his 19 regular-season ACC championships. The Tigers ultimately ended the 1958 postseason with a 5-1 record in elimination games.

"We really didn't have a tremendous amount of talent, but we had heart and we wanted to play," Spiers said. "We didn't quit, we didn't take off plays; we came after you for nine innings. Everybody did their jobs, everybody pulled for their teammates."

The NCAA District Tournament was held in Sims Legion Park in Gastonia, NC, where the Tigers had dispatched the Tar Heels two weeks earlier to win the ACC Championship. The Tigers drew Florida, the Southeastern Conference champions, while George Washington represented the Southern Conference, and Florida State was the independent entry.

In just one game Wilhelm figured out how quick it took to get backed into a corner. Stowe, who ended up owning 14 of Clemson's 22 wins that season, was the natural choice to open against the Gators. But he was yanked in the second inning after the lefty gave up three runs on three walks, a single, and an error.

Although Clemson rallied to score five runs in the sixth and seventh innings, Florida built a seven-run lead early in the game and hung on for an 8-6 win. In the meantime, the Seminoles had taken care of the Colonials, pitting George Washington against Clemson the next day, with the loser going home.

Wilhelm gave Stowe another chance. But it was not to be. Stowe served up a grand slam in the first and surrendered a three-run blast in the second as the Tigers found themselves seven runs down coming to bat in the second inning.

"That bus ride to Clemson seemed not far away," Spiers recalled feeling.

And then, what has been described by some as the "prettiest thunderstorm ever" came through and washed out that game as well as the FSU-Florida fracas, pushing everything back 24 hours.

Unlike now, any game that had not gone five innings had to start from scratch. Thus, George Washington's 7-0 lead was washed away with the storm.

The next day, Wilhelm started right-hander Ed Lakey, and the sophomore went out and sat the Colonials down on six hits as Clemson remained alive with a 4-2 victory.

The Tigers had to wait around for the outcome of the FSU-Florida affair and play the loser in another elimination game that night. Florida bumped the 'Noles into the loser's bracket and was in the driver's seat at 2-0.

Hendley started on the mound for Clemson and had a six-hit, 5-0 lead going into the last half of the seventh inning when a pair of doubles scored a run, causing Wilhelm to bring Stowe in from out of the bullpen.

After striking out a pinch hitter in the No. 9 slot, Stowe walked Dick Howser, whose name is synonymous with Florida State baseball, and then gave up a three-run homer to Charlie Rogers to close the gap to 5-4.

In the bottom of the ninth, Howser slashed a one-out triple, and then a single by Rodgers, his fifth hit of the game, tied the score at 5.

In the Clemson 10th, Bobby Norris hit one down the third base line, and pitcher Frank Slusser threw the ball into right field as Norris ended up on third on what Wilhelm often referred to as "a 30-foot triple."

FSU coach Danny Litwiler, who had been in the "Big Leagues" a number of years, ordered Slusser to intentionally walk Hendley and Fred DeBerry, Clemson's No. 1 and No. 2 hitters. While this was going on, Wilhelm was having a conversation with Spiers, the club's leading RBI man.

Wilhelm later said he told Spiers he didn't quite understand why Litwiler was loading the bases in the top of the inning, but that if he saw a pitch he liked, he should start swinging.

And he did.

"We didn't understand it then and I don't understand it now," Spiers said.

The result was a bases-clearing double up the left centerfield alley, giving the Tigers a 10-7 lead. A one-out single in the bottom of the 10th inning was all Florida State could muster as Clemson moved on to play Florida, and the Seminoles went back to Tallahassee.

After getting Sunday off—the NCAA did not play on Sundays in those days—Lakey got the starting nod against Florida, who liked him as well as Stowe. Lakey surrendered four runs in the top of the first thanks to a Charlie Smith grand slam, but Clemson got three runs of its own in the bottom half of the inning.

When the Gators scored four more runs in the second inning, Wilhelm made another walk to the mound. By the time Hendley relieved to start the sixth inning, the Gators were up, 10-5, and things were anything but promising for the Tigers.

But Clemson scored five runs in the sixth inning, another in the seventh, and took a 14-11 lead with a three-run outburst in the eighth. But Smith hit a three-run bomb in the top of the ninth to tie the game at 14.

Clemson was not done, though. The Tigers loaded the bases with two walks and an error in the bottom of the ninth, and Hendley drove in the winning run with a base hit for a 15-14 victory. First baseman Fred DeBerry had four hits that afternoon to lead the Tigers.

After the three-hour, 25-minute marathon, another game had to be played to decide the title because the winner had to be in Omaha, NE, on Thursday for the start of the College World Series.

In between games, Wilhelm looked down his bench, and there were Stowe, Lakey, and Hendley. They had all pitched in the first game. Stowe had a 12-3 season mark, and Wilhelm looked him in the eye and said, "You're my most dependable man. See what you can do."

Stowe literally pitched the game of his career, giving up only four hits, and though he walked four batters, he struck out a career-high 17 that evening. Clemson managed only two hits, both by Spiers, but three walks, a single, and an error chased in three runs in the third, and Stowe continued his mastery of the Gators, as he had at least one strikeout in each inning and fanned the side in both the second and seventh innings.

A two-out double and a single produced Florida's lone run in the eighth, as the Tigers advanced to their first College World Series with a 3-1 victory.

Stowe continued in Omaha where he left off in Gastonia, as he struck out 13 in a 4-1 win over Arizona in the first game of the CWS. But, Clemson's magical run finally came to an end in the two next two games.

"We were all dead tired, exhausted," said Stowe, who ended his junior year with a 14-4 record, which included 120 strikeouts.

Holy Cross ripped through the Tigers' pitching in the second game, pounding out 19 hits in a 17-4 win, while Western Michigan eliminated them in the third game with a 5-3 victory.

The 1958 Clemson team had only 15 players on its roster, while some teams in the College World Series—like top-seeded Southern Cal—had 16 pitchers on its roster alone.

"None of us expected to be in Omaha when the season began," said Spiers.

Nobody except Wilhelm, of course, who later admitted it was harder to do than he first thought after accomplishing it in his first two seasons at Clemson.

"I was so new to college baseball, maybe I didn't realize how hard it was," he said years later. "The College World Series wasn't as well known as it later became, but it was still a big deal.

"My 1958 team wasn't my best, but it was my first and we accomplished something memorable."

PLAYING FOR THE LOVE OF THE GAME

Ty Cline starred at Clemson from 1958-'60 and was an All-American his junior season, which happened to be his last at Clemson. In 1959, he helped the Tigers advance to the College World Series as well as making the 1959 US Pan Am Team. That year, he led Clemson in most hitting categories while compiling a 5-1 record as a pitcher. As a junior, he hit .348 and was named to the All-ACC and All-Atlantic Region teams to go along with his All-American selection.

Cline's career batting average at Clemson was .335, as he went on to play 12 years in the majors.

"Coach Wilhelm gave us pride," the All-American said. "He taught us how to handle ourselves. It is amazing what kind of man he was and what he has done for so many people who have gone through Clemson over the 36 years that he was there."

Cline was an outstanding athlete, and he was also offered a partial basketball scholarship from Norm Sloan at The Citadel, but Clemson upped the ante.

"Coach Bob Smith at Clemson called and they worked out a deal where I would come to Clemson on a half-baseball and half-basketball scholarship," Cline said. "After my freshman year, Coach Frank Howard, Coach Press Maravich, and Coach Wilhelm decided that I would be placed on a baseball-only scholarship."

After the 1960 season, Cline signed with the Cleveland Indians of the American League. His professional career lasted 12 seasons, 1960-1971, as he played for seven major league teams.

"It was probably one of the better eras in baseball that you are going to see. We played for the love of the game and not the money," Cline said.

THE STREAK

Rusty Adkins was not the kind of guy to just sit back and wait his turn. When he came to Clemson, he felt he could help the team right away. In 1964, however, the NCAA did not allow freshmen to play, so Adkins had no choice but to wait a year.

That was the last time he waited to play, and he made sure Wilhelm knew that.

"I told coach if I'm not good enough to play, you can have your scholarship back," Adkins said.

Wilhelm never requested it back because Adkins was more than good enough. His first career hit was a home run. He went on to earn All-ACC and All-District honors in all three seasons he played. He was Clemson's first, and still the only, three-time All-American (1965-'67).

Legendary Coach Bill Wilhelm (L) and Harold Stowe are pictured. Stowe helped lead Clemson to the 1958 College World Series in Wilhelm's first season at Clemson.

CLEMSON: Where the Tigers Play

Rusty Adkins had a 41-game hitting streak that spanned for the 1965 and 1966 seasons.

In 1965, Adkins hit .444 on the year and did not strike out in 126 at-bats. He had a career batting average of .379 at Clemson, and those were the days when the college game used wooden bats. Like his first career hit, his last career hit was a home run.

Baseball America named Adkins to its All-College Baseball Team for the 1965-'74 era.

"He was what you might call a 100-percenter," Wilhelm said of Adkins. "I never used the term 110 or 120 percent because 100 percent is all there is. Very few players approach 100 percent.

"Rusty was a good hitter with a good eye."

How good was that eye? Good enough to record at least one hit in 41 straight games, an NCAA record at the time.

The streak, which is still an ACC record, started in 1965 and carried over to the 1966 season. It was in serious jeopardy in the 32nd game of the streak against N.C. State. The game was in the ninth inning, and Adkins came to the plate for what was more than likely his final at-bat.

"The N.C. State catcher said, 'Well Rusty, this is it. It's ended.' I said, 'We'll see if it's over, it's been a good ride.' Then I hit the ball over the center field fence," Adkins said.

Adkins's 41-game hitting streak still ranks in the NCAA's all-time top 10 list. After finishing his Clemson career in 1967, the York County, SC, native signed with the Kansas City Athletics and played four years in their farm system before retiring.

The former second baseman was later inducted into the Clemson Hall of Fame as well as being named to the South Carolina Hall of Fame in 1995. He was then enshrined in the Clemson Ring of Honor in 1998 and became the inaugural member of the York County Sports Hall of Fame that same year.

In 2002, Adkins was named to the ACC's 50-Year Anniversary team.

WILHELM MAKES IT BACK TO OMAHA

Mahony will never forget the day when he hopped on his bicycle, tied his cleats to his handlebar, and rode down to Tiger Field for the first day of tryouts. It was in the fall of 1972, and the freshman was eager to continue playing the game that has meant so much to his life.

"I had my cleats on the bike. You know, those typical pictures you will see with a kid riding his bike to the baseball field. That was me," Mahony said. "Then I looked out on the field and I saw guys like Smiley Sanders, Charlie Ing, Pat Fitzsimmons, Richard Haynes, and Lin Hamilton. All of these guys were pretty good players, All-ACC Players and I said to myself, 'There is no way I can play with these guys.'"

And he didn't, at least not on the 1973 team.

That following summer, while scouting other players, Wilhelm saw Mahony pitching in an American Legion game in Maryland. Remembering his conversation with Mahony the year before, the Tigers' skipper encouraged the young player to give walking on another shot when he came back to Clemson for his sophomore year.

"I wanted to play third base, but Pat Fitzsimmons was already there and we already had some pretty good infielders, so I was not going to beat out anybody," Mahony said.

But because he loved the game, Mahony went back out there, and that's when his opportunity to make the squad at Clemson presented itself. During one early practice, Wilhelm asked for volunteer pitchers for batting practice, and Mahony graciously raised his hand.

"If I was going to make the team, I knew I had to do anything I could to make it," he said. "I pitched before, so I might as well go ahead and give it a shot. So I went out there and pitched batting practice, but I pitched like I was in a game. I was out there to impress somebody."

But instead, he started making the other players mad. Mahony did not seem to care, though. He wanted to show Wilhelm what he could do, so he kept on pitching like he was in a game, and eventually the legendary coach took notice.

"I remember the guys complaining and asking, 'Coach, is this guy pitching batting practice or are we in the bottom of the ninth here? What's going on?' After that batting practice session, Coach came up to me and said, 'I think we found a position for you. We can probably work you in.' Then he said, and I'll never forget this, 'But, when you hit, nothing exciting happens.'

"That's a typical Coach Wilhelm one-liner. I will never forget that. You know when you grow up playing baseball, you knew you could hit. But when he told me that I was like, 'Well, it looks like I better pitch.'"

But before he could pitch, Mahony had to get a haircut. Yes, a haircut. In the early 1970s, almost every man had long hair and a mustache. It was the style, along with bell-bottom corduroy pants and plaid shirts. But if you played for the Clemson baseball team, you played by Wilhelm's rules, and he did not like long hair on any of his ballplayers. His players were supposed to look sharp and respectable at all times.

"He said, 'If you are going to be a part of this program, you are going to get a haircut before you come to practice tomorrow. You will not be on the field again with that hair,'" Mahony recalls. "So as soon as I left the field, the first thing I did was get my hair cut. I came back the next day, and he gave me a chance.

"That's what you ask for, is just a chance."

Mahony made the best of his opportunity and lettered for Clemson from 1975-'76.

"Playing for Coach Wilhelm, you had to respect the way he was," Mahony said. "If you started taking the way he was personally, you would have a problem. I saw kids have problems because they took it personally.

"He would really get in your face. He would say some things that if you took it wrong, it could be mean. A lot of guys took it that way, and it affected the way they played. That was not good when that happened because he was not going to back off."

By the time Mahony was a senior in 1976, most of his teammates grew to understand and respect Wilhelm and his teachings. In 1975, the Tigers earned an at-large bid for the NCAA Mideast Regional after winning a share of the ACC Regular season title. It was the program's first NCAA Tournament bid since playing in the NCAA District III Playoffs in 1967.

"We didn't even know we had a bid. All of us had gone home," Mahony said. "We weren't even practicing and in fact some guys had already started playing on summer teams.

"Then we got called back and did not really practice very much. In fact, on our way to Ypsilanti, MI, because we did not fly up there, we played some teams on the way. Coach had set up some games to play because we had not practiced together."

But the scrimmages did not help. The Tigers were eliminated after losing to Eastern Michigan and Penn State in the first two games of the regional.

"That experience got us ready for the next year because we knew we were better than that," Mahony said. "Most of the guys on the 1975 team played on the '76 team with the exception of Denny Walling and maybe a couple of pitchers.

"In 1976, we knew we were good enough."

Of all his College World Series teams, the 1976 squad reminded Wilhelm a lot of his first one. There were no real superstars. There was no flash about them. They just worked hard, played harder, and were fundamentally sound.

"I see five reasons why [Wilhelm] was so successful and I use those lessons today," said Alan Hoover, the designated hitter on the '76 team. "First, surround yourself with talented people who are high in character. Second, be fundamentally sound in what you do. To become sound fundamentally you have to practice over and over. Third, keep it simple. Fourth, talk straight. Be honest in everything you do. Fifth, be aggressive and go down swinging."

The Tigers came out swinging all right. With guys like catcher Bill Foley, second baseman Billy Wingo, shortstop Kurt Seibert, third baseman Robert Bonnette, left fielder Dave Caldwell, and center fielder Steve Tucker, they opened the season winning eight of their first nine games. But then a stretch in which they lost nine of 12 games in a 10-day period came along. However, that did not set them back.

At 11-10, Clemson traveled to Newberry, SC, where it took care of business against the outmanned Indians to end a three-game losing streak with a 4-1 victory. That got the Tigers rolling, as they first put together an 11-game win streak and then a five-game winning streak to close the regular season.

"Coach Wilhelm was the leader and we wanted to win for him, but we also wanted to win for each other," Mahony said.

With a 29-13 overall record, including a 10-2 mark in the ACC, Clemson entered the ACC Tournament as the top seed. Thanks to pitchers like Ron Musselman, who had pitched a no-hitter against Virginia the week before, the Tigers extended their win streak to eight games by beating Wake Forest 2-0 and Maryland 2-1 and 3-2. It was the Tigers' first ACC Tournament Championship, which began in 1973.

"We were a team and that's what was neat," Mahony said. "I thrived on that when I was a player. I wasn't that great of a player, but I was made better because of the people around me.

"You see that in any sport. You see guys excel and become better players because of who they are surrounded by. I was fortunate to be surrounded by really good players and when I got up and pitched I didn't lose any sleep worrying if the guys behind me could play defense or if the team was going to score runs. I could take the mound pretty confident that these guys are going to help me get there."

By winning the ACC Tournament, Clemson earned an automatic bid to the NCAA Atlantic Regional, which was held in Columbia, SC. Archrival South Carolina, the last team to beat the Tigers, was the top seed and host.

Clemson whipped Furman in the first game, 13-2, setting up a rematch with the Gamecocks. The Tigers beat USC in Columbia on April 2 that year, before falling to the Gamecocks, 4-3, 11 days later in Clemson.

In the Atlantic Regional, Clemson tallied a 10-4 win to advance to the Championship round. Everyone expected Clemson and USC to meet at least one more time, but Furman came out of the loser's bracket with a stunning upset over the Gamecocks.

Clemson had no problem beating Furman for a second time, disposing of the Paladins 6-2 to win the regional and advance to the College World Series for the first time in 17 years.

"We knew we were good enough to get there, but that's almost where it stopped because we got there," Mahony said. "That was our goal. Get to Omaha. I think we were a little intimidated at first because we had not been there before.

"Coach had not been there since '59. So I think we were a little intimidated as a team by the surroundings."

The other seven teams in the World Series were Arizona, Arizona State, Auburn, Eastern Michigan, Maine, Oklahoma, and Washington State. Arizona was making its 10th trip to the CWS, while Arizona State was making its eighth and Oklahoma its sixth.

It didn't help that the Tigers flew to Omaha in a DC9 that made just about everyone on the plane sick, and to add insult to injury, it did not have air conditioning.

"It had propellers on both wings and real small back wheels," Mahony said. "I remember we had to stop in Evansville, IN. I will never forget that. We had to land there to get gas on our way to Omaha. We got out and it was so hot. We were all dying because we were burning up.

"Guys were getting sick. There was no air conditioning in the plane going out there and it was just bouncing around. But we thought it was normal. We didn't know any different at the time. We just got on the plane. 'Let's pack it up and go. We're flying to Omaha.'"

When the Tigers got there, a yellow school bus picked them up and took them to the hotel. After that, they unpacked, they headed over to a local high school to practice, and that's when they noticed they were a little out of place and thought they did not fit in.

Arizona State was finishing up its practice. The Sun Devils had come to Omaha on a commercial jet and were driven around on a charter bus.

"When we practiced, we wore almost our dress uniforms to practice," Mahony said. "Arizona State, all of their guys had shorts on, and they weren't wearing shirts in practice. They all looked like Greek Gods out there with their tans and everything else. Here we show up, and 'Here are the boys from Clemson. Country comes to town.' That's kind of what we felt like even though we knew we had a really good team. But this was all new to us."

For a little while the game seemed new to Clemson, too. The Tigers played Auburn in the first game and quickly fell behind. But then they settled down and started to rally.

"Once we got to playing, after two or three innings, we realized we could compete against anybody," Mahony said.

Clemson came back to beat Auburn 9-4 and advanced to play Eastern Michigan in the second game.

"That's the one we should have won. We let that one get away," Mahony said.

Two days after the Auburn win, Eastern Michigan beat the Tigers 3-2 in 10 innings. The next day, Clemson was eliminated by eventual national champion Arizona, 10-6.

Nearly 40 years later, Mahony looks back at 1976 with great pride. He and his teammates accomplished something only a few others have. They set a goal, achieved it, and then played in one of sport's greatest events.

"When you say you have played college baseball, to me that is fantastic," he said. "To say you played college baseball and you played at Clemson means a lot anywhere because of the tradition and everything that is here.

"I'm very proud of that, especially being a walk-on. To say that I played and ended up with a full scholarship because of Coach Wilhelm, I'm proud of that. But to say you played in Omaha, that takes the respect level to another level when you talk about guys that have been playing baseball. Everybody does not get that opportuni-

ty and there are very select programs that can make that statement—'We played in Omaha.'

"It gives you creditability that you have been there, regardless of when it was. Coach took the '58 and '59 teams to Omaha in his first two years as a coach, that's amazing. I can't even imagine that. It was awesome that we got to be the next [team], the first one in 17 years to do it. It was a special team."

SIMONS MAKES HISTORY

Neil Simons says he learned so much about baseball from Wilhelm that he will always be grateful. But don't think for a minute that Wilhelm wasn't grateful for what Simons did for him and the Clemson program, as well.

In his four years at Clemson, Simons is still the only player in Clemson history to be named to the All-ACC first-team all four years in college. Twice he helped the Tigers make it to Omaha for the College World Series, and three times he guided Wilhelm's teams to ACC Championships.

As a freshman in 1977, Simons hit a career-high .376 while guiding the Tigers back to the College World Series. Clemson got back to the CWS for a second straight season thanks to a 42-10 ledger, which included a 9-1 record in the ACC. The Tigers won the Coral Gables, FL, Regional that year with a thrilling 10-9 victory over the University of Miami in the championship game.

The 1978 and '79 teams won the ACC but fell just short of reaching Omaha, as Miami eliminated the Tigers both years at the Coral Gables, FL, Regional. Clemson finished the 1978 season 39-14 and was 10-2 in the ACC.

The 1979 team posted a 40-15 mark and was 10-1 in the ACC, as Simons, who now was a fixture in center field, hit .355, while catcher and designated hitter Dave Buffamoyer hit .343.

Though the Tigers struggled in the ACC regular season in 1980, there was no slowing them down in the tournament. As the No. 3 seed, Clemson swept the ACC Tournament for its third consecutive championship with wins over Wake Forest (4-0), Maryland (9-4), NC State (5-4), and North Carolina (12-3).

Led by Simons (.317), catcher Dave Lemaster (.315), leftfielder Billy Weems (.328), third baseman Frank Russ (.327), and second baseman Tim Teufel (.387), Clemson took Wilhelm back to the CWS for a fifth time. However, it was not an easy road.

In those days, the ACC Tournament was played at the end of April and was held two weeks before the NCAA Regionals began. Wilhelm, who learned from his experience in 1975, scheduled nine games in between to keep his team fresh. The Tigers, however, did not play too well in that stretch and lost five games, including four of the last five.

Luckily, it did not affect the selection committee's decision to award Clemson as a regional host for the first time, especially considering No. 2 seed South Carolina outscored the Tigers 10-2 in a two-game sweep in Columbia on May 10 and 11 of that year.

But home field advantage has a way of making a team feel better. Eleven days after losing to USC in the second game, the Tigers put up 22 runs in a first-round win over East Tennessee State. The next day, they took down the Gamecocks, 6-2, and then advanced to the CWS for a third time in five years with a 17-12 victory over their archrivals the following afternoon. In the three games combined, Clemson scored 45 runs.

Though there were many great moments for the Tigers in 1980, Simons said one of the best came in Clemson's win over Virginia in mid-April. In a tight game, Simons hit a ball off future major league pitcher Ricky Horton down the line. The ball curled about the foul pole and the umpire called it a home run. What happened next stunned Simons.

"After I crossed home plate I looked up and saw Coach Wilhelm at the plate arguing with the umpire that it was a foul ball," Simons said. "I couldn't believe he was arguing against a home run by one of his own players in his ball park.

"He told me in the dugout that he didn't want Clemson to get a reputation that we were a bunch of 'homers' and that Clemson would be a place where [the opposing team] would be treated fairly."

By the way, the umpire did not change his call.

Clemson finished the 1980 season 38-21 after losing the first two games of the CWS to Miami and California. Teufel was an All-American and joined Simons, pitcher Mike Brown, and shortstop Robbie Allen on the All-ACC team, as well.

YOU DO NOT NEED A 'JIMMY' WHEN YOU HAVE A 'KEY'

Jimmy Key was one of Wilhelm's all-time greats. He is the only baseball player in Clemson history to be first-team All-ACC at two positions in the same season. He played three seasons on the diamond in Tigertown and then went on to a successful 15-year major league career, including two World Series Championships.

"Gene Compton, a former Clemson payer who was living in Huntsville, kept telling me about this left-hander that I had to see," Wilhelm said. "He was being heavily recruited by all the schools, so I made the trip to Birmingham, AL, to watch him pitch in the state quarterfinal game in front of 4,000 people.

"He struck out 19 batters in 11 innings and won 1-0. I was so impressed that I went to him after the game and offered him a full scholarship. Without any hesitation and [without] ever seeing Clemson, he said, 'I'll take it.' He was certainly one of the easiest players I ever recruited."

He turned out to be one of Wilhelm's best players, too. In Key's freshman season, he led Clemson in starts and innings pitched. Though he was a freshman, he started in the opening game of the 1980 College World Series and finished the season 7-5 with a 2.99 ERA.

It became evident that season how effective Key was at getting batters out without overpowering pitches. He struck out only 52 batters but at the same time allowed just 85 hits.

In his sophomore season, Key impressed with his bat, hitting .317 in 167 at-bats, but he was 4-6 on the mound.

He turned things around his junior year, putting together perhaps the greatest all-around season in Clemson history, while garnering All-ACC honors as both a pitcher and as a designated hitter. He had an ACC-best nine wins to go along with seven complete games in 116 innings pitched.

At the plate, Key hit a team-best .359 and then a school record 21 doubles.

Key went on to play 15 seasons (1984-'98) in the majors, including nine with Toronto, four with the New York Yankees, and two with Baltimore. He accumulated a 186-117 record along with a 3.51 ERA and won at least 12 games in the 12 seasons in which he started at least 12 games.

Key was also a four-time All-Star and played on two World Series Championship teams, the Blue Jays in 1992 and the Yankees in 1996. Key, who wore a Clemson T-shirt underneath his uniform for good luck, even got his teammates to wear Tiger T-shirts.

HEFFERNAN RULES BEHIND THE PLATE

Bert Heffernan, who was a catcher for the Tigers from 1985-'88, was once described as looking like they used his uniform to drag the field before the game. It was not dirty because of ground maintenance; instead, it was because of his hard play and hustle at a position he loved.

"He got the job done behind the plate better than anybody I've ever seen in college baseball," said Wilhelm. "He's the toughest I've ever had.

"There are three things that make Heffernan stand out from any other player I've ever seen anywhere. One, he's not afraid of getting dirty and two, he's not afraid of getting hurt, and most importantly, he's not afraid of embarrassing himself. He has a good time playing this game."

Heffernan had a .337 career batting average at Clemson. He had 27 career home runs and 63 doubles in his four years. He played in 259 games in his four-year career.

"I don't know how I got put behind the plate," Heffernan said. "But, I've been there since I was eight years old. There's always something going on if you're the catcher. That's what makes it so much fun. I loved it."

SPIERS MEANS CLEMSON BASEBALL

Bill Spiers just couldn't get enough.

After hitting .345 in his first two seasons on the baseball diamond, he saw an ad in the school's student newspaper (*The Tiger*) from then-head football coach Danny Ford that caught his attention.

The ad read, "We are concerned about our punting situation. If there is a student reading, those who can punt, please call me at the office. We aren't looking for any Dale Hatchers, just someone who can average about 40 yards with a four-second hang time."

That ad led to Spiers trying out, making the squad, and becoming the starting punter for the 1986 ACC Champions, where he averaged 39.2 yards per punt. Despite playing on the gridiron for only one season, his average is one of the best in Clemson history.

But as much as he loved his football fame, baseball has always been Spiers's first love.

Spiers came from an athletic background. His brother Michael lettered four times in baseball at Clemson in the late 1980s and early '90s as an outfielder. Michael was also the 1991 ACC Tournament MVP.

Their father, Bud, was a shortstop, like Bill, for the Tigers from 1957-'59 and played on Wilhelm's first two College World Series teams.

As a freshman in 1985, Bill Spiers hit .380 in 171 at-bats at a variety of positions. In his sophomore year, his power numbers improved as he hit 11 doubles, five triples, 12 home runs, and stole 35 bases to go along with 53 RBIs and a .322 batting average.

In 1987, Spiers led the ACC with 11 triples, while hitting .290 and stealing 16 bases as the Tiger shortstop. The 11 triples still stand today as the most in a single season in Clemson history.

The *Sporting News* tabbed Spiers as a first-team All-American, while he was also a first-team All-ACC selection in 1987. He was also an All-ACC Academic Honor Roll honoree that year.

In his Clemson career, Spiers accumulated 17 home runs, 119 RBIs, 34 doubles, 17 triples, and 60 stolen bases in just three seasons. He was also a two-time ACC Academic Honor Roll member, the recipient of the Clemson Sportsmanship Award in 1986 and 1987, and a member of the 1986 and 1987 NCAA Tournament Teams.

Spiers was drafted in the first round (13th overall) by the Milwaukee Brewers in the 1987 June draft.

1991 WAS THE BEST

Although Wilhelm had many rewarding years at Clemson, the 1991 season was his most successful in terms of wins. The Tigers ran up a 60-10 record that season, the best record in the nation, captured the ACC regular-season title, and swept the competition in the ACC Tournament and the NCAA Northeast Regional to earn a berth to the College World Series.

The 60 wins set a league record for victories in a season, breaking the old record of 54, set by the 1987 and 1988 teams. His 1991 team ranked No. 4 in *Baseball America*'s final poll. The trip to Omaha marked the sixth and final one of his career, and the Tigers' ACC title was his 10th as head coach. He was named District III Diamond Coach of the Year along with the ACC Coach of the Year honor.

WILHELM LOVED HIS PLAYERS

In his 36 seasons as a head coach, Wilhelm, who passed away on Christmas Eve morning in 2010, amassed a record of 1,161-536-10 (.683), making him the fifth winningest coach in the history of college baseball at the time of his retirement in 1993.

For his remarkable career achievements, Wilhelm, who coached all 36 years at Clemson, was inducted into the National College Baseball Hall of Fame in 2011. He became the first person associated with Clemson to be inducted into the Hall of Fame in Lubbock, TX, which inducted its first class in 2006.

Wilhelm was also inducted into the state of South Carolina Athletic Hall of Fame and the Clemson Athletic Hall of Fame in 2012.

Wilhelm never liked the spotlight put on him. He always gave credit to his players for his success.

"Of all the people I played for in my lifetime, I rate Coach Wilhelm as the number-one coach I had," said 1960 All-American Ty Cline.

Despite a Hall of Fame career, Wilhelm graciously turned down acceptance into the Clemson Hall of Fame, the Clemson Ring of Honor, the South Carolina Athletic Hall of Fame, and the College Baseball Hall of Fame while he was alive.

He even disliked the banner current Clemson baseball coach Jack Leggett placed inside Doug Kingsmore Stadium that honors Wilhelm's career at Clemson.

"Coach had an enormous impact on the lives of countless baseball players," said Billy McMillan, who played for Wilhelm from 1991-'93. "He taught me more than just about the game of baseball. He taught me how to deal with people fairly, how to work hard, and the importance of discipline."

Serving as the head baseball coach at one school for an entire career is quite an accomplishment. Having 36 seasons under the belt is an even greater feat. But spending 36 years at one school and never having a losing season is unheard of.

What made Wilhelm so successful was the way in which he treated his players and what he demanded in return because of it.

"The two most important things in my life were my marriage and coming to Clemson," said Rusty Adkins, a three-time All-American from 1965-'67. "He brought me to Clemson and I had not even seen the school before I accepted a scholarship.

"I was close to him my entire career and it continued for 40 years. I loved the man."

One of the best examples of how Wilhelm treated his players is the story of Jeff Morris. His story is one of legend at Clemson because his grand slam in the eighth inning of the 1993 ACC Championship game secured Wilhelm's final championship.

For his heroics, Morris was named the Most Valuable Player of the 1993 Tournament. How he got to that point and the belief Wilhelm had in him is what makes his story so great.

A walk-on in the fall of 1988, Morris came to Clemson with the dream of playing for Wilhelm. It's the only reason he came. The 5-foot-8 skinny freshman from Pittsburgh, PA, knew it would be a hard climb, but he was willing to do anything he could to make his dream come true.

Morris became a Wilhelm fan after he attended Wilhelm's baseball camp while in high school. He loved the instruction he got from Coach Wilhelm and the other coaches there, plus he fell in love with Clemson.

"What impressed me so much when I went to Clemson's baseball camp was how involved Coach Wilhelm was," Morris said. "At the North Carolina camp the week before, [their coach] came out and talked to us and asked how we were doing, and then we did not see him again. He wasn't involved at all.

"Coach Wilhelm was actively involved. He spent some time with me and I remember he made one comment to me. He told me, 'You have a good little stick there.' That kind of told me I wanted to play for this guy."

When Morris finally got to Clemson, he discovered there were 34 kids just like him, trying to do the same thing. He worked his tail off. He was always the first to come to practice and the last one to leave. One by one, he noticed the other walk-ons getting cut. Wilhelm would call them into the office and would tell them straight up what the deal was.

"Coach was always a straight shooter. He told it like it was. He was very honest with you," Morris recalls. "I was struggling and I was one of the bottom-of-the-half guys, but for some reason he kept me around. I did not tell him this until later, but I broke my thumb before I came down so I was a little bit hindered and was just getting back in the swing of things."

Wilhelm stuck by Morris's side, even though assistant coaches Dave Littlefield and Joel Lepel were asking Wilhelm why he had not cut Morris.

"He came in one day and told them to leave him alone about Morris," said Sanford Rogers, a former assistant inside the Sports Information Department at Clemson. "He said to 'Leave him alone about it. He is a good kid, he works hard, and he is staying.'"

The reason Wilhelm was committed to Morris was the conversation the two had one day after practice.

After missing practice one day due to classes, Morris recognized all the freshmen and the few walk-ons that were left over; other than himself, they all had brand-new Converses with orange spikes. Wondering if this was a sign he had been cut, Morris waited until practice and approached Wilhelm about where his shoes were because his cleats were old and worn out.

"I was thinking he didn't have the heart to cut me so he was just waiting to cut me," Morris said. "I sat down with him, and I asked, 'Coach, do you think I can get a pair of those shoes?' He looked at me and said, 'No son. Jeff, that's not necessary.'

"So he looked at me and said, 'Why did you come to school here?' And I said, 'To play baseball for you.' But he told me, 'You can't play baseball for Clemson. You know you can't.' So I told him I can. I told him I was a late bloomer. That I was going to get bigger and stronger and drink my milk and work out. 'The cleats would really help me because I'm not getting out of the box and it is causing me to slip in the outfield. My thumb is just now getting better and I'm just now starting to swing the bat.'

"He said, 'Thumb! What did you do to your thumb? What's wrong?' So I told him what had happened and he said he would get me a pair of cleats the next day and then he would give me a couple of more days to see if I could make the team."

With the new cleats and his thumb finally healed, Morris connected on seven-straight extra base hits during team scrimmages and earned his roster spot in the process.

After taking infield practice with Bill Spiers later that week, Wilhelm gave Morris the news he had been waiting for.

"'Jeff, I'm not going to cut you. Go see Todd in the locker room, he has a locker for you,'" Morris recalls. "It's funny because all the lockers were taken so I had to share with one of the freshmen. I was happy with that, but I'm sure as a scholarship freshman he wasn't as happy about sharing his locker with a walk-on who should not have even made the team."

But, Morris proved his worth, as he had a career .313 batting average and will forever be linked to his grand slam in the 1993 ACC Championship game that gave Wilhelm his last title.

The ACC Tournament proved to be magical that year, as the Tigers went through the five-day tourney with a 5-1 record, including a come-from-behind 11-7 win over NC State in the championship game, thanks to Morris's grand slam.

Clemson received a No. 2 seed in the NCAA's Mideast Regional in Knoxville, TN, the sixth-straight year the Tigers were a No. 1 or No. 2 seed heading into NCAA play. In the regional, the 1993 team set a school record for wins against top-25 teams in a season with 13, so their overall 45 wins came against one of the toughest schedules in the country. Thirty-two of the 65 games were against teams that played in the NCAA Tournament.

In his last years at Clemson, Wilhelm took the Tigers to the NCAA Tournament seven straight times, while posting a 356-115-1 record, an average of nearly 51 wins a year. He took a team to the NCAA Tournament 17 times in his career.

Wilhelm's 1,161 career victories make up one of the highest totals in any sport by an ACC head coach. He posted a record of 378-158-1 in ACC regular-season games, a 70.5 winning percentage, and had at least a .500 league record in each of his final 21 seasons.

The Tigers captured 14 ACC titles outright, more than any other team, and Wilhelm was the mentor for 11 of them. Clemson has either won or tied for the regular season title 21 times, and Wilhelm was the head coach on 19 of those occasions. He had 10 consecutive years (1973-82) when the Tigers either won the ACC regular season or tournament title.

Wilhelm, a native of China Grove, NC, played at NC State for two years before signing with the St. Louis Cardinals in June of 1950. After one year of professional baseball, he entered military service, where he spent two years.

He played service ball and spent two more years in the professional ranks before returning to college, where he went to Catawba College (Salisbury, NC) and received his degree in January of 1957.

In 2012, Wilhelm was inducted into the Catawba College Sports Hall of Fame.

LEGGETT KEPT IT GOING

Few programs in the country have had as much uninterrupted success as the Clemson baseball program. Since 1958, only three head coaches have led the Tigers. In the 58 years prior to the 2016 season, Wilhelm and Jack Leggett combined for 2,116 wins, 20 ACC regular season titles, nine ACC Tournament titles, 38 NCAA Tournament bids, and 12 trips to the College World Series. In 2016, Monte Lee led the Tigers to an ACC Tournament Championship during his rookie campaign and took the Tigers to a NCAA regional.

"I don't know if there is anyone in the country that has gone that long and had that much success as we have had here with our baseball program," former Clemson athletic director Terry Don Phillips said.

Leggett was no stranger to success before he came to Clemson as Wilhelm's associate head coach and recruiting coordinator in 1992. As a player, he was the captain on Maine's 1976 College World Series team. He also was a two-time All-Yankee Conference honoree in football as a defensive back and placekicker and still holds the school record for the longest field goal, a 52-yarder.

As a coach, he spent five seasons at Vermont, where he first started the program, and then turned into a consistent winner. In 1977, he coached the Vermont club team and by 1978, he organized and coached the school's first intercollegiate team.

At age 23 and only two years removed from the college game as a player, Leggett was the youngest head coach in the country. In his first year, he guided Vermont to an 11-9 record. In his five seasons as the head coach at Vermont, Leggett had a 75-61 record.

In 1983, Leggett left Vermont for Western Carolina, where he spent nine years and compiled 302 victories. He led the Catamounts to five NCAA Tournaments from 1985-'89, five Southern Conference titles, and a top-30 ranking during his tenure as head coach.

Leggett's 1988 team set the school record for wins in a season, posting a 38-24 record, while the 1989 squad won its fifth consecutive Southern Conference title. The Catamounts averaged 33 wins a season during his time in Cullowhee, NC, and his teams played in the conference title game in eight of the nine seasons.

The 1991 Catamounts, his last team there, posted a 36-26 record. One of the 36 wins came in a 9-7 victory over Clemson on March 31, one of just 10 losses the No. 4 Tigers had that year.

Leggett, who was inducted in the Western Carolina Hall of Fame in 2001, produced 35 first-team All-Southern Conference players, six conference Players of the Year, and had 16 players sign pro contracts.

Like Clemson, Leggett's success in baseball continued. In his 22 seasons prior to 2013, he led Clemson to 955 (43.4 per season), 21 NCAA Tournament appearances, and six College World Series berths.

Clemson is the seventh winningest program in the nation during his time as head coach.

"Some of his characteristics are very similar to Coach Wilhelm's," said Bob Mahony, who now calls games on the Clemson Tigers Sports Network. "Jack respects the game. Now Jack has moved on from how the kids are treated and what the expectations should be from an administrative commitment standpoint. I think in that sense he has taken it to another level."

Of Leggett's 955 wins at Clemson, 244 have come against teams ranked in the top 25 of at least one of the three major polls. He also had 125 wins over top-10 teams, 68 victories in NCAA Tournament competition, and has directed Clemson to a winning record in ACC regular-season games in 21 of his 22 seasons in Tigertown.

For his accomplishments, Leggett was inducted into the American Baseball Coaches Association Hall of Fame on January 3, 2014, in Dallas, TX. Prior to 2016, he was the sixth winningest active coach in the country with 1,332 victories, which ranked 9th all-time in baseball history.

In 1994, Clemson won the ACC regular-season title and went on to win the tournament title, as well. In 1995, the Tigers repeated as ACC regular-season champions and won the NCAA East Regional title to advance to the College World Series.

The 1996 team, which had National Player of the Year Kris Benson on the mound, brought Clemson another NCAA Regional title and a second consecutive berth to the College World Series.

Leggett guided Clemson to the College World Series in 2000, 2002, 2006, and 2010, as well.

In 2006, the Tigers captured the Atlantic

Jack Leggett is one of the winningest head coaches in the nation.

Division title with a 24-6 record and then won the ACC Tournament Championship. Clemson also won regional titles in 1999, 2000, 2001, 2002, 2005, 2006, 2007, 2009, and 2010.

In seven of the 22 years Leggett was the head coach, the Tigers finished in the top 10 of all three major polls, and there was at least one top-25 final ranking in 16 seasons.

Leggett was named ACC Coach of the Year three times (1994, 1995, and 2006).

GOOD FROM THE START

It did not take Leggett long to prove to the Clemson faithful that the tradition Wilhelm began was not going to go anywhere under his watch.

"The expectations are always going to be high here at Clemson, but I think the thing that our fans have a hard time getting over is how good everyone else is," Mahony said. "How many other programs out there are really good? When Coach Wilhelm was here, Clemson was the best for a long time because everybody else wasn't that good. Now, the ACC is loaded. The top six or seven teams can compete for a national championship at any time and can compete with anybody in the country.

"It has not always been like that. Yet, since Jack came here, we have been to 18 regionals. He has only missed one year in 19 years and went to five Super Regionals since they began in 1999. His record is pretty good."

In his first year, Leggett led the Tigers to both ACC regular season and tournament championships. With just three starters returning in the field, Clemson was unranked in the preseason top 20, but it quickly reached the top 20 of every poll with a two-game sweep of No. 9 Tennessee. Those were the first two of 19 wins over top-25 teams.

The 1994 Tigers, which finished the year 57-18, won a record 13 straight ACC games to open the season and ended the year with a 20-4 mark in the conference. After two wins over Miami in April of 1994, Clemson ascended to the No. 1 ranking in the nation, according to *Collegiate Baseball*. It was just the second No. 1 ranking in school history, but the first of 20 weeks in which Leggett has had the Tigers on top of the polls.

After winning the 1994 ACC regular-season title, Clemson captured the ACC Tournament title by winning four games against top-20 teams. It was the fifth time in school history that the Tigers won the regular-season and ACC Tournament titles in the same year. As a result, Clemson was rewarded as a regional host for the first time in 13 years.

Clemson was eliminated in the NCAA Regional, but it concluded 1994 as the nation's winningest team. The summer following that season, Leggett was chosen to the University of Maine Hall of Fame.

TIGERS BACK IN THE COLLEGE WORLD SERIES

It did not take Leggett long to get Clemson back to the mecca of college baseball. In 1995, his Tigers had a 54-14 record due in part to an offense that was in the top 10 in the nation in scoring (8.4 runs per game).

The Tigers also had six players on that team that went on to play in the major leagues.

Clemson opened the year with 25 straight wins after suffering a season-opening loss to Oklahoma State. In the 25-game win streak was another two-game sweep of Tennessee as well as three-game sweeps against ACC foes Duke, Wake Forest, and Maryland.

The Tigers went on to have a 10-game win streak later in the season and cruised to another ACC regular season title with a 20-4 record. Clemson again hosted a regional, but this time it won it, winning every game by at least three runs. The Tigers easily disposed of Navy, Jacksonville, Winthrop, and Alabama to advance to the College World Series.

CLEMSON'S FIRST NATIONAL PLAYER OF THE YEAR

In 1995 Clemson advanced to the College World Series thanks to its hitting. In 1996, it made a return trip to Omaha, but this time it was due to a pitching staff that owned the best ERA (3.03) in the nation.

There was a big reason for that, actually two to be exact. The 1996 team produced eight major league draft picks, including seven in the first 17 rounds. Included in those selections were pitchers Kris Benson, the No. 1 overall pick, and Billy Koch, the No. 4 overall pick. It was only the second time in the history of the draft, which dates to 1965, that one school produced two of the first five picks.

The Tigers also had Ken Vining, the squad's No. 3 man in the weekend rotation. He had a 10-3 record with a 2.97 ERA, while Koch was 10-5 with a 3.14.

"I think pitching was definitely to our advantage," said Vining. "We had so much depth that any day we went there we could have a good day."

Benson was the ace of the staff, and for good reason. He had a 14-2 record to go along with a 2.02 ERA. He also had 204 strikeouts in 156 innings pitched over 19 starts.

By the end of the season, Benson was named the consensus National Player of the Year in college baseball and was the recipient of the Dick Howser Trophy and the Rotary Smith Award winner, given to the nation's best baseball player.

"I could not have written this season any better," said Benson.

The Clemson ace was also named the ACC Player of the Year and was selected as the ACC Athlete of the Year for all sports.

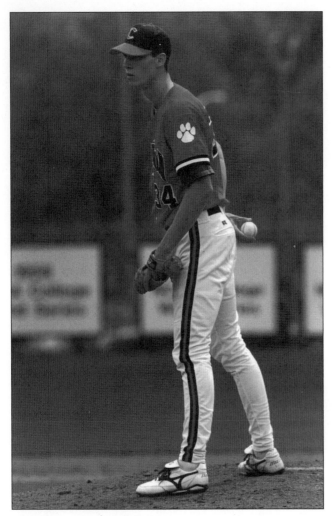

Kris Benson was named National Player of the Year in 1996.

"Kris is something special," Leggett said. "He has an ability to zero in on what he's doing and focus like no one I've ever coached. His pitching speaks for itself."

That summer, Benson was the No. 1 overall selection by the Pittsburgh Pirates of the major league Draft. He was the first Clemson athlete in any sport to be chosen number one in any draft.

Benson also pitched for Team USA in the 1996 Olympics in Atlanta, GA.

With Benson, Koch, and Vining on the mound, the Tigers posted a 51-17 record. The 51 wins ranked fourth in the nation. And though Clemson had a dominant pitching staff, it was not too shabby at the plate, either.

First baseman Jason Embler was one of five Tigers hitting over .300 in the lineup. He led the squad with a .357 average, while second baseman Doug Livingston was hitting .341, catcher Matthew LeCroy .316, shortstop Kurt Bultmann .304, and right fielder Jerome Robinson .303.

The Tigers finished second in the ACC that year to Florida State, though they swept the Seminoles at home in a three-game series. The sweep of FSU locked up Clemson for a regional site for a third straight year, and once again the Tigers took advantage.

Clemson rolled through the regional, beating up on Charleston Southern (9-1), Old Dominion (5-1), West Virginia (6-3), and Tennessee (12-5) on its way to another appearance in the College World Series.

"We feel confident. If we play like we did in the regional, we have a chance to win it all," Benson said at the time.

The Tigers did not win it all, but they came closer than they ever had before. After losing to Miami in the opener, 7-3, Clemson bounced back to beat Oklahoma State, 8-5, in 10 innings and then rallied to win a thriller against Alabama, 14-13.

Miami ended the Tigers' run the next day with a 14-5 victory. Ironically, after going the entire season without a loss, Benson suffered both defeats at the hands of Miami, but neither defeat made Leggett think differently about his ace.

"Kris Benson will always be the best college pitcher I've had or seen," Leggett said. "I'll remember all the games he won for us. He gave us all he had. He's as good a player as you'll see in college."

CLEMSON TURNS GREENE

In 2000, Clemson climbed to the No. 1 ranking by *Collegiate Baseball* after opening the season 23-3. The Tigers again traveled back to Omaha for the first time in four seasons.

Clemson went 1-2 in the College World Series that year after sweeping its way through the regional and super regional rounds. The Tigers ended the year with a 51-18 record and finished second in the ACC. Clemson claimed 14 wins over top-25 teams, including 11 wins against top-10 teams.

The 2001 season saw Clemson triumph over adversity. The Tigers suffered a five-game losing streak, along with the unexpected loss of seniors Patrick Boyd and Mike Proto to injury. But, again, Clemson finished second in the ACC and was a step away from Omaha before being eliminated by eventual National Champion Miami.

But the College World Series experience of 2000 and the rocky road of a 41-22 season in 2001 set the stage for one the Tigers' greatest runs. The 2002 team was loaded with power and future major league talent.

In all, eight players were drafted that year as Clemson went 54-17 and finished third in the College World Series, matching the 1996 team's two victories in Omaha.

The trio of Khalil Greene, Jeff Baker, and Michael Johnson combined to hit 77 home runs and drove in 265 RBIs. Greene was the patriarch of the three.

In the Tigers' 71 games, he set single-season records in home runs (27), RBIs (91), extra-base hits (61), slugging percentage (.877), and total bases (250). Greene was named the National Player of the Year and picked up the Dick Howser Award, the Golden Spikes Award, and the Rotary Award as college baseball's best player. He was the No. 13 overall pick by the San Diego Padres in the 2002 major league draft.

Greene's .470 batting average in 2002 was the best in ACC history. He also holds Clemson's all-time records for games played (272), at-bats (1,069), hits (403), doubles (95), RBIs (276), and total bases (668).

As good as Greene was at the plate, his skills at shortstop are often overlooked. He had a .961 fielding percentage in 71 games in 2002 and committed just 14 errors, this after having a .965 fielding percentage in 2001.

Greene went without an error in 24 ACC games. He will always be remembered for the way he threw his body into his craft, knocking down ball after ball with electrifying stops.

"He was like that every day," Leggett said. "He would get a big hit, two, or three it seemed like every day. And he would make two or three plays in the infield like that every day.

"You never knew what he was going to do. He was fun to watch."

And he was never better than on the big stage. In the first game of the College World Series, the Tigers drew Nebraska, whose loyal fans packed Rosenblatt Stadium with a sea of red and white.

With more than 24,000 fans pulling against him, Greene put on one of the greatest performances in Clemson history.

Besides making one incredible play after another at short, he also drove in five runs thanks to a two-run double and then a three-run home run that gave the Tigers a 10-8 lead in the bottom of the eighth inning.

Greene helped Clemson rally from a six-run deficit to beat the Cornhuskers, 11-10. Baker's RBI single in the bottom of the ninth lifted the Tigers to the win.

Greene continued his heroics in Clemson's next game against ACC rival Georgia Tech. He saved Clemson's 9-7 win by going airborne to take away a potential base hit in the bottom of the ninth inning.

While in Omaha, he broke the all-time NCAA's doubles record with his 95th, while becoming only the second player in Clemson history to hit over .400 for a season and the first one since 1941.

Greene also extended his 34-game hitting streak, third all-time in school history.

"He had the best start-to-finish offensive season I've ever seen," Leggett said.

No one before or since has ever capped off his career at Doug Kingsmore Stadium any better than Greene did. In his last at-bat, he cranked a solo shot over the left field wall to finish off Arkansas in the Super Regionals.

He celebrated by leaping into the arms of his teammates at home plate and then tossing his batting gloves into the stands along the first base side on his way back to the dugout.

"I wasn't going to use them again, so I just chucked them," he said after the game.

TIGERS ARE TOP CATS IN THE ACC, AGAIN

The 2005 Tigers played one of their toughest schedules in history, which included 42 of their 66 games against teams that played in the NCAA Tournament. Clemson still managed to come within one win of a trip to the College World Series, falling in three games at Baylor in the Waco (TX) Super Regional.

Clemson was 19-9 against top-25-ranked teams and won 21 ACC regular-season games, finishing in second place in the ACC standings. This success laid the foundation for what was to come in 2006.

In 2006, Clemson returned eight starters in its lineup as well as pitcher Josh Cribb, its most consistent pitcher over the two seasons. All the stars were lined up for Leggett to have one of his best teams in Tigertown.

And they did not disappoint, either.

Clemson posted its most ACC wins in history (24), went 53-16, and won the ACC Tournament title thanks to a seldom-used pitcher by the name of Sean Clark.

After undergoing surgery for a torn labrum the year before, Clark fell down the Clemson depth chart, thanks to a pitching staff that was loaded with strong arms. But the rigors of the ACC Tournament and two marathon games with Georgia Tech the night before led to a strong need for Clark's services.

If not for an injury to another teammate, Clark would not have been on the Tigers' 25-man postseason roster. Instead, he got his first start of his Clemson career in perhaps the biggest ACC game the program had been in since last winning a conference title in 1994.

"I never could have dreamed this up," Clark said afterward.

Clark gave up one run on four hits in eight-plus innings of work as he lifted Clemson to its ninth ACC Tournament Championship with an 8-4 victory.

"Coming back at the beginning of the year, I thought I could be the guy," said Clark, who pitched only 10 1/3 innings in seven appearances prior to the ACC Championship game. "When I wasn't, it was kind of discouraging."

Despite thinking about quitting, Clark stayed with it and found himself on the mound in the ACC Championship game.

"We had about three or four guys who hadn't pitched yet who were fresh," Leggett said. "The players have confidence in him, so of the people who were ready, he seemed like the person to give the opportunity to."

Clark sat down the first eight batters he faced and took a shutout into the ninth inning, when he was replaced after giving up a leadoff single.

Clark received a standing ovation from the crowd at The Baseball Grounds of Jacksonville in Jacksonville, FL, and a hug from his head coach. He then shared high-fives with each Clemson player as he headed to the dugout.

"For him to be able to do this in this arena will be something he'll remember for the rest of his life," Leggett said.

With the Clemson fans cheering above his dugout, Clark stepped back out for one last curtain call and a tip of his hat on what was an unforgettable afternoon.

"I was a little uncertain on what to do," he said. "I didn't know what to do, but I went with it."

Clark's performance inspired his teammates. It also earned him a second straight start in the Clemson Regional. He got the Tigers off to a great start by scattering three hits in eight innings of work, while shortstop Stan Widmann hit a two-run home run for a 3-0 victory.

The Tigers had no problems beating Elon in the second game and then won the Regional with an 8-6 victory over Mississippi State.

COLVIN CARRIES TIGERS TO OMAHA

Clark had already got the positive mojo heading in Clemson's direction with his performance in the ACC Championship Game, and in the first game of the Clemson Regional, outfielder Tyler Colvin brought it all the way over.

Oral Roberts was the best story of the NCAA Tournament at the time. The Golden Eagles won the Fayetteville, AK, Regional thanks to a win over host Arkansas and two over No. 2 seed Oklahoma State.

In the Clemson Super Regionals, they had a one-run lead on the host Tigers in the bottom of the ninth inning with one out. Oral Roberts had taken an 8-7 lead on the Tigers after closer Daniel Moskos, who went on to be the No. 4 overall pick of the Pirates in 2008, gave up three runs in the top of the ninth inning.

"We knew what we had to do. We've been doing it throughout the course of the season," Leggett said.

With one out, Herman Demmick singled up the middle, and the center fielder Brad Chalk laid down a perfect punt for an infield single down the third-base line. Third baseman Marquez Smith then lined a hit to deep short, loading the bases for Colvin.

"Coach told us going into that last inning that it's not over," Demmick said. "We had to get base runners and do what we can to push them around."

With Demmick 90 feet away representing the tying run, Leggett told his senior to run like crazy on anything hit on the ground and to be cautious on a fly ball. So when Colvin took reliever Sean Jarrett's 0-1 offering to deep right field, Demmick trotted back to third base to tag up. When he got to the bag and looked up, he saw Colvin's ball sailing over the fence in right field.

"As soon as I looked up, the ball is hitting the brick wall off the batting cages," Demmick said after the game.

Jarrett's second pitch was a slider that hung over the plate, and Colvin laid on top of it to lift the Tigers to an 11-8 victory. It was the first game-ending grand slam home run in Clemson history.

"I was going up there trying to hit it hard and hopefully find a hole. I just did my thing," Colvin said.

Colvin did a lot of things in 2006. The first-team All-American led Clemson with a .356 batting average, 100 hits, and 171 total bases, 23 of which were stolen.

The Tigers finished off Oral Roberts with another tight victory the next day, this time 6-5, to advance to their 11th College World Series appearance.

When it was all said and done, the Tigers finished ranked No. 5 in all three polls with a 53-16 record, including a 26-9 mark against top-25-ranked teams. Clemson's pitching staff had a 3.26 ERA, the sixth-best figure in the nation, one of many reasons Leggett was named ACC Coach of the Year.

Colvin and Andy D'Alessio were both first-team All-Americans, while Cribb earned third-team honors. Colvin (No. 13 overall by the Chicago Cubs) was one of 10 Tigers selected in the 2006 draft.

PARKER'S 20-20

The first time he went out onto the football field, Kyle Parker had no idea what he was doing.

"We were just little kids running around," he laughed.

Parker's dad, Carl, knew. The elder Parker, who played wide receiver in the NFL, had seen it in his son's arm, even at nine years old. He saw he could do some things with Kyle that most teams at that age could not.

"He would be out there spreading us around," Parker said. "Other teams would be out there running the Wing-T, but we would be out there throwing it deep."

With Kyle's team throwing the ball all over the place, other teams were confused. They got even more confused when Carl called for five wide receiver sets.

"They scrambled around trying to figure out what they should do, while we had receivers running wide-open all over the field. It was fun. We were pretty good," Kyle said.

Playing baseball was pretty fun for Kyle too, though success on the diamond for him did not come until a few years later. Spending the early parts of his life in South Georgia, where football is King, Kyle never really developed his skills as a baseball player.

That changed when he and his family moved to Jacksonville, FL, in the fourth grade. The game started coming to him easier, due in large part to the competition.

"A lot of the kids got into baseball, so I got into it," Kyle said. "I started playing AAU and ended up going to Miami it seemed like every weekend or South Florida playing ball all summer long."

From those experiences, Kyle developed into a two-sport athlete who shined in both at Clemson. In football, he was an All-America quarterback at Bartram Trail High School, where he was selected as an EA Sports Elite 11 Quarterback and played in the ESPN/Under Armour All-America game.

In baseball, he was an all-state and all-county performer and was named the County Player of the Year as a junior in high school. Parker, who stands just barely six feet and weighs 210 pounds, was a middle infielder in high school and usually, because of his athletic ability, played wherever he was needed.

But Parker wasn't known for his skills on the field, but instead he was known for his power hitting, which allowed him to become a first-team All-ACC selection as a true freshman at Clemson. That season, he hit .303 with 14 home runs and 50 RBIs, while playing in 57 games. He also had 12 doubles and had an on-base percentage of .400.

What made that feat more remarkable was the fact Parker could have been in high school that spring had he chosen to. Instead, he graduated from Bartram Trail in December and enrolled at Clemson that following January. Less than 60 days later, he was out on the baseball field in a Clemson uniform.

"He is a complete player," Leggett said. "He is strong and has great power and quickness in his bat."

Leggett described Parker the same way Clemson head football coach Dabo Swinney did.

"He's savvy," Swinney said.

Kyle seldom let things bother him. In the Clemson Regional in 2009, after striking out in his first plate appearance off the bench, he stepped up with two outs and down a run to Oklahoma State in the bottom of the eighth inning. With runners in scoring position, he delivered a two-run single that sent Clemson to the Super Regional Round.

On the football field, he also proved just how savvy he could be. After throwing an interception to Florida State cornerback Jamie Robinson, who returned it 52 yards for a first-quarter touchdown, Kyle simply walked by Swinney and said, "My bad, Coach."

After that, he went on to complete 18 of 30 passes for 242 yards and a career-high four touchdowns, clinching the Tigers' first ACC Atlantic Division Championship.

"He handles his emotions very well," Swinney said. "He doesn't let mistakes haunt him. He moves on. He doesn't let success get to him, either. He just plays."

Kyle plays because that's how he sees it. He is only having fun.

Carl says his son has always been that way. He doesn't let the stress and the pressures of what comes with playing both sports get to him. There was a time when his mom, Cathy, remembered picking Kyle up after a practice, and before getting into the car, he leaned over and vomited.

Her motherly instincts immediately took over, and she wondered if they were all pushing him too far. Kyle calmed those fears when he told both his parents he was having too much fun for it to be considered work.

"In football, there is nothing like Saturdays," he said. "That is so much fun. There is nothing you compare that to in all of sports. Just having all those people out there, it is something else.

"In baseball, you can enjoy the whole season. Football gets tough when you are over there doing two-a-days and practice all day just to play one game, but baseball

you get to go on the road and hang out with the guys and just go out there and play every day. That's the enjoyable part for me."

Both sports presented different challenges, both physically and mentally.

"I say the thing about baseball is that you don't really feel it until the end (of the season)," Kyle said. "Once you get to the end, you are like 'man this has been a long year.'

"In football you feel it every Sunday. You get beat up and you just have to shake it off and go back to work. They are both pretty physically tough on you, but you just have to know what you are doing."

Kyle had a lot of fun in the 2009-'10 academic year. He became the first Division I athlete in history to throw 20 touchdowns passes and hit 20 home runs in the same academic year.

On the football field, he threw 20 touchdowns and passed for 2,661 yards in leading the Tigers to its first appearance in the ACC Championship game. Later that spring, he hit 20 home runs and had 64 RBIs in leading Leggett's Clemson team back to the College World Series.

After he led the Tigers with a .344 batting average to go along with his 20 home runs, the Colorado Rockies drafted Kyle in the first round of the major league draft with the No. 26 overall pick.

Kyle, who was a first-team All-American on the baseball diamond, ultimately signed with the Rockies in July of 2010 but decided to play one more season of football.

"I just have so much fun playing both, that kind [of] stuff doesn't bother me," he said.

Kyle ultimately hung up his football cleats following a turbulent 2010 season in which he suffered an injury to his ribs. Despite some disappointments, he still had some good moments, like his 167 passing yards in a win over Georgia Tech and his 214 yards in a 14-13 victory over Russell Wilson and 23rd-ranked NC State.

"It's been awesome," Parker said about his time at Clemson. "I'm just glad I came here. I'm glad I got to be a part of this university where I got a chance to do this. Not many people would play both sports.

"If you were to ask me when I came here could I imagine all the things that happened and the success I and both teams had, I don't think I would believe it. I was extremely blessed to be in this situation."

2010 WAS AN UPSTREAM BATTLE

The Clemson baseball team fought its way upstream all year in 2010, and finally it reached the source of that river with an 8-6 victory over Alabama in the third and final game of the Clemson Super Regionals.

The Tigers advanced to the College World Series for the 12th time in the program's history—the 11th-best total in all of college baseball.

"I couldn't be more proud of my team," Leggett said afterward. "We came from the depths in the middle of the season. We kept our heads in the game and kept on battling and working at it. We had some adversity on the way. You just had to know the game was going to end like it did the way the season has been going."

Fittingly enough, Clemson's struggles throughout the 2010 season describe the origin of the city they have been trying to go to all along—Omaha. Omaha is an Indian name from the Nebraska Indian Tribe that means "upstream," presumably because at one time they lived upstream from their close relatives, the Quapaw.

Clemson, which finished the year 45-25, was fighting upstream when the season began that March. After starting the year 17-2 and becoming one of the sure-locks for Omaha by the middle of April, the Tigers dropped six of their next eight games and fell into a midseason slump that took another nine losses in 12 games to recover from.

At that point, most people wrote the Tigers off, but not their head coach. Leggett still had faith that his team would turn it around and would make a run.

"There were a lot of tough times in the middle of this season and if you don't believe something you can never achieve something," he said. "All this time, I said we just need to get our act together and believe we can still get to Omaha and be a team that's tough to beat at the end of the season.

"Coaches have a very powerful position on the team because the players feed off of us. I'm proud of what we have accomplished and I'm proud of the other coaches. Everyone on our coaching staff continued to work hard when some others gave up on us."

There were some who doubted Clemson in the Super Regional Finals. The Crimson Tide (42-25) had their ace— Nathan Kilcrease—on the mound. He had an 8-2 record with a 2.42 ERA.

After he yielded just two runs to No. 8 Georgia Tech in six innings to win the Atlanta Regional the week before, no one was giving Clemson much of a shot against the Crimson Tide.

But from the get-go, the Tigers attacked Kilcrease. After wasting a leadoff hit from Chris Epps in the top of the first, Clemson got on the board and took the lead for good in the second when John Hinson hit a home run to right field, which also scored Kyle Parker, who led off the inning with a base hit to left.

It was Hinson's fifth home run since the NCAA Tournament started the week before in the Auburn Regional.

"We were seeing the ball well today and hitting the pitches that we liked," Hinson said afterward. "We did well hitting the pitches that were mistakes."

The Tigers continued to get hits off Kilcrease in the third inning, as Epps and Freeman led off the inning with back-to-back singles, and then with two outs, shortstop Brad Miller, the 2011 ACC Player of the Year, doubled to the gap in right field to make the score 4-1.

Clemson wasn't done there. In the fourth inning, Richie Shaffer, who was picked No. 25 overall by the Tampa Bay Rays in 2012, homered for the second-straight game to lead off the inning, and then after a walk and an infield hit from Freeman, left fielder Jeff Schaus delivered with a two-out double to right field for a 6-1 lead.

"As an offense we just had a great approach to the game today," Shaffer said. "We were squaring up on pitches we like and John Hinson got us started to put us up 2-1 and we kept going from there. We just had a great approach at the plate all day and never backed off."

The Tigers eventually chased Kilcrease off by the sixth inning after tattooing him for six runs on 11 hits.

With one out in the seventh inning, and Hinson standing on base, Clemson eventually extended its advantage to seven runs when Shaffer hit a bomb to straightaway center field. It was his second home run of the afternoon and his third in the last two games.

"I thought we came out to play offensively and we did a great job of scoring two runs in the second inning, two in the third and two in the fourth to keep the pressure on Alabama," Leggett said. "We were swinging the bat really well and had some great at-bats on a good pitcher."

But it wasn't over yet, not even when Alabama had two outs in the bottom of the ninth and was down to their last strike. Brett Booth kept the Tide's slim hopes alive with a towering shot past the right field wall for a two-run homer that made the score 8-3.

After they loaded the bases with three-straight singles, Alabama's second baseman Ross Wilson drew a walk to bring home another run, which brought the tying run to the plate in first baseman Clay Hones. The game appeared to be over when Jones hit a hard roller straight to Miller at short, but Miller failed to get his glove down, and two more runs scored for an 8-6 margin.

Alabama's Jake Smith then came to the plate. He had already homered in Games 1 and 2, and any kind of hit could have tied the game or won it for the Tide. But Will Lamb, who normally would have started, forced Smith to fly out to left field, which subsequently started a dog pile on the infield as Clemson clinched yet another trip to the College World Series.

Clemson's Super Regional win over Alabama was a microcosm of the entire year, and through the ups and downs the team found its way in the end. And that made getting to Omaha that much more satisfying.

"The only way I can describe it, it's the most satisfying moment I have had," Hinson said. "It was incredible, with all the work we put into it. All the time and effort has paid off so far and we are going to Omaha to win.

"It is a big step to get there and we were able to reach it."

The 2010 Tigers tied the 1996 and 2002 squads with two wins in Omaha with wins over top-ranked Arizona State and Oklahoma. Clemson finished third in the CWS, tying its best finish with the 2002 team.

"It was definitely a special season," Freeman said. "It's not exactly how I wanted it to end in Omaha. I would have liked to have it end [in the Championship Series]. But getting here is something special.

"The whole event is something special. And then to share it with the guys on our team and such good friends and brothers that I've made along the way, it just makes it that much more special. And with this coaching staff, as much as they care about our players, it's awesome to come here and experience Omaha in its last season at Rosenblatt.

"So it's a special season, and coming to Omaha made it more special. It's tough to have to go away early, but it's a special season, nonetheless."

NEW FACILITY, NEW ERA FOR CLEMSON BASEBALL

There was a lot of excitement in the Clemson baseball program thanks to the new $9 million facility the baseball program moved into in the fall of 2015.

The new facility gave the players a brand new state-of-the-art clubhouse and locker room, area, while the coaches got new offices, a team meeting room, and a conference room. There is also a baseball museum as well as dining and kitchen areas.

"It gives you everything you need," Clemson baseball coach Monte Lee said. "The lockers are nice. It's very spacious. You can do all your laundry in that building. It has a pro locker room for the former players to come back and have a place to change, practice, and work out with us.

"It has a players' lounge with a ping-pong table and big screen TVs, and it has a full-service kitchen, which I think is unbelievable. We can feed the team there after practice, after games, and we can have alumni functions in that building. Then the coaches' offices are at the top and they are as nice as any offices I have ever been in."

Lee says opening up the new facility, along with a new era in Clemson baseball, brings the entire baseball family together at the same time.

"I'm concerned, really, with how it impacts the players. How it impacts recruiting," he said. "I want it to be a place where former players can come back, look and see the history of Clemson baseball, and see what they had a part in, too, when it comes to all the College World Series appearances, the ACC Championships, the first-round draft picks, the Big Leaguers . . . I want all of those teams and individual players to be recognized in some shape, form, or fashion in the building.

"I think we will get there."

Again, the two biggest impacts the new baseball operations center makes is the functionality that will be made available for the current players, and the influence it may have in recruiting.

"We can truly walk the kid through the facility," Lee said. "We will be able to walk those kids into the building now and show them what it is all about.

LANDING CLEMSON JOB IS DREAM DESTINATION FOR LEE

It took just 20 seconds for Monte Lee to tell the hundred or so people packed into the WestZone team meeting room how he felt about being named Clemson's new head baseball coach.

"This is a dream job of mine," he said during his formal introduction as the Tigers' new coach. "I don't know if I can even put into words how excited I am about this opportunity for my family, for my friends, and for myself. I'm extremely excited about it."

The excitement comes from Lee being a true South Carolinian. He was born in Spartanburg, raised in Lugoff, attended and played for the College of Charleston, was an assistant coach at the University of South Carolina, and then returned to Charleston as a head coach.

"I have been very fortunate in my career that I lived in South Carolina my whole life and I have coached in South Carolina my whole life. Not many people get that type of opportunity," Lee said.

Not many people get the opportunity to be the head baseball coach at Clemson, either. Lee is just the third head coach in 58 years to lead the Tigers' baseball program. He succeeded Jack Leggett, who won 955 games the previous 22 years and Bill Wilhelm, who won 1,161 games in the 36 years he led the program.

The Clemson baseball program is in the top 10 in all-time victories and has won more ACC titles than any other school.

"The tradition of Clemson is second to none," Lee said. "It has been led by two men over the last 58 years between Bill Wilhelm and Jack Leggett. When you look at what these two men accomplished in their careers here at Clemson, it's incredible. Two thousand, one hundred and sixteen wins at Clemson between these two men."

Lee followed those comments by spitting out statistic after statistic on Wilhelm and Leggett, while showing his respect for what each man accomplished in Tigertown.

Besides his 1,161 victories, Wilhelm won 17 regular season ACC Championships and seven tournament championships, which is an ACC record. He also had six College World Series teams, and his 1991 squad won an ACC-record 60 games.

"I don't even know how you do that," Lee said.

As for Leggett, whom Lee recognized as the one Wilhelm passed the torch to, he won three ACC Championships, earned six trips to Omaha, nine Super Regionals, and 21 Regionals. His 1994 team won 57 games, which is the second most in ACC history.

"That is tradition," Lee said. "And that is one of the main draws for me to be here at Clemson, to be able to follow two great men."

So who is Monte Lee? He is from South Carolina. He is married and has four daughters. He played baseball at the College of Charleston, was an assistant coach at the University of South Carolina, and was one of the more successful coaches in College of Charleston history.

Lee's seven teams in Charleston won 276 games, eclipsed the 40-win mark three times, earned four NCAA berths, advanced to a Super Regional, and won three conference titles.

"We don't have any professional sports in South Carolina," Lee said. "College baseball is huge in this state, and when you grow up in South Carolina, like I have, you are on one side of the fence or the other.

"This (South Carolina) rivalry is second to none in college baseball. I can tell you this. We are going to do our best here at Clemson to recruit the kind of kids that can come in here and knock down that fence to play for us. The kids of South Carolina will be our upmost priority, and we will recruit this state inside and out."

What else can anyone expect from a South Carolina boy from Lugoff who just landed his dream job?

A GROUP OF OVERACHIEVERS

There was truly one word for Monte Lee to use as he described his first baseball team at Clemson, "Over-achievers."

It was the perfect word to describe a team that was a preseason pick to finish fifth in the ACC's Atlantic Division, eighth in the conference, and would be considered lucky to make the NCAA Tournament. It was a team that had question marks at starting pitching, had to platoon at first and third base, had deficiencies in the outfield with adequate arm strength, and a defense that was prone to make errors.

No one expected the 2016 Clemson baseball team to do anything, no one except for themselves, of course.

"I can coach for the rest of my life and I may never have a more competitive group of players," Lee said following the Tigers' loss to Oklahoma State in the championship round of the 2016 Clemson Regional. "It's just an unbelievable group of kids that fought, clawed, and scratched and did everything they could to possibly put us in this position."

The position they put themselves in was a No. 7 National Seed, ACC Champions, and winners in 17 of their last 22 games.

The Tigers finished the season 44-20 overall, the most wins in one season since 2010. They won the program's first ACC Championship in 10 years, hosted a regional for the first time in five years, won a tournament game for the first time in three years, and won two tournament games for the first time in four years.

Yes, Clemson's goal is always to make it to Omaha and to play in the College World Series. But, let's be real here. No one outside of that Clemson clubhouse thought that could be true in Lee's first year, but they came closer than any of the previous four teams did.

"This is a group of overachievers, and I'm very, very proud of them," Lee said. "The relationships I developed here with this team and this group of players is something I will cherish for the rest of my life.

"Wins and losses come and go. Championships come and go, but at the end of the day it is about the relationships that you develop with your players, and that is why I got into coaching to begin with. It's about developing relationships and trying to make a difference in kids'

lives, and boy did they make a difference in my life. This team, I just can't say enough about their heart, their dedication to this program, to this school and to each other. It was a lot of fun."

The 2016 season was a lot of fun. The Tigers started it with a 21-7 record. A kid, who was still supposed to be in high school, took the college game by storm with his uncanny ability to see the baseball and to hit with power at the same time.

Seth Beer finished the season with a Clemson-freshman record 18 home runs and 70 RBIs. He led the Tigers in hitting (.369), slugging percentage (.700), and on-base percentage (.535) on his way to becoming the first freshman in the history of the ACC to earn the conference's Player of the Year Award.

But when teams started pitching around Beer midway through the season, it was All-America catcher Chris Okey who stepped up. Okey took advantage of his opportunities by hitting 15 home runs and driving in a team-high 74 RBIs. He batted .339 with a slugging percentage of .611 and an on-base percentage of .465.

"We came into this season with not many expectations, and to be able run out with these guys and have the year that we had, we came up a little short, but as coach said, it's about the relationships we built," Okey said. "We created some special ones here, and I'm so thankful to my teammates, and it is a close group to play with.

"It's fun being a Clemson Tiger. It was a heck of a year."

When Okey got going, so did the Tigers. After a midseason slump in which it won just two of nine ACC games, Clemson got rolling with series wins over Florida State and NC State, and then 10 straight victories that carried over into the ACC Championships and the Clemson Regional.

The Tigers concluded the year with 11 wins in their last 13 games.

"Right now, it is just kind of tough. There are a lot of emotions," Beer said. "There are a lot of good friends that I have made over time, and some of them are done here. They are done putting on this uniform. There are a lot of emotions going through my mind right now. That's the kind of stuff I'm thinking about.

"It's the end of the season, and it really kind of has not set in. As of right now, what comes first is my teammates and picking them up as they picked me up throughout the whole season. That's the kind of stuff going through my mind right now."

To show the kind of fight the Tigers had and how they always clawed back when things did not look good, consider this. They were 14-5 in one-run games, and 24 times they came from behind to win a game. In games following a loss, Clemson was 14-5. Not bad for a team many considered to be an average one at best prior to the year beginning.

"Obviously, I'm disappointed that it came to an end, but I could not be prouder of a group of kids," Lee said.

"This is definitely a group that I will always remember and be very, very proud of it."

HOWSER AWARD DRIVES BEER TO BRING TIGERS BACK TO OMAHA

Though he had just received the Dick Howser Trophy as the nation's top player in College Baseball in 2016, Seth Beer longed to be on the field at TD Ameritrade Park in Omaha, NE.

Instead, the Clemson outfielder had to watch from the press box as participating teams in the 70th annual College World Series took batting practice.

"I just wish I could be out there," Beer said after receiving the Dick Howser Trophy. "It just makes me so hungry to go out there and compete.

"It is kind of bittersweet. It is great to be here, but you want to be here playing. That is the ultimate goal and that is the ultimate experience . . . to be able to come to Omaha and take Clemson back."

Regardless, there is nothing wrong with being named the National Player of the Year as a consolation prize. Beer became the first freshman to ever win the award, and the third Tiger overall. Kris Benson received the trophy in 1996, and Khalil Greene won it in 2002.

"It's an incredible feeling," Beer said. "Obviously, there are so many great players in the country, in the ACC and even on the Clemson baseball team. To be able to get acknowledge as one of the best is an incredible experience. There are so many great players out there in college baseball."

And this year Beer was the best of them all.

Beer had an incredible season at Clemson under head coach Monte Lee in what should have been his senior year at Lambert High School in Suwanee, Georgia. After enrolling at Clemson in January, he posted remarkable numbers that earned him ACC Player of the Year honors, also a first by a freshman.

"It has been an amazing experience to be here in Omaha and accept an award like that on TV," Beer said. "It has been incredible for not only me, but for Clem-son baseball. It is just an awesome feeling to accept this award on behalf of Clemson."

In 2016, Beer batted .369 with 18 homers, 13 doubles, 70 RBIs, 57 runs, 62 walks, 15 hit-by-pitches, a .535 on-base percentage, and six outfield assists in 62 games. He also had a .700 slugging percentage, the best mark by a Tiger since Greene had a .877 slugging percentage when he won the Dick Howser Trophy.

It is incredible Beer is the National Player of the Year considering he did not enroll at Clemson until January, meaning he did not participate in any off-season conditioning program or in fall ball. He won the National Player of the Year Award literally as a kid straight out of high school, which leads to this question. How can he possibly top that?

"You have to be able to go out there every day and not lose that hunger for it," Beer said.

It helps to be in Omaha and watching teams like Miami and Oklahoma State—two teams the Tigers lost to this year—taking BP at TD Ameritrade Park.

"Every day of the year you have to try to get better, no matter what that is. It's one of those things where we had a taste of what it is like," Beer said. "We know what that feels like now and I think we will have a fire burning underneath us.

"We are a good ball club and we deserve to be there just like everybody else. I think there will be a chip on our shoulder this coming season."

Beer led the Tigers to a 44-20 record in 2016, a top-eight national seed in the NCAA Tournament, and Clemson's first ACC championship in 10 years.

"I think with the upcoming year, not only has this sparked a fire under me, but one under Coach Lee, too. He is going to do everything he can and the coaching staff can, and I will do everything I can to help our team get back (to Omaha)," Beer said. "You better believe I'm coming back. When I get back to school I will talk to my teammates and I will tell them that I have seen it and we have to get here. Everything you get to experience when you get here, and all that stuff, we need to get back here soon."

CLEMSON BASEBALL HISTORICAL TIMELINE

April 24, 1896—Clemson played its first baseball game, a 20-13 loss to Furman. The home games were played on Bowman Field in front of Tillman Hall. The Tigers' first head coach was R.T.V. Bowman.

May 12, 1899—Clemson played South Carolina for the first time. The Tigers won 21-8 in eight innings in Columbia.

1900—Legendary football coach John Heisman, who coached Clemson's gridders for four seasons, was named the Tigers' baseball coach. Heisman compiled a 28-6-1 (.814) record in three seasons (1901-03), which still stands today as the best winning percentage in Tiger history, slightly ahead of another legendary football coach, Frank Howard.

1904—Vet Sitton played in his first season at Clemson. The Pendleton, SC, native, a 5'11", 170-pound righty, played one season (1909) for the Cleveland Indians, where he was 3-2 with a 2.88 ERA in 50.0 innings pitched. He later was the Tigers' head coach in 1915-16 and compiled a 26-18-1 (.589) record.

April 12, 1913—Doc Ezell pitched Clemson's first no-hitter in a 5-0 victory over Erskine.

March 27, 1916—Clemson defeated West Virginia Wesleyan 4-2 in the first game played on Riggs Baseball Field. Clemson played on this field until the 1970 season.

April 29, 1916—Elmer Long pitched a no-hitter in a 2-0 win over Virginia Military.

1921—Clemson joined the Southern Conference and was a charter member.

1922—Flint Rhem, one of the Tigers' greatest players of the 20th century, played in his first season at Clemson. He played during the 1922-23 seasons and later went on to play 12 major league seasons with the St. Louis Cardinals, Philadelphia Phillies, and Boston Braves. He had a 105-97 career record with a 4.20 ERA and over 1,500 strikeouts. He was 20-7 with a 3.21 ERA with the Cardinals in 1926, his best season. He once pitched a no-hitter (in 1924, one year before his rookie season in the Majors) while playing for the Fort Smith (AR) minor league team. He struck out 16 batters in the game and made it in "Ripley's Believe It or Not" by not allowing a ball to be hit out of the infield.

April 30, 1923—Flint Rhem struck out 21 batters in a 3-3 tie with Furman that went 13 innings. The game was called because of darkness.

1923—Flint Rhem had a 7-2-1 record and completed all nine games. He had a total of 136 strikeouts for a 15.1 per game average. He also had two one-hit games that season and gave up only 40 hits all year, or 4.4 hits per game.

Historic Riggs Field was home to the Tigers from 1916-'69.

April 17, 1924—Lefty Smith pitched a no-hitter in a 6-0 win over South Carolina.

1931—Clemson's season was cut short due to an outbreak of meningitis on campus in April. Clemson finished 6-2.

1932—Legendary football coach Jess Neely, who coached the Tiger gridders for nine seasons (1931-39), coached his first season as Clemson's baseball coach. He compiled a 67-66-2 (.504) record in seven seasons (1932-38).

1932—Clemson won the state baseball championship.

1935—Clemson won the state baseball championship.

1941—Dude Buchanan set the school record for batting average in a season with a .485 mark (33-for-68).

1943—Frank Howard, the Tigers' career leader in football victories (165), coached the baseball squad for one season, compiling a 12-3 overall record. His career record is still the second-best of any coach in school history. There have only been five different baseball head coaches since his brief stint.

March 29, 1946—Joe Landrum pitched a no-hitter in a 6-0 win over Erskine.

June 12-20, 1947—Clemson participated in the NCAA Tournament for the first time. The Tigers advanced to the NCAA Eastern Finals and lost to eventual finalist Yale (and first-baseman George Bush) on June 20 at New Haven, CT.

1947—Joe Landrum was Clemson's first baseball All-American. He earned first-team honors from ABCA after posting a 12-2 record and 2.23 ERA. Landrum went on to pitch for the Brooklyn Dodgers. Clemson won the Southern Conference title with a 13-2 record.

May 5, 1950—Fred Knoebel hit for the cycle (the first by a Tiger) at South Carolina. He walked in the first, tripled in the second, singled in the fourth, and hit a home run in the fifth. Knoebel also doubled in the seventh and was hit by a pitch in the eighth. Clemson won the game 14-5.

The 1947 Clemson baseball squad was the first team to play in the NCAA Tournament.

June 8-9, 1950—Clemson played Alabama and Kentucky in the NCAA Tournament at Kannapolis, NC, losing both games.

April 4, 1952—Billy O'Dell struck out a Clemson-record 21 batters in a 5-2 win over South Carolina at Orangeburg, SC.

May 8, 1953—Billy O'Dell pitched a no-hitter in a 2-0 win over South Carolina. That same day, Clemson officially joined the newly formed Atlantic Coast Conference.

May 22-24, 1954—Clemson participated in the NCAA Playoffs in a home-and-home series with Virginia Tech but lost to the Hokies twice in as many games. Clemson lost the first game 11-10 on May 22. It marked the first NCAA Tournament event in any sport played at Clemson. The Tigers lost to Virginia Tech 7-1 two days later in Blacksburg.

1954—Clemson won the ACC title with an 8-4 ACC regular-season record in the conference's inaugural season. Bob Smith was also named ACC Coach of the Year.

Fall, 1957—From the advice of North Carolina head coach Walter Rabb, Frank Howard hired a 27-year-old assistant from China Grove, NC, named Bill Wilhelm.

March 24, 1958—Bill Wilhelm coached his first game and defeated Michigan State 7-5 in seven innings at Clemson.

May 19, 1958—Clemson defeated North Carolina 4-1 at Gastonia, NC, in a playoff game to determine the ACC Champion. Both teams had 11-3 records after the regular season, forcing the one-game playoff.

June 5-9, 1958—The Tigers won the NCAA District III Playoffs to advance to the College World Series. The Tigers lost their opening game of the NCAA Tourney to Florida 8-6. Therefore, the Tigers had to win five games in a row to advance to the College World Series in Omaha, NE, a destination never reached before by Clemson at the time. So the Tigers promptly defeated George Washington and Florida State to stay alive. The only problem was that Clemson had to defeat Florida twice on June 9 to advance. In the first game, the Tigers

won a thriller 15-14 when Bailey Hendley singled home Larry Wilson in the bottom of the ninth. Later in the day, Clemson won 3-1 to advance to Omaha. Harold Stowe, who went on to play for the Yankees, pitched a four-hitter to earn his 13th victory of the season. The two victories in one day still stands today as the only time that Clemson has won twice in one day to advance to the College World Series.

June 14-16, 1958—Clemson participated in the College World Series for the first time. Clemson defeated Arizona 4-1 on June 14 but lost to Holy Cross 17-4 on June 15 and Western Michigan 5-3 on June 16.

1958—Harold Stowe led the nation in appearances (21), innings pitched (127.0), strikeouts (126), and wins (14).

May 16-18, 1959—After the 1959 regular season, Clemson, Wake Forest, and North Carolina were tied for first place, forcing a playoff among the three. Clemson beat Wake Forest 4-2 at Thomasville, NC, on May 16 and downed North Carolina 9-7 at Gastonia, NC, to claim the ACC crown.

June 4-6, 1959—Clemson raced through the NCAA District III Playoffs at Gastonia, NC, downing Georgia Tech 9-6 and Florida State twice (24-2, 5-0) to advance to Omaha.

June 13-15, 1959—The Tigers lost to Arizona 3-2 on June 13 in 12 innings in their first game in Omaha. They bounced back and defeated Colorado State 7-1 the next day but were eliminated by Penn State 7-0 on June 15.

1959—Clemson was ranked #7 in the final *Collegiate Baseball* poll.

May 8, 1962—Clemson hit an ACC-record five homers in one inning (sixth) against South Carolina in a 27-17 win. Clemson also hit a Tiger-record eight homers in the game.

1962—Clemson led the nation in homers per game (1.6).

April 10, 1965-May 17, 1966—Rusty Adkins had a 41-game hitting streak. Adkins hit .438 during the streak that still stands as the longest in ACC history.

1966—Clemson led the nation in runs per game (9.1), home runs per game (1.28), and slugging percentage (.502).

May 6, 1967—Nelson Gibson and Charlie Watson combined to pitch a no-hitter in a 3-0 win over Georgia Tech.

June 2-5, 1967—Clemson participated in the NCAA District III Playoffs at Gastonia, NC. After losing the first contest against Florida State, Clemson rebounded with three straight victories. But Auburn ended Clemson's season by defeating the Tigers 6-5 in 13 innings in the championship game.

1967—The Tigers won the ACC title (11-2). Clemson was ranked #7 in the final *Collegiate Baseball* poll.

June 6, 1968—Lefthander John Curtis became Clemson's first first-round major league draft pick. He was the #10 overall pick in the secondary phase by the Boston Red Sox.

March 7, 1970—Clemson played its first two games at Doug Kingsmore Stadium. The Tigers defeated Louisville 10-0 and 8-1 in two seven-inning games. The field featured a "Crosley-like" terrace around the outfield fence that gave the field a more closed-in perspective and reduced maintenance for drainage purposes.

1970—Clemson was ranked #18 in the final *Collegiate Baseball* poll.

April 17, 1971—Dave Van Volkenburg pitched a no-hitter in an 11-0 win over Florida State in a seven-inning game.

1971—Clemson was ranked #22 in the final *Collegiate Baseball* poll.

March 16, 1973—Lindsay Graham pitched a no-hitter in a 3-0 win over Maryland in an eight-inning game.

1973—Clemson won the ACC regular-season title with a 10-2 record.

April 19, 1974—Chuck Porter pitched a Tiger and ACC-record 16.0 innings in earning the victory over Virginia 3-2 in the first game of a doubleheader at Clemson.

1974—Clemson won the ACC regular-season title with a 10-1 record.

April 22, 1975—Steve Tucker hit for the cycle at Georgia Tech. He doubled in the first, tripled in the fourth, homered in the sixth, and singled in both the seventh and ninth innings. Clemson won the game 18-3.

May 23-24, 1975—Clemson participated in the NCAA Mideast Regional in Ypsilanti, MI. Eastern Michigan and Penn State defeated the Tigers 5-3 and 5-4, respectively.

1975—Denny Walling led the nation with 1.58 RBIs per game. Clemson tied for the ACC regular-season title with a 10-2 record and was ranked #25 in the final *Collegiate Baseball* poll.

April 17, 1976—Ron Musselman pitched a no-hitter in a 9-0 win over Virginia.

1976—Clemson was ranked #5 in the final *Collegiate Baseball* poll.

April 23-25, 1976—Clemson won its first ACC Tournament Championship, as the Tigers defeated Wake Forest 2-0 and Maryland in two games (2-1, 3-2) at Clemson.

May 21-24, 1976—The Tigers won the NCAA Atlantic Regional in Columbia, SC, by downing Furman 13-2 in game one, defeating South Carolina 10-4 in the second game and beating Furman 6-2 to advance to Omaha.

June 11-14, 1976—Clemson participated in the College World Series. The Tigers defeated Auburn 9-4 on June 11 and lost to Eastern Michigan 3-2 in 10 innings on June 13. Arizona eliminated the Tigers 10-6 on June 14.

1976—Clemson won the ACC regular-season title with a 10-2 record.

February 26-March 27, 1977—Clemson opened the season with a 26-game winning streak, the longest winning streak in school history.

March 17, 1977—Brian Snyder pitched a no-hitter in an 8-0 win over North Carolina-Wilmington.

May 20-22, 1977—Clemson defeated Mississippi and won two of three games from host Miami (FL) in winning the NCAA South Regional to advance to the College World Series.

June 10-14, 1977—In the College World Series, Clemson lost to Arizona State 10-7 on June 10 but beat Temple 13-4 the next day. However, Cal State Los Angeles eliminated Clemson 1-0 on June 14.

1977—Clemson captured the ACC regular-season title with a 9-1 record. Clemson was ranked #5 in the final *Collegiate Baseball* poll.

April 22-24, 1978—The Tigers won the ACC Tourney title at Clemson. The Tigers swept through the tourney with wins over N.C. State (12-1), Duke (13-0), and Wake Forest (7-2).

May 19-21, 1978—In the NCAA Atlantic Regional at Coral Gables, FL, the Tigers beat host Miami (FL) 8-5 in the first game but lost to Marshall (9-3) and Miami (7-5).

1978—Clemson won the ACC regular-season title with a 10-2 record. The Tigers also started the tradition of wearing ankle-long white pants for every game. Clemson was ranked #25 in the final *Collegiate Baseball* poll.

April 7, 1979—Clemson's most productive offensive game came at N.C. State. The score . . . 41-9. The Tigers led 18-6 after four innings and capped off the day with 18 runs in the ninth. Robert Bonnette had three hits in the ninth, in which 22 Tigers batted. Neil Simons went 4-for-6 with three walks, six runs, three homers, and a Tiger record-tying 10 RBIs. Dave Buffamoyer also set a record with seven runs, while Bonnette and Tony Masone had five hits apiece. Future major leaguers Tim Teufel and Bill Schroeder batted fifth and sixth, respectively, and combined for five hits, nine runs, and nine RBIs.

May 18-20, 1979—In the NCAA Atlantic Regional at Coral Gables, FL, the Tigers defeated Georgia Southern 8-4 but lost to Miami (FL) 2-1 in the Tigers' next game. The next two games yielded the same results, as Clemson downed Georgia Southern 2-0 but lost to Miami 4-1.

1979—Clemson won the ACC regular-season title with a 10-1 record. There was no ACC Tourney that year. Clemson was ranked #9 in the final *Collegiate Baseball* poll.

March 10, 1980—Mike Brown pitched a perfect game in a 2-0 win over North Carolina-Wilmington in seven innings.

April 22-26, 1980—Clemson won the ACC Tournament held at Raleigh, NC, by winning four games in a row without a defeat. The Tigers downed Wake Forest (4-0), Maryland (9-4), N.C. State (5-4), and North Carolina (12-3).

May 22-25, 1980—In the NCAA Atlantic Regional at Clemson, the Tigers beat East Tennessee State (22-4) and South Carolina twice (6-2, 17-12) to advance to Omaha.

May 31-June 1, 1980—In the College World Series, Clemson lost to Miami (FL) 13-5 and California 6-4.

1980—Clemson was ranked #4 in the final *Collegiate Baseball* poll.

April 22-26, 1981—Clemson won the ACC Tournament held at Chapel Hill, NC. Clemson defeated North Carolina 7-5 in the championship game. The Tigers won four straight games after losing their second game of the tournament.

May 22-23, 1981—In the NCAA Atlantic Regional at Clemson, the Tigers lost to Wichita State (7-2) and East Tennessee State (2-1).

1981—Clemson tied for the ACC regular-season title with a 10-4 record.

March 5, 1982—Jeff Gilbert pitched a no-hitter in a 5-0 win over Western Carolina.

1982—Clemson captured the ACC regular-season title with a 10-2 record.

March 6, 1984—Scott Parrish pitched a no-hitter in a 6-0 win over The Citadel in a seven-inning game. The no-hitter is the last by a Tiger individual to date.

1984—Clemson tied for the ACC regular-season title with a 12-2 record.

May 13, 1985—The Tigers played host to the first night game ever at Clemson. The Tigers downed Furman 13-1.

1985—Clemson tied for the ACC regular-season title with a 9-4 record.

May 4, 1986—Clemson's longest streak of not being shutout (232 games) ended with a 5-0 defeat at the hands of South Carolina in Columbia.

May 21-24, 1987—The Tigers played in the NCAA South Regional at Huntsville, AL. The Tigers defeated West Virginia, Seton Hall, and Auburn but lost to Arkansas twice and were eliminated from the tournament.

1987—Clemson was ranked #10 in both the final *Baseball America* and *Collegiate Baseball* polls. The Tigers won 54 games, the first time Clemson had reached 50 wins.

May 26-30, 1988—The Tigers participated in the NCAA Northeast Regional at New Britain, CT. Clemson defeated Fordham 3-2 in game one in 19 innings. It still stands today as the longest game played in Clemson history. The Tigers also defeated Saint John's but lost to Rutgers and Kentucky and were eliminated from the tournament.

1988—The Tigers won the ACC regular-season title with an 18-2 record. Clemson was ranked #15 in the final *Baseball America* poll and #21 in the final *Collegiate Baseball* poll. Left-hander Mike Milchin was also a member of the United States Olympic team.

May 13-16, 1989—Clemson defeated Maryland, Georgia Tech, N.C. State, and North Carolina (twice) in winning the ACC Tournament title at Chapel Hill, NC. Clemson defeated the Tar Heels 12-4 in the championship game.

May 25, 1989—Brian Barnes won his 16th game in a 6-2 win over Stetson in the NCAA Atlantic Regional at Tallahassee, FL, setting the school record for wins. He also set the Tiger record and led the nation with 208 strikeouts.

May 25-28, 1989—The Tigers participated in the NCAA Atlantic Regional at Tallahassee, FL. Clemson defeated Stetson twice and Auburn once, but losses to Florida State and Auburn eliminated the Tigers from the tournament.

May 27, 1989—April 10, 1990—Brian Kowitz had a 37-game hitting streak, second-longest in Clemson history. Kowitz, who later played with the Atlanta Braves, hit .430 with 43 RBIs during the streak.

1989—Clemson was ranked #14 in both the final *Baseball America* and *Collegiate Baseball* polls. Brian Barnes ended his career with an ACC-record 44 wins.

April 29, 1990—Bill Wilhelm won his 1,000th career game in a 17-10 win over Georgia Tech at Atlanta, GA.

May 25-27, 1990—Clemson played in the NCAA Central Regional at Austin, TX. Clemson beat Texas-Arlington but lost to Creighton twice and was eliminated from the tournament.

May 11-14, 1991—The Tigers won the ACC Tournament held at Greenville, SC. The Tigers beat Georgia Tech 24-8 in the championship game, winning for the fifth time in as many games.

May 23-26, 1991—Clemson swept though the NCAA Northeast Regional at Orono, ME, and advanced to the College World Series. Clemson downed Princeton, Villanova, Mississippi State, and Maine.

June 1-3, 1991—In the College World Series, the Tigers lost to Creighton and Long Beach State.

1991—Clemson won the ACC regular-season title with an 18-3 record. Clemson was ranked #4 in the final *Baseball America* poll and #8 in the final *Collegiate Baseball* poll. The Tigers ended the season with a school record 60 wins. Eric Macrina hit a then-school record 24 home runs, and

Clemson led the nation in runs per game (9.97), winning percentage (85.7), and wins (60).

May 21-23, 1992—The Tigers participated in the NCAA Mideast Regional at Starkville, MS. Clemson defeated Yale but lost to UCLA and Oklahoma.

1992—Clemson won the ACC regular-season title with a 19-5 record. Clemson was ranked #7 in the final *Baseball America* poll and #10 in the final *Collegiate Baseball* poll.

April 20, 1993—Keith Williams hit for the cycle at Furman. He hit a home run in the first, doubled in the third, singled in the sixth, and tripled in the ninth. Clemson won the game 17-2.

May 15-19, 1993—The Tigers won the ACC Tournament at Greenville, SC. Clemson defeated N.C. State 11-7 in the championship game, a game that ended at 1:21 AM. Jeff Morris's grand slam propelled the Tigers to victory. It was just the senior's second career homer. Ironically, both of his homers were grand slams off N.C. State pitcher David Allen. Both came in the eighth inning with one out, and both gave Clemson the lead.

May 28-31, 1993—Clemson participated in the NCAA Mideast Regional at Knoxville, TN. The Tigers earned victories over Rutgers and Fresno State in their opening two games but then lost to Fresno State and Kansas.

July 2, 1993—Bill Wilhelm announced his retirement after 36 seasons with the Tiger program. His retirement press conference was fittingly held in the first-base dugout at Doug Kingsmore Stadium. He had a 1,161-536-10 (.683) record and never had a losing season. He was the fifth-winningest coach in NCAA history at the time of his retirement.

1993—Clemson was ranked #17 in both the final *Baseball America* and *Collegiate Baseball* polls.

March 19, 1994—Shane Monahan hit for the cycle at Hawaii-Hilo. He tripled in the first, singled in the second, and homered in the sixth. He also doubled in the eighth and singled in the ninth. Clemson won the game 13-5.

May 18-22, 1994—The Tigers won the ACC Tournament Championship at Greenville, SC. The Tigers defeated Florida State 4-1 in the championship game.

May 26-28, 1994—Clemson participated in the NCAA East Regional at Clemson. Clemson downed The Citadel and Old Dominion but lost to Notre Dame and Auburn.

1994—Clemson won the ACC regular-season title with a 20-4 record in Jack Leggett's first season as the Tiger head coach. Leggett received ACC Coach of the Year honors, as well. Shane Monahan set the ACC record and led the nation with 137 hits. He also led the nation in runs (97), and the Tigers led the nation with 57 wins. Clemson was ranked #4 in the final *Baseball America* poll and #9 in the final *Collegiate Baseball* poll.

February 18, 1995—Gary Burnham hit for the cycle at Texas-Arlington. He doubled in the first, tripled in the third, walked in the fifth, homered in the seventh, and singled in the ninth. Clemson won the game 18-0.

April 14, 1995—The greatest comeback in Clemson history took place on this date, the first game of a three-game series at N.C. State. The Wolfpack had just scored three and six runs in the seventh and eighth innings, respectively, to take a 15-4 lead. The Tiger leadoff batter struck out to start the ninth inning. Clemson then got three straight hits and two walks. Seth Brizek hit into a fielder's choice for the second out, as David Miller scored on the play to cut the deficit to 15-7. The next six Tiger batters all reached safely on hits, highlighted by Shane Monahan's three-run homer that cut the Wolfpack lead to just two runs. After two more hits and a walk, Matthew LeCroy tied the score with a clutch double. The Tigers went on to win 17-15 in 10 innings. Clemson did so being down 11 runs on the road with no runners on base in the ninth inning and one out, and without the benefit of a Wolfpack error in the ninth.

May 25-28, 1995—The Tigers won the NCAA East Regional held at Clemson with wins over Navy, Jacksonville, Winthrop, and Alabama.

1995—Clemson won the ACC regular-season title with a 20-4 record. Jack Leggett received ACC Coach of the Year honors. Paul Galloway became Clemson's first Academic All-American. Clemson was ranked #8 in both the final *Baseball America* and *Collegiate Baseball* polls.

April 21, 1996—Clemson played in one of the longest nonstop days of baseball in history. The Tigers and Georgia Southern were slated to play two nine-inning games, but the two games lasted a total of 28 innings. The first was a 10-inning affair, with Georgia Southern winning 8-6. The latter game also saw Georgia Southern win, this time 9-7 in 18 innings. The games combined for eight hours and 44 minutes in length (not counting the 31 minutes in between).

May 23-26, 1996—The Tigers won the NCAA East Regional at Clemson and advanced to the College World Series. Clemson recorded victories over Charleston Southern, Old Dominion, West Virginia, and Tennessee.

May 31-June 5, 1996—Clemson made its eighth College World Series appearance, Miami (FL) defeated the Tigers to open the tournament, so Clemson had to win to stay alive. The Tigers responded with a 10-inning, 8-5 win over Oklahoma State and next faced Alabama, the #1 seed. The morning of the game, Kris Benson and Billy Koch learned they were the #1 and #4 overall picks, respectively, of the major league draft. The Tigers, though, sent out Ken Vining, who was 10-3, to face a potent Crimson Tide hitting attack. But it was the Tigers who jumped out to an early 5-0 lead. Alabama battled back to take a 12-10 lead after eight innings. Gary Burnham and Jerome Robinson led off the ninth with singles. Then, 5'8" second-baseman Doug Livingston hit an opposite-field double to give Clemson the lead. But the Tigers, who led 14-12, had to contain the hot Alabama bats in the bottom of the ninth. Brett Taft led off with a double. Rusty Loflin flied out to Livingston and Drew Bounds singled. On came Koch, who was making a rare relief appearance. He struck out David Tidwell and seemed to throw a game-ending groundball off the bat of Joe Caruso, but the ball went through the legs of shortstop Kurt Bultmann, plating Taft and putting runners on first and third. But Koch got Dax Norris to bounce out to first baseman Jason Embler, who made a spectacular grab ranging to his right and looking into the sun. Embler flipped to Koch to record the final out of the game, as the Tigers won 14-13 and advanced further in the College World Series than it ever had before.

1996—Clemson led the nation with a 3.03 ERA. Clemson was ranked #5 in the final *Baseball America* poll and #4 in the final *Collegiate Baseball* poll. Kris Benson was named national Player of the Year by *Baseball America* and *Collegiate Baseball*. One of the most decorated players in Tiger history also received the Dick Howser Trophy and the Smith Award. He won his first 14 decisions and had a 2.02 ERA in 156.0 innings pitched. He allowed 109 hits and 27 walks while striking out 204 (7.6-to-1 strike-out-to-walk ratio), easily a Tiger record. He had seven complete games and four shutouts, as well. Benson was the #1 overall pick of the 1996 draft (Pirates), becoming the first Tiger to be picked at that position. He donned the Red, White, and Blue for Team USA in the Centennial Olympics in Atlanta in 1996, earning a bronze medal. Tiger teammates Billy Koch and Matthew LeCroy joined Benson on the Olympic team.

May 22-24, 1997—Clemson played in the NCAA Central Regional at Lubbock, TX. Clemson defeated Nevada in its opener but lost to Rice and Texas State.

1997—Matthew LeCroy hit 24 homers and set a Tiger record with 53 career homers. Kurt Bultmann set a Clemson record with 31 doubles, a mark later eclipsed by Khalil Greene.

March 21, 1998—Clemson scored 19 runs in one inning against Maryland. Ironically, Clemson did not score in any other inning of the game. The run total set an NCAA record for most runs in a third inning. In the inning, Clemson sent 23 batters to the plate and had 12 hits and six walks. Like the 11-run comeback in the ninth inning at N.C. State in 1995, the first Tiger to bat in the inning was retired. The next 17 batters reached base safely. Patrick Boyd and Kurt Bultmann both reached base in all three plate appearances and scored three runs in the inning.

April 24, 1998—Rusty Adkins had his jersey retired and was inducted into the Clemson Baseball Ring of Honor, joining Bill Wilhelm in the elite company.

May 21-23, 1998—Clemson hosted the NCAA East Regional. Clemson lost to South Alabama in 16 innings and eventual National Champion Southern California.

1998—Clemson was ranked #21 in the final *Baseball America* poll and #23 in the final *Collegiate Baseball* poll.

March 8, 1999—Clemson's streak of 146 weeks being ranked in one of the major polls ended. The last time the Tigers were not ranked was at the end of the 1990 season. Clemson had a 407-138 (.747) record over that span.

May 28-30, 1999—In the NCAA Fayetteville (AR) Regional, Clemson lost to Missouri State 23-5 in the first game and needed to win four games in two days to advance. The Tigers came through with wins on Saturday over Delaware and host Arkansas. Clemson had to beat Missouri State twice on Sunday and did just that by scores of 8-7 and 7-5.

June 4-6, 1999—Texas A&M won two of the three games in the NCAA Super Regional at College Station, TX. Despite coming up short, Clemson battled back after a 20-3 defeat in the opening game and had the lead entering the ninth inning in game three in a hostile environment.

1999—Clemson was ranked #17 in the final *Baseball America* poll and #13 in the final *Collegiate Baseball* poll.

March 20, 2000—Clemson was ranked #1 by *Collegiate Baseball* after opening the season 19-3. The Tigers spent two weeks as that poll's top team.

May 26-28, 2000—Clemson played host to Middle Tennessee, Illinois, and Old Dominion in regional play and claimed wins over Middle Tennessee (4-0, 21-3) and a win over Illinois (9-3) to earn the right at hosting the first-ever super regional at Clemson.

June 2-3, 2000—The Tigers defeated Mississippi State 11-4 and 9-4 in the Clemson Super Regional to earn their ninth trip to the College World Series.

June 9-14, 2000—Clemson made its first appearance in the College World Series since 1996. The Tigers beat San Jose State 10-6 before losing to top-ranked Stanford 10-4 to fall into the losers' bracket. Clemson was then eliminated by Louisiana-Lafayette 5-4.

2000—Clemson had a 51-18 record and was ranked #7 in the final *Baseball America* poll, #6 in the final *Collegiate Baseball* poll, and #5 in the final *Sports Weekly* poll.

May 25-27, 2001—The Tigers drew a #2 seed in the Clemson Regional and played host to South Alabama, William & Mary, and Seton Hall, claiming wins over William & Mary (4-1) and Seton Hall (24-4, 8-2) to advance.

June 1,2, 2001—Clemson met Miami (FL) in the Coral Gables Super Regional and was eliminated with a pair of losses (10-8, 14-6). The Hurricanes went on to win the national title.

2001—The Tigers finished 41-22 and were ranked #17 in the final *Baseball America* poll, #13 in the final *Collegiate Baseball* poll, and #14 in the final *Sports Weekly* poll.

February 22-March 15, 2002—Clemson opened the season with 13 straight wins to vault to #2 in the polls. The Tigers defeated Auburn (3), South Carolina (2), and Purdue (3) during the stretch.

March 12, 2002—Clemson set the school record for batting average (.522) in a game in defeating Georgia Southern 20-8. The Tigers had 23 hits in 44 at-bats.

March 17-April 5, 2002—Clemson won 13 more games in a row to start 26-1. The winning streak helped the Tigers rank #1 in all three polls for seven straight weeks.

April 3, 2002—Jeff Baker hit a walkoff homer against Winthrop to give Clemson a 6-4 win. It was his third homer of the game, as he became the first Tiger to hit three homers in a game since 1993 and the first to do it in the history of Doug Kingsmore Stadium.

April 16—June 14, 2002—Khalil Greene had a 34-game hitting streak, the third-longest streak in Tiger history. He batted .519 with 48 RBIs during the streak. The streak ended against Georgia Tech in the College World Series.

May 12, 2002—Khalil Greene set the ACC record for career hits with his 367th at Virginia. He went on to total 403 hits, second-most in NCAA history. In the series, he also went eight straight at-bats with a hit and 13 consecutive plate appearances reaching base safely.

June 7-9, 2002—After sweeping through the Clemson Regional the weekend before, the Tigers fell to Arkansas in the first game of the Clemson Super Regional. But the Tigers fought back to win the final two games and advance to Omaha for the 10th time in school history. Khalil Greene homered in his last at-bat at Doug Kingsmore Stadium.

June 14-21, 2002—Clemson had its most successful run in the College World Series when it won the first two games over hometown favorite Nebraska and Georgia Tech. Against the Cornhuskers, Clemson overcame a 7-2 deficit before rallying to win 11-10. Khalil Greene's dramatic three-run homer in the seventh inning gave the Tigers the lead late in the game. Jeff Baker broke a 10-10 tie with a walkoff double. Michael Johnson then went 3-for-3 with a home run in Clemson's eight-run second inning against Georgia Tech, as the Tigers won their second straight game 9-7. Clemson then lost to South Carolina twice. Clemson had defeated the Gamecocks three out of four times in the regular season. The final game saw Greene start his 269th consecutive game, believed to be an NCAA record. He also played in his 272nd straight game, or every game he was a Tiger. He broke the NCAA record for career doubles (95) during the College World Series, as well.

2002—Clemson had a 54-17 record and was ranked #3 in all three final polls. The Tigers set school records for

homers (112), fielding percentage (.971), and saves (26). The trio of Jeff Baker, Khalil Greene, and Michael Johnson combined for 77 homers and 259 RBIs. They were three of eight Tigers selected in the major league draft, including Greene, who was a first-rounder, and Johnson, who was picked in the second round. Greene went on to earn national Player of the Year honors from all six services that gave the award.

March 4-24, 2003—The Tigers won 14 games in a row. The streak was the seventh-longest in school history and helped catapult Clemson to a #10 national ranking.

April 23 & 25, 2003—Michael Johnson hit a three-run, walkoff homer to beat East Tennessee State 6-3 in 12 innings on April 23. In the next game, against Georgia Tech, Brad McCann hit a two-out, three-run homer in the bottom of the 10th inning to give Clemson a 9-7 win.

2003—Clemson extended its streak to 17 consecutive NCAA Tournament appearances, with defense being the key to many wins. The Tigers had a .969 fielding percentage for the season. Clemson also fell one win short of its 18th-straight 40-win season. Michael Johnson was Clemson's lone first-team All-ACC selection, while left-hander Robert Rohrbaugh earned freshman All-America honors.

April 21-24, 2004—In three games during this span, Clemson won with a walkoff play. On April 21 against Western Carolina, a Catamount error gave the Tigers an 8-7 victory. Two days later, Russell Triplett lined a walkoff single to give the Tigers a 2-1 win over N.C. State. Then the following game, Zane Green, who was hitless in his previous 23 at-bats, hit a single to the wall in right-center to give Clemson a 4-3 win over the Wolfpack.

June 6, 2004—Trailing 9-2 and on the verge of having its season end in the Athens (GA) Regional, Clemson rallied for a 10-9 victory at Georgia, capped by Lou Santangelo's grand slam in the seventh. The seven-run comeback tied the Tiger record for the biggest deficit overcome to gain victory in an NCAA Tourney game. In game two that day versus the Bulldogs, Clemson led 6-4 entering the ninth. But against Tony Sipp, who had been nearly unhittable in the regional, Bobby Felmy and Jason Jacobs hit solo homers to tie the score, then Clint Sammons hit a solo shot in the 10th for the game-winner.

March 19, 2005—Kris Harvey hit two home runs and pitched 7.0 scoreless innings of one-hit ball to lead the Tigers to a 9-1 win over #9 North Carolina. A school record four times during the 2005 season, he hit a long ball and earned the win on the mound in the same game.

April 23, 2005—Taylor Harbin had one of the best games by a Tiger in history. Against the Wolfpack in Raleigh, he went 5-for-5 with three homers, eight RBIs, and five runs to lead the Tigers to a 16-9 win. The three long balls came on consecutive pitches over three at-bats. Harbin added a triple and single and only lacked a double for the cycle. The three home runs tied a school record held by many, while his 16 total bases broke the Clemson record of 15 that was set by Dick Hendley in 1951.

June 3-5, 2005—The Tigers swept their way through the Clemson Regional with wins over North Carolina A&T, College of Charleston, and Oral Roberts by a combined score of 26-5. Andy D'Alessio had the nation's highest batting average in a regional, as he earned Clemson Regional MVP honors thanks to going 7-for-9 (.778) with four doubles, a homer, and four RBIs.

June 11-13, 2005—Clemson traveled to Texas to play #6 Baylor in the Waco Super Regional. The Tigers won game one 4-2 but fell in the last two games by scores of 7-1 and 6-1. The Bears advanced to the College World Series.

2005—Clemson came one win away from a trip to the College World Series. The Tigers finished in the top 20 of all three polls, with a high ranking of #13 by *Collegiate Baseball*. Clemson won 21 ACC regular-season games, finishing second in the standings. The Tigers, who were 19-9 against top-25-ranked teams, started the season 15-13 but went 28-10 the rest of the way. They did all this while playing a difficult schedule, which included 42 of its 66 games against teams that played in the NCAA Tournament. Kris Harvey earned first-team All-America honors and tied for second in the nation with 25 home runs. Freshman Taylor Harbin earned second-team All-America accolades by *Collegiate Baseball*, as he hit an ACC-best 28 doubles, also second-most in the nation.

February 6, 2006—Clemson had its earliest #1 ranking in school history when *Baseball America* put the Tigers atop its poll.

April 22-May 25, 2006—Clemson had a 17-game winning streak, its longest since 1995. The streak included 15 straight victories over ACC teams.

May 18, 2006—Clemson defeated #22 Wake Forest 26-1 at Doug Kingsmore Stadium thanks to 25 hits, including seven home runs. It set a new mark for largest margin of victory (+25) at Doug Kingsmore Stadium.

May 24-28, 2006—Clemson captured the ACC Tournament crown in Jacksonville, FL with a 4-1 record. Sean Clark made a surprise start in the title game against N.C. State and pitched 8.0 masterful innings of one-run and four-hit ball in his first career start in the 8-4 victory. Tyler Colvin earned ACC Tournament MVP honors.

June 2-4, 2006—Clemson won all three of its games in the Clemson Regional, with wins over North Carolina-Asheville, Elon, and Mississippi State, to advance to the super-regional round. Taylor Harbin was named tourney MVP.

June 9-10, 2006—The Tigers won two close games in the Clemson Super Regional over #14 Oral Roberts to advance to the College World Series. Tyler Colvin's walkoff grand slam, the first in school history, gave the Tigers

an 11-8 win in the first game, then Clemson scored three runs in the eighth inning to beat the Golden Eagles 6-5.

June 16-20, 2006—Clemson made its 11th trip to the College World Series. It was also the Tigers' 20th straight NCAA Tournament appearance. Clemson defeated Georgia Tech in its opening game but fell to North Carolina and Cal State Fullerton.

2006—The Tigers drew 184,946 fans for their 39 home dates, an average of 4,742 per date. Jack Leggett was named ACC Coach of the Year after leading the Tigers to a 53-16 overall record, including a 26-9 mark against top-25-ranked teams, an ACC regular-season and tournament title, and a trip to the College World Series. Clemson finished #5 in all three major polls. Josh Cribb and Andy D'Alessio were named to *Collegiate Baseball*'s All-America team. Three Tigers were named to the NCBWA All-America team, including D'Alessio and Tyler Colvin as first-team players and Cribb on the second team. Colvin had a 26-game hitting streak, as Clemson had a 25-1 record during that stretch. Ten Tigers were taken in the major league draft, highlighted by Colvin's first-round pick by the Chicago Cubs.

February 12, 2007—Clemson moved to #1 in the *Baseball America* and *Collegiate Baseball* polls before it played its first game of the season.

March 25, 2007—Clemson's 5-0 win at Maryland gave Head Coach Jack Leggett his 1,000th win in his 28th season as a Division I head coach. He became the 29th head coach in Division I history and second-youngest at age 53 to reach the 1,000-win mark.

May 11-13, 2007—Clemson defeated #2 Florida State twice in three games at Tallahassee, FL. It was the Tigers' first series win at Florida State since 1993. The Seminoles entered the series with a 32-2 home record and had not lost back-to-back games all year until the Tigers won the final two games of the series.

May 26, 2007—David Kopp pitched a complete game, the only by a Tiger in 2007, in Clemson's 5-1 victory over #3 Florida State in the ACC Tournament at Jacksonville, FL. The Florida native allowed just six hits, one unearned run, and no walks with seven strikeouts against the nation's best-hitting team. It also came against Seminole starter Bryan Henry, who entered the game with a perfect 14-0 record but suffered his first loss of the season. The Tigers went 2-1 in the ACC Tourney but did not advance to the finals.

June 1-4, 2007—Clemson won all three of its games in the Myrtle Beach (SC) Regional, with one win over St. John's and two victories over host Coastal Carolina to advance to the super-regional round. In the first game, Brad Chalk hit a two-out, run-scoring single in the ninth inning to give Clemson the walkoff win after it trailed 2-1 entering the bottom of the ninth inning. Four Tigers had at least three hits apiece in each of the two wins over the Chanticleers. Andy D'Alessio was named regional MVP.

June 8-9, 2007—The Tigers lost two close games at Mississippi State by scores of 8-6 and 8-5 in the Starkville (MS) Super Regional in front of 26,335 combined fans.

2007—Clemson averaged 4,810 fans for its 34 home dates and had 163,537 fans in all visit Doug Kingsmore Stadium. Marquez Smith was the Tigers' lone first-team All-ACC selection after Clemson had a 41-23 overall record and 18-12 mark in ACC regular-season games. Clemson finished ranked in the top 15 of all three major polls. Andy D'Alessio tied the school record with 59 career home runs. Brad Chalk had a streak of 50 straight games reaching base via a hit, walk, or hit-by-pitch that started in 2006 and ended in 2007. Eleven Tigers were selected in the major league draft, highlighted by Daniel Moskos, who was the #4 overall pick of the draft. Five Tigers were selected in the first three rounds, as well.

February 24, 2008—For the fourth time in school history, a player hit two home runs in one inning. In the third inning against Mercer at Doug Kingsmore Stadium, Wilson Boyd hit a one-out, solo homer. Later in the frame, he belted a two-out, three-run homer in the Tigers' nine-run inning. Clemson won the game by a score of 10-3.

March 9, 2008—In the second game of a doubleheader against Wake Forest at Hooks Stadium in Winston-Salem, NC, freshman Kyle Parker went 5-for-5 with three homers, a double, five runs, seven RBIs, and 15 totals bases. His last homer, a three-run shot, tied the score in the ninth inning in a game Clemson won by a score of 12-11. Parker had just one homer and two RBI in his career entering the game.

April 20, 2008—Clemson and Duke played to a 6-6 tie in 10 innings at Jack Coombs Field in Durham, NC. It was the Tigers' first draw since 1987. Clemson scored four runs in the ninth, capped by Ben Paulsen's two-out, three-run homer to tie the score. After a scoreless 10th inning, Kyle Parker blasted a two-run homer with no outs in the 11th inning. Immediately thereafter, inclement weather halted play. The game was eventually called due to unplayable field conditions, meaning that Parker's long ball did not count.

2008—Clemson finished the season with a 31-27-1 record and did not advance to the NCAA Tournament for the first time since 1986, ending its 21-year streak. Doug Hogan also had a 24-game hitting streak that started in 2007 and ended in 2008.

March 18, 2009—Five right-handers combined to pitch Clemson's first no-hitter since 1984 in a 14-0 victory over South Carolina-Upstate. Justin Sarratt, Scott Weismann, Kyle Deese, Tomas Cruz, and Matt Vaughn combined to allow just two base runners, one on an error in the outfield on a routine fly ball and one on a walk in the eighth inning. The five pitchers also combined to face only one batter over the minimum.

April 5, 2009—Jack Leggett won his 700th game as Clemson's head coach in the Tigers' 10-1 win over Duke at Doug Kingsmore Stadium.

April 11, 2009—In a memorable day for Kyle Parker, he led the White squad to a win in the football Spring Game by completing 13-21 passes for 171 yards and a touchdown. Then he rushed over to Doug Kingsmore Stadium to play a doubleheader against #5 Miami (FL). Although he did not make it in time to start the first game, he went a combined 3-for-7 with two homers and five RBI in the doubleheader.

April 21, 2009—Jeff Schaus hit a two-out, walkoff grand slam to lift Clemson to a 5-3 win over #19 Coastal Carolina at Doug Kingsmore Stadium.

May 29-June 1, 2009—Clemson won three games facing elimination in a two-day span to capture the Clemson (SC) Regional title and advance to the Tempe (AZ) Super Regional. The Tigers won their opener over Tennessee Tech 5-4 thanks to Jeff Schaus's two-run walkoff double in the ninth inning. After falling to Oklahoma State 3-2 in the next game, Clemson eliminated Tennessee Tech with a 10-0 victory. The Tigers then topped the Cowboys 15-1 and 6-5 to win the regional. The former was Head Coach Jack Leggett's 1,100th career win. In the championship game, Clemson rallied from a 5-1 deficit to score five combined runs in the seventh and eighth innings, capped by Kyle Parker's two-out, two-run single in the eighth inning. Chris Epps was named Regional MVP.

June 6-7, 2009—The Tigers lost two games at #2 Arizona State by scores of 7-4 and 8-2 in the Tempe (AZ) Super Regional.

2009—Clemson had a 44-22 overall record and 19-11 ACC mark, third-best in the league. The Tigers finished in the top 16 of all three major polls. Clemson did not lose more than two games in a row all season. Clemson's 3.68 ERA was fifth-best in the nation, its best finish since 1996. Jeff Schaus (OF) was Clemson's lone first-team All-ACC selection. Nine Tigers were selected in the major league draft, highlighted by Ben Paulsen, who was chosen in the third round. The Tigers also averaged 4,727 for their 36 home dates.

March 7, 2010—Clemson defeated #15 South Carolina 19-6 at Carolina Stadium in Columbia behind two grand slams, one by Chris Epps and one by Phil Pohl. It was the first time the Tigers hit two grand slams in one game since March 3, 1991.

March 17, 2010—Clemson totaled 16 extra-base hits in its 22-6 victory over Georgia Southern at Doug Kingsmore Stadium. The Tigers amassed nine doubles, one triple, and six home runs. Clemson hit four homers in an eight-run first inning. The Tigers also hit back-to-back home runs three times in the game.

April 21, 2010—John Hinson went 5-for-6 with three home runs and seven RBIs in Clemson's 22-4 win over South Carolina-Upstate at Doug Kingsmore Stadium. He hit a solo homer in the second inning, a three-run homer in the third inning, and another three-run homer in the sixth inning.

May 20-22, 2010—Entering the final regular-season weekend trailing Florida State by three games in the ACC standings, the Tigers swept the Seminoles in a three-game series at Doug Kingsmore Stadium to finish in a tie with Florida State in the ACC Atlantic Division standings. However, Clemson was crowed division champion thanks to the tiebreaker of sweeping the series. Clemson won by scores of 9-8, 8-4, and 8-3.

June 4-7, 2010—Clemson won three of its four games in the Auburn (AL) Regional to capture the title. The Tigers trounced Southern Mississippi 10-1 in their first game and faced host Auburn in the winners' bracket. Behind Casey Harman's first career complete game, Clemson topped Auburn 5-2. The Tiger lefty allowed just five hits, two runs, and one walk with eight strikeouts against one of the nation's best offensive teams. After Auburn advanced to face Clemson again, Clemson was one strike away from advancing before Creede Simpson hit a dramatic three-run homer to give Auburn an 11-9 lead. Clemson rallied to cut Auburn's lead to 11-10 but fell short. In the final game of the regional, Clemson came up with several key defensive plays and outlasted Auburn 13-7 to advance to the Clemson Super Regional. John Hinson was named Auburn Regional MVP.

June 12-14, 2010—After falling to Alabama 5-4 in the first game of the Clemson (SC) Super Regional at Doug Kingsmore Stadium, the Tigers rebounded with a 19-5 win in game two to even the series. Then, the Tigers held on to defeat the Crimson Tide 8-6 in game three to advance to the College World Series.

June 21-26, 2010—Clemson made its 12th trip to the College World Series and went 2-2 in four games to finish in a tie for third in the nation. The Tigers topped #1 Arizona State 6-3 in their opener and then defeated #6 Oklahoma 6-4 to improve to 2-0. However, #5 South Carolina downed Clemson twice by scores of 5-1 and 4-3 to end the Tigers' season.

2010—Clemson had a 45-25 overall record and 18-12 ACC mark in winning the ACC Atlantic Division title. The Tigers finished the season ranked #4 in the polls after winning the Auburn (AL) Regional, Clemson (SC) Super Regional, and earning a bid to the College World Series, where it finished tied for third in the country with two wins in Omaha and advanced further than any other ACC team. Kyle Parker was named a first-team All-American and was picked in the first round of the major league draft. Head Coach Jack Leggett was named ABCA Atlantic Region Coach of the Year. The Tigers also averaged 4,694 fans per date for their 35 home dates.

May 17, 2011—Clemson totaled 23 hits and tied a school record for batting average (.523) in a game in its 19-0 win over Davidson. The Tigers scored in all eight of their innings in which they batted. There was also a 127-minute rain delay. During the delay, both teams conducted multiple skits on the field.

July 3, 2011—Bill Wilhelm, Clemson's head baseball coach for 36 seasons from 1958-'93, was one of seven members of the 2011 class inducted into the National College Baseball Hall of Fame. He became the first person associated with Clemson to be inducted into the National College Baseball Hall of Fame. He passed away on December 24, 2010, at the age of 81.

2011—Clemson had a 43-20 overall record and 17-13 ACC mark. The Tigers finished the season ranked as high as #16 in the nation after hosting the Clemson (SC) Regional. After starting the season 14-12, the Tigers won 29 of their final 37 games. The Tigers were sixth in the nation in batting average (.318) and 15th in runs per game (7.1). Clemson led the ACC in batting average (.318) by 14 points and had an ACC-high 106 steals. The Tigers had eight draft picks, led by second-round picks Brad Miller and Will Lamb. Miller, who was 16th in the nation and first in the ACC with a .395 batting average, was named ACC Player of the Year and was a first-team All-American along with earning the Brooks Wallace Shortstop of the Year Award. Lamb had a 25-game hitting streak, the longest by an ACC player in 2011. The Tigers averaged 4,393 fans per date for their 36 home dates.

February 25-26, 2012—Clemson overcame deficits of 4-0 and 6-0 to defeat Maine in both games at Doug Kingsmore Stadium. The Tigers defeated the Black Bears 9-5 after trailing 4-0 on February 25, then rallied from a six-run deficit for a 9-6 win the following day.

March 21, 2012—Jack Leggett won his 1,200th career game as a head coach in the Tigers' 4-2 win over Elon at Fluor Field in Greenville, SC. He became just the 15th head coach at a Division I school to reach that mark.

April 13,17, 2012—Thomas Brittle hit a walkoff single in the 12th inning to give Clemson a 7-6 win over #17 N.C. State on April 13. Four days later, he hit another walkoff single in Clemson's 3-2 win over Charleston Southern. Both walkoff singles scored Tyler Slaton.

May 12,14,25, 2012—Clemson notched three wins over top-ranked Florida State, including its first-ever top-ranked victory at home on May 12. Jon McGibbon's three-run walkoff homer in the ACC Tournament on May 25 gave Clemson a 9-7 win over the Seminoles. The Tigers won three of their four games against #1 Florida State, who went on to play in the College World Series.

2012—Clemson had a 35-28 overall record and 16-14 ACC mark. The Tigers lost just two games by more than four runs and had 19 comeback wins. Clemson led the ACC in fielding percentage (.973). The Tigers had seven draft selections, led by first-round pick Richie Shaffer, who tied for third in the nation in walks (63) and was a first-team All-America player. Thomas Brittle had a 22-game hitting streak, the longest by an ACC player in 2012. Shortstop Jason Stolz committed just four errors in starting all 63 games. The Tigers averaged 4,406 fans per date for their 33 home dates.

April 1, 2013—Clemson defeated No. 1 North Carolina 5-4 in 11 innings on the road. Scott Firth stranded runners at second and third in the eighth, 10th, and 11th innings without allowing a run, while Garrett Boulware's groundout scored Jay Baum for the winning run. It was the first of Clemson's 11 wins in a row, its longest winning streak since 2006.

May 14, 2013—Trailing 7-5 with one out in the ninth inning against USC Upstate, Kevin Bradley hit an opposite-field, three-run homer to give Clemson an 8-7 win. It was his first career homer, while he entered the game with just two career RBIs. He became the first Tiger since 1988 to have his first career long ball be in walk-off fashion. He only started at the last minute due to Jon McGibbon's illness.

May 31-June 3, 2013—Clemson participated in the NCAA Regional at Columbia, S.C. Clemson lost to Liberty 8-3 and defeated St. Louis. Clemson was eliminated by Liberty 3-1.

2013—Clemson had a 40-22 overall record and an 18-12 ACC mark. The Tigers, who were ranked No. 25 in the final *USA Today* poll, totaled an ACC-high 111 steals, 16th-most in the nation. After starting the season 16-11, Clemson won 23 of its next 27 games thanks to winning streaks of 11 and nine games. Garrett Boulware led the team in homers (8) and RBIs (45), while Shane Kennedy led the team in batting average (.317), on-base percentage (.408) and steals (22). Daniel Gossett became the Tigers' first double-digit winner since 2002, as he was 10-4 with a 2.56 ERA. Freshman Matthew Crownover had a 7-3 record and team-best 2.19 ERA, while he led the ACC in ERA (1.73) in league games.

January 3, 2014—Head coach Jack Leggett was inducted into the ABCA Hall of Fame in Dallas, Texas. He was one of seven inductees during the annual convention.

May 17, 2014—Clemson rallied from a 9-2 deficit to defeat Boston College 10-9 in 13 innings. The Tigers were down 9-4 entering the ninth inning but scored five runs, including four with two outs, to tie the score. Jon McGibbon's two-out, three-run double tied the score, then Jay Baum's two-out double scored Garrett Boulware for the winning run. The victory gave Clemson a winning ACC regular-season record.

May 22, 2014—Clemson defeated No. 3 Miami (Fla.) 3-2 in the ACC Tournament, giving head coach Jack Leggett his 1,300th career win. The Tigers trailed 2-0 before

rallying for the walk-off win on Steve Wilkerson's run-scoring single in the ninth inning.

May 30-31, 2014—Clemson lost to Oregon 18-1 and to Xavier 6-4 at the NCAA Regional in Nashville, TN.

2014—Clemson had a 36-25 overall record and 15-14 ACC mark. The Tigers were ranked in the top 25 most of the season and led the ACC with 89 steals and 116 doubles, the latter of which was tied for 18th in the nation. The Tigers were also tied for 20th in the nation in steals and 11th in strikeouts per nine innings pitched. Clemson won 11 of its last 15 games pre-NCAA Tourney games, including two wins in the ACC Tournament, to earn an NCAA Tournament berth. Tyler Krieger led the team in batting average (.338) and was one of seven Tigers who earned All-ACC honors. Daniel Gossett, a Golden Spikes Award semifinalist, had a 7-2 record, 1.93 ERA and 107 strikeouts to earn second-team All-America and first-team All-ACC honors. Matt Campbell added a team-high eight saves, an 0.84 ERA and a .144 opponents' batting average. Clemson averaged 4,379 fans for its 33 home dates.

March 2, 2015—Junior righthander Brody Koerner pitched a four-hit shutout with seven strikeouts in Clemson's 7-0 win at No. 8 South Carolina. Koerner, who won the Bob Bradley Award, was the biggest reason South Carolina did not score a run in a home game for the first time since 1998. He also became the first Tiger to pitch a shutout in Columbia since 1968.

May 12, 2015—Facing Furman at Fluor Field in Greenville, S.C., Clemson trailed 10-0 after two innings but rallied for a 23-15 win. The Tigers scored in each of the last seven innings, including eight runs in the seventh inning. Tiger batters totaled 22 hits, 15 walks, and two hit-by-pitches. The nine-inning game lasted 4:42, and it was the most runs scored by the Tigers since 2006.

May 14-16, 2015—Clemson swept No. 8 Florida State in a three-game series at Tallahassee, FL, by a combined score of 20-7. It was Clemson's first-ever sweep at Florida State. The Tigers won by scores of 4-1, 7-0, and 9-6, while the Seminoles scored five runs in the bottom of the ninth inning of the series finale. Clemson handed Florida State, who was 27-4 at home entering the series, its first three-game sweep at home since 2006.

May 18, 2015—Junior lefthander Matthew Crownover was named ACC Pitcher of the Year in a vote by the 14 ACC head coaches as announced by the league office. Crownover was Clemson's first-ever ACC Pitcher of the Year, as the ACC first named one in 2005. Kris Benson was the last Tiger hurler to earn ACC Player of the Year honors in 1996.

May 28, 2015—Junior lefthander Matthew Crownover and sophomore catcher Chris Okey were named All-Americas by *Collegiate Baseball*. Crownover was a first-team selection, while Okey was a second-team pick.

May 29-30, 2015—Clemson lost to Arizona State 7-4 and Pepperdine 10-8 at the NCAA Regional in Fullerton, CA.

2015—Clemson had a 32-29 overall record and a 16-13 ACC mark. Clemson had an 8-5 record against top-25 teams and a 7-4 record against top-10 teams, including a 4-0 record on opponents' home fields. Matthew Crownover, a first-team All-American and ACC Pitcher of the Year, had a 10-3 record and 1.82 ERA. Chris Okey earned first-team All-America honors by hitting .315 with 12 homers and 57 RBIs, while freshman Reed Rohlman was a third-team All-American who batted .356 with three home runs and 58 RBIs. Clemson averaged 4,251 fans for its 28 home dates.

June 4, 2015—Clemson parted ways with head coach Jack Leggett, who led the program to 21 NCAA Tournament appearances in 22 seasons and six College World Series berths. He also recorded 955 wins and was the seventh-winningest coach in the country during his tenure in Tigertown.

June 10, 2015—Sophomore catcher Chris Okey was named a first-team All-American by NCBWA. Okey joined junior left-hander Matthew Crownover as first-team All-Americans from the 2015 team. Crownover was named a first-team All-American by *Collegiate Baseball*. It marked the first time since 2006 that Clemson had multiple first-team All-Americans on one team. Crownover earned second-team All-America honors by NCBWA, as well.

June 18, 2015—Clemson hired Monte Lee to become just its third head coach since 1958. Lee served as head coach at College of Charleston from 2009-'15.

May 8, 2016—Clemson defeated No. 9 NC State 2-1 behind Pat Krall's complete-game victory in his first career start to win the series 2-1. With the victory, the Tigers won back-to-back series against Florida State and NC State, meaning Clemson won two top-10 series in a row. It marked the first time since 1994 and just the second time since the ACC went to a three-game series format in 1990 that Clemson accomplished the feat.

May 23, 2016—Freshman outfielder Seth Beer was named ACC Player of the Year, as announced by the league office. Beer is the first freshman to be voted ACC Player of the Year since the award was established in 1969. Beer is the 13th Tiger to earn ACC Player of the Year honors and the first since shortstop Brad Miller in 2011.

May 26-29, 2016—Clemson won all four of its games in the ACC Tournament at Durham (NC) Bulls Athletic Park to capture the ACC title. The Tigers defeated four teams who all played in the NCAA Tournament, including three teams that hosted a regional. The Tigers edged Virginia 5-4, Louisville 5-3, and Wake Forest 5-4 before defeating Florida State 18-13 in the ACC Championship Game. Mike Triller was named ACC Tournament MVP.

June 3, 2016—The Tigers won their 10th game in a row by defeating Western Carolina 24-10 in the Clemson Regional. Clemson tied a Tiger NCAA Tournament record with 24 runs and set the school NCAA Tourney record with seven home runs. The 10-game winning streak started with a 17-4 win at Georgia Southern on May 15. During the stretch, the Tigers were 8-0 away from home.

June 3-5, 2016—Clemson defeated Western Carolina twice, 24-10 and 15-3, but lost to Oklahoma State twice, 12-2, and 9-2, at the NCAA Regional in Clemson, SC

June 8, 2016—Outfielder Seth Beer was named national co-Freshman of the Year by *Collegiate Baseball*. He became the first Tiger freshman to win a national award. He joined Tennessee Tech's Kevin Strohschein as recipient of the honor.

June 15, 2016—Seth Beer, Chris Okey, and Pat Krall were named All-Americans by NCBWA. Beer and Okey were first-team selections, while Krall was a second-team choice.

June 27, 2016—Seth Beer, Chris Okey, and Pat Krall were named All-Americans by *Perfect Game*. Pat Krall and Seth Beer were named to the first-team and Chris Okey was named to the second team.

June 17, 2016—Freshman outfielder Seth Beer was named the 30th recipient of the Dick Howser Trophy, presented annually to the national Player of the Year. The Dick Howser Trophy committee and National *Collegiate Baseball* Writers Association presented the award on Saturday, June 18, at a national news conference at TD Ameritrade Park prior to the opening game of the 70th annual College World Series. Beer is the first freshman to win the award.

2016—Clemson had a 44-20 overall record and 16-14 ACC mark. The Tigers, who were ranked in the final polls as high as No. 15 by *USA Today*, then won the ACC Tournament title at Durham, NC, with a 4-0 record before hosting a regional as the No. 7 national seed. Clemson had 24 come-from-behind wins and set a school record with 14 one-run victories. Seth Beer, Pat Krall, and Chris Okey earned first-team All-America honors, the first time in history Clemson had three first-team All-Americans in one season. Beer became the first freshman to win the Dick Howser Trophy as national Player of the Year and was the ACC Player of the Year, also a first by a freshman, after hitting .369 with an ACC-high 18 homers, 70 RBIs, and a .535 on-base percentage. Clemson averaged 4,664 fans for its 35 home dates.

MEN'S
Basketball

When basketball first hit the Clemson campus in 1912, the sport provided the corps of cadets an activity to witness and in which to participate during the winter season. This new branch of athletics soon grew in popularity among students, and shortly thereafter it became a favorite amongst intramural sports.

From a modest four-game inaugural season in 1912 to today's rigorous ACC schedule, the Clemson basketball program has reached new heights in advancing to post-season play during the decade of the 1980s, '90s, and the school's most successful run from 2008-'11.

Basketball at Clemson has become the entertaining indoor activity Dr. Naismith, the inventor of the game, intended.

THE FIRST SEASON

Clemson first fielded a basketball team in the winter of 1912. The Tigers won two games on their first day of play (February 9), defeating Furman 46-12 and the Butler Guards 78-6. Both games were played at Furman.

In the first game of the day, against Furman, Clemson's center and captain, James Erwin, scored 22 points, while his brother John scored 20 points to lead the Tigers to victory.

In the second game of the day, Clemson defeated the Butler Guards 78-6. James Erwin scored 58 points, while brother John scored 16 in leading the Tigers to victory. The 58 points still rank as a single season record by a Clemson player over 100 years later.

Frank Dobson was the Tigers coach during the first two seasons of basketball, and he also coached the Tigers football team.

Clemson's first basketball team was formed in 1912.

ERWIN BROTHERS WERE THE FIRST STARS

Two of the early stars of Clemson basketball were brothers John and James Erwin. Their impact on Clemson athletics at that time was immeasurable. Not only were they tennis champions, but great basketball players.

James Erwin was born on December 14, 1892, in Spartanburg, SC, to James and Margaret Caldwell Erwin. His father ran a laundry in the city.

On the basketball court, he played in the 1911-12 and 1912-13 seasons. James graduated from Clemson in textiles in 1913. He died on February 6, 1978, in Spartanburg, SC.

Clemson tennis and basketball great John Watson Erwin was born on April 5, 1894.

He graduated from Clemson in 1914, the same year that Frank Johnstone Jervey (the man that the Jervey Athletic Center is named for) graduated. He majored in textiles and put together a very impressive athletic résumé.

John was on the Clemson tennis team in 1912, 1913, and 1914. He served as the president of the State Intercollegiate Tennis Association his senior year in 1914. This position was in charge of running the annual state college tennis tournament in which various state teams competed.

Like his brother, John was on the first basketball squad that Clemson fielded and played forward in 1912, 1913, and 1914. He was also the head coach of the 1914 basketball team, holding the distinction of being the only player-coach in Clemson basketball history.

The 1913 Taps yearbook called him "a fine point getter and very aggressive in every play."

A veteran of World War I, John was president and owner of Erwin Wholesale Co., a grocery wholesaler in Spartanburg. He died on March 3, 1972, in Spartanburg.

FIRST COURTS

The Tigers played their first home basketball games on Bowman Field when weather permitted. When inclement weather was in the area, the games were played in the basement of Sikes Hall.

Clemson began playing its games in the newly completed YMCA in 1916.

Clemson played its first game at the YMCA (currently the Holtzendorff YMCA building), tying Presbyterian 39-39 on February 1. Audley H. Ward, a Clemson professor, coached the Tigers.

During the fall of 1921, the Clemson student body helped level the ground for the new facility. This new building was located south of Riggs Field. The building was a quasi hut and provided Clemson a larger regulation indoor basketball court. Clemson lost to Georgia 24-16 in the dedication of a new basketball arena on January 13, 1922.

Athletic Director Mutt Gee and Josh Cody were instrumental in the building of the Fike Field House, which gave Clemson a state-of-the-art basketball arena during that day. The gymnasium was built at a cost of $60,000 and was the first stage of Fike Field House to be built.

Cody was the head coach for both the football and basketball teams in 1927-31, the last coach in Clemson history to coach the two revenue-producing sports.

The rest of Fike was built from the receipts of the 1940 Cotton Bowl, the first bowl game that a Clemson football team attended.

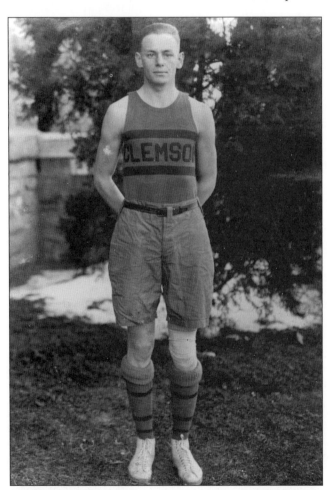

John Erwin was a player-coach for the Tigers in the 1913-14 season. He was also the head coach after he graduated in the 1914-15 season.

Bowman Field—This is a picture of what is thought to be Clemson's very first home game on March 9, 1912.

Holtzendorff YMCA was Clemson's home court from 1916–'21.

This basketball court was the Tigers' home in 1922-29. It was located above and south of Riggs Field. This was where the tennis courts were located, as well. The frat quad is located there now.

Clemson played in Fike Field House from 1929–'68.

Furman defeated Clemson 34-28 in the first game played at Fike Field House on January 7, 1930.

BANKS MCFADDEN LEADS CLEMSON TO CONFERENCE CHAMPIONSHIP

In 1939, Clemson belonged to the old Southern Conference, a 20-team league at the time. The conference consisted of all the schools now in the Atlantic Coast Conference, along with South Carolina, Davidson, The Citadel, Washington & Lee, VMI, and a few others. Because there were so many members, only the top eight teams were invited each year to participate in the conference tournament.

Banks McFadden, Clemson's only two-sport All-American and retired intramurals director, was a junior center on the 1938-39 team.

"The previous season, we had been runner-up in the conference for the first time and we had a pretty good team coming into the 1938-39 season," he remembers. "But we didn't get off to a good start at all that year, and for a while it looked as if we wouldn't even be invited to the tournament.

"Most of our starters were also on the football team and since the two seasons almost overlapped, it seemed we always got off to a poor start. By the middle of January, we were 2-2 in the conference. Back then we couldn't miss class for athletics so our coaches decided we would go to the state of North Carolina one weekend and play all three teams. We did and we lost on three consecutive nights to UNC, N.C. State, and Duke, making us 2-5 in the conference with only five conference games left to play."

But the Tigers made an amazing comeback and won 10 of their next 11 games and managed to win an invitation to the tournament. At the time, only 10 players could travel with the team. Retired Dean of Student Affairs George Coakley was selected as one of the 10 for a very unusual reason.

"Our coach, 'Fearless Joe' Davis was very superstitious," Coakley said. "I believe that the only reason I got to go to the tournament is that I sat next to him during those games! I had an identical twin on the team and he didn't get to go."

The Southern Conference Tournament was always held in Raleigh, NC. This year, instead of the usual eight participants, 11 teams were asked to the tournament, because five teams were tied for seventh and eighth place. Clemson was one of these teams, so the Tigers had to play an extra game before making it to the final eight.

The first contest was on Wednesday night against the North Carolina Tar Heels, who had beaten the Tigers the previous season in the final game. UNC led until the final seconds of the game, when a Banks McFadden basket put Clemson ahead to stay and the Tigers won by one point.

The following night, the Tigers faced number-one-seeded Wake Forest. Once again, the Deacons held the

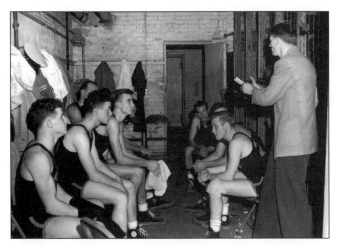

Banks McFadden, standing, was a basketball All-American in 1939. He led Clemson to the Southern Conference Championship in 1939. He also coached the Tigers in 1946-56.

lead until late in the second half, when McFadden put the Tigers ahead. This time the margin of victory was two points. On Friday night, the Tigers took a fairly easy victory from Davidson, winning by 16 points. The team was tired, but excited about being in the finals.

"Every night after the games, the team would walk downtown for a while," Coakley said. "We would walk past a sporting goods shop that displayed the conference trophy in the window. We would eye that thing each time we walked by, but we never expected we would win it since we had to win four games to do it."

Before the Tigers could win that trophy, they had one more team to defeat.

"The class of the whole tournament was a team called Maryland," said McFadden. "They weren't very big, but they had very good ball handlers. We surprised even ourselves and won by 12 points."

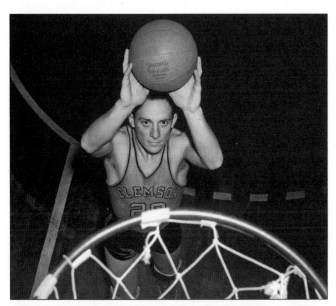

Dude Buchanan was a standout basketball and baseball player. He was a member of the 1939 Southern Conference basketball team. He was the first scholarship athlete who was not a member of the football team.

The Tigers were the Southern Conference Champions and returned to Clemson. However, the team had to leave the trophy in Raleigh to be repaired.

"I remember we were so happy and I had the trophy," said Dude Buchanan, a star on the 1939 team. While we were celebrating, I dropped the trophy and we had to leave it back in Raleigh to get repaired. We got to campus and the cadets welcome us back to campus with a pep meeting. Everyone was anxious to see the trophy and was asking to see the cup. Coach Davis stared at me and told them 'You can't see it, Buchanan dropped it and it's back in Raleigh getting fixed.'"

Traditionally, the conference champ was invited to the National Invitational Tournament, but instead of the Tigers receiving an invitation, Maryland went to the tournament in Madison Square Garden.

"We expected to get an invitation, but we were so elated with the championship that we really didn't question it. After all, we were just some overgrown football players who had managed to play well as a basketball team!" McFadden said.

Years later, McFadden and Coakley found out that the 1939 basketball squad had indeed received an invitation to the NIT, but that it had been turned down by Athletic Director Jess Neely, who also happened to be the football coach.

"I almost passed out!" said McFadden. "But he said that our bread and butter was football and since most of us were football players, we had to get back for spring practice."

Spring practice must have gone well since that year's football team was invited to the Cotton Bowl.

YARBOROUGH: LONE DIAMOND IN CLEMSON ROUGH

Bill Yarborough of nearby Walhalla first played on the 1952-53 Clemson basketball squad when freshmen were eligible. He earned a second letter for his play during the first semester of his sophomore season, 1953-54, but dropped out of school for the second semester. Yarborough then resumed play at Clemson during his junior year (1954-55) and played during what normally would have been his senior season (1955-56).

Prior to the 1956-57 season, North Carolina Coach Frank McGuire requested an extra year of eligibility for Tar Heel Jerry Vayda, who, like Yarborough, had sat out one semester for academic reasons. When the vote came before the ACC athletic directors, Frank Howard of Clemson suggested that Vayda be granted the extra year of eligibility only if the same grace year were given to Yarborough.

Perhaps figuring that the return of a star player could make hapless Clemson more competitive within the league, the athletic directors bought Howard's idea, and Yarborough returned for a fifth season.

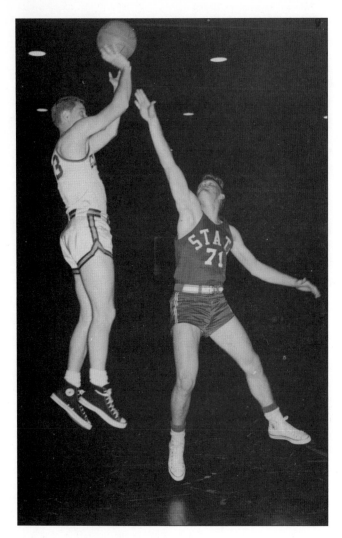

Bill Yarborough was fourth in the nation in scoring with a 28.3 ppg. average in the 1954-55 season.

Yarborough's return actually didn't help the Tigers' cause much. Their record was 7-17, which fell right in line with the other marks during his career: 8-10, 5-18, 2-21, and 9-17.

Those marks accurately reflect basketball's place on the Clemson athletic department pecking order during the early days of the ACC. Basketball, as an intercollegiate sport, rated only slightly above crew in Howard's view. Howard, who doubled as Clemson's athletic director and football coach, once said of crew that he would not fund a sport in which people "sat on their butts and moved backward."

Howard wasn't much interested in a sport that was not revenue producing, and basketball at Clemson did not make enough money "to pay the gymnasium's light bill," according to Yarborough.

Banks McFadden was one of Howard's chief assistants in football and filled his spare time during the winter coaching basketball. Many of the basketball players were actually football players who merely wanted to stay in shape year-round.

Yarborough was an exception. After leading Walhalla High School to 33 straight wins and the South Carolina

Class C high school championship in 1952, he was recruited by Wake Forest and Clemson. He selected Clemson only because Wake Forest Coach Murray Greason thought that the 6-foot Yarborough was too small to play forward.

Yarborough played guard at Clemson and developed into the Tigers' top reserve as a freshman. He was a starter the remaining four years and eventually earned second-team All-ACC honors in 1955 and 1956. His two-hand set shot from outside the key was deadly, and he eventually copied the running one-hand shot of his hero, N.C. State's Sammy Ranzino.

Yarborough's 46-point effort against South Carolina in 1955 remains the modern-day scoring record at Clemson and was never topped in Clemson's old Fike Field House.

Yarborough finished the year fourth in the nation in scoring with a 28.3 figure.

"That game was actually one of my biggest disappointments," says Yarborough. "We didn't win, and that really taught me a lesson about one player not being good enough to beat an entire team.

Yarborough learned to lose at Clemson. In his five seasons, the Tigers were 31-83, including a woeful 4-47 mark against ACC competition. Clemson lost its first 26 games in the ACC before defeating Virginia for its lone league win in 1956.

"I thought we'd never win that first one," Yarborough recalls. "It was a tough go at Clemson in those days, but it was an educational experience."

MAHAFFEYS DEALT CLEMSON FOUR OF A KIND

Probably no other university in the nation has the distinction that Clemson does when it comes to brothers playing basketball. And there are even some father-son duos. A.C. Swails (father) and Jack Swails (son) played roundball for the Tigers over 30 years apart. The Krajack brothers, George and Eddie, had their career overlap two seasons, while Clarke and Ed Bynum were cousins and missed overlapping one season.

Twins George and Francis Coakley played both baseball (1939-41) and basketball, and later on, George's son John lettered three years, 1968-71, on the hard court.

In 2009, Devin Booker joined his older brother, Trevor, at Clemson, and the two became the fourth-highest scoring brother combination in ACC history. They were also one of three sets of brothers in ACC history to both be named to the all-conference team.

But the most unusual occurrence was the arrival of the Mahaffey brothers.

Clemson had four brothers from LaGrange, GA, bring their talents, and there was at least one brother on the varsity team for 12 consecutive seasons (1959-1970). In football, there were four Ducworth brothers (Ronnie, George, Thomas, and C.H.) who earned a total of eight letters, but they were not consecutive like the Mahaffeys.

The Mahaffeys' father, Howard T. Mahaffey, graduated from Clemson in the early '30s, and even though he was nearly as tall as his sons, the father played baseball for the Tigers.

The story goes that Mr. and Mrs. Mahaffey brought their sons to Clemson once on a visit, approaching town from the west on Highway 123. About two miles from campus, the road tops a hill for a panoramic view of the university. It is said that on this visit, Mr. Mahaffey stopped the car as Clemson came into view.

He had the boys exit from the car and said to them: "Now this is where you are going to college."

Working as a ball boy at local tennis tournaments in La Grange, GA, during the early l950s, eight-year-old Tommy Mahaffey's pay was an old basketball.

"They were getting ready to discard it," Tommy said. "I took the ball home. Finally, the next Christmas, we talked our dad into giving us a basketball goal. He put it up on the garage, and we got another three or four years out of that old basketball."

Mr. Howard Mahaffey's 1955 Christmas gift of $35 for a basketball goal ultimately paid for four college educations. It was a gift that kept on giving! Tommy, Donnie, Randy, and Richie Mahaffey all learned the game in the family driveway. They all played the game at Clemson University.

The first son, Tommy (6-foot-7), enrolled at Clemson in 1958-59. Donnie (6-foot-8) enrolled as a freshman in 1960-61, Randy's freshman year was 1963-64, and the last one, Richie (6-foot-7), came aboard in 1966-67. Tommy's senior year overlapped Donnie's sophomore season, and

that is the only time during these dozen years that two of the brothers were on the varsity team together.

The Mahaffey family was represented at Clemson in 1959-70. At least one of the four brothers played for Clemson every year in those 12 seasons, and one brother led Clemson in rebounding for nine straight seasons, 1960-68. Each brother broke the previous brother's Clemson career rebound record.

Over the 12 seasons, the Mahaffeys collectively played 300 basketball games, scored 3,555 points, and had 2,728 total rebounds. Their names still rank prominently in the Clemson record book in many areas. All four graduated from Clemson.

Randy is the only one of the quartet to play pro ball. He was picked in the second round of the draft by Los Angeles but ended up playing for the Kentucky Colonels, New York Nets, and Carolina Cougars of the old ABA.

PRESS MARAVICH AND BOBBY ROBERTS

Clemson's basketball coach in 1957-62 was Peter "Press" Maravich. During this time, he led Clemson to a 55-96 record. However, at that time the Tiger basketball team was not giving the full allotment of scholarships, but he did well considering the limitations.

Maravich grew up in the steel mill town of Aliquippa, PA, right outside of Pittsburgh. Press was born in 1915 to his parents, Vajo and Sara Maravich. They first lived on the south side in Pittsburgh. Press's father worked as a locomotive engineer in the steel mills. There were seven children, including Press. Of the seven, only Press survived infancy. Two years later, his father was killed in a train accident. His mother married again, and they moved to Aliquippa.

As a boy, he got the nickname "Press" because he always had an opinion on every topic. His cousin, Bob Maravich, said he was just like the *Pittsburgh Press Newspaper*. Most Aliquippans of that time, especially the Serbs, had nicknames, and Press's stayed with him the rest of his life.

Of course, Maravich's famous son Pete grew up in Clemson and was here through his junior high years.

In 1958, Maravich hired Bobby Roberts as an assistant coach. The two would go through Pennsylvania, especially the Beaver Valley, and met many Serbs of Aliquippa.

The finest moment for Coach Maravich at Clemson was in 1962, when Clemson upset N.C. State and Duke in the ACC Tournament and advanced to the ACC Championship game for the first time in the school's history. Clemson lost to Wake Forest in the finals, 77-66.

After Maravich left Clemson, Roberts became the head coach for eight years in 1962-70. He followed in Maravich's footsteps, recruiting players in the Pennsylvania area, and found one of Clemson's best players in Aliquippa—Butch Zatezalo.

In 1967, The Tigers defeated all four Big-Four North Carolina schools in an eight-day period, including number-four ranked North Carolina. Jim Sutherland was

Randy Mahaffey was one of four brothers to play for Clemson. He was first-team All-ACC in 1967.

Press Maravich was the first coach in school history to guide the Tigers to the championship game of the ACC Tournament. In 1962, the Tigers lost to Wake Forest in the ACC title game.

Bobby Roberts was the Clemson coach in 1962-70. He was the head coach when Littlejohn Coliseum opened in 1968.

named ACC Student-Athlete of the Year (Jim Weaver Award) and was the recipient of the Norris Medal (Clemson's Outstanding Student).

Sutherland also was fourth in the nation in free-throw percentage (89.7). He was the winner of an NCAA post-graduate scholarship. Randy Mahaffey was chosen as a first-team All-ACC player.

Also under Roberts's era at Clemson, Littlejohn Coliseum opened its doors, as Clemson defeated Georgia Tech 76-72 in the first game in the new arena on November 30, 1968.

POSTSEASON PLAY STARTS FOR CLEMSON

At the end of the 1975 season, freshmen Skip Wise and Tree Rollins led Clemson to the Tigers' first-ever postseason bid. Although the Tigers lost to Providence in the first round of the NIT, the foundation was laid for Clemson's greatest era in basketball.

The 1974-75 Tigers finished the season 17-11 overall and tied for second in the ACC at 8-4. Clemson finished ranked 19th in the final UPI Coaches' poll.

Five years later, under then-Head Coach Bill Foster, the Tigers went to the NCAA Tournament for the first time and advanced to the Elite Eight, losing to eventual champions UCLA.

TREE PLANTED SEEDS OF TIGERS' HOOPS GROWTH

Wayne "Tree" Rollins was perhaps the most significant basketball signee in the history of the Clemson program.

As a high school All-America in Cordele, GA, Rollins was recruited by more than 200 schools. He visited 11 before selecting the Tigers, instantly making them a threat to win the ACC championship for the first time.

"That was an exciting time," says Rollins, who once was crafty enough to schedule visits to Florida State and Clemson on the same weekend. "Each weekend I could go somewhere different. For a high school guy to travel that way was a tremendous educational experience."

Four years later, Rollins had taken Clemson out of the ACC's basement and into its upper echelon. Although the Tigers failed to win a league crown, Rollins left Clemson as the best center in the school's history and one of the best ever in the ACC.

In 110 games from 1974 through 1977, Rollins averaged 13.3 points and 11.9 rebounds. Twice he led the ACC in rebounding, and three times he was second-team All-ACC.

Before Rollins departed Clemson for a lengthy career in the NBA, his jersey No. 30 was the first retired by the school. His 1,311 career rebounds and 450 blocked shots remain school records.

Tree Rollins was a three-time second-team All-ACC selection.

"More than basketball, the biggest thing about him was that he was such an unselfish guy and had such a great attitude," says Bill Foster, who succeeded Tates Locke as Clemson's coach for Rollins's final two seasons. "He's a super person, just a fine guy."

In the end, Rollins chose Clemson because of his liking for Locke and because Clemson was a short drive from Cordele.

"The people at Clemson were great to me. It was a nice, small town and just a great experience for me."

In his second game at Clemson, Rollins scored 22 points to go with 20 rebounds and nine blocked shots against St. John's. From the outset, Rollins was an intimidator. He picked up the nickname "Tree" as a 6-foot-8 junior high student and continued to stand out like a tree both on and off the court at Clemson.

"If someone shouted, 'Hey, Wayne,' on campus, I probably wouldn't even turn around," Rollins said.

The only area in which Rollins did not stand out was on offense. He scored 20 or more points in a game 19 times at Clemson, and three times ranked among the ACC's top 10 field goal shooters. But Rollins barely averaged 10 field goal attempts a game for his career.

His forte was rebounding and blocking shots, and nobody did that better than the kid with a 42-inch sleeve. He registered the only statistical triple-doubles (double figures in three categories) in Clemson history with 20 points, 14 rebounds, and 10 blocked shots against Presbyterian as a junior and 16, 15, and 10, respectively, against Duke as a senior.

Rollins's play was instrumental in taking Clemson basketball to new heights. The Tigers had their first winning season (14-12) since 1967 when Rollins was a freshman. Then they were 17-11, 18-10, and 22-6 from 1975 through 1977, marking the first time in more than 50 years that Clemson had four consecutive winning seasons. Within the ACC, Rollins' presence made Clemson a title contender.

The Tigers finished tied for second in 1975 and 1977 and came within inches of reaching the title game of the '75 ACC Tournament. A follow-up shot by Rollins missed at the end of regulation, and Clemson dropped a 76-71 overtime decision to UNC in the semifinals.

"It rolled around the rim and out," Rollins says. "It actually went in, but wouldn't stay down."

Shortly after that loss, Clemson accepted its first postseason tournament bid but lost to Providence in the first round of the NIT.

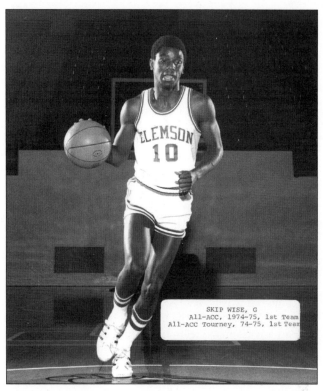

Skip Wise was the first freshman in history to be named first-team All-ACC.

"We just weren't able to win the big one when I was there," says Rollins. "Even when we went to the NIT, we went up to New York with the attitude that it was second-best."

Foster talks at length of Rollins's rebounding and shot-blocking abilities. But his most vivid memory of Rollins is that of a senior in 1977 who was the first to help the freshmen carry the team luggage on road trips.

"He was very coachable," Foster said. "His attitude was just unbelievably good." In the 1974-75 season, Clemson advanced to the NIT and finished 17th in the final UPI poll, as Skip Wise became the first freshman in league history to make first-team All-ACC. The Tigers defeated three top-10 teams (#3 Maryland, #4 N. C. State, and #10 North Carolina) along the way.

BILL FOSTER MAKES CLEMSON ELITE

In Bill Foster's first season at Clemson, he led the Tigers to consecutive road wins over fifth-ranked Wake Forest and second-ranked Maryland. Greg Coles's behind-the-back shot from 15 feet away contributed to the win at Maryland and thus started one of the best runs in Clemson basketball history.

In 1977, Tree Rollins added to that when he was chosen third-team AP All-American and was the 14th overall pick by the Atlanta Hawks in the NBA draft. Rollins had his number 30 retired before his last home game. The team was ranked as high as tenth in the country that year, the highest ranking achieved by a Clemson team at the time.

The Tigers won 22 games to set a Clemson record and was the first Tiger team to win at least 20 games in a season. Then, in 1979, the Tigers were chosen for the NIT and went to Rupp Arena and beat Kentucky 68-67, in overtime.

In 1980, Bill Foster's team was selected to the NCAA Tournament for the first time ever and advanced to the finals of the Western Regional. Clemson reached a high ranking of 10 at one junction of the season. The Tigers also defeated six top-20 teams over the course of the season, including fourth-ranked UNC and top-ranked Duke in the same week. It was Clemson's first win over a #1-ranked team in basketball.

Billy Williams was a Helms Foundation All-America and first-team All-ACC. Bobby Conrad was named the ACC's Student-Athlete of the Year (Jim Weaver Award) and recipient of the Norris Medal (Clemson's Outstanding Student).

Though it was their first time in the NCAA Tournament, the Tigers' run to the Elite Eight that year is still the deepest any Clemson team has advanced in the national tournament. That year, Clemson knocked off Utah State and then a Danny Ainge-led BYU team to reach the Sweet 16 Round.

The Tigers then knocked off Lamar, 74-66, to advance to the Elite Eight and West Regional Final, where UCLA beat the Tigers, 85-74, to end the season. Clemson closed the year with a 23-9 record. The 23 wins at the time were the most for any Clemson team in history.

The Tigers went 20-11 in 1981, and afterward Larry Nance was chosen in the first round of NBA Draft by the Phoenix Suns. The Tigers won the Rainbow Classic in Hawaii and beat eventual National Champion Indiana in the process on the way to a 12-1 start.

In 1983-84, Bill Foster coached his final season at Clemson. The Tigers ran to an 11-2 start, including a 72-71 win over South Carolina and a 66-61 overtime victory over Marquette. Clemson then defeated defending NCAA Champion NC State by 63-61 on January 9th, followed by a victory over a Mark Price-led Georgia Tech team. But the Tigers lost 12 of their last 15 games, and the Foster era ended with a 14-14 mark.

In his nine years at Clemson, Foster had only one losing season, while posting a 156-106 record. He is third in Clemson history in win percentage, and his 16 wins against top-20 teams is tied for the most in school history. He owns the record for most overtime victories with 13.

BIG GAME, LARGE CROWD

It was the perfect night for an upset.

On January 9, 1980, one of Clemson's biggest landmark basketball wins occurred before the largest crowd in Littlejohn Coliseum.

The Clemson students were back in town from their Christmas and holiday break on this Wednesday night. Number-one Duke was in town and everyone wanted to see the 18th-ranked Tigers tangle with the Blue Devils that night.

The Blue Devils had its share of household names: Gene Banks, Kenny Dennard, Mike Gminski, Bob Bender, and Vince Taylor. But so did Clemson, as Larry Nance, Horace Wyatt, Moose Campbell, Bobby Conrad, and Billy Williams rounded out the starters for Clemson. These Tigers would eventually make up the team that advanced to the NCAA's Elite Eight later that season.

There was a Clemson women's game prior to the men's game that night. Fans were coming into Littlejohn in droves. For the women's game there were 9,000 people, a Clemson women's attendance record that still stands today. With that many people in Littlejohn that early, how many more would squeeze into the arena? When all was said and done, there were 13, 864 people in Littlejohn Coliseum, which had a seating capacity of 10,638.

They were sitting and standing everywhere; in the aisles, around the concourse that separates the lower bowl and the upper sections of Littlejohn, and everywhere else where a person could see the court. They probably would have sat on the rafters and catwalks above the court and around the ceiling, but there were not enough ladders to go up there.

"At that time, if a student had an activity card, we did not turn them away," said longtime Clemson Athletic Ticket Manager and current Game Management Director, Van Hilderbrand.

"This is not to say we weren't safety conscious," said Hilderbrand. "Duke is a high- profile program and we had no classes the next day. I remember the student line going from Littlejohn Coliseum down the hill to the football stadium, up the street going toward Fike Field House, going pass Howard's rock and all the way to gate one of the football stadium.

"I also recall how orderly the students were that night, and they understood our predicament. With that said, all the fans in general understood that we were going to have a large crowd and it was going to be packed and crowded. We started letting students sit in the aisles, one per step. We were in constant contact with then-Athletic Director Bill McLellan and the Fire Marshall and kept them informed of the situation," said Hilderbrand.

"We did not turn any students away. The decision was made in cooperation with the appropriate officials to let all the students in that wanted to come to the game. We did not oversell the seats, we simply had more students that night and it seemed as if all the Clemson students wanted to come to the big game—and they did. We didn't have any complaints from the large crowd that night.

"Although we changed our policy on the number of people that were allowed in the coliseum later on, we had a good and a very cooperative crowd, and I think the packed house helped the Tigers that night," said Hilderbrand.

The record crowd had great expectations for the clash between the top-ranked Blue Devils and the Tigers, and the two teams did not disappoint.

In regulation, Duke built its largest lead of the game, a five-point advantage, 57-52, with 12:17 left as Taylor made two free throws. However, Clemson went on a 6-0 run and took a 58-57 lead over two minutes later when Nance hit a hook shot. Duke took a 66-62 advantage with 4:54 left when Banks hit a jumper from the baseline.

Clemson's Campbell made a layup 10 seconds later. Clemson then got the ball back, and Gminski fouled Campbell, sending him to the line for a 1+1 opportunity. He calmly made both with 4:26 remaining, tying the score at 66-66.

After this point, there was no more scoring in regulation. Duke decided to hold the ball for a last shot, as there was no shot clock in college basketball in those days. Duke called a timeout with 13 seconds left to set up the last-second shot. Clemson then called a timeout after Duke took the floor so the Tigers could set up their defense. What happened in this timeout helped send the game into overtime thanks to longtime Athletic Communications Director Tim Bourret.

"I'm from Hartford, CT, and during the Christmas break I saw Duke play at Providence," explained Bourret. "Duke was in the same situation at that particular time, they needed a bucket at the end of the game and what they did was to let Chip Engelland throw the inbound pass to Gminski and the defense collapsed on him and he would get the ball back to an open Chip Engelland, who was a great shooter. It worked perfectly for them in the Providence game.

"I was not working for the Clemson radio network that season and I saw Engelland check into the game," said Bourret. "I immediately went to the Clemson bench and told Tiger Assistant Coach Dwight Rainey to have someone guard Engelland and stay with him.

He was going to inbound the ball to Gminski and he would get a quick pass back to Engelland and he would have an open shot. When Engelland inbounded the ball from midcourt, he threw the ball to Gminski.

"Gminski threw the ball back to Engelland, but he was being guarded closely by a Tiger defender and he didn't get the open shot like he wanted and he ended up heaving a desperation attempt that missed and the game went into overtime. So much of the time whoever inbounds the ball gets forgotten about and is left wide open. I was glad I could contribute and do my part for Clemson that night."

In the overtime period, the Tigers gained the upper hand, then put on a free-throw-shooting clinic to gain the victory.

After a Campbell layup and two free throws by Banks of Duke, Clemson got the lead for good when Billy Williams hit a 15-footer. After a Duke miss, Bobby Conrad hit two freethrows to put the Tigers up 72-68. Duke fought back, pulling to within two on two occasions, but the Tigers free-throw shooters were near perfect down the stretch. Clemson made 15 of 17 free throws in the overtime period.

The Tigers upset number-one ranked Duke 87-82, giving the Tigers their first victory over a number-one ranked team.

"We knew we had to hit our free throws down the stretch," said Bobby Conrad. "We didn't do that in an earlier loss to Oregon State when we were in the same position. Tonight, all of the guys did a great job at the line and we were able to keep the upper hand," said Conrad after the win.

For the game, Campbell paced the Tigers with 23 points and seven rebounds. Williams had 19 points and seven assists. Larry Nance had 14 points and 11 rebounds. Bobby Conrad finished with 10 points including being 8-8 from the free throw line in the overtime period.

Banks, who scored 31 points, and Gminski, who added 30 points, led Duke.

It was one of many special games for the Tigers that season. Clemson lost to UCLA in the NCAA Tournament's Elite Eight, and this 1979-80 team is considered by many to be one of the best, if not the best, in Clemson history.

The "big win before the large crowd" will always be a Clemson classic.

CLIFF ELLIS AND HIS BIG MEN

In his last game at Littlejohn Coliseum, Cliff Ellis bent down at midcourt and kissed the orange Tiger Paw to show his appreciation for his 10 years as the Tigers' head coach. That afternoon, February 26, 1994, his Tigers defeated Maryland 73-67 to send him out as a winner in his final game there.

"I have great feelings for Clemson. Clemson is very dear to my heart," Ellis said. "I'll be pulling for Clemson every game from here on out, every single game. This is a special place."

Ellis helped make Littlejohn Coliseum and Clemson a special place in men's basketball during his tenure as head coach from 1985-'94. He was responsible for coaching the Tigers' first and only ACC Player of the Year in Horace Grant. He was also responsible for bringing in and coaching future NBA talents in Elden Campbell, Dale Davis, and Sharone Wright.

All four players are listed in Clemson's top 25 players of all time as part of the All-Centennial team, which was honored by the university in 2012.

Head Coach Cliff Ellis won 177 games during his career in 1984-94. Under his leadership, he led the Tigers to eight postseason tournaments.

Campbell and Davis played a big role in Ellis's 1990 Clemson team that won the program's only ACC Championship, while advancing to the Sweet 16 Round of the NCAA Tournament.

Ellis led Clemson to a 177-128 mark in 10 years (1984-94), and the Tigers went to eight postseason tournaments—three NCAAs and five NITs. He coached Clemson to the ACC regular season title in 1989-90, the only regular-season ACC title in Clemson history. The Tigers had a 24-8 record that year. His 1986-87 Tiger team won a record 25 games.

"There is an ACC Championship here. That had never happened. This is a special place," Ellis said. "Clemson holds a dear place in my heart."

The Cliff Ellis era began in 1984-85 at Clemson, and the Tigers were chosen for the NIT. Clemson defeated three top-20 teams in the regular season, including #8 Georgia Tech in Atlanta in Ellis's first ACC game and #11 North Carolina as Chris Michael hit a jumper with two seconds left.

In 1985-86, Clemson advanced to the Final Eight of the NIT. Horace Grant finished 10th in the nation in rebounding with a 10.5 rpg. mark.

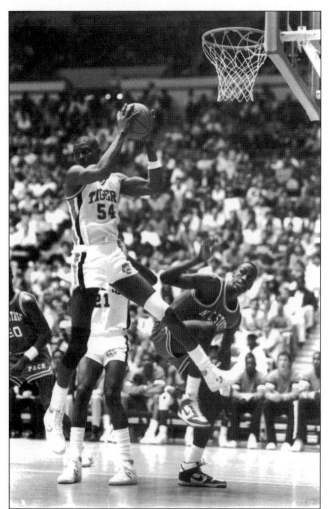

Horace Grant was the ACC Player of the Year in 1987.

The 1986-87 team was selected as the number-four seed of the Eastern Regional of the NCAA Tournament and was ranked 13th in the final AP poll. Clemson set the school record for most wins overall (25) and in league play (10), and the team also reached an AP ranking of number 10, which tied the school's best mark at the time.

Horace Grant won the ACC Triple Crown of basketball and was Clemson's first ACC Player of the Year, and first-team All-ACC. He was the #10 pick of the NBA draft by Chicago and was chosen second-team AP All-American. Grant was third in the nation in field goal percentage (65.6) and won the Frank McGuire Award as the top athlete in South Carolina.

Ellis was named ACC Coach of the Year and was sixth in the AP National Coach of the Year voting.

Elden Campbell finished 10th in the nation in field goal percentage, (62.9), and eighth in blocked shots per game (3.1), as he won third-team All-ACC honors in 1987-88.

Dale Davis set an ACC record for field goal percentage (67.0) in a season and finished third in the nation in that category in 1988-89. He was a major reason Clemson advanced to the NCAA Tournament that year. Also that year, Campbell ranked ninth in the nation for blocked shots (3.1).

The 1989-90 season brought on numerous firsts for the Clemson basketball team. The Tigers won their first-ever Atlantic Coast Conference regular season championship by posting a 10-4 record. They also advanced to the Sweet 16 in the NCAA Tournament before losing to UConn 71-70 on a last-second shot.

Clemson defeated LaSalle in the second round of the NCAA Tournament to reach the 26-win mark, a school record. LaSalle had won 22 in a row and was ranked 12th in the nation coming into the game. Clemson battled back from a 16-point deficit, the largest halftime deficit overcome to lead to a Clemson victory in school history.

Both Dale Davis and Elden Campbell were named first-team All-ACC players, a first for Clemson. Also, head coach Cliff Ellis was named ACC Coach of the Year. The Tigers finished the season ranked 17th in the final AP and UPI polls. Campbell was a first-round pick of the Los Angeles Lakers.

In 1991, Dale Davis was a first-round pick of the Indiana Pacers, the #13 pick of the entire draft. He finished his career sixth in ACC history and second in Clemson history in total rebounds, with 1216. He averaged 12.1 rebounds per game, ninth in the nation, and was the recipient of the IPTAY Athlete of the Year.

Clemson's 1992-93 team boasted three future NBA players in Sharone Wright, Devin Gray, and Chris Whitney. The Tigers finished the season strong with a victory over 12th-ranked Wake Forest, 10th-ranked Florida State in the ACC Tournament, and SEC rival Auburn in the NIT.

Whitney was a second-round draft choice of the San Antonio Spurs in the June draft and played the rest of the decade in the NBA.

Clemson again had a winning season and advanced to the NIT in 1993-94. In January, Ellis announced this would be his 10th and final season as Tiger head coach.

In the Rainbow Classic that year, Sharone Wright improved his NBA draft status by leaps and bounds, nearly recording a triple-double in a head-to-head matchup with Bryant Reeves of Oklahoma State. Clemson defeated the 20th-ranked Cowboys 68-65, while Wright blocked eight of Reeves's shots.

Late in the season, Clemson upset second-ranked North Carolina by a 77-69 score. Wayne Buckingham had a career-high 14 points in the Clemson victory.

In the postseason, Clemson defeated Southern Mississippi and West Virginia to advance to the Final Eight of the NIT. The victory over West Virginia would be the 177th and final of Cliff Ellis's career.

Eighteen years after he kissed the floor at Littlejohn, Ellis greeted it with another kiss at midcourt after Clemson University honored him with a plaque before its game against Ellis's new team at the time, Coastal Carolina. The plaque was given to Ellis in appreciation for all the good he did for Clemson basketball.

"It was weird being on the [visitors'] side of the court," Ellis said. "It was weird early, but I'm very appreciative of Clemson for the warm welcome I received."

Those are all reasons why Clemson is so special to Ellis and why he chose to kiss it once he came back to Littlejohn.

"The last time I walked off this court, I kissed it. When I came back, I kissed it. I love this place," he said. "I really do. I have a lot of friends here. I have 10 extended families here. I love the players that played for me all of those years. It was a great run."

1990 ACC REGULAR SEASON CHAMPIONS

There was a feeling of anticipation and excitement on the Clemson campus late in February, over 25 years ago.

A Tiger victory over fifth-ranked Duke in Littlejohn Coliseum on February 28, 1990, would give #20 Clemson at least a share of the ACC Regular Season Championship. There was a chance for history to be made, as this would be Clemson's first ACC Championship in men's basketball. It was billed as "the most meaningful regular season game in Clemson history."

Tickets were being scalped, students camped out for prime seats, and the Clemson team would wear orange jerseys that night.

It was a Wednesday night, and there was a demand for tickets like never before as the crowd sensed that this would be the Tigers' big night. The home crowd wanted to make sure that they would do their part, inspiring the Tigers to victory by being loud all through the game.

It was reported that a record 182 media passes were issued for the game that was televised nationally by ESPN. An orange pompom was draped across each seat for the fans, adding to the color and pageantry . The 12,500 fans in attendance were not disappointed.

Clemson trailed Duke 53-51 at the half. In the second half, Clemson started getting the ball inside to the "Duo of Doom," Elden Campbell (6'11", C) and Dale Davis (6'11", F). The Tigers opened an 81-72 lead on Kirkland Howling's jumper with 6:55 left to go in regulation.

Then Duke lived up to its #5 ranking. The Blue Devils went on a 14-6 run, narrowing Clemson's lead to 87-86 as Phil Henderson grabbed a loose ball and drove down the court for a dunk with 1:29 left to go.

Starting Clemson guard Marion Cash converted on two free throws to give the Tigers an 89-86 advantage. Campbell scored as he gathered a rebound and tipped the ball in from close range, giving the Tigers a five-point lead, 91-86.

Duke's Bobby Hurley hit a three-pointer from the right side, and the Blue Devils were within two points of the Tigers. Young hit both free throws, giving the Tigers a 93-89 lead with 27 seconds left. Robert Brickley made a layup and was fouled by Campbell, but he missed the free throw as 19 seconds was showing on the game clock.

The Tigers' Kirkland Howling hit two free throws with 17 seconds left. Duke's Bill McCaffrey hit a 15-footer on the left baseline, and Clemson held a 95-93 lead. Howling was fouled with four seconds left, and he calmly made both free throws, making the score 97-93. This would be the final score, and when the buzzer sounded, the Clemson fans stormed the court greeting their heroes.

Clemson had made history! Eventually Clemson won sole possession of first place in the ACC standings. Tiger Head Coach Cliff Ellis was hoisted on the shoulders of his players. Clemson even cut down the nets with the help of the fans. It was big night, and it would go down as one of the biggest regular season victories in Clemson basketball history.

"It's a perfect ending to a perfect season at home," Clemson center Elden Campbell said after scoring 22 points and blocking four shots as the Tigers improved to 10-3 in the ACC and 23-5 overall. The win topped a 14-0 home schedule and gave the 20th-ranked Tigers 24 straight victories at Littlejohn Coliseum. "We'll celebrate tonight, and tomorrow we'll get ready for the next game." Two students succeeded in picking up Campbell and carried him to the basket, where he helped cut the net down.

"We're going to enjoy this moment," said Clemson Head Coach Cliff Ellis. "This is the regular season championship, and I'm proud.

"This is a big win for our program, I thought we played inspired and I think we played with a lot of confidence . That's exactly what you want to see when you go down the stretch."

Duke Head Coach Mike Krzyzewski was also impressed by the play of his team and the Tigers in his postgame comments. "It was a great game, I'm just sorry we lost," said Krzyzewski. "I was really impressed with our team and the play of Clemson . There were so many big plays especially down the stretch. They made them and we did too.

"Cliff has done a great job," said Krzyzewski. "The two big guys have really asserted themselves at the highest level. Dale Davis is exceptional and Campbell is right there with him. They are good kids and I like their team and how Cliff coaches them."

That evening in late February of 1990 will go down as one of the memorable nights in Clemson athletic history.

"I'm proud and happy tonight for everybody," said Ellis after the game. "It's a great time for Clemson."

RICK BARNES AND GREG BUCKNER ERA

Rick Barnes was named Clemson head coach in late March of 1994. Within the first two weeks of the announcement, Sharone Wright decided to turn professional.

Wright was the sixth overall pick of the NBA draft, the highest selection in Clemson history. Then, Devin Gray, the ACC field goal percentage champion of 1994, suffered a heart attack.

Despite those setbacks, Barnes created interest and enthusiasm in the program and led the Tigers to 10 consecutive wins to open the season. The most amazing was a victory at Duke on January 4th. The Blue Devils were ranked ninth in the nation and had been to the NCAA championship game the year before. Six different Tigers made a three-point goal, and Clemson shot 55 percent from the field overall in Clemson's 75-70 victory.

Led by the Slab Five (Merl Code, Bruce Martin, Bill Harder, Rayfield Ragland, and Andy Kelly), Clemson advanced to the NIT and won 15 games. It was quite an accomplishment, especially since it was picked to be the worst ACC team in history prior to the season.

In the ACC Tournament, Barnes and North Carolina coach Dean Smith exchanged words at the scorer's table late in the game. Barnes was accusing Smith of talking to his players while play was in progress. Smith felt Clemson's players were too aggressive. Standing up to Smith, especially in this theater, made Barnes even more popular than he already was with the Clemson faithful.

Seven new freshmen joined the 1995-96 team in Rick Barnes's second year, and they helped bring Clemson to a new level over the next four seasons. Clemson won 18 games in 1995-96 and gained victories over every other ACC team, something that had not happened since the 1989-90 season.

Clemson defeated Minnesota in December in Littlejohn Coliseum, a game that really sparked the masses. A three-point win over 19th-ranked Duke, Clemson's third-straight win over the Blue Devils, gave the young Clemson team confidence. Even a season-ending torn ACL to junior guard Merl Code failed to dampen the momentum.

The Tigers defeated a Stephon Marbury-led Georgia Tech team 73-70. That Tech team tied for the ACC title

with Wake Forest, whom Clemson thrashed with an incredible defense, 55-41.

Clemson had beaten every ACC team in the regular season, except North Carolina. In the ACC Tournament it looked as if the Tar Heels would make it three in a row, as Dean Smith's team held an 8-point lead.

But Clemson battled back in the closing minutes. With 0.6 seconds remaining, Harold Jamison fed Greg Buckner, who dunked the ball over the outstretched arm of Antawn Jamison, giving Clemson a 75-73 victory. It was the first time Clemson had ever beaten North Carolina in the ACC Tournament and the first time Clemson had beaten North Carolina in the Tar Heel State since 1967.

The victory sent Clemson to the NCAA Tournament, Clemson's first appearance in that event since 1990. Clemson was the youngest team in the 64-team field, starting four freshmen and a sophomore. Georgia, the oldest team in the tournament, won the battle 81-74, but the groundwork had been set.

In 1996-97, Clemson began the season with the school's first Midnight Madness, an event that attracted 4,500 fans. It was a start to a landmark season for Clemson.

The Tigers won 16 of their first 17 games and reached a #2 national ranking, the school's highest on record. Clemson opened the season with a victory over third-ranked and defending national champion Kentucky in the Hoosier Dome in Indianapolis. The 79-71 overtime victory was among the most exciting in school history, and it was certainly the highest-ranked non-conference victory in school history.

Harold Jamison scored 20 points to lead Clemson, while Iker Iturbe was the key to breaking Kentucky's vaunted full-court press.

Clemson raced to a 5-0 start, including a victory over ninth-ranked Duke and a win at 11th ranked-Maryland. Wake Forest and National Player of the Year Tim Duncan came to Clemson for the most celebrated regular season game in the history of Littlejohn Coliseum. The tension was at a zenith the entire game. Clemson was called for an offensive foul on its last possession and Wake Forest won 65-62, but Clemson fans had seen ACC basketball at its best.

Clemson went on to a 23-10 record that season. The Tigers defeated Miami (OH) and Wally Szczerbiak in the first round before beating Tulsa in the second round, sending Clemson to the Sweet 16 for the first time since 1990.

Minnesota, who had beaten Clemson in the regular season, was the opposition in the round of 16. The Tigers fell behind by as many as 17 points in the first half but cut the lead to two with nine minutes left. Trailing by a bucket with 10 seconds left, Tony Christie drove the length of the court to hit a diving shot at the buzzer and send the game to overtime. Clemson had a six-point lead in the first overtime, but Minnesota hit a shot to force a second OT. The Gophers then went on a minirun and held on for a 90-84 victory.

The Tigers concluded the season ranked eighth in the final *USA Today* poll, the highest final ranking in Clemson basketball history. The Tigers were 14th in the final AP poll. Rick Barnes was named one of 10 finalists for National Coach of the Year by AP. Clemson was ranked every poll of the season, a first in school history.

Based on its fine 1996-97 season and the return of 11 lettermen and four starters, Clemson was ranked #5 in the preseason AP poll. Rick Barnes set up a challenging schedule. But injuries forced Clemson into some early-season losses to Gonzaga and Kentucky. Victories over Maryland and South Carolina, both top 20 teams, were noteworthy.

With a healthy McIntyre, Clemson won six of eight down the stretch. Greg Buckner had 29 points on his Senior Night in Littlejohn Coliseum, resulting in a 14-point win over Georgia Tech. Buckner started 122 consecutive games in his Clemson career. Clemson defeated Wake Forest in the first round of the ACC Tournament, only to face #1-ranked Duke again.

Once again, Clemson battled with a top-five team to the wire. But William Avery scored with under a second left to give Duke a 66-64 victory, denying Clemson its second trip to the finals in ACC Tournament history.

Clemson suffered a disappointing 75-72 loss to Western Michigan in the first round of the NCAA Tournament. It was the ninth time Clemson had lost by five points or less in 1997-98. After the season, on Easter Sunday, Rick Barnes resigned to become head coach at Texas.

LARRY SHYATT AND FOUR SENIORS

Larry Shyatt, who spent three years as Barnes's associate head coach at Clemson and one as head coach at Wyoming, became Clemson's head coach in April of 1998.

In that first year, he had four seniors back on the roster whom he had helped recruit as freshmen in 1995. Clemson raced to an 11-1 record in Shyatt's first year, including a 70-66 win over rival South Carolina, Clemson's fifth-straight win over the Gamecocks.

Clemson struggled in January but came on strong in February and March. A highlight was a 78-63 victory over North Carolina, Clemson's largest victory margin over the Tar Heels in 19 years.

The Tigers were dominant at home in February and March, winning their last six home games by an average of 23 points per game. The regular season concluded with a 28-point victory over Georgia Tech on Senior Night.

Clemson moved into the NIT and had the greatest postseason run in school history. First, the Tigers defeated geographic rival Georgia by 20 points, then downed Rutgers on the road by 10. Clemson then beat Butler by 20 points, behind 17 points and 17 rebounds from Tom Wideman. Jamison had a career-high 26 points, including seven dunks. McIntyre also had a memorable game, with 21 points and 11 assists.

The third-round win sent Clemson to Madison Square Garden for the semifinals. The Tigers thrashed Xavier, a 26-win team, by 24 points for the first 25 minutes of the game, then held on for a 79-76 victory.

Clemson came one possession short against California. The Tigers, leading by two, blocked a California shot, but three Clemson players ran past the ensuing loose ball. Geno Carlisle hit a field goal with four seconds left and was fouled on the play. The extra point gave California a 61-60 victory.

The seniors of 1999 had made quite an impact on Clemson basketball. They recorded 79 victories, made three NCAA appearances, and were part of a finalist team in the NIT. Thirteen of the 79 wins were over ranked teams.

McIntyre concluded his career second in school history in both scoring and assists. Jamison left as the school's career leader in field goal percentage, and Wideman was perhaps the most decorated student-athlete in school history.

Will Solomon led the ACC in scoring and ranked 16th in the nation with a 20.9 average in 1999-2000. He made first-team All-ACC, the first Tiger to make first-team since 1990, and was the first Clemson sophomore to do so in 30 years.

In 2000-01, Clemson defeated number-one North Carolina 75-65, the school's second win over a nation's top-ranked team. Solomon turned pro a year early and was the second-round pick of the Memphis Grizzlies.

The next season, Ed Scott earned third-team All-ACC honors and was third in the nation in assists per game with a 7.93 mark.

In 2002-03, Scott was named first-team All-ACC, the first Clemson point guard in 43 years to be a first-team selection. He was third in the ACC in scoring (17.7). He was the ninth player in ACC history to reach 1000 points, 500 assists, and 400 rebounds in a career.

PURNELL GUIDES TIGERS TO POSTSEASON PLAY

Oliver Purnell coached for seven seasons at Clemson and guided the Tigers to six postseason appearances, including three consecutive NCAA Tournaments in his final three years with the program.

His teams at Clemson compiled a 138-88 record for a .611 winning mark. Purnell became only the second coach in ACC history to improve his team's winning percentage in five consecutive seasons, from 2004-'09.

In 2004-05, Clemson advanced to the postseason for the first time since 1999. Sharrod Ford had a game-winning dunk at the buzzer on Senior Night to lift Clemson to a victory over Virginia Tech.

The 2006-07 team matched a school record by winning 25 games. This team also set a Clemson standard with a 17-0 start to the season and advanced to the championship game of the NIT.

Purnell coached the 2007-08 team to a berth in the ACC Championship game, just the second in history for the Tigers. The team won 24 games, including 10 in the regular-season ACC race to match a school record.

His 2008-09 team went 23-9 overall, 9-7 in the ACC, and handed a top-10 Duke team their worst loss in 19 years when Clemson won 74-47 over the Blue Devils at home. It was the signature victory during the Purnell era.

The 2009-10 team followed with another 9-7 mark in league play, making it the only time in Clemson history the Tigers posted three consecutive winning seasons against ACC competition.

Trevor Booker was a first-team All-ACC forward in 2010 and was a first-round draft pick (#23 overall) by the Washington Wizards.

THROWING DOWN THE "BOOK" AT CLEMSON

It depends on who you talk to, but Trevor Booker will say he can beat his brother in a game of one-on-one, and Devin Booker will say the same.

"I can't let my younger brother beat me," Trevor said. "I'm not going to let that happen."

Trevor likes to let everyone know he is the best Booker. When he heard his younger brother Devin claimed to have beaten him one-on-one several times over the years, but could not remember exactly when those moments occurred, Trevor said there was a good explanation for that.

"He probably can't remember because it didn't happen. That's why he can't remember," he said laughing.

Devin says he can beat his older brother four out of 10 times in a game of 21. Trevor claims it has never happened once and that it never will.

"There is no way I can let my younger brother beat me," he said. "It is not in my blood. I mean it was hard for my cousin, Jordan, to beat me and he did not do it too many times, but my younger brother, I can't let that happen. Not yet. Not until we are like 60."

And even then Trevor does not think it will happen. In fact, he says Devin has never dunked on him. And besides an occasional block or something, he pretty much has his way with his little brother.

"He might hit a jumper in my face every now and then, but I'm definitely not getting dunked on," Trevor said. "If I see he has a wide-open dunk, I'm just going to let him dunk it. I'm not going to jump with him."

The Booker brothers have been playing basketball since they were kids, playing on a goal right down the street from their home in Whitmire, SC. Sometimes they played with each other, and other times they played against each other.

"All of that has paid off," Devin said.

The brothers' competitive drive and their eagerness to be better than the other has led them to where they are now. Trevor is in the NBA playing for the Washington Wizards, while Devin capped his Clemson career by being named to the All-ACC squad as a member of the third-team.

Trevor was the original "Book" at Clemson, garnering that nickname from Purnell during his freshman season. Devin assumed the nickname when his brother left for the NBA.

The Booker brothers scored 2,879 points at Clemson from 2006-'13, the fourth-best brother scoring combination in ACC history. In fact, they are one of only five brothers in the history of the ACC to score at least 1,000 points each in their careers.

Trevor tallied 1,725 points from 2006-'10, while Devin recorded 1,154 points in his four years. Not only were Trevor and Devin great scorers for the Tigers, but also they did a lot of other things. Only 12 players in Clemson history have accumulated more than 1,000 points and 700 rebounds, and the Booker brothers are two of them.

"As you can see, we have made a name here at Clemson, and we just try to do what we can to make Clemson proud," Devin said.

In that seven-year span, at least one Booker brother was in the Tigers' starting lineup for 227 of the 230 games played during that time.

When they became teammates, they became the first brother duo in basketball at Clemson since Horace and Harvey Grant in 1983-84.

Before his little brother got to Clemson, Trevor was already an All-ACC second-team selection in 2009, as he became the first player since Wake Forest's Tim Duncan in 1997 to lead the conference in rebounding and field goal percentage, and the first underclassman at Clemson to do it since Dale Davis did the same in 1990.

"He gets things going with the way that he plays the game," Purnell said. "He plays it with tremendous energy and he is obviously effective, but he is exciting on both ends of the floor with the shot block on the defensive end and with the dunk on the offensive end."

Trevor started every game of his 134-game career at Clemson, which is a record for both starts and consecutive starts. He was a first-team All-ACC selection his senior year, the first post player at Clemson to earn that accolade since Campbell and Davis in 1990.

He finished his college career third in Clemson history in rebounding and fifth in points, while leading the Tigers to three-straight NCAA Tournament appearances and to the ACC Tournament Championship Game in 2008, the first for the school in 46 years.

Trevor joined former Wake Forest and NBA great Tim Duncan as the only players in the history of the ACC with at least 1,500 points, 1,000 rebounds, 200 block shots, and 200 assists. Trevor ranks in the ACC's top 10 in scoring, rebounding, blocked shots, and field goal percentage.

Trevor was named to Clemson's 100th Anniversary Team in 2012 for his accomplishments.

"He may be the best all-around player to have played at Clemson and there have been some pretty good ones there," Purnell said. "He is one of the best to play in the ACC and there have been a lot of great, great, great players in the league."

Trevor Booker was a first-team All-ACC selection in 2010.

On his own, Devin helped guide the Tigers to the 2011 NCAA Tournament and the program's first win in the tournament since the 1997 Sweet 16 run. In 2011, Clemson posted a 22-12 record and a 9-7 mark in the ACC, the program's fourth-straight winning record in conference play.

Like his brother did his final year at Clemson, Devin had an All-ACC season, averaging 13.1 points and 7.5 rebounds per game in 2012-13, while developing a reputation as one of the more physical post players in the conference.

"I think Devin played consistently at a very high level," current Clemson head coach Brad Brownell said. "He certainly has done, as I like to term it, the heavy lifting. He has done a lot of the things you need done in basketball.

"Some of that does not show in the statistics. He has been a fixture in our low post for a long time and he has certainly played very well."

Though he is sticking to his side of the story that he has indeed beaten his older brother on the basketball court, Devin admits playing against and competing for playing time against Trevor in high school and later in college only helped him grow as a basketball player.

"Playing against him all this time has just made me better," Devin said. "Him being [an NBA] player makes me want to work harder to get to the level that he is at right now."

McDANIELS IS AS HUMBLE AS THEY COME

Brad Brownell calls K.J. McDaniels one of the more humble players he has ever coached. How humble? Clemson's leading scorer and rebounder from the 2013-14 team was taking a nap when the Atlantic Coast Conference announced he was a first-team All-ACC selection, only the 12th player in Clemson history to own such an honor.

"I got a call from Coach Steve Smith to congratulate me," McDaniels said. "I didn't know because I was in the bed asleep. It was surprising to me, honestly."

McDaniels surprised everyone in the ACC in 2014. He was one of the most improved players in the conference, averaging 17.1 points and 7.2 rebounds per game in the regular season, and for a second straight year he led the conference in blocks per game (2.8).

"I saw a lot of tweets saying if K.J. McDaniels isn't first-team All-ACC then something is wrong," the junior said. "I was not too worried, but I was surprised I made first-team ACC with these calibers of players. It's an honor."

McDaniels deserved the honor. He finished fourth in the ACC in free throw percentage (.847), fifth in scoring, sixth in field goal percentage (.452), and seventh in rebounding. He was the only player in the country to lead his team in scoring, rebounding, three-pointers, blocks, and steals. He became only the second player in ACC history to do it, joining Wake Forest's Josh Howard who did it in 2002-03.

Devin says he does not mind being compared to his brother. He understands that comes with being a Booker, but he admits he never really thought about it when he decided to come to Clemson out of Union County High School in 2009.

"I actually did not figure that out until I got here," he said laughing. "That's when it really hit me. Before then, I knew Clemson was where I wanted to be. It was close to home, it's a great atmosphere, and in the ACC I knew it was going to get me better because there are some tough individuals to play against.

"But, when I first got here, that's when all the questions started hitting me about my brother."

The Tigers recorded 144 wins with a Booker in the lineup, or 20.6 wins per year, while posting an 83-25 mark at home during those seven seasons, a .768 winning percentage. They also helped the Tigers win 57 ACC games, the most in a seven-year span in Clemson history, and carried the program to four straight NCAA Tournaments from 2008-'11—a first in the program's history.

"[Trevor] had his time here at Clemson with his four years and I have had my time here with my four years," Devin said. "He put in the work and did all he could and I've done the same thing."

The Clemson forward was also voted as the ACC's Defensive Player of the Year.

"He has improved as much as anybody that I have ever coached," Brownell said. "We knew he had a high ceiling when we recruited him. That's one of the things that attracted us to him. He was an NBA talent athletically. The basketball part of it just had to come."

It has been a process to get McDaniels to that point, but it was a process Brownell and his staff enjoyed being a part of. When he signed with Clemson in 2011, McDaniels was a raw talent that had more athletic ability than any player Brownell has ever coached.

In that first year, he averaged only 3.9 points and 1.8 rebounds per game. But he first showed his potential earlier that year when he scored 14 points, grabbed eight rebounds, and had five blocked shots at Virginia Tech. The only downside of his game that afternoon was at the foul line, where he missed all three of his attempts in what turned out to be a 67-65 loss.

"His freshman year, it was his skill level that needed improvement. But it was also physically just being strong enough," Brownell said. "And then there is a big part of the pace and the mental aspect of the game. There is just so much to learn, especially when you are transferring to a wing position."

A month later at Florida State, McDaniels topped his effort at Virginia Tech when he dropped in 16 points, had eight rebounds, four steals, and two blocked shots.

"He had flashes of great play and then his sophomore year I thought he was much more consistent and he was our second or third best player on the team and became a double-figure scorer," Brownell said. "He made a huge jump for us."

After starting one game as a freshman, McDaniels became a regular starter for the Tigers in the 2012-13 season. He played in 28 games—missed two games because of an ankle injury—and started 25 of them. His points per game average went up to 10.9, while he led the ACC in blocks per game and increased his rebounding average to five per outing.

"Because of the success he had last year, I think that really motivated him or excited him to where he was 'Hey! I can be really good.' You saw a guy take another huge step, and I think he will take another big step or two before he is done playing basketball," Brownell said.

McDaniels's confidence took off in 2013-14. Twelve times he scored 20 or more points, including a career-high 30 at Notre Dame on Feb. 11. Five times he scored at least 20 points and grabbed at least 10 rebounds in the same game.

Duke head coach Mike Krzyzewski called McDaniels "the best athlete in the ACC" after he grabbed 10 rebounds, blocked three shots, and scored 24 points in a 72-59 Clemson victory.

"He is still a guy that can get better and it is really important to him," Brownell said. "I'm just really excited and happy for him because I know it is a heck of an honor to be named All-ACC, especially when you are in a

K.J. McDaniels scored over 1000 points in three seasons. He was first-team All-ACC in 2014.

league with 15 teams now as opposed to the old eight or nine or 12 teams.

"He is doing it in a league with 15 teams and a bunch of really good players."

And really, isn't that all McDaniels has done since he first stepped foot on Clemson's campus in 2011?

"Our best player is as humble as they come," Brownell said. "He is an All-ACC guy, but he does not act any different than anybody else. He spends as much time as anybody else working."

BILL FOSTER—MORE THAN A BASKETBALL COACH

With the news of Bill Foster's death on May 27, 2015, the memories of some of Clemson's greatest basketball victories soon come to mind.

Foster passed away in Charlotte, NC, after a long battle with Parkinson's Disease. He was 79.

He was known as a program builder, and he continued his forte at Clemson after he guided UNC Charlotte to an 87-39 record in five years. What also comes to mind was his ability to build quality citizens.

"He was much bigger than basketball," said Bobby Conrad in a recent interview. Conrad played point guard under Foster from 1976-'80. "You could be a Division I ACC player under him, and still have a life outside of basketball, and a lot of us really appreciated that.

"He was all about teaching life lessons and was very much excited about seeing his players succeed in life. Coach Foster was a very influential, very impactful person in the lives of all of his players," said Conrad.

NEW LITTLEJOHN COLISEUM: AN UNBELIEVABLE FACILITY

When he first came to interview for the Clemson job back in 2010, Brad Brownell did everything he could to get the job, including reaching across former athletic director Terry Don Phillips's desk to beg him to hire him as the Tigers' new coach. Phillips ultimately did just that.

"Terry Don and Billy D'Andrea are the guys that brought me to Clemson and I will never forget that," Brownell said as Clemson officially opened the new Littlejohn Coliseum with a ribbon-cutting ceremony on Oct. 14. "I had to crawl over the table just begging Terry Don to hire me. 'Come on Terry Don give me a chance. I'm going to work for you,' and I have never forgotten that he gave me the opportunity. For him to take that risk on me it means a great deal and it always will."

It did not take Brownell long to begin talks with Phillips on what his program needed to be a successful one. What it needed was a new arena. Littlejohn Coliseum was outdated, especially the players' amenities as the Tigers were falling behind especially when ACC rivals Virginia, NC State, Georgia Tech, and now Louisville and Pitt have some of the best arenas in the country.

When Terry Don retired in 2012, new athletic director Dan Radakovich picked up were Phillips left off and with IPTAY's Aaron Dunham and the athletic department's business manager Graham Neff, getting a new area quickly took off. Three years later, Littlejohn is brand-new and the Swann Pavilion, where the men's and women's programs are now housed, is one of the best practice and players' facilities in the country.

"Dan has done this before so things got moving quickly," Brownell said. "He did not take a lot of convincing to say, 'Hey, we need to move forward in basketball.' Obviously, having done things at Georgia Tech, Dan knew what to do, but I think he took it to another level here."

Brownell's says basketball's new digs has the Tigers on par with just about everyone in the ACC and has created a certain level of excitement and positive momentum in the program.

"It takes some time to get to. There were times a few years ago where I was telling [the media] there were a lot of really good things happening behind the scenes within the program that do not always show up in wins and losses and in those days, there was a lot of time spent to make this day a reality."

Brownell says he gets a lot of satisfaction in seeing the new facility.

"It's something that I kind of challenged myself to get done. Very early on I knew I wanted to do this," he said.

"Aaron Dunham, and I got together, and I just talked to him about it. 'Hey, we need to make this happen.' Clemson basketball can't have the success that people want without making facility improvements.

"We had to convince people that this is what we need and we have to find a way to figure out how to do it. I was certainly willing to do what I needed to do make it happen and he took me up on that."

Jaron Blossomgame, a first-team All-ACC performer in 2016, described the renovated Littlejohn Coliseum, and the Swann Pavilion, as "unbelievable," while saying he was grateful and appreciative to all of those Clemson fans and supporters who donated to the project.

The Clemson forward said the players' lounge—which has two big-screen TVs, video games, couches, a pool table, arcade games, and a kitchen and dining area—and the locker room is where he spends most of his time these days.

The new Littlejohn and the Swann Pavilion, with the new coaches' offices, weight room, training room, and a state-of-the-art practice facility puts Clemson on par with other new arenas in the ACC and across the country.

"The old Littlejohn, it was hard to compete and get recruits when you have places like Duke and North Carolina with top-of-the-line facilities. The Littlejohn we had really did not have an advantage," Blossomgame said. "But with what we have now, kids will come here and see all the nice and new shinny things we have and they are attracted to that type of stuff. That, plus being in the ACC, obviously, gives us an advantage with some kids.

"It is an unbelievable place and I'm sure everyone will love it once they get to see it."

Brownell met with all kinds of different people and went to different places to create momentum. The Clemson coach said he remembers meeting one fan at a Prowl and Growl event when he first got hired, and she whispered to him, "I like basketball more than football." Brownell asked her, 'Why are we whispering? You can talk out loud about that. That's not a bad thing. That is a good thing.'

"You just had to go find some of those folks and get them excited about it . . . Thankfully we have some great folks at Clemson."

MEN'S BASKETBALL HISTORY

February 9, 1912—Clemson won its first two basketball games played on its first day of competition. Under the direction of Coach Frank Dobson, the Tigers defeated both Furman and the Butler Guards in games played in Greenville, SC. Clemson defeated Furman by a score of 46-12 in the first game. In this game James Erwin scored 22 points, while his younger brother, John, added 20 points. Then thanks to a school record 58 points on 29 field goals by James Erwin, Clemson defeated the Butler Guards 78-6. At the half, the score was 40-0 in the Tigers' favor.

March 9, 1912—Clemson defeated Wofford 56-13 in the Tigers' first-ever home game. James Erwin scored 30 points in this match. Clemson played its home games in the basement of Sikes Hall or on Bowman Field in front of Tillman Hall when the weather was mild. Frank Dobson was the Tigers' coach curing the first two seasons of basketball. During this time, Dobson also coached football and baseball. James Erwin averaged 31.0 ppg. for the year, while his younger brother John averaged 17.0 ppg.

January 18, 1913—James Erwin scored 47 points in the 69-19 win over Furman in Clemson, SC. Because of inclement weather, the game had to be moved to the basement of Sikes Hall. This was the first indoor game played on the Clemson campus.

February 7, 1913—Brothers James and John Erwin scored all 26 points in leading the Tigers to a 26-22 win over Georgia Tech in Atlanta, GA. James scored 14 and John finished the night with 12.

1914—Clemson was coached by a player during the 1914 season. John Erwin served as the captain and coach. He finished his career averaging double figures for three seasons, including a 16.3 PPG average his senior season.

February 1, 1916—Clemson began playing its games in the newly completed YMCA (Currently the Holtzendorff YMCA Building) as the Tigers and Presbyterian played to a 39-39 tie. Audley H. Ward, a Clemson professor, coached the Tigers.

February 17, 1916—J.W. Stribling scored 50 points as the Tigers defeated Erskine 72-13 at Clemson, SC. This effort is only the second 50 or more scoring performance in school history.

February 15, 1919—Julian Robertson scored 31 points in the Tigers' 73-34 victory over Piedmont.

February 25, 1921—Clemson played in its first postseason basketball tournament, the Southern Intercollegiate Athletic Association (SIAA) Tournament in Atlanta, GA. The Southern Conference Basketball Tournament grew from this event, and it's the oldest postseason basketball tournament in the country. Auburn defeated Clemson 45-25. The game started at 9:00 p.m., and up until this time, this was the latest that Clemson had ever started a basketball game in its history.

March 5, 1921—Clemson won its 10th game of the year with a 25-15 victory over Wofford in Spartanburg, SC. Colbert scored seven points in the Tigers' win. With this win, the Tigers claimed the state championship. This marked the first time that the Tigers won 10 or more games in a season.

January 13, 1922—Clemson lost to Georgia 24-16 in the dedication of a new basketball arena. During the fall of 1921, the Clemson student body helped level the ground for the new facility. This new building was located south of Riggs Field. The building was a quonset hut and provided Clemson a larger regulation indoor basketball court.

February 28, 1924—Clemson won its first posttournament game with a 17-15 victory over Florida in Atlanta, GA. The next night, the Tigers lost to Vanderbilt.

January 6-9, 1926—The Tigers played four games, against St. Stanislaus, New Orleans Y, and Tulane twice, to open the season. At the time, this was the farthest the Tigers had traveled for a basketball game. It was very similar to a holiday tournament, participating in four games in New Orleans, LA.

1927-31—Josh Cody was the head coach for both the football and basketball teams, the last coach in Clemson history to coach the two revenue-producing sports. Athletic Director Mutt Gee and Josh Cody were instrumental in the building of the Fike Field House, which gave Clemson a state-of-the-art basketball arena. The gymnasium was built at a cost of $60,000 and was the first stage of Fike Field House to be built. The rest of Fike was built from the receipts of the 1940 Cotton Bowl, the first national bowl game for the Clemson football team.

January 7, 1930—Furman defeated Clemson 34-28 in the first game played at Fike Field House.

February 14, 1931—Clemson defeated Kentucky at Fike Field House on the Clemson Campus. This was a great win for the Tigers considering that some of the Clemson schedule was cancelled due to a meningitis quarantine on the Tigertown campus.

January 8, 1932—The Tigers at one point kept the Gamecocks from scoring for over 15 straight minutes in the first half in building a 15-3 lead at intermission. The Tigers were never threatened and won the game 31-22 in Columbia, SC. Pat Calhoun scored eight points, as did Joe Sherman. Sherman later became the alumni secretary for the Tigers.

February 20, 1935—The Tigers defeated Presbyterian 39-23 at Clemson, SC, in clinching the state championship. Swails scored 17 points in this game to lead the Tigers to victory. Clemson finished the season with a 15-3 record, still the best single-season winning pct (.833) in Clemson history.

January 11, 1936—Clemson defeated Georgia Tech 35-32. Brown, although scoreless, played a great defensive game, which included a steal in the closing seconds to secure the game for the Tigers. Pennington, a 6-2 forward for the Tigers, led all scorers with 11 points.

February 15, 1936—Clemson defeated South Carolina 43-30 in Columbia, SC, to clinch the State Championship. Clyde Pennington scored 20 points for the Tigers.

February 26, 1936—The Tigers' Kitchen scored a field goal in the last 15 seconds of play in leading Clemson to a 20-19 win over Wofford in the Terriers' Field House in Spartanburg, SC.

February 23, 1937—The Tigers' Wister Jackson's free throw with 30 seconds remaining in regulation clinched a 31-29 win for the Tigers over the South Carolina Gamecocks at Clemson, SC.

February 25, 1937—McGee, a substitute forward, grabbed a loose ball and looped in a long field goal as the buzzer sounded to give the Tigers a 33-32 win over Wofford at the Terriers' Field House in Spartanburg, SC.

February 19, 1938—The legendary Banks McFadden scored a career-high 27 points in a 58-39 victory over rival South Carolina.

February 28, 1938—Clemson defeated Wofford 52-24 in Spartanburg, SC, as the Tigers clinched the State Championship for the third time in the last four years. Sophomore Banks McFadden scored 20 points in the rout of the Terriers.

March 3-5, 1938—Clemson advanced to the Southern Conference Championship in Raleigh, NC. Clemson defeated Richmond 35-32 in the first round and Washington & Lee 38-33 in the semifinals. In the championship game, Duke defeated the Tigers 40-30. Banks McFadden scored 13 points in this game.

1939—The Tigers won the Southern Conference Tournament title and won eight of their last nine games. This is the first and only conference tournament title in Clemson history. Banks McFadden was chosen to the Helms Foundation All-America team. His number 23 was retired years later. Clemson won four games in the Southern Conference Tournament even though they never led at the half in any of the games.

February 28, 1952—With a 76-64 victory over rival South Carolina, Clemson won its 11th Southern Conference game of the season. The 11 conference wins still stands at the most ever by a Clemson men's basketball team.

December 17, 1954—Bill Yarborough scored 40 points against Virginia at Clemson, SC.

January 19, 1955—Bill Yarborough scored 46 points against South Carolina at Clemson, SC.

February 21, 1955—Tommy Smith had 30 rebounds in a 105-94 victory over Georgia at Clemson, SC.

December 28-29, 1955—Clemson defeated LSU 100-95 and South Carolina 94-87 as the Tigers won the Gator Bowl Tournament in Jacksonville, FL.

January 11, 1956—Bill Yarborough scored 38 points in a 109-80 loss to sixth-ranked Duke at Clemson, SC.

December 17, 1960—Choppy Patterson scored 39 points in a 78-68 win over The Citadel at Clemson, SC.

January 3, 1963—Donnie Mahaffey had 25 rebounds against Georgia in a 93-73 victory at Clemson, SC.

January 8, 1963—Mike Bohonak inbounded a pass to Gary Burnisky, who scored with one second left to lift Clemson to a 66-64 win over Furman in Greenville, SC.

January 14, 1963—Donnie Mahaffey had 24 rebounds in a home game vs. The Citadel.

December 3, 1963—Mike Bohonak made a 10-foot shot with two seconds left as the Tigers defeated North Carolina 66-64 in Clemson, SC.

December 29-30, 1965—Clemson defeated Mississippi 85-57 and Manhattan 77-67 as the Tigers claimed the Poinsettia Classic in Greenville, SC.

February 19, 1966—Joe Ayoob hit a 45-foot shot with one second left in overtime as the Tigers defeated N.C. State 76-74 in Charlotte, NC.

December 29-30, 1966—Clemson defeated LSU 92-82 and Furman 83-66 as the Tigers won the Poinsettia Classic in Greenville, SC.

February 18, 1967—Clemson defeated fourth-ranked North Carolina 92-88 in Charlotte, NC. The Tigers also defeated Wake Forest, Duke, and N.C. State during the week. It marked the first time the Tigers defeated the Big Four Schools from North Carolina in consecutive games. The victory was the seventh in a row for the Tigers in conference play, still a school record.

February 28, 1968—Clemson lost to Georgia Tech 80-51 in the Tigers' last home game in the storied Fike Field House.

November 30, 1968—Clemson defeated Georgia Tech 76-72 in the first game played at Littlejohn Coliseum. Dave Thomas of Clemson hit a jump shot at the 18:37 mark of the first half to score the first points in the new arena.

February 18, 1969—Butch Zatezalo scored 46 points against Wake Forest in a 100-84 loss to the Demon Deacons in Winston-Salem, NC. This set a Clemson ACC game record for most points scored by a player.

February 27, 1969—Butch Zatezalo scored 38 points against Wake Forest in a 112-104 double-overtime loss to the Demon Deacons at Clemson SC.

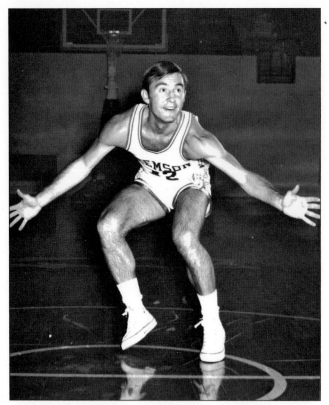

Butch Zatezalo was the first three-time All-ACC player in Clemson history. He scored 1,761 career points.

May 18, 1969—Athletic Director Frank Howard announced that Craig Mobley would become the first African-American student-athlete at Clemson. Mobley was signed by then-Head Coach Bobby Roberts.

February 14, 1970—Butch Zatezalo scored 43 points against N.C. State as the fifth-ranked Wolfpack defeated Clemson 102-84 as part of the North-South Doubleheader in Charlotte, NC.

December 29-30, 1971—David Angel had 22 rebounds in the Auburn game played at Greenville, SC, as part of the Poinsettia Classic. Clemson defeated Holy Cross 67-49 and Auburn 77-67.

November 30, December 1, 1973—Playing in his second game as a Tiger, freshman Tree Rollins had 22 points, 20 rebounds, and nine blocked shots in a 68-58 victory over St. John's. The Tigers defeated Auburn 87-72 and Saint John's 68-58 to claim the IPTAY Invitational.

December 28-29, 1973—Clemson's Tree Rollins had 24 rebounds vs. Delaware in a game played at Greenville, SC, as part of the Poinsettia Classic. The Tigers defeated Delaware 78-63 and Furman 75-67 to claim the championship.

November 30, 1974—The Tigers' Skip Wise scored 38 points against Pennsylvania at Clemson, SC, in a 76-75 loss to the Quakers in the IPTAY Invitational.

January 22, 1975—Behind 25 points from Skip Wise, Clemson defeated third-ranked Maryland 83-82 at Clem-

son, the program's highest-ranked victory in history at the time.

February 1, 1975—Clemson defeated Phil Ford and North Carolina by an 80-72 score in Littlejohn Coliseum, giving Clemson two wins over top-10 teams within a 10-day period.

February 4, 1975—Clemson achieved its first national ranking after defeating 10th-ranked North Carolina 80-72 just three days prior. The Tigers entered the UPI poll at 15th and finished the season with a number-19 ranking.

February 22, 1975—Clemson defeated fourth-ranked and defending national champion N.C. State by a 92-70 score in Littlejohn Coliseum.

March 13, 1975—Clemson was ranked 19th in the final UPI poll, its first final top-20 ranking in history.

November 28, 1975—The Tigers' Tree Rollins had 22 rebounds in a victory over Harvard in the season opener and in the IPTAY Invitational in Clemson, SC.

December 6, 1975—Tree Rollins had 22 rebounds vs. Charleston Southern at Clemson, SC.

December 13, 1975—Tree Rollins had the Tigers' first-ever triple-double vs. Presbyterian, finishing with 20 points, 14 rebounds, and 10 blocked shots in Clemson's 103-64 victory at Clemson, SC.

December 28-29, 1975—Clemson defeated Boson College 80-60 and Davidson 72-54 in claiming the Charlotte Invitational in Charlotte, NC.

February 28, 1976—Clemson hit 70 percent of their shots (48-68 from the field) in a 122-79 win over Florida Southern.

November 26-27, 1976—The Tigers defeated Yale 104-50 and Florida State 108-92 en route to claiming the IPTAY Tournament at Clemson, SC.

December 11, 1976—Tree Rollins had 23 rebounds vs. Tennessee Tech. The Tigers won this game 133-78. The 133 points is the most points scored in a single game by a Clemson team.

December 14, 1976—The Tigers' Derreck Johnson had 16 assists vs. Buffalo in Clemson's 98-67 win at Littlejohn Coliseum.

December 16, 1976—Clemson's Tree Rollins had 10 blocked shots in a 59-54 victory over Jacksonville at Jacksonville, FL.

December 28, 1976—Derreck Johnson had 18 assists in Clemson's 128-76 win over Boston College as part of the Dairyland Classic in Milwaukee, WI.

January 19, 1977—Tree Rollins had 23 rebounds against ACC foe Maryland as the Tigers upset the 13th-ranked Terrapins 93-71, at Clemson, SC.

February 23, 1977—Tree Rollins had a triple-double, as he had 16 points, 15 rebounds, and 10 blocked shots vs. Duke in the Tigers' 67-63 upset win over the 18th-ranked Blue Devils at Clemson, SC.

February 26, 1977—Tree Rollins became the first Clemson athlete to have his jersey retired. His No. 30 was hung before the Roanoke game, his final home game as a Tiger. Rollins was Clemson's first Associated Press All-American in basketball.

November 25-26, 1977—The Tigers defeated Texas Christian 125-62 and Rhode Island 82-75 in winning the IPTAY Invitational in Clemson, SC.

December 1-2, 1978—Clemson defeated Brown 73-57 and Kent State 72-52 as the Tigers claimed the IPTAY Tournament Championship.

December 28-29, 1978—The Tigers defeated Texas-El Paso 68-57 and Texas Tech 58-57 as the Tigers won the Sun Bowl Carnival in El Paso, TX.

February 21, 1979—Clemson beat Duke 70-49 in Littlejohn Coliseum. The Blue Devils, who had been to the NCAA Finals the year before, were ranked sixth in the nation entering the game.

November 30-December 1, 1979—The Tigers defeated Siena 90-72 and Middle Tennessee 94-61 as the Tigers claimed the IPTAY Tournament Championship in Clemson, SC.

January 2, 1980—Clemson began a terrific week in Littlejohn Coliseum with a 93-76 victory over sixth-ranked North Carolina and Head Coach Dean Smith.

January 9, 1980—Clemson defeated number-one-ranked Duke in overtime 87-82. A Littlejohn Coliseum record crowd of 13, 863 was in attendance. Bobby Conrad made eight of eight free throws to clinch the victory for the Tigers.

February 9, 1980—Clemson defeated fifth-raked Maryland 90-81 at Clemson. It was the third win over a top-six team at Clemson in the 1979-80 season. Billy Williams, Larry Nance, and Horace Wyatt all had 20-point nights for the Tigers, who moved into the top 10 in the nation after the victory.

March 1, 1980—Clemson was invited to the NCAA Tournament for the first time in school history. The Tigers were the number-four seed in the West Regional.

March 6, 1980—Clemson participated in its first NCAA Tournament game with a 76-73 win over Utah State in the West Regional at Ogden, UT.

March 8, 1980—Clemson defeated Brigham Young 71-66 in Ogden, UT, in the First Round of the NCAA Tournament in the West Regional.

March 12, 1980—Clemson defeated Lamar 74-66 at Tucson, AZ, in the NCAA's round of 16. This was the 23rd win of the season for the Tigers, a school record at the time.

March 15, 1980—UCLA defeated Clemson 85-74 at Tucson, AZ, in the NCAA's West Regional Final, (Final Eight).

November 28-29, 1980—Clemson defeated Cornell 82-64 and Fairfield 99-71 as Clemson won the IPTAY Tournament at Clemson, SC.

December 29, 1980—The Tigers defeated eventual national champion Indiana 58-57 in the semifinals of the Rainbow Classic. Indiana was ranked 15th in the nation entering the game, and it was the first time Clemson had beaten the eventual national champion.

December 30, 1980—Clemson claimed the championship at the Rainbow Classic following a 75-71 overtime victory over hometown favorite Hawaii. The tournament victory contributed to the Tigers' 12-1 start that year.

November 27-28, 1981—Clemson defeated Bowling Green 809-91 and Stetson 79-72 as the Tigers won the IPTAY Tournament in Clemson, SC.

November 26, 1982—Clemson's Milan Belich nailed the first three-pointer in ACC history when he hit one at the buzzer against Texas A&M to send the game into overtime. Clemson ultimately won the Alaska Shootout contest 82-79 in double overtime. This was the first year the three-point shot was deemed legal under NCAA rules.

November 26-27, 1983—Clemson defeated Wagner 105-55 and Marquette 66-61 in overtime to claim the IPTAY Invitational in Clemson, SC.

February 29, 1984—Coach Bill Foster won his last ACC game, a stunning 77-76 victory over 15th-ranked Duke in Cameron Indoor Stadium. Clemson had a 76-61 lead with seven minutes left, then held on as Johnny Dawkins missed a potential game-winning 15-foot jumper. Horace Grant, then a freshman, was a big key for the Tigers, with 16 points.

November 30-December 1, 1984—Clemson defeated Campbell 90-55 and South Alabama 79-69 as the Tigers won the IPTAY Invitational. Former Clemson Head Coach Press Maverich was an assistant coach at Campbell.

January 8, 1985—Clemson defeated eighth-ranked Georgia Tech 90-81 in Atlanta. The contest marked the first ACC game for new coach Cliff Ellis. Vincent Hamilton scored 27 points to lead the Tigers to victory.

January 30, 1985—Clemson defeated 11th-ranked North Carolina 52-50 on a jump shot by Chris Michael with only three seconds remaining.

November 25, 1985—The Tigers' Grayson Marshall set a NCAA record with 20 assists against Maryland-Eastern Shore in an 83-57 win at Clemson, SC.

November 29-30, 1985—Clemson defeated East Tennessee State 92-67 and South Florida 70-60 as the Tigers won the IPTAY Invitational Championship at Clemson, SC.

December 2, 1985—Clemson's Larry Middleton was 12-13 from the field in a 101-63 win over Rider.

November 28-29, 1986—The Tigers' Horace Grant was 12-13 from the field in 108-91 victory over Georgia State. The Tigers also defeated Boston University to win the final IPTAY Invitational Championship.

March 13, 1987—Southwest Missouri State defeated Clemson 65-59 in Atlanta, GA, in the NCAA Tournament's Southeast Regional.

November 28, 1987-January 20, 1987—Clemson won 17 games in a row. This set the school record for the most consecutive wins to start the season.

January 20, 1987—After defeating Georgia Tech on a jumper by Michael Tait with three seconds left, the Tigers improved their season mark to 17-0. Clemson achieved a high national ranking of 10th before falling to Duke four days later in overtime.

February 18, 1987—Clemson defeated Wake Forest 87-71 to improve its record to 24-2, the best 26-game record in Clemson history.

February 25, 1987—Clemson defeated Georgia Tech 88-77 for its 10th ACC win of the season. The 10 ACC wins are tied for the Clemson record for league victories in a season. Horace Grant played his final game at home and had 30 points and 11 rebounds in a dominating performance.

March 2, 1988—Dale Davis had 23 points and 17 rebounds to lead Clemson to a 79-77 upset of ninth-ranked Duke.

March 5, 1988—Clemson upset 13th-ranked Georgia Tech 97-94 in double overtime at Littlejohn Coliseum. It gave the Tigers consecutive wins over top-15 teams in Littlejohn Coliseum.

January 7, 1989-December 15, 1991—Clemson won 29 consecutive games at home. The streak started with a 75-58 victory over Maryland and ended with a 108-100 loss to UNC-Charlotte on December 15, 1991. This streak included 13 victories over ACC teams; five of those teams were ranked in the AP top 25.

March 4, 1989—Dale Davis was 12-13 from the floor vs. 25th-ranked Georgia Tech as the Tigers defeated the Yellow Jackets 81-79 in overtime at Clemson, SC.

February 28, 1990—Clemson defeated Duke 97-93 for its 10th conference win of the season. The victory clinched at least a tie for the ACC title, and the Clemson fans stormed the court while the Tigers cut down the nets. The following Sunday, North Carolina gained a victory at Duke to give Clemson the outright league title, its first ACC regular season championship in history. It was the

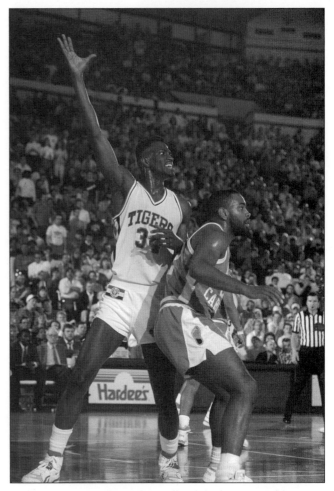

Dale Davis was a three-time All-ACC player over his career.

final home game for Clemson career scoring leader Elden Campbell.

March 17, 1990—Clemson advanced to the Sweet 16 of the NCAA Tournament after defeating La Salle, who had won 22 straight entering the contest, by a score of 79-75. The Tigers erased a 16-point halftime deficit, the largest halftime deficit overcome to gain victory in Clemson history.

March 22, 1990—Clemson fell just short of advancing to the Elite Eight after Tate George hit a turnaround jumper at the buzzer to give UConn a 71-70 victory. Clemson had overcome a 19-point deficit to take a 70-69 lead.

December 20-21, 1990—Clemson defeated Coppin State 71-70 and Florida Atlantic 99-89 as the Tigers won the Florida International Tournament in Miami, FL.

December 12, 1992—Clemson's Sharone Wright had a triple-double vs. UNC Greensboro as he had 21 points, 15 rebounds, and 10 blocked shots in the Tigers' 88-62 victory.

January 26, 1993—The Tigers' Shorone Wright had his second career triple-double as he had 12 points, 14 rebounds, and 10 blocked shots in an 82-72 win over Maryland at Clemson, SC. Wright finished second in Clemson history in career blocks and was the Tigers' highest-ever draft pick at number six in 1994.

January 4, 1995—Head Coach Rick Barnes quickly generated enthusiasm in the basketball program his first season by upsetting ninth-ranked Duke 75-70 in Cameron Indoor Stadium.

March 8, 1996—Clemson knocked North Carolina out of the ACC Tournament with a 75-73 victory, its first ever in the tournament versus the Tar Heels. Greg Buckner took a pass from Harold Jamison and dunked the ball over Antawn Jamison with just 0.6 seconds remaining. Buckner's dunk remains one of the Tigers' most famous plays in history. The win was the first by Clemson over North Carolina in the Tar Heel state since 1967.

November 15, 1996—Clemson shocked the college basketball world with a thrilling 79-71 upset over defending national champion and third-ranked Kentucky. The upset still stands as the highest-ranked nonconference victory in Clemson history.

January 7, 1997—Clemson, ranked number five in the Associated Press poll at the time, defeated number-10 Duke 86-82 in overtime. The meeting was the first ever between two schools ranked in the top 10 at Littlejohn Coliseum. The Tigers trailed by six with 54 seconds remaining but sent the game to overtime, and Greg Buckner sealed the victory with a steal and a subsequent dunk.

January 23, 1997—Clemson played Wake Forest in the first meeting between two top-five schools in Littlejohn Coliseum history. The Tigers were ranked number two by the Associated Press, still its highest ranking ever obtained. A capacity crowd watched as Tim Duncan and Wake Forest held on for a 65-62 victory.

March 16, 1997—Clemson shut down All-American Shea Seals and the Tulsa Golden Hurricane to advance to its first Sweet 16 NCAA appearance since the 1989-90 season.

March 20, 1997—Clemson battled number-one seed Minnesota into double overtime, before falling 90-84 in the NCAA Round of 16. Tony Christie hit a driving layup at the end of regulation to send the game into overtime for the Tigers. The Tigers ended the year ranked number eight in the final *USA Today* poll, their highest in history.

March 23, 1999—Clemson downed Xavier 79-76 to advance to its first NIT Championship game.

January 15, 2000—Clemson's Will Solomon scored 43 points against Virginia at Littlejohn Coliseum. The Cavaliers defeated the Tigers 98-91. Solomon's total marked the most points ever scored by a Clemson player in the arena's history.

September 9, 2000—Dale Davis became the charter men's basketball member in Clemson's Ring of Honor. Davis was the first player in ACC history to lead the league in rebounding and field goal percentage in consecutive

years and was a first round pick in the 1991 NBA draft by the Indiana Pacers.

January 24, 2001—The Tigers' Will Solomon scored 41 points against Georgia Tech in a 111-108 loss to the Yellow Jackets.

February 18, 2001—Clemson shocked the college basketball world again as it defeated number-one ranked North Carolina 75-65 in Littlejohn Coliseum. It was only the second time Clemson had ever defeated the top-ranked team in college basketball. Will Solomon led the Tigers with 25 points, and Tony Stockman clinched the victory with a pull-up three pointer in the last minute.

February 13, 2002—Clemson's Ed Scott had 16 assists vs. Wake Forest in a 118-115 triple-overtime victory over the 19th-ranked Demon Deacons at Clemson, SC. Scott also scored 30 points, and this was the second time a player has scored at least 30 points and dealt out 15 assists in an ACC game.

January 31, 2004—Clemson made 11-13 three-point goals, a Clemson record and the sixth-best three-point shooting pct game in NCAA history in an 81-72 victory over 12th-ranked North Carolina at Littlejohn Coliseum. Shawan Robinson scored a career-high 24 points and made 5-6 three-points shots.

December 4, 2004—Clemson won 63-62 over South Carolina on a three-pointer by Cheyenne Moore in the final seconds of overtime in Columbia, SC.

March 1, 2005—Olu Babalola and Sharrod Ford scored five points in the final 10 seconds on Senior Night, and Ford delivered the game-winning slam at the buzzer as Clemson defeated Virginia Tech 66-64.

December 19-21, 2005—Clemson won the San Juan Shootout title with a 66-59 win over Akron. The Tigers also defeated PR-Mayaguez 101-60 and Holy Cross 71-48 in the tournament.

November 10, 2006-January 6, 2007—Clemson won 17 consecutive games. This tied the school record for most victories to start the season.

January 6, 2007—Clemson improved to 2-0 in ACC play and 17-0 after back-to-back last-second wins at Florida State and home versus Georgia Tech. Cliff Hammonds made a high-arching layup with under three seconds left in Tallahassee, then James Mays hit a left-handed driving layup to give the Tigers the last-second win over the Yellow Jackets. The Tigers matched a school record with a 17-0 start after defeating N.C. State three days later.

January 13, 2007—Clemson defeated Arkansas State 83-44, Monmouth 77-65, and Old Dominion 74-70 in winning the Old Dominion Classic in Norfolk, VA.

March 21, 2007—Clemson got a 29-point effort from K.C. Rivers and downed Big East power Syracuse 74-70 on national television in the quarterfinals of the NIT at Clemson, SC.

March 27, 2007—The Tigers matched a school record with 25 wins after defeating Air Force 68-67 in the semifinals of the NIT at New York in famed venue Madison Square Garden. It marked the second time in school history that Clemson advanced to the championship game of the NIT.

March 29, 2007—West Virginia defeated Clemson 78-73 in the finals of the NIT Tournament in Madison Square Garden in New York, NY.

March 2, 2008—Clemson rallied from a 20-point deficit to pull out a 73-70 win over Maryland in College Park. It was the largest second half deficit overcome by Clemson. Terrence Oglesby hit the game-winning three-pointer with 2.3 seconds left.

March 15, 2008—Clemson upset second-seeded and seventh-ranked Duke in the semifinals of the ACC Tournament in Charlotte, NC, earning the program's second-ever berth in the championship game and first since 1962. It was the school's 24th win of the season, giving the Tiger program a record 49 wins in back-to-back years.

November 14-16, 2008—The Tigers defeated Hofstra 98-69, Texas Christian 70-58, and Temple 76-72 in winning the College of Charleston Invitational in Charleston, SC.

February 4, 2009—Clemson upset third-ranked Duke by a score of 74-47. It was the largest margin of defeat ever for Clemson against a ranked opponent. It was also Duke's largest margin of defeat since the 1990 championship game.

November 29, 2009—Clemson knocked off eventual NCAA runner-up Butler 70-69 in the 76 Classic in Anaheim, CA. Demontez Stitt hit a pair of go-ahead free throws in the final seconds, while Trevor Booker blocked a three-point attempt at the buzzer.

January 23, 2010—Clemson played host to ESPN College Game Day for the first time in history of the popular weekly series. Over 4,000 fans were in attendance for the show, which preceded the Tigers' game against Duke later that night.

January 25, 2011—First-year Head Coach Brad Brownell led the Tigers to a thrilling come-from-behind 60-50 victory over N.C. State after trailing by 19 points (31-12) in the opening half of play.

March 15, 2011—Clemson defeated Alabama-Birmingham 70-52 in the "First-Four" round of the NCAA Tournament in Dayton, OH.

March 18, 2014—Clemson defeated Georgia State 78-66 in the first round of the NIT at Clemson, SC. K.J. McDaniels led the Tigers with 30 points.

March 23, 2014—The Tigers defeated Illinois 50-49 at Littlejohn Coliseum in the NIT. Rod Hall scored the game-winning layup with 9.3 seconds left.

March 25, 2014—Clemson won over Belmont 73-68 at Clemson, SC, in the NIT quarterfinal round.

April 1, 2014—SMU Defeated Clemson 65-59 in the NIT semifinals in New York, NY.

February 6, 2015—At its Winter Quarterly meeting, the Clemson Board of Trustees gave final approval to begin construction on the renovation project of Littlejohn Coliseum with a targeted start date, pending state agency approvals, of later in the spring of 2015. The Board gave its final approval for the renovation of Littlejohn Coliseum, including reconstruction of the seating areas, along with new practice facilities, locker room, meeting rooms, and coaches' offices for both the men's and women's basketball programs. The trustees also approved the athletic facilities bond resolution for the project, which is slated to cost $63.5 million to be financed completely by the athletic department and IPTAY.

March 18, 2015—Clemson Athletics received final approval from the South Carolina Budget and Control Board to begin renovation of Littlejohn Coliseum. The Board approved the construction project and issuance of bonds for the project, which is slated to cost $63.5 million to be financed completely by the athletic department and IPTAY. The project previously received approval from the Clemson Board of Trustees and the Joint Bond Review Committee. The Budget and Control Board's sign-off is the final step in the approval process, and construction is slated to begin following graduation on May 8.

April 16, 2015—Clemson University and the city of Greenville formally announced a partnership to host 2015-16 men's basketball home games and commencement ceremonies, beginning in August. The announcement took place at the brand-new Clemson entrance at the Bon Secours Wellness Arena.

January 5, 2016—The 74-73 win at Syracuse was Clemson's first overtime triumph on the road in ACC play since 1986-87, Horace Grant's senior season. It was Clemson's first-ever road win over a team that made the Final Four in the same season.

January 10-16, 2016—For the first time in program history, Clemson defeated three consecutive top-25 opponents. It happened over the course of a calendar week as the Tigers beat Louisville, Duke, and Miami. Clemson was the only team in the country to defeat all three this season. The Tigers beat top-10 opponents Duke and Miami in consecutive games in this stretch, and this has not been achieved by a Clemson team since the 1975-76 season.

November 11, 2016—Clemson defeated Georgia 76-64 in the opening night in the newly renovated Littlejohn Coliseum. The win came in front of a capacity crowd of 9,000.

WOMEN'S
Basketball

NCAA Final 8:

1990-91

NCAA Final 16:

1988-89, 1989-90, 1990-91, 1998-99

NCAA Appearances:

1981-82, 1987-88, 1988-89, 1989-90, 1990-91, 1991-92, 1992-93, 1993-94, 1995-96, 1996-97, 1997-98, 1998-99, 1999-2000, 2000-01, 2001-02

ACC Champions:

1995-96, 1998-99

ACC Regular Season Championship:

1980-81

Top-25 Seasons:

1980-81 (20th), 1987-88 (20th), 1988-89 (13th), 1989-90 (19th), 1990-91 (8th), 1991-92 (19th), 1993-94 (22nd), 1995-96 (14th), 1996-97 (21st), 1997-98 (14th), 1998-99 (10th), 2000-01 (22nd)

Women's basketball was first played at Clemson during the 1975-76 season. The Lady Tigers had the prestige of playing in the inaugural NCAA Tournament in 1982 and made many return trips in the late 1980s along the way through to the new millennium.

The first women's coach was Mary Kinnerty, who also coached the women's tennis team. She would only coach the Lady Tigers for one season (1975-76), and then Annie Tribble from nearby Anderson College would take the reins.

THE TRIBBLE ERA

Annie Tribble is proud of her career at Clemson and what she did for elevating women's sports.

At both Anderson Junior College (now Anderson University) and Clemson, she helped start and developed the women's basketball programs, winning three National Championships at Anderson and carrying Clemson to postseason play, including the inaugural NCAA Tournament in 1982.

During her career she not only coached women's basketball, but she also played. She played basketball, field hockey, and softball during her high school days at Anderson Girls' High in Anderson, SC. She went on to play basketball, track and field, and tennis at Anderson Junior College in her late 20s when she was a housewife.

After earning a degree at Anderson, she graduated from Clemson with a BA in English. She joined the Anderson College staff in November of 1965 as intramural director and instructor of physical education. She was soon named the first-ever women's basketball coach at the school.

Tribble's coaching career with the women's team at Anderson started in the 1967-68 campaign. During her nine-year career, she led the Trojans to an impressive 155-33 record. She led Anderson Junior College to three National Championships and one runner-up finish.

With so much success at nearby Anderson Junior College, it was only natural that Clemson would contact her to coach the Tigers and their fledging program.

"I was excited when Clemson contacted me," said Tribble. "I was a Clemson graduate and I had always hoped they would start a program."

Tribble took over the Lady Tigers' second season when Clemson's first coach Mary Kinnerty decided after coaching two sports in her first year that she would devote her time as the women's tennis coach.

"I knew some of my former players had transferred to Clemson as they had a team a year before I had arrived. It was an exciting time for me. The ACC had not started the tournament yet and I remember going to meetings to help get that started. It was fun to see the tournament get started and be a part of that process. We used to play on campus sites in the earlier years and then they moved the tournament to a neutral site at Fayetteville, NC, a few years later. We played for the 1982 championship in Raleigh and got beat by Maryland.

"The biggest disappointment when we first started was the lack of support. Looking back, I should have asked for more such things as assistant coaches. Jimmy Howell, a graduate assistant, and I were the only coaches for the first few years. I really enjoyed my career and I really enjoyed recruiting."

When talking about star players, she had many. Two that come to mind are Donna Forester and Barbara Kennedy. "I can't imagine how many points they would have scored if the three-point field goal would have been in existence! They were probably two of the best players to come out of the state of Georgia."

Tribble remembers many classic games while she coached the Tigers. "We had great battles with N.C. State, and Maryland was always a tough game. When you beat Maryland, it was a big accomplishment in those days.

"I believed in playing tough competition. We played Tennessee, Louisiana Tech, Old Dominion, and Georgia. I believed in playing tough competition as it made the team better and it gave the team valuable experience."

During her stint with the Tigers, Tribble coached five All-Americans and eight All-Atlantic Coast Conference players. She led Clemson to seven 20-plus-win seasons and took her Lady Tiger teams to seven postseason tournaments. She led Clemson to a 200-135 record in 11

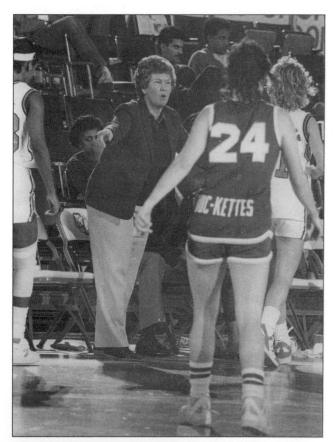

Annie Tribble was the head coach at Clemson for 11 seasons and had a 200-135 record.

seasons. During her career she was 355-168 in 20 years of coaching. She coached Clemson to the 1980-81 ACC regular-season championship and served as a member of the US Olympic Committee.

During this time she also raised a family with her husband Glenn and they had two sons, John and Andy. They now have 11 grandchildren.

Probably, the thing that sets Tribble apart from other coaches is her down-to-earth attitude. She took a personal interest in each of her player's lives and studies. Annie Tribble was not just a winner, but she inspired young people to become winners, as well.

"It was good to be on the ground floor and help get the Clemson program started. I really love young people. It was fun seeing them grow, and later hearing that they had families and were successful and productive citizens," said Tribble.

Annie Tribble brought to Clemson one of the best players to have ever played in the Atlantic Coast Conference, the legendary Barbara Kennedy.

BARBARA KENNEDY

The 1982 season was the last year Lady Tiger Barbara Kennedy-Dixon donned a Clemson uniform, but she still holds many school and Atlantic Coast Conference records, including the records for most points (3,113) and rebounds (1,252).

How she got started in basketball and how she ended up at Clemson was via perseverance and determination.

"In the sixth grade I tried out for the cheerleading squad that was going to cheer for the junior varsity basketball team. From that point, I fell in love with the game of basketball. The guys made it interesting. After cheering that one season, I decided to try out for the girls' junior varsity team and I made it my first year. I really did not know what to do and I made a lot of mistakes that first year. I learned a great deal. I also played pickup basketball games with other guys and this is what helped improve my game.

"Playing basketball in college was a goal for me, but it was a goal I did not think I could reach. I did not know how that process worked. I did not know if I wanted to leave home or not. As I finished my junior year and received some praise from opposing coaches, I got interested. Different coaches would tell me to concentrate on the books as well as my game.

"In my senior year I started realizing there may be an opportunity. I started concentrating on my studies, and working on my basketball skills. I thought I made some progress as I started getting some contacts from college coaches. My first contact was Coach Annie Tribble from Clemson and that solidified that there was maybe a chance for me to compete at the next level.

"I really wasn't recruited that heavily," said Kennedy-Dixon. "West Georgia, South Carolina, and Clemson were the only schools that were interested in me. The reason I chose Clemson had nothing to do with the school because I had never been there and I did not know where it was. The person that first called me was Coach Tribble. I remember my first phone call from Coach Tribble and how pleasant she was, how complimentary she was and how encouraging she was. She continued to show interest. She was very much like my mom as she had a caring and loving personality. She conveyed that on the telephone.

"I remember when she came for a visit at one of our games. I tried so hard—maybe too hard. I was trying to prove to her that I could play. Things went terrible! I think she started backing off. But I did not. I was waiting for her phone calls. She called me one day and told me she had used all her scholarships. She also told me if I made the test scores and wanting to come she would bring me in on a volleyball scholarship. I took the SAT and made the required score. I told Coach Tribble I made the test scores and here I come! I came to Clemson on a volleyball scholarship. Coach Tribble was the motherly-type coach—the characteristics I needed to be successful.

"Once I arrived at Clemson I thought I was close to Heaven! I saw this campus with its beauty and everyone was friendly. I was in awe of the facilities, the administrators, the professors and how friendly and helpful they were. It was a dream come true! I was surrounded by people who cared for me not only as an athlete, but

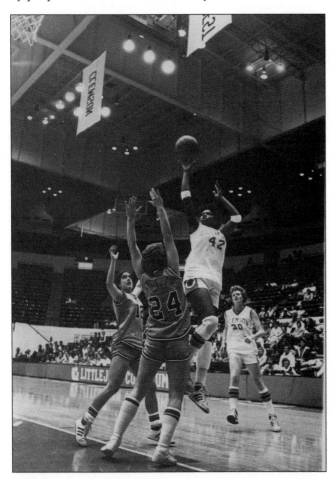

Barbara Kennedy was a two-time All-American who led the nation in scoring in 1982.

as a person. I must have known in the back of my mind that this was the place for me. I wanted to play for Coach Tribble.

"The most memorable game that sticks out in my mind was the North Carolina game on February 23, 1982. This was the first game my mom had a chance to see me play on the collegiate level. She got a chance to hear me sing the National Anthem for the men's game after our game. It was a very emotional day as it was the last home game for me at Clemson. I had other family members there too. It was a most memorable day."

JIM DAVIS LEADS CLEMSON TO FOUR NCAA FINAL 16s AND ONE NCAA FINAL EIGHT.

After Coach Tribble retired in 1987, Jim Davis came to town and carried Clemson to 14 NCAA Tournaments and two ACC Championships in 1996 and 1999.

According to Davis, There's nothing stronger than the family bond.

To create this strong link and make it successful involves an untiring work ethic and enduring teamwork.

These two elements are consistent with a winning basketball team. Clemson head basketball coach Jim Davis bases his coaching philosophies on these two family principles—both hard work and teamwork.

"I am the 10th of 12 children [seven boys and five girls] in my family," said former Clemson Head Coach Jim Davis. "We are blessed that all 12 are still living. All the sisters and brothers have all been successful in the careers they have chosen. I attribute what little success I have had to the principles my mother and father taught me. I also learned a lot from my older brother and sisters.

"There is no substitute for hard work. My dad worked two jobs, the L& N Railroad and of course the hard job of being a farmer. He would work 3 p.m.-11 p.m. on the railroad and then would get up at the crack of dawn to start his farm work. Hard work was a principle he instilled in all of us. He worked hard at providing for us, and made it possible for us to participate in athletics.

"Teamwork was another valuable lesson. Everyone had chores to do and they had to accept the responsibilities of getting them done every day, or our family could not function. Everyone had a part to play."

Davis's absorption of the principles of hard work and teamwork paid off at Clemson, as his teams' trips to the postseason became customary and the Lady Tigers became a staple in the rankings.

In 1987-88, his rookie campaign at Clemson, Davis gave the words "turn around" a new meaning. In one short year, he tripled the number of wins of the 1986-87 team by turning a 7-21 club into a 21-9 squad in 1987-88, and it was also the best turnaround season in the history of the ACC.

In his 18 years at Clemson, the Lady Tigers were 355-197. He had 16 postseason appearances, 14 NCAA

Jim Davis led Clemson to 355 victories in 18 seasons.

Tournament appearances, 11 top-25 seasons, and 11 seasons when the Lady Tigers won 20 or more games. He finished with 51 victories against ranked competition and coached 16 All-ACC players.

"In any area of life you learn to depend upon each other and that is what players on teams have to do for strength. Sometimes you don't feel like doing work, but you have to perform your duties by encouragement from others.

"My dad is responsible for me getting in coaching. We would be out playing ball and if there was work to be done he would say 'you better leave that ball alone—you can't earn a living with that ball.' I guess I wanted to prove him wrong in that one instance. I have a love for athletics. I knew I wanted to be a basketball coach in the seventh grade."

There are many athletic departments that are glad he did, as Davis has been successful everywhere he has been.

Davis spent six successful years at Roane State Community College in Harriman, TN. Davis put together one of the most successful stints ever in the junior college ranks by coaching Roane State's Raiderettes to 127 wins against only 35 losses, which represents a .784 winning pct. His 1984 team finished 27-2 and won the National Junior College Athletic Association National Championship.

"At one time, a high school coach was the most respected person in the community. He performed many roles in the high school, and they looked to the coach for discipline. If anybody got sick or injured, they would get the coach. If anyone needed counseling, the faculty would call on him. He was the most respected person around, and I wanted to be a part of that. The coach was always right.

"Another principle my parents instilled in me was to never, never, never quit—always see things through to the end. I played football and there were times I wanted to quit, but my dad would not allow that. I try to instill in my players to never quit.

"Along the way I have made some good friends in the coaching profession. I consider every coach in the ACC a friend. Although we compete on the floor and in recruiting, I want to walk off the floor and be friends.

"I loved coaching women's basketball at Clemson. I did everything I could to support and help our players. I wanted to be there when they needed me. I tried to teach each one of them the philosophy of working hard, nothing is free in this world, and if it's worth working for, you will appreciate it more. We encouraged them to be the best they can be on and off the floor and simply do what is right. If you give the best effort in doing what is right, everything will be all right, win or lose."

A native of Englewood, TN, Davis is married to the former Bobbie Henderson, and they have one son, Todd, and a daughter-in-law, Rhonda.

"When I was offered the job at Clemson, what jumped out at me was the family atmosphere—Clemson is one big family. The alumni, friends, fans, and the Orange Brigade members all make up this family. The love, support, and care of our Clemson family is a constant reminder of the love, support, and care I received when I was growing up."

Looking back on the entire Clemson experience, the people are what made it so special.

As far as memories of games, Davis has plenty.

"I remember one game we were playing Rutgers and we came back from a 20-point deficit in the 2nd half and won their tournament. The night before we beat Texas on a last-second shot as Dana Puckett hit a three-pointer. I also remember Peggy Sells hitting the shot that put us in the NCAA Final Eight.

"Yes, I remember us beating the number-one and number-two ranked teams, I remember the ACC Championships and those will always be there, but what stands out to me were the people, the players, the fans, and how special Clemson was as an institution. I wish I would have won more games and maybe I would have stayed longer.

"Clemson sold itself," said Davis. "If we could get the person on campus when recruiting I felt that we had a great chance of signing that person. Clemson was never a tough sell, because I love the place so much. Once you get orange blood, you never get rid of it. That's why I used to tell my players time and time again, 'Once a Tiger, Always a Tiger.' I also encouraged my players to join IPTAY after they graduated and give back to the school that helped you.

"I think about the sacrifices that people like Dr. R.C. Edwards, Coach Frank Howard, Harvey Gantt, [and] Walter M. Riggs made and how they shaped the school and their love for Clemson—it's amazing."

Coach Davis feels at home in Tigertown, at home with his Clemson family.

One of his players who starred for Davis in the early 1990s was Cheron Wells from Dayton, OH.

SURE SHOT

Excitement and enthusiasm are expressed in a variety of forms.

For Clemson's Cheron Wells, the excitement she brought to Lady Tiger basketball centered around her winding acrobatic moves toward the basket, a successful, left-handed jump shot in the closing seconds of a game, and a crisp, sharp pass to an open teammate.

Wells's enthusiasm for basketball and life were displayed by her warm friendly smile, a winning attitude, and a unique closeness to her family, teammates, and friends.

She brought excitement and enthusiasm to Lady Tiger basketball in 1990-91 and 1991-92. She was a junior college transfer from Kilgore Junior College in Tyler, TX. She was the leading scorer (14.1 PPG) on the Clemson team that advanced to the NCAA Tournament's Final Eight in 1990-91. She became the first Lady Tiger to be named to an All-Region team and was also the first Lady Tiger since 1982 to be named to the ACC All-Tournament team as she led the Tigers to the championship game, another first since the 1982 season.

Clemson was the only team in the nation to defeat both a number-one- and a number-two-ranked team (Virginia and N.C. State, respectively) during that season, and Wells eclipsed the 25-point mark in each game.

In 1991-92, Wells averaged 15.0 points per game and led the Tigers to the NCAA Tournament's second round. She was named second-team All-ACC and was named a third-team All-American. She also participated in the 1992 US Olympic Trials. She finished her career scoring 930 points in only two years of play.

As her career continued, Wells became the focal point of nearly every team's defensive strategy. For her explosiveness and ability to change the momentum of a game, she was unmatched by few in the country.

Wells attributed her fine play to being enthusiastic and excited about playing the game she loves the most.

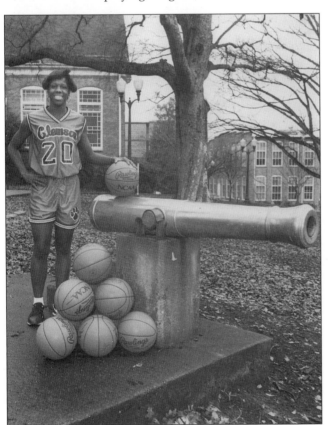

Cheron Wells led the Tigers to the NCAA Final Eight in 1991 and was named to the NCAA East Region team that season.

"I was an enthusiastic player and this made me play harder," said Wells. "When the adrenaline was flowing and you were out there in front of the crowd playing the game you loved the most—there was nothing better.

"Basketball is a unique sport; there are so many things you can do with the ball such as driving to the basket, creating scoring opportunities with good passes, and making the big play on defense. When we were playing, I saw the crowd getting excited and the players are getting motivated; it's like a continuous cycle. There is nothing better, it is indescribable.

"I fell in love with Clemson on my first visit. On the initial trip I met so many friendly people, and with Clemson's academic reputation, I knew this was the right place for me. Jim Davis was a great coach and he helped me in a number of ways. He knew the game of basketball and he brought my game a long ways defensively."

"Cheron was one of the finest guards in the ACC," said Davis. "She was among the best guards that I have coached in my career."

Wells brought some exciting moments to Clemson basketball with her quickness, and her upbeat personality that was created by her genuine love for the game.

BARR IS A STAR

A post player who "starred" for Jim Davis was Jessica Barr.

The Clemson promotional material for Jessica Barr declared the short and powerful statement "Barr is a Star!"

Was she ever! Jessica Barr developed into one of the most heralded players to play at Clemson since Barbara Kennedy.

Barr transferred to Clemson from Georgia and played for Clemson for two seasons, the 1992-93 and the 1993-94 campaigns.

During the 1994 season, she was the first Tiger to be named ACC Player of the Year. She was named first-team All-ACC and All-ACC Tournament. She was the third Lady Tiger ever to lead the team in scoring, rebounding, and field goal percentage in the same season. And she led the ACC in scoring with a 19.8 average, scoring 594 points as a senior.

She capped off her senior campaign by being one of 10 players to be named a Kodak All-America and a *Basketball America* All-America. Later on, she was named the State of South Carolina Amateur Athlete of the Year by the S.C. Athletic Hall of Fame.

Barr was an accurate shooter during her career, as she hit 53 percent of her shots and finished in third place on the Clemson career list for the best accuracy. She was also a threat from the outside, hitting 38 percent of her shots beyond the three-point line. The 6-2 forward/center was a Batesburg, SC, native.

After her senior season, she was invited to try out for the United States National team.

Jessica Barr was a 1994 All-America player.

TWO ACC CHAMPIONSHIPS

When thinking of Clemson's best team, the 1999 squad soon comes to mind.

It would probably be the overwhelming choice by fans, as well. The team consisted of four seniors, Natasha Anderson, Nikki Blassingame, Amy Geren, and Itoro Umoh. These four players became household names to the Clemson faithful.

This senior class helped win the school's very first ACC Championship their freshman year in 1996 and finished their career with another ACC Championship Trophy in 1999. It's no wonder that this group of seniors became the school's winningest class in history with a record of 93-33 for a .738 pct.

The year started with a bang as the 1999 squad won the first 11 contests. The team started the season unranked and appeared in the polls at the number-25 spot after winning the first four contests of the season. Clemson won two ACC contests by defeating N.C. State and Maryland in the month of December. After wins over Dartmouth and South Carolina, Clemson had an impressive win over Louisiana State in Myrtle Beach, SC, on December 20. Umoh's driving layup with 3.1 seconds left gave Clemson the victory over the Tigers from Baton Rouge, LA.

Clemson's four seniors in 1999 Natasha Anderson, Itoro Umoh, Amy Geren, and Nikki Blassingame led Clemson to the 1999 ACC Championship.

After being ranked 14th during the middle of December, the win over LSU must have impressed the voters, as the Lady Tigers moved up to 10th in the polls. Clemson lost two straight to Virginia and North Carolina, but the Lady Tigers rebounded with wins over Florida State and Georgia Tech. Clemson lost to Duke in Durham but reeled off four straight wins, including a victory over 14th-ranked Iowa State on January 24. This win proved to be costly, as Erin Batth went down with a knee injury. But she miraculously returned to the lineup five games later.

On January 17, Itoro Umoh had 12 points, 11 rebounds, and 10 assists in recording a triple-double en route to Clemson's 78-38 win over Wake Forest. This was only the fifth time a player in the history of the ACC had recorded a triple-double, the second time in Clemson history. Clemson defeated Maryland and lost to Virginia on the road. After a home loss to North Carolina, Clemson won four straight to finish the regular season with a 21-5 record.

On February 27, fourth-seeded Clemson defeated fifth-seeded N.C. State 52-51 in the quarterfinals of the ACC Tournament, in Independence Arena in Charlotte, NC. This was the first quarterfinal game ever televised.

Batth went down with another injury that required six stitches in her chin. It was questionable if she would play the next day, but she played in the Duke matchup in the semifinals. Clemson defeated the eighth-ranked and top-seeded Blue Devils 76-71, in the semifinals.

On March 1, Clemson routed 11th-ranked North Carolina 87-72 in the finals. Umoh was named the MVP of the tournament, and the injured Batth played in the Championship game, probably the most courageous effort in Clemson women's basketball history.

Clemson played host to the first two rounds of the NCAA Tournament. The Lady Tigers were seeded second in the Mideast Regional, the highest seed in school history.

Clemson defeated Florida A&M in the first round 76-45. The Lady Tigers advanced to the Final 16 with a 63-51 victory over Illinois.

This marked the fourth time that Clemson had advanced to the final 16 under Head Coach Jim Davis.

Eventual Final Four participant Georgia defeated the Lady Tigers 67-54 in the semifinals of the Mideast region in Cincinnati, OH, to end the season.

Clemson finished the season with a 26-6 record and ranked 10th in the final Associated Press poll. The 26 wins are a school record for most victories in a single season. Other accolades included the guard tandem of Itoro Umoh and Amy Geren being named first-team All-ACC. Coach Jim Davis was named Coach of the Year and Itoro Umoh was named All-Region in the Women's Basketball Coaches Association District II.

Clemson had three 1,000 point career scorers on the 1998-99 squad—Itoro Umoh (1,402), Amy Geren (1,402), and Natasha Anderson (1,033). Geren led the team in scoring with a 13.5 PPG, and Nikki Blassingame led the team in rebounding with a 7.9 RPG. Umoh led the team in assists (182) and steals (63).

Geren, known for her three-point shooting ability, won the National Three-Point Shooting Contest in the Spring of 1999.

WOMEN'S BASKETBALL HISTORY

September 7, 1975—It was officially announced that Clemson would compete in women's basketball as a varsity sport for the 1975-76 season.

December 6, 1975—Clemson played and won its first game with a 55-51 win over Davidson at Clemson, SC.

January 10, 1976—Cookie Blackney had a school-record 25 rebounds against South Carolina.

January 17, 1976—The Lady Tigers won their first-ever overtime game with a 68-66 win over Baptist College.

May 28, 1976—Annie Tribble was named the second head coach of Clemson women's basketball.

February 12, 1977—Donna Forester tied the school record with 25 rebounds in the Columbia College game.

February 26, 1977—Clemson scored a school record 136 points against Gardner-Webb.

March 12, 1977—Clemson claimed its first win over a ranked opponent. The Lady Tigers defeated 16th-ranked Memphis State 79-72, in the AIAW Region II Tournament in Memphis, TN.

December 12, 1977—Donna Forester was 12-12 from the field against Claflin. The perfect game from the field set a school record.

January 14, 1978—Clemson won its own Lady Tiger Invitational at Clemson, SC, with a win over South Carolina, 79-66, in the championship game.

January 16, 1978—The Lady Tigers' Debra Buford converted two free throws with two seconds remaining to lift Clemson to a 73-71 victory over Francis Marion.

January 11, 1979—The Lady Tigers won their own Lady Tiger Invitational at Clemson, SC, with a 61-60 win over East Carolina.

January 17, 1979—Drema Greer had a school record 17 assists in the Wake Forest game.

January 23, 1979—Clemson appeared in its first Associated Press poll. The Lady Tigers were ranked 20th with an 11-5 record.

November 28, 1979—Clemson's Bobbie Mims hit both ends of a 1-1 with eight seconds left to give Clemson an 83-81 victory over Georgia.

December 20, 1979—Clemson won the Carolina Christmas Classic with an 80-77 win over host North Carolina in the championship game.

January 9, 1980—Clemson defeated Duke 111-56 in front of 9,000 fans at Littlejohn Coliseum, the largest crowd to date to see a Lady Tiger home game.

January 12, 1980—Clemson won its own Clemson Lady Tiger Invitational with a 94-74 win over the University of Mississippi for Women.

February 8, 1980—Bobbie Mims hit both ends of a 1-1 with eight seconds remaining to give Clemson a 78-76 victory over Virginia in first round of the ACC Tournament.

February 23, 1980—Clemson won its 100th all-time game with a 77-69 win over the College of Charleston.

February 24, 1980—Barbara Kennedy scored a school record 45 points against Claflin.

March 20-22, 1980—The Lady Tigers participated in the NWIT in Amarillo, TX. Clemson won one game and lost two in the tournament.

January 10, 1981—Clemson won its own Lady Tiger Invitational at Clemson, SC. The Lady Tigers defeated Alabama 79-72 in the championship game.

February 2, 1981—The Lady Tigers defeated Duke 67-54, which made Clemson the regular season champions of the ACC with a 6-1 league record.

February, 10, 1981—Clemson defeated second-ranked Old Dominion 73-64, at Clemson.

February 12-14, 1981—The Lady Tigers played host to the fourth annual ACC Tournament. Clemson defeated Wake Forest in the opening round and lost to N.C. State in the semifinals.

March, 26 1981—Clemson finished 20th in the final Associated Press poll, its first top-20 ranking in a final poll.

November 28, 1981—Clemson defeated Missouri 68-52, in the championship game of the Wayland Baptist Queens Classic at Plainview, TX.

December 19, 1981—Clemson won the South Florida Invitational at Tampa, FL, with a 74-59 win over Miami in the championship game.

February 1, 1982—Jenny Lyerly hit 1-2 free throws with four seconds remaining to give Clemson a 79-78 victory over Tennessee Tech.

February 28, 1982—Maryland defeated Clemson 93-81 in the championship game of the ACC Tournament.

March 12, 1982—Clemson played in the inaugural NCAA Tournament. The Tigers lost to Penn State at University Park, PA. This was the first women's NCAA Tournament game ever played.

Barbara Kennedy played in her last game as a Lady Tiger and scored 43 points against Penn State in an NCAA first-round loss at University Park, PA. She also scored the first points in the history of the women's NCAA Tournament. Kennedy completed her career with 3,113 points and 1,252 rebounds. The 43 points against Penn State is still the second-most points scored in an NCAA Tournament game. She also led the nation in scoring with a 29.3 ppg. average for the 1981-82 season.

March, 1982—Barbara Kennedy was named first-team All-American by Kodak, the Women's Basketball Coaches Association, and *Basketball Weekly*.

April 17, 1982—Barbara Kennedy had her #42 jersey retired at a ceremony at the annual Orange-White Spring football game.

January 5, 1983—Peggy Caple became the first player in ACC and Clemson history to finish a game with a triple-double. Caple had 19 points, 10 rebounds, and 10 blocked shots vs. Kansas State.

March 4, 1983—Clemson's Mary Anne Cubelic tipped in a missed shot at the buzzer from underneath to lead Clemson to a 93-92 victory over Duke in the first round of the ACC Tournament at Fayetteville, NC.

November 26, 1983—Clemson won the Wayland Baptist Queen's Classic at Plainview, TX, with a 95-75 win over S.F. Austin in the championship game.

March 22-24, 1984—Clemson participated in the NWIT at Amarillo, TX. The Lady Tigers finished in third place.

Nov. 23-24, 1984—The Lady Tigers defeated Nebraska 99-84 in the championship game of the Nebraska Invitational in Lincoln, NE. Clemson shot a school record .642 (43-67) from the field.

December 7, 1985—The Lady Tigers won their 200th all-time game with a 62-61 win over South Carolina at Clemson, SC.

January 11, 1986—Melinda Ashworth made 18 free throws (attempted 20) against Virginia. The 18 made free throws and the 20 attempted free throws set single-game school records.

January 22, 1987—Annie Tribble announced her decision to retire as head coach of the Lady Tigers, effective at the end of the season.

February 21, 1987—Clemson defeated Wake Forest 95-83 in Annie Tribble's last home game as head coach of the Lady Tigers. This was also her 200th win at Clemson.

February 28, 1987—Annie Tribble coached her last Clemson game. N.C. State defeated the Lady Tigers, 79-58, in the ACC Tournament. Tribble finished her career with a 200-135 record at Clemson and a 355-168 record as a head coach.

April 1, 1987—Jim Davis was named head coach of the Lady Tigers.

November 28, 1987—Clemson won the Georgia Southern Thanksgiving Classic at Statesboro, GA, with a 64-52 win over Georgia Southern in the championship game.

March 19, 1988—James Madison defeated Clemson 70-63 in the second round of the NCAA Tournament at Harrisonburg, VA.

March, 1988—Clemson finished 20th in the final *USA Today* poll.

December 30, 1988—Clemson defeated St. Peter's 67-63 in the championship game of the St. Peter's Tournament at Jersey City, NJ.

January 6, 1989—The Lady Tigers defeated fifth-ranked Maryland 69-67 at Clemson.

March 18, 1989—Clemson defeated Georgia 78-65 in the second round of the NCAA Tournament at Clemson, SC. The Lady Bulldogs were ranked number 10 in the country.

March 23, 1989—Auburn defeated Clemson 71-60 in the semifinals of the Mideast Regionals in the NCAA Tournament at Auburn, AL.

March, 1989—The Lady Tigers finished 13th in the final *USA Today* poll.

December 30, 1989—Clemson defeated Montana State 80-53 in the championship game of the Brigham Young Invitational.

March 14, 1990—Clemson defeated Manhattan in the first round of the NCAA Tournament's East Regional.

February 24, 1990—Peggy Sells hit one of two free throws with six seconds remaining in lifting Clemson to an 80-79 victory over North Carolina.

March 17, 1990—The Lady Tigers won over Connecticut 61-59 in the second round of the NCAA Tournament's East Regional.

March 22, 1990—Tennessee won over Clemson in the semifinals of the East Regionals in the NCAA Tournament at Norfolk, VA.

March, 1990—Clemson finished 19th in the final *USA Today* poll.

November 25, 1990—Clemson won the Kansas State Invitational at Manhattan, KS. The Lady Tigers defeated Kansas State 68-61 in the championship game.

January 2, 1991—Clemson defeated second-ranked N.C. State 82-73 at home.

January 8, 1991—The Lady Tigers were ranked 12th in the Associated Press poll. This was the highest Clemson had ever been ranked in this poll.

February, 22, 1991—Lady Tiger Head Coach Jim Davis won his 100th career game. Before arriving at Clemson, he coached one year at Middle Tennessee State and had a 19-8 record in 1986-87.

March 2, 1991—Jackie Farmer tipped in the winning basket underneath as time expired in leading Clemson to a 60-58 win over Duke in the first round of the ACC Tournament in Fayetteville, NC.

March 3, 1991—Clemson upset number-one ranked Virginia 65-62 in the semifinals of the 14th annual ACC Tournament, for Clemson's first win over the number-one ranked team in women's basketball. Cheron Wells scored 26 points to lead the Lady Tigers.

March 4, 1991—N.C. State defeated the Lady Tigers 84-61 in the championship game of the Atlantic Coast Conference tournament.

March 16, 1991—Clemson defeated Providence 103-91 in the second round of the East Regional.

March 21, 1991—Clemson's Peggy Sells scored the winning basket at the game-ending horn to give Clemson a 57-55 win over James Madison in the semifinals of the East Regional in the Palestra in Philadelphia, PA.

March 23, 1991—Connecticut defeated Clemson 60-57 in the East Regional Finals. This was the farthest Clemson had ever advanced in a women's postseason tournament. Cheron Wells was named to the NCAA East Regional All-Tournament team.

March, 1991—Clemson was ranked eighth in the final *USA Today* poll and 21st in the final Associated Press poll.

November 22, 1991—The Lady Tigers won their 300th game with a 66-54 win over UNC Charlotte in the Vanderbilt Tournament.

December 16, 1991—Shandy Bryan was named National Player of the Week by *Sports Illustrated* for the period of December 9-15. She appeared in the December 23rd issue of the magazine.

December 21, 1991—Clemson defeated South Florida 90-83 in the championship game of the South Florida Tournament, in Tampa, FL. Shandy Bryan went 12-12 from the floor in this game.

February 12, 1992—Clemson head coach Jim Davis won his 100th game at Clemson with an 81-69 win over South Carolina.

February 15, 1992—Clemson upset number-one-ranked Maryland 72-55 at Clemson.

March 18, 1992—Clemson defeated Tennessee-Chattanooga 76-72 in the first round of the NCAA Tournament's East Regional.

March 22, 1992—West Virginia defeated Clemson 73-72 in the second round of the NCAA Tournament's East Regional.

March, 1992—Clemson finished 19th in the final *USA Today* poll and 20th in the final Associated Press poll, the first time Clemson has been ranked in the final top 20 in both polls.

December 27, 1992—Dana Puckett scored 22 points and had the game-winning buzzer shot as the Lady Tigers defeated 11th-ranked Texas 78-75 in the first round of the Rutgers/Bell Atlantic Classic.

December 29, 1992—Jessica Barr scored on a 16-foot shot with 3.8 seconds left to give the Lady Tigers a win over Rutgers and the Rutgers/Bell Atlantic Championship.

March 12, 1993—Shandy Bryan was named to the District III Kodak All-America team.

March 17, 1993—Tara Saunooke tied a NCAA Tournament record for three-point goals made in a game in leading Clemson to a 70-64 victory over Xavier (OH) in the first round of the NCAA Tournament at Clemson, SC. She hit six in the contest.

March 21, 1993—Stephen F. Austin defeated the Lady Tigers 89-78 in the second round of the Midwest Regional in the NCAA Tournament.

January 8, 1994—Jaci Stimson hit a left-handed hook shot with 1.3 seconds left to beat 24th-ranked Maryland 54-52 at Clemson, SC.

February 25, 1994—Clemson broke the school record for the most ACC wins in a season with a 55-51 win over Georgia Tech.

March 2, 1994—Jessica Barr was named Atlantic Coast Conference Player of the Year.

March 16, 1994—Clemson defeated 19th-ranked Florida International in the first round of the NCAA Tournament.

March 19, 1994—Number-one ranked Tennessee defeated Clemson in Knoxville, TN, 78-66 in the second round of the NCAA Tournament.

March 24, 1994—Jessica Barr was named to the Division III Kodak All-America team.

April 1, 1994—Jessica Barr was named to the Kodak All-American team.

April 4, 1994—Clemson finished 22nd in the final *USA Today* poll.

November 27, 1994—Clemson began its 20th season of women's basketball with a 94-86 double-overtime loss to Western Kentucky at Murfreesboro, TN.

December 17, 1994— Head coach Jim Davis won his 150th game at Clemson with a 99-59 win over East Carolina.

Dec. 19-21, 1994—The Lady Tigers defeated Army, Providence, and UCLA in winning the Northern Lights Invitational in Anchorage, AK. This was the first time the Lady Tigers had played outside the continental United States.

Jessica Barr was named ACC Player of the Year in 1994.

December 29, 1994—Tara Saunooke broke the Atlantic Coast Conference record for most three-point field goals made in a career in the S.C. State game. She concluded her career with 252 three-point field goals.

March 23, 1995—Northwestern State defeated Clemson 80-64 in the first round of the National Women's Invitational Tournament in Amarillo, TX.

March 24, 1995—Clemson defeated Pacific 80-75 in the consolation semifinals of the NWIT.

March 25, 1995—Clemson shot .603 from the floor, seventh-best in school history, as the Lady Tigers defeated East Tennessee State 107-66 in the consolation finals of the NWIT.

November 28, 1995—Clemson overcame a 12-point deficit in the last 1:35 in regulation to tie the score to claim a 77-74 overtime win over UNC-Charlotte.

December 19, 1995—The Lady Tigers defeated Texas-Arlington 85-72 in the championship game of the Texas-Arlington Tournament in Arlington, TX.

February 17, 1996—Clemson's Stephanie Ridgeway scored on a 16-foot jump shot with 4.3 remaining in lifting Clemson past Wake Forest 59-58 at Winston-Salem, NC.

March 1, 1996—Clemson claimed its 400th all-time victory with a 67-49 win over North Carolina in the ACC Tournament.

March 1-3, 1996—Clemson defeated North Carolina 67-49 in the first round of the ACC Tournament. The Lady Tigers defeated Virginia 75-67 in the semifinal round. In the Championship game, Clemson defeated Duke 71-54. Laura Cottrell was named Tournament MVP.

March 11, 1996—The Lady Tigers finished 14th in the final Associated Press poll.

March 16, 1996—Clemson defeated Austin Peay in the first round of the NCAA Tournament at Clemson, SC.

March 18, 1996—Stephen F. Austin defeated Clemson in the second round of the NCAA Tournament with a 93-88 overtime margin.

March, 26, 1996—Dory Kidd won the Robin Roberts/ WBCA Sports Communications Scholarship Award.

April 2, 1996—Clemson finished 17th in the final *USA Today* poll.

December 22, 1996—Clemson defeated Florida 52-50 in the championship game of the Boise State Tournament in Boise, ID.

December 29, 1996—The Lady Tigers defeated Hofstra 69-59 in the championship game of the Dartmouth Tournament in Hanover, NH.

January 11, 1997—Head Coach Jim Davis became Clemson's all-time winningest women's basketball coach with

201 wins at Clemson with a 74-63 victory over Florida State.

March 2, 1997—North Carolina defeated Clemson 62-58 in the championship game of the Atlantic Coast Conference Tournament.

March 10, 1997—Clemson finished 21st in the final Associated Press poll.

March 15, 1997—Marquette defeated Clemson 70-66 in the first round of the NCAA Tournament at Clemson, SC.

April 1, 1997—Clemson finished 25th in the *USA Today* poll.

December 22, 1997—Clemson defeated Temple 65-39 in the first round of the Sun Splash Shootout at Nassau, Bahamas. This marked the first game the Lady Tigers had ever played outside of the United States.

December 23, 1997—The Lady Tigers defeated Idaho State 58-50 in the Sun Splash Shootout Championship game at Nassau, Bahamas.

January 2 & 5, 1998—Clemson defeated fifth-ranked North Carolina 77-63 on January 2. On January 5, Clemson defeated ninth-ranked Virginia 74-67. This is the first time in Lady Tiger history that they had defeated two top-10 teams in consecutive games. The two games were 72 hours apart.

January 8 & 11, 1998—N.C. State defeated Clemson 73-51 on January 8. On January 11, Clemson defeated Maryland by the same score. This is the first time in Lady Tiger basketball history that consecutive Clemson games have resulted in the same score.

February 27, 1998—Head Coach Jim Davis won his 250th career NCAA Division I game with an 85-68 win over Florida State.

March 1, 1998—North Carolina defeated Clemson 81-50 in the championship game of the Atlantic Coast Conference Tournament.

March 9, 1998—Clemson finished the year ranked 14th in the Final Associated Press poll.

March 14, 1998—Clemson defeated Miami (FL) 60-49 in the first round of the NCAA Tournament. With this win, Clemson won its 25th game of the season, setting a new school record for most wins in a single season.

March 16, 1998—Louisiana Tech beat Clemson 74-52 in the second round of the NCAA Tournament.

March 31, 1998—Amy Geren finished the season leading the ACC in three categories: best free throw pct. (.876), best three-point field goal pct. (.409), and the most three-point goals per game (2.1). She is the third Clemson player in history to lead the league in three categories in a single season.

March 31, 1998—Clemson finished 21st in the Final *USA Today* poll.

December 20, 1998—Itoro Umoh's driving layup with 3.1 seconds left gave Clemson the victory over LSU at the ACC-SEC Challenge in Myrtle Beach, SC.

January 17, 1999—Itoro Umoh had a triple-double vs. Wake Forest. She had 12 points, 11 rebounds, and 10 assists as she led Clemson to a 78-38 win over Wake Forest at Clemson, SC. This was the fifth time in the history of the Atlantic Coast Conference a player had recorded a triple-double, and the second time in Clemson history.

January 28, 1999—Head coach Jim Davis won his 250th game at Clemson with a 55-45 win over Maryland in Cole Field House.

February 27-March 1, 1999—Clemson defeated N.C. State 52-51 in the quarterfinals of the ACC Tournament. The Lady Tigers defeated top seeded Duke 80-75 in the semifinal round. In the championship game, Clemson defeated North carolina 87-72. All three games were televised by the ACC Regional Network (Sports South, Florida Sunshine, and Home Team Sports). Clemson vs. N.C. State was the first quarterfinal game ever televised.

March 9, 1999—Itoro Umoh was named to the Associated Press Honorable Mention All-American team.

March 12, 1999—Head coach Jim Davis was named the Women's Basketball Coaches Association (WBCA) District II Coach of the Year. Itoro Umoh was named to the All-District II team. Clemson also defeated Florida A&M 76-45 in the first round of the NCAA Tournament.

March 14, 1999—Clemson defeated Illinois 63-51 in the second round of the NCAA Tournament. This was also the 26th win for the Lady Tigers in the 1998-99 season. The 26 wins is a school record for most wins in a single season.

March 20, 1999—Georgia won over Clemson 67-54 in the NCAA Tournament's Final 16 in the Mideast Regional semifinals in Cincinnati, OH.

March 25, 1999—Amy Geren won the women's three-point shooting contest at St. Petersburg, FL. From a field of the nation's top women's three-point shooters, Geren edged Kelly DeLong of Western Michigan 21-15 in the finals. In the "Battles of the Sexes," Geren defeated the men's champion, Jason Terry of Arizona 18-16. Terry was the Pac-10 Player of the Year and was the CBS National Player of the Year. This contest was televised by ESPN.

March 17, 2000—Clemson defeated Drake 64-50 in the first round of the NCAA Tournament at Storrs, CT.

March 19, 2000—Connecticut defeated Clemson 83-45 at Storrs, CT, in the Second Round of the NCAA Tournament. Connecticut eventually won the 2000 NCAA Championship.

November 29, 2000—Head coach Jim Davis won his 300th career game with a 56-43 win over South Carolina in Columbia, SC.

March 13, 2001—Clemson finished 22nd in the final Associated Press poll.

March 16, 2001—Nuria Forns hit two free throws with 0.8 seconds remaining in leading Clemson to a 51-49 win over Tennessee-Chattanooga in the first round of the NCAA Tournament at Cincinnati, OH. This was in the Mideast Region.

March 18, 2001—Xavier defeated Clemson 77-62 in the second round of the NCAA Tournament in Cincinnati, OH, in the Mideast Region.

April 2, 2001—Clemson finished the season ranked 22nd in the final *USA Today* poll.

November 16, 2001—Head Coach Jim Davis won his 300th game at Clemson with a 67-53 victory over East Carolina at Clemson, SC.

March 15, 2002—Arkansas defeated Clemson 78-68 in the first round of the NCAA Tournament in the Mideast Region at Manhattan, KS.

December 21-22, 2002—Clemson won the Nassau, Bahamas, Tournament with a 45-37 win over Marshall and a 70-67 victory over Oakland.

March 7, 2003—Chrissy Floyd hit two free throws with under one second left to give Clemson the win over Maryland in the quarterfinals of the ACC Tournament at Greensboro, NC.

March 17, 2004—Clemson lost to UNC Charlotte 78-71 in the first round of the WNIT at Clemson, SC.

December 20, 2005—Susan Yenser hit a short jumper as the buzzer sounded to give Clemson a one-point win over Winthrop 52-51.

April 18, 2005—Cristy McKinney was named head coach of the Lady Tigers.

November 30, 2005—The Lady Tigers set the school record for blocks in a single game when they recorded 16 against the Furman Paladins in Greenville, SC. Khaili Sanders totaled eight blocked shots in the contest, which ranked her second all-time for blocks in a game for an individual.

January 16, 2006—Clemson converted 20 of 21 free throws against Wake Forest at Littlejohn Coliseum. The .952 percentage was the highest mark a Clemson women's basketball team had achieved in history. Tasha Phillips went to the line most often that afternoon and converted all six of her attempts. Julie Talley was 4-4; Amanda Frist was 3-3; and Maxienne White was 2-2. Tasha Taylor missed the only free throw of the game for the Lady Tigers, as she was 3-4 from the foul line.

November 23-24, 2007—Clemson defeated Rice 62-59 and Siena 77-67 in winning the Coors Classic, in Boulder, CO.

March 1, 2008—The Clemson women's basketball team posted its 600th program win, doing so in dramatic fashion. The Lady Tigers erased a 14-point deficit and defeated Florida State 72-70 on a buzzer-beater by Morganne Campbell.

November 30, 2008—Clemson defeated Washington 85-67 in the championship game of the Washington Husky Classic, in Seattle, WA.

December 3, 2009—Kirstyn Wright drilled a three-point field goal with just under three seconds to play to win the ACC/Big Ten Challenge game over Northwestern in Evanston, IL.

February 18, 2010—Lele Hardy's shot with 3.5 seconds left sent the Clemson/Miami game into overtime. Hardy's layup with 0.8 seconds left in overtime clinched the game for the Tigers 73-72.

March 29, 2010—Itoro Coleman was named the fifth head coach in Clemson women's basketball history. Coleman played at Clemson from 1996-'99 and won two ACC championships as a player.

November 8, 2010—Itoro Coleman earned her first win as Clemson's head coach despite missing the contest due to the recent birth of her third daughter. Coleman would return to the team on Nov. 26, a 20-point win over Furman.

February 17-24, 2013—The Lady Tigers win three straight conference games for the first time since the 2003-04 season.

March 8, 2013—Itoro Coleman was relieved of her duties as Clemson's head women's basketball coach. Coleman completed her third season at the helm of the program, compiling a 25-63 record overall and a 10-38 mark in the ACC.

April 8, 2013—Director of Athletics Dan Radakovich announced that Audra Smith has been named the head women's basketball coach. Smith, a 1992 Virginia graduate, was the head coach of the Alabama-Birmingham program for nine seasons prior to her arrival at Clemson.

April 18, 2013—Former Clemson head women's basketball coach and Hall of Famer Annie Tribble passed away after a battle with cancer. Tribble was 80. During her 11-year career, she coached the Tigers to a record of 200-135 and one ACC regular-season championship. Tribble served as clemson's women's basketball coach from the 1976-77 season through the 1986-87 season. She led the Lady Tigers to at least 20 wins seven times. The Lady Tigers advanced to postseason play seven times, including the inaugural NCAA Tournament in 1982. The Clemson graduate posted 22 wins over top 25 teams, including victories over seventh-ranked Tennessee, 13th-ranked South Carolina, and second-ranked Old Dominion in a two-week period during the winter of 1981.

November 10, 2013—Audra Smith gained her first victory as head coach at Clemson with a 72-50 win over Wofford at Clemson.

January 31, 2014—Nikki Dixon reached the 1,000-point plateau in the Lady Tigers' 80-79 overtime victory over Georgia Tech in Atlanta, GA. She capped the night with the game-winning basket on an end-to-end layup with eight seconds left to give the Tigers the win, its first in Atlanta since 2004.

November 14, 2014-January 2, 2015—The Lady Tigers win nine straight home games, the 6th longest streak in school history and best since 1997-98.

February 6, 2015—At its Winter Quarterly meeting, the Clemson Board of Trustees gave final approval to begin construction on the renovation project of Littlejohn Coliseum with a targeted start date, pending state agency approvals, of later in the spring of 2015. The Board gave its final approval for the renovation of Littlejohn Coliseum, including reconstruction of the seating areas, along with new practice facilities, locker room, meeting rooms and coaches' offices for both the men's and women's basketball programs. The trustees also approved the athletic facilities bond resolution for the project, which is slated to cost $63.5 million to be financed completely by the athletic department and IPTAY.

March 18, 2015—Clemson Athletics received final approval from the South Carolina Budget and Control Board to begin renovation of Littlejohn Coliseum. The Board approved the construction project and issuance of bonds for the project, which is slated to cost $63.5 million to be financed completely by the athletic department and IPTAY. The project previously received approval from the Clemson Board of Trustees and the Joint Bond Review Committee. The Budget and Control Board's sign-off is the final step in the approval process, and construction is slated to begin following graduation on May 8. The Clemson women's basketball team played the 2015-16 home games at the Jervey Gymnasium.

November 11, 2016—Clemson defeated Coastal Carolina 64-57 in the newly renovated Littlejohn Coliseum.

CLEMSON
Boxing

NEW SPORT ARRIVES AT CLEMSON

Although boxing had a short life as an official sport at Clemson, it was very popular among fans and cadets.

Oftentimes the basketball games would start early on a Saturday evening and the boxing match would begin afterward in front of capacity crowds in Fike Field House in the Big Gym. Clemson enjoyed rivalries with local teams such as The Citadel, Georgia, and South Carolina. It also had fierce fights with foes from Maryland, North Carolina, Virginia Tech, LSU, and Florida.

Clemson fielded boxing for 17 seasons, beginning in 1928 until 1948 with a four-year interruption due to World War II. The Tigers were very competitive in this sport, winning eight individual Southern Conference Championships plus two Southern Conference Team Championships in 1938 and 1940.

THE FIRST YEAR

Clemson participated in its first boxing match on February 10, 1928, as the Tigers met South Carolina in Columbia, SC, at Carolina Field House. The Gamecocks won 4-3. A.P. "Dizzy" McLeod was the Tigers' first-ever coach. The former Furman athlete was later head coach of the Paladins' football and basketball teams in the late-'20s and during the decade of the '30s.

Clemson played host to its first boxing match at Fike Field House on February 16, 1928. Clemson defeated Georgia 4-3 in a very exciting match. With the scored tied 3-3, Joe Robinson of Clemson won a decision in the extra round of the heavyweight tilt over Gene Haley of Georgia.

PRO FOOTBALL AND COLLEGE FOOTBALL HALL OF FAMER TAKES OVER

In 1929, Pro and College Football Hall of Famer Joe Guyon coached the Tigers through the 1932 season. He was also an assistant football coach with the Tigers under head coach Josh Cody. The 1929 season saw the Tigers participate in the Southern Conference Tournament for the first time. The young program showed signs of prospering. During the 1929 season, Fletcher Cannon and Robert Torchia were both 4-1 on the year. The Tigers were 3-3 overall.

A highlight of the 1930 season occurred when the Tigers won a close match with Presbyterian College. On January 30, 1930, the Tigers' Ruben Seigle defeated Blackley at the heavyweight class to give Clemson a 4-3 victory over Presbyterian.

The 1931 campaign saw much of the boxing season cancelled due to the meningitis quarantine on the Clemson campus. Clemson lost to LSU and Tulane in Louisiana in mid-January in the only bouts of the year.

One of the featured moments of the 1932 season was when Clemson boxed Florida in nearby Greenville, SC, at Textile Hall. On February 9th, Ruben Siegel defeated Leo Bilinski of Florida by decision in the heavyweight class in leading Clemson to a 4-3 win over the Gators. This allowed the Tiger fans in the upstate city to see college boxing for the first time in this

Joe Guyon, who is a member of both the College and Pro Football Halls of Fame, was the head boxing coach in 1929-31. He also was the head coach for the Tiger baseball team.

area. This is the same arena where Frank Selvy scored his 100 points against Newberry.

In 1933, Clemson finished the season with a 4-1 record, losing only to South Carolina in Columbia. Captain Pete Heffner coached both the 1932 and 1933 squads.

COACH BOB JONES LEADS THE TIGERS TO TWO CONFERENCE CHAMPIONSHIPS

Coach Bob Jones, a former Clemson football and basketball player and assistant football coach, took over the program in 1934. The Tigers finished 5-1 during the season and had impressive wins over Florida, Duke, and two victories over Georgia.

Clemson went unbeaten for the first time in 1935, when the Tigers were 3-0-2. Clemson recorded two wins over Georgia and one over South Carolina. The Tigers tied Duke and Presbyterian.

Clemson had another impressive season in 1936 with a 4-1-1 record overall. They followed this with a 3-2 mark in 1937.

In 1937 Clemson entered two boxers in the NCAA Tournament for the first time. Paul Waller of Washington State won the decision over Ripper Murray in the 125-pound weight class. Russell Dorn was defeated in the semifinals of the 155-pound class. Clemson finished in 16th place at the NCAA meet with one point.

Clemson finished the year with a 4-1-1 record and won the Southern Conference Championship in 1938. Clemson was first with 16 points, followed by The Citadel with 11, and Duke with 10. Maryland, North Carolina, and South Carolina tied for fourth with eight points, and N.C. State was seventh with three points. Russell Dorn was conference champion in the 155-pound weight class, while Harvey Ferguson and Harvey Dorn won the 175-pound conference title.

NATIONAL RUNNER-UP

Another feature of the 1938 season was John "Ripper" Murray advancing to the finals of the 125-pound weight class in the NCAA Boxing Championship. Defending 135-pound National Champion Ben Alperstein of Maryland defeated Murray in the finals. Clemson finished tied for eighth in the NCAA meet with four points.

Clemson boxing head coach Bob Jones led the Tigers to the 1938 and 1940 Southern Conference Boxing Championships.

John Murray has the distinction of being a finalist in the NCAA Tournament in the 125-pound weight class. Murray, a 125-pound boxer from Charleston, SC, stood 5'1" and was a very successful fighter.

In 1937, he reached the finals of the Southern Conference Championships and lost in a controversial bout with Tom Birmingham of Maryland. Birmingham won the decision, which met the disapproval of the crowd. He also hit Murray after the bell after the second round.

That year, Murray went to the NCAA Tournament and finished sixth in the 125-pound class in 1937 in Sacramento, CA.

During his senior season in 1938, Murray reached the semifinals of the 125-pound class in the Southern Conference Tournament.

On April 2nd, he fought his way through the NCAA Tournament and lost to Maryland's Ben Alperstein in the NCAA championship bout in Charlottesville, VA.

He became Clemson's second athlete to finish second in a NCAA competition. Track standout Ross O'Dell finished second twice in the pole vault during his career in 1926-28.

Murray graduated with two degrees from Clemson. He started his academic career at the College of Charleston but decided to transfer to Clemson. After transferring to Clemson, he joined the boxing squad and soon made a name for himself.

He enrolled at the Medical University of South Carolina in 1938 and graduated in 1942. During World War II, he was a doctor on board Navy ships, transporting troops in preparation for the D-Day invasion. Because of a shortage of medical personnel during that time, he also performed dental work and was even called on to become a psychiatrist.

He would talk with his soldiers and play board games and card games to help get the troops' minds off of the war. In 1942 and 1943, he was an intern at Staten Island Hospital. He was stationed at Newport, RI, in 1944-45.

After the war, he worked in public health in Washington State. There he worked with Native Americans and at the Reservation of Neah Bay, located near the Canadian border. After noticing sickness and various problems among his patients, he was the first doctor to realize that there was an outbreak of tuberculosis there. After vaccinations, and a little time, the health of the Native Americans improved, and he was credited with saving scores of lives there.

John "Ripper" Murray was the National Runner-Up in the 135-pound class at the NCAA Boxing Meet in Charlottesville, VA.

During the war, he had a friend burned to death in an accident. He also did research on burns while studying in Charleston. This fascinated him, and he wanted to improve the treatments when a person was burned.

During the late-1940s, he was in Rese, Florida, at the Rayford Prison Hospital Ward. There he worked and invented a lotion that would, as some observers described, turn "a third-degree burn into a suntan."

"I wish we would have got this location analyzed and put it on the market to help people, but he died before he could do much with his invention," said John Murray, a son.

"He was also a chiropractor and medical doctor. He believed in providing drugs and doing prevention for better health. He also believed in going the least invasive way when dealing with treatment. He encouraged liquid vitamins and I remember growing up we were never ill, and I think it was because of the vitamins and prevention."

While in Florida, he started a hospital along with another doctor, as he performed his duties at the prison.

On January 26, 1948, he died of a heart attack at Raeford, FL.

"He loved Clemson," said John. "He graduated first in his high school class. Russell Dorn, a boxing teammate of my father, was my godfather."

In 1939, the Tigers finished the year with a 4-1-2 record overall. Clemson had wins over Florida, Georgia, Presbyterian College, and The Citadel. Clemson and Loyola tied to start the season, as did the Tigers and the Gamecocks. Clemson lost to Georgia in a rematch. The Tigers finished fourth in the Southern Conference Championships in a rebuilding year.

WARREN WILSON COMES TO THE AID OF CLEMSON FOOTBALL TEAM AT THE COTTON BOWL

Earlier in the year, Clemson was boxing in the Sugar Bowl Tournament in New Orleans in late December of 1939. Wilson received word to go from there to Dallas,

TX, where the Tigers were going to play in the Cotton Bowl on January 1, 1940. Although not on the varsity football roster and having played some earlier, he took a train to Dallas, TX, and was ready to play in the Cotton Bowl if Clemson needed him. It is not known if he played in the game, but he was ready if the Tigers needed him. This is very similar to the 12th-man story at Texas A&M.

In 1940, Clemson went 4-1 overall and won the Southern Conference Tournament. Ferguson won the light-heavyweight division, and Warren Wilson defeated Baxter of South Carolina to win the heavyweight class.

In 1941, Clemson defeated South Carolina and lost to Virginia Tech in the only matches of the season. The Tigers finished sixth in the Southern Conference Tournament, and Wilson again won the heavyweight championship.

Wilson had a brilliant career at Clemson, finishing with a record of 14-4-1, with three wins by knockout and one by a technical knockout in three years of work. He is second on the Clemson career list for most wins with 14. He was such a revered boxer that some opponents would forfeit the match against him. Once, when Clemson was losing a match one bout after another, he was warming up for his match, and he kept hitting the heavy bag harder and harder because Clemson was losing the match. His opponent kept hearing his warm-up session get louder and louder till finally he forfeited his match in the heavyweight class. His opponent was heard to say, "I'm not getting in the ring with him."

WARREN WILSON—WORLD HEAVYWEIGHT CHAMPION?

Warren Wilson could have been a heavyweight-turned-pro after his senior season, but due to World War II and an accident he suffered before the War, he gave up thoughts about a professional career. Former World Heavyweight Champion and boxing great Jack Dempsey once wrote Wilson and said that he would be the next heavyweight champion of the world, as no one hit harder than he did.

In 1942, the Tigers went 1-3 under Head Coach Walter Cox. Clemson did not field boxing in the years 1943-1946, due to World War II.

In 1947 and 1948, Clemson fielded boxing once again under Head Coach Bob Jones before dropping the sport after the 1948 season. Many schools dropped the sport during this time, and the NCAA eventually gave up staging championships in the

Warren Wilson was the Southern Conference Heavyweight Champion in 1940 and 1941.

The 1940 Boxing Team won the Southern Conference Championship.

early-1960s. In the two years after the war, Jerry Orr won the Southern Conference Title in the 130-pound class, and Carl Pulkinen won the 135-pound title as Clemson finished second in the 1947 Southern Conference Tournament.

Clemson was very competitive in this sport and had many great athletes and coaches. It proved to be a fan-favorite, as Fike Field House would be packed to cheer the Tigers on to victory. Although the sport was short-lived at Tigertown and across the country, Clemson proved to be a true champion in the college boxing arena.

BOXING HISTORY

February 10, 1928—Clemson participated in its first boxing match as the Tigers met South Carolina in Columbia, SC at the Carolina Field House. The Gamecocks won 4-3. The Tigers were coached by Dizzy McLeod, who was also the school's baseball coach in the spring of 1928.

February 15, 1928—Clemson played host to its first boxing match at Fike Field House. Clemson defeated Georgia 4-3. With the match score tied 3-3, Joe Robinson of Clemson won a decision in the extra round of the heavyweight tilt over Gene Haley of Georgia.

January 22, 1929—The Tigers announced the 1929 schedule. The schedule featured Presbyterian College, Florida, Georgia, South Carolina, and The Citadel. The 1929 team was coached by Joe Guyon, the famous pro football and baseball player. A total of 40 Clemson cadets went out for the squad in the Tigers' second year of boxing.

March 1 & 2, 1929—Clemson first boxed in the Southern Conference Tournament. The tournament was held in Memorial Gymnasium in Charlottesville, VA.

January 30, 1930—Ruben Seigle defeated Blackley at the heavyweight class to give Clemson a 4-3 victory over Presbyterian.

1931—Much of the boxing season was cancelled due to the meningitis quarantine on the Clemson campus. Clemson lost to LSU and Tulane in mid-January to start the season. These were the only two matches of the season.

1932—Clemson entered the 1932 season with a new coach, Captain Pete Heffner. Later in 1934, Captain Heffner was one of the first men to meet to discuss ways Clemson could help its football program get back on track. On October 16, 1934, Clemson suffered a surprising 6-0 loss against The Citadel in a football game played in Florence, SC. After the game, Captain Frank J. Jervey, Head Coach Jess Neely, Assistant Coach Joe Davis, and Captain Heffner of the university military staff met. The meeting started the ball rolling toward the establishment of the IPTAY Foundation.

February 9, 1932—Ruben Siegel defeated Leo Bilinski of Florida by decision in the heavyweight class in leading Clemson to a 4-3 win over the University of Florida at Textile Hall in Greenville, SC.

1932—Clemson finished the season with a 4-1 record, losing only to South Carolina in Columbia.

1933—The Tigers were 4-2 overall, with wins over North Georgia, Georgia, South Carolina, and Presbyterian College. The Tigers lost to Florida and the second match against Georgia.

1934—Coach Bob Jones, a former Clemson football and basketball player and assistant football coach, took over the program in 1934. The Tigers finished 5-1 during the season and had impressive wins over Florida and Duke and two victories over Georgia.

January 13, 1934—Clemson overcame a 3 ½ to 2 ½ deficit and won the last two matches to edge Duke in Durham, NC, 4 ½ to 3 ½. Clemson's William Medlin scored a technical knockout over Joe Jester in the 175-pound match and Dick Henley won by default at heavyweight to give the Tigers the victory.

1935—Clemson went unbeaten for the first time ever, as the Tigers were 3-0-2. Clemson recorded two wins over Georgia and one over South Carolina. The Tigers tied Duke and Presbyterian.

1936—Clemson had another impressive season in 1936, finishing with a 4-1-1 record overall.

April 2 & 3, 1937—Clemson entered two boxers in the NCAA Tournament for the first time ever. That year's event was held in Sacramento, CA. Paul Waller of Washington State and Pacific intercollegiate 135-pound champion won a decision against Ripper Murray in the 125-pound weight class. Russell Dorn was defeated by Steve Wilkerson of Mississippi in the semifinals of the 155-pound class. Clemson finished in 16th place at the NCAA meet with one point. For the season, the Tigers finished with a 3-2 mark in the dual matches.

1938—The Tigers finished the year with a 4-1-1 record overall.

February 25 & 26, 1938—Clemson won the Southern Conference Boxing Championships at College Park, MD. Clemson was first with 16 points, followed by The Citadel with 11, and Duke with 10. Maryland, North Carolina, and South Carolina tied for fourth with eight points, and N.C. State was seventh with three points. Russell Dorn won the junior middleweight class. Harvey Ferguson won the light-heavyweight class.

April 1 & 2, 1938—Another feature of the 1938 season was Ripper Murray advancing to the finals of the 125-pound weight class in the NCAA Boxing Championships in Charlottesville, VA. Defending 135-pound National Champion Ben Alperstein of Maryland defeated Murray in the finals. Clemson finished tied for eighth in the NCAA meet with four points.

1939—Clemson finished the season with a 4-1-2 mark overall.

February 23-24, 1940—Clemson won the Southern Conference Boxing Championship on February 23rd and 24th in Columbia, SC. Light-heavyweight Harvey Ferguson and heavyweight Warren Wilson won their respective weight classifications. Clemson was first with 13 points, while The Citadel and North Carolina tied for second with 10 points. Maryland was fourth with six points. Duke and Virginia Tech were tied for fifth with three points, and N.C. State finished seventh with 0 points.

February 28-March 1, 1941—Heavyweight Warren Wilson defeated Kimball of North Carolina by knockout with 25 seconds elapsed in the third round as Wilson won the heavyweight title for the second-straight season. He became the third Tiger to win two Southern Conference Titles.

1942—Walter Cox coached the Clemson boxing team this season, while Bob Jones was in the service during World War II. Cox, who was an assistant football coach, also coached the baseball team.

1943-1946—Clemson did not field a boxing team during these years due to World War II.

January 31, 1948—Clemson played host to its last home match, and the Tigers defeated The Citadel 4.5-3.5.

February 27, 1948—Clemson and South Carolina tied 4-4 in the last boxing match in history for the Tigers. The match was held in Columbia, SC.

MEN'S
Cross Country

ACC Champions:

1978, 1980, 1981, 1982, 1983, 1987, 1988

NCAA Meet Finishes:

1977 (20th), 1978 (25th), 1980 (8th), 1981 (9th), 1982 (8th), 1983 (4th), 1984 (13th), 1987 (11th), 1988 (4th)

EARLY SUCCESS

Clemson first started cross country in the fall of 1915. Clemson, Presbyterian, and Newberry participated in the inaugural State Cross Country Championships held at Clinton, SC.

The three teams competed for the State Cup on Thanksgiving Day in 1915, just prior to the Presbyterian-Newberry football game. The Tigers finished third in the meet that day. Clemson's team was composed of James Dick, C. Hughes, David Sullivan, H.C. Salter, and Walter Herbert.

The Tigers won the state meet in 1916 over Presbyterian, Newberry, and South Carolina. Roy Ellison, Sullivan, Herbert, and Oliver Going were members of the team.

In 1917, Clemson was successful in winning the Cup for the second consecutive year. Roy Ellison of Clemson won the individual title. The state meet was not held in 1918 or 1919. The Tigers won the State Cup again in 1920, 1921, and 1922, five times in the seven years. Former South Carolina Statesman, Strom Thurmond, was a member of the 1922 team.

In the 1922 season, Clemson also defeated Georgia in a dual meet in Athens and finished second in the Southern Intercollegiate Athletic Association Meet.

W.D. Reed served as coach of the Tigers in 1922-24 and enjoyed success during those years. He coached the Tigers to the State Championships in 1922 and 1924 and had a dual meet win over Georgia and a second-place finish in the SIAA meet in 1922.

In 1926, Clemson continue to dominate the state cross country scene. The Tigers defeated Furman and Wofford

and had a win over Georgia. The Tigers lost to Georgia Tech that season.

During the 1927 season, Clemson won the state title. In 1928, Clemson ran in a meet with Georgia Tech that finished at halftime of the Georgia Tech-Notre Dame football game at Grant Field.

Clemson didn't field a cross country team after 1931. This hiatus lasted until the 1954 season (the ACC was started in 1953). One of the reasons for the long interruption may have been the lack of staff, as the track coaches during that time were assistant football coaches, and also the lack of interest by the student body.

THE EARLY ACC ERA

In 1957, the Tigers had two top-10 finishers who propelled Clemson to a second-place finish in the Atlantic Coast Conference Meet. Walt Tyler finished fourth and Dale Tinsley finished 10th for Head Coach Bank McFadden's Tigers. Tyler finished ninth in the 1958 championships.

Jim Morehead was also a star for the Tigers in the late-1950s and early-1960s. In 1959, he finished fourth at the ACC meet. In 1960, he finished eighth, and in 1961, he finished fifth in the ACC meet for the Tigers.

In 1963, Ernie Drown was a third-place finisher for the Tigers in the ACC Meet.

LATE-1970s AND 1980s—THE TIGERS REIGNED SUPREME

Clemson started to become a stalwart program during the late-1970s and 1980s. In 1976, Dean Matthews became the first Tiger to win the ACC individual title.

In 1977, the Tigers finished 25th at the NCAA Meet in Wisconsin. During the next 11 years, the Tigers would finish in the top-25 nine times and the top 10 five times, including two fourth-place finishes at the NCAA Meet.

During this era of success, Hans Koeleman was the ACC Meet's individual champion three times, the NCAA District Meet individual champion three times, and a

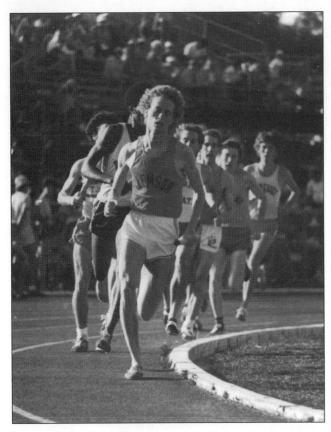

Dean Matthews was the individual champion at the ACC Cross Country Meet in 1976.

three-time All-America, the most in school history. He finished third in the 1982 NCAA Meet.

HANS KOELEMAN—THE MOST DECORATED CLEMSON CROSS COUNTRY RUNNER

Hans Koeleman is considered one of the most decorated and revered distances runner in Clemson history.

How he got to Clemson was very fortunate for him and Clemson. "A Dutch friend [a high-jumper] was transferring from New Mexico Junior College to Clemson. I was traveling through Europe with him in the fall of 1979 and he asked me if I would be interested in joining him. I told him to give my details to the Clemson Head Coach, Sam Colson, who called me right away and had me hooked and committed in five minutes."

Colson did not have to do much persuading to sign Koeleman. "Adventure in general: life in the US has an incredible attraction. More specific: living in a small college community and learning new things, get a good education. More athletic-specific: the almost continuous warm weather, hills and woods. Sam Colson told me in the phone call that 'we have sun, hills and a few nice bars. Think you'll like it.' He was right," Koeleman said.

When talking to Koeleman about key people in his life, he is quick to mention his mother and coaches. "My mother was a huge influence in my life, for giving me complete freedom to pursue my dreams; my Dutch coach Bob Boverman, for being an inspiring and very knowl-

edgeable coach; Sam Colson, for giving me the opportunity to give my whole life a massive twist and boost. As a tribute to the latter, I named my son Sam. He's now 6 and last year met with Sam Colson. They got along very well," said Koeleman.

Some of his most memorable moments as a student-athlete were during the cross country season at Clemson. "At Clemson, I loved the cross country season. My 1982 District III Cross Country Championships at Furman stands out [I won in a course record time] as well as the NCAA Cross Country Championships of that same year when I finished third. The 1980 Indoor ACC track and field meet at Greensboro is also a memorable one. I doubled in the two-mile and mile runs within a half-hour and won both. Also, our ACC team track championship of 1980 was fantastic. We ended Maryland's 24-year reign.

"Internationally, there is no doubt that the 1984 and 1988 Olympics stand out. Nothing can beat competing in an Olympic arena."

Koeleman has been very busy after his Clemson days. "I moved to Durham, NC, to train and prepare for the 1988 Games and then moved to Los Angeles to attend the University of Southern California. After that I moved back to Amsterdam and worked at Nike's European headquarters for 16 years.

"What I remember most about Clemson is the spirit. It is tangible and something I take with pride. At the 1983 Commencement ceremony our president told all graduates to never forget what Clemson stood for: an ever-present positive attitude. He was right and his words have stayed with me to this day. On a more mundane level: the small-town color, the hills, and the Blue Ridge Mountains in the distance."

"I am still in touch with many who live in Clemson and try to visit every few years. I still call it home—well, one of the three places I consider 'home': Clemson,

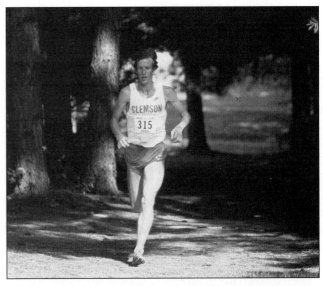

Hans Koeleman was a three-time All-American in cross country in 1980, 1982, and 1983.

Itay Magidi, who later qualified for the Beijing Olympics, won the individual championship at the 2006 ACC Cross Country Meet.

Amsterdam, [and] Los Angeles. Talking and thinking about Clemson makes me happy."

OTHER STANDOUTS

The 1980s boasted a slew of All-America standouts. Jim Haughey was an All-America runner in 1981 and 1982, Stijn Jaspers was an All-America honoree in 1983, Dov Kremer was a two-time All-America runner in 1987 and 1988, and Yehezkel Halifa received All-America accolades in 1988, as he finished second at the NCAA meet.

Julius Ogaro won the ACC individual championship at the conference meet in 1981, while Robert deBrouwer won the individual title in 1984 and Martin Flynn won the ACC Meet in 1986. Kremer won the title in 1988 with a virtual tie with teammate Yehezkel Halifa, as both runners crossed the finish line at the same time.

In the 1990s, Cormac Finnerty won the individual championship at the ACC Cross Country Meet in Chapel Hill, NC, as the Tigers finished fourth as a team.

In 1994, Kevin Hogan won the individual championship at the ACC Cross Country Meet in Atlanta, GA.

In 2003, Scott Shaw was named an All-America, and Itay Magidi won the individual championship at the 2006 ACC Cross Country Meet at Charlottesville, VA.

MEN'S CROSS COUNTRY HISTORY

November 25, 1915—Clemson ran in its first cross country meet ever in the State of South Carolina Cross Country Meet in Clinton, SC. Businessmen of Clinton and Newberry had donated the trophy for the four-mile meet, which was held before the Presbyterian College-Newberry football game on Thanksgiving Day. Newberry finished first in the meet, followed by Presbyterian and Clemson.

November 30, 1916—Clemson won the State of South Carolina Cross Country Meet in Newberry, SC. The team composed of Roy Ellison, David Sullivan, Walter Herbert, and Oliver Going won the cup in the annual cross country meet between Newberry, Presbyterian College, South Carolina, and Clemson. Clemson's Roy Ellison finished first overall in the meet.

November 29, 1917—Clemson won the State Cross Country Meet for the second year in a row just before the Presbyterian-Newberry football game on Thanksgiving Day in Clinton, SC. Clemson finished first, followed by Presbyterian and Newberry. For the second year in a row, Ellison finished first overall in the meet. The Tigers' L.M. Morecock was third, Going fourth, and Pint Corwell seventh.

November 25, 1920—The Tigers won the State Cross Country Meet at Clinton, SC, after an interruption due to World War I.

November 24, 1921—Clemson won the State Cross Country Meet on Thanksgiving Day at Newberry, SC. Clemson's second team lost to Georgia in a dual meet on the same day.

1922—Against Georgia, Clemson won a dual meet 20-35 in Athens, GA.

November 30, 1922—On Thanksgiving Day, Clemson won the state meet in Clinton, SC. Captain Young of the Tigers came out first. This was the third consecutive year that the Tigers had won the State Championships. South Carolina finished in second place, followed by PC, Wofford, and Newberry.

December 16, 1922—Clemson finished second in the Southern Intercollegiate Athletic Association Meet and fourth in the Birmingham Athletic Club Meet, which were run simultaneously.

November 3, 1923—Clemson ran its first-ever cross country meet at Tigertown. The Tigers defeated Georgia 28-29. The race finished at Riggs Field.

The 1922 Clemson cross country team finished second in the Southern Intercollegiate Athletic Association (SIAA) Meet. W.D. Reed was the Head Coach.

November 17, 1923—Clemson finished fourth at the first-ever Southern Conference Meet in Atlanta, GA. The race started and ended at Grant Field. The runners crossed the finish line during halftime of the Georgia Tech-Kentucky football game.

November 23, 1924—Clemson won the State Championship, with a perfect score. Buck, R.E. and E.C. Sease, and Tommy Hart, all seniors and running their last race for Clemson, were ahead of the field. They all joined hands and crossed the finish line together.

1954—Clemson started the cross country program again, after not fielding a team since 1928, with two dual-meet wins over South Carolina.

November 18, 1957—Walt Tyler finished fourth and Dale Tinsley finished 10th at the ACC Cross Country Meet in Winston-Salem, NC, to be the first Clemson athletes to be named All-ACC in cross country.

November 16, 1959—Jim Morehead finished fourth in the ACC meet in Durham, NC, and was named All-ACC. This was his first honor. He was the first Clemson athlete to be named three-time All-ACC in Cross Country, having subsequently earned the honor in 1960 and 1961, too.

November 22, 1971—Larry Rush was the first Tiger to participate in the NCAA Cross Country Championships. Rush finished 196th at the 285-individual meet, held in Knoxville, TN.

October 23, 1976—Dean Matthews won the South Carolina State Cross Country individual championship. The Tigers finished second in the team competition at Furman University in Greenville, SC.

November 6, 1976—Dean Matthews was the individual champion at the ACC Cross Country Meet at Charlottesville, VA. The Tigers' Dave Geer finished fifth. The Tigers finished fourth at the meet.

November 22, 1976—Dean Matthews finished 56th at the NCAA Cross Country Meet in Denton, TX. There were 256 runners who finished the meet.

Oct. 22, 1977—Scott Haack won the South Carolina State Cross Country individual championship at Greenville, SC. The Tigers also claimed the team title.

November 21, 1977—The men's cross country team finished 20th at the NCAA meet at Washington State University. This was Clemson's first top-20 finish in cross country.

October 21, 1978—Clemson won the South Carolina State Championship held at Furman in Greenville, SC. Scott Haack of Clemson was the individual champion. The Tigers turned in a perfect score of 15, as Tigers took the first five places in the final results. Haack set a new course record over the five-mile course with a time of 24:51.0

November 4, 1978—Clemson won its first-ever ACC Championships in cross country. The Tigers' Scott Haack finished second in the meet at Raleigh, NC. Tim Frye was fourth, and Bill Stewart was eighth.

November 20, 1978—The Men's cross country team finished 25th at the NCAA meet in Madison, Wisconsin.

November 1, 1980—Hans Koeleman won the individual championship and Clemson finished first in the Atlantic Coast Conference Cross Country Championships at Winston-Salem, NC. The Tigers' Terry Goodenough was third, while Julius Ogaro placed fourth and Jim Haughey placed eighth. As a team, this was the first of four straight ACC Cross Country Championships Clemson won in 1980-83.

November 24, 1980—The Men's cross country team finished eighth at the NCAA Meet at Wichita, KS. Hans Koeleman led the Tigers with an 11th-place finish and Terry Goodenough was 24th as both men earned All-America honors.

October 31, 1981—Clemson won the ACC Championships behind Julius Ogaro's first-place finish. Teammate Hans Koeleman finished second, only 3/10 of a second behind Ogaro. The Tigers' Jim Haughey placed third.

November 23, 1981—The Men's cross country team finished ninth at the NCAA Meet at Wichita State in Wichita, KS. Jim Haughey was named an All-America.

October 30, 1982—Clemson won the Atlantic Coast Conference Cross Country Championships in College Park, MD. Hans Koeleman won the ACC individual championship.

November 22, 1982—Clemson finished eighth at the NCAA Cross Country Meet at Bloomington, IN. Hans Koeleman finished third in the meet, while teammate Jim Haughey finished 34th. Both men earned All-America honors.

October 29, 1983—Hans Koeleman won the individual title as he led Clemson to the team championship at the ACC Men's Cross Country Championships at Charlottesville, VA. Teammate Stijn Jaspers finished second. This was the third time Koeleman won the individual championship at the ACC Cross Country Championships.

November 21, 1983—Clemson finished fourth at the NCAA Cross Country Championships. Hans Koeleman was the top finisher for Clemson, finishing seventh in the meet. Stijn Jaspers placed 16th. Both Koeleman and Jaspers were named All-Americas.

October 27, 1984—Robert deBrouwer won the ACC individual championship at the ACC Cross Country Championships. The Tigers finished second as a team.

November 19, 1984—Clemson finished 13th as a team at the NCAA Cross Country Meet at Penn State.

November 1, 1986—Martin Flynn won the ACC Individual Championship at the ACC Cross Country Meet at Clemson, SC. The Tigers finished fourth as a team.

October 31, 1987—Clemson won its sixth ACC Men's Cross Country title in school history as the Tigers defeated 18th-ranked N.C. State and 20th-ranked Wake Forest. Yehezkel Halifa paced Clemson with a third-place showing.

November 23, 1987—The Clemson men's cross country team finished 11th at the NCAA Cross Country Meet. Dov Kremer finished 22nd in the race and earned All-America honors.

October 29, 1988—Clemson won the ACC Cross Country Championships at Winston-Salem, NC. Dov Kremer won the individual championships and teammate Yehezkel Halifa finished 2/10 of a second behind, in second place officially. Both Kremer and Halifa finished the meet at the same time. After a discussion between the two, they decided that Kremer would finish first and Halifa would be second. Clemson's Bob Pollock was named ACC Cross Country Coach of the Year.

November 21, 1988—The Tigers finished fourth at the NCAA meet behind Yehezkel Halifa's second place finish. Halifa finish 1/10 of a second out of first place. Dov Kremer finished in sixth place. Both Tigers earned All-America honors. The second-place finish by Halifa was the highest place by a Clemson runner.

November 2, 1991—Clemson's Cormac Finnerty won the individual championship at the ACC Cross Country Meet in Chapel Hill, NC. Clemson finished fourth as a team.

October 29, 1994—The Tigers' Kevin Hogan won the individual championship at the ACC Cross Country Meet in Atlanta, GA.

November 24, 2003—Scott Shaw was named an All-America runner and finished 34th at the NCAA Cross Country Meet at Waterloo, Iowa.

October 28, 2006—Itay Magidi won the individual championship at the ACC Cross Country Meet in Charlottesville, VA.

October 27, 2007—Matt Clark was eighth in leading the Clemson runners to a fourth-place finish at the ACC meet in Charlottesville, VA.

October 29, 2011—Ty McCormack was eighth at the ACC Cross Country Meet held at Clemson, SC. The Tigers finished 10th in the team race.

WOMEN'S
Cross Country

THE EARLY YEARS

The Clemson women's cross country team established itself as one of the nation's elite programs in the decade of the 1980s.

In the fall of 1978, the first coach of the women's cross country team was Sam Colson. Starting with a last-place finish in the ACC that first season, Colson took the Lady Tigers to a sixth-place finish in the nation in 1981.

Cindy Duarte had many firsts for the women's cross country and track & field teams.

She was the first Tiger to participate in a national meet in cross country, indoor track and field, and outdoor track and field.

"I was very happy to go to Clemson and be part of the early beginnings of the cross country and track programs," said Duarte. "As you enter college, the level of training and competition rises. I really loved the town of Clemson, the university, and the facilities. I came from a rural area, and I liked the size of Clemson and the wide-open spaces for training.

"We were a new program and everyone was supportive and did what they could to help. It was a great feeling participating in the inaugural NCAA meets. I think that it was fun being part of a new program. It's a wonderful feeling earning All-America honors. I am so thankful that I had the opportunity," said Duarte.

During her career, she earned many honors. She was the first Tiger to be named All-America in indoor track, outdoor track, and cross country as a female athlete. She participated in the AIAW Championships in the 3000 me-

ters in 1981, the first Lady Tiger to compete in a national outdoor and indoor track meet.

She was named an All-America runner in cross country at Clemson in 1981 along with Kerry Robinson, the first female All-America runners in Clemson cross country history.

She was also a two-time All-Region performer in cross country in 1980 and 1981, and she was also the first two-time All-District cross country performer in Clemson history. For her outstanding career, she was named a member of the ACC 50-Year Anniversary cross country team.

WAYNE COFFMAN—CONSISTENCY IN PROGRAM

When it comes to Clemson's women's cross country team, one of the most prominent earlier coaches was

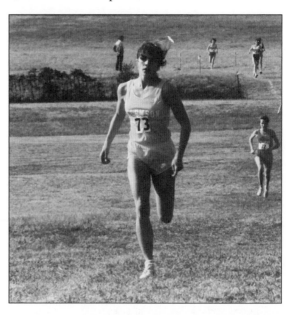

Cindy Duarte was the Tigers' first All-America runner. She, along with Kerry Robinson, was named an All-America runner at the inaugural NCAA Women's Cross Country Meet in 1981.

Wayne Coffman. Coffman served as an assistant coach (1978-85) and was subsequently the head coach (1985-98) of the women's cross country/track program.

Coffman led the cross country and track teams to much success and transformed the early track team from a distance-only program to the full program of field events, jumps, and sprints during his career.

"I happened to be finishing my eligibility at Clemson, as I had just completed my senior season and I had one more year to finish my degree. I started working with the women's program. After I graduated, Sam Colson [then-head coach] asked me if I wanted to work on my Master's degree and help coach the women's program. So I stayed and did my graduate work.

"The Athletic Director at that time, Bobby Robinson, hired me in 1985. We took it to a full program in 1987. That first year, Jeannie Burris was our first field event athlete, and then we signed Marcia Fletcher Noad as our first sprinter/hurdler. We starting adding more athletes and we won the 1991 ACC Outdoor Track and Field Championship. That was a crowning moment for us, as we accomplished a lot in such a short time.

"I guess what I am most proud of was the consistency in our program, especially in cross country—we finished in the top 20 for so many years. I remember former head coach Sam Colson and I talking about getting an NCAA trophy. They would give trophies to the top four cross country team finishers at the NCAA meet. We kept saying we need to win a trophy. So in 1990, we finished third at the NCAA Championship in Knoxville, TN, and we got our first trophy! I thought we could finish in the top 10, but I had no idea we could finish as the third-best team in the country. We really ran well that day.

"Our first All-American, Cindy Duarte, helped get our distance program rolling. She was an All-American in track and cross country and this helped us build momentum for our young program. Our early success attracted more recruits and the success built on itself. We also had scholarships with the support of IPTAY and the administration."

Another early star who helped put Clemson on the map in women's cross country and track was Tina Krebs, who ran from Clemson in the '80s.

"I think that Tina Krebs helped set the tone of the program with her work ethic," said Coffman. "She was an architect student and she worked so hard. I can still see her biking to practice with rolled-up drawings from architecture in her backpack. This characteristic is what

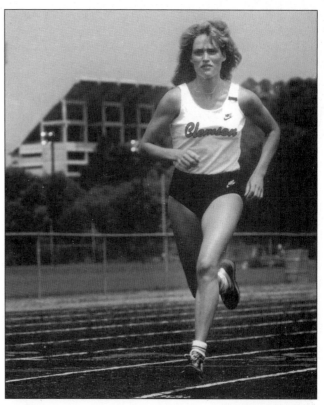

Tina Krebs was a two-time cross country All-America runner.

we tried to instill in our program from the beginning— academics first, athletics second. We worked hard in the classroom and kept the GPA high.

"I feel as a coach I was able to give people confidence," said Coffman. "I always wanted our teams to be well prepared and I was very thorough with details. I did not want to leave any rock unturned. I preached academics and fundamentals to our athletes. I was a blue-collar type coach that was concerned with details, and I think it paid off in the long run," added Coffman.

In 2010-12 seasons, the Tigers finished in the top 10 at the NCAA region meets.

In 2010, Kim Ruck became the first female at Clemson in 17 years to participate in the NCAA Cross Country Meet. Ruck has been named NCAA All-Region in 2009, 2010, and 2011. Alyssa Kulik was named NCAA All-Region in 2010 and 2011.

Grace Barnett became the 10th Clemson runner to be named Cross Country All-American as she finished ninth at the 2016 NCAA Cross Country meet at Terre Haute, IN.

WOMEN'S CROSS COUNTRY HISTORY

September 16, 1978—Clemson participated in its first women's cross country event, the Stone Mountain Invitational, in Stone Mountain, GA. Shelly Wooldridge, from Camden, SC, was the first-ever women's track and field/cross country scholarship athlete. Sam Colson coached the team.

October 28, 1978—Clemson participated in the first-ever ACC Cross Country Meet in Winston-Salem, NC.

October 25, 1980—Cindy Duarte was Clemson's first All-ACC Cross Country performer, as she finished ninth.

Nov 2, 1980—Cindy Duarte finished 14th at the AIAW Regional Meet in Charlottesville, VA, and qualified for the national meet.

November 15, 1980—Cindy Duarte participated in the AIAW National Meet in Seattle, Washington.

October 31, 1981—For the second year in a row, Cindy Duarte was named All-ACC, as she finished fifth. Kerry Robinson finished sixth to earn her first All-ACC honor.

November 23, 1981—Clemson finished sixth at the first-ever NCAA Women's Cross Country meet at Wichita, KS. Kerry Robinson and Cindy Durate were named All-America runners. Robinson finished 25th and Duarte 30th in the inaugural meet.

October 30, 1982—Four Tigers finished in the top 10 at the ACC Meet and earned All-ACC honors at College Park, MD. The four Tigers included Stephanie Weikert (4th) Kerry Robinson (6th), Tina Krebs (7th), and Judith Shephard (10th).

November 13, 1982—Four Tigers were named to the All-District team at the District meet at Greenville, SC—Tina Krebs (4th), Kerry Robinson (5th), Stephanie Weikert (7th), and Judith Shephard (11th).

November 22, 1982—Women's cross country finished fifth at Bloomington, IN, at the NCAA Cross Country Meet. Stephanie Weikert was named All-America, as she finished 16th.

October 29, 1983—Clemson had three runners finish in the top 10 at the ACC meet at the University of Virginia. Tina Krebs, Kerry Robinson, and Stephanie Weikert were all named All-ACC.

November 12, 1983—Tina Krebs was named to the All-District team for the third-straight season, as she finished third in the race. The Tigers took third place at the Boscobel Golf Course in Pendleton, SC.

November 21, 1983—The women's cross country team finished seventh at the NCAA meet in Lehigh, PA. Tina Krebs was named All-America, as she finished seventh in the race.

November 10, 1984—Clemson finished second at the NCAA District III Cross Country Meet in Greenville, SC. Tina Krebs placed third and Kirsti Voldnes was eighth.

November 19, 1984—The Tigers finished fifth in the NCAA Meet in University Park, PA. Tina Krebs was named All-America, finishing fifth overall.

November 16, 1985—Clemson finished third as a team at the NCAA District III Championships in Greenville, SC, and the Tigers' Ute Jamrozy finished third in the race.

November 25, 1985—The women's cross country team finished 15th at the NCAA Meet in Milwaukee, WI.

November 1, 1986—Clemson won the ACC Women's Cross Country Championships in Clemson, SC. Three Tigers finished in the top 10—Ute Jamrozy(1st), Elsa Breit (3rd), and Joanne Power (10th).

November 15, 1986—Clemson finished third in the NCAA District III Meet in Greenville, SC. Jamrozy was fifth in the race as the Tigers' highest finisher. Breit placed 14th, and Joanne Power was 19th in the race.

November 24, 1986—The Tigers finished fifth at the NCAA Meet in Tucson, AZ. Jamrozy finished in fourth place overall and earned All-America honors at the meet.

November 14, 1987—Clemson finished third at the NCAA District III Meet. Michelle Kalikin(16th), Kris Salt (17th),and Helen Rogers were among Clemson's top finishers(18th).

November 23, 1987—Clemson finished 13th at the NCAA Cross Country Championships in Charlottesville, VA.

November 12, 1988—Clemson was third at the NCAA District III Meet. Clemson did not receive an NCAA team bid that season but finished 18th in the final national poll.

October 28, 1989—Clemson head coach Wayne Coffman was named ACC Cross Country Coach of the Year. The Tigers finished second at the ACC meet. Anne Evans was Clemson's top finisher, as she finished fourth.

The 1986 Clemson Women's Cross Country team won the ACC Championship that was held in Clemson, SC.

November 11, 1989—Clemson finished third in the NCAA District III Meet in Greenville, SC. Anne Evans was a seventh-place finisher.

November 20, 1989—The Tigers finished seventh at the NCAA Cross Country Meet at Annapolis, MD. Evans was named an All-America runner, as she finished 19th.

October 27, 1990—Evans won the individual championship at the ACC Cross Country Championships in Charlottesville, VA. Mareike Ressing was third, and Kris Salt finished fifth. Clemson finished second at the meet.

November 10, 1990—Clemson won the NCAA District III Meet for the first time ever. Evans was Clemson's top finisher with a second-place mark. Ressing was fifth and Salt ninth for the Tigers.

November 19, 1990—Clemson finished third at the NCAA Cross Country Meet at Knoxville, TN. Evans finished seventh, and Ressing was 15th overall. Both women were named All-Americans.

November 16, 1991—The Tigers finished fifth as a team at the NCAA District III Championships in Greenville. Michelle Scholtz was the top finisher for the Tigers, as she finished in ninth place.

November 13, 1993—Clemson finished third at the NCAA District III Meet in Greenville. Ressing finished fifth in the race and Tina Jensen was 12th to lead the Tigers. Karen Friedrichsen was 20th, and all three Tigers were named to the All-District team.

November 22, 1993—The Tigers finished 16th at the NCAA Cross Country Meet in Bethlehem, PA.

November 16, 1996—Clemson finished seventh at the NCAA District III Meet in Greenville, SC. Jensen was a top-10 finisher, placing ninth in the race.

November 14, 1998—The Tigers finished fifth at the NCAA District III Meet in Greenville, SC. Beth Ahern was 19th in the meet and was named All-District.

November 13, 1999—Clemson was ninth at the NCAA District III Meet in Greenville, SC.

November 15, 2008—The Tigers finished 10th at the NCAA Southeast Region Meet in Clemmons, NC. The Tigers' Jenna Baker had an All-Region performance, finishing 12th in the meet.

November 14, 2009—Kim Ruck finished 11th at the NCAA Southeast Region meet in Louisville, KY, for the best finish for a Tiger since the 1993 season. As a team, the Tigers finished in 12th place.

November 13, 2010—Kim Ruck became the first female at Clemson in 17 years to earn a trip to the NCAA Cross Country Meet after finishing sixth at the NCAA Southeast Regional in Louisville, KY. The Tigers finished in eighth place as a team. Along with Ruck, Alyssa Kulik was also named NCAA All-Region. It was the first time since the 1993 meet that the Tigers produced two All-Region performers.

November 22, 2010—Ruck finished 90th at the NCAA Cross Country Meet in Terre Haute, IN.

November 12, 2011—The Tigers finished fourth at the NCAA Southeast Regional Championships in Louisville, KY, the program's highest finish at a regional meet since the 1993 squad had placed third. Two runners received All-Region honors. Alyssa Kulik finished eighth and Kim Ruck was 25th.

November 9, 2012—Clemson finished seventh at the NCAA Southeast Regional Championships in Charlotte, NC. Kate Borowicz and Erin Barker earned All-Region honors at the meet. Borowicz finished 21st and Barker was 24th.

October 30, 2015—Grace Barnett was 10th at the ACC Cross Country Meet at Tallahassee, FL.

October 28, 2016—Grace Barnett finished third at the ACC Cross Country Meet in Cary, NC. It was the best finish for a Clemson runner since 1997, when Tina Jensen finished third at the conference meet.

November 11, 2016—Grace Barnett finished fourth at the NCAA Southeast Region Cross Country Championships at Earlysville, VA.

November 19, 2016—Grace Barnett became the 10th Clemson runner to be named Cross Country All-American as she finished ninth at the NCAA Cross Country Meet at Terre Haute, IN.

WOMEN'S
Diving

DIVING HISTORY

April 30, 2010—Athletic Director Dr. Terry Don Phillips announced that Clemson would begin a two-year phaseout of its men's swimming and diving and women's swimming programs at the end of the 2011-12 academic year. Phillips said the women's diving program would continue.

July 1, 2012—Leslie Hasselbach Adams was named the head women's diving coach. She was previously an assistant coach at Clemson.

September 11, 2012—Clemson released the first schedule in program history. The slate included nine events.

October 13, 2012—Clemson participated in the first-ever meet for the diving-only program. The Tigers defeated the College of Charleston and lost to Georgia Tech in Atlanta, GA.

February 9, 2013—The Clemson women's diving team participated in its first-ever home meet when Davidson came to McHugh Natatorium. The Tigers defeated the Wildcats 106-58.

February 23, 2013—Four Clemson divers scored and picked up 12 points at the Atlantic Coast Conference Women's Swimming and Diving Championships at the Greensboro Aquatic Center. Elizabeth Tatum finished 10th in the three-meter competition. Chelsea Uranaka also scored in the event for the Tigers and finished 16th. Jessica Resler finished 16th in the one-meter competition and was 15th in the platform. Emily Howard was 16th in this category.

March 11-13, 2013—Four Tigers competed in the NCAA Zone B Championships in Knoxville, TN. Megan Helwagen, Elizabeth Tatum, Emily Howard, Juliana Melchionda, and Chelsea Uranaka represented Clemson at this event.

February 8, 2014—Senior captain Emily Howard set the three-meter school record for the second straight week while fellow senior Heather Britt set career highs in both the one-meter and three-meter events at McHugh Natatorium at Clemson, SC. Clemson defeated both Davidson and James Madison to finish the dual meet portion of the schedule. The Tigers finished 10-1-1 overall, including a perfect 7-0 record at home.

February 20-22, 2014—Danielle Reitsma finished 17th at the ACC Championships in the one-meter competition at Greensboro, NC . Teammate Juliana Melchionda was 19th. In the three-meter competition, Melchionda was 17th and Chelsea Uranaka was 19th. In the platform competition, Reitsma was 10th and Sarah Braun was 14th.

March 10-12, 2014—Senior Emily Howard finished 24th overall to lead the Clemson women's diving team in the one-meter diving of the NCAA Zone B Championships at the Greensboro Aquatics Center. Teammate Megan Helwagen finished 28th overall to finish second among her teammates with a score of 241.95. In the three-meter diving, Sarah Braun was 21st and Chelseas Uranka was 25th. Danielle Reitsma was 26th in the event. Freshman Danielle Reitsma advanced to the finals of the platform diving to finish 12th. Reitsma is the first member of the women's diving only program to advance to the finals of any event at NCAA Zones.

April 9, 2014—Senior Emily Howard was named to the All-ACC Academic Swimming and Diving Team. She is the first member of the women's diving program to receive the honor.

February 19-21, 2015—The Clemson diving team concluded competition at the 2015 ACC Championships with three top-20 performances in the platform. Sophomores Sarah Braun and Danielle Reitsma and junior Megan Helwagen placed 15th, 16th, and 17th, respectively, for the Tigers in the tower event. Helwagen was Clemson's top performer in the three-meter, finishing 22nd, while Reitsma placed 24th in the event. Braun recorded the Tigers' best score in the one-meter competition.

March 9-11, 2015—At the NCAA Zone B Championships in Athens, GA, Sarah Braun finished 18th in the one-meter finals. In the three-meter competition Megan Helwagen was 23rd . In the platform finals, Sarah Braun was 14th and Megan Helwagen was 17th.

April 28, 2015—Sophomore Sarah Braun and freshman Allison Brophy were named to the 2015 All-ACC Academic Women's Swimming and Diving Team, as announced by the conference office.

February 17-19, 2016—The Clemson diving team totaled 86 points and finished seventh in the Atlantic Coast Conference Meet in the diving category at the Greensboro Aquatic Center, in Greensboro, NC. The Tigers recorded a program-best finish as a team, as well as by an individual. The seventh-place finish was Clemson's best finish at the conference championship meet since 2012, when the program became a women's diving program. Sophomore Danielle Reitsma advanced to the finals of the platform competition, placing sixth overall, becoming the Tigers' first finalist in any event at the ACC championship meet. In the one-meter competition, Clemson's Danielle Reitsma was the Tigers' top finisher, earning 12th place. Caylin Hirapara was 16th and junior Sarah Braun was 23rd. In the three-meter competition, Braun finished 19th and Helwagen was 21st.

March 7-9, 2016—At the NCAA Zone B Meet at the Georgia Tech Aquatic Center in Atlanta, GA, Megan Helwagen advance to the finals in the one-meter competition and finished 16th in the finals. In the three-meter portion of the meet, Caylin Hirapara was the top performer for Clemson, finishing 20th. Not far behind Hirapara was fellow freshman Sarah Blank, who garnered a 22nd place finish. Sarah Braun finished in 14th place in the platform event. Helwagen qualified for the zone meet in all three events, all four years of her collegiate career, the only diver in Clemson program history to do so.

April 25, 2016—Junior Sarah Braun was named to the 2015-16 All-ACC Academic Women's Swimming and Diving Team as announced by the conference office.

March 14, 2017—The Clemson Women's Diving program was discontinued, as announced by Clemson Athletic Director Dan Radakovich. The decision comes five years after the Clemson swimming teams and the men's diving team were discontinued. It was also announced that softball will be added by Clemson as a collegiate sport by the year 2021.

MEN'S
Fencing

NCAA Meets:

1966 (15th), 1968 (38th), 1969 (25th), 1970 (13th), 1971 (41st), 1976 (15th), 1977 (13th), 1978 (4th), 1979 (9th), 1980 (5th), 1981 (4th), 1982 (2nd)

ACC:

1979 Champions

ACC Regular Season Champions:

1979, 1980

HAL COOLEDGE STARTS THE FENCING PROGRAM

Professor Hal Cooledge of the Architecture Department started Clemson Fencing as an outlet for his students. Still considered a club program, the Tigers finished tied for 15th in the 1966 NCAA meet in Durham, NC.

Cooledge joined the Clemson faculty in 1956 and retired in May 1996. During his 40-year association with the College of Architecture, he was a well-respected teacher, researcher, and author. He was instrumental during the 1960s in the effort to restore Thomas Green Clemson's collection of paintings and also funded a professorship in architecture.

A Georgia native, Cooledge graduated from Harvard University. After World World II, he held a research position with an oil company until the Texas City Disaster in 1947, the deadliest industrial accident in US history, which involved a chain reaction of fires and explosions that killed almost 600 people.

He returned to graduate school at the University of Pennsylvania to study art and architectural history and taught at several other institutions before accepting his Clemson position in 1956.

Music was one of Cooledge's passions. He was considered a superb pianist and was a member of the Metropolitan Opera Guild. He was also cast in a speaking role as Dean Collins in *The Midnight Man,* a 1974 murder

mystery movie filmed on the Clemson campus and in the surrounding communities.

Although considered a club program, the Clemson fencing team had early success in the NCAA Tournament. Wayne Baker, a football player, was the first Tiger to place in the top 10 at an NCAA meet, finishing ninth in the Sabre in 1969 in South Bend, IN.

The Clemson Athletic Department and the Atlantic Coast Conference started to sponsor men's fencing in 1970.

Hal Cooledge started the men's fencing program at Clemson.

CHARLIE POTEAT TAKES OVER

Charlie Poteat was named the Clemson head fencing coach prior to the 1975 season. The Poteat era showcased constant improvement and top-25 finishes in the NCAA Championships. After his rookie campaign, the Tigers were top-25 finishers in the NCAA event, placing as high as second in the 1982 campaign. He won four consecutive ACC Regular Season Championships, from 1979 to 1982.

Clemson finished fourth as a team in the 1978 NCAA Meet and ninth in the 1979 NCAA Championships.

In 1980, Clemson was tied for fifth in the NCAA Meet. Clemson finished fourth in the 1981 NCAA Championships and second in 1982. Clemson was 16-0 vs. the ACC in the last three years of competition. In the last four years of the program, the Tigers were 56-7 in dual match competition.

Poteat was the National Coach of the Year after guiding the Tigers to a second-place national finish in 1982, the final year of the program. The team finished in the nation's top 10 for the last five years of his tenure. They also finished in the nation's top five four out of the last five years the Tigers fielded a fencing team. They won the Atlantic Coast Conference Tournament in 1979. Poteat's Tigers defeated his opponents by an average score of 19-8 over his last four seasons. He finished with a career record of 89-22 in eight years as the head fencing coach at Clemson, for a .802 pct.

After he left Clemson, Poteat went to Lincoln Memorial University in the fall of 1984, serving as head resident at a dormitory, teaching physical education, and coaching men's tennis.

Poteat decided he would stay local and purchased a small farm in the Speedwell area that he quickly called home.

Athletically, throughout nineteen seasons at the helm of the Railsplitter program, Coach Poteat's teams reached the NCAA Men's Tennis Tournament six times and the NAIA Tournament once, earning respect not only in the Gulf South Conference as one of its top programs, but also throughout the entire southeast United States.

During the 2004 spring season, which turned out to be his last, Coach Poteat guided his team to a third-place Gulf South Conference Eastern Division finish, while completing the year with an 11-5 record, which ended in the NCAA South Regional Tournament.

Poteat died of cancer on July 14, 2004, at the age of 54. On October 14, 2011, the tennis building at the Lincoln Memorial University Tennis Center was named in his honor.

STEVE WASSERMAN AND OTHER OUTSTANDING FENCERS

Steve Wasserman, a three-time All-American, reflected back on the program.

"I guess I ended up at Clemson by accident," said Wasserman. I had won the state championship in New Jersey my junior and senior seasons. I was also set to go to the University of Pennsylvania. I had heard of the Clemson program. Coach Poteat started recruiting me and I took a visit to Clemson.

"I loved what I saw," said Wasserman. "Clemson had academically what I wanted to study and when he offered me the scholarship, I accepted. I'm glad I made that decision.

"Coach Poteat was young—not much older than we were. He was energetic. He had fenced at North Carolina. He was dedicated to the team and its success. It was an honor to be on the team. He was a great recruiter.

"In my senior season [1982], we knew we had a good team. We had the people to compete. We believed we could compete for the National Championship. We had done well in dual meets and in the tournaments we had that year.

"We went to the NCAA National Tournament and we fell short. We finished in second place. It was a great year. Sure you want to win it all, but we had a lot of success that season.

"We were surprised when we received the news that they were ending the program. We were disappointed. We had developed into one of the best programs in the country."

Clemson dropped men's fencing in 1982 after Wasserman's senior season. The Tigers finished second in the NCAA meet, the highest finish for the program.

"Looking back, I was happy with my decision to attend Clemson," Wasserman said. "My sister graduated from Clemson and she did really well. I also met my wife at Clemson. There's no question that some decisions change your life forever. I graduated with an economics degree and later went to law school. I still come back for Clemson football games and stay very active with Clemson. I simply fell in love with the place."

Other outstanding Clemson fencers include three-time All-America athlete Jay Thomas (1979-82) and three-time All-America honoree Steve Renshaw (1977-80).

Renshaw was a 1980 Atlantic Coast Conference champion in the Sabre. Thomas was a 1980 conference champion in the Épée.

FENCING HISTORY

March 25-26, 1966—Clemson finished tied for 15th in the NCAA meet in Durham, NC, on the Duke campus.

March 28-30, 1968—The Tigers finished 38th as a team in the NCAA meet in Detroit, MI, on the campus of Wayne State University.

March 27-29, 1969—Clemson finished in a tie for 25th as a team at the NCAA meet in Raleigh, NC. N.C. State University served as the host of this event.

March 19-21, 1970—The Tigers finished 13th at the NCAA Championships in South Bend, IN, on the Notre Dame campus. Wayne Baker, a Tiger football player, became the first Clemson fencer to finish in the top 10 in the individual competition, with a ninth-place finish in the Sabre. The Tigers' Tom Gambill finished 22nd in the Épée and Paul Ferry was 23rd in the Foil.

March 18-20, 1971—Clemson finished the NCAA Tournament in 41st place at the annual event at the US Air Force Academy at Colorado Springs, CO. Wayne Baker finished 25th in the Sabre competition.

September 4, 1974—Charlie Poteat was named the head coach. Poteat came to Clemson from the University of North Carolina, where he earned his BA in chemistry in 1972 and his MA in physical education two years later. He was a two-time All-ACC pick with the Tar Heels. He also served as an assistant for North Carolina in 1973 and 1974.

March 17-18, 1976—At the Historic Palestra in Philadelphia, PA, Clemson finished 21st at the NCAA Meet, where the University of Pennsylvania played host. Jim Walters finished tied for 15th in the Épée, as did Jim Heck in the Sabre. Frank Cava finished in a tie for 30th in the Foil.

February 26, 1977—Clemson's George Podgroski finished first in the Épée competition, and Steve Renshaw and Jim Heck finished second and third,respectively, in the Sabre at the Atlantic Coast Conference Championships in Chapel Hill, NC. The Tigers finished third as a team.

March 24-26, 1977—The Tigers finished 13th overall at the NCAA Fencing Championship held at the University of Notre Dame in South Bend, IN. Steve Renshaw finished fifth in the Sabre. Because of his performance, he was named second-team All-American. George Podgorski finished 18th in the Épée.

February 25, 1978—Clemson finished in second place in the ACC Meet held in Clemson, SC. Don Fletcher, Jim Heck, and Steve Renshaw received first-team All-ACC honors. Guy Johnson and Frank Seva earned second-team All-ACC honors.

March 16-18, 1978—Clemson finished fourth in the NCAA Championships in Kenosha, WI, on the campus of the University of Wisconsin-Parkside. This was the first time that the Tigers finished in the top 20 in all three weapons. Steven Renshaw finished third in the Sabre, Frank Ceva finished eighth in the Foil, and Don Fletcher finished 20th in the Épée. Head coach Charlie Poteat was runner-up in National Coach of the Year voting.

February 17, 1979—Clemson set a school record for most victories in a season with 15. The Tigers also set a school record for the largest margin of victory with a 26-1 win over South Carolina on February 17th in Clemson, SC. The Tigers also had a 5-1 record in the ACC and won the ACC regular season title.

February 24, 1979—Clemson won the Atlantic Coast Conference Championship at Carmichael Gymnasium at N.C. State. A total of seven Clemson men were named All-Atlantic Coast Conference. The Tigers' Steve Renshaw (Sabre), Jay Thomas (Épée), Mark Wasserman (Sabre), Guy Johnson (Foil), and Craig Vecchione (Foil) were all named to the first team. Jim Heck (Sabre)and Don Fletcher (Épée) were named to the second team. This marked the highest number of Tigers named to the All-ACC team in one season.

March, 1979—Clemson finished ninth at the NCAA Tournament in Princeton, NJ. Renshaw and Thomas were both named second-team All-Americans.

The 1979 Clemson team won the ACC Championships.

February 3, 1980—The Tigers defeated Virginia 20-7 and North Carolina 15-12, as the Tigers clinched the ACC regular season title. Clemson finished 6-0 in the ACC.

March 1, 1980—Clemson finished second at the ACC Championship in Clemson, SC. Renshaw won the Sabre event and Thomas finished first in the Épée.

March 13-15, 1980—Clemson finished in a tie for fifth at the NCAA Championship at Penn State University. Thomas finished fifth in the Épée and Renshaw finished seventh in the Sabre. Thomas was received second-team All-America honors, and Renshaw was named an honorable mention All-American.

February 26, 1981—The Tigers wonthe ACC regular season, as Clemson finished with a 5-0 record in the ACC.

March 19-21, 1981—Wasserman finished sixth in the Sabre and was a second-team All-American. Vecchione and Thomas were honorable mention All-Americans. The Tigers finished fourth in the NCAA Championship at Kenosha, WI.

March 16-18, 1982—Clemson finished second in the NCAA Tournament at the University of Notre Dame. Thomas finished second in the Épée, Wasserman finished sixth in the Sabre, and Johnson finished 11th in the foil. Coach Poteat was named National Coach of the Year in a vote by his peers. Clemson dropped the Fencing Program in the Spring of 1982.

Coach Charlie Poteat led Clemson to an NCAA second-place finish in 1982. He led the Tigers to five top-10 finishes at the NCAA meet.

WOMEN'S
Fencing

NEW PROGRAM

Although Clemson fielded women's fencing for only seven seasons, the Tigers accomplished so much during this short time. From the humble beginnings of putting together a team in 1975 to its trip to partaking in the inaugural NCAA Tournament in 1982, Clemson made a good showing on the strip.

"I remember before the first year, we went around and had flyers put under dorm doors and around student areas to get people to come out for the team," said Bill Shipman, the first coach of the women's fencing team.

"We had 25 or so come out for the first practice and about 12 or so stayed for the first team. We had great athletes out for the team. We practiced at Fike Recreation Center. Everything was new and at the time we had good facilities.

"It was a challenge to start a program, but it was also fun," said Shipman. "I was happy with the turnout and the effort of our first year."

Prior to the second season, Clemson started officially recruiting young ladies, and the program started to develop. Clemson was 2-13-1 in its first year and made a tremendous turnaround the next season, finishing 5-3 overall under Shipman.

"We struggled our first season," said Shipman. "We had a chance to recruit prior to the second season and things started coming together. My second year we took a group of novices and we defeated an older N.C. State team. We were also fortunate to defeat Ohio State and William & Mary that season.

"We recruited fencers from the East, and the program started to develop. I was also an assistant on the men's

The 1975-76 team was the first Clemson women's fencing team.

fencing team. I was thankful to Clemson and Coach Poteat for the opportunity to coach at Clemson.

"Overall it was fun and a great experience being on the ground floor and getting the women's program started. Clemson is a great place, and I really enjoyed my time there."

THE INAUGURAL NCAA TOURNAMENT

Clemson had the honor of fencing in the first-ever NCAA Tournament that was held in Fresno, CA. Clemson participated as a team, and they also had an individual entry in Debbie Wasserman.

"I came to Clemson for different reasons. First I was recruited, and second my brother Mark was already on the men's fencing team, so I knew about Clemson already," said Wasserman. "I fenced at Morris Hills High School and had success there. I thought the facilities and everything about Clemson was just gorgeous. I remember I came in as a freshman and it was a fun time.

"We had a good team. The football team had just won the National Championship and it was an exciting time my freshman season. We went to the NCAA Tournament in California. I was a participant in the individual tourna-

The 1982 team participated in the first-ever NCAA Fencing Championships.

ment. I thought it was awesome that we were on the big stage and it was historical being in the first NCAA Meet."

Clemson finished eighth at the first-ever NCAA Tournament in 1982. Wasserman was defeated in the first round. She finished the season with a 38-14 individual record and led the team as a freshman.

The final year of the women's varsity fencing program was 1982.

"I was disappointed when Clemson dropped the program," said Wasserman. "However, I had a great time at Clemson and received a wonderful education. I graduated and went to Emory Medical School, and I am now a pediatrician. There's no doubt that Clemson prepared me for my future."

Wasserman is an IPTAY member and comes back to Clemson for football games and other activities.

WOMEN'S FENCING HISTORY

January 17, 1976—Clemson participated in its first collegiate dual competition as the Tigers faced Georgia Southern and Florida State in Statesboro, GA.

1977—Bill Shipman's Tigers finished with a 5-3 record overall in just its second season.

1978—Dave Griffin's Tigers posted a 6-3 record, and Teresa Wallen received second team All-Region recognition.

1979—The women's fencing team finished the 1979 season with a 14-2 victory over South Carolina. Clemson ended the season with an 8-7 record overall. Clemson was on the losing end of duels against William Patterson and North Carolina. Each opponent won on touches after an 8-8 draw.

1980—Clemson finished the season with a 7-7 record overall and 2-2 mark vs. Atlantic Coast Conference teams.

January 29-30, 1981—Clemson defeated MIT, Harvard, Brown, Brandeis, and

Coach Bill Shipman and fencer Teresa Wallen.

Wellesley on the road and improved its overall record to 8-6.

March 8, 1981—Clemson finished third in the AIAW Regional Meet at Chapel Hill, NC. The Tigers qualified for the AIAW National Meet that was held in South Bend, IN. Jayne Komoski was named first-team All-Tournament, and Renshaw was named to the second team. Komoski finished fourth at the Championships and qualified for the National Individual Championships.

April 1-4, 1981—Clemson finished 16th nationally in the AIAW National Meet at South Bend. Komoski finished 41st at the AIAW Individual Tournament.

March 25-27, 1982—Clemson finished eighth in the first-ever NCAA Women's Fencing Championships. Debbie Wasserman had a 38-14 record overall and Kathy Renshaw was 35-17 on the year to lead the Tigers. Wasserman was also a participant in the inaugural NCAA Individual Tournament.

Debbie Wasserman participated in the inaugural NCAA Fencing Championships.

WOMEN'S
Field Hockey

Clemson played its home matches at Historic Riggs Field. Joanne Baines, a graduate of Winthrop College and in charge of starting the program at Clemson, coached the Tigers for the full five years of the program's existence. After a slow start during the inaugural season, the Tigers had an 11-5-3 record in 1978. The Tigers played in the AIAW Regional Tournament (a forerunner to the NCAA Tournament) in 1979 and 1980. In the first year of the NCAA Tournament in 1981, Clemson was ranked in the top 10 nationally during the season. However, the number of teams that participated in the first NCAA Tournament was small, and the Tigers barely missed making the tournament.

Coach Baines coached one All-America player, Barbara Johnson, a midfielder, in 1981. That season, Johnson scored 24 goals, and Clarke Jones scored 12. Clemson finished the season with a 14-4 record overall.

Many schools in the local area began dropping field hockey. Because of the lack of local competition and the expense of traveling to play opposition, Clemson decided to drop the program after the 1981 season.

"It was a challenging opportunity," said Joanne Baines when asked what it was like starting the field hockey program at Clemson. "I was hired by Mr. McLellan [then-athletic director at Clemson]. I was young, I had played field hockey at Winthrop, and I was ecstatic to take the challenge. I remember the first season, I was in grad school at Clemson as well, [and] we started out using local players and players that were already enrolled in school that had played in high school. We didn't have a chance to recruit for the first year.

"After we went through the first season, we started recruiting, and we started to learn the ropes and we did better our second season. We had a lot to learn, and at the same time we were having a great time," said Baines.

"We focused our recruiting on the Eastern Seaboard and we had a lot of success bringing players to Clemson. I was very proud of our first All-American, Barbara Johnson. We had great support from the university with scholarships, budget, and facilities. Clemson was very supportive. Recruiting was great, as Clemson was and still is an easy sell. We had great assistants along the way and I was very happy and again we had a lot of fun. The road trips were long because of the distance, but we had fun and this helped build team character and camaraderie.

"The program was dropped because the local competition were dropping their programs, and we started to have to travel a long way to play. We would be gone for three or four days traveling by vans and sometimes cars.

"We worked hard and had fun. We grew up together and I feel we had a good time. The experience and coaching at Clemson was very rewarding," said Baines.

After leaving Clemson, Baines taught physical education and worked with children with special needs. She is also very active with the Special Olympics program in South Carolina.

The 1981 Clemson field hockey team finished the year with a 14-4 record.

Joanne Baines was Clemson's field hockey coach when Clemson fielded the sport.

FIELD HOCKEY HISTORY

September 19, 1977—Clemson played at Appalachian State in the first-ever field hockey match for the Tigers.

November 4, 1978—Clemson completed the season with a 1-0 win over Catawba. The Tigers finished the season with an 11-5-3 mark overall.

November 4, 1979—The Tigers completed an undefeated regular season with a 4-0 win over Pfeiffer at the Deep South Tournament at Winthrop in Rock Hill, SC.

November 16-17, 1979—Clemson lost to William & Mary and Eastern Kentucky at the AIAW Region II Tournament in Williamsburg, VA.

November 7-8, 1980—The Tigers lost to Virginia 2-1 and Longwood 2-1 in the AIAW Region II Tournament. The Tigers finished the season with a 12-5-2 record overall.

September 23, 1981—The Tigers were ranked eighth in the NCAA Division I Field Hockey poll. This was the first time ever that the Tigers were ranked nationally in this sport. This was also the first season that the NCAA started conducting championships in women's sports.

November 10, 1981—Midfielder Barbie Johnson, a Greene, NY, native, was named All-America for the 1981 season. She is Clemson's first and only player to receive this honor. She finished the year with 24 goals, including five against Davidson and three against Catawba. She scored in 16 of 17 matches she played in that season.

Barbie Johnson scored 54 career goals and scored 24 in 1981.

CLEMSON
Football

THE MEETING THAT STARTED FOOTBALL

On a still, balmy September night in 1896, on the young and undeveloped Clemson College campus, a group of cadets met in the barracks to discuss the feasibility of organizing a football team to represent the all-male military school. Other state schools had football, and the question was raised—why not Clemson?

From this group, three students were appointed to consult an engineering professor, Walter M. Riggs, as to the management of a football team and to ask his aid as coach. Legend has it that only one of these 30 players had ever seen a football.

It was only appropriate Riggs would coach the Clemson Tigers. Riggs originally came to Clemson from Auburn. He graduated with top honors in 1892 with a BS degree in electrical and mechanical engineering. At Auburn, he was captain and catcher of the baseball team as well as the manager and left end of the football team. He also served as class president and was the director of the Glee Club.

Upon his graduation at Auburn, he was an assistant to the president of the college until 1896, and then he made his trek to Clemson.

WALTER RIGGS, THE FATHER OF CLEMSON ATHLETICS

Walter Riggs could easily be called the Father of Clemson Athletics.

He coached the football program at Clemson, not only because he had football experience, but he was also one of only two people on the Clemson campus to have ever seen a football game when the sport started in 1896. (The other person was Frank Thompkins, who played in the backfield on Clemson's first-team in 1896.)

In an article written by Riggs, he describes his arrival at Clemson in the late 1800s.

"In 1896, Clemson College was quite a different-looking place to what it is now. The campus was more or less covered with underbrush. There were no well-defined paths and very poor roads. There was only one barracks and only three other principal buildings—the Main Building, the Chemical Laboratory, and the Mechanical Hall. The Agricultural Laboratories and classrooms were in the main building. The post office was a little one-room wooden house to the right of the road as you pass the Mechanical Hall, and about halfway between the road and the Calhoun Mansion. On the grass sward in front of this little post office, football had its beginnings.

"When leaving Auburn, I had 'sworn off' from athletics. But when the fall of 1896 came around and the Clemson boys wanted to get up a football team, the 'call of the wild' was too strong, and again I found myself in a football suit, and the single-handed coach of the first Clemson football team.

"There was only one man in college who had ever seen a football, and that was Frank Tompkins. The players had to be taught everything. They had never seen a gridiron or a football game, and had no idea what to do or how to stand.

"The first game was with Furman University in Greenville, and it was the first time the Clemson eleven lined up on a full-sized gridiron. Furman, who had been playing for several seasons, was confident of victory—Clemson won the game 14 to 6."

THE IMPORTANCE OF FOOTBALL

"In looking back over a service of several years, I regard the introduction of intercollegiate football into Clemson College as one of the most valuable steps in the development of the institution. Long before its graduates could spread its fame as an institution of learning, its football teams had made the name of Clemson College known and respected throughout the nation.

"In a well-rounded college life, play is just as indispensable to healthy growth as is work. Athletics should not interfere with studies, nor should studies exclude athletics; each should have a proper and legitimate place in the thought and life of the students."

Riggs stepped down as football coach after the first season because the players wanted him to devote all of his time to being a professor in the engineering department.

Clemson athletics and Riggs, however, could not be split. Although not given the title, Riggs also was the equivalent of an athletic director, managing money and making contracts with other teams as he served as president of the Athletic Association.

Riggs could easily be called a loyal man, as he answered the need of the Clemson football team again in 1899. The Clemson Athletic Association was low on money and could not afford to hire a coach. So Riggs once again answered the call of the school and became the coach of the 1899 team for free.

Riggs later became president of Clemson on March 7, 1911, and in 1915, a new football stadium with other athletic facilities was named in his honor as Riggs Field. It is currently the home of the Tiger soccer team. In two years of coaching, Riggs guided the Tigers to a career record of 6-3.

After starting the Clemson program and coaching the team in 1896 and 1899, he headed the Clemson Athletic Association (athletic director) and was a key administrator of the Southern Intercollegiate Athletic Association (an early southern athletic conference with several schools as members).

THE FIRST GAME

There is something to be said about the "old college try."

On October 5, 1896, Clemson began practice on a 50x200-foot field in front of the college. It is believed that

Walter Riggs arrived at Clemson in the late-1800s.

this field was located in front of what is now the student union building (the area between Tillman Hall and the Trustee House) on campus.

Also, the first football team had training rules to be followed to the letter. They were as follows:

(1) Will report promptly to all practices prescribed by the coach unless physically disabled or prevented from attending on account of college duties.

(2) That in any of the above instances, we will report the facts beforehand, when possible to the coach.

(3) That we will not, without the consent of coach and trainer, eat anything at any time except at the training table; will not drink an alcoholic beverage or spirituous liquors or soda water.

(4) Will not use tobacco in any form or engage in any form of dissipation.

(5) Will retire not later than 11:00 p.m. unless permission is granted by coach and trainer or prevented by college duties.

(6) Will obey the directions of the coach and captain on the field of play as before specified, and use our influence to promote discipline both on and off the field of play.

Practice continued, and as one description put it, "a hardy group of early Tigers who cared little for their skin and bones turned out for practice and began enthusiastically slamming each other to the rock-strewn practice field."

Without any capital, the team's first equipment was personal property, but other necessary equipment was purchased with money that was willingly contributed by members of the faculty and student body.

Equipment in the early years consisted of very little padding except at the knees and elbows. Tightly fitting and laced leather or canvas jackets were the main bodily protection against the crashing effects of mass plays and left little for a tackler to grab. A few had nose and shin guards. Due to the lack of helmets and need for head protection, they wore long hair.

After gruelling practices, the first-ever Clemson game day finally arrived.

On October 31, 1896, Clemson traveled to Furman more than likely by train. This was the first time that many of the Clemson players had seen a full-sized gridiron.

George Swygert, center on the first Clemson football team, recalls the Furman game and the first season as follows:

"With Professor Riggs as our coach, we got in shape fairly well. Our first game was with Furman, the biggest men I have ever seen, and believe it or not we won that game! We had a few trick plays. One was when the play ended near the sidelines, our lightest end would hide the ball under his sweater and as the two teams moved toward the center of the field for the next play, he appeared to be injured, [and] then when things were clear, he would made a bee-line for the goal. This worked maybe once a game; it worked against Furman our first game."

Very few details of the Clemson-Furman game are known, but it is known that Charlie Gentry scored Clemson's first touchdown in history.

The Tigers defeated Furman 14-6 in Greenville, SC.

Clemson's upset win over Furman was a monumental milestone for the school. Furman was considered at the time an experienced team, having played the game since 1889 (the year Clemson was founded).

A member of Clemson's first football team, Shack Shealy was the head coach of the Tigers in 1904. He holds the distinction of being the only Clemson player to have coached his alma mater. Shealy coached Clemson one year and guided the Tigers to a 3-3-1 record overall, which included wins over Alabama, Georgia, and Tennessee.

BRINGING HEISMAN TO CLEMSON

Before he came to be known as one of the best coaches in college football history, John Heisman was a tomato farmer somewhere in Texas. President Riggs once recounted how he brought Heisman back to football.

"In the spring of 1894, I was a graduate manager of the football team at Auburn. It fell to my lot to find a coach for the season of 1895, and as the University of Pennsylvania had that year one of the most successful as well as originial teams in the east, I wrote to Carl Williams, the Penn '94 captain, asking him to suggest a suit-

able man. He replied, recommending J.W. Heisman, an ex-Penn player, and an old coach of his while at Oberlin. He did not know Heisman's whereabouts at the time, but he had his home address.

"After several weeks, I got into communication with Mr. Heisman, finding him in Texas engaged in raising tomatoes. It seems that he was only an indifferent farmer and having sunk about all of his capital in the tomato venture, he was glad to go back to his old love and we readily came to terms. The salary was as I remember it, in the neighborhood of $500.00, and we thought that figure high.

"I shall never forget my first impressions of Heisman while I met him at the depot in Auburn. Looking at his rather small stature and begrimed [appearance], as he was with the travel stain of a long journey, I could not but feel that we had again made a mistake in the selection of a coach—we had made several before.

"But it did not require many days of practice to show that the Auburn team was in the hands of a master, and with the decisive defeat of the University of Georgia at the Exposition Grounds, which closed our season of 1895, we felt that in Heisman we had found the right man.

"I left Auburn that winter to ally myself with Clemson College, then the newest of the A and M colleges. No football had ever been played there, and only one student had ever seen the game played. There on a little field only one-third [in] size [which] overlooked the white columned homestead of the great John C. Calhoun, the first football scrimmage took place in the fall of 1896.

"From that first kick, it was a four-year struggle to lay a foundation that might enable me to realize an ambition that he had cherished ever since leaving Auburn to get Heisman at Clemson. By 1899, the Clemson football team had risen steadily until its talent was equal to that of any southern college, and the time had come to put on the long-planned finishing touch. I went to Birmingtham to compete with Auburn of Heisman's services, and came back with a contract.

"During the four years that Heisman had coached at Clemson, I have not missed ten practices nor a single match game. I have had no closer person or athletic friend than Heisman, and I know his methods thoroughly, therefore I feel that in speaking of him both as a man and as a football coach I am speaking from an actual and intimate knowledge. As a coach, there is no other like Heisman."

JOHN HEISMAN COMES TO TIGERTOWN

A name synonymous with not only the early years of Clemson football but also the collegiate game as a whole is John Heisman.

A stern disciplinarian, he expected his players to be of high character and performance both on the football field and in the classroom.

Heisman's ingenuity in originating plays was one of his strong points. He usually had something new up his sleeve for every game.

It is said he used everything in the book and a lot that was not. Coach C. R. "Bob" Williams said it availed little to case one of his (Heisman's) games, for he rarely used the same trick over again. As he often introduced new plays before each game, he had little use for players who could not quickly learn his signal system and remember the intricate and changing plays. This eliminated much otherwise eligible material. Heisman used very few substitutes (3 or 4 at best) notwithstanding the 35-minute halves. This may have been due to scarcity of first-class material, or the expense of travel and upkeep and extra equipment. Also, the rules of the game limited return to the game. A player had to have stamina to remain the full 70 minutes of the game.

Heisman coached the Tigers in 1900-03 and was responsible for putting the Clemson name among the annals of the great early collegiate teams.

The 1900 team was Clemson's first undefeated team.

He invented the hidden ball trick, the handoff, the double lateral, and the "flea flicker." He pioneered the forward pass and originated the center snap and the word "hike" (previously the center used to roll the ball on the ground to the quarterback).

Heisman took Clemson to a 19-3-2 record in his four seasons. His .833 winning pct. is still the best in Clemson history. He was also the Clemson baseball coach between 1901-04.

Clemson was a powerhouse during his tenure and was a most-feared opponent. His secret was that he depended on smart, quick players rather than large size and brawn.

Another favorite Heisman story was the speech he used to make before a season began. Heisman would face his recruits holding a football. "What is it?" he would sharply ask. Then he would tell his players "a football is a prolate spheroid, an elongated sphere, in which the outer leather casing is drawn up tightly over a somewhat

smaller rubber tubing." Then after a long pause he would say, "Better to have died as a small boy than to fumble this football."

Heisman broke down football into these percentages: talent 25%; mentality 20%; aggressiveness 20%; speed 20%; and weight 15%. He considered coaching as being a master-commanding, even dictatorial. He had no time to say "please" or "mister," and he had to be occasionally severe, arbitrary, and something of a czar.

On November 29, 1900, Clemson defeated Alabama 35-0, which allowed Heisman's team to finish the season undefeated with a 6-0 record. This was Clemson's first undefeated team and was the only team to win all of its games in a season until the 1948 squad went 11-0. The Tigers only allowed two touchdowns the entire 1900 season and were the Southern Intercollegiate Athletic Association champions.

Clemson opened the 1901 season with a 122-0 win over Guilford. The Tigers averaged 30 yards per play and a touchdown every minute and 26 seconds. The first half lasted 20 minutes, while the second half lasted only 10 minutes. Legend has it that every man on the Clemson team scored a touchdown in this game.

The Guilford captain was so distraught over the way his team had played. "We missed everything today, tackles and blocks. One thing we won't miss is the train back home."

In 1902, John Heisman played the trick of all tricks on Georgia Tech and their followers.

"We had already won a couple of games, and word drifted to Clemson that Georgia Tech would spare nothing to beat us," said Heisman. "When the train with the Clemson team and baggage arrived in Atlanta the day before the game, the Tech supporters made it a point to entertain our players royally.

"The Tech supporters marveled at the ease with which they were able to get our players to sneak out that night and participate in the wild parties around town. There was quite a lot of eating and drinking and the more the Clemson men indulged in such pastime the more were the Tech men willing to back with money their belief that they would win the next day. Boy, did we clean up the Tech money. Clemson won 44-5. The Tech people wondered at the hardiness of the Clemson men after a night of revelry, until they discovered that Coach Heisman had sent a bunch of bohunks to Atlanta with the team's equipment and kept the varsity at Lula, GA, a small town some miles from Atlanta, the night before the game."

In the Furman game on October 24, 1902, Clemson defeated Furman 28-0. But how Clemson set up one touchdown was quite interesting.

Heisman made use of the handoff or lateral slightly backward pass, as the forward pass was against the rules in that day. It seems that an oak tree stood a few feet inside the sideline on the Furman playing field, which for sentimental reasons had not been removed. Heisman, observing this, instructed the quarterback, "that if a line of scrimmage occurred near this tree, to signal for a lateral pass, from one back to another back to pass or run between the tree and the side line." The ruse worked so well that a long gain was made that set the stage for a touchdown.

On November 27, 1902, Clemson played in the snow for the first time in a game against Tennessee. The Tigers won the game 11-0 and claimed the Southern Intercollegiate Athletic Association crown (an early conference that had several southern colleges and universities as members).

In Heisman's final season in 1903, Clemson defeated Georgia Tech 73-0 on October 17, 1903. Clemson rushed the ball 55 times for 660 yards, while Tech ran the ball 35 times and collected 28 yards. The second half was shortened to 15 minutes.

John Heisman's 19-3-2 record is still the best in Clemson history on a percentage basis. The man after whom the famous trophy that each year honors the best player in college football was named holds the distinction of building the foundation of Clemson's football tradition.

JIM LYNAH—A SECOND CHANCE

An early Clemson football star, Jim Lynah made the most of his "second chance."

Lynah was born in Charleston, SC, and grew up in Savannah, GA.

He was a two-year starter for Head Coach John Heisman at right end for the Tigers in 1900 and 1901. The 1900 team was Clemson's first undefeated team, and they were also the Southern Intercollegiate Athletic Association (SIAA) champions.

The 1900 Tigers rolled over teams that season that included Davidson 64-0, South Carolina 51-0, Georgia 39-5, Alabama 35-0, Wofford 21-0, and Virginia Tech 12-5. The Tigers were 6-0 that season and surrendered just 10 points the entire year.

The 1901 team finished 3-1-1, and during this season Heisman's Tigers defeated Guilford 122-0 and had a 29-5 victory over Georgia.

Lynah was about to graduate from Clemson in June of 1902. To add merriment to the occasion of the upcoming graduation, he and some others "borrowed" a turkey from Clemson professor William Shannon Morrison's farm.

They had a fine celebratory turkey dinner at the expense of the bird owned by Professor Morrison. The guilty participants were caught, and Lynah, the ringleader in this prank, was expelled from school the week before graduation.

In the fall of 1902, Lynah enrolled at Cornell and began college again, where he was regarded as one of the top players in the East and captained the 1904 team under Hall of Fame Coach Pop Warner.

He played primarily the position of quarterback on the football squad and was a member of the Quill and Dagger society as well as Sigma Phi. He was described a "powerful runner who was dangerous with the ball."

Lynah is one of the two players known to have played for two of the most famous and legendary football

James Lynah played for John Heisman at Clemson and Pop Warner at Cornell.

coaches to ever pace the sidelines, John Heisman and Pop Warner.

The other player that both men had the opportunity to coach also had Clemson ties. Joe Guyon played for Warner at Carlisle Military Institute in 1912 and 1913, and he later played for Heisman at Georgia Tech in 1917 and 1918. The Yellow Jackets won the National Championship in football in 1917. Ironically, Guyon was later the Tigers' head coach in baseball and boxing during the late-1920s and early 1930s. Guyon is a member of both the NFL and the College Football Halls of Fame.

After graduating from Cornell in 1905, with a degree in mechanical and electrical engineering, Lynah joined the construction department of the E.I. DuPont Company as an electrical engineer.

In 1922, 20 years after he was to have graduated from Clemson, the class of 1902 had a reunion, and the school presented Lynah with a diploma from Clemson. In the registrar's office, he is indicated as having received a Bachelor of Science degree in engineering.

That same year, he started work at General Motors in Detroit, MI, and for the next several years he proved to be an ingenious asset for the company. At GM, Lynah directed the general purchasing and manufacturing staffs, and at the young age of 48, he retired to his Savannah home in 1929.

A year later he was appointed chairman of a committee for the expansion and development of the College of Engineering by the Cornell University Board of Trustees.

In 1935, Lynah was named the first full-time director of athletics at Cornell and served in this capacity until 1944.

While athletic director at Cornell, Lynah still had time to perform a major service for his country. In July of 1940, with World War II already started in Europe, he took a dollar-a-year job as coordinator of specifications for the nation's huge national defense program serving under William S. Knudson, chairman of the National Defense Commission. Also during World War II, Lynah ran the Brunswick Shipbuilding Company in Brunswick, GA.

During his tenure, he put Cornell athletics on a sound financial basis. He took the lead in organizing what became the Eastern College Athletic Conference (ECAC).

He instituted the plan for a central office of the ECAC and became its first chairman. He was also a strong proponent for a stronger Ivy League.

The ECAC is a college athletic conference comprising schools that compete in 19 sports. It has 303 member institutions in NCAA Divisions I, II, and III. Most or all members belong to at least one other athletic conference.

Most member schools are in other conferences as well, but through the ECAC they are able to participate in sports that their main conferences do not offer. Its headquarters are located in Centerville, MA, on Cape Cod.

Each year the ECAC currently awards the James Lynah Distinguished Achievement Award. The award is bestowed annually to a maximum of four former ECAC athletic administrators who have achieved outstanding success in their respective careers or have made great contributions in the interest of intercollegiate athletics, the NCAA, and the ECAC.

Lynah organized Cornell's department of athletics, physical education, and women's physical education into a single department.

As chairman of a university committee for the development of athletic facilities, before and after he served as director, he set plans in motion that brought about Moakley Club House at the Cornell Golf Course, Teagle Hall, and an indoor ice skating and hockey rink, which was completed in 1957 after Lynah's death in February, 1956, and was named in his honor.

Lynah Arena at Cornell is an iconic building that is used by Cornell's hockey teams. It was constructed for $500,000 with a donation from Walter S. Carpenter, Jr., whose gift came with the stipulation that he did not want his name on the building.

In 1948, Lynah was named chairman of the NCAA enforcement panel, which became known as the "NCAA Sanity Code." He played a key role in the investigations of alleged violations of the code by any of the member universities and colleges. Fearless in his convictions, he took a strong stand on control of recruiting and devoted many years to improving procedures of the NCAA.

Lynah was also a significant proponent in forming the Ivy League in football, established nearly six months after his death in 1956.

He is a charter member of the Cornell Athletic Hall of Fame and was named to the Greater Savannah Athletic Hall of Fame posthumously in 1978.

Lynah was a person of intellect and diversity. He was a member of the American Association for the Advancement of Science, the American Academy of Political and Social Science, the American Society of Mechanical Engineers, the Society of Automotive Engineers, and the Army Ordnance Association.

For many years, a fund established by Lynah was awarded to Clemson students with high scholastic rating and who possessed outstanding qualities of character and leadership. The award was given in memory of the distinguished professors who were teaching at Clemson when the 1902 class were undergraduates. This list of professors included William Shannon Morrison, the owner of the turkey that Lynah "borrowed" in 1902.

Lynah in his professional career was a noted industrialist, national and local leader, and legendary sports figure.

A newspaper article by *Savannah News Press* sports editor Frank Tilton summed up Lynah's life this way: "When Lynah died the morning of February 24, 1956, at his residence, he left behind a splendid record of achievement in all that he endeavored to do, whether it was serving his fellow man, or country's business, cultural, or national affairs, or promoting the integrity of sports."

1903—CLEMSON'S FIRST BOWL GAME

On November 24, 1903, Clemson participated in its "First Bowl Game." The game between Clemson and Cumberland was billed as the game to decide the "Championship of the South," as the winner would be the champion of the SIAA. The SIAA crown was a formidable title in this day and age, "as there were many collegiate powers prowling the playing fields of the south."

Although it was not officially a modern postseason extravaganza similar to what football fans enjoy today, the 1903 Clemson-Cumberland game had met some of the criteria of being Clemson's first bowl game, 87 football seasons ago.

In this particular season, Clemson was considered the best in the Atlantic Coast Region, as the Tigers had defeated Georgia, Georgia Tech, N.C. State, and Davidson. The only loss came to the hands of North Carolina. Clemson had outscored its opponents 156-11, including a 73-0 win over Georgia Tech.

Cumberland was considered the best team in the western part of the southern region, as it had defeated powers such as Vanderbilt, Tennessee, and Sewanee and had scored 304 points.

Originally, the two teams' seasons would have drawn to a close in early November, but the interest surrounding college football to decide which was the best football team in the South could not be ignored by players on both sides, not to mention the fans. The result was Clemson and Cumberland officials agreeing to meet on November 26th, in Montgomery, AL.

Like today's bowl games, a contract was signed, and the game was to take place at a neutral site and on a holiday, Thanksgiving Day. The contract, drawn up just two weeks before the game, stated that the contest was to be played at Oak Park in Montgomery, AL. The game was to begin promptly at 3:00 p.m. and end at 5:00 p.m. sharp.

The game had added significance, as it was the Tigers' first opportunity to prove itself as a southern power, as this was only the eighth year Clemson had fielded a football team.

It would be a battle between Cumberland's backfield of giants charging the Clemson line and Clemson's smaller, swifter backs making long runs around the end. The average height and weight of the Clemson starting 11 was 5' 9 1/2" and 163 1/2 pounds. Cumberland was the heavier team, as the average height and weight was 5' 11" and 172 pounds.

Some interesting notes on some of the members of Clemson's 1903 football team: halfback Fritz Furtick and Jock Hanvey were also track stars for the Tigers; quarterback John Maxwell was the catcher on the Tiger baseball team; right end Hope Sadler was Clemson's record holder in the broad jump and the 440-yard dash; left end C.V. Sitton was named All-Southern end on the 1902 team and was recognized as the best college baseball pitcher in the South; J.A. Forsyth, a right guard, had played every down for the last three years as a Tiger; and J.A. McKeown was Clemson's largest player on the 1903 team, at 6'2" and 194 pounds.

Cumberland dominated the game in the early going, as the Bulldogs jumped to an early 11-0 lead. Cumberland's first score was made by line plunges eight minutes into the game. Minturn scored from a short distance, and M.O. Bridges kicked the extra point, giving Cumberland a 6-0 lead (in 1903, touchdowns were worth five points, while extra points were worth one point).

Four minutes later, Cumberland struck again as left halfback J. Allen Head crossed the goal line and M.O. Bridges failed to convert on the extra point.

After a 10-minute halftime, Cumberland kicked off to Clemson. The Tigers' John Maxwell took the ball at his own 10-yard line and raced 100 yards to score Clemson's first touchdown of the game (the fields were 110 yards in length in 1903). The extra point was no good, and Cumberland led 11-5.

Clemson then took advantage of a Cumberland fumbled punt on the Bulldogs' 35-yard line late in the game. With less than a minute to go in the contest, darkness hovered over the field, and the hundreds of spectators who had braved the cold afternoon were quiet, anxiously awaiting the last play of the game. Clemson had one last chance, and of course Cumberland was expecting a trick play.

"25-86-3-14 hike!" rang out Maxwell's voice as he gave signals for the last play. After the ball was centered, a Clemson man dressed in a gold jersey was seen with the ball unexpectedly running up the middle through Cumberland's defense for 35 yards and into the end zone with little if any interference.

Fritz Furtrick, the Tigers' right halfback, had scored the tying touchdown by simply running up the middle over center as time expired. Jock Hanvey kicked the extra point (two-point conversions were not legal in 1903). The game was over, and Clemson and Cumberland had tied 11-11. The Tigers were cochampions of the South and the SIAA conference, probably the first major milestone in the history of Clemson football.

The 1903 team was the cochampion of the South.

When word reached Clemson that the game had ended in a tie, the Clemson students and local townspeople built a bonfire and paraded around campus.

Then came the dispute for the coveted game ball. The ball always goes to the winning team, but the score was a tie. Captain Suddarth of Cumberland insisted on Captain Sadler of Clemson taking the trophy, while Captain Sadler was equally as insistent that Captain Suddarth should have the ball. A compromise was finally reached after 10 minutes. The ball would go to Patrick J. Sweeny, the patrolman who had been efficiently guarding the entrance to the sidelines by warning the media, substitutes, and fans to "get down in front" so the spectators could see the game, or Clemson's first unofficial bowl game.

This game had another bit of irony to it. This was John Heisman's last game as the Tigers' head coach, as he accepted Georgia Tech's head coaching job later that night. Heisman concluded his Clemson coaching career with a player scoring on the last play of his final game as the Tiger coach.

From this touchdown play in Montgomery, AL, a winning bowl tradition was started, and Clemson established itself not only as a southern power but as a national power when bowl games are played.

ROBERT C. "DADDY" POTTS—CLEMSON'S FIRST NFL PLAYER

The first-ever player to play for Clemson and go to the NFL was Robert C. "Daddy" Potts. Potts was a three-time football letterman at Clemson from 1917-'19.

Potts took an interesting route on his way to the pro ranks as he first attended graduate school at Washington and Lee in Lexington, VA, after graduating from Clemson in 1920. While at Washington and Lee, Potts again played football and was a standout wrestler. In those days, graduate students were eligible to play varsity sports.

The first game Potts ever saw was a game he played in as a ninth grader at Fort Mill (SC) High School in 1912. Nobody on the Fort Mill team had ever seen a football game, for that matter, and they were beaten 72-0 by Winnsboro. The Fort Mill team began to understand the game as the season progressed and actually won a rematch with the same Winnsboro team at the end of the season.

It was already apparent that Potts might have a future in football, as he was the largest player on that Fort Mill team. He was dominant on both sides of the ball, and after a stellar prep career, he was on his way to Clemson on an academic scholarship, as those were the days before IPTAY and athletic scholarships.

At Clemson, Potts started at left tackle for Head Coach Edward "Jiggs" Donahue. During the three years, the Tigers went 17-6-2, including a perfect 3-0 record against rival South Carolina. Potts was named to the All-State team in 1918 and 1920 and was also on the All-Southern team in 1920.

Potts was a teammate of Clemson Athletic Hall of Fame members Bertie "Stumpy" Banks, Frank "Boo" Armstrong, and James "Susie" Owens.

It was during his time at Clemson that Potts received the Nickname of "Daddy." The 1920 edition of Taps had this description of Potts: "'Daddy,' our term of endearment, implies the sense of strength and leadership, and to say that he deserves it is putting it mildly."

After graduating from Clemson in 1920, Potts chose to further his education at Washington & Lee. He played football, wrestled, and was a member of the crew team while at the Virginia school. Potts stayed at Washington and Lee until 1923, before moving to Florida to work as an engineer.

While working in central Florida, Potts was asked to play on local football teams that scrimmaged nearby professional teams. These scrimmages and training sessions were similar to today's spring training for major league Baseball teams in Florida.

At the end of one of the training sessions, Potts was signed by the NFL's Frankford Yellow Jackets. They were a team based out of the Philadelphia suburb for which they were named. The franchise would eventually become today's Philadelphia Eagles.

The 1926 team was the only year Potts played professionally. He definitely picked the right year to play, as Frankford went 14-1-2 and won the NFL Championship. Those were the days well before the term "Super Bowl."

The league champion was crowned based on the won-loss record achieved in the regular season. On the way to the championship that year, Frankford beat George Halas and the Chicago Bears.

Against the highly regarded New York Giants, Potts intercepted a pass and almost returned it for his only career touchdown before being tackled on the two-yard line. The 14 wins by Frankford in 1926 were the most in the regular season by an NFL team until 1984, when the San Francisco 49ers had a record of 15-1.

Potts was a tackle on that Yellow Jacket team and got to play against NFL legends Jim Thorpe, Red Grange, and Curly Lambeau during the championship run. At 235 pounds, Potts was the heaviest player on the team, and at age 28, he was the second-oldest player behind only Coach Guy Chamberlain, who also played.

A teammate of Potts on those Yellow Jacket teams was Houston Stockton from Gonzaga. There would be another famous Stockton to come out of Gonzaga named John, the longtime Utah Jazz point guard who was the grandson of Houston.

After his lone professional football season, Potts moved to Whiteville, NC, and married Blanche Dyson. After World War II, they moved to Loris, SC, where they opened Potts Jewelry Store. Potts was very active in Loris, and returning to South Carolina enabled him to keep up with the Tigers and travel to Clemson games when possible.

"Daddy" Potts was the foundation for the Tigers' tradition of sending players to the NFL. He was an ambassador for Clemson in many ways other than just being the first Tiger to play in the NFL. Potts passed way in August of 1981 just prior to Clemson winning the National Football Championship. Somewhere, Daddy Potts was looking on with a very big smile—his Tigers were the champions.

E.J. STEWART, AN INNOVATOR IN COLLEGE FOOTBALL

Forty-four-year-old Edward James (E. J.) Stewart served as head coach at Clemson in 1921 and 1922. He also made stops at other noted schools during his career.

Stewart played football and baseball at Scio College and played football, basketball, baseball, and ran track at Western Reserve University. He was the first athlete to win letters in all four sports in the same school year at Western Reserve. Upon his graduation, he played, organized, and served as head coach of the Massilon, OH, professional football team.

He began coaching college athletics at Mount Union College in Alliance, OH, and in 1907, papers rated his team as the strongest in Ohio. The basketball team that he coached was without a doubt the best in the state.

In 1908-09, Stewart left Mt. Union College and was named head basketball coach at Purdue University. After four consecutive losing seasons, the first-year coach directed Purdue to an 8-4 season and a second-place finish in the Big 10 Conference.

He coached at Oregon State in 1911 and won the Pacific Coast Championship in basketball his first season. He built the football, basketball, baseball, and track programs, and the Oregon State Aggies ranked athletically with the best of the Pacific Coast.

E.J. Stewart was Clemson's coach in the early-1920s. He is thought to be the first coach to use communications between the press box and the field among coaches.

Stewart left Oregon State and was hired as the head football and basketball coach at the University of Nebraska. At Nebraska, he led the Cornhusker football team to a combined record of 11-4 in 1916-17. They also won the Missouri Valley Conference title both seasons. He gave up the position when he left for World War I. He also served as basketball coach for three seasons, compiling a 29-23 record. After leaving the service, he entered the automobile business as president and treasurer of the Stewart Motor Co. Because of the economic conditions at the time, he decided to go back into coaching, and this time he took a job at Clemson.

In the Spring of 1922, Stewart coached the baseball and track teams while conducting spring football practice. In the fall, Stewart's football team went 1-6-2, but he improved to a 5-4 mark in 1922. It was in the 1922 season that Clemson had its first homecoming game, a 21-0 loss to Centre on September 30. He coached the track teams in 1922 and 1923. He was also the head basketball coach in 1922 and 1923 and had a 19-19 record for both years. In 1923, he had an 11-6 mark.

He was also signed to coach a third year at Clemson, but a larger school, The University of Texas, came calling, and he was to coach there for four seasons.

At Texas, he had an 8-0-1 mark in 1923 and a 5-3-1 record in 1924. In 1925, he had a 6-2-1 record, and in his final season, he compiled a 5-4-0 mark. The 1923 and the 1925 teams finished second in the Southwest Conference.

After his stint at Texas, he went to the University of Texas El Paso for two seasons, 1927 and 1928. In 1927, he had a 2-2-2 record, and in 1928, he finished with a 3-4-1 mark. Stewart was tragically killed in a hunting accident in Texas on November 18, 1929.

Stewart is believed to be one of the first coaches to use communication from the press box or top of the stands to the field while the game is in progress. Eastern coaches, such as those at Harvard, thought that they had come up with the idea in the late-teens and early-20s. The idea of using a telephone during a football game was evolved by Stewart during his regime at the Oregon Agricultural College (Oregon State). He first tried it during the Oregon-Oregon State game in 1913 and used the telephone plan repeatedly in subsequent important contests on the Oregon State schedule.

After he went to Nebraska to assume the head coaching position, he reverted to his telephone scheme during the Nebraka-Syracuse game on Thanksgiving Day, 1917. Seated on the top of a covered stand at the north side of the Nebraska field, a vantage point that enabled him to get a better view of every play and player than if he were on the sidelines, Stewart used a telephone in passing information to his aides on the Cornhusker bench. It is not known if he used this technique at Clemson or not, but everyone around the country on all levels of football uses this scheme today.

Stewart seemed to enjoy his days at Clemson and remarked about the school and the wonders of the student body support in a letter to the student newspaper, *The Tiger.*

"I know that Clemson is filled with a spirit that cannot be conquered, and I know that they are given the most devoted backing possible. The student body and alumni pick the teams up and makes them win against odds that are seemingly against them. I know of no other school in the country whose men fight harder and [more] whole-heartedly than the Clemson Tigers."

MR. TOUCHDOWN, BERTIE CECIL "STUMPY" BANKS

Bertie Cecil "Stumpy" Banks holds the distinction of earning five varsity letters from Clemson, as he played in 1915-19. The reason he got to play the extra year is that he missed part of one season due to his service in World War I.

He actually was part of the program for six seasons, since he entered Clemson in 1914 and played on the freshman team that fall. He came to Clemson as a five-foot, five-inch, 105-pound running back. By the time he graduated, he gained 50 pounds. He was also the starting catcher on the Tiger baseball teams in 1918 and 1919.

On the football field, he scored five touchdowns against Furman on October 13, 1917, in a 38-0 Tiger victory and set the school record that is still in existence today. He also caught two touchdowns against South Carolina on October 26, in Clemson's 27-0 win. He was the captain of both the 1918 and 1919 teams.

Banks was one of six brothers to graduate from Clemson. After graduation, he was a mainstay at all Clemson games, as he manned the sideline chains for 35 years. This included all of the games with South Carolina on Big Thursday in Columbia. He started the first-down chain duties in 1920 and missed only three games until his death in 1961.

Banks was named All-State three years and All-Southern in 1919 by the legendary John Heisman. He was listed on the All-Clemson team covering the period from 1896-1935. In 1975, he was inducted into the Clemson Athletic Hall of Fame.

JOSH CODY LEADS CLEMSON TO SUCCESS

Although a lot of changes have taken place in college athletics since Josh Cody paced the sidelines as head football and basketball coach in the late-1920s and early-1930s, some principles he stressed should never change.

After leaving Clemson after the 1930 season with a 29-11-1 record, Cody coached at Vanderbilt, Florida, and Temple, which was his final stop in coaching and administration. At one time or another, he coached both the football and basketball teams at these schools.

Cody played football at Vanderbilt. He remains the only Commodore to earn All-America honors three times (1915, '16, and '19). The 1920 Vanderbilt graduate was selected as an All-Time All-America player by the Football Writers Association. The Commodores had a 23-9-3 record, as he was a devastating lineman on both sides of the ball under legendary Head Coach Dan McGugin.

On occasion, he played in the backfield and was both a great passer and drop-kicker. He once converted on a 45-yard drop-kick against Michigan.

As one teammate recalled, "He would tell the running backs on which side of him to go, and you could depend on him to take out two men as needed. He was the best football player I've ever seen."

Cody also played basketball, baseball, and was on the track team at Vanderbilt, earning 13 varsity letters in all. And, if this were not enough, he was a lieutenant in World War I in 1917 and 1918.

Another teammate who witnessed his greatness once said, "He was a farm boy and he had no polish, but he was very honest and sincere. He didn't have a scholarship—we had none in those days—but he had a real job. He cleaned the gym every day, cleaned up the locker rooms and the showers, and tended to the coal furnace after practice."

There were also many documentations to his toughness. Teammates remember that he did not like to wear pads, so he cut up an old quilt and sewed it into the shoulders of his jersey.

Upon graduation, Cody started his coaching career at Mercer in 1920 as coach of all sports and athletic director. In 1923, Cody came back to Vanderbilt as head basketball and baseball coach, and as an assistant in other sports. In 1926-27, the Commodores finished 20-4 and won the Southern Conference basketball title under his tutelage.

In his first year as head football coach at Clemson (1927), he led the Tigers to a 5-3-1 record, then guided Clemson to back-to-back 8-3 seasons in 1928 and 1929.

Cody was a popular man among the Clemson student body. He was nicknamed "Big Man" because of his large stature. According to one account, when he was seen on campus and the name "Big Man" was yelled, he would turn and wave and smile the largest grin. He loved and respected the students at Clemson, and they loved him.

This probably was best exemplified when it was rumored he was leaving after three years at Clemson. To show their appreciation for his fine record (including a then-3-0 mark against South Carolina), the students, faculty, and staff acted quickly and took up a collection to buy him a brand-new black Buick and presented him this new car in front of the steps at Tillman Hall on May 6, 1929. He would stay for one more year after this kind gesture. In 1930, the Tigers finished with an 8-2 mark in his final football season at Clemson, the first time in history the Tigers had won at least eight games in three consecutive years.

Cody is the only coach in Tiger history who has been around more than two years who never lost a football game to South Carolina. He also defeated Furman three-straight seasons, had a 13-0-1 home record, and had a 72-percent winning mark overall, fourth-best in Clemson history. He also coached Clemson's first All-America player, center O. K. Pressley. Cody also coached basketball at Clemson for five years and led the Tigers to a 16-9 slate in 1930. During the 1928-30 seasons, he guided Clemson to a 22-4 mark at home on the hardwood.

While Cody was coaching the football and basketball teams, he had a capable assistant in Joe Guyon, who also coached the baseball and boxing teams. Guyon was a Native American who had attended Carlisle Indian School (1912-13) with the great Jim Thorpe, the greatest athlete in the first 50 years of the 20th century, according to the Associated Press.

Guyon played two years under John Heisman at Georgia Tech (1917-18), including the Yellow Jackets' 1917 National Championship team. Guyon also had the distinction of playing both pro football and baseball and was named to the National Foundation Football Hall of Fame and the NFL Hall of Fame in Canton, OH. An injury in baseball ended his playing career, and so he came to Clemson as a coach.

Upon leaving Clemson, Cody returned to Vanderbilt as an assistant football coach and head basketball coach.

He was the head football coach and athletic director at Florida from 1936-'39.

In 1940, Cody was a line coach at Temple and was appointed head basketball coach in 1942. He held that post until he became athletic director in 1952. During his tenure as basketball coach, Cody racked up 124 victories and guided the Owls to the NCAA Tournament in 1944, the first NCAA Tournament appearance in the history of the program. That team reached the Elite Eight of the tournament.

In 1955, he coached the football team at Temple after the original coach resigned on the eve of the season. The Owls were winless that year (0-8), but Cody never complained and instead stressed, "They were improving and trying hard."

During his career, Cody had a few guiding principles he developed that he thought were important.

At that time, Cody had African Americans playing at Temple on the basketball team. When asked before the NCAA Tournament what he would do if segregation became an issue and his team could not stay in the same hotel or eat in the same restaurant, he simply replied, "We will not play in that city. We go together as a team or not play at all."

Such was Cody—he loved his players and respected them, and they did the same.

"I've always tried to treat a player the way I'd expect my son to be treated," was another of his guiding principles.

Another rule he lived by: "It's important to realize how much influence a coach can have on his youngsters," he once said.

Cody retired to a farm in New Jersey. He died of a heart attack on June 19, 1961, in Mount Laurel, NJ, at the age of 69. He was inducted into the College Football Hall of Fame as a player in 1970 and the Tennessee Sports Hall of Fame in 1999.

Cody enjoyed a wide reputation as athlete, coach, administrator, and gentleman. Although many things have changed in the last 80 or so years since Cody was at Clemson, some things that he stressed, like the importance of character and respect for others, will never change.

CLEMSON'S FIRST ALL-AMERICA PLAYER, O. K. PRESSLEY

The record book never gives the complete story.

Although a typical record book lists the accomplishments of former greats in various categories, it never tells of an athlete's character, integrity, leadership, dedication, or his love for the game and Clemson. Those accomplishments are etched in the minds of his family, friends, and those he or she has touched during their lives.

Former Clemson football great O. K. Pressley is listed in the Clemson record book as the Tigers' first football All-America player in 1928. The Tiger archives also tell of him being All-Southern in 1928 and captain of the first

Clemson football team to win eight games in a season (1928). He was a unanimous choice for All-State honors in 1928 and named to the All-Southern team.

But most important, according to the records (memories) of family and friends, he was also an All-America honoree in the game of life.

"O. K. Pressley was like his initials—he was O. K.!" said Henry Asbill, who was an end on the Clemson teams in the late-1920s.

"O. K. was a dedicated player. He played the game because he loved football and his school. He would help his team play better and harder by encouraging us. He would yell to us on defense, 'Lets go boys, let's hold them here, we can do better than that,' or 'Good play.' He never complained if he got hurt."

O. K. Pressley was the starting center and linebacker on the Clemson varsity football team in 1926-28. Back in those days, a player participated on both offense and defense. He was named third-team All-American, according to Newspaper Enterprise of America, John Heisman, and Walter Trumbull teams.

"He was a great player and person. He gave it his all," said Bob McCarley, who was a running back on the Clemson teams in the late-1920s. "He was an inspiration to all of us. He played clean and was a good sportsman who represented Clemson well. We all admired him."

"A better center than Captain O. K. Pressley of Clemson is hard to find," said former South Carolina Head Coach Billy Laval.

Pressley was a dedicated family man. As his son Kirk explains,"My father was a great father and an All-American in every aspect of his life."

O. K. Pressley almost did not make it to Clemson, as his brother Tom tried to get him to go to Wofford with him and play football. Tom got off the train at Spartanburg and tried to convince his brother, but O. K. insisted he needed to go to Clemson. After he had gone 10-15 miles up the track toward Clemson, he almost jumped off the train and ran back to Spartanburg, but something inside of him told him to go on and be a Tiger—thus beginning one of the greatest football careers ever at Clemson.

When O. K. arrived at Clemson, he began playing for the local YMCA team. Too modest to tell of his high school exploits, he remained on the YMCA team until he was discovered by the Clemson varsity coaches.

The YMCA team and varsity would scrimmage quite often on Bowman Field in front of Tillman Hall. He was playing defensive tackle in the first scrimmage, and he was an instant star. At first, the varsity put their best blocker on him, and then they started double- and triple-teaming him, and he was still making tackles.

The Clemson varsity team claimed he was stealing their signals, and Pressley challenged the varsity team to have their huddles at Tillman Hall, then come and play. A star had been found, and immediately he was asked to join the Clemson football squad.

Pressley was not only a great football player, but at times served as trainer, publicist, and friend—anything to help the Clemson Tigers win.

As a trainer, Pressley helped team doctor Lee Milford. "It was in the South Carolina game in 1928 on the opening kickoff, that two of our boys ran together and both of them had severe cuts over their eyes," recalled Pressley in a 1983 interview. "They could barely see out of them. Dr. Milford came running out on the field and said, 'We got to take these boys out.' Those were the days when you couldn't substitute. If you left the game, you were finished for the day. We didn't have anybody else to put in the game. I told him to give me some tape so I could work on one while he worked on the other. We patched them up so they could see out of their eyes and remain in the game."

Pressley acted as a publicist when he kept the Winthrop University campus informed of the Tigers' exploits, especially his hometown girlfriend and later wife. Still in pads after a ball game, he would walk to the Western Union Office and send a telegram to her at the Winthrop campus and tell of the Clemson fortunes. Several Winthrop students would wait anxiously for the news of the Clemson Tigers, (Back in those days, Clemson was the state's all-male school and Winthrop was the state's all-female college. Winthrop was consided Clemson's sister school.)

O. K. loved his teammates and was willing to share with them as any good friend would. The day before an Auburn game, the players went downtown in Auburn, AL. O. K. Pressley had 50 cents for the trip and bought a banana split for 25c. Pressley insisted on 12 spoons so his teammates could share in this special and unusual treat. It must have had some special power, as Clemson upset Auburn 6-0. It was in this game that Pressley suffered a severe hand injury.

He was in a great deal of pain on the train trip back home, but he never complained. He would miss the next game against N.C. State, and he was being held out of the South Carolina contest.

In the South Carolina game, the Gamecocks were driving. O. K. Pressley knew he could help his team, but head coach Josh Cody did not want to play him because of his injury. South Carolina kept driving. O. K. went to Cody and begged to be put in, and the coach firmly said, "No." South Carolina was on the Tigers' 10-yard line. O. K. looked at the coach with pleading eyes.

Cody looked at O. K. and then looked at the field with an approving nod of the head as if to say, "Please go in and stop the Gamecocks." Pressley charged out onto the field. On the first play, he tackled the South Carolina player for an eight-yard loss. The next play, Pressley tackled the South Carolina ball carrier for a seven-yard loss. The next two plays, Pressley tackled the Gamecocks' ball runners for a five- and seven-yard loss, respectively. It was probably the greatest one-man defensive stand in the history of Clemson football. Pressley must have given the Tigers a charge, as

Clemson defeated the favored Gamecocks 32-0. Both teams came into this game with undefeated records of 5-0.

College graduation in 1929 didn't end Pressley's football-playing days in that he entered the Marine Corps and served as a player/coach for some seven years. He went on to become a much-decorated military figure before he retired with 20 years of service to his credit in 1949 and returned to his native Chester County. He taught in the public schools there for several years and retired to his farm near Chester.

He was honored at Clemson in 1983, over 50 years later, by being inducted into the Clemson Hall of Fame, along with other Clemson greats. Pressley died on September 22, 1984.

Clemson's first All-America football player continued to be an All-America player long after his Clemson career and made his mark in many people's record books.

JESS NEELY LEADS CLEMSON TO THE COTTON BOWL

Perhaps one of Clemson's most beloved coaches was Jess Neely.

Neely's influence and inspiration are still present today, as the IPTAY Scholarship Club was founded during his coaching tenure. IPTAY is the lifeblood of the Clemson Athletic Department. It provides funds for athletic scholarships and capital improvements.

Neely was head coach at Clemson from 1931 through 1939 and spent the next 26 years at Rice University in Houston.

Neely coached Clemson to its first bowl game, the 1940 Cotton Bowl, where the Tigers capped a 9-1-0 season by beating Boston College 6-3. Clemson ended the season ranked 12th in the final Associated Press poll, its first top-20 season in history. Boston College was ranked 11th going into the game, and it was Clemson's first win over a top-20 team in its history. The team featured the play of Banks McFadden, Clemson's first Associated Press All-America player. Clemson had a 43-35-7 record during Neely's tenure.

Neely coached Rice to four Southwest Conference Championships and six bowl appearances, the last being a trip to the Bluebonnet Bowl in 1961.

During 40 years of college coaching, he compiled a record of 207-99-14. Neely was eighth in college football history in victories heading into the 1994 season. For his accomplishments, he was inducted into the College Football Hall of Fame.

Neely graduated from Vanderbilt in 1924, after lettering three years in football and serving as captain of the 1922 team. He coached a year of high school football before returning to his alma mater to obtain a law degree. But he never practiced law.

He coached four years at Southwestern College in Clarksville, TN, and then went to the University of Alabama in 1928. It was there that he met Frank Howard. Neely brought Howard to Clemson as line coach in 1931.

Howard replaced him in 1940 and remained as head coach for 30 years. In 1967, Neely returned to his alma mater as athletic director. He officially retired in 1971 but continued to coach golf until 1981, when he moved back to Texas.

"If I didn't look in the mirror every day, I wouldn't know how old I am," Neely once said. "Working with the boys makes you feel young, I feel that in athletics the boys learn a sense of loyalty and sacrifice and values they don't learn anywhere else.

"They learn to compete," he said "and that is what life is all about—it's competition.

"If they make good in football, chances are they'll be successful elsewhere. I like to see that those boys make something of themselves. That's my reward.

"The boys go to college to study and get that degree. Playing football is a side activity. When fellows go to a school first to play football, they get an entirely wrong sense of values.

"And when you start them off with the wrong sense, it isn't difficult for them to go astray," said Neely.

Neely died at the age of 85 in 1983, but his landmark accomplishments in the 1930s at Clemson contributed significantly to Clemson's outstanding football tradition.

THE 1939 SEASON

Perhaps one of the most significant seasons in Clemson's football history is the 1939 season. This squad played and defeated Boston College 6-3 in Dallas's 1940 Cotton Bowl.

So much of the history and heritage of Clemson football documents 1939 as a cornerstone season. Not only was it Clemson's first bowl team, but also it was Clemson's first-team to be ranked and the first to end a season in the national top 20 (12th in the final AP poll).

Clemson opened the year with its annual victory over Presbyterian, then suffered its only loss, a 7-6 squeaker, to Tulane in New Orleans. The Tigers would win their next seven (only nine regular season games were played back then) and would accept their first bowl bid.

Oddly enough, that only loss to the Green Wave saw Banks McFadden first rise to national prominence. Many observers say that is where McFadden made the All-America team on his punting exhibition, especially on his quick-kicks from the single-wing tailback position. He averaged over 43 yards a kick in 12 punts that afternoon and had six punts of at least 50 years, still a single-game record today.

Starting out with a 1-1 record after two games, few would even hazard a guess that Clemson would play in its first bowl game at the end of the season. Few also figured that Coach Jess Neely would move on to Rice at the end of the season, where he would remain for the next 27 years.

It might seem ironic that Neely's first winning season, 1934, was the year that IPTAY was founded. Neely had asked for $10,000 from IPTAY to boost the program.

But Neely fought adversity with slow and well-thought-out solutions. How many coaches today could win 36 games in six seasons with only 14 out of 56 games played at home? Only once did Clemson play as many as four games at home during Neely's stay, and only twice were there three home games in a year. Thirteen of the 56 games were played on neutral sites.

Even this '39 team only played two games at home, opening the season with an 18-0 win over Presbyterian, and then in the seventh game, downing Wake Forest 20-7.

With the exception of the Tulane loss, the Tigers were only behind twice during the entire season, and there was one tie, although it didn't last long. Players went both ways and only gave up 45 points in the 10 games, counting the Cotton Bowl.

In the third game, the Tigers defeated N.C. State 25-6 in Charlotte, with the Pack's lone score coming in the final period. Clemson played Navy at Annapolis, then went back to the nation's capital the next Saturday and downed George Washington, 13-6.

There were many stars on this team. McFadden and Joe Blalock were both All-America players and joined George Fritts and Shad Bryant on the All-Southern Conference team. That quartet, along with Walter Cox and Bob "Red" Sharpe, were members of the All-State squad. Payne, Tom Moorer, and Carl Black were the only three to start all 10 games.

They suddenly found themselves—a group of players from small-town environments, playing big-time football. Neely rewarded the team for its efforts by taking all 51 players to Dallas for the game. The trip was made by train.

While in Dallas for the bowl game, talk was rampant that Neely would leave Clemson for the head coaching job at Rice. Bill Sullivan was the publicity man for Frank Leahy and Boston College, and he said that he was in the hotel room in Dallas when Neely told a small group that he would definitely take the Rice offer.

Frank Howard, who was Neely's line coach, spoke up and said: "Well, I'm not going with you." And according to Sullivan, Neely said: "I hadn't planned to ask you."

When Howard was confronted with this, he denied it and said that J.C. Littlejohn, Clemson business manager, had promised him the Clemson head coaching job if Neely left. Sullivan, incidentally, is the same Sullivan who used to own the New England Patriots and Sullivan Stadium in Foxboro, MA.

1940 COTTON BOWL

"That McFadden put a lot of these gray hairs on my head," Neely told *Boston Post* reporter Gerry Hern in an article prior to the Cotton Bowl. "I don't discourage him any. He's a smart tailback; and if he feels he has worked the team into a bad spot, I like to see him get reckless.

"We've scored a few touchdowns on plays I've never seen before."

Neely never had an issue allowing McFadden to improvise; if a player came back to the huddle and told McFadden that a certain play might work, the All-America star would instruct his teammate to see if the defensive player made the same mistake twice. If he did, McFadden would expose him on the next play call.

"Every now and then they would make [a play] up on the field," Neely said. "If I don't recognize a play, I'm sure Boston coach Frank Leahy won't."

Jess Neely's last Clemson team won eight games in the regular season with just one loss, to Tulane. The 8-1 Tigers were rewarded with an invitation to play Boston College in the fourth Cotton Bowl, but Clemson first had to get permission from the Southern Conference, which they immediately granted. The 1939 season not only resulted in Clemson's first bowl appearance, but also the Tigers' first first-team All-America player, Banks McFadden.

On the last play of the first quarter, Bru Trexler punted to BC's Charlie O'Rourke, who fielded the punt on the Clemson 40 and returned it to the 13. Two running plays lost 10 yards, but on third down Frank Davis gained six. Alex Lukachik then kicked a 34-yard field goal to put the Eagles up 3-0.

Clemson's scoring drive began when McFadden returned an Eagle punt to the 33. Charlie Timmons rushed for 15 yards in two plays, and two plays after that, McFadden hit Wister Jackson with a 16-yard pass to the Eagle 20. Timmons ran the final 20 yards in three carries, but Shad Bryant missed the extra point.

Later in the period, a 51-yard punt by McFadden started Boston College at its 20. The Eagles fumbled on first down, and Clemson's George Fritts recovered at the 24. The Tigers could do nothing with the gift, however, as Joe Blalock fumbled after a short pass.

The game turned into a defensive struggle in the second half, although Boston College did penetrate deep into Clemson territory on two occasions. The Eagles took the opening kickoff to the Clemson 19, but a holding penalty and an incomplete pass ended the threat, and BC was forced to punt.

Late in the game, the Eagles drove to the Clemson 11, but Bryant and McFadden each broke up two passes, and Clemson took over on downs.

McFadden effectively bottled up the Eagles other than those drives with his punting. His 44-yard average on nine kicks, including two boots for 51 and 55 yards in the second half, prevented Boston College from getting good field position, and the Clemson defense made the 6-3 score stand.

Timmons led Clemson with 115 yards on 27 carries. Defensively, McFadden, who averaged 43 yards per punt on the day as well, reportedly went sideline to sideline knocking down Charlie O'Rourke's passes.

The Eagles finished the afternoon completing only four of 23 passes, with one interception. As a whole, Boston College netted only 102 yards of total offense.

"Clemson is every bit as good as they were cracked up to be," Leahy told reporters after the game. "We lost to a great team, one of the best I have ever seen. I have the satisfaction of knowing that while we were beaten, the game wasn't lost on a fluke."

JOE BLALOCK, TWO-TIME FOOTBALL ALL-AMERICA PLAYER

Joe Blalock was a three-sport athlete, but Walter Cox believes his one-time teammate "could have been a five-sport man had he had the time. He played football, baseball, and basketball, but he would have been a heckuva track man or a boxer," Cox surmised.

The Charleston native "was the best football player we had at Clemson at the time," recalls Howard. "I was a young football coach [in 1940] and hadn't had any experience. But Joe was a versatile player in the fact that he was a good pass receiver, he could come around from his right end position and pass [left-handed], and sometimes he wouldn't pass the ball but would keep it and run on an end around."

McFadden remembers a game against Furman, in which the Tigers were trailing 3-0 at halftime. "Joe threw me a touchdown pass in the end zone and I dropped it. I was so wide open that I looked like a player who came out at two o'clock when practice had been called for three." But McFadden did score a touchdown later in the game, and the Tigers won 14-3. Clemson received a bid to play Boston College in the Cotton Bowl after this victory.

Howard was quick to correct anyone who would mention that Blalock was "a good football player": "I remember that he was a great football player—not a good one—but a great one."

McFadden played on the '39 team with Blalock, then was in pro ball (with the old Brooklyn Dodgers) for one year before returning to Clemson. By then, Blalock was a senior, but McFadden was coaching the secondary and really had no opportunity to tutor him as an offensive player.

"He is one of the most outstanding athletes Clemson ever had," McFadden said without reservation. "He was one of these natural-type people."

Joe Blalock was a two-time All-American.

"Blalock could have played any number of positions," McFadden believes. "Back when I played, you didn't start sophomores. But we had both Blalock and George Fritts [an interior lineman] my senior year starting as sophomores."

"Joe was the easy-flowing type . . . it didn't seem for him to take any effort in doing anything," McFadden continued. "He could do all of the things kind [of] effortlessly. I had to work like a dog to get things out of myself."

"Joe was exceptional," McFadden's praise went on. "He could have played most any position on the team, except interior line, and he might have been able to play that. And Joe was not the flashy type. He was easy-going, quiet, always had a little smile, and always had something nice to say about people. Boy, what a wingback he would have made on the old single wing formation."

Blalock helped vault the Tigers into national prominence during the '40 season with an effort that started him on the way to his All-America rating.

Clemson and Wake Forest were both undefeated (3-0) when 15,000 crowded into Riggs Field for the Southern Conference showdown. The first quarter ended at 0-0, but the Tigers put 13 points on the board in each of next three quarters for a surprising 39-0 triumph.

"Joe [Blalock] proved himself, and nothing ordinary, understand," one description in a newspaper said.

First, he blocked a punt to put his team in scoring position. On the following play, he came back from end to pitch a touchdown pass. A little later, he ran for a touchdown on an end around and wound up the day by intercepting a pass and reeled off 45 yards to the goal line.

But the quiet, unassuming Blalock thought nothing about it. He seized the opportunity every chance he had to help his team to greater heights, be it on the gridiron, basketball court, pitcher's mound, or batter's box.

His work, not his words, spoke for him, which was just one reason that he became Clemson's first two-time All-America football player.

BANKS MCFADDEN, CLEMSON'S GREATEST ATHLETE, KNOWN AS "THE GREAT"

Banks McFadden is regarded as Clemson's greatest all-around athlete in its sports history.

McFadden, also known as "Bonnie Banks" or "The Great," was a standout at Clemson in football, basketball, and track, earning three letters in each sport from 1936-'40. He earned All-America honors in both basketball (1938-39) and football (1939) and was named the nation's most versatile athlete in 1939.

On the basketball court, McFadden led Clemson to the 1939 Southern Conference Tournament Championship, the only postseason tournament title in Clemson basketball history. The Tiger center was Clemson's top scorer each season and finished his career with a then-Clemson record 810 points.

Banks McFadden was named the nation's most versatile athlete for 1939-40.

In track, McFadden won three events in the state track meet in one afternoon, setting state records in all three of them. Earlier in the same year, he placed first in five events in a dual meet, scoring 25 points, while the opposing team's total score was 28 points. His senior year, he also pitched in one game for the Clemson baseball team.

On the gridiron, McFadden was a triple-threat player, leading the Tigers to a 9-1 record and Clemson's first-ever bowl bid. With McFadden batting down four passes in the second half, and averaging 44 yards on 11 punts, the Tigers defeated a Frank Leahy-coached Boston College team, 6-3, in the 1940 Cotton Bowl in Dallas, TX.

"I had seen safety men play centerfield in a football game and cover a lot of defensive territory, but that was the only time I saw it done from a halfback postion," Howard said in *The History of Clemson Football*. "McFadden put absolutely everything he had into that effort—ability, speed, heart, endurance, determination, and a sixth sense of where the ball was going."

McFadden held the Clemson single-season punting record (43.5 in 1939) for 40 years, and his 22 punts of at least 50 yards in 1939 still stand as a Clemson single-season record.

At the conclusion of his career, he was a first-round draft choice of the Brooklyn Dodgers of the NFL, the fourth selection of the draft, which to this day is tied as the highest draft choice in Clemson history, along with that of Gaines Adams in 2007 and Sammy Watkins in 2013. He played one year in the NFL with the Dodgers and led the NFL in yards per rush before returning to Clemson.

In 1959, McFadden became the first Clemson football player inducted into the College Football Hall of Fame.

After coaching Clemson's defensive backs under second-year head Coach Frank Howard in 1941, McFadden joined the Army Air Corps and spent four years in North Africa and Italy. He was discharged as a colonel.

McFadden came back to Clemson after his service and was again the secondary coach, this time for four seasons (1946-49), and then took over as head freshman football coach for five years before returning to coach defensive backs in 1955, a spot he held until Howard retired following the '69 season.

Besides his football coaching years, McFadden also put in a stint as varsity track coach, freshman basketball coach, and for 10 years, 1946-47 through 1955-56, he was Clemson's head basketball coach. From 1947-'48 through 1951-52, McFadden improved its conference victory total each year, the first coach in the history of college basketball to realize a conference victory improvement five consecutive years. The streak was culminated with an 11-4 Southern Conference record in 1951-52, still the Clemson record for conference wins in a season.

After Howard resigned as head football coach in 1969, McFadden took over the university's intramural department, which he directed for 15 years.

McFadden came to Clemson in a 6' 3" frame and a skinny 165 pounds. Frank Howard said, "If McFadden drank a can of tomato juice, they could have used him as a thermometer." Howard was an assistant coach under Jess Neely when McFadden came to Clemson in 1936.

"I can remember the first time I saw him on the practice field," Howard recalled. "He looked like one of those whooping cranes. I thought sure as the devil that Coach [Jess] Neely had made a mistake by giving this boy a scholarship. But he proved me wrong."

McFadden was granted a long list of honors throughout his career. In 1966, he was presented with Clemson University's Distinguished Alumni Award. He was a charter member of the Clemson Athletic Hall of Fame and the South Carolina Athletic Hall of Fame. In 1987, both his uniform numbers—23 in basketball and 66 in football—were retired by Clemson University.

In 1994, he was inducted as a charter member of the Clemson Ring of Honor at Clemson Memorial Stadium.

Of all of the honors he received as an athlete, he said the 1939 football team MVP award was his highest honor. "To me, when your teammates vote you something, then you feel pretty good. That award meant more than anything else [to me]."

McFadden is the only Clemson athlete to have both his football jersey and basketball jersey numbers retired. In 1995, the Banks McFadden Building at Jervey Athletic Center was dedicated in his honor.

FRANK HOWARD—THE LEGEND

An era ended at Clemson University on June 30, 1974, when Howard officially retired from the payroll. But instead of playing golf or fishing every day as most men do after retirement, Howard never truly left Clemson, as he came to his office seven days a week in the Jervey Athletic Center, beating most of the employees in every morning.

Clemson's most antimated figure retired from coaching December 10, 1969, after 39 years on the Clemson coaching staff, 30 of which were as head coach. He was also athletic director during this time, and he kept this position until February 4, 1971, when he was named assistant to the vice president of student affairs at the university. He held that post until the mandatory retirement age of 65 rolled around in 1974.

"I had to do it [retire from football] sooner or later," he liked to joke. "The reports would get out every year that I was retiring, and it would ruin my recruiting. The only way we're going to build this place up is to get a coach in here who isn't retiring every year."

At his press conference when he announced his retirement, he said, "I'm retiring because of health reasons; the alumni got sick of me."

Shortly after his retirement when he reached the age of 65, the Clemson Board of Trustees named the playing surface of Memorial Stadium ("Death Valley") as "Frank Howard Field" in honor of his long service to the university. It was only the third time that a building or installation had been named by the trustees for a living person.

Howard was a charter member in both the South Carolina Athletic Hall of Fame and the Clemson Athletic Hall of Fame. During his career, he was chosen as a member the NATA (National Athletic Trainers Association) Hall of Fame, the NACDA (National Association of Collegiate Directors of Athletics) Hall of Fame, Helms Athletic Hall of Fame, State of Alabama Hall of Fame, Orange Bowl Hall of Honor, National Football Hall of Fame, Mobile (AL) Athletic Hall of Fame, Mobile High (Murphy) Hall of Fame, and the Gator Bowl Hall of Fame.

Howard has also been presented the Order of the Palmetto, the highest honor that the governor of the state can bestow. Clemson University also recognized Howard once more with the presentation of the Clemson Medallion, which is the highest public honor bestowed by the university to a living person who exemplifies the dedication and foresight of its founders.

Clemson's "Legend" stepped onto the rolling hills of Clemson in August, 1931, fresh from the varsity football ranks at the University of Alabama, where he was a first-stringer on Coach Wallace Wade's 1930 team that drubbed Washington State 24-0 in the 1931 Rose Bowl. Howard was known as the "Little Giant" of the Tide's "Herd of Red Elephants."

The bald veteran came to his first coaching post under Jess Nealy as a line tutor. "At least that was my title,"

Howard recalls. "Actually, I also coached track, was ticket manager, recruited players, and had charge of the football equipment. In my spare time I cut the grass, lined tennis courts, and operated the canteen while the regular man was out to lunch."

Howard was not only track coach from 1931-'39, but also he served as baseball coach in 1943, and his 12-3 record that year is still the best percentage for a season in Clemson history.

Howard held the line coaching post until Neely went to Rice University as head coach in 1940 following Clemson's 6-3 victory over Boston College in the 1940 Cotton Bowl. When the Clemson Athletic Council met to name a successor to Neely, Professor Sam Rhodes, a council member, nominated Howard to be the new head coach.

Howard, standing in the back of the room listening to the discussion after being interviewed by the council, said: "I second the nomination." He was given the job and a one-year contract, which he lost after about three months. He never had another contract his entire career.

Altogether, he served Clemson for 43 years. When he retired as head coach following the 1969 season, he was the nation's dean of coaches, having been a head football coach at a major institution longer than anyone else in the United States.

Howard had the reputation of being a jokester, hillbilly, and country bumpkin. A thick Alabama drawl helped the effect. In reality, Howard was one of the nation's most successful coaches. When he retired, he was one of five active coaches with 150 or more victories.

While line coach in 1939, the Tigers' record (8-1) was good enough to merit a trip to Dallas, where Clemson met undefeated Boston College under the late Frank Leahy in the fourth annual Cotton Bowl (1940). The 1948 team's mark of 10-0 carried Clemson to the fourth annual Gator Bowl (1949), and two years later, a 9-0-1 record sent the Tigers to Miami's 17th annual Orange Bowl (1951).

The Country Gentlemen were champions in their first three bowl ventures. Boston College fell 6-3 in the Cotton Bowl, Missouri was beaten in the Gator Bowl 24-23 (Howard said this was the best football game he ever witnessed), and Miami felt the Tiger claws, 15-14 in the Orange Bowl. The total point spread in these three bowl wins was five points. Howard said, "We humiliated all three of 'em."

The seventh annual Gator Bowl beckoned the Tigers again in January 1952, and by being conference champions in 1956, Clemson played in the 23rd annual Orange Bowl and again in 1957. Miami downed Clemson 14-0 in the second Gator Bowl trip, and Colorado led Clemson 20-0, then trailed 21-20, before finally defeating the Tigers 27-21 on Clemson's second trip to Miami.

The Tigers then played in the 25th annual Sugar Bowl (1959) and held No.1-ranked Louisiana State to a standstill before losing 7-0.

The invitation to play in the first annual Bluebonnet Bowl in Houston in December 1959 was the eighth bowl that Howard had been a part of either as a player (one), assistant coach (one), or a head coach (six). It was the seventh bowl trip for a Clemson team and the sixth in 12 years.

Howard says that Clemson's 23-7 triumph over Texas Christian in the Bluebonnet was the best performance he ever witnessed by a Clemson team. By playing in that Bluebonnet Bowl, Clemson became the first-team to play in two bowls in the same calendar year. The Tigers played LSU January 1, 1959, in the Sugar Bowl and the Horned Frogs in the Bluebonnet December 19, 1959.

The Tigers' victory over TCU was their fourth success in seven postseason appearances. In all seven, Clemson was the established underdog.

Howard served on the coaching staff of the Blue-Gray game in Montgomery, AL, in 1941, 1952, 1959, and 1966; was on the East staff of the annual East-West Shrine game in San Francisco, CA, in December, 1960, and again in December, 1962; and was named coach of the South squad in Miami's 1961 and 1969 North-South game. He coached in the 1970 Hula Bowl, which was his ninth postseason all-star game.

While Howard has not been active on the sidelines since that Hula Bowl game, he still kept his hands in football. Each year he served as the recruiter of the Gray team players of the Blue-Gray game. The Blue recruiter was Don Faurot, whom Howard defeated in the 1949 Gator Bowl. Howard also served as one of 15 voting members of the important rules committee of the NCAA for a period of three years while in the active ranks. A single-wing expert for 22 seasons (including nine as line coach), Howard changed to the T-formation and its many variations in 1953. Still another major change in the offense was installed in 1965 with the "I" and pro-type set.

In his 13 seasons as head coach using the single-wing, Clemson won 69, lost 47, and tied 7 games. In 12 years of "T" teams, the Tigers won 71, lost 47, and tied 4. Using the "I" in his last five years of coaching, Clemson recorded a 25-24-1 record.

In his 30 years as a head coach, Howard won 165, lost 118, and tied 12 contests. In addition to heading up the Clemson football program, Howard also had the job of directing the school's entire athletic program and at the same time raising all of the required scholarship funds. The athletic department was always on a sound financial footing under the guidance of Howard.

In 1959, the Tigers presented Howard with an 8-2 season, which led to the Sugar Bowl Invitation. One of these 1959 wins was the 100th of Howard's coaching career. That came against the late Jim Tatum of North Carolina, a coach whom Howard had never beaten. And the Tigers had to come from behind three times to win 26-21.

Howard was named Southern Conference Coach of the Year in 1948. In 1958, he was named Atlantic Coast Conference Coach of the Year and was accorded that honor again in 1966.

Howard, who coached nowhere else but at Clemson, won ACC championships six times (1956-58-59-65-66-67) in the first 15 years of the conference.

In 1966, Howard recorded his 150th collegiate victory when the Tigers defeated Maryland 14-10.

Howard was born in Barlow Bend, AL (three wagon greasin's from Mobile), March 25, 1909. He spent his early days on the farm playing mostly cow pasture baseball because there were not enough boys around the community to form a football team. Howard said he left Barlow Bend walking barefooted on a barbed wire fence with a wildcat under each arm.

He graduated from Murphy (now Mobile) High School, where he played football, baseball, and basketball and served as president of both the junior and senior classes.

After graduating from Murphy High, Howard entered the University of Alabama in the fall of 1927 on an academic scholarship provided by the *Birmingham News*. He played guard as a reserve his sophomore year. During his junior year, he started every game but two, and an ankle injury sidelined him then. Again, his senior year he was a regular.

Howard was president of the freshman class at Alabama, was a member of Blue Key, and was president of the "A" Club.

After coming to Clemson, Howard married the former Anna Tribble of Anderson, SC, August 23, 1933. They were the parents of a daughter, Alice (Mrs. Bobby McClure of Gastonia, NC), and a son, Jimmy, of Clemson.

For over five decades, Howard was in great demand both as a banquet speaker and a clinic lecturer. Few states have escaped his homespun oratory, which has brought the house down on many occasions. Many have felt his digs, especially if they have been to the podium before Howard.

Many stories have been told on Howard, but for every one poked toward him, he can fire two back. People have found that it's best not to throw too many darts in Howard's direction, especially if he is given the opportunity to have the microphone again.

Most stories told on Howard are true, and some of them classified as fiction have been told so many times that even Howard believed they were true.

"When I die, I want to be buried up there on that hill [Cementary Hill] behind the stadium," Howard would say. "I want to be there so I can hear all them people cheering my Tigers on Saturday and where I can smell that chewing tobacco in every corner of the stadium. Then, I won't have to go to Heaven. I'll already be there."

Howard died in January, 1994, and left behind a legacy that will probably never be equaled in the annals at Clemson. His honesty and down-to-earth sense of humor will be remembered for other generations to pass on. And, as he wished, he is buried behind Death Valley, where he can hear the roar of the crowd cheering for his Tigers on Saturdays in the fall.

FRED CONE—"THE GREATEST PLAYER I'VE EVER COACHED"

It is perhaps the most unusual story concerning an athlete's journey to Clemson in school history. Fred Cone was visiting his sister in the Magnolia State at Biloxi, far from the haunts of his hometown, an obscure place called Pineapple, AL.

Another place, Barlow Bend, and just about as remote as Pineapple, but with only about 50 miles between them, had already sent one of her sons out into the athletic world to Clemson, and like Cone, he would also make a name for himself.

His name was Howard, Frank by first name, and to him would also come some fame, thanks to the efforts of Cone and a strong supporting cast.

Unbeknownst to Howard, Cone's sister lived next door to Howard's sister, Hazel, in Biloxi. On years when Clemson would play Tulane in New Orleans, Howard would send Hazel a pair of tickets.

"One year she sent the two tickets back," Howard remembered, "and said she'd like to have four tickets because she wanted to take the next door neighbor to the game."

That was in 1946, Cone's senior year in high school. Howard remembers that after Cone graduated, Hazel wrote him and said: "Brother, I have you a good football player, but he's never played football."

Howard recalled that he had told the Clemson registrar to save him 40 beds in the barracks and that he would turn in that many names on September 1st.

"When Hazel wrote me about Fred Cone, I had 39 names on that list. So I just wrote 'Fred Cone' in as the 40th name and that was that," Howard recalled.

"And that's how I got probably [one of] the best, if not the best, football player I ever had." Howard should have made his sister recruiting coordinator.

Some of this reasoning might be sentimental, because when the 1947 team was 1-5, a committee of students tried to get Howard to resign.

"Yeah, they came over to my office and wanted to fire me," Howard remembered on one occasion. "But I told them how we were going to win the last three from Furman, Duquesne, and Auburn, and we did win those last three. The students probably thought I knew what I was talking about."

Those three victories were the start of a 15-game winning streak, which is still a school record.

Cone graduated from Moore Academy in Pineapple and came to Clemson in 1947 as a freshman, but first-year players were not eligible to play then. It was probably best for Cone because he had not played high school football. He needed a year to get acclimated. When Cone became eligible for the varsity team in '48, the football program took on a different air.

The Tigers had an undefeated season in 1900 (6-0 under John Heisman) and in 1906 (4-0-3 under Bob Williams) and had had only four other campaigns with only one loss, and three of those were under Heisman. The other one-loss season was 1939 (7-1-1 under Jess Neely), when Howard was line coach.

Howard, who was named head coach in 1940, was 36-34-3 his first eight seasons but was actually 33-34-3 when this committee of students came to him about resigning.

But this was BC (Before Cone) and Gage, and Mathews, and Prince, and Salisbury, and Gillespie, and a host of other small-town players playing big-time football.

But '48 couldn't have been any better. Just like the 1981 National Championship season, there were some close calls, there were some favorable calls that may never happen again, the ball bounced right on almost every occasion, and the luck of the horseshoe was never stronger.

In the second game of '48 against N.C. State, Cone had the first of his eight 100-yard career rushing games, although the only score was a 90-yard punt return by Bobby Gage, with Tom Salisbury throwing the last key block. The defense held the 'Pack three times on the one-yard line.

Later at South Carolina, Phil Prince broke through and blocked a punt that Rabbit Thompson picked up and ran in for a score and a 13-7 win. The Tigers withstood 42 Butch Songin passes in Braves Field against Boston College and then had to battle the weather elements and a tough Auburn team before grabbing a 7-6 victory in Mobile.

But the nail-biter of the year was yet to come.

Around 21,000 Clemson fans trekked to Jacksonville for the fourth annual Gator Bowl, and these Tiger followers helped set a new attendance record (35,273) and put this young, fledgling bowl in the black for the first time. Clemson became a friend for life.

Clemson ended up on the long end of a 24-23 game, which saw Gage named the game's MVP with 137 yards of total offense. Jack Miller kicked Clemson's only field goal of the entire season, and sophomore Fred Cone rushed for 72 game yards and scored twice in the first quarter.

Of all the thrills that Howard had as a player at Alabama and as an assistant coach and head coach at Clemson, Cone is involved in the play that stood out in Howard's mind the most, and it was against Missouri in the Gator Bowl.

Clemson held a one-point lead and faced a fourth-and-three at the Mizzou 45. It was either gamble for a first down, or punt and give Missouri another chance to score. As Howard would say later: "We hadn't stopped them all day, so I took my chance with a running play."

Cone hit a stone wall at left tackle but kept digging and slid off a little more to the outside, found a little wiggle room, and mustered six yards and a first down at the Missouri 39. Clemson retained possession those few remaining minutes and ran out the clock.

Cone scored seven touchdowns rushing and gained 635 yards on the ground that sophomore year, and there

were great expectations for '49. But the likes of three-sport star Frank Gillespie, school career offensive leader Bobby Gage, and blocking back Bob Martin were out of the picture, and the Tigers broke even (4-4-2).

One of those ties (7-7) was with Mississippi State, and one of the Bulldog star linemen was present-day country and western comedian Jerry Clower. On one of his many records, Clower recalls playing at Clemson and how he was coached to stop Cone. But he admits being run over by Cone once and, "that number 31 [Cone's number] just kept getting smaller and smaller as he was running down the field."

Despite the down year in '49, Cone gained more yards (703) rushing and scored more touchdowns (9) than he did during his sophomore year.

But 1950 was to bring about another undefeated season. Cone, Bob Hudson, Dick Hendley, Jackie Calvert, and Mathews were still around, while Glenn Smith, Billy Hair, Pete Manos, Dan DiMucci, and Jack Brunson were coming into their own.

After the expected win over Presbyterian to start the season, Clemson faced preseason No. 17 Missouri on the road. On the first play from scrimmage, Calvert dashed 80 yards to score, and Clemson was off to a 34-0 romp. Cone gained 111 yards in 21 attempts, one of three Tigers over the 100-yard mark that day.

The Tigers always departed from Anderson Airport on road trips then, and an Anderson merchant, the late Sarge Murchison, was always there to wish the team good luck. On that particular day, Murchison had a farmer friend bring a Missouri mule to the airport. Cone was pictured in the papers the next morning on the day of the game riding the mule.

Big crowds were always on hand at the airport when the team returned after the game. Howard, in his pre-game dressing room remarks, told his players: "If you don't win this game, the only thing that'll be at the airport tonight to meet you will be that jackass."

That victory over Mizzou apparently put everybody in step. The Tigers enjoyed another undefeated season; the only scar was a 14-14 tie with South Carolina. Cone had his third 100-plus-yards rushing (in four games) and scored twice against the Gamecocks, but Steve Wadiak was unstoppable that day, outgaining the entire Clemson team with 256 yards rushing.

However, Cone played most of the game with a busted lip after taking a shot to the face by a USC defender. In those days, there were no facemasks on helmets, and just before halftime he was hit right on the right side of his mouth as he tried to make a cut.

At halftime, the team doctor sewed him up without the help of any novocaine, stitching him up with just a needle while Frank Howard was talking to the team.

"It wasn't too painful because I was too excited about the game," Cone said. "In this game, you just didn't feel pain."

These 1948 and 1950 seasons marked the only time in Clemson football history that there have been two undefeated seasons over a period of three years. Cone and Ray Mathews were the only common denominators in the starting lineup on those two teams.

In '50, Clemson scored 50 points in three different games, but Cone saved his best until the last regular season game against Auburn. Rumor had it that if Clemson scored over a certain number of points on Auburn, the Orange Bowl bid was in its pocket. The South Carolina Tigers took the Alabama Tigers 41-0. Cone gained 163 yards, two total yards shy of a five-yard average, and scored three touchdowns on the ground, and his only pass reception, good for 28 yards, also went for a score.

Icing on the cake this time came against Miami in the Orange Bowl. Sterling Smith's tackle of Fred Smith in the end zone for a safety brought a 15-14 victory Clemson's way, and Cone gained 81 yards on the ground, scored once, punted four times, and returned one kickoff. It was a great climax of Cone's career.

His number of carries (184), yards gained rushing (845), and 15 touchdowns were all school season records at the time. Also, he became Clemson's first 2,000-yard rusher (2,183), and his 31 career touchdowns were also a school best, as were his 189 points scored.

A seven-year career with the Green Bay Packers was so impressive that he was inducted into their Hall of Fame in 1974. He was also a member of the Dallas Cowboys in their first year of existence in 1960. Later, he returned to Clemson as its chief recruiter for 10 years beginning in 1961.

After Cone completed his Clemson career, Howard was still stumped as to how his sister could predict that her neighbor's brother would be such an outstanding football player. "He just looked so athletic jumping off of that diving board," Hazel said, without skipping a beat.

Hazel never sent Frank another player. She didn't have to. She saved his neck one time with Cone, and that lasted 22 more seasons.

THE LEGENDARY DUMB-DUMB WYNDHAM

One of the most ferocious players in Clemson history has to be Stephen F. "Dumb-Dumb" Wyndham. He had another nickname, Wyndie, but Dumb-Dumb is the one that everyone remembers with fondness.

His play as a blocking back and his reckless style at linebacker helped propel the Tigers to an undefeated season in 1948 and an unbeaten season in 1950. The Tigers also won the 1949 Gator Bowl with a 24-23 victory over Missouri and a 15-14 thriller over Miami in the 1951 Orange Bowl.

Dumb-Dumb Wyndham got his nickname at practice one day. When he first came to Clemson, everybody called him Friendly.

"I didn't know at first why they called him Friendly, because he was the most unfriendly boy on the team, but I later found out that Friendly was actually his given middle name," said Clemson Head Coach Frank Howard.

"He got confused on a play I called at practice, I finally straightened him out. I told him, 'Boy you're so dumb you ought not be one, you ought to be twins.' After that, all his teammates didn't call him Dumb, but Dumb-Dumb because of my remark about twins.

"I remember we were playing Missouri in the second game of the 1950 season," said Howard. "It was hot that day. I remember kicking off after we scored a touchdown. It was a high but short kick. They had a big tackle, he was 6-6 and weighed almost 290 pounds, and that was big in those days. That big tackle had his hands up to catch the kickoff. The second the ball touched his hands, Dumb-Dumb hit him right in the stomach and knocked him cold.

"They recovered the ball and went on offense. The right halfback ran with it. Dumb-Dumb tackled him and knocked him out. The fullback ran with it on the next play, and Dumb-Dumb knocked him out. Then the left halfback ran with it, and he knocked him out. He knocked four players out on four consecutive plays. The Missouri captain went up to the referee and asked him to get that wild 'so and so' out of this game, before he kills every one of us."

In the 1949 Gator Bowl game against Missouri, Harold Entsminger was the Misssouri quarterback. He pitched the ball to one his halfbacks. Entsminger was leading the sweep coming around the end. Dumb-Dumb was playing linebacker and ran over the quarterback to get at the ball carrier, and he knocked both of them out. "Dumb-Dumb was a killer," said Howard.

Howard told another story about Dumb-Dumb. "We were going up to play Boston College. I was showing a Boston College film to Dumb-Dumb. The year before, this fellow from Boston College had made a lot of good runs against us.

"So I told Dumb-Dumb, 'We got to stop that boy this Saturday.'

"He said, 'Coach, the third time I hit him, he'll be out of the game for keeps.'

"I didn't pay much attention to that. I thought it was a boy talking big.

"We kicked off to Boston College to start the game. That boy, caught the ball and started up the field. Dumb-Dumb hit him so hard the kid's shoes came off. He threw the football down on the ground, staggered off the field, and never came back in the rest of the game.

"I asked Dumb-Dumb coming back on the plane how he knew he was going to knock that boy out of the game.

"He said, 'Coach, I told you it would be after the third time I tackled him just to protect myself, but I really figured the first time I hit him, he would come out of there.'

"Dumb-Dumb was the reason I got one of my best players from Greenwood, SC. His name was Harvey White.

"Harvey's father was the sheriff in Greenwood," said Howard. "Some of his prisoners got out one night, and he called for the bloodhounds to track them down. Dumb-Dumb was a South Carolina law agent. He was the one who brought the bloodhounds to Greenwood. The dogs got to running and barking when they picked up the scent of the prisoners. Dumb-Dumb was right behind them, running with the dogs.

"Mr. White later told me that when those prisoners saw that fellow chasing those dogs, they surrendered. They said they weren't scared of the dogs, but they didn't want that wild fellow behind the dogs to get a hold of them. The sheriff later told me that Dumb-Dumb was one of the main reasons he sent his son up to Clemson."

Wyndham was named All-South in 1950, his teammates voted him best defensive player, and he served as cocaptain of the 1951 Orange Bowl Champions.

Wyndham, from Moncks Corner, SC, went on to become a lieutenant in SLED (State Law Enforcement Division) in Columbia. He was inducted into the Clemson Athletic Hall of Fame in 1980.

Wyndham passed away on October 29, 1983, at the age of 54.

"Dumb-Dumb was a real terror," said Howard. "He was a great one."

FRANK GILLESPIE—THREE-SPORT STAR

Frank Gillespie was the model student-athlete during his career at Clemson. He was an excellent student, double-majoring in electrical engineering and textile engineering. As if that weren't enough, he was a starter on three teams, football, basketball, and baseball. He was also the student body president.

In the 1947-48 season, he won the McKelvin Award as the Athlete of the Year in the Southern Conference.

Coach Howard remembers Gillespie when he came to Clemson on a visit.

"When I was younger, I'd put on the pads and work out with the players some," said Howard.

"I remember a boy I tried out, which was legal in those days. His name was Frank Gillespie. He was from Beckley, WV. I hadn't heard much about him, but he wanted to come to Clemson. I said come on down, and I'll work you out. I put on the pads with him. I lined up in front of him and told him to charge into me. Whomp! Bam!

"I said, 'That's enough, son.'

"'Coach, I thought we were going to work out,' he told me.

"'We have, welcome to Clemson.' I signed him on the spot.

"He went on to be one of the finest we've ever had. He was a great leader and athlete and could do pretty much whatever he wanted."

1948 TIGERS FINISH SEASON UNDEFEATED & RANKED NO. 11

The 1948 team was one of the most talented in Clemson history, especially when you consider it was a unit with just 37 players on the travel squad. Eight players on this club are in the Clemson Hall of Fame. The team was a perfect 11-0, including a school record seven wins away, and a #11 final Associated Press ranking.

Clemson was one of just three undefeated, untied teams and had the most wins in the nation that year. Michigan and Notre Dame were also undefeated, but neither team played in a bowl game.

It was a club that was dominating on defense (allowing just 76 points) and had a precision single-wing offense that performed in the clutch. Five of the 11 wins were recorded by a one-touchdown margin or less, more "close" wins than any team in Clemson history. It might have been the greatest squad in school history in terms of special teams.

The perfect season of 1948 was as much a surprise to Clemson fans as the perfect season of 1981. Both years, the Tigers were coming off mediocre seasons. In 1947, Clemson was just 4-5 and had to win the last three games to do that.

"Entering the 1948 season, we didn't think we would be as good a team as the previous year because Henry Walker decided not to come back," recalled Phil Prince, captain of the 1948 Tigers. "He had been our leading receiver the previous year and would have been one of the top players in 1948. He had already earned one degree from Virginia and then got another from Clemson in the spring of 1948. He was offered a job in the textile industry and decided to take it. He went on to become president of the company."

Many teams in recent Clemson history have had a formula that featured talented youth and wise veteran players. According to Prince, that was one of the reasons for the success of the 1948 Tigers.

"We had an interesting mixture of seniors and sophomores. The difference in the 1948 team compared to 1947 was the sophomore class. That group of sophomores was the greatest group of athletes Clemson had had in one class up to that point. At the same time, we had some experienced players in the senior class. It just seemed that the leadership of the seniors jelled with the athletic talent of that sophomore class."

Fred Cone, a sophomore in 1948 who is among just four players in the Clemson Ring of Honor, agrees with Prince. "We had a lot of great athletes on that team. Bobby Gage, he could run, he could pass, he did everything. He called the plays, he ran the team, he gave everyone confidence.

"Frank Gillespie, Phil Prince, Gene Moore, they were all great team leaders who set an example for the sophomores. We were lucky to have such a group of leaders.

"We also had an outstanding coaching staff," continued Cone. "Coach Howard was our leader, but the assistants were very good. I remember Goat McMillan drilling us on how to hide the ball when we were practicing the spin for the single-wing offense. He taught us all the tricks of hiding the ball from the defense."

Prince summarized another important team characteristic. "Vince Lombardi once said, 'To be a successful team, you have to love each other.' We were always there for each other. To go undefeated and untied, we had to stay together. We had a lot of cliff-hangers in that season and we had to stay together to pull them out. We didn't have any quit in that team."

The 1949 Gator Bowl is still considered one of the most exciting games in the bowl's history.

"From a spectator's standpoint, I still think it is the most exciting game I ever saw a Clemson team play," Howard said. "We couldn't stop them and they couldn't stop us. That's the reason we went for it on fourth down late in the game.

"I was afraid to let them have the ball back. I guess we were fortunate, but we had some good players and they came through for us."

For Clemson, it jump-started an era that saw the football program go to six bowl games in 12 years, including two trips to the Orange Bowl and one Sugar Bowl appearance.

"I don't think that I have ever had more satisfaction out of one season than I did in 1948," Howard said.

FORMATION OF THE ACC

The formation of the Atlantic Coast Conference in 1953 gave Clemson a chance to prosper and be more competitive on the national stage.

Two of the reasons a new league was formed was there were 17 teams in the Southern Conference. Many of the larger schools thought it was simply too many. At the time, the Southern Conference also had a ban on bowl games. After the 1951 regular season, Maryland and Clemson both defied the conference ban and went to bowl games anyway. Maryland went to the Sugar Bowl and won the National Championship, and Clemson went to the Gator Bowl.

The Southern Conference put Clemson and Maryland on probation for one year. They could play each other but were forbidden to play other Southern Conference teams unless it was state law that two teams should play. Legislators in South Carolina immediately made it state law for one year that Clemson and South Carolina play in football during the 1952 season.

Actually the new conference was formed, and an agreement was reached to start the new league at the Clemson House in Clemson, SC, at the Southern Conference Winter Meetings on December 12-13, 1952. Representatives from 17 schools were in attendance.

The schools withdrawing from the Southern Conference also met and conducted business and made plans. It was decided that the conference would not be formed or announced in Clemson and it would be initiated at the Southern Conference Spring Meetings in Greensboro, NC, on May 8-9, 1953.

With that Spring Meeting at Sedgefield Country Club, a new era in Clemson athletics occurred. Tagged "the Seceding Seven" by the media, Clemson, South Carolina, North Carolina, N.C. State, Duke, Wake Forest, and Maryland made plans for a new league of "big" schools only and formally withdrew from the Southern Conference.

The ultimate goal of the new seven-team conference was to be intraconference rivalries among all member teams in all sports.

On June 14, there was a meeting of the seven schools in Raleigh, NC, to form definite plans.

"I am hoping that we will be able to work out all of the common problems, and form this new compact organization, give it an appropriate name, and start to work on what I consider will be one of the best if not the best conference in the United States," said Clemson Head Coach Frank Howard.

"The new conference should work out to everyone's benefit. For the past 20 years, we have been trying to schedule athletic contests with some of the schools but haven't had too much success. Since we all belong to the same conference, we will have six football games scheduled ever year and will be at liberty to schedule three or more nonconference games each season. In this manner a true conference champion can be decided.

"I feel sure that schools in the new conference will feel more kindly toward each other, as they will have more in common. An organization like this is what our alumni and friends wanted. We are going to have to work hard in this new league and IPTAY will have to raise more money and get more members for us to be successful."

IPTAY did grow, and more members joined. It is one of the most successful scholarship clubs in the nation. In the ACC, there are now 15 members, 14 that play football.

DOCTOR LEE MILFORD—PIONEER OF THE ACC

Dr. Lee W. Milford, Sr. was one of Clemson's most influential and highly regarded leaders in the late-1920's through the 1950s.

Dr. Milford came to Clemson on January 1, 1926, and was hired as the school's medical doctor. In this role, he was the physician for the student body and the various Tiger sport teams. The 1917 Emory Graduate was the Clemson town doctor, as well. It's hard to imagine how many people he helped during his practice.

In addition to his medical duties, he had the unique responsibility of also being the chairman of the Athletic Council at Clemson and a faculty representative to the Southern Conference for 26 years. He was a three-time Southern Conference president and was instrumental in the organization of a booking office for conference football and basketball officials.

During his Clemson career, the Tigers went to their first bowl game; Banks McFadden was a two-sport All-American; Frank Howard was hired as head football coach and athletic director; and the Atlantic Coast Conference was formed.

In the early-1950s, Milford was a leader in the organization of the Atlantic Coast Conference and was one of four people to write the conference's constitution and by-laws.

One of his first moves, when he arrived at Clemson in 1926, was the purchase of an X-ray machine. "I wouldn't try to practice medicine without it," he said in a 1956 interview.

Head Football Coach Frank Howard credits him with countless "game-winning" decisions made over injured players and helping with their recovery.

One of the oddest football injuries he believes he ever saw took place when a player had a fracture of the trachea (windpipe). "It took a long time for him to recover from this," said Milford.

Dr. Milford was well respected in the medical profession. He was the founder of the Southern College Health Association and served as the president of the organization for eight years. He also served as vice president of the National Health Association. He was a member of the American Medical Association, the American Academy of General Practice, the Southern Medical Association, the Southern Surgical Congress, and the South Carolina Medical Association.

He retired from Clemson in 1956 after a 30-year career. When he retired, he held the title of Director of Student Health Services.

Dr. Milford's son, Lee, Jr., played basketball and tennis for Clemson before he graduated in 1943. Like his father, he became a doctor and graduated with a medical degree from Emory in 1946.

Dr. Lee Milford, Jr. was recognized as one of the world's best hand surgeons and a pioneer in that field. He authored a book titled *The Hand*, and it went through multiple printings and was published in four languages. His son, Dick, was a tennis standout for Head Coach Chuck Kriese in 1977-80, making him the third generation to be part of Clemson athletics.

Dick was one of Kriese's first recruits. He was a four-year starter and won 61 singles and 69 doubles matches in his career. He was also a member of the 1980 ACC Championship team.

Dr. Milford, Sr. died on Saturday, January 5, 1980, at the age of 88. He had a long, distinguished career of helping others and serving Clemson.

1958 TEAM—SUGAR BOWL-BOUND, BLUE-CLAD TIGERS

Frank Howard's 1958 Clemson football team does not hold a lot of school records. There are teams with more yards rushing, more yards passing, more points scored, and the same goes for defensive high-water marks. For the season, this ACC Championship team ranked 12th in the final AP poll yet outscored the opposition by just 31 points.

But the 1958 team does have one important distinction—four times that season, Clemson overcame a deficit in the final period to gain victory. The Tigers had comebacks against North Carolina, Virginia, Vanderbilt, and N.C. State.

What was this team's secret to success? One need only look to the example set by team captain Bill Thomas. This club put the team first in every manner. Thomas even delayed his wedding until after the season in accordance with Coach Frank Howard's wishes.

"We didn't play very well against Colorado in the 1957 Orange Bowl," recalled Thomas, who was a sophomore in 1956. "A lot of the players had gotten married that year and brought their wives to Miami for the bowl game. We went down 21-0 in the first half and Coach Howard thought the players' minds weren't on the football game.

"He said he didn't want me to get married until after the bowl game. I wanted to get married in December and have a honeymoon in New Orleans at the Sugar Bowl, but Coach Howard said no."

That is just one example of the self-sacrifice and the "team first" attitude of the 1958 Tigers. It was a true team, the deepest of Frank Howard's career. Clemson won the ACC title but had just one first-team All-ACC player and no All-America players.

This team had talent, but it was balanced. Eight players off the 1958 Tigers made it to the NFL, including five who played at least five years and two who were first-round draft choices (Lou Cordileone and Harvey White). Harold Olson, a tackle, went on to make All-Pro in the AFL.

The statistics from that season document the incredible level of balance. Clemson led the ACC in rushing with 225 yards a game, yet no one had over 500 yards, and only one player, quarterback Harvey White, had a 100-yard rushing game.

Eight different players had at least 100 rushing yards for the year. The team completed 69 passes for the season, but to 15 different players. No receiver had over 60 yards in any game, never mind a 100-yard game. Twelve different players returned kickoffs, and another dozen returned a punt. Three different quarterbacks ran the attack, and seven different players had interceptions.

"Coach Howard played two full teams and sometimes three," said Thomas. "That depth was the big reason we were able to dominate the fourth period and win games in the final quarter."

Clemson opened the season with a victory over Virginia at Death Valley. This was a special opening day because Memorial Stadium had been enlarged over the summer to hold 40,000 fans. There was a new press box, a new scoreboard, and the team ran down the hill on a rug for the first time.

Clemson dominated the action, gaining 384 yards on the ground and winning the total offense battle, 438-300. Additionally, Clemson intercepted four passes, by four different players, but gave up 174 in the air on 13 completions, a high total for those days. Lowndes Shingler scored on a one-yard run with 14 minutes left, and the Tiger defense held Virginia in the final moments.

After the game, Howard said he was disappointed with his pass defense, something that was apparent to a lot of people, even his wife. "I tried to get my wife [Anna] interested in football for 15 years," said Howard in a newspaper account the week after the game. "Then our son Jimmy started playing and she went to all his games. When I saw her after the game, she asked me what I was going to do about that pass defense. I've created a back-seat driver."

Game Two was against North Carolina, and it might have been the biggest game of the season. A record 40,000 fans jammed Death Valley on a 93-degree day. Concessions ran out of soft drinks and ice in the third period. It was so hot that the North Carolina team warmed up in just T-shirts; they didn't put their pads in until just before game time.

This was a day on which team depth would be the difference. Howard had nine different players rush the ball, and Harvey White and Shingler split the quarterback duties. Mrs. Howard was satisfied with the pass defense on this day, as North Carolina gained just 145 yards in the air. Clemson, on the other hand, had its most efficient day of the year, hitting 9-14 passes for 110 yards.

The game went back and forth with many clutch plays. Clemson scored early on a blocked punt. North Carolina attempted a quick kick by Don Coker, but Jim Payne raced through the line to block the attempt. Jim Padgett got to the ball first and raced 28 yards for a touchdown.

One of the biggest plays took place right before halftime, when George Usry scored a touchdown on a one-yard run on the last play of the half. Clemson was sending its kicking unit on to the field to try for the PAT, but when North Carolina's Jim Tatum argued over the allowance of the late score, the Tar Heels were hit with a delay of game penalty, moving the ball to the one-yard line. Howard then tried to go for two, but the attempt failed, and the score was tied at the half. That is one of the few recorded times in history that getting a penalty helped a team directly on the scoreboard.

The second half went back and forth until the Tigers drove 80 yards for the lead score. With 2:52 remaining in the game, George Usry scored from a yard out to put Clemson up 26-21, and that would be the final score.

This was a landmark day for Howard. First, he finally defeated fellow future Hall of Fame Coach Jim Tatum after five straight losses. Second, it was the 100th head coaching victory for Howard, still the only Clemson coach with 100 wins (he would end his career with 165). After the game, he was presented the game ball and proudly stated it was going to be placed prominently on his mantle at home next to a picture of Fred Cone, who was a key player for Howard in the 1948-50 era.

"I think the smartest thing I did today was substitute every five minutes," said Howard. "I knew depth was going to be a factor in this heat." Howard also singled out the play of Jim McCandless, a fine player who would go on to the pros. McCandless was playing for the first time

after breaking his neck in a swimming accident two years previously.

While Game Three won't go into the books as a game decided by a touchdown or less (seven points), in actuality it was decided by just one touchdown. Clemson scored just one touchdown and then made a two-point conversion to gain an 8-0 triumph over Maryland in College Park. This was Clemson's first victory over Maryland since the formation of the ACC.

White connected with Wyatt Cox on a 50-yard scoring pass in the third period, and then George Usry scored the two-point play. You will notice that there were a lot of two-point conversion attempts in this season. The 1958 season was the first year of the two-point play in college football. Coaches at that time, including Frank Howard, thought it would be easy to score from the three. Clemson scored 25 touchdowns that season and went for two 20 times, converting eight times.

While Clemson did not have a star system in 1958, the Vanderbilt game produced the single-best performance of the year by a Tiger. Harvey White gained 105 yards rushing in just 14 carries and completed 8-12 passes for 60 yards. Additionally, White scored both of Clemson's touchdowns in the final period of a thrilling 12-7 victory in Nashville.

Clemson trailed 7-0 going into the final period, thanks to five turnovers over the game's first 45 minutes. But White and Rudy Hayes, who had 99 yards rushing on the night, led Clemson back. Trailing 7-6 with just 6:30 left in the game, White took the Tigers on a breathtaking drive that included a fourth-down conversion at the Vanderbilt 10 with 53 seconds left.

Finally, with nine seconds remaining, White burst over the goal line from three yards out. This remains the latest fourth quarter touchdown score in Clemson history that decided the outcome of a game. For his heroics, White was named Associated Press National Back of the Week.

"With Harvey White, you knew he was going to get the job done," recalled Thomas. "He could take a team down the field in the clutch." The scores of the games to this point backed up Thomas's statement. It was the third victory by exactly five points for the Tigers in the first four games and in reality the fourth straight win by a touchdown.

Clemson hit a midseason slump, losing to South Carolina, gaining victory over Wake Forest, and then losing to Georgia Tech. The Wake Forest game was a 14-12 Clemson victory. One of the highlights was a touchdown by Johnny Mac Goff, who is now superintendent of education for the state of Ohio. He scored what proved to be the winning touchdown in the fourth quarter.

His score gave Clemson a 14-6 lead. However, Wake Forest came back behind the passing of future NFL star Norman Snead, who scored a touchdown on a five-yard run that culminated an 88-yard drive with just four minutes left. But, on the touchdown play, Snead was injured, and reserve Charlie Carpenter had to come off the bench cold to try for the two-point play. His pass was incomplete, and Clemson had another close victory.

Clemson closed the regular season with three consecutive victories. A 13-6 victory in Raleigh clinched the ACC Championship. Bill Mathis, who later became the first former Clemson player to win a Super Bowl Championship ring (with Joe Namath and the New York Jets), was the top rusher against the Pack, going 13-75. Usry and Bobby Morgan scored the touchdowns, as again Clemson scored both of its touchdowns in the fourth period.

After the team's most convincing victory of the season, 34-12 over Boston College, Clemson clinched a Sugar Bowl bid with a 36-19 win over Furman. Furman outscored Clemson 19-6 in the second half, and Clemson players and coaches wondered if they had blown the Sugar Bowl bid in the process.

Immediately after the game, Coach Howard went to his office and called the bowl committee to get a reaction. The committee offered Clemson the bid. Howard went into the dressing room to inform the team, "We got it." The Tigers were matched with undefeated and number-one-ranked LSU and 34-year-old coach Paul Dietzel.

Clemson's invitation was met with disdain by many of the national media. "A lot of people thought SMU should have been LSU's opponent," said Thomas. "We were not shown much respect, but we came to play."

The Tigers put in many hours of practice at home and in Biloxi, MS, in preparation for Billy Cannon, the 1958 Heisman Trophy winner. Coach Howard kept all the articles that ridiculed the Clemson program and showed them to the players prior to the game in an effort to fire up the team.

Since both teams' jerseys were light-colored, and because of everyone in America having black-and-white televisions, something had to be done about the players' attire. LSU wore a gold uniform and Clemson, the visiting team, was going to wear white. NBC-TV executives wanted one team to wear a darker jersey so the viewers would be able to distinguish the team on the field. Clemson decided to wear a dark-blue jersey for this game.

His ploy worked, as Clemson gave LSU its toughest game of the season. LSU's high-powered offense gained just 182 yards of total offense and just nine first downs. The LSU Tigers had to score on a halfback option pass in the third period after a Clemson fumble at its own 11.

Clemson drove 17 plays from its own 17 to the LSU 28 late in the game, but a fourth-down pass from White to George Usry went incomplete, and LSU held on to win the game 7-0. Clemson had shown America that they deserved to be in the Sugar Bowl.

Never has a Clemson team gained so much respect from a loss. "I wish we could line up and play LSU again . . . today," said Thomas.

It was this type of spirit, which still lives on today, that made the 1958 Clemson team one of Clemson's most successful and respected teams in history.

FRANK HOWARD—THE DISCOVERER

Some of the best discoveries are made by accident. And for Clemson fans over 50 years ago, it was fortunate that the great Clemson football scientist Frank Howard happened to stumble across a place kicker in spring practice of 1962.

A rising and unknown senior, Rodney Rogers, happened to be playing with the football one day before a practice session that involved kicking extra points and field goals.

It was one way Rogers satisfied a desire to get his hands and feet on the football, since he did not see much action as a defensive back. Howard observed that Rogers was quite talented at splitting the uprights. "Son," Howard said, "I want you to keep practicing them kicks; you might be the answer to our problems this fall." The discovery on this warm spring afternoon turned out to be one of the most rewarding in Howard's 30 years as master of the Tigers.

As the 1962 season progressed, Rodney Rogers almost became a forgotten man. In Clemson's first eight games, he kicked four field goals and several extra points. In the ninth game against Maryland just a week before the South Carolina contest, Rogers kicked a 23-yard field goal against the Terrapins with only 1:24 left in the game to give the Tigers a 17-14 Atlantic Coast Conference win.

Rogers thought this was the biggest kick of his life, until . . .

On November 24, against South Carolina, Rogers proved to be a hero again, and the discovery Howard made proved to be a sure-patented product the Tigers would be proud to market and put on the shelves with some of the greatest football games in ACC history.

Clemson was clad in blue jerseys for the annual war with the Gamecocks. The jerseys were four years old, as they were bought for the Sugar Bowl game against LSU in 1959. LSU, as host team, said it would wear white. Clemson's familiar orange jerseys did not offer enough contrast to keep the television people happy, and the

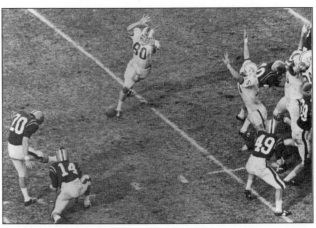

Rodney Rogers kicks the winning field goal against South Carolina in 1962.

other Clemson jerseys were white, so Frank Howard ordered a couple of sets of dark-blue jerseys for the classic.

After the Maryland game, the Clemson players started thinking about the South Carolina game, and someone remembered the blues. A couple of the Clemson players asked Coach Howard about wearing the blue against Carolina, and soon the whole team joined in and finally Howard said OK.

Clemson took an early 7-0 lead against the Gamecocks in the ACC classic, as Charlie Dumas scored from two yards out. South Carolina evened the score at 7-7 when Dan Reeves completed a 44-yard touchdown pass to Sammy Anderson. Reeves became a star player for the Dallas Cowboys and was later the head coach of the Denver Broncos and the Atlanta Falcons. After the two teams swapped field goals, South Carolina took a 17-10 lead, as Reeves scored on a six-yard rush with 1:47 left to go in the first half. Clemson tied the score late in the third quarter, as Jim Parker pitched to Elmo Lam for a 14-yard touchdown.

With 8:51 left to go in the game, Clemson started a 17-play, 71-yard drive that would consume 7:09 on the clock.

Rogers kicked the winning field goal from 24 yards out and 1:42 left to go in the game, to give the Tigers the eventual winning margin of 20-17.

Clemson's defense held the Gamecocks, and the Tigers took over on downs.

"I thought the Maryland game the week before was my biggest thrill, but now that was nothing compared with the South Carolina game. I'm from South Carolina, and nothing is better than beating them in football—if you play for Clemson."

"Before the field goal, I kept saying over and over, 'I have got to make this one,'" said Rogers. "I have just got to make it," he said.

When the ball sailed through the uprights, Rogers erupted with joy. One of his wildest dreams had come true.

Rogers had been part of a great discovery that could never be improved or changed with the passage of time.

THE DAY KENNEDY DIED

Two buses transporting 60 Clemson football players, along with 20 coaches, administrators, and student managers, pulled out of the parking lot at Fike Field House just after noon on November 22, 1963.

It would be a three-hour ride to Batesburg, SC, the road headquarters for the Tigers during the era when Clemson played South Carolina in Columbia.

Head Athletic Trainer Fred Hoover and Line Coach Bob Smith were riding together in the front seat of the first bus.

"We went through a lot of little towns to get to Batesburg," said Hoover, then in his sixth season of a 40-year career. "It was a much longer ride in those days, because I-26 had not been built yet.

"We were riding through Saluda, and as we passed the post office, Bob noticed that the American flag in front

of the building was at half-staff. We thought that was odd, because it took a major event for that to happen."

Something major had in fact taken place. At 12:30 p.m. (central time), President John F. Kennedy had been shot at Dealey Plaza in Dallas, TX, while riding in an open-car motorcade. He was pronounced dead at Parkland Hospital at 1:00 p.m., and 33 minutes later, a press conference was held to tell the world.

"We obviously didn't have cell phones in those days, and I don't even know if the bus had a radio," said Hoover.

The team continued its trip and arrived at the hotel in Batesburg at 3:00 p.m.

"None of us knew of the assassination until we got off the bus and someone from the hotel staff told us."

Similar to the events of September 11, 2001, it took a while for the gravity of the situation to sink in within the sports world. (Clemson and most other college football teams practiced on the afternoon of September 11, 2001, after the Twin Towers were attacked, and games for the next weekend were not postponed until the next day.)

"We didn't know if the game would go on or not," recalled Hoover, who still helps out at Clemson home football games as a liaison between the football office and Tiger opponents. "We had a practice scheduled at a local high school, so we went ahead and did the workout."

However, it was not much of a practice.

"We were up for the game, but after our boys heard of the president's death, things started to happen," said Head Coach Frank Howard in an interview with Jake Penland of *The State* the next day.

"There were busted signals with two boys running together . . . things like that. They didn't have their mind on football."

When the team returned from practice to the hotel, the game had not been cancelled. In fact, Clemson President Robert C. Edwards and South Carolina President Thomas F. Jones had released a joint statement saying the game would go on as scheduled.

In retrospect, some in the media of the era speculated that the game was not postponed immediately because CBS was planning to televise the Saturday afternoon contest on a regional basis.

It was to be just the second regular-season game televised in Clemson history, and it was to be shown on 50 CBS affiliates in 11 states. Each school was to be paid $53,000 for the appearance. Some believed CBS had an influence on the two university presidents.

So, the Clemson team had dinner at the hotel and monitored television coverage provided by Walter Cronkite on CBS.

The television coverage was dramatic, and speculation had the country wondering if the United States was going to be attacked by a foreign country. Remember, we were just 18 years removed from World War II, and the Cuban Missile Crisis had taken place the previous year (October 16-28, 1962).

N.C. State and Wake Forest were actually scheduled to play a game Friday night, and that game went on.

But as the evening continued, more and more schools announced postponements or cancellations.

At 9:30 p.m., Howard received a call from Dr. Edwards, who informed him the game would be postponed until the following Thursday, Thanksgiving Day.

At 10:00 p.m., Clemson and South Carolina released a joint statement.

"The Clemson vs. South Carolina football game scheduled for November 23, 1963 has been postponed due to the death of President John F. Kennedy. We regret any inconvenience that may be caused to individual fans, but we feel this action is in accord with the solemnity of the hour."

Coach Howard called the players together, and one of the players suggested the team return to Clemson that night and practice on Saturday. Howard agreed, and the team was back on the road to Clemson by 10:30 p.m.

The teams played in relative anonymity the following Thursday on Thanksgiving Day, as the game was not televised on CBS. A Detroit Lions game had priority. The Tigers defeated the Dan Reeves-led Gamecocks by a score of 24-20 thanks in part to a touchdown by Howard's son, Jimmy.

Similar to the way sports helped heal the country after September 11, 2001, the games helped put the nation on the path to healing in 1963.

1963 CLEMSON-GEORGIA, "THE HAIL GAME"

The most unusual weather occurrence in Clemson football history took place on October 12, 1963. A beautiful day had shaped up for the Clemson-Georgia game at Death Valley: it was sunny and 84 degrees. However, when the Georgia band took to the field at halftime, the skies grew dark, and halfway through the Georgia band's show, hail and heavy rain suddenly bombarded the field, bouncing off tubas and taking its toll on the drums, many of which were immediately torn. Fans were seen running, taking refuge underneath the North and South Stands.

The Georgia band made a hasty retreat to the shelter of the west end zone seats. A group of Clemson students, including many Tiger band members offered the 125 rain-soaked Redcoat band members shelter in nearby dormitories for a drying out and some fresh clothes.

The torrential hailstorm hit at 2:50 p.m. and caused temperatures to plummet from 84 degrees to 57 degrees in 45 minutes. Almost an inch of hail poured in a 20-minute period, and the game was delayed.

Clemson Head Coach Frank Howard and Georgia Head Coach Johnny Griffith met under the stands and delayed the start of the second half for 30 minutes. The field looked like a sheet of ice. Clemson's grounds crew cleared the field as much as possible.

The Tigers dealt with the conditions the best during the second half and tied the score 7-7 in the third quarter, which ended up being the final score. Clemson also blocked two Georgia field goal attempts to preserved the tie in this memorable game.

A TOUGH DECISION—BRUCE McCLURE

The Horned Frogs came to Tigertown very highly touted in 1965, and it was going to take a great Clemson performance to knock off TCU in this meeting. TCU played in the Sun Bowl at the conclusion of the 1965 season. For Clemson lineman Bruce McClure, it was the most memorable game of his life.

It wasn't the hype of the football game that McClure remembers, nor was it the fact that a member of the old Southwest Conference was coming to town for the first time. Instead, it was the events surrounding this late October weekend that forced him to make the hardest decision in his young life.

McClure, a native of Charlotte, NC, came to Clemson from Myers Park High School. Coach Whitey Jordan recruited him in high school. Clemson found out about Bruce McClure from Hap Carr, who also was a Myers Park graduate and had played football at Clemson and was also a baseball manager. He told the Clemson coaches about McClure, and the Tiger coaches were very much impressed.

"Coach Jordan gave me a scholarship in the fall of 1961, and when I started I was on the 12th team. I worked my way up and I ended up on the first unit on the freshman team," said McClure, who is the owner of Seven Products Plus, a contractors supply company in Anderson, SC.

McClure was in his fifth year at Clemson in the 1965 season, having redshirted the 1962 season due to a knee injury. McClure said that on this particular Friday morning before the TCU game, he got a message in his dorm that Coach Howard wanted to see him and fast. McClure said he was wondering why in the world Coach Howard wanted to see him, and the thought entered his mind, *I wonder what I have done?*

"I went as fast as I could to his office in Fike Field House. His secretary announced that I was there. He told me to come in and I sat down. He simply said, 'Boy, your Momma is dead.' I was shocked. I knew she had been sick with leukemia, but I thought there was more time. She had been coming to the games. At that time they were coming out with new innovations in treatment and we were very encouraged. But during surgery she had a brain hemorrhage and died.

"I was numb; I didn't know what to say. Coach Howard went on to say, 'We need you to play tomorrow, but we also understand if you don't. But we need you.'

"By the time I left his office, I knew I would play in the game. I told him I would play but I was going to Charlotte that night [to] spend time with my family.

"I was shocked and hurt and other thoughts were going through my mind. I was the oldest brother; I have to take care of my family. I had to go and tell my brother, who at that time was a freshman at Clemson. I ran into Dean Cox, and he was a big help to me. I knew I had to get home. I drove up to Charlotte with my brother, and it was the longest drive I have ever made in my life. I drove back to Clemson with a family friend early Saturday morning and we got back to campus around 2:00 a.m. and I went to my dorm room. I didn't sleep for maybe two hours.

"I kept thinking, *I just talked to Mom and she had said 'go back to school' on a previous visit*. I wanted to stay home and make sure she was all right just days before. She told me whether she lived or died that I had my own life to live. 'You will get in trouble if you stay at Charlotte and you'll get behind on your studies.' One thought that kept going through my mind is she told me to fulfill your commitments under any circumstances. I loved my parents and they had made many sacrifices for the family. I was going to fulfill my commitment to Clemson and my teammates.

"I got up on game day and met the team for the pre-game meal. Coach Howard, Coach Don Wade, and Coach Whitey Jordan all came and talked to me.

"I went to the field house to get dressed for the game. I went in the dressing room, and trainers Herman McGee and Fred Hoover were very helpful. I remember both of them talking to me. The rest of the team pretty much let me have my time to myself."

In the press box, McClure's name was not included on the depth chart for the TCU game; as Clemson's longtime Sports Information Director Bob Bradley explained, "we didn't put his name on the depth chart because we didn't figure he would play, given the circumstances."

"I didn't start, but I got in late in the first half," Mc-Clure said. "I started thinking about football. At the half, Coach Howard asked if I was doing OK. He talked about my situation and me during the halftime talk. I played most of the second half. It was senior day and I had a sponsor—there was so much going through my mind. All that was so difficult, but I knew somehow everything would work out. Back in those days you played both ways, on offense and defense.

"I played really hard and we defeated TCU 3-0."

According to the *Charlotte Observer*, McClure figured strongly in Clemson's 3-0 upset victory over the Horned Frogs.

During the final seconds of the game, Clemson was running out the clock. Quarterback Thomas Ray ran a sneak to kill the clock. When the mass of Texas Christian players climbed off him and the finals seconds were counting down, he scrambled to his feet and dashed to the Tiger player dressed in uniform number 68 on the field, Bruce McClure. Ray thrust the ball into McClure's hands. It was the game ball. "Take this," Ray said. "We won this one for you."

McClure said after the game, "It would have been Mom's wish that I play. She wanted me to live up to my commitments. That's the only thing that enabled me to do it. "

HOWARD'S ROCK AND ITS MYSTICAL POWERS

It was fortunate for Clemson that former IPTAY Executive Secretary Gene Willimon acted when he did. Otherwise, Clemson might not have beaten Virginia 40-35 on Sept. 24, 1966, in the season opener for the Tigers.

S.C. Jones gave Head Coach Frank Howard a rock from Death Valley, CA.

It was Willimon's idea to put a rock from Death Valley, CA, on a pedestal on top of the hill during the summer of 1966, where the Tigers make their famous stadium entrance. Alumnus S.C. Jones gave Howard the rock after a visit to Death Valley, CA. Jones must have thought it to be an appropriate gift to Howard, as the stadium has been called Death Valley by friend and foe alike for many years prior to 1966.

Howard told Willimon to do something with the rock. Willimon had a brainstorm and immediately came up with the idea of putting it on a pedestal overlooking the playing field where it still sits today, over 25 years later.

Even though the players did not begin touching the rock for good luck until a year later, the rock must have brought the Tigers good luck, or as Frank Howard stated, "mystical powers" in the 40-35 win over Virginia in 1966. The Tigers managed to win, despite losing five fumbles and giving up 429 yards total offense. It was obvious some kind of strange powers must have been with the Tigers on this particular day.

It also did not hurt the Tigers' chances that Buddy Gore rushed for 117 yards in this game, and Clemson's Jimmy Addison was 12-19 in passing for 283 yards.

The Tigers went ahead in the ACC contest early in the second period on the strength of a 68-yard punt return by Frank Liberatore, a touchdown pass from Addison to Phil Rogers, and the running of Buddy Gore. The second and third quarters belonged solely to the Bob Davis-led Cavaliers, and with the help of Clemson fumbles, Virginia took a 35-18 lead with 3:06 left to go in the third quarter.

Edgar McGee, Phil Rogers, and Wayne Bell caught key passes to bring Clemson to a 35-33 deficit with about three minutes to play.

Faced with a third down and short yardage on Clemson's 25-yard line, the Tigers were driving for the go-ahead score.

"We called a pass play that had resulted in several earlier completions to our split end Wayne Bell," recalled Clemson quarterback Jimmy Addison. "Wayne found an open spot between the linebackers, and the Virginia cornerback came from his deep position to cover the open receiver."

Jacky Jackson, who had run from his tailback position down the left sideline, made a beautiful catch behind that cornerback and outran the safety man to the end zone. That gave the Tigers a 40-35 advantage with 3:49 left and proved to be the winning touchdown. "I remember this play distinctly", said Addison, who later would attend law school at the University of Virginia. "I thought I had overthrown Jackson, but he put it in second gear and ran underneath the pass." However, the Cavaliers had one more chance, and Davis marched Virginia down the field. With 1:49 left to go in the game, the Cavaliers had a second and 10 situation on the Tigers' 14-yard line. Davis's pass was intercepted by Phil Marion, and the Tigers proceeded to run out the clock.

Jimmy Addison was the Associated Press Back of the Week, while Virginia's Quarterback Bob Davis was named *Sports Illustrated*'s Back of the Week. It is probably the only time two opposing players in the same game have been named national players of the week in the history of college football.

Davis set the Atlantic Coast Conference's record for most passes attempted and completed, records that have since been broken. He finished the game hitting 26-48 passes for 312 yards, while the Tigers' Addison was 12-19 in passing for 283 yards and three scores. Addison is still third on the Clemson individual highest single-game passing efficiency list for his performance against the Cavaliers with a 240.39 mark, but he is first among Tiger quarterbacks who have thrown at least 15 passes in a game.

"As someone suggested on the sidelines during the fourth quarter," continued Addison, "the university should have run everyone out of the stadium before the fourth quarter and made them pay to reenter."

It was truly a ball game worth two admissions.

WAS IT THE SHOES?

On a windy November day in 1967, it probably was the shoes that enabled Clemson to upset 10th-ranked N.C. State 14-6 in Clemson's first-ever win over a top-10 team in Death Valley.

Coming into this Atlantic Coast Conference classic, the Wolfpack was enjoying a fabulous year, defeating its first eight opponents. After the Pack defeated Virginia in Charlottesville in the eighth game, Penn State and Clemson remained, both on the road.

Before the Nittany Lions game, there was talk that N.C. State had the Sugar Bowl bid wrapped up, provided there was at least a split in the last two games. The Wolfpack lost to Penn State 13-8, making the Clemson-N.C. State game even more crucial for the Wolfpack's New Year's Day bowl hopes.

The Wolfpack had become nationally famous in 1967, because of their tenacity and their distinctive white shoes. At this time, every team in the nation, along with N.C. State's offensive unit, was wearing black shoes.

N.C. State started wearing the white shoes on defense when left cornerback Bill Morrow noted a member of the Kansas City Chiefs wearing white shoes.

Morrow, who scored the first touchdown for N.C. State in the new Carter-Finley Stadium when he intercepted a pass in 1966, went to cocaptain Art McMahon with the idea. Linebacker Chuck Amato said he would paint his shoes white, and the idea spread throughout the Wolfpack defense. State was ranked number one in the ACC in defense coming into the Clemson game and was a sure bet to beat a 4-4 Clemson team.

A few of the Clemson players, the week before the game, wanted to paint their shoes orange to counteract the perceived intangible advantage of N.C. State's white shoes.

"I remember a lot of players got together and we decided to paint our shoes orange," recalled former Clemson tailback Buddy Gore.

"Our trainer Herman McGee rounded up the orange paint needed for our idea and we went to the dorm that week and painted our game shoes orange, said Gore. "I have no idea where he got the orange paint. Coach Howard did not know what we were doing until that Saturday morning. I think he liked our plan."

Gore was one of Clemson's greatest backs ever, and in 1967, he was named the Atlantic Coast Conference's Player of the Year.

Assistant Coach Don Wade was also involved in the scheme. "We got the paint from eight or nine different places," Wade explained. "It's tough to find orange paint that would be suitable for shoes."

N.C. State jumped ahead 6-0 after Gerald Warren hit two second-quarter field goals from 37 and 47 yards out with his back to a gusty 22-mph wind.

Gore scored what proved to be the winning touchdown for the Tigers early in the third quarter. With a third-and-11 situation facing the Tigers on N.C. State's 27, Clemson was obviously facing a throwing situation.

"N.C. State was in a defense that would provide double coverage on the wideouts and forced the linebackers to cover the man coming out of the backfield," remembers Gore.

"I was not the primary receiver by any means," Gore continued. "After all, I only caught seven passes my entire career. I was in the flats around the 12-yard line and I was open after beating the linebacker. The cornerback and the safety were with our wide receiver. I will never forget when I was open in the flats. I looked at our quarterback Jimmy Addison and he stared right back at me and he threw me the ball and I went in for the touchdown."

Clemson went on to win the game 14-6, ensuring the Tigers at least a tie for the ACC crown. The Tigers defeated South Carolina the next Saturday to clinch the championship outright.

"How many tackles did those orange shoes make, coach?" a sportswriter asked Coach Frank Howard after the game. "None," Howard replied in a word. "But I tell you, there is something about football that makes boys believe in something that will help them. When they believe they can do something, they usually do it."

On that particular day, it must have been the shoes!

ACC DOMINANCE IN THE MID-TO-LATE-SIXTIES

Clemson won the Atlantic Coast Conference in 1965, 1966, and 1967. The Tigers were 16-4 in the league during this time.

Also in this era, the Tigers had two All-America players—offensive tackle Wayne Mass and offensive guard Harry Olszewski.

Number-44 Buddy Gore was a star player in the 1960s. The tailback was known for being a workhorse in Coach Howard's running attack. Another hard-nosed back in the 1960s was Ray Yauger.

PARKER RESURRECTS "RUNNING DOWN THE HILL"

When his Tigers ran out of the dressing room and onto the field at Memorial Stadium for the first time on September 8, 1973, against The Citadel, Red Parker remembered the atmosphere was pretty stale that day.

In fact, as the former Clemson head coach recalled, there was no energy at all in the stadium. And due to that, his Tigers played stale as they squeaked out a 14-12 victory.

"When I went to Clemson, attendance was way down," said Parker, who coached at Clemson from 1973-'76. "It was just a period of time when the enthusiasm was not the way it is now. It was kind of a difficult time out on that football field before the game and during the game.

"It was not something that was fun."

That following Monday morning, Parker went to then-Athletic Director Bill McLellan and said they needed to do something to get the spirit and enthusiasm back in Death Valley.

"I thought about a lot of things I had heard about Clemson before I went there," Parker said. "One of the things that struck me as being a gold mine of potential was the Tigers running down the hill in the east end zone. I saw that as a spirit uplifter.

"Coach Howard had done it for years, and I felt like it did all that he wanted it to do. He accomplished a great deal with that, and keep in mind running down the hill was Coach Howard's deal."

Clemson had stopped running down the hill in 1970 following Howard's final year as head coach. There were several reasons why it did that, but the main reason had to do with the new dressing rooms in the west end zone.

"When I came to Clemson, I was astounded that running down the hill was dropped," Parker said. "It really, really disappointed me. Well, at that point right there, after the first home game, I went to Bill McLellan, and I said, 'Bill, there is not enough spirit and enough energy and enthusiasm in the stadium. There is just not enough to have what you have to have to play major college football. That is just the way it is.'

"He said, 'What do you want to do?' And I said, 'I want to run down the hill.' Bill at that point said, 'We can't run down the hill because the reason we quit is because we spent thousands and thousands of dollars on a new dressing room on the [west] end of the stadium.' Which was true, they did. They did spend a lot of money on those dressing rooms, which they had to have. It was an absolute must. They had to have those dressing rooms down there, so I went back to my office and I got to thinking."

And during that period of thought was when "The most exciting 25 seconds in college football" was reintroduced to Tiger fans. However, it wasn't done the way they remembered it.

"When I first started coming to Clemson games in 1964, they did not run down the hill like they do now," Clemson Senior Associate Sports Information Director Sam Blackman said. "When Coach Howard was here, they dressed inside old Fike Field House and would leave to go to the stadium from there. They would walk down Williamson Road. I can still see those helmets bouncing up and down now as they were coming down the street. You could see the tip of the orange helmets just over the fence.

"Coach Howard had them enter the stadium through a fence that they used to sit at the top of the hill and they would come down the hill and into the stadium. They did it as convenience more than anything else.

"My father and I always went to watch that," Blackman continued. "There wasn't much fanfare then as there is now. Maybe a couple hundred people, if that many. But, keep in mind, they came down the hill in those days prior to warm-ups. A lot of the fans were still tailgating at that time and had yet to enter the stadium."

Learning how Howard's teams ran down the hill, and why they did it, helped Parker get creative. Knowing he had to use the west end zone locker rooms, Parker thought of a plan that has been used by every Clemson coach since.

What Parker created is one of the best motivating events in sport, and one of the best recruiting tools in college football.

Clemson's next home game in 1973 did not occur until October 6th. The Tigers were coming off back-to-back road losses to Georgia and Georgia Tech, and Parker was anxious to see how the crowd would respond as Clemson ran down the hill prior to its battle with Texas A&M.

"I don't mind thinking far-fetched at times, so I decided at that point it would be worthwhile for me to figure out a way to run down the hill because you always have a little bit of dead time before the game," he said. "I thought it would be a worthwhile opportunity to seize this and move on with it. We always used two buses to go to the motel where we stayed for the pregame meal, and then we bused into the stadium and dressed for the game. Well, after we got on the field and warmed up, we came back in the dressing room and did everything we needed to do.

"At that point, instead of going out onto the field for the game, we had the players get on the buses. We then drove them around the stadium to the other end of the field, got them off the buses, and came down the hill together. That made a big difference in our stadium. It got people excited."

And it still does today. Nobody in college football has such a unique entrance as Clemson does!

"In my opinion, running down the hill is one of the greatest motivators in all of college football," Parker said. "In fact, when I was at Clemson, we believed if we could get the prospects there on a Saturday afternoon when the Tigers ran down the hill, we had a chance to recruit them. And we brought in a lot of them."

BENNIE CUNNINGHAM—TWO-TIME ALL-AMERICA PLAYER IN 1974 AND 1975

Before the start of the 1968-69 school year, Bennie Cunningham, Jr. was a tall skinny kid who played the clarinet in the band at the old Blue Ridge High School in Seneca, SC. Though he enjoyed playing the clarinet, he did not like the work that went along with it.

What he loved to do was play football. Cunningham was a natural at it. He was lean, he was fast, and, more important, he was good at it. So before his freshman year of high school, Cunningham decided he was going to quit the band and play football instead.

A few weeks into practice, however, Cunningham realized football wasn't all it was cracked up to be. He

discovered he hated practice. He didn't like the fact he had to condition his body and lift weights, and learning the playbook was like having extra homework.

He discovered he was working harder in football than he ever did in the band, so the week before the first game, he told the coaches he was quitting the team.

"I got fed up with football because I didn't realize how hard it was to play football," Cunningham said.

The coaches were puzzled by Cunningham's decision. Since the start of practice, he did nothing but succeed. They had already penciled him in as a starter, though he had never played the game before he came out for the squad.

But none of that mattered, as he still quit the team.

That afternoon, Cunningham went back home and did his homework and studied like everything was okay. Life was good. He was getting what he wanted out of it, or so he thought.

Later that evening when his dad came home and discovered his son quit the team, it was time for a good heart-to-heart conversation.

"My father came to me upset and said, 'Listen, you quit the band because it was tough and now you have quit the football team because it was tough. I don't care what you do in life, there are going to be times when things get tough. You can't quit every time something gets tough,'" Cunningham recalled.

"So that's when I decided to go back out for the team and prove to myself and everybody else that I can do this."

And did he ever prove it. After integration moved him to Seneca High School, Cunningham went on to become a three-time All-State player for the Bobcats, which led to Shrine Bowl honors and a football scholarship to Clemson.

During his time with the Tigers, Cunningham became the most decorated tight end in Clemson history and the ACC, for that matter. He became Clemson's first consensus All-America player in 1974 and then the Tigers' first two-time first-team All-America player the following year.

In 1974, the Tigers were 7-4 and had a 6-0 record at home with wins over Georgia, Georgia Tech, and South Carolina. In 1975, Cunningham was also chosen on many first teams as a senior, despite a down season at Clemson. He was also a two-time first-team All-ACC pick and was selected to play in the Hula Bowl, the Japan Bowl, and the East-West Shrine game after his senior year.

In 1976, Cunningham was taken in the first round by the Pittsburgh Steelers.

After the 1985 season, Cunningham decided to call it a career after 10 years with the Steelers, where he amassed 2,879 yards and 20 touchdowns, plus blocking for most of Franco Harris's 91 career rushing touchdowns. In 2007, when the Steelers celebrated their 75th Anniversary, the Pittsburgh fans voted Cunningham on the all-time roster, the only tight end on the team.

FROM FULLER TO SPILLER

As you walk into Dabo Swinney's office inside the WestZone of Clemson Memorial Stadium, you will notice the life-size poster of former running back C.J. Spiller on his wall. The poster, which was used as a promotional item for Spiller's Heisman Trophy Campaign in 2009, is just one of the many collectibles Swinney has on display.

His most prized possession sits on his desk, a glass paper weight with a business card inside. On the back of the business card is a written agreement between Swinney and Spiller that says, "I, C.J. Spiller, agree to visit CU on the 13th of Jan. 06."

It's an informal contract Swinney made on the spot when he visited Spiller in Lake Butler, FL. Swinney, then the wide receivers coach at Clemson, knew Spiller was a man of his word, and drawing up this impromptu contract would guarantee the five-star running back was going to at least come and visit Clemson.

Spiller kept his commitment and visited Clemson on the day he said he would. Three weeks later, he slipped his mother, Patricia Watkins, a note as he walked to the podium to make his announcement on where he was planning to play college football. Then in front of all of his high school peers, and an auditorium full of Florida fans, he told them he was coming to Clemson.

The rest is history, you might say. Spiller broke countless Clemson and ACC records and even a few NCAA records in his four years in Tigertown, but what the running back and former ACC Player of the Year actually did was greater than that. This young man from Lake Butler, FL, who was recruited by just about every school in the country, took a chance to come to a school that had not won much of anything in the recent years prior to his arrival, and in doing so he changed the program, much like Steve Fuller did in 1975.

In 1974, Fuller, who played high school football at nearby Spartanburg, was one of the more coveted high school products in the state of South Carolina. Everyone wanted him, but he chose to come to Clemson, a program that appeared to be on the rise under then-Head Coach Red Parker.

The Tigers were coming off a 7-4 season, including a perfect 6-0 mark at home. Clemson might have gone to the Peach Bowl that year had it not been for a controversial play in a 29-28 loss at No. 20 Tennessee.

Though his first two years at Clemson didn't go too well, ultimately Fuller led the Tigers to an 8-3-1 season in 1977 and to an 11-1 year in 1978. The 1977 season was Clemson's first bowl appearance in 18 years, while the 1978 year marked the first time since 1967 that the Tigers won an ACC Championship.

Fuller was named ACC Player of the Year after both seasons, one of two players in ACC history to do so. But like Spiller, Fuller's legacy was more than just about setting records and winning games. His presence and

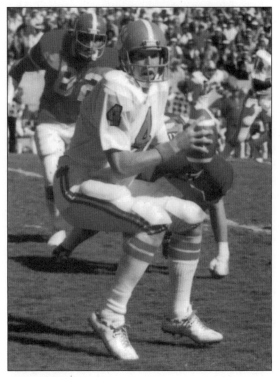

Steve Fuller was named ACC Player of the Year in 1977 and 1978.

then his success at Clemson led to other big-time athletes following in his footsteps—guys like running back Lester Brown, fullback Marvin Sims, defensive tackle Jim Stuckey, linebacker Bubba Brown, safety Rex Varn, offensive tackle Lee Nanney, wide receiver Perry Tuttle, defensive tackle Steve Durham, linebacker Jeff Davis, quarterback Homer Jordan, running back Chuck McSwain, fullback Jeff McCall, and . . . you get the point.

Fuller's presence and the amount of success he was able to have at Clemson allowed other top athletes to believe the same could happen for them at Clemson. Eventually, the Tigers were signing some of the best players in the country, and the results showed on the football field.

From 1977-'91, Clemson won 133 games, did not have a losing record for 15 straight seasons, won seven ACC Championships, appeared in 11 bowl games, won seven bowl games, recorded six 10-win seasons, and most important won the program's only National Championship in 1981.

Clemson had seen this act before in its lustrous history. Cone, whom Howard called his greatest player, had the same effect in the late-1940s, which was a decade that saw the Tigers post a perfect season in 1948, win three ACC Championships, and play in six bowl games, while winning three of them.

Before Cone, there was McFadden, who led Clemson to the program's first bowl appearance and victory following the 1939 season with a 6-3 victory over Boston College. McFadden is still considered by many the greatest athlete to play at Clemson.

Since Spiller put on the orange and white in 2006, the Tigers have won 109 games, won the program's first ACC Championship since 1991, won the ACC Atlantic three times, played in the ACC Championship game twice, played in seven bowl games, played in a BCS game, and has posted back-to-back 10-win seasons.

THE GAME THAT STARTED A NEW ERA

Though most of the 54,129 fans who walked through the gates an hour before kickoff were hoping to see their Clemson Tigers warm up prior to their 28-9 victory over archrival South Carolina, instead, all they saw was an empty half of the field, while the Gamecocks went through their pregame warm-ups.

"We didn't know where they were," said Sam Blackman, who was 14 years old at the time. "We were sitting on the Hill, and I kept wondering, 'Where are the Tigers?'"

It was easy to see why someone might think the Tigers were going to be a no-show. Clemson was 2-6-2 coming into the Palmetto State's annual battle, while the Gamecocks were 6-4. The only thing that stood between them and a Peach Bowl invitation was a victory over Clemson.

But the Tigers weren't warming up in Death Valley because they were scared to play South Carolina. Instead, they were at a field adjacent to Memorial Stadium that was used as a practice field for the soccer team. The lot is now known as Lot 2 for game day parking and is used as an intramural field the rest of the year by the university.

"We were very relaxed for the pregame," Parker said. "We did not want to waste any emotion until we got to the top of the Hill. It was a very casual warm-up. If someone thought he had enough, he went over and sat down.

"You could not have done that down at the stadium. We were well prepared. We had to eat it for a year, and I know we were ready to play."

Whatever happened on that soccer practice field that morning, it worked. Clemson held the Gamecocks' powerful offense to 124 rushing yards and forced five turnovers, including three interceptions. The Tigers rushed for 280 yards and got 127 from Warren Ratchford and 98 from fullback Tracy Perry.

"We did not know what they were doing, but we heard afterward that they had a pretty spirited practice," Blackman said. "Whatever it was, obviously it worked. We had not seen them play like that all year."

The Tigers did not touch the playing surface in Death Valley on that cold and rainy afternoon until they came storming down the Hill just before kickoff. Their entrance energized what was at the time the largest crowd to see a football game at Memorial Stadium.

The emotion in the stadium sparked the Tigers as Fuller, then a sophomore, led an 81-yard drive that was capped by Perry's three-yard run. South Carolina tried to answer the Tigers' score, but Ron Bass's pass to the end zone was picked off by Clemson's Brian Kier.

Ratchford, who had 92 yards rushing on five carries in the first quarter, broke off a 54-yard run on the ensuing possession, and then Perry scored his second touchdown, this time from 12 yards out, for a 14-0 lead.

"After the first drive, I thought we were in pretty good shape to have them come to us and try to beat us," Parker said. "There were a lot of things we could have done and did not do."

But they did do a lot of them. One was capitalizing on South Carolina mistakes. Leading 14-3 in the third quarter, Clemson recovered a bad snap that sailed over the punter's head at the South Carolina 16. Four plays later, Fuller capitalized on the gift with a 5-yard run for a 21-3 lead.

Later in the third quarter, O.J. Tyler intercepted another Bass aerial at the Clemson 29. Forty-four yards later, Fuller made the Gamecocks pay again, with a 27-yard scamper that electrified the sellout crowd and put the Tigers on top 28-3.

"Steve Fuller played a gutsy ball game," Parker said.

After a South Carolina score, Clemson was going in for another touchdown when reserve quarterback Mike O'Cain fumbled near the goal line. None of that mattered, though, as the Tigers beat South Carolina and ended their season in Death Valley.

"This is the greatest experience of my life to be around a group of kids like this," Parker said. "Our seniors have taken the position that they are willing to do anything to prepare this team for the future, and I just want to thank them.

"I hated [the fact that] we fumbled on that last drive. I thought Mike O'Cain would get one in. We made only one change this week and that was to put Joe Bostic at center. He is only a sophomore, and he is going to be a great one."

And he was, as were a lot of other guys. Parker, who was 17-25-2 in four seasons at Clemson, was not allowed to stick around to find out. He was fired the following Monday, and a few weeks later a guy by the name of Charlie Pell was hired from Virginia Tech. Pell brought with him a 29-year-old coach by the name of Danny Ford to coach the offensive line.

But Parker was right—the future was bright at Clemson. The victory over South Carolina propelled the Clemson program into the future, as the next season the Tigers began a streak of 15-straight winning seasons in which the program won 133 games, a national championship, seven ACC titles, eight bowl victories, 10 bowl appearances, and 11 Top-20 seasons.

THE CATCH

It all started following Clemson's 7-6 victory over Georgia in Athens. As the Tigers were making the 70-mile hike back to Clemson, Pell asked the bus driver to pull over. Pell wanted to savor the victory, considering it was Clemson's first win at Georgia since 1914.

So as the legend goes, Pell went into a convenience store and bought every player on the team a cigar to commemorate the win. The cigar celebration became a big part of the 1977 season, as the Tigers used the Georgia win to jump-start a great run.

Pell and the Tigers went on to win seven straight games, and after each victory, they lit up a cigar. Well, sort of. Clemson wide receiver Jerry Butler chose not to smoke his cigars and instead he scribbled the score and the date on each of his. There was just one place left in his collection back at his dorm—for the South Carolina game.

But South Carolina wanted no part of this so-called rite of passage. The Gamecocks were still smarting from the previous year's loss in Clemson when the Tigers, despite winning just two games prior to it, pounded USC, 28-9, knocking it out of contention for a possible Peach Bowl bid.

The roles were reversed this time around. The Game-cocks were sitting at 5-5 and knew their season was over regardless of the outcome, but Clemson (7-2-1) was in the running for a Gator Bowl invitation and needed a victory over their archrival to secure the bid and go bowling for the first time since 1959.

During the first two-and-half quarters, everything was pretty much going according to plan. The Tigers had a veteran team that was hungry and had a head coach who got them believing in themselves. The Gamecocks were young and unsure of what they could accomplish.

The Tigers jumped out to a 17-0 lead by halftime, thanks to a Warren Ratchford touchdown, a 30-yard field goal by Obed Ariri, and a Lester Brown touchdown from the one. When fullback Ken Callicutt rumbled 52 yards midway through the third quarter, Clemson found itself up 24-0 and well on its way to victory.

"Dwight Clark and I did the unpardonable; we started talking about how great we had played," quarterback Steve Fuller said to *The* (Columbia) *State* newspaper back in November of 2002.

It was about that time when South Carolina's Spencer Clark raced untouched for a 77-yard touchdown to cut the lead to 24-7. Over the next eight minutes, the Tigers could do nothing right, and USC could do no wrong.

On Clemson's next three possessions, it fumbled the ball, went three-and-out, and then shanked a punt 10 yards. USC took advantage of each mistake to crawl back in the game with two Steve Dorsey touchdowns to make the score 24-20.

With 7:02 to play, South Carolina again gained possession of the football and had a chance to take the lead for the first time all night as they moved the ball to the Clemson 40.

"We called a pass route we had not run all day," South Carolina receiver Phil Logan said years later. "The defense backpedaled and I curled."

When Logan curled, quarterback Ron Bass delivered a strike. It was fourth and 10 at the Clemson 40, and USC

seemed desperate to make one last play to at least extend the drive. What Logan did not expect was to be so wide open.

"I expected to be hit, but nobody was there," he said. "I cut across the field, got some blocks, and I was never touched."

Logan's 40-yard touchdown gave the Gamecocks a 27-24 lead with one minute and 48 seconds to play. Logan and his teammates were so confident the game was over, Logan was seen lifting his jersey to the crowd revealing a garnet T-shirt underneath with white letters that read, "No Cigar Today."

"That kind of ticked this old boy off," Butler said.

It appeared to motivate the entire Clemson offense. Facing a third down and seven from the Clemson 36-yard line, Fuller hit Rick Weddington for 26 yards to the South Carolina 38-yard line and a first down. After an incompletion, Fuller found Clark across the middle for 18 yards, setting Clemson up at the 20.

The Tigers quickly rushed to the line to run another play, when Fuller noticed South Carolina's defense was confused and they had trouble getting players onto the field. The play called for Butler to cut to the corner, but USC put pressure on Fuller and forced him to throw the ball earlier than he would have liked.

"I saw the ball headed toward the middle of the field," Butler said. "He was dumping the ball out of the end zone, but I jumped and got my hands on the ball, and I knew if I got my hands on the ball, I could catch it."

Butler made a leaping, twisting catch that no one else could have made in that game, and no one else has made since.

"It was a first-down play. We had plenty of time, and I threw it where he would catch it or it would be incomplete," Fuller said. "Nine times out of ten, it would have been incomplete."

Instead, it's a play simply known as "The Catch." The 20-yard pass play gave Clemson the lead, and with the extra point Clemson led 31-27, with :49 left. The Tigers held on to defeat the Gamecocks.

THE 1978 SEASON

Most times in life, it takes failure in order to reach great success. Expectations entering the 1978 season were at the highest at any point in the last 20 years. The Tigers were coming off an 8-3-1 season in which they went to their first bowl game in 18 years and finished the year ranked 19th in the final Associated Press Top 20 poll.

Clemson began the 1978 season looking as if it were going to exceed its lofty expectations. The ACC's preaseason favorite rolled over The Citadel in the season-opener, as eight different Tigers scored in a 58-3 victory.

"It was easy because we worked hard for four weeks to make it look easy," fullback Marvin Sims said. "I wasn't surprised we did this well; I expected it."

The eighth-ranked Tigers expected to do the same thing in Week 2, when they rolled down the road to Ath-

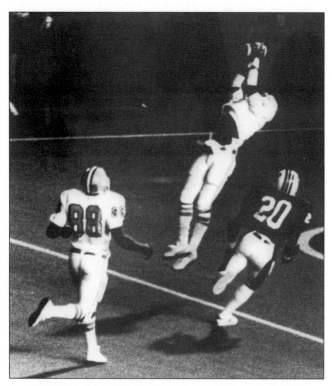

Jerry Butler made "The Catch" on November 19, 1977. It was a 20-yard pass from Steve Fuller to Jerry Butler with just 49 seconds remaining and gave Clemson a 31-27 win over South Carolina in Columbia.

ens, GA, to play unranked Georgia. The Bulldogs were still smarting from the 1977 matchup when Clemson knocked down a two-point conversion on the last play to sneak out of Athens with a 7-6 win.

But the Clemson players were feeling good and felt this was their year to shine. Georgia quickly brought them to Earth. The Bulldogs forced six Clemson turnovers and kept the Tigers out of the offense, while limiting the strong running game to 156 yards.

The defense held its own, limiting Georgia to two first-half field goals, but the Bulldogs opened the second half with an 80-yard drive, capped by a 13-yard Jeff Pyburn touchdown pass to flanker Carmon Prince. Georgia had seized control of the game and finished the afternoon with 205 rushing yards against Clemson's proud defense.

"We gave a good solid Georgia team a chance to whip us," Pell said.

The Tigers were stunned. Just three hours earlier they were boasting about being unbeatable and being the best in the country, and suddenly they were left trying to figure out what went wrong.

"We learned our lesson quick," linebacker Bubba Brown said. "After The Citadel game we were on top of the world, and when we went to Athens as the favorite, I think we were beginning to believe all the stuff people were saying about how good we were.

"The Georgia game brought us back down to Earth. We learned that even though we had talent, we had to work for everything we got."

This was when aguably the best Clemson team ever assembled was born. A look to the final NCAA statistics from that season tells the rest of the story.

The Tigers of 1978 finished fifth in the nation in scoring offense at 32 points per game and fifth in the nation in scoring defense, allowing just 10.5 points per game. Clemson was fourth in the nation in total offense at 436.7 yards per game, and 15th in total defense, allowing 254 yards a game. The Tigers were sixth in the nation in rushing, averaging nearly 300 yards per game, and fifth in turnover margin. The passing game, led by Fuller, completed 54 percent of its passes and threw just five interceptions.

Even the special teams were among the best, as the Tigers finished second in the nation in punt returns, and recent Clemson Hall of Fame inductee Obed Ariri was 12th in the nation in scoring.

A look at the future NFL stars on that 1978 team gives more evidence that this was the most talented team in Clemson history. No less than six players (Butler, Fuller, Jim Stuckey, Jeff Bryant, Perry Tuttle, and Terry Kinard) were first-round NFL draft choices. Seventeen players on the team were drafted, and 18 played in the NFL. Eleven of the 18 played at least five years in the NFL.

The players on Clemson's starting offense that year played a combined 61 years in the NFL. Just look at the offensive line alone. Jeff Bostic, the center, played 14 years in the league. His brother, Joe Bostic, was a starting guard who started nine years in the league and was an All-America player in 1978. Steve Kenney, a starting tackle, played for the Philadelphia Eagles and Detroit Lions for seven years.

Fuller played 10 years in the league, while his favorite targets, Butler and Clark, both were All-Pros and played nine years in the league. That does not even include second-team wide receiver Perry Tuttle, who was a first-round draft pick and All-America athlete in 1981.

The character of the team started to take over in the third game, and the result was a 31-0 victory over Villanova, a team led by future All-Pro Howie Long. A Clemson Homecoming crowd enjoyed a 38-7 victory over Virginia Tech in the season's fourth game, as Fuller ran 75 yards for a touchdown on the game's second play from scrimmage, still the longest run by a Clemson quarterback in history.

The offense continued its dominance of the offensive line in Week Five, when the Tigers gained 419 yards rushing in a 30-14 win over Virginia. Lester Brown, known as "the Rubber Duck," had 178 yards rushing, including a 59-yard touchdown run on Clemson's first play from scrimmage.

A 28-8 victory over Duke followed, thanks to the play of Randy Scott, who had three takeaways out of Clemson's seven total forced turnovers.

The NC State game in Raleigh was a battle of the Browns. N.C. State was led by Ted Brown, a senior running back who had rushed for 227 yards and four touchdowns against Clemson as a freshman. The Tigers featured Lester Brown, who would end the season as Clemson's second 1,000-yard rusher in history and who also had a record 17 touchdowns.

The key to the game? Clemson had one more Brown than the 'Pack. It was Clemson linebacker Bubba Brown who earned National Player of the Week honors from *Sports Illustrated*. Clemson's all-time leading tackler finished the day with 18 tackles and almost personally limited Ted Brown to 70 yards in 21 carries and no touchdowns in Clemson's 33-10 victory.

Clemson rushed for 247 yards, including 118 yards and two touchdowns by Lester Brown. Rex Vain returned an interception 93 yards for a touchdown, his second ninety-plus-yard return of his career. It was a big victory for Clemson over a team that would end the season with a 9-3 record and a top-20 final ranking.

"This was a great team victory," said Pell. "I can't express in words how much this victory means. It is the greatest team effort I've been a part of since I first put on a football uniform in 1958."

It was also a proud day for Clemson fans. In one of the most incredible showings of spirit in college history, the 5,000 or so Clemson fans forced N.C. State quarterback Scott Smith to back away from the line of scrimmage and ask the referee for time because of crowd noise—noise caused by the visiting Clemson fans.

The winning streak continued the next week on Tobacco Road with a 51-6 scorching of Wake Forest. For the sixth time in eight games, Clemson scored on its first possession of the game. The Tigers rushed for 342 yards and gained 208 yards passing. Lester Brown led the way with a 117-yard rushing performance, and Tuttle caught his first career touchdown pass, ironically in his hometown of Winston-Salem, on a 42-yard pass from Fuller.

The defense showed how much improvement it had made over the previous two years. In 1976, Wake Forest running back James McDougald had rushed for 249 yards against the Tigers. The entire Wake Forest team had just three yards rushing in 25 attempts on this afternoon.

The rivalry with North Carolina was one of the strongest in the ACC in the late-1970s and 1980s. Clemson was a heavy favorite against a young North Carolina team that featured a sophomore linebacker named Lawrence Taylor. The outside linebacker would go on to be considered one of the NFL's greatest defensive players of all time, as he helped lead the New York Giants to two Super Bowl Championships in the late-'80s and early-'90s during his Hall of Fame career.

The Tar Heels were 3-5 when they came to Death Valley, but they were as talented as any team Clemson had faced that year. They were a young team that was still finding itself under first-year head coach Dick Crum.

"They're due and we know it," Pell said during the week leading up to the game.

With 13:14 left in the game, North Carolina was proving Pell's point. The Tar Heels held a 9-6 lead, and Clemson's dreams of a championship season and top-10 finish were in jeopardy.

Fuller directed a precise 80-yard drive, and Lester Brown scored on a one-yard run with 9:48 left. The Clemson defense took over from there.

"It wasn't pretty football on our part," Pell said. "The important thing was that our players did what they had to do to get a victory after they fell behind. That's an important step—and that's what we are most proud of as coaches."

While Clemson had been racing to an 8-1 record, Maryland had been doing the same. A battle of top-12 teams met in College Park for the championship of the ACC on November 18, 1978. It proved to be as exciting as a heavyweight championship fight.

It was a game of big play after big play. At one juncture, there were three consecutive scores from at least 60 yards out. Maryland scored on a blocked punt that was recovered in the end zone by Mike Carney. On the next possession, Jerry Butler got loose in the secondary and sped 87 yards for a score.

Broadcaster Jim Phillips simply said, "And Butler is off to the races."

Maryland countered with a 98-yard touchdown run by Steve Atkins, still the longest run in ACC history. But, Clemson got off the mat when Fuller hit Clark over the middle and the future NFL Player of the Year raced 67 yards for a touchdown.

That score tied the game at 21 after three quarters. Clemson's winning 70-yard drive came in the fourth quarter and culminated with a five-yard run by Brown. Maryland then drove to the Tiger seven, but on third down, Clemson's Bubba Brown stopped Maryland's Dean Richards for a loss, and the Terps settled for a field goal with 1:56 left.

Chuck Rose recovered the ensuing onside kick and when Fuller guided the Tigers to a pair of first downs, the game ended with a 28-24 victory, an ACC title, and a bid to the Gator Bowl to meet Ohio State.

"The story of today's game is more than what happened on the playing field," Pell said afterward. "It's something that was two years in the making, and it took an unbelieveable amount of work and dedication from our coaches and players.

"Last year, we learned how to win. This year, mainly in the last two weeks, we've shown that we have what it takes to win by coming from behind."

Clemson fans knew what they had done, and the folks at the Greenville-Spartanburg Airport were not ready for what happned next. When the Tigers' charter airplane from Washington, D.C., landed, more than 8,000 fans were there to greet them. For over a mile, cars were parked on both sides of the road leading to the airport all the way to I-85.

The regular season finale in Death Valley featured one of the most dominant rushing performances in Clemson history on a team basis. For only the third time in school history, three different Clemson backs rushed for at least 100 yards as the Tigers thrashed rival South Carolina 41-23.

The list of 100-yard rushers included Fuller (108), who was later named ACC Player of the Year for the second time at season's end, Sims (104), and Lester Brown (121). In all, the Tigers rushed for 397 yards on 70 carries.

"We basically ran four plays all game," Pell said. "We had more than that in our game plan, but there was never any reason to use it.

"It was a simple game plan, and we executed it well. We had so many players making super plays that it's hard to single any one person out."

FULLER TO BUTLER

Jerry Butler and Steve Fuller came to Clemson with few characteristics in common. Actually, Butler was in school on a track scholarship, while Fuller was one of the most highly recruited football players ever to come out of the state of South Carolina.

Butler came from the state's smallest athletic program (1-A classification) at Ware Shoals and Fuller's 4-A Spartanburg High Vikings was the highest classification. Butler's coach was Joe Burgess, and Fuller's mentor was Bill Carr. Spartanburg High was state runner-up to Spring Valley of Columbia in 1973, Fuller's junior year.

While their backgrounds were different, Fuller and Butler had one thing in common—they were both athletes. One could throw the football and the other could catch it.

No doubt the most famous completion in Clemson football history is Butler's winning catch, which Fuller threw, against South Carolina in 1977, when both were juniors. The Tigers had led at one time 24-0, but the Gamecocks had rallied to go ahead, 27-24. A six-play, 67-yard drive by Clemson, which took 59 seconds, ended with that spectacular 20-yard completion that left 56,410 limp.

In the second game that season, when Clemson had edged past Georgia 7-6 in Athens, Tiger Head Coach Charlie Pell had started a ritual when Clemson won—passing out cigars to players in the dressing room afterward.

That night in Columbia, after Phillip Logan had scored on a 40-yard pass play from Ron Bass to give the Gamecocks their three-point lead, several of the South Carolina players pulled up their game jersey to reveal another shirt that was imprinted with "No Cigars Tonight" on it.

Little did they know that one of the many Fuller-to-Butler passes was just a few minutes away, which would turn their zenith of happiness into the darkest of dreams.

But this pair would leave memories in the minds of Clemson fans that would be difficult to erase.

Their last three years, the duo had completions of over 50 yards three different times. Butler caught at least one pass in 35 consecutive games, had five games with over 100 yards in receptions, and set school records in career receptions (139) and career reception yardage (2,223).

Fuller set many school records. He had over 100 yards passing in 21 games. His 1,655 yards passing in 1977, his total offense (2,164) in 1978, and his career total offense yardage (6,096) were new school marks.

The Fuller-Butler connection would be successful for 10 touchdowns during the pair's parallel careers at Clemson, three in their sophomore season of 1976. But then the corner turned in '77, and the Tigers would go to their first postseason game in 18 years when the Gator Bowl beckoned.

Butler's longest reception from Fuller came against Maryland at College Park in '78 in a game many still say is the best ACC game ever. The league championship was on the line, and there were 7-, 14- and 21-all ties before the Tigers came out a 28-24 winner. Clemson's first three scores knotted the game each time, and the one that tied the game at 14 was an 87-yard strike. Butler caught the only touchdown in a 7-3 win over N.C. State in '77, in addition to his winning catch against the Gamecocks.

But the game where Fuller and Butler would hardly let anyone else play with the ball was against Georgia Tech in Atlanta in '77.

Fuller ran the ball 13 times and only had a net gain of 13 yards. But two of the rushes were for scores. He only passed nine times, and completed five (163 yards), but Butler was on the receiving end of all five catches.

Those 163 yards receiving at the time were the most ever by a Clemson player in a game. In that memorable Maryland game, Fuller threw for 216 yards on just eight completions, and Butler had five of those for 140 yards.

In the 1977 Yellow Jacket contest, a 31-14 Tigers victory, an opening drive taking five minutes off the clock resulted in a 37-yard field goal from Jimmy Russell.

Steve Fuller and Jerry Butler helped start Clemson back to national prominence with that performance in 1977. In the next several years, the Tigers would play in many bowls and claim a National Championship in 1981.

Fuller and Butler were both first-round draft choices out of college.

Most Clemson fans believe this pair is still No. 1. The seed planted by them in 1975—their freshman year—continues to produce a harvest.

FORD TAKES OVER

As the seventh-ranked Tigers began prepping to play No. 20 Ohio State in the Gator Bowl Classic, the headlines in the local newspapers started to change daily. Florida had fired head coach Doug Dickey and was searching for a new coach to lead the Gators' program.

Pell, who first came to Clemson as an assistant head coach to Parker in 1976, was an ideal candidate. Pell had taken a Clemson program that had a lot of talent and taught them how to become champions. At first, he dismissed rumors he was talking to Florida and that he was being named its next head coach.

Upon leaving to accept the Florida job and to begin recruiting there, Pell recommended that his former assistant head coach, Danny Ford, become Clemson's new head coach. Within 24 hours, Clemson's Board of Trustees agreed and approved the former Alabama tight end as their next head coach.

"No other candidate was considered or discussed," board chairman Paul McAlister said.

Intially, Pell wanted to finish what he started in 1978 and asked if he could coach the Tigers in the Gator Bowl, but Clemson boosters were not so happy about his departure, and they asked for his resignation immediately. Many believed Pell betrayed the university and its backers, and they insisted that he not be allowed to coach in the Gator Bowl.

When Pell returned from Florida, he met with his staff and players in a series of meetings and ultimately decided it was best for all parties that he turn over all preparations to Ford. The new Clemson coach, who was only 30 years old at the time, was able to retain all but two of the coaches on the staff, for the others—defensive coaches Dwight Adams and Joe Kines—went to Florida with Pell.

Ford quickly went to work preparing for the Gator Bowl and recruiting. Knowing he was about to lose 26 seniors, he knew he had to keep the kids who had already committed to the program on board and not follow Pell to Florida. Luckily for Clemson, Ford was the recruiting coordinator and had great relationships with several blue chip recruits like running back Chuck McSwain.

McSwain remembers vividly what Pell said to him in hopes of getting him to back off on his pledge to the Tigers.

"Charlie was here when I was first recruited here," McSwain said. "Charlie decided to leave and he said the reason he decided to leave and go to Florida is because Clemson can't win a national championship. He said, 'Why don't you come with me to Florida?' I thought about it to a point, until I found out most of the Clemson coaching staff was going to stay. Then I decided I was going to Clemson, and three years later we win the National Championship.

"It was funny because he said that was the reason why he was leaving. He said, 'It will never happen at Clemson.'"

With recruiting going well, Ford's next task was getting his team ready to play the Buckeyes in less than three weeks in Jacksonville, FL. His first game as head coach wasn't an easy one, either.

He was coaching against future Hall of Fame coach Woody Hayes. His Buckeye program was one of the more respected and biggest programs in the country.

"Before the game, I didn't know if I was going to be able to make it to the game," said Ford. "I almost lost my guts about four o'clock. But, when we started the game, I forgot about it. It was just like lining up and playing for the first time."

The 1978 Gator Bowl was a landmark game in Clemson and college football history. Clemson won a narrow decision 17-15, its first win ever against a Big Ten team.

Freshman Cliff Austin, who had started the season on the junior varsity squad, scored what proved to be the winning touchdown. Four years later, he scored the first touchdown in Clemson's National Championship victory over Nebraska.

Ohio State scored late and went for the tie, but Jim Stuckey broke through the line and stopped freshman quarterback Art Schlichter short of paydirt. Ohio State had one more chance in the final minutes. The Buckeyes drove to the Clemson 40. But, on a second-down play, Charlie Bauman intercepted a Schlichter pass, the only interception of the second-team middle guard's career.

Bauman had dropped into the passing lane to make the theft and was then run out of bounds at midfield on the Ohio State side of the field.

When Bauman stood up, he was struck in the throat, shockingly, by Hayes. A fight ensued, and when it was sorted out by the officials, Clemson was given possession of the ball, and Ohio State was charged with a 15-yard unsportsmanlike penalty.

"I think he may have hit me," said Bauman after the game. "I was face to face with him. There was a lot of commotion and in the excitement I think he may have hit me. I just want to see the film."

The film revealed that Hayes indeed hit Bauman, throwing a forearm punch right into Bauman's throat.

Clemson ran out the clock to gain the victory. The next day, Hayes was fired by Ohio State and never coached again.

"Coach Hayes is a great football coach and a great man. I hate to see it happen, and I hate that Clemson was involved in it," Ford said in a press conference the morning after the game. "He's done a lot for college football, and I'm sorry that we had to be involved at the end."

The bizzare ending might have taken some of the attention away from Clemson's victory, but the Tigers finished the year ranked sixth in the final Associated Press Poll thanks to an 11-1 record, the highest in Clemson history at the time.

THE MYSTIQUE OF THE ORANGE PANTS

Danny Ford was searching for something to spark his football team. Prior to the 1980 season, Ford had his team manger order a special pair of pants for the Tigers to wear against archrival South Carolina in the season finale. Ford wasn't sure how he was going to introduce the pants to the team or if he would even wear them at all that year.

But after falling to Maryland 34-7 the week before the Palmetto State's big game, Ford knew it was time to break out these so-called special pants. It was either now or never.

Entering that year's South Carolina game, Ford found himself in a pinch. After losing their last two games in 1979, and then to fall to 5-5 through the first 10 weeks in 1980, Clemson fans became restless, and some were calling for Ford's job.

"It did not look real good for us that week," Ford said.

It looked even worse with No. 14 South Carolina coming to town. The Gamecocks were already Gator Bowl-bound, and they featured the best running game in the country thanks to running back George Rogers, who went on to win the Heisman Trophy.

Knowing he would need to get a spark in the locker room, Ford called his two defensive leaders, cornerback Willie Underwood and linebacker Jeff Davis, into his office before a practice that week. That's when the former Alabama player pulled out a pair of burnt-orange pants. The pants took Underwood and Davis aback for a second, but they agreed to wear them.

Ford asked that Underwood and Davis keep it quiet because he was going to surprise the team after the team meal the Friday night before the game.

"We knew something was up, but we didn't really know what," said running back Cliff Austin.

When dinner was done, Ford came up front, where he said a few words about the game and then reached down and held up the orange pants.

"This is what we are wearing tomorrow," Ford said.

"When he did that, the room went crazy," said Davis. "That's all the guys could talk about was wearing those orange pants with the orange jersey and the orange helmet and how the fans were going to love it. Coach Ford was a master motivator. He knew how to push the right buttons.

"That moment relaxed us. All of sudden, we weren't thinking about having to win this game to save his job or about how we were going to stop George Rogers or any of that. We were just looking forward to playing the game."

To surprise the fans, Ford asked his players to put their thigh pads in their orange pants and to wear their orange jerseys over their white pants for pregame warm ups. With the thigh pads already in place, it would make the transition of changing the pants faster when they got back in the locker room.

"We all knew we were going to change into the orange pants when we got back in the locker room so we were pumped up and ready to go," Davis said. "We knew how excited the fans were going to get when they see us come to the top of the Hill wearing all orange."

When the fans saw the Tigers gather at Howard's Rock dressed in all orange for the very first time, the sell-out crowd of 64,000 in Death Valley got extremely loud.

"When the fans saw us, they went absolutely crazy," Davis said. "We knew we were going to win."

It did not appear as if Clemson was going to win late in the third quarter, when the Gamecocks drove the football to the Clemson 16 and was in position to take their first lead of the day. But with 32 seconds remaining in the quarter, Underwood stepped in front of a Garry Harper pass and raced 64 yards down the sideline before stepping out of bounds at the USC 24.

Six plays later, quarterback Homer Jordan called his own number from the one-yard line as the Tigers took a 13-6 lead.

Though Rogers carried the ball 28 times for 168 yards, Clemson kept him at bay, and out of the end zone.

"Our goal was to keep him from breaking the ball outside and make someone else beat us," Davis said.

There was no one else.

On South Carolina's next possession, Harper again tried to go outside with a pass, but the pass was again cut off by Underwood, who this time made sure he did not step out of bounds as he raced 37 yards down the sideline to give Clemson a 20-6 lead.

The two interceptions were the first of Underwood's career, a span of 41 games.

Later on, the Tigers got a 15-yard Jeff McCall touchdown to end the scoring in the 27-6 victory. Underwood finished his day with 101 return yards, which is still a Clemson record. He also recorded 17 tackles and was named the National Player of the Week by Sports Illustrated.

The win over the Gamecocks lifted Clemson to its perfect run in 1981, which ended with a 22-15 victory over Nebraska in the 1982 Orange Bowl, sealing the Tigers' first and then-only national championship in football.

Clemson went on to post a 16-2 record under Danny Ford when it wore orange pants.

CLEMSON EARNED ITS NATIONAL CHAMPIONSHIP

Thanks to its victory over 14th-ranked South Carolina, Clemson finished the 1980 season with a 6-5 record. It was not a mark really to brag too much about, but to hear the players coming back from the 1981 season tell it, they felt as if they won the National Championship.

"What Willie did, and that game, motivated us the entire off-season," Austin said. "We were changing. That spring, we were changing from being a loser to a winner. We were fueled by our upset win over South Carolina to end the season and it just kept going.

"We came out of that spring a better football team. Our confidence level was high. That was the roughest spring, but the best spring that I went through during my time at Clemson."

When the Tigers got back to Clemson that summer, the tough times continued in camp as they prepped for the upcoming season. The offense was led by a potent rushing attack that featured Austin, Jeff McCall, Kevin Mack, and McSwain. Then there was All-ACC quarterback Homer Jordan and All-America wide receiver Perry Tuttle that gave the Tigers just enough of a passing threat to keep defenses honest.

The defense was led by Davis, defensive tackle Jeff Bryant, defensive tackle William Devane, defensive tackle Dan Benish, and All-America safety Terry Kinard. Clemson also had a freshman phenom at nose guard named William "The Refrigerator" Perry, who dominated opposing centers with his raw and dynamic athletic ability.

Overall, the Tigers finished second nationally in scoring defense, seventh in rushing defense, seventh in turnover margin and eighth in total defense. Clemson led the ACC in total defense, rushing defense, scoring defense, and interceptions.

In a 13-3 victory over No. 4 Georgia in Week 3, they forced nine turnovers, still a Clemson record for one game.

"I can remember when we played that if the offense lost the ball we go tell them that we are going to get the ball back," said Davis, who led the Tigers in tackles and was an All-Amercian in 1981. "I can remember that most of the time, that is exactly what happened."

Overall, Clemson only allowed three teams to score more than 10 points in 1981—Wake Forest, South Carolina, and Nebraska—and it went 18 quarters without giving up a touchdown during one stretch.

"We didn't want people to score on us, and we wanted to physically dominate people," Davis said. "In a sick way, that was our joy. Yeah, we may not have beaten everybody by 21 points, but your body and your mental state of mind said we beat you by 21 points.

"That's the kind of football we played. We had no reason for how great we were playing."

But that reason was Ford. Just 33 years old, Ford became the youngest coach in college football history to win a national championship, which still holds true today.

Ford was a fiery coach who coached off his players' emotions.

A player's coach, Ford knew what buttons to push to motivate individuals and his team.

"He was a tough guy," Davis said. "He was very well respected. He had fire in him, and we fed off of that. He basically took what Charlie Pell started and took it to the next level.

"When we played for him it was hard for us to look ahead. It was hard for us to think too highly of ourselves because he had a way of pulling us back down."

Davis recalls if it wasn't for Ford and his staff keeping them grounded, especially after the 13-3 win over Georgia, things might have been different in 1981.

"The coaching staff did a good job of keeping us focused, keeping our goals out there and understanding that some great things can happen if we keep on playing the way we had been playing," he said. "I think that's why we won the national championship because we never really bought into the hype.

"We never bought into how great we were. It was more important for us to prove how great we were game in and game out."

With every passing week, critics from around the country predicted this would be the week the Cinderella story from the small upstate town would end. But each week the Tigers found a way to win. When the offense finally got things going in the second half of their 21-3 victory over Kentucky, Clemson became a runaway train that ran over anything in its path.

"It was about the business at hand," Davis said. "That is what our team focused on. It was the business at hand."

After the win over Kentucky, the Tigers steamrolled over Virginia 27-0. Then scored 31 points in the second and third quarters in a 38-10 win at Duke.

The offense then rushed for 304 yards in a 17-7 victory against N.C. State, before the record-setting 82-24 afternoon against Wake Forest on Halloween.

But the game that told the team, the coaching staff, and the national media that 1981 was the year of the Clemson Tigers—was their 10-8 win in Week 10 at North Carolina. On that afternoon, the Tigers won a hard-fought, tough and physical football game, against a North Carolina team that finished the year 10-2 and ranked in the Associate Press Top 10.

"We knew we played some great football and we knew we played a tough brand of football," Davis said. "We had been tested and tried. We hand been in the tough football games. We had been in the 10-8 games. If I had to say there was one game when we started thinking about the national championship, I would say it was that game."

Clemson went on to capture the ACC Championship—its first goal—the following week in a 21-7 win against Maryland. It was just the Tigers' second victory in 10 years against the Terps and first since a 28-24 victory, which wrapped up the ACC title in 1978.

The following week against rival South Carolina, Clemson closed a perfect regular season for the first time since 1948 with a 29-13 victory in Columbia, bringing everything full circle and setting the stage for the greatest moment in Clemson football history.

"That [1980] season balanced our attitude even though we had success early. There was no reason for us to get the big head," Davis said. "There was still a lot of work to be done and we were fortunate to be in the position we were in."

Game 1: Clemson 45, Wofford 10

The Tigers did not look perfect when they opened the season at home against Wofford. The Terriers were an NAIA school at the time and was a late addition to the schedule when Villanova dropped football in March of 1981.

Not knowing much about Wofford, the Tigers struggled early on. At the end of the first quarter the score was tied at 3-3. Not exactly the start one might imagine for a team that went on to win a National Championship four months later.

In the second quarter, the Tigers got going as Jordan hit Tuttle with an 80-yard touchdown pass for Clemson's first touchdown of the season. Jordan later added a 14-yard run by halftime to give Clemson a 17-3 lead at the break.

"If we hadn't thrown that big bomb, it could have been 3-3 at halftime," Ford said.

Clemson won the second half 28-7, but the Terriers' wingbone offense gained 165 yards on the ground. Only Nebraska had more yards rushing against Clemson that season.

"They had an excellent game plan in the first half and ran us ragged with their misdirection plays," Ford said. "We just had a whole lot more depth than they did."

Game 2: Clemson 13, Tulane 5

Clemson played its first-ever game indoors, defeating Tulane in a defensive struggle. All five Clemson defensive backs had at least one interception as the Clemson defense forced seven turnovers overall.

Tulane scored on a field goal and a safety to take a 5-0 lead at the end of the first quarter. But Clemson's defense allowed just 40 yards rushing in the game and just 177 yards of total offense altogether.

Davis had 20 tackles, while Terry Kinard had 12 tackles and an interception.

"When you go back and look at what happened in that season, there were several times we were behind," Ford said. "We won some close games. We weren't that good yet. We found ways, like against Tulane, to win."

Clemson did not get on the scoreboard until midway through the second quarter, when defensive end Joe Glenn fell on a Tulane fumble at the Green Wave 25-yard line. Moments later, Austin ran it from the four to give the Tigers a 7-5 lead, which they carried into halftime.

Tulane fumbled the kickoff to open the second half, but a mishandled snap prevented Clemson kicker Bob Paulling from a 33-yard field goal attempt. The Tigers ended the third quarter with a nice drive, and this time Pauling was able to get off a 31-yard field goal that was true for a 10-5 lead.

On the ensuing possession, Clemson picked off a Tulane pass, and a few minutes later, Paulling added his second field goal of the night, a 37-yarder for a 13-5 lead that because of the way the defense was playing made it seem like a two-touchdown lead.

"It was a rough game," Tuttle said. "They were a real physical team, and I'm glad that we got out of this one the way we did."

Game 3: Clemson 13, No. 4 Georgia 3

Clemson forced a school-record nine turnovers, including five interceptions, on its way to a 13-3 victory over No. 4 and defending National Champion Georgia.

An interception by strong safety Tim Childress set up the game's only touchdown, an eight-yard pass from Jordan to Tuttle in the second quarter. Donald Igwebuike booted two field goals of 39 and 29 yards to counter Georgia kicker Kevin Butler's 40-yard kick in the third quarter to cap the win.

"This was probably the biggest game we are going to play this year," Davis said afterward. "When we lost to Georgia last year, we kind of lost our morale. It hurt us the rest of the season.

"We know the rest of the games are important, but we had to win this one."

The win propelled the Tigers into the national rankings the next week at No. 19 in the Associated Press Poll and No. 18 in the Coaches Poll.

Game 4: No. 14 Clemson 21, Kentucky 3

Kentucky, which was coming off a near upset of SEC heavyweight Alabama, completely stymied the Clemson offense in the first half and led 3-0 at the break thanks to a 40-yard field goal in the first quarter.

But the Tigers took control of the game on the opening possession of the second half. Clemson drove 83 yards in 13 plays, which was capped by an 11-yard Kevin Mack touchdown. After recovering a Kentucky fumble on the Wildcats' ensuing possession, Jordan took the football in from the three for a 14-3 lead.

"We didn't play worth a lick in the first half, offensively or defensively," Ford said. "We couldn't establish anything in the first half. We were lucky to be down 3-0."

The Tigers put the game away in the fourth quarter with a 94-yard drive which consumed nearly six minutes of the clock. McSwain capped the drive with a 3-yard plunge. Clemson amassed 213 yards in the second half, while holding Kentucky to 97.

"The team came out and played like Clemson should play in the second half," Ford said.

Game 5: No. 9 Clemson 27, Virginia 0

The No. 9 Tigers had little trouble against a Virginia team that was 0-20 against Clemson all-time coming in. The Tigers racked up 265 yards rushing in their ACC opener and finished the afternoon with 426 yards of total offense.

The Cavaliers, on the other hand, were limited to 237 total yards and never sniffed the Clemson end zone. The Tigers got two Cliff Austin touchdowns and one from Jeff McCall in the 27-0 victory.

"Our goal was to keep them from scoring," said defensive end Bill Smith. "Anytime a defense can keep a team from scoring, it's got to help your offense. They ran to our weak side in the second half and did a good job until we adjusted, but we really got serious when they got near the goal line."

Game 6: No. 6 Clemson 38, Duke 10

A young offensive coordinator by the name of Steve Spurrier stunned Clemson in Death Valley the year before in a 34-17 victory. The Blue Devils were 0-5 coming into that contest, while the Tigers were 4-1. And to make matters worse, it came on Homecoming.

That loss humiliated Clemson and was the beginning of its downfall during the 6-5 season. The players didn't forget and neither did Ford, who said in the week leading up to the game that Duke would rather beat Clemson than any other team, including its archrival North Carolina.

"They don't like Clemson," he said. "They're not impressed with Clemson and don't have any reason to be impressed with Clemson."

By the end of the third quarter, Duke was completely impressed with Clemson. The Tigers jumped out to a 31-3 lead in the third quarter on its way to a 38-10 victory.

"This was my best game at Clemson," Jordan said. "The receivers ran great routes and I had a good day throwing the ball."

The Clemson offense rolled up 563 total yards with 323 of that coming on the ground. Jordan completed 13 of 19 passes for 198 yards and a touchdown. Austin ran for 178 yards and two touchdowns on just 19 carries.

"We were not ready to play last year, but we were ready this year," Austin said. "I think it showed."

Game 7: No. 4 Clemson 17, N.C. State 7

Clemson needed its defense more than ever before as it hosted N.C. State in the first Textile Bowl. After giving up its first rushing touchdown of the season in the first quarter, the Clemson defense smothered the Wolfpack the rest of the day, holding them to a mere 201 total yards.

The Clemson offense didn't have a great day, but it did rush for 304 yards, controlling the line of scrimmage and the football for much of the afternoon. Jordan rushed for a career-high 104 yards, while Austin and McCall each scored touchdowns in the 17-7 win.

Trailing 7-3 late in the second quarter, the offense finally got something going as Jordan accounted for 44 of the 65 yards on a scoring drive Austin capped with a one-yard plunge into the end zone.

The score remained 10-7 until midway through the fourth quarter, when Jeff McCall broke loose off tackle and rumbled 15 yards for the game-clinching score.

"We weren't sharp today," Ford said afterward. "We weren't clicking on 12 volts. Our defense did the job in the second half. At the same time, our offense took control of the line of scrimmage and we were able to move the ball pretty good, though we didn't score the points we would have liked to."

Game 8: No. 3 Clemson 82, Wake Forest 24

Scoring was not a problem when Clemson came back home to play Wake Forest on Halloween. The Tigers set ACC records for total yards (756), rushing yards (536), margin of victory (58 points), and points scored (82) in the 82-24 victory in Death Valley.

"We've really been needing a game like that," offensive tackle Lee Nanney said. "Hopefully, it will silence the critics who said we didn't have an offense."

Nine Tigers scored on the day, including three touchdowns by McSwain and two by Austin.

Game 9: No. 2 Clemson 10, No. 8 North Carolina 8

Ford knew Game 9 of the 1981 season would be the toughest one left on his schedule. He also knew it would be the one with the most distractions, too.

Clemson, 8-0, was ranked No. 2 by the Associated Press and No. 3 by United Press International (the Coaches Poll) coming into its November 7, 1981, clash at North Carolina. The Tar Heels were 7-1 and ranked No. 8 in both major polls.

"The North Carolina game did more for us winning the national championship than any other game," Davis said. "It was the ultimate test for us. We expected to win in Death Valley and we expected teams to already be behind when the whistle blew in Death Valley. But, to go into the backyard of a top 10 football team with everything at stake, and win, that did it for us.

"Remember, North Carolina had everything to play for. It's right there for them. You can think there were people wondering 'Can Clemson stay focused?' And we beat them in a fight. It was an all-out brawl. May the best man win! It was man-on-man."

This was the first time in the history of ACC football that two of its schools clashed in a battle of top 10 teams. With an ACC Championship and a major bowl bid at stake, it was dubbed the biggest game to ever be played in the state of North Carolina.

"(North Carolina) came to play," Bryant said. "They were at home and they were a top 10 team. We both were striving for that goal which was to win the ACC and take it further from that.

"It was a very physical game. I can remember being sore for a couple of days after that."

It was also Homecoming Weekend in Chapel Hill, NC, and it was the last game at Kenan Stadium for UNC's seniors—a class that had helped the Tar Heels win an ACC Championship the year before and beat traditional powers such as Texas and Oklahoma along the way.

To top things off, there were bowl representatives from eight bowl games in attendance, more than at any other game that afternoon across the country. *Sports Illustrated* had been at Clemson all week to chronicle the Tigers' magical run and was in Chapel Hill on that afternoon. ABC was broadcasting it as part of their regional coverage and carried the game throughout most of the country.

All of America's eyes seem to be placed on this small school from the foothills of South Carolina, and Ford knew he had to do something to turn his team's focus to what was really important—beating the Tar Heels.

So the 33-year-old coach put up "Carolina On My Mind" posters on just about every available space in the Jervey Athletic Center that week.

"Were we excited about the hype? Yes! We wanted the stakes high," said Davis. "It didn't get better than this. This was another opportunity for us to do something in Clemson football history that had not been done.

"We took all of that into consideration. We would not have approached that game any other way because there was the crown jewel of college football standing right in front of us. We could almost touch it.

"The world was watching. We had a great opportunity. It was everything that a young man and a young student-athlete could want."

Nobody loved playing North Carolina more than Davis. A native of Greensboro, NC, he has a distain for the "Powder Blue" like no one else.

"North Carolina, for me, was a big game," he said. "I'm from North Carolina, and I want to beat them more than anyone else we play. This was my last opportunity to make a statement in North Carolina that I made the right decision in coming to Clemson."

It also didn't help that the Tar Heels had taken down Davis and the Tigers the year before in Death Valley. It was the first time he had lost to North Carolina and the 223-pound linebacker did not like the taste it left in his mouth.

It also stung because the Tar Heels were clearly the more physical team in 1980, thanks to a future Hall of Famer named Lawrence Taylor, who had sacked Jordan for a nine-yard loss during a goal-line stand to preserve UNC's 24-19 victory.

"We didn't like them and they didn't like us," Davis said. "We both knew it was going to be a hard-fought physical game. They had some very good athletes and they were a very good football team. We were going into their backyard. It was going to be tough."

Ford knew it was going to be tough too, and though he didn't tell his team, he had some doubt whether they could stand up to the Tar Heels' physicality.

"I was concerned about how we can play physically with this team," he said. "We were outmuscled in 1980, which did not happen too often with our football teams. Their game plan in 1980 was to outmuscle Clemson, and I think they did it.

"We knew that's what they were going to try and do again."

He was right. North Carolina came out to hurt Clemson. It wanted to be the intimidator. It wanted to be more physical. The Tar Heels did that in some way. They knocked McCall out of the game in the fourth quarter with two broken ribs as well as defensive tackle Dan Benish with a sprained knee.

McCall had a game-high 84 yards before he left and scored the game's lone touchdown—a seven-yard run with 6:54 to play in the second quarter.

But, don't think North Carolina went untouched. The Tigers removed UNC quarterback Rod Elkins in the second quarter after he led his team on a field goal drive. Elkins had sprained his ankle two weeks before against South Carolina, and though he did not start the Clemson game, he was soon put in after starter Scott Stankavage was sacked once and fumbled twice on the Tar Heels' first two drives.

On the very next play from scrimmage following McCall's touchdown, Elkins reinjured his ankle and did not return. With North Carolina's best quarterback now out of the game, the Tigers could concentrate more on shutting down The Tar Heels' potent rushing attack.

UNC ranked second in the country running the football coming in, but Clemson held the Heels to 84 yards on 42 carries. Stopping the run had been the Tigers' ammo all season. With new defensive coordinator Tom Harper at the helm, Clemson led the ACC in rushing defense and ranked second in the country.

"We would put a goose egg on our [defensive] board before every game," Davis said. "We didn't do it as a

mark or just to put something up there. No, we actually believed it. It was symbolic to us. You were not going to score on us. Even if you get in our territory, you might have a chance to get a field goal, but you can forget about scoring on us.

"We took pride in that. You were not supposed to score on us. We even took pride in goal line [situations] in practice. I don't care how close you put the ball you were not going to score on our defense. We believed that. That was not some tough guy talk or something to motivate people. We believed it."

North Carolina running back Kelvin Bryant believed it. In his first game back after arthroscopic knee surgery five weeks earlier, he gained just 31 yards on 13 carries, as did fellow running back Tyrone Anthony on eight carries.

"When I see Kelvin, he likes to joke that he gets a headache right when he sees me because we were hitting him so hard that day," Davis smiled.

Bill Smith is sort of the unsung hero. The play everyone remembers is Jeff Bryant having the presence of mind to jump on what appeared to be an incomplete pass with 57 seconds to play.

The pass was ruled a lateral, and by jumping on the loose football, Bryant secured Clemson's 10-8 victory in front of a then-record crowd at Kenan Stadium of 53,611. But what people don't recall is who actually caused the fumble.

That would be Smith. After moving the ball out from the shadow of their own goal line, the Tar Heels found themselves with a first down at their own 40 thanks to a 12-yard scramble by Stankavage on third-and-10 from the two, then a 9-yard pass to wide receiver Ron Richardson and a 14-yard pass to Anthony.

With just over a minute to play and one timeout left, the Tar Heels called a screen pass to fullback Alex Burrus. Stankavage threw the ball behind the line of scrimmage, and when Burrus went to make the catch, Smith met him, knocking the ball to the ground.

The ball rolled 15 yards backward toward the Clemson sideline, and that is where Bryant jumped on the football at the UNC 25-yard line.

"They were moving the ball down the field, and all they needed was a field goal to win," Smith said. "That was just a timely play that happened."

Timely indeed; in fact, it was perhaps the calling-card of the 1981 defense. In 1981, Clemson ranked seventh in the nation in turnover margin and led the ACC in forced turnovers with what is still a school record 41.

"That play epitomizes our football team," Davis said. "We are talking about Bill Smith, a guy when people talk about our national championship team, they don't think about. Those were the type of players we had that made plays when plays needed to be made. He makes that play and then Jeff Bryant was the only guy on the field that had the sense of mind to know that was a lateral and 'I'm getting on this thing.'

"That's the kind of football team we were. We did the little things. We played hard and we tackled hard."

No team that season learned that any better than the Tar Heels. Twice, North Carolina had first-and-goal inside the Clemson 10, and both times it was held to short field attempts by Brooks Barwick.

Early in the second quarter, North Carolina appeared to have a possible touchdown on a third-down swing pass in the flats to Anthony, but Clemson All-America safety Terry Kinard came out of nowhere to drag him down at the five. The Tar Heels settled for a 22-yard Barwick field goal and led 3-0.

Now trailing 10-5, following a Donald Igwebuike 39-yard field goal, UNC took its second drive of the third quarter and marched down to the Clemson four thanks to a 21-yard halfback pass from Anthony to Griffin. But Davis and Kinard stuffed Kelvin Bryant for a five-yard loss on the next play, and then Stankavage threw incomplete on second and third down, forcing the Tar Heels to settle for a 26-yard Barick field goal.

In the fourth quarter, North Carolina again had an opportunity to take the lead following a muffed punt by Billy Davis at the Clemson 37. After gaining just four yards on first and second down, the Tar Heels' hopes for taking the lead were dashed when freshman nose guard William Perry broke through and sacked Stankavage for a 10-yard loss.

"With the kind of defense we had, we never panicked," Jeff Bryant said. "We are going to make the big play. It was always role call to the ball."

Following a Clemson punt, UNC again moved into Tiger territory to the 39, but again the defensive stiffened, with a tackle for a loss and two incomplete passes.

Unable to move the ball, Clemson punter Dale Hatcher then pinned the Heels deep in their own territory at the two-yard line with 2:19 to play, setting up the final dramatics in one of the biggest victories in Clemson history.

Jeff Bryant, who played 12 seasons in the NFL, had a stellar career at Clemson, but it wasn't until Tom Harper became the defensive coordinator in the spring of 1981 that he finally realized what kind of player he could be.

Harper did wonders for Bryant's play. He helped him become sound fundamentally. He helped him with his technique. He helped him become a better football player, and a better person.

"Tom Harper was very instrumental in my development," Bryant said. "He was a great guy. I wish I had Tom Harper all four years. I'm thankful I had him when I did though because he really made a difference with me."

Bryant credited Harper's instruction as one of the reasons he stayed alert and recognized the lateral on North Carolina's final drive.

"I was coming up field pretty hard because I figured they were going to pass the ball. I had a good rush on and I was about as deep as the quarterback," he said. "I noticed him throwing the ball, and I saw the hit, but I noticed he threw the ball behind him.

"Bill made a great hit and I saw the ball coming out so my thinking was to rush over there and get on it because no one else thought it was a lateral. I thought it was one because of the angle I was at because I was right there behind the quarterback as he threw the ball."

Smith, who admits he did not know it was a lateral at the time, sometimes wonders about the "what ifs" had Bryant not jumped on the loose ball.

"Who knows what would have happened had we lost that game, but thank goodness we can say 'what if' all we want because we didn't lose it," he said. "We won it and we did all we could do to win it. That was the mentality of that team all year."

After Jordan fell to the ground three times to run out the final 57 seconds, a mass celebration broke out on the Clemson sideline. As Tar Heel fans made their way to the exit, the Clemson players and the 10,000 or so Tiger fans who traveled up to Chapel Hill stayed and enjoyed what they had accomplished.

"We knew that anything was possible at that point," Bryant said.

With a victory over the No. 8 Tar Heels behind them, Clemson for the first time admitted the possibility of going undefeated and playing for a National Championship was on its mind.

"It was important because we started thinking a little bit now about being undefeated," Davis said. "Until that point, we were not trying to touch it. There might have been a few rumblings here and there, but we were all about one game at a time.

"At that point, and where we were at, you were going to have to do something phenomenal to beat us."

Game 10: No. 2 Clemson 21, Maryland 7

It was Jordan that played phenomenal in clinching the ACC Championship for Clemson, and Maryland had Tulane head coach Vince Gibson to thank for that. After beating the Terrapins the previous week, Gibson said, "Clemson won't defeat Maryland because of the lack of a consistent passing game."

Jordan was anything but inconsistent against Maryland. He was responsible for 312 total yards—the third highest total in Clemson history at the time—including three touchdown passes, while completing 20 of 29 passes.

"I didn't read it, but I heard about it," Jordan said.

Thanks to Jordan's play, the Tigers wrapped up their second ACC title in 14 years and their eighth overall with a 21-7 victory on Senior Day in Death Valley.

"Our primary goal before the season was to win the ACC Championship," Ford said.

Two of Jordan's touchdown strikes went to Tuttle, who had 10 catches for 151 yards to become Clemson's all-time reception leader, while the other went to Jerry Gaillard, who ended his Clemson career with his first touchdown catch.

The Tiger defense held Maryland to 236 yards and only allowed a touchdown after the Terrapins recovered a fumble at the Clemson seven.

Game 11: No. 2 Clemson 29, South Carolina 13

Ford was a little ahead of his times when it came to using running backs. In the late-1970s and '80s, it was common for college football teams to have one running back to carry the load. South Carolina did it with George Rogers during his Heisman Trophy campaign, as did Georgia with Herschel Walker.

Ford, who only thought about the forward pass if he was forced to do so, believed in having a stable of running backs at his disposal. When it came to using running backs, no one was better than Ford.

"One guy would start a game, but the other guy might end it," Austin said.

Austin, along with McSwain, played tailback for the Tigers in 1981. Austin led the Tigers with 824 yards and scored nine touchdowns that season, while McSwain was second on the team with 692 yards and seven scores.

Clemson also used McCall (457 yards and five touchdowns) and Kevin Mack (287 yards and two touchdowns) at fullback, giving the Tigers four All-ACC-caliber running backs who could carry the rock at any time.

"Back then, we did not get but nine carries a game," McSwain said. "Cliff would get nine, and then I would get nine. We might not have had a bunch of yards, but it might have been 75 yards or so for Cliff and 70 for me.

"But, what we did was pound the ball and pound the ball and wear people out. We didn't score very many points, other than the Wake Forest game, so we would just keep the ball away from people."

Regardless, it worked for Clemson, and when the Tigers got down to the end of the season, their talented depth in the running game came to the forefront. McCall, who scored Clemson's only touchdown at No. 8 North Carolina that year, went down in the same game with broken ribs and missed the Maryland and South Carolina games.

However, Mack stepped in, and the Tigers did not miss a beat the following two weeks.

Against South Carolina, Austin tweaked his ankle midway through the contest, and McSwain took over. All he did was carry the ball 25 times for a career-high 151 yards, while scoring two second-half touchdowns in the Tigers' 29-13 victory over the Gamecocks.

"I was fortunate in the South Carolina game because Cliff got hurt," said McSwain, now an athletic director and football coach in his home state of North Carolina. "That is the only reason I got that many [carries]. That's three of four ball games for me.

"I was raising my hand that I wanted out. Those were too many carries."

Though he may have been tired, he did not look it, especially when he plowed over several USC defenders on his way to a 23-yard touchdown in the fourth quarter that sealed the Clemson victory and wrapped up a perfect 11-0 regular season.

What made it even more special for McSwain was the fact his little brother, Rod, blocked a punt in the first quarter that changed the momentum of the game. The ball rolled into the end zone where Johnny Rembert fell on the ball for the Tigers' first score.

Though Clemson missed the extra point and still trailed 7-6 at the time, every one of the 56,971 fans could feel that the Tigers were going to end their special season with a win in Columbia after that play.

"You could not ask for a better way to end the year than to be down there and have Rod block a punt and then I had the day that I had," Chuck McSwain said. "When I look back, it brings back good memories. We were very fortunate."

From there, Clemson got a 24-yard field goal from Paulling, and then Jordan scampered off the left side for an 11-yard touchdown to put the Tigers in front 15-7 at the break.

After South Carolina appeared to make things interesting with a Gordon Beckham 10-yard pass in the third quarter, the Tigers, behind McSwain's running and Jordan's passing, went right back down the field and seized control of the game with a one-yard run by McSwain.

McSwain then added on with his 23-yard scoring run in the fourth quarter to send Clemson on to the 1982 Orange Bowl.

"Rod blocked a punt and I had a couple of long runs. It was a great day for the McSwain brothers," he said.

Game 12: No. 1 Clemson 22, No. 4 Nebraska 15

The Tigers moved into the No. 1 spot a week after they concluded the regular season. Penn State beat Dan Marino and previously undefeated and No. 1 Pittsburgh, 42-14, that week, propelling Clemson to the No. 1 position as it headed to play Nebraska in the Orange Bowl on New Year's Day.

"We know we have one more thing to do," Ford said. "I'm just like everybody else, I want to see how good Clemson is. We've proved already that we're a great football team. The only thing that stands in our way now is Nebraska.

"Georgia can't do nothing. Alabama can't do nothing. And Penn State can't do nothing. That's the way it ought to be. This team has done its own business all year long. They just went ahead and did it all themselves. Now they have a chance to do it again."

The 1982 Orange Bowl was Clemson's first Orange Bowl appearance in 25 years. Jordan, the game's Most Valuable Offensive Player, completed 11 of 22 passes and had 180 yards total offense in leading the Tigers, while Davis, the Defensive MVP, had 14 tackles. Smith, now on the Clemson Board of Trustees, had a career-high 10 tackles to lead the linemen.

Clemson allowed just one pass completion in the second half.

"No matter what they say, nobody else in the country has done what we've done this year," Ford said after the game. "We beat the No. 2 team (Georgia), the No. 4 team (Nebraska) and we beat the No. 8 team (North Carolina).

We've beaten three teams in the top 10 and nobody else has beaten even two.

"We played 11 and whipped 11 to get to be No. 1. Now, we've played 12 and whipped 12."

Nebraska took the opening kickoff, but three plays later, Clemson middle guard William Devane recovered a Mark Mauer fumble at the Nebraska 33.

Jordan drove Clemson to the Nebraska 24 before the drive stalled, and Igwebuike drilled a 41-yard field goal to put the ACC Champions up, 3-0.

The Cornhuskers came right back, however, as the Big Eight Champions drove 69 yards in eight plays to score on a 25-yard halfback pass from Mike Rozier to Anthony Steels. Kevin Seibel's extra point gave Nebraska the lead at 7-3 with 6:43 to go in the first quarter.

After an exchange of punts, the Clemson offense moved from the Nebraska 42 to the 21 to set up Igwebuike's second field goal on the night. The 37-yard boot narrowed the score to 7-6.

Davis recovered a second-quarter Phil Bates fumble that gave Clemson the ball at the Nebraska 27. The running combination of Jordan, Kevin Mack, and Cliff Austin moved the ball to the Cornhusker two.

Austin, who had been stuck in a hotel elevator for two hours earlier in the day, scampered in for the score that gave Clemson a 12-7 lead that it would not relinquish.

On its second possession of the second half, Clemson drove 75 yards in 12 plays to score its final touchdown of the night, a 13-yard pass from Jordan to All-America receiver Perry Tuttle in the corner of the end zone. For Tuttle, it was his eighth touchdown grab of the season, which set a school record. Bob Paulling's extra point put the Tigers ahead 19-7.

Now in control of the game, Billy Davis returned a punt 47 yards to set Clemson up in great field position, again. Jordan moved the ball to the Nebraska 20, where Igwebuike kicked a 36-yard field goal, his third of the evening, to put Clemson ahead 22-7 with two-and-a-half minutes left in the third stanza.

The Cornhuskers were down but not out, though. After a near interception by Rembert, Mauer engineered an eight-play, 69-yard drive that was capped by a 26-yard run by Roger Craig. After a penalty, Craig ran in the two-point conversion from eight yards out to close the gap to 22-15 with nine minutes to play.

"When Nebraska tried to come back, we had a little talk," nose tackle William Perry said. "We had come too far, worked too hard, and had too many people cheering for us.

"When we went out there in the fourth quarter, we just took it to them. There was too much riding on this for us to blow it."

The Clemson defense shut down the Big Red offense on their final extended drive, then the Tigers' offense held on to the ball for nearly five-and-a-half minutes to run down the clock to six seconds. Andy Headen deflected Mauer's desperation pass to preserve the win and the National Championship.

"We earned that thing," Davis said. "Not in a sense that we beat everybody or were more talented. We earned that thing on the practice field. That's where we won our national championship.

"We didn't win the national championship in the Orange Bowl in Miami. We won that thing on those practice fields. Coach Ford worked us. If I could say anything that could define us, I would say that was it. We knew how to work. When you know how to work, there is no give up and there is no satisfaction when you know how to work.

"The only thing you know is that I have to work until this last whistle and that's the mindset," Davis continued. "Hard work equals mental toughness. Mental toughness means you do the little things. Doing the little things means that you are detailed and anything that is excellent is detailed.

"That thing has marked us for the rest of our lives. I know it has for me, anyway. No matter what it is, the car business, the ministry, the fundraising—I expect to be the best at what I do. That is how you know it is real."

Clemson began the 1981 season unranked and unproven, but when it was all said and done, the Tigers were the only undefeated and untied team in the country. They may not have looked perfect at times, but their 12-0 record said otherwise.

"They were a terrific group and they set out to accomplish one goal, and that was to be perfect," Ford said.

TERRY KINARD, PLAYING IT DEEP

Few defensive backs in Clemson's rich history have made an impact the way Terry Kinard did in his Clemson career.

The Sumter, SC, native was a two-year member of the All-ACC team. He is still the all-time Clemson leader in career interceptions with 17, a mark that tied an ACC record at the time. He also holds the Clemson record for tackles by a defensive back, with 294 in his career.

"Clemson gave me the opportunity," Kinard said. "I was very fortunate. I could not have picked a better place to go to school. I played with a lot of great players at Clemson, especially guys on our defense like Jeff Davis, Jeff Bryant, and many others.

"I certainly could not have made it to the Hall of Fame without the great players we had at Clemson at that time."

Kinard, who was the starting free safety on the Tigers' 1981 National Championship team, was inducted into the College Football Hall of Fame in 2001. He played for the Tigers from 1978-'82 and was named National Defensive Player of the Year by CBS Sports after his senior year, the first national award won by a Clemson football player.

The Clemson safety was also the first Clemson player to be a unanimous All-America pick. He was the first two-time Clemson All-America defensive back and a first-team AP All-America player two years in a row, the only Clemson player to do that. He was chosen to the *USA Today* All-College Football Team in the 1980s.

Kinard was honored in a ceremony at the College Football Hall of Fame in South Bend, IN, in August of 2002. Ironically, he burst on to the national scene in South Bend in 1979.

Just a freshman at the time, Kinard had two fourth quarter interceptions and seven tackles overall to lead Clemson to a 16-10 victory over the Irish. The College Football Hall of Fame is located just two miles from Notre Dame Stadium.

"This was a dream come true," Kinard said. "It is something you don't expect, but when it does happen you are thrilled. It is a great honor when you consider that only one other Clemson player has been named to the Hall of Fame. To be alongside a great legend like Banks McFadden means a great deal.

"I also have to thank Coach Ford and the other coaches. I especially have to thank Coach Willie Anderson, who recruited me. Years later, he gave me the opportunity to go to Oklahoma and serve on his [high school] coaching staff.

"He impressed upon me the importance of finishing my degree, which I did. It has made a world of difference. I am sure it made a difference in me getting into the Hall of Fame. He cared about me many years after I left Clemson, and it says a lot about him and the people at Clemson."

Kinard was a first-team Associated Press All-America player in 1981 and 1982.

After leaving Clemson, Kinard was a first-round pick of the New York Giants in 1983, the 10th overall. *Sports Illustrated* named him to College Football's Centennial Team in 1999.

He played and started for the Super Bowl Champion New York Giants in 1986 and was with the club until 1989. During that time, he played in the 1988 Pro Bowl Game. He then left the Giants and played with the Houston Oilers in 1990, his last year in the NFL.

THE JUDGE—JEFF DAVIS

During Clemson's magical run through the 1981 season, the Tigers' defense was known as a hard-hitting bunch that played football like it was meant to be played. They were rough and tough. If there was a blade of grass to defend, they defended it, and usually they were successful in doing so.

The defense got its attitude from its captain, Jeff Davis, who led the team in tackles, forced fumbles, and fumble recoveries.

"He was the best I ever had," said Ford. "No linebacker I played with or coached hits as hard as he did."

With Davis leading the way in 1981, the Tigers finished second nationally in scoring defense, seventh in rushing defense, seventh in turnover margin, and eighth in total defense. Clemson led the ACC in total defense, rushing defense, scoring defense, and interceptions.

The 1981 defense forced what is still a school record 41 turnovers, with some of those coming after their own offense turned the ball over.

"There were times when our offense would turn the ball over, and as we were walking onto the field, I would find Homer [Jordan] and tell him, 'Don't sit down. We were going to get you the ball right back.' Then we would go out there and do it," Davis said.

Davis, who currently works for Clemson as an assistant athletic director, was inducted into the Clemson Ring of Honor in 1995, and the centennial football team in 1996.

The North Carolina native was a first-team All-America player in 1981, when he led the Tigers in tackles. Davis was also named MVP of the ACC and was the Defensive MVP in the Orange Bowl victory over Nebraska, the game that clinched the national title for the Tigers.

Davis has the third-best mark in career tackles in Clemson history and has also caused the most fumbles and recovered the most fumbles in team history. He was a fifth-round draft pick of the Tampa Bay Bucs and played for them from 1982-'87. He led the Bucs in tackles and was the captain of the team for four seasons.

Along with being in the Clemson Ring of Honor, Davis was inducted into the Clemson Hall of Fame in 1989 and the South Carolina Hall of Fame in 2001. Also in 2001, he was honored with the "Use Your Life" Award from Oprah Winfrey's Angel Network for his work with the "Call Me Mister" program at Clemson.

Davis was inducted into the College Football Hall of Fame in December of 2007, joining his teammates Terry Kinard and Banks McFadden as the only three Clemson players in the College Football Hall of Fame.

THE PERRY BROTHERS—THE "FRIDGE" AND MICHAEL DEAN

Michael Dean Perry will never forget the first play of his college career. It was in the season opener against Appalachian State in 1984.

He lined up alongside his older brother, William, who was already a two-time All-America player at middle guard for the Tigers and was a part of Clemson's National Championship team in 1981.

"Playing next to William was exciting in and of itself," Michael Dean said. "We grew up playing alongside each other in middle school, junior high, and high school, and now I get the opportunity to play with him at the next level in a big-time college environment.

"It was a great feeling, and I enjoyed every minute of it."

Especially the first play of the game, when William broke though the line, sacked the quarterback, stripped the football, and Michael Dean recovered it for a touchdown.

"It was so exciting. It was without a doubt the most memorable play of my career," the younger Perry said.

It did not take long for Michael Dean to be a part of another great moment involving his brother. Nine weeks later, the Tigers hosted Virginia Tech in a game that featured the greatest matchup of defensive linemen in the history of Death Valley.

Besides the Perry brothers, the Hokies themselves had 1984 Outland Trophy winner and future Pro Football Hall of Famer Bruce Smith.

"How many big-time players were in that game? I know William was in it and Bruce was in it, but who was the third one? I didn't have anything on those two guys at the time," Michael Dean said.

But the freshman had the better game.

"I remember all the hype and buildup surrounding it that week," said Michael Dean, who played at Clemson from 1984-'87. "But if I recall correctly, I believe I had a pretty good game that day. Now that I look back at it, that game might have been the day when I started coming into my own."

Michael Dean came into his own, all right. Though he is the little brother to William "The Refrigerator" Perry, Michael Dean was never one to live in the shadows of his brother. He made a name for himself and broke all of his brother's records.

"We don't really talk about the records when we get together," Michael Dean said. "We actually just sit around and catch up on what has been happening in our lives. Believe it or not, we rarely even talk about football."

Michael Dean is no longer all alone as the school's all-time sack leader with 28, but he still solely holds the record for tackles for loss, with 61.

During his time at Clemson, he was part of a defense that ranked among the best in the nation in 1986 and in 1987, plus he helped guide the Tigers to two ACC Championships, while earning All-ACC and All-America honors both times.

Before C.J. Spiller took home the ACC's top honor in 2009 as the conference Player of the Year, Michael Dean was the last Clemson player to earn such an honor—an even more special feat considering he was a defensive tackle.

After Clemson, Michael Dean went on to play 10 seasons in the NFL after being drafted by the Cleveland Browns in the second round of the 1988 NFL Draft. While playing for Cleveland, Denver, and Kansas City, he earned All-Pro honors eight times—a record for a former Tiger—and played in six Pro Bowls over the course of his career.

Michael Dean has since been named to Clemson's All-Centennial team, a member of the ACC's 50-year Anniversary Football Squad, and inducted into the Clemson Athletic Hall of Fame.

As for William, he finished his career with 60 tackles for loss and 27 sacks, while earning All-America status in 1982, 1983, and 1984. He was a consensus first-team All-America player in 1983 and a first-team selection in 1984. He is still the only Clemson player to be named All-American three times in his career.

William was a member of two ACC Championship teams (1981 and 1982) as well as the 1981 National Championship team. His Clemson teams posted a 37-6-2 record in his four years in Tigertown.

After Clemson, William was drafted No. 22 overall in the 1985 NFL Draft by the Chicago Bears. He made the All-Rookie team and was a part of the Bears' Super Bowl title run that year, where he scored a touchdown in Super Bowl XX.

At more than 300 pounds, he is still the biggest man to score a touchdown in a Super Bowl. William went on to play 10 years in the NFL, for the Chicago Bears and the Philadelphia Eagles.

Like Michael Dean, William is a member of the Clemson Hall of Fame, was named to Clemson's All-Centennial team, and to the ACC's 50-year Anniversary football squad.

CLEMSON THREE-PEAT

Clemson won the ACC Championship three times from 1986-'88, which began a stretch that saw the Tigers compile four straight 10-win seasons from 1987-'90. In fact, starting with Clemson's 1986 ACC Championship team, the Tigers won at least eight games for six straight seasons—the best six-year stretch in the program's history. Clemson posted a 57-12-3 record during that period of time.

In 1986, the Tigers were 5-1-1 in ACC play. Heroic efforts by quarterback Rodney Williams and tight end Jim Riggs and a 20-yard David Treadwell field goal with 20 seconds left forced a 17-17 tie with Maryland, giving the Tigers the conference crown.

Both Clemson coach Danny Ford and Maryland coach Bobby Ross coached the game from the press box, due to suspensions imposed by the ACC. The Tigers capped the season with a 27-21 victory over Stanford in the Gator Bowl that season. The Tigers scored all 27 points in the first half.

Clemson finished 17th in the final Associated Press Poll.

In 1987, the Tigers again won the ACC and finished the year with a 10-2 record. Clemson surprised the football world with a 35-10 win over Penn State in the Citrus Bowl. It was the largest margin of victory against a Joe Paterno squad in a bowl game.

Instead of depending on the running game, the Tigers took to the air and dominated the Nittany Lions. Clemson gained 499 yards. Williams was named the Player of the Game as he threw for 214 yards. Running back Terry Allen rushed for 105 yards, and wide receiver Keith Jennings caught seven passes for 110 yards, giving Clemson a 200-yard passer, 100-yard rusher, and 100-yard receiver in the same game for the first time since 1969.

Clemson was ranked No. 10 in the final UPI Poll.

In 1988, Clemson won the ACC and finished the season with a 10-2 record. The Tigers again defeated a perennial power in the Citrus Bowl. This time the Tigers won an exciting 13-6 game over No. 10 Oklahoma.

Clemson became the first ACC team to defeat Oklahoma. The Tigers held the Oklahoma offense without a touchdown for just the second time in the decade of the 1980s.

Clemson was ranked No. 8 by the UPI, No. 9 by the Associated Press, and No. 10 in the *USA Today* Coaches Poll when the finals rankings came out.

LAST-MINUTE HEROICS BY A WALK-ON KICKER

David Treadwell will always be remembered for beating Georgia inside the last 10 seconds in 1986 and 1987.

On September 20, 1986, Clemson defeated Georgia 31-28, as David Treadwell kicked a 46-yard field goal with no time left on the clock in Athens, GA. The next season on September 19, 1987, Treadwell booted a 21-yard field goal with two seconds left to beat Georgia on national TV 21-20 in Death Valley.

Treadwell was a consensus first-team All-America player in 1987. He won or tied games six times in his career inside the last three minutes of the fourth quarter. He was a place kicker with the Denver Broncos and the New York Giants in the NFL.

ROD-NEY! ROD-NEY!

The chant started from one end of Frank Howard Field, and soon it filled the whole stadium. "Rod-ney! Rod-ney! Rod-ney!"

The scoreboard above the west end zone stands even got into the act.

"It sounded a lot better this time," Clemson quarterback Rodney Williams said after his Tigers beat rival South Carolina 29-10.

The year before, Williams was greeted with a similar chant at Williams-Brice Stadium in Columbia. Except on that night, it had a negative connotation to it. His last pass—which was intercepted and returned for a touchdown by safety Brad Edwards—lifted the Gamecocks to a 20-7 victory, which got the 77,000 fans in Columbia that night to chant, "Raaahhdnee! Raaahhdnee!"

A Columbia, SC, native and a graduate of Irmo High School, that night, and that chant specifically, haunted the Tigers' signal-caller for a whole year. But with 10:44 left in the 1988 tussle, Williams spun into the end zone to cap Clemson's final scoring drive of the afternoon.

It was fitting that Williams scored the game-clinching touchdown, and that he did it the way those who remember watching him play know him for—running Danny Ford's triple-option offense to near perfection.

"It was just a regular option," Williams said. "We had been running it to both sides during the game, but we decided to run it to the weak side then.

"I came down and faked it to Tracy [Johnson]. The defensive tackle took Tracy and the defensive end took Terry [Allen], and the tackle did a great job blocking the outside backer and making a seam for me."

Williams had 43 of the Tigers' 225 rushing yards on that wet afternoon in Clemson. His seven-yard touchdown, on his final carry in Death Valley put Clemson securely in front 29-7. Usually calm and reserved, which sometimes Ford wished he was not, Williams finally showed some emotions by pumping his fist to the crowd and then hugging Ford as he came over to the sideline.

"Scoring on my final play was a great thing to happen," Williams said.

Williams, who won more games (32) at Clemson than any other Tiger quarterback, threw for 192 yards in his final game at Death Valley.

"Rodney played well, and he has excelled for us for a lot of different reasons," Ford said after the game. "He has had a great four years with us, and we're glad all of our seniors went out winners."

But few in the history of Death Valley have gone out the way Williams did. With a little more than four minutes to play, Ford let Williams take the field to start the last drive of the game, and then after one play, he substituted him for backup Chris Morocco.

As Williams jogged over to the sideline and was greeted with hugs and high-fives from his teammates and coaches, the 84,000 fans who were wearing orange in Death Valley stood to their feet and gave him a standing ovation, and soon the chants of "Rod-ney! Rod-ney! Rod-ney!" filled the stadium once again.

"I definitely like to know that they know my name," Williams said. "But it means even more when they're yelling your name because they appreciate you."

ORANGE PANTS II

Woody McCorvey was in shock when he and the rest of the Clemson football team walked into the locker room and saw the infamous orange pants sitting in each of the players' lockers.

The Tigers had just returned from pregame warm-ups as they prepared to play South Carolina at Williams-Brice Stadium in Columbia that night.

"That was something that was very uncharacteristic of what Coach Ford did because it was always a tradition that we wore them at home," said McCorvey, who is now an associate athletic director at Clemson. "The only other time they wore them on the road was when they won the national championship in 1981."

Clemson had not worn orange pants since losing to Florida State in 1988 in a game that is known as "Puntrooski." Ford would only allow them to be pulled out for what were deemed special games. He used them as motivation, and it worked.

Clemson was 15-2 at the time in the orange pants, which first debuted in a 27-6 victory over South Carolina in 1980. The two losses were a one-point defeat by the Gamecocks in 1984 and the three-point loss to the Seminoles in 1988.

The Tigers would have to earn the right to wear orange pants by the way they practiced. The seniors would request to wear the special britches the Monday before a big game, but players never knew if they would get to wear them until they came in from pregame warm-ups.

McCorvey remembers the emotions in the locker room that night when the players saw the pants.

"When we went back into the locker room and saw that they were out, it went crazy in there," he said. "You could not believe the sense of the locker room when those kids saw those pants. We went back out there and played with a lot of enthusiasm and a lot of emotion.

"It was pretty much a complete ball game by us that night."

The Tigers rushed for 335 yards and finished the night with 446 total yards in a 45-0 victory. The defense held the Gamecocks to 155 total yards, while forcing five turnovers in the series' last shutout.

"Clemson played a perfect game," then-South Carolina head coach Sparky Woods said. "I think the turning point took place when we kicked off. We just got beat throughout the entire game."

The 15th-ranked Tigers scored on their first four possessions, while totaling 302 yards before halftime. Running back Terry Allen scored on two first-quarter runs and had 97 yards before reinjuring his knee late in the second quarter. That was the last time he played in a Clemson uniform.

But Allen's injury was a sidebar to the kind of night it was for Clemson. The Tigers physically dominated the game on offense, defense, and special teams.

Some say that the 1989 game is still the best game a Clemson team has ever played against the Gamecocks.

"I was not here for the 63-17 game [in 2003], but during my seven years, that night in 1989 might have been our most complete ball game that we played," McCorvey said. "We had a lot of good ball games in those years, but I can't remember a one from the beginning to the end where our players played that way the entire game.

"You talk about playing four quarters on offense, defense, and special teams—that was a four-quarter football game."

And it all started because of a change in pants, special orange pants, that is.

"We had no idea and still to this day, I have never asked or talked to Coach Ford about it," McCorvey said. "I don't know what made him do it. A lot of times he would meet with the seniors and they would talk about things in there.

"Whether they talked about it that week, I don't know. We did it, though, and it was something I will always remember and I know those players will remember it, too."

FORD RESIGNS

Following Clemson's victory over South Carolina, the Tigers accepted a bid to play West Virginia in the 1989 Gator Bowl. It was to be one of the finest hours in Clemson's illustrious bowl history.

Once again, the Clemson running game was magnificent, while the defense was even better as the Tigers defeated West Virginia and Heisman Trophy Finalist Major Harris 27-7.

Harris came into the game ranked eighth nationally in total offense and ninth in passing efficiency, but the Clemson defense, led by outside linebacker Levon Kirkland, enabled the shifty Harris to gain only 17 yards on the ground and 119 yards in the air.

Kirkland was named MVP for the game after he recorded nine tackles, a sack, caused a fumble, and had three quarterback pressures.

Clemson held the Mountaineers, powerful offense to 237 total yards, while the Clemson offense got a workman-like 257 yards on 61 carries.

The Tigers wore West Virginia down and scored 17 unanswered points in the fourth quarter to put the game away. As a matter of fact, Clemson scored the game's last 27 points after the Mountaineers opened the night with a 90-yard touchdown drive.

Defensive tackle Chester McGlockton, who led the ACC in sacks, stripped Harris of the ball near his goal line and then fell on the ball in the end zone for one of the Tigers' three touchdowns. Fullback Wesley McFadden and tailback Joe Henderson had the other two scores.

Placekicker Chris Gardocki kicked field goals of 27 and 24 yards.

Henderson led Clemson with 92 yards, while quarterback Chris Morocco had 65 yards and Kennedy had 57.

Clemson finished the year ranked 11th in the UPI Poll and 12th in the Associated Press and *USA Today* Coaches Polls.

"We have gone through a lot of adversity this year and you have to give credit to our seniors. They held us together. This was their 38th win in four years.

"They have been a part of a great four years and a significant period in Clemson history. I'm going to miss this bunch."

That was Ford's last interview as Clemson's head coach. He stepped down as head coach on Jan. 19, 1990. No one, including Ford himself, knew that the Gator Bowl, like his first, was his last game as Clemson's coach.

In his 11 years at Clemson, Ford produced a 96-29-4 record, which included a 6-2 bowl record and a 7-3-1 ledger against the Gamecocks. At the time, he left Clemson as the third winningest coach in the country in terms of win percentage. He was only behind Nebraska's Tom Osborne and Penn State's Joe Paterno.

SOLID DEFENSE STARTS THE TIGERS OFF IN THE DECADE OF THE 1990s

In 1990, the Tigers finished the year with the top-ranked defense in terms of total yards allowed and were also one of the nation's best in scoring defense, rushing defense, and passing defense. The Tigers finished 10-2 that season and concluded with a 30-0 win over Illinois in the Hall of Fame Bowl in Tampa, FL.

That defense was one of the main reasons why the Tigers were picked to win the ACC in 1991 as six starters and several key reserves returned from that unit, including Kirkland.

"Coming into a game, we felt like we were going to win every one of them," said Levon Kirkland, who was a two-time All-America player at Clemson.

There was good reason to think that. Joining Kirkland on that 1991 team were future NFL starters in defensive tackle Brentson Buckner, defensive tackle Chester Mc-Glockton, outside linebacker Ashley Sheppard, outside linebacker Wayne Simmons, strong side linebacker Ed McDaniel, and cornerback James Trapp.

The offense wasn't too bad either, as wide receivers Terry Smith and Larry Ryans, and running backs Rodney Blunt and Ronald Williams, joined DeChane Cameron.

"I think the difference with our teams back then is that if we lost a game it was almost guaranteed that we would make a run at some point in time," Kirkland said. "When we lost a game, we kind of knew the next game was going to be our game."

Clemson finished the 1991 season 9-2-1 and ranked 18th in the final Associated Press Top 25. It marked the sixth straight year in which Clemson only lost two games and the sixth straight year it finished ranked in the AP poll.

THE PRIDE OF ALLENDALE—RAYMOND PRIESTER

Raymond Priester holds Clemson marks for career rushing, single-game rushing, most 100-yard games, and most carries. He also holds the marks for most 100-yard games in a season and consecutive 100-yard games.

Priester came to Clemson from a little town in the lower part of South Carolina called Allendale. He left there in 1993 as Allendale-Fairfax High School's all-time leading rusher with 5,673 yards and 71 touchdowns. He was a four-year starter and earned a spot on South Carolina's 1993 Shrine Bowl team.

Both Clemson and South Carolina asked for his services, but he chose Clemson because recruiting coordinator Rick Stockstill promised him a chance to play running back, and USC was more interested in him playing linebacker.

Though he was playing running back, Priester discovered it was not going to be as easy as he first thought it was. There was a lot of competition at tailback, and after fall camp he fell to third on the depth chart.

For a little while, he thought hard about transferring, but his mother, Rosella, told him without hesitation that he was staying put and he was going to work it out.

"I told him he was going to stay right there and wait his turn," she said. "You don't play by yourself, you play as a **team**."

It turned out that the 6-foot-1, 230-pound running back did not have to wait long to get his turn. After a 1-2 start to the 1994 season, Clemson head coach Tommy West decided to shake things up. In practice, he told Priester he was getting his shot, and later that week he started and rushed for 88 yards in the Tigers' 13-0 victory over Maryland.

Priester never left the starting lineup again. His first 100-yard game came against Florida State in 1995, the first of three straight games in which he eclipsed the 100-yard plateau. He finished the 1995 season with five 100-yard games, but what happened on November 11, 1995, against Duke is still the best single-game rushing mark in Clemson history.

After rushing for 263 yards on 32 carries, Priester's offensive linemen wanted to carry him off Clemson's Frank Howard Field.

"I asked them not to do it," he said. "They're the ones who are basically responsible for it, so why should they carry me off?"

The 263 yards allowed Priester to top the 1,000-yard mark, the first running back at Clemson to do it since Allen in 1988. The very next week against South Carolina, he shattered Flagler's single-season mark against South Carolina and finished the year with 1,322 yards and six touchdowns.

As impressive as he was at running the football in 1995, the numbers he put up in 1996 were even better. Priester went over the 100-yard mark a record seven times in 1996, including four consecutive times to end the year.

His four-straight 100-yard games is also a single-season record.

"We take pride in Raymond's accomplishments," said one of his offensive linemen, Jim Bundren. "It's a unique situation, but when Raymond breaks a record we really feel a part of it, and Raymond always gives us credit."

Priester was giving Bundren and the boys up front a lot of credit then. He closed out 1996 by rushing for 100 or more yards five times in the last six games. The one time he did not it was because the Tigers were comfortably ahead of Maryland in a 35-3 victory. West pulled him out after gaining 85 yards on 19 carries.

The next week, he began the greatest four-game stretch for a running back in Clemson history.

First he rushed for 122 yards in a 24-16 victory at No. 15 Virginia and then for 146 yards in a 40-17 rout of N.C. State. The following week against South Carolina, he broke off a 65-yard run—the longest of his career—and rushed for 137 yards on 18 carries. He capped off the year with 151 yards against LSU—still a Clemson bowl record—in the Peach Bowl on New Year's Eve.

The 556 yards he gained in the last four games allowed Priester to break his single-season record by 23 yards (1,345), while it also allowed him to pass Kenny Flowers as the all-time leading rusher at Clemson. He also became the first running back in Clemson history to rush for 1,000 yards in back-to-back seasons.

"Blocking for Raymond Priester adds to our motivation," said lineman Glenn Rountree. "We take a lot of pride in the records he breaks because when Raymond is running the ball well, we win."

Never was that more evident than on October 25, 1997. Though Maryland and everyone else in the college football world knew what Clemson's game plan was on this particular afternoon—give the football to Priester—the Terrapins could not stop him.

Priester ran for 204 of the Tigers' 245 yards that afternoon, while tying a single-game record with 36 carries in the 20-9 victory. He also scored both of Clemson's touchdowns.

In the first quarter, he carried the ball seven consecutive times and gained 50 of the Tigers' 63 yards on the touchdown drive. Like he started, he finished the Terps off in the fourth quarter with nine straight carries (10 total) or 81 yards on a 94-yard touchdown drive.

"Ask any back in the nation how many times they want the ball, and they'll tell you as many times as they can," Priester said.

Nobody at Clemson has gotten the ball more than Priester. He finished his career with a school record 805 carries and is still the all-time leading rusher with 3,966 yards. His 15 100-yard rushing performances are also a program best.

And though Clemson fans may not think of his name right at first when they think of the Tigers' all-time best running backs, that does not bother him. He never was all about that. Priester enjoyed his time at Clemson and he enjoyed the fact he was a Clemson Tiger, and he would not change a thing.

"I consider myself lucky," he said. "So many guys haven't had the chance to do what I've done. I'm blessed to have walked that road. I'm happy today. I'm happy tomorrow. I'm happy the next day. I wouldn't change a thing."

THE BEST LINEBACKER AT LINEBACKER U

When he first came to Clemson, Anthony Simmons wanted to be like the great linebackers who came before him. When he left after his junior year in 1997, he arguably could have been called the best.

In his three years at Clemson (1995-97) Simmons recorded 486 tackles, only 29 off the school record Bubba Brown recorded in four years from 1976-'79. The middle linebacker also recorded 52 tackles for loss, which is fourth all-time.

"Every player wants to be able to say, 'I left my mark here,'" Simmons told *Sports Illustrated* in 1997.

Simmons definitely left his mark at Clemson. He is just the second player in Clemson history to earn All-America status three straight years, including consensus first-team status in 1997 when he was a finalist for the Butkus Award, which is given to the nation's best linebacker.

In his last season in Tigertown, Simmons recorded 158 tackles, 25 tackles for loss, and had eight sacks. He even

broke up four passes on those rare times he dropped back into coverage.

"He's the greatest pure hitter I've ever seen in college," said Reggie Herring, Simmons's defensive coordinator at Clemson. "Against Maryland he hit a guy so hard on the goal line it was like a cannon had gone off."

Clemson had its fair share of great linebackers in the day, such as Brown, Davis, Kirkland, and McDaniel. But as good as they all were, none of them made the impact Simmons made from the moment he stepped foot on campus.

Just five days into fall camp, the Spartanburg, SC, native was in the starting lineup, one of two true freshmen whom longtime Clemson sports information director Tim Bourret can remember starting so soon.

During his freshman year, the inside linebacker earned third-team All-America honors with 150 tackles, including 11 tackles for loss. In his sophomore year, he set a single-season record at the time with 178 tackles, including 16 for loss as he became a first-team All-America player.

After his junior season, he became the first Clemson player to be named first-team All-ACC as a freshman, sophomore, and junior.

One can only wonder what damage Simmons could have done had he not decided to enter the NFL draft after his junior season.

Simmons was picked 15th overall by the Seattle Seahawks in the 1998 NFL Draft and played seven years and in 87 games during his career.

PRO FOOTBALL HALL OF FAME AWAITS BRIAN DAWKINS

One of the best memories Brian Dawkins has from his career at Clemson is an interception he made against North Carolina in 1995.

The Tigers were up 10-0 at the time, and the Tar Heels were threatening, which is when he stepped in front of a North Carolina pass and took it back for a touchdown. It was his only touchdown of his four-year career at Clemson. And it turned out to be a big one, too, as UNC rallied to score the last 10 points of the game.

"That was a memorable play because of the significance of the game," he said. "At the time they were making a comeback on us and to make that play, it put the game away. That's something I will always remember."

That following week, the Clemson star had three interceptions in one half against Duke, which is tied for a Clemson record.

The strong safety finished the 1995 season with six interceptions and nine passes broken up. He also caused one fumble and recovered two, while recording 60 tackles. At the end of the year, his season rewarded him with All-ACC and All-America status.

During his career at Clemson, Dawkins dug into a lot of teams. He finished his career with 247 tackles and 11 interceptions. He earned his way on to three All-ACC teams, including first-team status during his All-American season in 1995.

Dawkins was named the first-team strong safety on Clemson's All-Centennial team in 1996—the active student athlete named to the team at time—and was selected to their Athletic Hall of Fame in 2009.

Dawkins credited former Clemson defensive backs coach Charlie Harbison for helping him get to All-America status as well as prepping him for the NFL.

"He did so much to get me to where I am," Dawkins said. "Coach Cheese has blessed me so much with my passion. He is a passionate guy too and he loves what he does and he loves the guys he is teaching. He is fathering his guys. He is not just a coach. He loves to love us.

"That speaks volumes about Cheese. He cares about the person and not just the player. . . . The coaching that I got here with Cheese and what he taught me, it prepared me and he had me where I needed to be.

"When I got to the NFL I knew the technique. I didn't have to learn as much technique-wise."

Dawkins learned enough under Harbison to become one the best and most feared safeties in the game. A second-round pick in the 1996 NFL draft by the Philadelphia Eagles, he started 13 of the 14 games he played in, recording 75 tackles, a sack, and three interceptions. During his Eagles career, Dawkins earned seven Pro Bowl selections in 1999, 2001, 2002, 2004, 2005, 2006, and 2008. He played in five conference championship games and one Super Bowl, as well.

He was also a Pro Bowl selection in 2009 and 2011 as a member of the Denver Broncos. In all, he played in 224 games during a 16-year career. His 16 seasons in the NFL is tied with former kicker/punter Chris Gardocki for the most years by a Clemson player in the NFL.

"I don't know anyone that comes in this league and expects to play 16 years," Dawkins said.

"There are some that say they are going to play that long, but that's not me. I wanted to make the team and have a successful career. The thing I always told myself is that I wanted to be a consistent player throughout the duration of my career. Whatever the length of that is, I want to be a consistent player. It just so happens that the Lord blessed me to be able to be that way for 16 years. That's a blessing."

Physically, Dawkins kept himself in the game by doing all the right things with his body. He still watches what he eats, he does workouts on a regular basis, he takes vitamins, and he receives massages. The biggest thing, he says, is the power of prayer and staying true to his faith.

"You actually say, 'How can you do this physically this long in the beginning?' You hear stories about some of the guys who have played and retired and the way that some of the guys are walking or not walking," he said. "Looking at some of the guys who have played this game, you wonder, *what is it going to take to get it done early?*

"As you start to play a little bit, you start to research and you ask guys who have played a long time what do they do. You make your own plan from there."

That plan has helped Dawkins do many things in his career. In a 2002 game versus the Houston Texans, he became the first player in NFL history to record a sack, interception, force a fumble, and catch a touchdown pass in a single game.

During the 2008 season, he became the 10th member of the 20/20 interception and sack club and broke the Eagles' record for games played by surpassing Harold Carmichael, who had 180.

When he finished his career with the Eagles, he had started 182 of 183 games, recorded 898 tackles, 34 interceptions, and 21 sacks—good enough to almost assure a spot waiting for his bust in the NFL Hall of Fame.

If that happens, it will be an accolade no former Clemson player before him has ever had bestowed upon him.

"It has crossed my mind and Lord willing if it does, that would be a tremendous accomplishment for myself and my teammates that have helped me along and believed in me from Little League all the way up to the NFL," Dawkins said. "To know that would be the case, with all the great athletes that have come through Clemson, and that I would be the one to hold that mantle up high for this university, that would be an honor.

"To know that I have played this long and accomplished the things I have accomplished like all the pro bowls and playing 16 years and all of those things. That means it will all be worth it, and when they say 'Brian Dawkins,' and they say 'Clemson University' with it, that will be a special thing to me."

"CATCH II"

Except for the 10,000 or so South Carolina fans who had made the trip up from Columbia, there was an eerie silence in Clemson Memorial Stadium in 2000, when tight end Tommy Hill fell on a Derek Watson fumble in the end zone to give the Gamecocks a 14-13 lead with 59 seconds to play.

For most of the 84,500 who were in attendance on that cold and damp evening, all had felt lost. But Clemson quarterback Woodrow Dantzler was not among them. As South Carolina set up to kick the football off, Dantlzer gathered the offense up and sent them a message.

"I told them that this is not about to happen," he said to reporters afterward. "We're not going to let this happen to our seniors."

It took a controversial catch from one of those seniors, All-America player Rod Gardner, to make the 98th battle of the Palmetto State's two biggest schools one of the best and most talked-about games in the long-standing rivalry.

With only 19 seconds left, Dantzler led the Tigers back on the field following a timeout, while staring at a third down-and-12 situation from their own 42. When he took the shotgun snap, Dantzler rolled to his left, drawing the safety away from Gardner. He then stopped and threw a high, deep lob to the right.

Gardner, who caught the decisive 29-yard touchdown the year before against the Gamecocks on a fourth-down play, ran a go-route down the far sideline. South Carolina had cornerback Andre Goodman underneath in coverage and safety Deandre Eiland deep as the ball went sailing through the air.

"It was in slow motion," Gardner said. "I wasn't even thinking about the defender. I just knew I had to make a play, and when it dropped into my hands, oh man."

Everyone in the stadium held their collective breaths as Gardner leaped high to haul in the 50-yard pass, while falling backward. When he settled to the ground, Clemson had the football at the South Carolina eight with 10 seconds left and needed just a 25-yard Aaron Hunt field goal to win the game.

"I'm still trying to figure out what happened," Dantzler said.

Hunt was true on his kick, and Clemson celebrated into the night with a dramatic 16-14 victory.

"The rivalry, I didn't even really know about it until I got here," said Hunt, who was a freshman from Tennessee that year. "So it was all talk up until tonight. Now I know what it's really like. It's a privilege to have a chance like that, and it's awesome to make the kick."

The Gamecocks, on the other hand, were beside themselves and felt as if they were robbed of a victory by the officials. Goodman and Gamecock fans alike said Gardner pushed off to create separation.

"I looked at the ref and I knew he was going to pull the flag," Goodman said. "He looked at me and smiled. I said, 'You had to see that.' He just smiled and shook his head. That rule is so funny. Sometimes it is called and sometimes it isn't."

Gardner saw it differently.

"I didn't touch him. I was playing the ball," he said.

Other than Gardner, everyone involved was surprised there was no flag thrown on what turned out to be the biggest single play in the history of the rivalry since Jerry Butler's leaping touchdown reception in the final seconds gave the Tigers a victory in 1977.

Prior to Gardner's catch, the two teams were flagged a combined 20 times for 111 yards. Clemson was called for four pass interference penalties that night, and former Head Coach Tommy Bowden admitted by the way the game was being called, he was surprised he did not see one on that play.

"I know we probably had four interference calls and they had one. I was really surprised," he said. "From what I saw earlier, yeah, I was surprised. If it's up in the air there was an interference call. Any time we threw a pass up, I thought there would be a flag called."

Former South Carolina Head Coach Lou Holtz was extremely angry following the game. He would later say Gardner's push-off was blatant. Because of the way the game was officiated, the Gamecocks coach never felt they

had the game won when Hill landed on Watson's fumble in the end zone with 59 seconds to play.

"You never think you have it won. Not as long as there are twenty-nine people on the field," he said.

The way Gardner saw it, it wasn't the officials who won the game; he just made a play when the opportunity came.

"I knew I had to make a play to win the game," he said. "We didn't want to lose the game like that."

Gardner finished his Clemson career as the all-time leading receiver in receptions (166) and yards (2,498) and was the first receiver in school history to record back-to-back 1,000-yard seasons. He was drafted 15th overall by the Washington Redskins in the first round of the 2001 NFL Draft.

He played in 91 games during the course of his NFL tenure.

In 2001, Dantzler became a Heisman Trophy candidate after tallying 418 total yards in a 47-44 overtime win at Georgia Tech and then 517 total yards a week later as the Tigers won at N.C. State 45-37.

At the end of the year, Dantzler became the first player in Division I history to throw for 2,000 yards and run for 1,000 more, as he threw for 2,578 yards and ran for another 1,061.

THE GAMECOCK-DOMINATOR

Charlie Whitehurst is simply known as the guy who beat South Carolina four times, the only quarterback on either side in the 111-year history of the rivalry to go 4-0 against his archrival.

"I kind of downplayed it early," he said. "It's a team honor. I guess my name gets put on it."

Whitehurst beat the Gamecocks in all kinds of ways, so he deserved to have his name on it.

In 2002, his first game against USC, he rallied the Tigers from a 20-13 deficit after Dondrial Pinkins gave the Gamecocks the lead with a 4-yard run and 3:04 to play in the third quarter.

From that point on, the game belonged to Whitehurst. A freshman at the time, he calmly led Clemson down the field, converting on two third-down plays—first passing 21 yards to Airese Currie on third-and-eight from the USC 32, and then scoring on an 11-yard scramble on third-and-10.

On the touchdown, Corey Jenkins chased Whitehurst out of the pocket on a safety blitz, but Whitehurst spun to the left, going toward the sideline, and then outran the USC defense to the end zone with 13:52 to play.

When Clemson got the ball, the freshman continued to make big plays, as he led the Tigers on the game-winning drive. First Whitehurst hit Derrick Hamilton for 22 yards and then tight end Bobby Williamson for six more before completing a 30-yard pass to Jackie Robinson that moved the football to the USC one.

Moments later, running back Bernard Rambert took a pitch from Whitehurst and ran around the right side to score from two yards out for a 27-20 lead.

The Gamecocks tried to answer the Tigers' two scores, as they drove to the Clemson 30 on their next possession, but Eric Sampson knocked down kicker Josh Brown's fourth-and-five pass on a fake field goal to give the ball back to the Clemson offense.

From there, the Tigers pounded the ball with running back Yusef Kelly and ran out the final 6:25 to win the game. Kelly carried seven times for 48 yards on the final drive.

"That's the hardest I have seen him run," Whitehurst said afterward. "But up front we were giving him holes, too. . . . There was a question in the media on who was the tougher team, and I think we proved who it was on the last drive."

Whitehurst also proved he was going to be a problem for the Gamecocks for another three years, as he completed 27 of 38 passes for 287 yards. If they had not figured it out by then, they figured it out the next year in Columbia.

The 2003 game is simply known as "63-17" by Clemson fans, but it should be noted that it was perhaps Whitehurst's finest hour as the Tigers' quarterback. He completed 18 of 26 passes for 302 yards and four touchdowns, while also rushing for 43 more yards.

He established new records against the Gamecocks for passing yards, touchdown passes, and total offense in the victory.

The 63 points were the most scored by either team in the rivalry, and that mark still stands today. It also was a statement game for the entire Clemson team, who after the game said they were playing to make sure Bowden stayed on as head coach.

Rumors had swirled after losing to Wake Forest three weeks earlier that Bowden would be gone, but the Tigers beat No. 3 Florida State—the first win against the Seminoles since 1989—then drilled Duke before humiliating South Carolina in front of its home crowd.

"We proved our point, that he's our coach and he's going to be the coach here," senior linebacker John Leake said afterward.

But the story of the night was again Whitehurst, who continued to chop up South Carolina. He completed the first 10 passes he threw, three of them for touchdowns on the Tigers' first three drives of the game, and then his fourth touchdown to Duane Coleman in the third quarter tied a Clemson record.

The 2004 game unfortunately was outshined by the fourth quarter brawl that embarrassed both schools and the state, but on the field, Whitehurst again owned the Gamecocks. Though his numbers weren't as dominant as the year before, the now-junior still completed 15 of 28 passes for 151 yards as the Tigers routed USC, again, 29-7.

Clemson outgained the Gamecocks 313 to 197 and were 8 of 17 on third down, while USC was 4 of 16. The Tigers scored a minute into the game after recovering a fumble on the opening kickoff and cruised from there.

They rushed for 162 yards on 48 carries and controlled the clock with a time of possession of 36:23. Running back

Reggie Merriweather led Clemson with 125 yards and three touchdowns.

"They never really stopped us today," Whitehurst said. "If you can run the ball, whenever you can do that, you're going to be at an advantage. When we threw the ball, guys were wide open and we were able to get big chunks that way."

The Tigers knew it was not going to be easy to beat South Carolina in 2005, but like always their leader found a way to get it done, even if he did need 35 yards to pick up a first down. Whitehurst got Clemson out of the long-distance situation and drove his team down the field in the final moments to beat South Carolina 13-9 in Columbia on a James Davis touchdown run with 5:58 remaining.

Following clipping and holding penalties on back-to-back plays, the Tigers found themselves buried at their own 22-yard line and needing to get to the USC 43 for a first down. But Whitehurst completed three passes in a row, the last a 28-yard strike to Curtis Baham on third-and-12 from the 35.

The pass moved the ball to the South Carolina 27. Davis then rolled off a 23-yard run to the 4-yard line and then rushed two yards before scoring the game-winner on the next play.

"At the end, put the game in Charlie Whitehurst's hands, and he comes through," Bowden said.

After Davis's score, the Tigers intercepted USC quarterback Blake Mitchell twice. The last came when defensive end Charles Bennett picked off a Mitchell pass that was deflected by defensive tackle Rashaad Jackson.

South Carolina had one more chance to get the ball back, but once again, fittingly enough it was Whitehurst who dashed the Gamecocks' hopes. On third-and-nine from midfield, he called his own number on a quarterback draw and picked up 10 yards to seal the win.

As he got up, Whitehurst got to one knee and used his index finger on his right hand to signal first down, sending the 10,000 or so Clemson fans at Williams-Brice Stadium into celebration mode.

"It's the sweetest feeling I have ever known in sports," Whitehurst said.

Whitehurst finished his career against the Gamecocks by completing 77 of 118 passes, for 912 yards. He completed 65.4 percent of his passes, and more important, he was 4-0 against the Tigers' archrival.

BOWDEN LEFT HIS MARK

On December 2, 1998, Tommy Bowden was named the head football coach at a school he called "his dream job."

Ever since the day he first visited Clemson's Death Valley as a young assistant coach at Duke University, Bowden pointed to Clemson as one of the 10 schools he would love to be a head coach at one day. He got that opportunity when Clemson parted ways with West following a turbulent 3-8 season in 1998.

Bowden, who was 18-4 at Tulane from 1997-'98, was known for his high-flying offense at the time, which led to the Green Waves' 11-0 record in 1998 and top-10 national ranking.

He stated his biggest goal at Clemson was to improve the school's perception on the field, in the classroom, and the facilities. For the most part, Bowden did all of those things.

"Tommy has done some marvelous things for our program, and we have had some good success," former Athletic Director Terry Don Phillips said.

In his nine-and-a-half years at Clemson, Bowden's teams won 61.5 percent of the time. His 72 wins rank third all-time in Clemson history behind Howard and Ford, while his nine-and-a-half seasons at the school rank as the third-longest tenure for a Clemson coach.

Bowden also won 13 games against Top-25 teams, the third-best mark in school history, including three of Clemson's top six road victories of all-time—wins at No. 9 Georgia Tech (2001), No. 10 Miami (2004), and No. 9 Florida State (2006).

All nine of Bowden's previous teams were bowl-eligible, as he took the Tigers to two Peach Bowls and at least one appearance in the Gator Bowl, Chick-fil-A Bowl, Champs Bowl, Tangerine Bowl, Music City Bowl, and Humanitarian Bowl.

The eight bowl appearances are the most by a Clemson coach. He was 7-2 against rival South Carolina.

Twice Bowden was named ACC Coach of the Year (1999, '03), joining Howard, Charley Pell, and Ford as the only two-time recipients of that award in Tiger history.

But it wasn't just wins and losses that defined what Bowden had accomplished in his time at Clemson. Off the field, his players rarely got in trouble, and Clemson graduated nearly 80 percent of its seniors in his nine years.

"There is not a better man," said Vic Koenning, who served as Bowden's defensive coordinator for three years. "I don't think there is a classier guy. I don't think he could have worked harder and done more for the school and for these kids. I just can't say enough about him and what he did here."

Clemson's graduation success rate of 94 percent in 2005 was fourth-best among the 119 Division I-A programs. In 2003, Clemson was 11th in the nation in graduation success rate among these programs, including second among public institutions.

"Our off-the-field issues and academic issues and the many, many other things he has represented this university in, he did in a very positive fashion," Phillips said.

But there was one thing Bowden could not bring Clemson. And though he tried as hard as he could, Bowden could never take the Tigers to the next level. He could not get his program over the hump and win that elusive ACC Championship.

"The program is pretty stable, but, and here comes the proverbial 'but,' we are surely not satisfied because we have not been to the BCS and haven't won or played in

the championship game, much less won it," Bowden said prior to the start of the 2008 season.

"So yeah, there is some stability in the program. Now, you have to evaluate is the program better. Are all of those things better? Look at the facilities I inherited 10 years ago. Is that better? You have to look at all of those things.

"The graduation rate, it is the highest ever, but winning the championship, that 10th win, playing in the BCS and playing in the conference championship game, that's a big piece of the puzzle. While it is stable in all of those other areas, that's the one that's frustrating and that's the one we have not done."

And that in a nutshell described Bowden's legacy at Clemson. Though he did a lot of good things, he never won a championship, and that ultimately led to his resignation after the Tigers started the 2008 season with a 3-3 overall record, including a 1-2 mark in the ACC.

Clemson entered the 2008 season as the No. 9 team in the country, but a 34-10 loss to Alabama to start the season on national television and then back-to-back defeats to Maryland and Wake Forest spelled the end to the Tommy Bowden era at Clemson.

Of all the numbers Bowden accumulated during his career at Clemson, the good and the bad ones, the most telling one of them all, and the one that defined him the most, was the nine losses as a ranked team to an unranked team.

"Until you win a championship it is always, 'why did you lose it?', 'how do you lose to a team you should have beaten?' That's always going to be the case until you win a championship," Bowden said.

COCK-A-DOODLE-DOO

Seconds after Chris Chancellor intercepted South Carolina quarterback Chris Smelley late in the fourth quarter, Clemson running back James Davis started to lead a chant that could be heard clear into the night sky.

"Dabo! Dabo! Dabo!"

That was the chant most of the 81,500 fans dressed in orange shouted, with Davis and many other Clemson players, following the Tigers' 31-14 victory over South Carolina.

The chant was not just a yell for celebration in Death Valley, but it was a message to Clemson Athletic Director Terry Don Phillips to make then-interim head coach Dabo Swinney the school's permanent head coach.

"That was awesome," Swinney said. "It was great. We have great fans. It is a very humbling thing when people give you credit and all that stuff and appreciate something you have tried to do."

Phillips did appreciate what Swinney did, and a week later he removed the interim tag in front of head coach, making Swinney the Tigers' permanent head coach. Since then, the Tigers have won five ACC Atlantic Division Titles, three ACC Championships, one National Runner-up, and one National Championship.

What Swinney did to the Gamecocks in 2008 was serve up a big helping of Davis and C.J. Spiller. The "Thunder & Lightning" backfield combined to rush for 179 yards and three touchdowns—all three scores coming from Davis, who scored on runs of 1, 20, and 2 yards.

The senior finished the afternoon with 91 rushing yards and exited Death Valley by blowing the student section kisses as the final seconds of the clock ran off.

Clemson totaled 383 yards in its most balanced offensive effort of the season—184 rushing and 199 passing. The defense held USC to 92 rushing yards and picked off Smelley four times.

It was an impressive performance because it allowed Clemson to close the regular season with a 4-2 record after Swinney took over for Bowden the Monday prior to the Georgia Tech game on October 13, 2008.

"Through Coach Swinney's leadership and the assistant coaches, I can't say enough good things about the job they did. They rallied and fought back and gave great effort," Phillips said. "I think as history goes along, and as Coach Swinney told the team in there, and I will copy off his words, this team is going to be remembered in history.

"This was a team that was written off and our kids gave great effort and you can't say enough of how proud we are and I can't say enough of how proud I am of Coach Swinney. He is a man of character. I have had a chance to observe him for six years, and certainly I have observed him in one of the more difficult places that you can place a coach in."

If there was any doubting what Swinney could do as a head coach, it ended with the beatdown he handed the favored Gamecocks.

"Clemson was the better team today," USC head coach Steve Spurrier said. "They had better coaches and players. The team we played today is an ACC Championship team. They thoroughly beat us."

The Tigers used a little trickery to build a 17-0 lead midway through the second quarter. Following Smelley's second interception, this time from safety Chris Clemmons, Clemson used a play called Cock-a-doodle-doo to add on to its lead.

The play called for wide receiver Jacoby Ford to stay near the sideline and act like he was tying his shoe where the defense doesn't see him. And no one did.

The Gamecocks blitzed quarterback Cullen Harper, and safety Emanuel Cook had Harper by the ankles when he went to throw the ball Ford's way.

"We were supposed to block that guy on the edge," Harper said.

But Harper stayed with the play and got out of Cook's grasp enough to get the ball to Ford, who was wide open near the 30, like the play had been drawn up. After catching the ball, the speedster took it to the end zone for 17-0 lead with 8:33 left in the first half.

"We had certain personnel on the field. Two people came in and three of us ran to the sideline," Ford said. "Coach [Brad] Scott acted like he was chewing me out, and I kind of bent down like I was tying my shoe. I

peeked a little bit to see if they could see me, then he gave me the little go signal, and after that I ran off."

The Tigers then used a third Smelley interception, this time a Michael Hamlin pick, to set up Davis's 20-yard run off left tackle for a 24-0 lead.

After two USC touchdowns cut the lead to 24-14 at the half, Clemson put the game away as Davis and Spiller rumbled down the field, the last being Davis's third and final touchdown of the afternoon for a 31-14 advantage.

Clemson later used a seven-minute drive in the fourth quarter to ice the game.

"That's where we have grown as a football team," Swinney said. "Our kids went back to work and snatched the momentum back. . . . To be able to run the ball like we did and stop the run like we did, that's how you win football games."

SWINNEY NEVER STOPS BELIEVING

When a speaker comes to talk with the Clemson football team, Swinney will tell his players to give three claps as the distinguished guest comes in the room, out of honor and respect.

When Swinney walked into the meeting room at the McFadden Building on December 1, 2008, to tell the team he was going to be named Clemson's 25th head coach, safety Michael Hamlin asked the team to stand up and give Swinney three claps.

"I thought that was a great moment," Davis said. "That's a guy with great courage and he always believes in himself and in the team. He always puts the players first and that is what you want out of a coach."

It was an emotional day for Swinney, who somehow fought through the ashes of what looked like a season gone down in flames after Bowden's resignation and came out a winner. But in seven short weeks, Swinney rallied the team, the school, and the community and persevered through it all.

As Swinney sets to enter his ninth full season at Clemson in 2017, he has the program back where it once proudly sat. The Tigers have since won a National Championship and played for it one other time. They've won five Atlantic Divisional Championships, three ACC Championships, and played in three Orange Bowls. They also recorded six straight 10-win seasons and won 70 games between 2011 and 2016.

"When I first walked into that meeting room on that first day, I sat that word 'Believe' carved out in wooden block letters right in front of them. I pointed to the sign, and I told them that's what I do. I told them I believe in them. I believed in our coaches. I believed in our program.

"I told them I wanted them to believe in each other. Not to believe in me necessarily, but to believe in each other. Ever since then, I carry that sign to every team meeting and sit right in front of the room for them to see it."

Swinney's first team, his interim team, did believe, as they turned around what could have been a disastrous season and earned a Gator Bowl invitation by season's end. Don't think the current players don't feel the same way. Look at the 2011 Chick-fil-A Bowl for a reference.

"The [2012] seniors, there [weren't] many of them, but when this group came to Clemson four years ago, there wasn't really much to sell them on," Swinney said. "All I could say [was], 'Hey, here is my plan. I believe. I just need you to believe. This is where we are going. This is how we are going to do it.'"

FULFILLING A LEGACY

Spiller isn't the only dynamic athlete to come out of Union County High School or the small area of Lake Butler, FL.

Before Spiller, Gerard Warren helped start a state championship run that lasted three years before heading to Florida and then to the NFL, where he played defensive tackle for the Denver Broncos. Then there is Andrew Zow. All he did was help quarterback Alabama to an SEC Championship in 1999.

But before them, there was a young man by the name of Clarence Brown, Jr., who has been described as perhaps the best overall athlete to ever play at Union County High School, including C.J. Spiller.

"He was probably a better basketball player than I was," Spiller smiled with pride.

Brown was also an outstanding football player and was on his way to perhaps becoming the first person from Union County to make it big as a professional athlete.

Unfortunately, he never got that chance.

Brown, a high school senior at the time, was stabbed in the neck when Spiller was just two months old. He was the younger brother of Spiller's mother, Patricia Watkins.

On the day of his death, Watkins tried to warn her brother that the man who killed him, a former boyfriend of the girl he was dating, heard him slip out the back door and went after him.

With Spiller in her arms, she saw the fatal stabbing that stole her brother's life. She laid Spiller down on the ground that long afternoon of Oct. 27, 1987, and ran to her brother's aid. There was nothing she could do as he died in her arms.

"He was on schedule to go to college and he probably would have been the first one to have played in the NBA or the NFL," Spiller said. "She says I show so much resemblance of him. If you look at old pictures, we are so much alike."

Spiller is especially like him on the athletic fields, where Watkins says she saw her brother in Spiller at a very young age. She thinks God, through Spiller, has given her family a second chance to see what it might have been like for him.

She is convinced that is where Spiller gets his ability and has picked up where her brother left off.

"From the pictures I can tell that he was very athletic," Spiller said. "He just had that shape. . . . It is just some-

thing that I carry. His life was taken, so I just take that burden and try to make that accomplishment for her to see what he could have had if he was able to go to college and then one day to the NFL or NBA."

Spiller has always carried that burden with him. Even in his developmental days as a young football player he wowed people with his ability and natural instincts. They were instincts that reminded all of them of Brown.

"C.J. was just a little guy, but he had a burst that nobody else had," Spiller's high school coach Buddy Nobles said. "It was like he was playing touch football and wouldn't let people touch him. He was definitely the talk of the town."

Spiller was also the talk at another small town—Clemson. From the first time he touched the ball, it was easy to see the burst Nobles was talking about. In his freshman year at Boston College, he took a swing pass in the flats and cut back to the middle of the field, where he made one would-be-tackler miss and raced 82 yards for his first career touchdown.

Later that year against Georgia Tech on ESPN, with College Game Day in the house, he got the entire country's attention where again he caught a pass in the flats, juked two Yellow Jacket defenders within a two-yard radius of tackling him. Twice he faked going inside and then cut back outside while racing down the sideline 50 yards for the score. It didn't even look as if he moved.

He also had a 52-touchdown run in the 31-7 victory, the first player in Clemson history to score two touchdowns of 50 yards or more in the same game.

"He is the fastest kid I've coached," Nobles said. "The reason he is the fastest kid is because within two steps he is full speed where it will take me and you eight to 10 steps and by that time he already has 10 or 12 yards on you and then with him being God-given fast, he is leaving you and making you look like a crazy fool for even trying to run after him."

That's what Spiller made Auburn look like in the 2007 Chick-fil-A Bowl. He took a handoff at his own 17, made one move, bounced it outside, and he was off to the races. Three Auburn players gave chase and when Spiller saw one might catch him while looking at the big video board in the Georgia Dome, he turned the speed up another notch.

"I just love seeing him on the field, I really do," said Watkins. "Just talking about him puts a smile on my face. He is something."

It also put a smile on Watkins's face when she saw her son graduate from college in three-and-a-half years.

"Graduating was my main goal when I came to college," Spiller said. "That's one that I can take off [my list], and it's something no one can take from me. In football, sooner or later you will have to put the cleats up and put them in the closet, but you will always have your degree. Nobody can take that away from you. So all the hard work I have put in has paid off."

Eleven months earlier, there were some who doubted Spiller's decision to come back to Clemson when he was a shoo-in first-round selection in the NFL draft. But Spiller firmly believed he was sent to Clemson for more than just being a football player.

He put his trust in God and let his faith guide him. To him, earning his degree was more important than anything he accomplished on the football field. He also wanted to be a good role model to his younger sister LaShey Mitchell and his daughter Shania.

"I'm the type that I don't want to tell someone else to do something if I have not done it," Spiller said. "I could not go out and speak to people about getting an education and getting their college degree if I had not finished.

"Of course I also want my daughter [Shania] to understand that money can get you a lot of things, but it cannot buy you happiness or anything like that. It would have been a joyful time to play in the NFL, but I'm pretty sure the NFL isn't going anywhere anytime soon, so it will always be there. But to come back and play one more season with your friends and then play in this great stadium, which I think is the best one in the country, and then having Coach [Dabo] Swinney as my head coach. There were a lot of things that played into me coming back."

But none of it was more instrumental than his faith.

"My faith has always paid off," Spiller said. "You just have to believe. That's the thing Coach Swinney always talks about, and that's something that I kind of learned from him. He always believes in his faith and it plays a role in every decision he makes, and it should.

"Your faith is never going to let you down. Like I have said, my faith and every decision that I make always goes to The Man Upstairs. He always has the right answer for you; whether you like it or not he is going to have the correct answer."

Spiller's faith guided him to one of the most prolific individual seasons in Clemson football history. His 2,633 all-purpose yards were a single-season record, as was his 20 touchdowns. His numbers,, including 1,212 rushing yards, 503 receiving yards, and five kick returns for touchdowns, allowed Spiller to become a unanimous first-team All-America player, the third in Clemson history at the time.

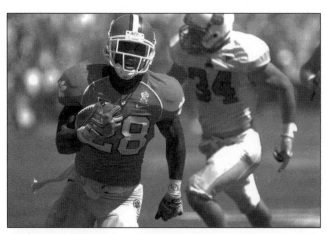

C.J. Spiller was the first Tiger in history to return a kickoff for a touchdown in consecutive games.

He also was named ACC Player of the Year, and after rushing for 233 yards in the ACC Championship game, he was named the game's Most Valuable Player.

Spiller established over 30 Clemson game-, season-, and career records, as well as several ACC records and two NCAA records. He is the first player in college football history to eclipse 3,200 rushing, 2,000 kickoff, 1,000 receiving, and 500 yards in punt returns.

"C.J. is very talented, but he just doesn't get by with his talent," Swinney said. "There are a lot of guys who have talent, but he is a rare guy. . . . It is such a rare thing to see a guy have that kind of ability and that kind of talent and then you get the best out of him. I mean he can notch it down quite a bit and still be pretty good.

"There are a lot of talented guys in the NFL that are good, but could be great if they had that kind of commitment all the time."

Spiller's commitment isn't just admired by his head coach. As he walked across the Littlejohn Coliseum stage to receive his degree, members of the Clemson Board of Trustees in attendance rose in near unison to give Spiller a standing ovation. No one in the Clemson athletic department can remember a time when the Board of Trustees gave a student-athlete a standing ovation at a Clemson University graduation ceremony.

The act by the Board of Trustees, which was spontaneous, triggered a louder ovation from the nearly 10,000 students and family members in attendance.

"It was a very humbling honor," Spiller said. "You don't realize how many lives you really touch or who is watching everything you are doing both on and off the field, so that's why I'm very careful in what I do and how I present myself.

In 2010, the Buffalo Bills drafted him No. 9 overall in the NFL Draft. He has not disappointed them, either. In 2012, he rushed for 1,244 yards and scored six touchdowns, while also catching 43 passes for 459 yards and two more scores on his way to being named to the AFC Pro Bowl Roster.

When Spiller is running for a touchdown, he isn't just succeeding for himself. He knows when he puts on the helmet and pads, his mother sees his uncle in him.

"That's how I try to take it. I try to live his legacy through me," Spiller said. "I'm pretty sure we are similar in a lot of ways."

KEEPING HIS WORD

When he saw the buses coming down the road on Highway 78 in Bamberg, SC, Da'Quan Bowers could hardly contain himself. Like a little boy waving down the Ice Cream Man on a hot summer day, Bowers darted into the middle of the busy highway to show the bus drivers where to park.

When the buses finally came to a stop, the 6-foot-4, 280-pound defensive end greeted each of the 70 or so teammates individually who made the three-hour bus ride from Clemson to Bamberg to be there for him when he laid his father, Dennis, to rest.

"It just means so much to me to see all of you here," Bowers told the team and coaches later in the church. "You guys all showed me how much you really care for me, my dad, and of course my family. This means the world to me. Thank you so much."

Later on that evening, Bowers promised to make this day up to his teammates. He was so touched that they were there for him in one of the worst moments of his life that he wanted to repay them by being the best teammate and leader he could be.

In 2010, no one in the country was better at both than Da'Quan Bowers. A former top prospect coming out of Bamberg in 2008, Bowers made offensive tackles and quarterbacks fear him. The Clemson defensive end registered 73 tackles, had 15.5 sacks, and 26 tackles for loss.

His 15.5 sacks, which led the nation, set a record for a Clemson defensive end and ranks second all-time in Clemson history. His 26 tackles for loss also rank second all-time, and it was the second-best mark in college football.

"When you look at what Da'Quan did, you can tell there was something different about the way he approached this year," Swinney said. "He made a promise to his dad, even before his dad passed away, that he would dedicate this season to getting better and proving he was the dominant player we all knew he was.

"When his dad died, he stayed committed to following out his father's wishes and dedicated the season to him. I'm so proud of the way Da'Quan has handled himself through all of this."

The most telling of that came after the Florida State game that year. Clemson was officially eliminated from the ACC Championship race after FSU kicker Dustin Hopkins nailed a 55-yard field goal as time expired in a 16-13 loss.

Though heartbroken his team would not have a chance to defend their ACC Atlantic Division Title, Bowers stood up in front of his teammates and challenged them to continue to play hard, finish the season strong, and earn themselves a bowl invitation.

"I learned a long time ago with the tragedies I have had to go through, not to ask why," Bowers said. "It's all in God's plan. He has a plan for us all, and He is trying to show us something."

His teammates listened. The next week, Clemson went out and beat Wake Forest 30-10 to become bowl-eligible for the 12th consecutive season. Bowers contributed by recording two sacks. At the time, it was his ninth consecutive game with at least one sack—a Clemson record.

"He really became a good leader for us," former Clemson safety DeAndre McDaniel said. "He would even get into the offense's huddle when he would come over to the sideline and would encourage those guys. He let them know he had their backs, too."

On January 5, 2011, Bowers decided it was time to fulfill his and his father's dream of playing in the NFL and

announced he was going to forgo his senior season and make himself eligible for the 2011 NFL Draft.

It wasn't a decision Bowers made hastily. After leaving Charlotte following the Meineke Car Care Bowl on New Year's Eve, he returned home to Bamberg, where he scheduled a meeting with his mother and sisters.

"I talked to Mom about it a couple of times on the phone," he said. "Me, her, my sisters, everybody sat down. We talked about it, prayed about it. One by one, I went around the room and asked them what they thought. They all gave me their reasons why I should stay and why I should go. I gave them my reasons. And I came up with a decision.

"The cons, basically, were leaving Clemson, not getting my degree on time, leaving my family, my team, and leaving on a bad note with a 6-7 year. The pros, I get a chance to fulfill a dream that I've always had. It was my father's dream for me to play in the NFL.

"I can live his dream. A great friend of mine, Gaines Adams, didn't have the career that he planned, because of his passing. I can let his dream live through mine.

"The ultimate goal, we all play football to play in the NFL. I just had the opportunity right now. I'm not promised this opportunity ever again in life, so I had to take it."

In 2010, Bowers became the first Clemson player to win multiple national awards in the same season—the Nagurski Award as the top defensive player in college football and the Ted Hendricks Award as the top defensive end in college football.

He was the fourth unanimous All-America player in the program's history and was the first Clemson player to win either of those national awards. Bowers was drafted No. 51 overall by the Tampa Bay Buccaneers in the 2011 NFL draft.

"I'm happy with the decision I made," Bowers said. "I thought I had a great career at Clemson."

DWAYNE ALLEN WINS NATIONAL AWARD FOR COUNTRY'S BEST TIGHT END

Dwayne Allen is one of the best-ever tight ends in Clemson history. His dedication and hard work enabled him to be named the nation's best tight end of the year in 2011.

"A lot of credit goes to the coaching staff we have here at Clemson. Coach Swinney does a great job preparing guys for the next level. In my decision to leave last year, Coach Swinney came to me and said, 'Dwayne, I think you are doing the right thing. I hate to see you go, but you are doing not only the right thing for you, but for your career.' That's the type of guy Coach Swinney is."

Allen's footprint is firmly imbedded in Clemson history, as well. Thanks to former players like Spiller, Thomas Austin, and Michael Palmer to name a few, Allen saw what it meant to be a Clemson Tiger and why Clemson was a family.

While he was just a redshirt freshman at the time, the 2009 seniors, and especially Palmer, showed Allen how much of a family the Clemson football program really is, to appreciate what your teammates mean to you, and how to do things the right way.

"When a player matures at Clemson, he really understands what it means to be a Clemson Tiger," Allen said. "In my case, I was very fortunate to open my eyes up and mature enough to the point where I was able to see it before I decided to move on with my career.

"Being a Clemson Tiger, you want your team to be successful more than anything in the world. You want your fans to be happy more than anything in the world. I had more joy signing autographs and taking pictures with the fans than I did scoring touchdowns or catching passes. That is the honest truth. Being a Clemson Tiger, it is all about giving back to Clemson and to the community of Clemson."

Allen gave back both on and off the field. On the field, he had 93 receptions for 1,079 yards and 12 touchdowns in his three-year career. His 93 receptions and 12 touchdowns tied the Clemson career records for a tight end with former Tiger and Pittsburgh Steeler John McMakin, who did the same from 1969-'71.

In 2011, Allen had the most prolific season by a tight end in Clemson history and one of the top five years in ACC history. He became the first Clemson tight end to catch 50 passes in one season for a record 598 yards, while also catching a record eight touchdowns.

Thanks to his hard work and dedication to get better, Allen became the best tight end in the country, as he was the consensus first-team All-America in 2011 and was the winner of the John Mackey Award as the nation's top tight end.

He was also the first Clemson tight end to make an All-America team since Bennie Cunningham in 1975. Cunningham went on to win two Super Bowl titles with the Steelers in the late-1970s.

Off the field, Allen gave a lot back to the community, as he spoke to children at area elementary schools and did as much community service projects as he could during his four years at Clemson. In the classroom, he was one of the best students on the team and needs just one more class to earn his degree from Clemson University.

"We are so proud of him," Swinney said. "What a tremendous example to all of us coaches on why we got into this profession. He is an example of why. That's my favorite part about coaching. To see a guy that develops into a man, to mature and learn a lot about life and is prepared; he is prepared for whatever comes his way.

"He is going to be a great player, but Dwayne Allen is a good young man too, and he is prepared to have a great future."

2011 ACC CHAMPIONS

Twenty years of frustration was cured in one night on December 3, 2011, in Charlotte, NC, as 20th-ranked Clemson scored 21 points in the third quarter to beat No. 3 Virginia Tech 38-10, winning its first ACC Championship in 20 years.

"We're a championship program and tonight we added to a great tradition," Swinney said. "And I think this was our 18th [conference title] overall and 14th ACC Championship.

"It's our first time to win 10 games in 20 years. It's our first time to win an ACC Championship in 20 years, first time to go to the Orange Bowl in 30 years. . . . So it's just great to be a Tiger, and we're 10-3, and we're excited about representing the ACC in the Discover Orange Bowl."

With the game tied 10-10 at the break, Clemson forced the Hokies to a three-and-out in its first possession and then used a 10-play, 87-yard drive to regain a lead it would not relinquish the rest of the night. Clemson quarterback Tajh Boyd, who was named the Most Valuable Player of the Game, threw his second of three touchdown passes with an 8-yard pass to tight end Dwayne Allen in the corner of the end zone to cap the drive.

That gave Clemson a 17-10 lead with 10:45 to play in the third quarter. Allen and Boyd hooked up for a 24-yard touchdown in the first quarter, as well. Boyd finished the night 20 of 29 for 240 yards and three scores. In the process, he set Clemson single-season records for total yards and passing yards.

It was a nice comeback for Boyd, who had struggled the previous two weeks.

"Somewhere you've just got to dig deep inside yourself, and work through things," the Clemson quarterback said. "Obviously, you do get a sense of complacency, and if you let it, if you let the outside world influence how you carry yourself and how you act, I mean, that's just one of the life lessons learned.

"I feel like that's one of the things that happened, and it happened for a reason, to let you know that all you can really do is believe in yourself and your family, which is my teammates. I mean, I'm just proud to be here."

Boyd got even prouder on the Tigers' next possession, as he hit Sammy Watkins in stride for a 53-yard touchdown pass that gave Clemson a 24-10 lead.

After another three-and-out forced by the Clemson defense, which held ACC Player of the Year David Wilson to 32 yards on 11 carries, the Tigers scored again, this time on a 29-yard touchdown run by Andre Ellington.

The Clemson running back finished with 125 yards on 20 carries. This was a week after the Hokies held Virginia to 30 yards rushing. Clemson finished with 217 yards.

"I'm proud of our running back, Andre Ellington," Swinney said. "He was a big-time player tonight on a big stage. He was one of the big keys in the game for us because we were able to run the football."

Boyd added his fourth touchdown responsibility of the night to cap the night's scoring with a one-yard plunge with 13:04 to play. From that point on, the celebration was on.

BECOMING A CONSISTENT WINNER, AGAIN

Swinney has talked about building a consistent winner ever since he took over the program in 2008. He wants to build one that, year in and year out, is competing for national and conference championships and consistently is being talked about.

Clemson's young coach seems to be well on his way to doing that. After winning their first ACC Championship in 20 years in 2011, Swinney's Tigers followed that up with an 11-win season—the school's first in 31 years—and its first final top-10 ranking since 1990.

Thirty-five times prior to the 2012 Chick-fil-A Bowl, that senior class had walked off the football field victorious. And though those 35 wins were sweet, it's hard to imagine any of them being as sweet as Clemson's 25-24 victory over No. 7 LSU in the Chick-fil-A Bowl that night in Atlanta, GA.

"This was special," senior defensive end Malliciah Goodman said.

It was special, as were the 11 scholarship seniors who capped off one of the more accomplished careers in Clemson history with a monumental win. Like the 1978 team's victory over Woody Hayes's Ohio State Buckeyes and like the 1981 squad's win over the big-bad Cornhuskers of Nebraska, no one gave Clemson a realistic shot at beating LSU in the Georgia Dome.

LSU is from the powerful SEC. They played for the National Championship just a year ago, and they were realistically just one play away from playing for it for a second-straight year. Clemson came into the Chick-fil-A Bowl still wondering if they belonged.

They wondered if they were as good as the Alabamas, LSUs, and Floridas of the world. Or were they just a top-15 team that couldn't compete with the big boys of college football?

They found out they could.

"This is a football team that got better all year long," Swinney said about his 2012 bunch. "Tonight we kind of grew up from some of the challenges we've had earlier in the year. I'm just so proud of our team, our staff, for their preparation. I'm proud of them for their commitment and their toughness, just their overall performance against a great LSU team."

That season's senior class was the smallest since 1999, but they accomplished more than any class in the last 21 years. Their 36 wins rank as the sixth-most in school history and the most since the 1991 team won 39.

They accomplished the most ACC wins in a four-year stretch with 23. They won the Atlantic Division title three times in four years. They won the program's first ACC Championship in 20 years when they won the 2011 ACC Title. They recorded back-to-back 10-win seasons, the first senior class to do that since the 1992 seniors. The list goes on and on and on.

"Man, those guys, they've taken this program where it hasn't been in 31 years," Swinney said. "They won more

games than any senior group in forever. Set a record for conference wins. Set a school record for home wins. The thing I'm the most proud of is that every single one of them has their degree."

It's no coincidence that in the biggest moment of their careers, the one that will define their legacy at Clemson for years to come, seniors like Goodman, cornerback Xavier Brewer, safety Rashard Hall, center Dalton Freeman, wide receiver Jaron Brown, and tight end Brandon Ford all made plays in the come-from-behind win over LSU.

"This is how I wanted to go out," Brewer said. "I wish we could have played for a national championship, but we let two slip away, but this is definitely the next-best thing. To beat a top-10 team in the Georgia Dome on New Year's Eve was awesome."

It was also the final step in putting Clemson back on top as one of the nation's best college football programs. Four years prior, Swinney asked this senior class to believe, to believe in him and in his vision for Clemson football.

Now, for those who follow that year's 2013 seniors, they will not have to just believe anymore, they will know. They now know winning at the highest level can be done at Clemson.

"We've been in this situation our whole careers," Ford said. "We've always had to prove people wrong and proving people wrong is a good thing. Tonight, we put it all together and accomplished a lot."

4TH-AND-16

Boyd describes kicker Chandler Catanzaro as "Money," and for good reason. Boyd said he never doubted Catanzaro's ability when the junior kicker lined up for a 37-yard field goal with two seconds to play in the 2012 Chick-fil-A Bowl.

"When (LSU) called the timeout to ice him, it meant nothing. I wanted to go up in the stands and celebrate already because I knew he was going to kick it through those uprights," Boyd said.

And that's exactly what Catanzaro did. The Greenville, SC, native calmly drilled the 37-yard field goal through the uprights as time expired, giving 13th-ranked Clemson a 25-24 victory over No. 7 LSU.

"I just love that guy," Boyd said. "He is a warrior. He is one of the strongest people I know, and he just comes through in the clutch."

Boyd, the 2012 ACC Player of the Year, came through in the clutch, too. The Chick-fil-A Bowl's MVP led the Tigers on a 10-play, 60-yard drive in the final 1:39, and it was not easy.

After being sacked on third down, Clemson faced a fourth down-and-16 from its own 14-yard line. It appeared LSU had Clemson right where it wanted them, but so did Boyd.

Clemson ran a switch play with two seams, with the receivers crossing. When Boyd walked up to the line, he saw the coverage and noticed someone had the inside guy. Wide receiver DeAndre Hopkins, who crushed just about every receiving record in 2012, then got past the inside guy, and Boyd delivered a perfect strike for 26 yards and a first down.

The play is now simply known in Clemson lore as "4th-and-16."

"Nuk kind of squirted by one high and I didn't really know he was going to get on top of him like that so I kind of released a little bit earlier, but again, being the kind of receiver he is, he always finds the ball in the air," Boyd said. "It was just a ridiculous play. I could not really see it because some of these guys are 6-5 and 6-6, so just hearing the roars of the Clemson crowd was a great feeling and a great sound."

After the first-down catch by Hopkins, Boyd found his favorite target for seven yards, and then Hopkins drew a pass interference penalty from LSU safety Eric Reid that moved the football to the LSU 42. On second-and-seven from the 39, Boyd found Hopkins along the right sideline for a 13-yard gain to the 26, and then he hit Humphries on a slant that got the ball to the 16.

Two plays later, after Boyd positioned the football in the middle of the field on a keeper, Catanzaro was true with the fourth game-winning kick in Clemson history.

"I knew right when it left my foot that it was good," Catanzaro said. "I want to say I didn't even see it hit the net. I just took off like I did against Wake Forest, except this time I fell, which was good. Everybody dog-piled me, which was pretty cool."

What made it even cooler was the fact that Clemson had rallied from an 11-point deficit in the fourth quarter to win the game. Trailing 24-13, Boyd, who completed 36 of 50 passes for 346 yards, led the Tigers on a 13-play, 63-yard drive that took 5:26 off the clock. Catanzaro capped the drive with a 26-yard field goal to pull Clemson within eight points, 24-16 with 9:46 to play.

After the Clemson defense—which held LSU to 219 total yards—stopped the SEC Tigers on three plays, Boyd again engineered a scoring drive, this time ending with a 12-yard touchdown pass to Hopkins, the second time the two teamed up for a score.

Following a failed two-point conversion try, the Clemson defense stepped up big again by forcing another three-and-out, giving the football to the offense at its own 20 with 1:39 to play and all three timeouts remaining. Playing against one of the best defenses in the country, Boyd found Hopkins for the 26-yard gain a few moments later, and he knew then they were about to make history.

"When we crossed the 40, I knew we were good to go," Hopkins said. "We can't throw a pick; just go out there, drive the ball, and go win the game."

And that's what they did.

LEARNING HOW TO WIN

Prior to pregame warm-ups for the 2014 Discover Orange Bowl, Clemson offensive coordinator Chad Morris gathered his players and asked them to raise their hand if they were a part of what happened two years before in the Orange Bowl loss to West Virginia.

"I told them it wasn't any fun. Ten minutes into the third quarter it wasn't any fun. It was a bad taste, but we have a chance to go out there and do something about it," Morris said. "Coach [Dabo] Swinney talked about, 'We're going to be back. We're going to be back.' And we got back.

"To see our guys do what they did, it was great."

What the Tigers did was rally from a nine-point third-quarter deficit to beat No. 7 Ohio State 40-35.

It happened pretty fast, too. Clemson scored two touchdowns in a two-minute-and-15-second span to grab a 34-29 lead with 32 seconds to play in the third quarter. And it all started with a change of possession, just like the free fall in the game against West Virginia two years before.

In front 29-20 with a little under four minutes to go in the third quarter, Ohio State wide receiver Corey Brown went back to field a Bradley Pinion punt at his own 37, but he took his eye off the ball just long enough to drop it, allowing the Tigers' Robert Smith to fall on it at the OSU 33.

Three plays later, from the 30-yard line, quarterback Tajh Boyd and wide receiver Sammy Watkins made them pay as Watkins leaped up and snagged the ball over the head of Ohio State's Doran Grant for the touchdown.

On the Buckeyes' next possession, while scrambling to avoid a sack from defensive end Vic Beasley, quarterback Braxton Miller rolled to his left and tried to throw the ball to a receiver along the Clemson sideline; instead, Tiger safety Jayron Kearse stepped in front of the ball, and the Tigers were in business again, this time at the Ohio State 38.

Four plays later, highlighted by a 15-yard run by Boyd, the Clemson quarterback threw a three-yard touchdown pass to Martavis Bryant, who made an acrobatic catch while getting two feet in bounds to give the Tigers a 34-29 lead.

"Two years ago we were a very young team. We had won games, but we did not understand success and what came with it," Boyd said. "For us it was all about the transition and continuing to move forward. You see the accumulation of it in what we are now, just a driven team that knows how to win games in the clutch."

Clemson did it in coming from 11 points down in beating LSU in the 2012 Chick-fil-A Bowl and did it again in the season opener against Georgia. Those experiences came up big for the Tigers in the final moments of this Orange Bowl Classic.

After the Buckeyes rallied to take the lead on a Miller-to-Carlos Hyde 14-yard touchdown with 11:35 to play, the Tigers responded with a 10-play, 75-yard drive, capped when Boyd threw his fifth touchdown pass of the night—a five-yard throw back to tight end Stanton Seckinger with 6:16 to play.

"We had enough mistakes to probably lose it, some critical errors, but our guys showed lot of heart and they got it done," Swinney said.

Ohio State had two more chances to win the game, but Clemson's defense forced a Miller fumble and then an interception from linebacker Stephone Anthony on its final two possessions to win the game.

Suddenly, in that moment, the memories of the 2012 Orange Bowl were finally in the past, and Clemson was once again an Orange Bowl Champion, the first time since the 1982 Orange Bowl Classic.

"It means we are one step closer to our goal, which is to be the best team in the country," Swinney said.

A GUTTY PERFORMANCE

Deshaun Watson limped onto the field at Clemson Memorial Stadium with an injured left knee and helped Clemson do something it had not achieved in five years—he led the Tigers to a win over archrival South Carolina in 2014.

As we all found out from Head Coach Dabo Swinney in the moments after the game, Deshaun Watson's feat was more courageous than we all had thought. He took down the Gamecocks and head coach Steve Spurrier, not just on a bad knee, but on one that had a torn ACL.

Even with a torn left knee, the freshman quarterback threw for 269 yards and two touchdowns, while running for two more in No. 21 Clemson's 35-17 victory over South Carolina on Saturday.

"I wasn't really in a lot of pain. I just could not move it that much," Watson said afterward.

Watson went out of the game twice. On the Tigers' opening drive, after Clemson moved the football from its own three to the South Carolina 26, but following an incomplete pass to Germone Hopper, he took himself out of the game.

That drive ended with a missed field goal.

Leading 21-7 with just under three minutes to play in the first half, the Gainesville, GA, native left the game again when the Tigers moved the football to the USC 49. Again, he took himself out of the game, this time after running back Wayne Gallman ran off left guard for three yards.

That drive ended when backup Cole Stoudt threw an interception two plays later.

"My knee locked up on me. I was not used to the brace," Watson said. "It was real tight on me. That's how the brace is, but at the moment it locked up, so I had to come out."

Swinney said the brace was cutting off the circulation in Watson's calf, so they took him into the locker room just before the end of the first half, took the brace off and readjusted everything.

Watson returned in the third quarter and did not leave the game again. He led the Tigers to two more touchdowns after that, including rushing for a one-yard score in the fourth quarter that sealed the victory.

"Deshaun Watson, he is a mental and genetic freak. That's all I can say," Swinney said. "There is no other way I can say it to be honest with you."

Swinney said they thought Watson tore his ACL in the Georgia Tech game, but the MRI came back that it was an LCL—the same injury he suffered in high school—and he returned to limited workouts the week of the Georgia State game. But that Thursday prior to the game, he fell down in practice while running a passing drill through cones.

That Friday, they did another MRI and discovered he tore his ACL this time.

"This kid just played this whole game with a torn ACL," Swinney said. "And when he shot off and ran for that touchdown, that was just unbelievable. The only issue he had today was that his brace was so tight it was making his calf go to sleep."

Watson did not actually score a touchdown on the play Swinney described, but it was a gutty effort nonetheless. From the South Carolina 10, he ran nine yards on a scramble that put the ball at the one, and he scored on the next play—his first of his two rushing touchdowns. That gave the Tigers a 21-7 lead with 4:55 to play in the second quarter.

"This guy is special, he really is," offensive coordinator Chad Morris said. "He is a winner and I think the future is so bright for that young man. Obviously, we are a different team when he is in there. He is calm and he is understanding, and that is just what he does."

Watson is not the first Clemson quarterback to play with a torn ACL. Tajh Boyd played with a torn ACL his senior year of high school and led his team to a state championship. Former Tiger quarterback Mike Epply played the entire 1983 season with a torn ACL.

Swinney said Watson had already told him he wants to play in the Tigers' bowl game and he will have surgery soon after. Swinney said he should be back in time for summer workouts.

But Saturday was about beating the Gamecocks and ending the five-game losing streak to their rivals. And with his 14-of-19 passing, Watson was one of the main reasons why.

"He was great. I will tell you, I'm amazed," Swinney said. "I watched him all week in practice and I really could not believe what I was seeing. It was like, 'Hey, let's go!'

"The confidence he brings to everybody else is special. He makes everybody else better."

And he did it with a torn ACL.

IT WAS B.Y.O.G. BRING YOUR OWN GUTS AGAINST NOTRE DAME

It had been 38 years since the "Golden Domers" last visited Clemson's Death Valley. On that day, a guy named Joe Montana rallied No. 5 Notre Dame from 10 points down in the fourth quarter to break No. 15 Clemson's heart.

Few expected the same kind of ending when the Irish brought a freshman quarterback named DeShawn Kizer into Death Valley on October 3, 2015 for a prime-time game that was being seen nationally on ABC.

Kizer, who was barely wet between the ears as a college quarterback, was no Joe Montana.

He was not even the starting quarterback when the season began. That honor belonged to Malik Zaire. But when Zaire broke his foot in the fourth quarter at Virginia, Kizer was thrown into action. He did have a Montana-like moment in that game when he threw a 39-yard touchdown pass to wide receiver Will Fuller with 12 seconds to play to beat the Cavaliers.

But No. 11 Clemson is not Virginia. If the Tigers are able to get out to a two-score lead on the Irish in the second half this time around, there will be no miraculous comeback.

Kizer played well in beating Georgia Tech and UMass the two weeks before the journey to Clemson. He was completing 67.7 percent of his passes for 541 yards and five touchdowns to go against two interceptions.

But Clemson is his first game on the road as the starter. It's Death Valley. There are 85,000 people screaming at him, not for him. How will he handle it? If Clemson can take away the running game, which will be defensive coordinator Brent Venables's game plan, can the freshman make the necessary plays to beat the Tigers when he has to throw the ball in obvious passing situations?

As for Clemson and quarterback Deshaun Watson, they were looking for respect. Heading into their clash with No. 6 Notre Dame, all they heard was how great the Irish were and how Clemson would not be able to match their physicality on either side of the ball.

In a way, he felt like Clemson was getting disrespected or not the credit it deserved for beating teams like Oklahoma, Ohio State, and LSU in the previous three seasons.

"From what I have been seeing we have kind of never had that respect, and for some reason we can't get over that hump," Watson said.

There was a reason why the media and the so-called experts were thinking Clemson could not beat the Irish. In the first two weeks, Clemson took out FCS foe Wofford 49-10 and then beat App State 41-10. Not exactly powerhouses, to say the least.

Then the Tigers struggled at Louisville in Week 3, escaping with a 20-17 victory to open up the ACC season.

In each of the last two weeks, Clemson had fallen in the polls despite the fact it had not lost a game. After beating Louisville, the Tigers dropped from No. 9 in the Amway Coaches poll to No. 10. After having the week off, they again dropped in the coaches' poll to No. 11.

They also slipped from No. 11 to No. 12 in the Associated Press poll.

"They have said we played two bad teams and then we struggled with Louisville," defensive end Shaq Lawson said. "We pretty much try not to pay attention to that because at the end of the day, if we do our job and

execute on the field and win, we are going to move up eventually."

Clemson and its fan base got the respect they were seeking when 82,415 fans sat in a driving rain storm and watched the Tigers build a 21-3 lead through three quarters.

Clemson jumped out to a 14-0 lead right off the bat thanks to a Watson-to-Jordan Leggett six-yard touchdown pass on the game's opening drive, which Watson followed up with a 13-yard touchdown pass to wide receiver Artavis Scott on the next possession.

Just six minutes and 17 seconds into the game, the Tigers already owned a two-score lead. Clemson led 14-3 at halftime.

It did not take long for the Tigers to extend the lead to 18 points in the third quarter. On the kickoff, kicker Ammon Lakip stripped C.J. Sanders of the football, and C.J. Fuller recovered it at the Notre Dame 29.

On third-and-two from the 21, Watson ran up the middle, broke one would-be tackle, and walked into the end zone for a 21-3 advantage.

"Give credit to Clemson. I thought they came out fresh and aggressive and made things difficult for us early on," Notre Dame head coach Brian Kelly said. "Certainly, they carried the play in the first half."

But the game was far from over. Kizer was no Joe Montana, but he sure did his best to impersonate him.

Kizer, who threw for 321 yards and two touchdowns, first hit running C.J. Prosise for a 56-yard touchdown on a wheel route that was perfectly executed down the far sideline.

Following a Greg Huegel 35-yard field goal to extend Clemson's lead to 24-9 with 10:56 to play, Kizer ran three yards for a second score and finally found Torii Hunter, Jr., for a one-yard score to pull Notre Dame within two points with seven seconds to play.

Kizer threw for 202 yards in the fourth quarter on 9 of 12 passing.

"I wish we could have supported him better," Kelly said. "I'm really proud of him and the way he competed. He played well enough for us to win."

Clemson finally stopped Kiser on the next play when Watkins blew through a double team and helped Ben Boulware make the game-winning tackle on the Irish's two-point attempt to tie the game as the Tigers hung on for a 24-22 victory.

For a second straight game, the defense found a way to make one more play at the end. When it was over, an emotional Swinney delivered one of the best postgame interviews of all time to ABC sideline reporter Heather Cox.

"It ain't always perfect. But what I told them tonight was, listen, we give you scholarships. We give you stipends, and meals, and a place to live. We give you nice uniforms. But I can't give you guts. And I can't give you heart. And tonight, hey, it was B.Y.O.G. Bring your own guts. And they brought some guts and some heart and they never quit 'til the last play."

And luckily, Kizer was not Joe Montana.

2015 WAS CLEMSON'S SEASON OF HARVEST

In front of him sat Nick Saban, the one guy Dabo Swinney and the rest of the college football world has been chasing for more than a decade. Also in the room were some of college football's other greats such as running backs Eddie George and Marcus Allen, wide receiver and Super Bowl MVP Desmond Howard, and quarterbacks Danny Wuerffel, Ty Detmer, Tim Tebow, and the great Doug Flutie, to name a few.

This was the Who's Who of College Football. This was the Heisman Trophy Presentation in New York. This is where all the greats in the history of college football come together each year to form a brotherhood unlike no other.

And there sat Dabo Swinney among them all. There he was supporting his quarterback, Deshaun Watson, a Heisman Trophy Finalist who in just two short years had taken little ole Clemson and put it at the top of the College Football Landscape.

Though Watson was a Heisman Finalist, December 12, 2015, was not about him or Swinney. No, it was about Clemson. Here it was, a program in the midst of a historical season, one in which it ran through the regular season and the Atlantic Coast Conference Championship Game undefeated. One in which it debuted in the top spot of the College Football Playoff Rankings and never let it go.

Here was little ole Clemson rubbing elbows with the elite in college football. Here was Clemson getting the respect it, and its fiery head coach, had been clamoring for.

As Swinney so eloquently said at the World's Largest Pizza Party the Sunday after the Tigers won its second ACC title in five years, "This is a celebration of this special team, and it is a celebration of Clemson University and what this place stands for and what it is all about.

"I am going to give you a little word and it is something I believe in. It comes from Galatians 6:9. It says, 'Do not grow weary from doing what is right and good. For at the appropriate time you will reap a harvest of blessings if you do not give up.' This team has not grown weary. They have stayed the course and they have overcome all kinds of obstacles. What I want you to know is that this is our season of harvest, but it is just getting started."

In 2015, Clemson's harvest definitely came in. It was an unprecedented run of honors and awards in the program's history. The 14 wins in a season was a first for the program, as was the six straight weeks the Tigers ranked No. 1 in the country.

Watson was Clemson's first Heisman Finalist as well the winner of the Davey O'Brien Award as the nation's top quarterback. He along with Swinney and defensive end Shaq Lawson were named the ACC's MVP, Coach and Defensive Player of the Year.

Swinney also won the Eddie Robinson Award, the Walter Camp Award, as well as several other National Coach of the Year honors. Watson and Lawson were named Consensus first-team All-Americans, while a record six players were named to some kind of All-America team.

The other All-Americans included safety Jayron Kearse, cornerback Mackensie Alexander, tight end Jordan Leggett, and kicker Greg Huegel.

A record 18 players, including the entire offensive line, were named on one of the three All-ACC Teams put out by the Atlantic Coast Sports Media Association (ACSMA). Ten of those 18 players were named first-team All-ACC by ACSMA, the Associated Press, or the league's coaches.

And three times—after only gracing the cover one other time in the program's history—a Clemson player was on the cover of *Sports Illustrated*, Watson on the first two and Lawson on the third.

"For these young men here, our season of harvest is for several years to come and we are going to enjoy every single second of it," Swinney said.

CLEMSON LETS ITS PLAY DO THE TALKING AGAINST OKLAHOMA

It started before Oklahoma and Clemson even arrived in South Florida. Sooners quarterback Baker Mayfield, who did not play in the Tigers' 40-6 victory, said what happened in the 2014 Russell Athletic Bowl was not going to happen this time around.

Mayfield, like Clemson quarterback Deshaun Watson, watched the Russell Athletic Bowl from the sidelines. The former walk-on was a transfer from Texas Tech, and he felt as if things would have been different had he been able to play that evening in Orlando, FL.

Meanwhile back in Clemson, the Tigers were downplaying the Russell Athletic Bowl victory, calling this a different year with two entirely different teams. Clemson went about its business and kept its nose to the ground and kept working like it has most of the season.

But the Sooners kept chirping, especially when they got to Miami.

"We say that it is never going to happen again," Oklahoma running back Samaje Perine said. "Last year, it looked like we did not want to be there. They were the better team last year and Coach [Bob] Stoops brings that up and tells us that it is a different atmosphere now. Whether we liked our position or not, we still had to show up and we did not show up, and they did.

"This year it can't happen like that and it is not going to happen like that."

The trash talk did not end there. Perine called out the Clemson defense. He did not think they were as good as the year before and that the Sooners were going to prove that in the Capital One Orange Bowl.

The Tigers came into the national semifinal game ranked seventh nationally in total defense, while leading the country in pass percentage defense, third-down defense, tackles for loss, and three-and-outs. But down the stretch of the season, Clemson's defense struggled to stop inferior teams such as Syracuse and South Carolina, especially in the running game.

Oklahoma, after all, was averaging 235 yards a game on the ground as Perine and fellow running back Joe Mixon gained more than 2,000 yards combined. During their seven-game winning streak leading up to the Orange Bowl, the Sooners averaged nearly 300 rushing yards and 52 points a game.

"There is always a crease with this offense," Perine said confidently. "There is always a crease somewhere and over the period of time we watched film on them, there was always a crease somewhere that can be exposed and we plan on exposing them."

Perine continued his verbal abuse on Clemson's defense by saying it was not as big or as strong as the unit last year that limited the Sooners to 278 total yards.

"Obviously, it is a correct statement. We were better last year. We were No. 1 in the nation and now we are No. 7 so it is what it is," Clemson linebacker Ben Boulware said with sarcasm and contempt.

Boulware apologized to Perine for being just the seventh-ranked defense and for allowing 295.7 yards per game, 128.8 of which comes on the ground despite the poor showings at Syracuse and South Carolina.

"Hopefully, they don't expose us," Boulware said with a grin. "I'm not one to try to make any controversy or make any big headlines. He can say what he wants to say, but they cannot talk their way into a win. You have to play on Thursday. You have to play the game so they can talk all they want to. Obviously, that is how they are trying to win the game, but you have to play the game. You have to line up and beat the man in front of you so we will see come game day."

Clemson safety Jayron Kearse did not care about making headlines.

"I'm not surprised [they are running their mouth]. They lost 40-6 last year," he said. "They need to talk junk. They need to boost themselves up, they need to give themselves confidence and talk their way into a win.

"We don't have to talk. We put it on film last year and we put it on film these 13 games this year, and we are going to go out and do the same thing on Thursday."

Things heated up even more after the Coaches' Luncheon the day before the game. As the players were loading up on their respected buses, verbal blows were exchanged.

"They have a lot of weaknesses and we will expose them, too," Clemson's All-America defensive end Shaq Lawson said.

Early on, it looked as if the Tigers might get exposed. The Sooners took the opening drive of the game and shoved the football right down Clemson's throat, going 75 yards in 10 plays. Perine carried the ball five times and gained 33 yards on the drive, including a one-yard touchdown with 11:16 to go in the first quarter.

To compound matters, Clemson lost Lawson to a knee injury on the second drive, leaving people to wonder if Clemson could keep up with the Sooners.

"He felt real bad that he was not going to be able to play and contribute to this big game," defensive end Kevin Dodd said. "Shaq is a real good competitor. He wanted to play in this game, but he couldn't, unfortunately.

"I knew I had to step it up so I went to the backups and said, 'It is just football at the end of the day. Do what you do and it would not be any different than practice."

Lawson's backup, Austin Bryant, took Dodd's advice and went out and did his job. The true freshman held his own against the Sooners. Bryant finished the game with eight tackles and helped with one of Clemson's five sacks on the day.

Though the Tigers defense settled in, the offense was still dealing with a little nervousness. Clemson totaled just 47 yards in the opening quarter and had just a field goal. But then head coach Dabo Swinney reached into his bag of tricks and pulled out a fake punt for the ages.

Following a 46-yard run by quarterback Deshaun Watson to move the ball to midfield early in the second quarter, the drive bogged down at the Oklahoma 44. It seemed as if the Tigers were going to try to pin the Sooners deep when punter Andy Teasdall rolled to his right, but then he stopped and threw the ball back to 315-pound defensive tackle Christian Wilkins, who ran a wheel route on the play and was wide open down the sideline. The gain went for 31 yards to the Oklahoma 13, and two plays later Watson was in the end zone and the Tigers were in front 10-7 with 12:45 to play in the first half.

"It was a great play, and I thought a spark that we needed," Swinney said afterward. "I felt like we were a little stagnant right there, a little tight, and we needed something—I wanted to send a message to the guys, 'Listen, we're here to play, and let's cut it loose.'"

It got Clemson's offense loose, all right. The Tigers totaled 258 yards in the second quarter. Though Mayfield led the Sooners on a late touchdown drive to grab a 17-16 lead and Watson threw an inexplicable pass that was intercepted in the end zone with 13 seconds left in the first half, Clemson was still in control.

"On offense, we were pretty balanced," said Watson, who totaled 332 yards and two touchdowns. "We have a great rushing game and a great passing game, so if you want to stop the running game, then we can pass the ball. You want to stop the pass, then we can run the ball. It doesn't really matter what the defense does. We just focus on us and our job and just really focus on that one play, and if it's a run play, we dominate the line of scrimmage, and if it's a pass play, the receivers get open and make competitive plays."

Clemson sent a message on the first play of the second half. Gallman broke a run off the right side and ran over a defender on his way to an 11-yard gain.

"We could tell at that moment that they were done, physically, maybe even a little bit mentally," left guard

Eric Mac Lain said. "We were just running all over them, and thankfully Wayne and Deshaun both were over 100 yards and just really dominated."

Gallman gained 111 of his 150 yards in the second half, while Watson rushed for 145 yards on 24 carries and also scored a touchdown. Gallman scored on a one-yard plunge to complete the opening drive in the third quarter. That gave Clemson a 23-17 lead at the time. His fourth quarter touchdown from four yards out put the game away.

"Wayne Gallman was relentless in the second half, and that's how we played," Swinney said.

The Tigers finished the afternoon with 530 total yards, including 312 on the ground. It marked the 10th straight game Clemson's offense totaled 500 yards. Watson also threw for 187 yards, including a 35-yard touchdown pass to Hunter Renfrow that was a dagger into the Sooners' hearts.

The Clemson defense was relentless, too. The Tigers quieted the Sooners, first by knocking Perine and Mixon from the game, and later by harassing Mayfield into five sacks and two interceptions.

When it was all said and done, the Sooners finished the game with 378 total yards. They were held 165 yards under their season average, while gaining just 67 yards on 33 rushes.

"There was a lot of talking but they kind of got quiet going into the third and fourth quarter," Clemson cornerback Cordrea Tankersley said.

Oklahoma got quiet because there was nothing left for them to be loud about. The Tigers outscored the nation's top-rated offense 21-0 in the last 30 minutes, limiting Oklahoma to 121 total yards.

"We just came together as a unit and did what we do best," Tankersley said. "We tried to lock everything down and we challenged each other, and it paid off."

It paid off with a 37-17 victory, advancing the top-ranked Tigers to the National Championship Game against No. 2 Alabama.

"We just came out and did what we do best. We just wanted to show the world what we are capable of and that we are still not finished," Tankersley said.

And they did it with their play, not by running their mouth.

WATSON PROVES HOW SPECIAL HE REALLY IS

Following it heartbreaking loss to Alabama in the National Championship Game, Clemson quarterback Deshaun Watson was asked, "Where do you most need to improve heading into next season?"

Without any hesitation, senior left guard Eric Mac Lain chimed in.

"Nowhere," Mac Lain said.

Watson smiled and the reporters in the room laughed, but it was not a laughing matter. Mac Lain was being serious.

It's hard to find a flaw in Deshaun Watson's game. Thanks to his 405 passing yards against Alabama's top-rated defense, Watson became the first player in FBS history to throw for 4,000 yards and run for 1,000 more in the same season.

The Crimson Tide had no answer for him as he threw four touchdown passes and ran for 73 yards. In all, Watson totaled 478 yards—a new championship game record at the time.

"He's special. He really is," Clemson head coach Dabo Swinney said. "We had 550 yards of offense. I'm really pleased with how he played. That's one of the things Coach [Nick] Saban was talking to me about after the game.

"This guy, he's special. Again, he's got great toughness, great heart, a great mind for the game, and just made some huge plays all the way to the end. What a great throw and catch by he and [Jordan] Leggett on the last touchdown there."

Watson completed 37-of-47 passes and four touchdowns to only one interception. The sophomore helped Clemson rack up a season-high 550 total yards against Alabama's vaunted defense, while converting on 6-of-14 third downs.

"We thought, to be honest with you, that we could do a better job against their quarterback than what we did. He did a fantastic job in the game," Saban said.

Like anyone who has played Watson, it was difficult for Alabama to contain him and force him to stay in the pocket. It was almost as if Watson were one step ahead of the Crimson Tide all night.

"You know, we like to play more man-to-man, but when you play against such an athletic quarterback and you're playing man-to-man, nobody is looking at the quarterback so that makes it tough, and when we did play zone tonight we didn't do a very good job,' we didn't tackle very well, break on the ball like we needed to. He extended some plays and made some big plays, but the guy is a fantastic player."

As for the original question, "Where do you most need to improve heading into next season?"

"I mean, just my whole game. I mean, it will really start when we get back to school, start watching this film, fix some of the mistakes I made and just get back rolling," Watson said. "Putting on some weight, getting in the weight room some more, and taking that next step in my game and level. I talked to Derrick Henry after the game, and we're going to try to link up after the off-season and learn from him and just really build that relationship. He's the Heisman winner, national champion, so I'm trying to do the same thing and just learn from guys that have been there and have done it."

Watson would have won the 2016 National Championship game had it not been for a breakdown in Clemson's special teams.

It was bound to happen at some point. All year long Clemson has gotten away with one special teams blunder after another. However, on the biggest stage in college football, it came back to bite them.

The call of the game came early in the fourth quarter, when Alabama surprised Clemson with an onside kick after tying the game at 24 with 10:34 to play. Marlon Humphrey caught the ball out of the air to give the ball to Alabama, and a couple of plays later, quarterback Jake Coker hit tight end O.J. Howard with a 51-yard touchdown pass to take the lead 31-24 with 9:45 to go.

Later in the quarter, Alabama's Kenyan Drake returned a Greg Huegel kickoff 95 yards for a touchdown with 7:31 to play in the game. It was the Crimson Tide's 10th nonoffensive touchdown of the season and the one that ultimately ended Clemson's magical season in disappointment as Alabama beat the Tigers 45-40 to win its fourth national title in seven years.

"Championship football is really just a game of a few plays and that is really what this one came down to, just a few plays," Swinney said.

Clemson had just cut the Tide's lead to 31-27 when Huegel angled the kickoff toward the left sideline. Drake took the ball, broke to his left, and then found the sideline before diving into the end zone for a 37-27 lead with 7:31 to play.

"Obviously, the two special teams plays were huge momentum plays," Swinney said.

The Tigers responded with a 15-yard touchdown pass to Artavis Scott with 4:40 to play in the game. But Alabama, which used big plays all night, used a 63-yard pass to Howard to set up Henry's one-yard touchdown with 1:07 to go to put the game out of reach.

Watson threw a 24-yard touchdown pass to Leggett with 12 seconds to play, but Alabama recovered the onside kick to secure the victory.

"Obviously, we wanted to win the game and we came up a little short, but I think at least the nation saw tonight why we've been so successful," Swinney said. "They saw the heart of our team. This team just has an incredible will to win and heart, and I think they gave us everything they had."

Watson threw for 405 yards and four touchdowns, but it was not enough.

"Going into the game, I was expecting to win. I thought we should have won," Watson said. "But like Coach Swinney said, there were a few plays we did not capitalize on, and I missed some throws, we dropped some balls and just had some missed miscues.

"At the end of the day, I wanted the W," Watson continued.

A year later, he got his chance again to get one.

FINISH WITH NO REGRETS

In 2015, Clemson had the opportunity do something no team in college football has done—go 15-0.

After three quarters in the College Football Playoff Championship Game against Alabama, it looked as if Clemson were going to do just that. Wayne Gallman's one-yard run with 4:48 to play in the third quarter gave the Tigers a 24-21 lead, a lead they carried into the fourth quarter.

But thanks to a brilliant onside-kick call from Nick Saban and a 100-yard kickoff return from Kenyan Drake, the Crimson Tide scored 24 fourth quarter points to beat the Tigers 45-40, ending the perfect season and the quest for the program's second national championship.

"We played 15 games and lost the last one. We were 14-0. We were almost perfect and we let it slip out of our hands," Clemson linebacker Ben Boulware said.

All of a sudden, the Tigers, like everyone else in college football, were back at square one. They were looking up at defending National Champion Alabama and had to climb that preverbal mountain again, and all the things that come along with it, to get back to where they were just seven months ago with a national championship staring them in the face.

"I will not say we went to the bottom of the mountain, but even if we would have won the game, we still would have had to start over. It isn't any different," quarterback Deshaun Watson said.

The difference is being the defending national champion or the runner-up.

"It's probably easier, to be honest with you. We have a highly motivated team," Clemson Head Coach Dabo Swinney said. "I think it's just the culture of our program. Regardless of whether we won 10 or won 14, it's always about what's next."

In 2016, Clemson was one of the favorites to make it make back to the College Football Playoff, but was that enough? Was winning a second straight ACC Championship enough? Was making it to the CFP good enough? Is just making it to the National Title Game, again, enough?

"We didn't win the game. We finished with some regrets. We want to finish with no regrets," Swinney said.

To finish with no regrets, the Tigers first had to start with some. In the 49 previous times Clemson entered a fourth quarter with the lead prior to the 2015 title game, the Tigers had not lost under Swinney's direction. It also marked the first time in the program's history it lost a game when gaining 500 or more yards.

"It is definitely motivation. We have a nice chip on our shoulder," Boulware said.

That chip had been on Clemson's shoulder during mat drills in February and during spring practice during March and April. Even in this summer the Tigers have not forgotten how close they were and how far they had to go in order to get back there, again.

"We have to start all the way back over. New class, new group . . . seniors and juniors left for the NFL. It is a whole new year," Watson said.

In the previous five years, Clemson had proven itself to be one of the best in the country in college football, winning 56 games and posting five straight 10-win seasons. But as the 2016 season began to rise, it had to prove it all over again.

"We've got to go prove it and earn it all over again with our daily commitment. We start over," Swinney said. "New team, new chemistry, new leadership . . . pay the price all over again with a humble and hungry spirit."

The overall success of the program since 2011 had been incredibly consistent, but Swinney said the 2016 team had been the easiest to motivate. There already seemed to be a sense of urgency in place.

"We are going to reload and do it all over again. It's not that difficult," Boulware said. "It sucks losing the last game, but you learn from it and grow from it, then you get back to work."

This time they want to finish with no regrets.

Game 1: Clemson 19, Auburn 13

Already thin at defensive end with the losses of Shaq Lawson and Kevin Dodd jumping a year early to the NFL, Dabo Swinney and defensive coordinator Brent Venables were a little uncomfortable about the lack of inexperience it had on the edges.

The Clemson coaches felt okay with Austin Bryant and Clelin Ferrell as their two starters off the edge, but they weren't sure about those they had behind them. Bryant was their most experienced player after having a monster performance in the Tigers' Orange Bowl win over Oklahoma, while Ferrell was a redshirt freshman with a ton of potential.

Behind them were two redshirt sophomores in Richard Yeargin and Chris Register, who had very little experience, while the coaches desperately wanted to redshirt freshman Xavier Kelly.

In the spring, the coaching staff came up with an idea to cross-train defensive tackle Christian Wilkins at defensive end. Though he was 6-foot-4 and weighed 305 pounds, Wilkins—outside of wide receiver Hunter Renfrow—was perhaps the most athletic guy on the team.

As a freshman, Wilkins found himself blocking in short yardage and goal line situations for the offense, and in the Orange Bowl he caught a 31-yard pass on a fake punt to set up the Tigers' first touchdown that afternoon. In the off-season, it was commonplace to see the jovial defensive tackle on Instagram or Twitter dunking a basketball or catching footballs while riding a bicycle.

Wilkins spent the last half of spring practice working on the outside, and to no one's surprise he excelled. However, when fall camp began three and half months later, Wilkins was back at his natural position of defensive tackle, where he was supposed to start alongside senior Carlos Watkins.

With the development of Ferrell, as well as Yeargin and Register, the coaching staff felt comfortable with what they had at defensive end barring injuries. All was well until Bryant fractured the fifth metatarsal in his right foot during the Tigers' first full scrimmage of camp, which was three weeks before they were set to kick off at Auburn.

It's a good thing the coaching staff planned ahead. With so much depth on the interior of the defensive line, it was easy for Wilkins to move outside until Bryant's return, which was not for another five weeks. However, Wilkins had just two weeks to get adjusted and a lot to do before the second-ranked Tigers opened the season.

"You are playing to more space for one, and two, there are a lot more things that can happen," said Wilkins as he tried to explain the differences of playing defensive end as compared to defensive tackle. "You have down blocks from the tackles. You have sniffers and fullbacks coming at you, you have to watch the quarterback. There are just so many different things.

"You may have to drop in coverage. There are a lot more things that I will have to do that I'm not used to doing when I play defensive tackle."

Wilkins went to work and attacked his new role hard as he tried to gain as much knowledge as possible.

"It is a little different than playing inside. You have a lot more responsibilities and you have to find ways to beat guys. Really, I'm just going to get in the film room, study as hard as I can and get with the other defensive ends and Coach (Marion) Hobby and just pick up everything I can to make sure I do an efficient job out there."

Swinney had a pretty good idea how he was going to do. During the Atlantic Coast Conference's weekly coaches' teleconference call with the media earlier in the week, Swinney said Wilkins was going to play a major role in the outcome of the game.

He was right.

From the outset, Auburn tried to use its speed and trickery to test the big guy. And every time they did, they wished they hadn't. Wilkins did a marvelous job of setting the edge on the outside, and if he could not get the tackle, he funneled things back inside, where linebackers Kendall Joseph, Ben Boulware, and Dorian O'Daniel were waiting.

"Overall, our defense was tremendous," Swinney said. "I thought we controlled the line of scrimmage. Those guys were disruptive. Christian Wilkins was the player of the game. I can't say enough about him."

Overall, Clemson had 14 tackles behind the line of scrimmage, four sacks, forced a fumble, and had two interceptions as the defense, not the offense, led the Tigers to a 19-13 victory. The Tigers held Auburn to 87 rushing yards, the lowest for a Gus Malzahn-coached team.

For his efforts Wilkins was named as the team's defensive MVP for the game.

"I really feel like it was a team effort tonight. It was a good job by our defense," Wilkins said. "We were tough tonight. We showed our guts, and that we were not afraid to compete."

Wilkins just did not get it done on defense. He also helped on offense too, as he was the lead blocker for the Tigers on fourth-and-goal from the one midway through the second quarter. The play had Wilkins offset from the line on the right side of the formation, which includes fellow defensive tackle Dexter Lawrence and his 6-foot-5, 340-pound frame.

Lawrence went in motion from the fullback spot and set up right behind Wilkins just before the ball was snapped. Led by Wilkins, the two plowed open a lane big enough for a truck to go through as running back Wayne Gallman called it the easiest touchdown of his life.

"That was fun. I like that," Wilkins said afterward. "I'm glad that the offensive coaches have enough confidence in us to go out there and do that and let us play a little offense."

When it comes to Wilkins, the coaching staff has all the confidence in the world in his abilities as Swinney even joked if the sophomore keeps catching the ball like he has done, they might just move him to slot receiver.

"I'm just having fun out there and just doing whatever it is the coaches ask me to do," Wilkins said.

Game 2: Clemson 30, Troy 24

To say the 30-24 victory over Troy by the nation's second-ranked team was an ugly win is an understatement. Clemson receivers dropped seven passes, quarterback Deshaun Watson threw two interceptions, and Ray-Ray McCloud let go of the ball at the one-yard line on what would have been a 75-yard punt return for a touchdown.

The defense even had its moments as it allowed a 66-yard touchdown run on a fourth-and-one play. It just wasn't pretty, but despite all the mistakes, the Tigers still found a way to win.

Watson bounced back from one of his worst performances to throw two touchdown passes in the fourth quarter, one to defensive lineman Christian Wilkins from one yard out, and the second one, a 23-yard pass to Deon Cain.

Watson finished the game with three touchdown passes overall, while completing 27 of 53 passes for 292 yards.

With Clemson clinging to a three-point lead early in the fourth quarter, the Tigers brought in its jumbo package on third-and-goal from the one-yard line. Watson faked the handoff to running back Wayne Gallman and then threw it to a wide-open Wilkins in the end zone for a 20-10 lead with 13:50 to play in the game.

Watson threw his third touchdown pass when he found Cain for a 23-yard strike with 10:00 to go.

Game 3: Clemson 59, S.C. State 0

No one is surprised Clemson rolled over S.C. State in Death Valley. However, the nearly 80,000 that were on hand were glad to see it.

After struggling to find any offensive rhythm in the first two weeks of the season, the third-ranked Tigers

got things going early and often against the Bulldogs in a 59-0 victory. The offense totaled 555 yards, and the defense held S.C. State to 102 total yards while pitching its first of three shutouts in the season.

Quarterback Deshaun Watson, who apologized earlier that week for having a bad attitude, came out focused as he completed 12 of 15 passes for 152 yards and three touchdowns. Watson found wide receiver Ray McCloud on touchdowns of seven and 36 yards, while hitting Deon Cain on another that covered 17 yards.

In all, Watson, Nick Schuessler, and Kelly Bryant threw five touchdown passes. It marked the first time since 2010 the Tigers had three different quarterbacks toss a touchdown pass in a single game.

Schuessler threw a 45-yard touchdown pass to freshman Diondre Overton, while Kelly hit Trevion Thompson for a seven-yard score in the third quarter.

Freshman running back Tavien Feaster had a four-yard touchdown run in the third quarter.

The Tigers (3-0) led 45-0 at the break, the most points scored by a Clemson team in one half since they did the same at Duke in 2012. Clemson scored 31 points in the first quarter, the most points ever in the first quarter by a Clemson team.

Game 4: Clemson 26, Georgia Tech 7

The last time Clemson won a football game at Bobby Dodd Stadium, Dabo Swinney's youngest son was just born. Clay Swinney is now 13 years old.

"He had a bottle in his mouth. It has been long enough," Clemson Head Coach Dabo Swinney said.

Swinney was just a young wide receivers coach himself back then, and in the five meetings that followed, Clemson found different ways to lose each of those football games. But it seemed as if the Curse of Bobby Dodd Stadium were lifted on a late September Thursday night in Atlanta.

After the Tigers had just stonewalled Georgia Tech on its first possession, Ray-Ray McCloud took a punt at the Clemson 42, made one guy miss, and then ran up the middle of the field 11 yards, where a Tech defender tackled him and poked the football out of his arm.

Here it was, one of those crazy plays that always seem to bounce Georgia Tech's way when the Tigers play on Grant Field. This was the early break the Yellow Jackets needed. But it never happened. Reserve linebacker Chad Smith was "Johnny on the Spot" as he jumped on the loose football, and Clemson continued to move forward.

Smith's recovery was the proof the Tigers needed that they weren't cursed, as they rolled to a 26-7 victory.

"Really, as a team, we were tired of hearing how it had been 13 years since we won down here and everything," defensive lineman Christian Wilkins said afterward. "So we just took it as a personal challenge to end that streak and come out with a win."

With Clemson already in front 14-0, again it was obvious there was no curse when late in the second quarter Georgia Tech's Lance Austin intercepted a Deshaun Watson pass in the end zone after Mike Williams ran the wrong route. Austin ran the ball out of the end zone when Williams grabbed him, and as he was trying to pull him to the ground, Austin's own teammate knocked the ball out of his arm while trying to jump over him. The ball bounced into the end zone, where Austin recovered the ball.

After a brief meeting, the officials ruled the play as a safety for Clemson. Instead of Tech getting the ball at the 20, and maybe having another momentum play, the Tigers got the ball back, and Watson orchestrated a last-second scoring drive in the final seconds—a 9-yard touchdown pass to Jordan Leggett—to conclude the first half for a 23-0 lead.

The defense proved there was no curse with one of the more impressive defensive performances in recent history. Clemson held the previously undefeated Yellow Jackets to 124 yards of total offense and limited their running game and the triple option to just 95 yards on 38 carries.

"That's a good job by our defense. Hats off to our defensive staff, they got us ready and hats off to all the other guys. They really bought in and were focused this week," Wilkins said.

Georgia Tech had just 22 total yards in the first half.

"I just think speed, quickness, size. . . . Those big guys inside can really move," Georgia Tech Head Coach Paul Johnson said.

And maybe that's why the curse was lifted? Or maybe there was never a curse after all. Regardless, Clemson made sure there was not one on Thursday night in Atlanta.

Game 5: Clemson 42, Louisville 36

Before the 2016 season had even began, Louisville quarterback Lamar Jackson was already stealing some headlines from Deshaun Watson, not that the Clemson quarterback cared or even noticed.

Though Jackson was not quite ready to be the passer Bobby Petrino likes in his pro-style offense, the Cardinals' head coach could no longer keep the heralded athlete under wraps. He had to let Jackson be who he was, and then hope to tame him later on.

In the 2015 regular-season finale against Kentucky, Petrino unleashed Jackson on a Wildcats team that was not prepared for what was about to happen. He let Jackson be Lamar Jackson, and the result was 316 total yards and three touchdowns, including 186 and two scores on the ground.

With a month to prepare for the Music City Bowl, Petrino fit the offense around Lamar Jackson's talents, and ever since then, the Pompano Beach, FL, native has been unstoppable. The freshman lit up Texas A&M for 453 total yards and three touchdowns, including an ACC-

record 226 rushing yards for a quarterback in a 27-21 victory.

And though Watson, the reigning ACC Player of the Year and a finalist for the Heisman Trophy in 2015, was still the media's darling at the ACC Football Kickoff last July, Jackson was starting to get his own little following.

Thanks to his two performances to close out the 2015 season, the media was intrigued. They wanted to see his personality, what made him tick. They wanted to know if he believed he was the best player in the ACC.

However, Jackson did not have to answer. His teammate did it for him.

"He is the best player in the country. He just does stuff that I have not ever seen before. I'm glad we only have to face him in practice," Louisville linebacker Keith Kelsey said. "He is going to surprise a lot of people this year, though it will not surprise any of us."

While reporters were trying to figure out who Lamar Jackson was, Deshaun Watson was on the other end of the building receiving all the pats on the back and the accolades from the previous year. Watson was again picked to win the ACC Player of Year Award, while he and the Tigers were the overwhelming favorite to win the ACC for a second straight season.

So without either one knowing, battle lines had already been drawn between the savvy veteran from Clemson, whom everybody loved, and the upstart from Louisville, who had shown flashes of greatness, but there was still too small of a sample size to know his full potential.

When the season finally kicked off, Jackson did not disappoint. He totaled 405 yards and eight touchdowns, while averaging 11.1 yards per play, in a 70-14 rout of Charlotte. He followed that up with 610 total yards and five touchdowns in a 62-28 win at Syracuse.

It took just two games, but Jackson caught the attention of the college football world. He was throwing and running for touchdowns and even hurdling defenders. He was literally a human highlight film that resembled a computer-generated player on a PlayStation game more than a human being.

But against Florida State in Week 3, there was no way Jackson was going to put up eye-popping numbers, or so they said.

They were wrong.

Jackson totaled 362 yards against FSU, while totaling five touchdowns in a 63-20 thumping of then-No. 2 Florida State.

"He not only welcomed this national stage, but he seized it," said ABC play-by-play announcer Chris Fowler.

Meanwhile, back in Clemson, the Tigers were undefeated, but Watson and the Clemson offense were not putting up the numbers everybody was expecting. Some questioned Clemson's offense and wondered if they could up keep with Jackson and the Cardinals.

As fourth-ranked Louisville came into Death Valley to play No. 3 Clemson, the roles flipped from what they were at the ACC Football Kickoff back in July. Jackson was now the favorite to win the Heisman, while Watson was barely in the conversation after his slow start to the season.

"Everyone loves to talk about Lamar, and Deshaun has kind of been in the background," Clemson linebacker Ben Boulware said. "I was like, 'We have a pretty good quarterback here, too.'"

But none of that bothered Watson.

"All of that talk is for the fans to draw attention to this game. It is for the media. It is for the money," the All-American said. "All of that stuff. At the end of the day, it is Clemson vs. Louisville. We are going to focus on what we have to do at Clemson and do what we want to do. We can't worry about what Louisville is doing or what Lamar Jackson is doing, we have to focus on what we are doing and prepare throughout the week and go out there on Saturday and execute."

Though Watson said he was not worried about what Jackson was doing, he did admit it was fun as a competitor to go against a player of Jackson's ability.

"It's competition. If you play this game, and all the great ones love the great competition going against the best regardless," he said. "He has to do what he has to do and I have to do what I have to do.

"We are both going against two good defenses on both sides so we just have to go out there and do what we have to do and be ourselves."

Watson and Jackson did not disappoint. In a game you could argue was one of the best of 2016, the two Heisman Trophy candidates put on a show for the ages.

Clemson head coach Dabo Swinney described Jackson as one of those few great players who makes you hold your breath every time he touches the ball. Since he is the quarterback, Swinney, along with Clemson defensive coordinator Brent Venables, was holding his breath a lot during Clemson's 42-36 victory in Death Valley.

"I was pretty dizzy holding my breath. I held it a lot," Venables said jokingly after the game. "I needed oxygen. He is pretty scary. He is pretty frightening."

Jackson lit up the Clemson defense, which came in ranked No. 3 in the country in total yards allowed at the time, with 457 yards of total offense, while running for two scores and throwing for a third.

"He is the real deal," Venables said.

Though his quarterback had just thrown his third interception of the game, Clemson cooffensive coordinator Tony Elliott was not going to let that effect the way he was going to call the final seven minutes and 52 seconds.

Following Artavis Scott's 77-yard kick return, which set the Tigers up at the Louisville 23-yard line, Elliott stayed aggressive with his play calling. He knew when it came to shaking off bad plays, he had the best quarterback in the business.

Before Scott's 77-yard return, Watson's last pass was intercepted, setting up a Cardinals touchdown that stretched their lead to eight points with just under eight minutes to play. Then Scott returned the ensuing kick 77 yards, which opened up Elliott's entire playbook and changed the complexion of the game entirely.

"When you flip the field like that, and you are down in the red zone, obviously you feel confident in your kicker that you have at least three points, plus everybody's defensive philosophy changes a little bit when you get in the red zone," Elliott said. "Obviously, when you are backed up and the way the flow of the game is, you want to make sure you sustain the drive. Whereas down in the red zone, you have some specific things you want to get to, and you can be a little bit more aggressive."

Earlier in the game, the Tigers found themselves in the same situation, and Elliott was true to his philosophy. He called a post to wide receiver Mike Williams, who was open for what looked like a sure touchdown. However, Watson, on first-and-10 from the Louisville 15, was off the mark on his throw and threw the ball behind Williams instead of leading him to the goal post. The result was an interception in the end zone, one of two red zone turnovers for the Tigers.

Flash-forward to the fourth quarter, and with a second down-and-seven from the Louisville 20-yard with just over seven minutes to play, Elliott trusted his quarterback, despite his two earlier mistakes, and called the same post-play he had called earlier to Williams.

"I had the confidence to come back with it and say, 'Deshaun, Yeah you threw the ball inside, but we are going to go at it again because structurally it should work and I have the confidence you can make it.' The guys went out and they executed it," Elliott said.

They executed it to perfection as Watson hit Williams in stride around the five-yard line, and then the 6-foot-3, 225-pound junior did the rest to get into the end zone for six points, cutting the Cardinals' lead to two points with 7:05 to play in the game.

Now with his quarterback back in the flow of the game, and playing with confidence, it was Watson's turn to steal the headlines from Jackson. Still trailing by two points, Clemson got the ball back at its own 15-yard line with 6:11 showing on the clock.

Earlier in the week, Swinney said Watson was one of those guys who did not let the moment get to him. He could throw three touchdown passes and never be too high or he could throw three interceptions and was never too low.

Against Louisville, he did both, but when the Tigers took over the ball late in the fourth quarter and had 85 yards to go for the winning score, Watson was just Deshaun Watson. He was not caught up in the moment. He had already shrugged off the three interceptions and was not even thinking about the four touchdown passes he had thrown. All he did was stay calm, and in doing so, he kept his teammates calm.

On the Tigers' final possession, with everything on the line, Watson completed 4-of-5 passes for 74 yards, including a 24-yard pass to Deon Cain on third-and-five from the Clemson 45 that he threaded between three defenders to keep the drive alive. On the following play, he found tight end Jordan Leggett on a throwback to the left, which turned out to be the game-winning 31-yard touchdown pass with 3:14 to play.

"For me, it was a simple throw. But he made it great. He finished the play. Before the drive I told him, 'Let's be great.' And that's what he brought," Watson said.

Watson finished the game with 397 total yards and five touchdown passes, but he had to sit on the sideline, and, along with Swinney and Venables, he had to hold his breath the final 3:14 as Jackson marched the Cardinals inside the Clemson 10-yard line with 40 seconds to play.

Like back at the ACC Football Kickoff, Jackson was the obvious up-and-comer. However, the light still shined on Watson and the Tigers as defensive back Marcus Edmonds shoved Louisville's James Quick out of bounds on a fourth-down play that was a yard short of the sticks with 33 seconds to play to secure the Clemson victory.

"He played well. He played hard till the very end," Watson said of Jackson's performance. "He did what he had to do for his team."

And so did Watson for his team, except his performance was just a little better than Jackson's in the end.

Game 6: Clemson 56, Boston College 10

Clemson had not had a play of 50 yards or more in the first five games of the season, but in the opening half of its 56-10 victory against Boston College, the Tigers had three in the first quarter.

After a Ray-Ray McCloud muffed punt set up a 21-yard Boston College field goal with 11:08 to play in the first quarter, the Tigers got a 59-yard touchdown run by Wayne Gallman on the ensuing possession, and then on the next offensive possession, Mike Williams made a diving catch at the five-yard line of a Deshaun Watson pass and later scored on a nine-yard toss by Watson for a 14-3 lead.

On the Tigers' next offensive possession, Watson hit Jordan Leggett down the seam, and then the tight end did the rest as he cut back inside and down the boundary for a 56-yard touchdown.

The Boston College defense, which led the nation in total yards allowed coming in, gave up 201 total yards in the opening quarter on 14 plays.

Clemson finished the game with 499 total yards. Watson led the Tigers with 266 passing yards and four touchdowns, while completing 14-of-24 passes. Gallman rushed for 109 yards on nine carries to lead the running attack.

After the offense slowed down in the second quarter, the defense stepped up and had a goal line stand to stop one BC drive, and then Ben Boulware hit quarterback

Patrick Towels high on a scramble, forcing a fumble that the Tigers' Dexter Lawrence recovered.

Watson extended the Tigers' lead in the third quarter with touchdown passes of 29 and 16 yards to Deon Cain for a 35-3 lead with 5:18 to play in the third quarter.

After an Eagles touchdown, Clemson's Tyshon Dye had a three-yard touchdown, Tavien Feaster had a 45-yard run for a score, and Mark Fields intercepted a pass and returned it 42 yards to conclude the scoring.

Game 7: Clemson 24, N.C. State 17 (OT)

Just before he went up and caught Ryan Finley's pass to end a 24-17 overtime victory over N.C. State, Clemson cornerback Marcus Edmond said he knew he was going to intercept the pass.

"After I caught it, I kind of blacked out," Edmond said afterward.

That might have had something to do with the fact he was mobbed by his teammates after he jumped in front of Bra'Lon Cherry to snag Finley's pass in the end zone.

"I almost died. Everyone kept on piling, and I'm trying to get up, and everybody kept on piling on top," Edmond said afterward. "I'm like, 'I can't breathe! I can't breathe!' Everybody just kept on piling on. I almost died."

Clemson fans almost did, too. The 81,200 that showed up on Saturday watched as the third-ranked Tigers did everything they could to lose the game but somehow found a way to win it. Clemson turned the ball over four times, three times in the red zone and the other was a pick-six to start the third quarter.

Clemson was also stopped by the 'Pack on a fourth-and-goal from the one-yard line.

Of course, N.C. State kicker Kyle Bambard helped the Tigers win it. The sophomore lined up to attempt a winning kick at the end of regulation, but it sailed wide right, sending the game into overtime. It was the first time since 1991 that an opposing kicker missed a field goal that would have beaten the Tigers in regulation.

Scott Session missed a 44-yard kick for Georgia Tech in a 9-7 Clemson victory that afternoon.

"I really didn't watch the kick. I just watched the student section," Clemson head coach Dabo Swinney said. "When I saw them going crazy, I was like, 'So you are saying there is a chance. We still have some life in us.'"

Artavis Scott, who ended up catching the winning touchdown, said he felt helpless watching Bambard line up for the possible winning kick with two seconds to play.

"That was tough. I was like, 'Dang!' But I still had faith that he was going to miss it. I knew something was going to happen. I knew we were going to get another shot," he said.

After a brief celebration, Scott said his first thought was "Let's go win it."

But again Clemson tried to lose it first. After a false start penalty to open overtime, the Tigers faced a fourth-and-one play from the N.C. State 16. Swinney decided to go for it, and C.J. Fuller, who was in for the injured Wayne Gallman, ran for two yards to keep the drive alive.

Then on second-and-eight from the 12, quarterback Deshaun Watson found tight end Jordan Leggett, who made sliding catch for an 11-yard gain to the one. But on first-and-goal, the snap popped off Watson's hands and went over his head, where he chased it down and fell on the ball at the 10-yard line.

"We had the ball at the one and I guess we felt like we needed to back it up to the 10-yard line," Swinney said. "We just kind of wanted to keep the rhythm of the day going."

However, Watson made up for it on the next play when he hit Scott on a skinny post on the next play for a 10-yard touchdown, which turned out to be the game winner.

"As soon as they called it, I knew we were going to score. It was huge. It was exciting," Scott said. "All we had to do was have our defense go out there and make a stop. And they got a stop for us."

Actually, it was Edmond that got the stop, jumping in front of Cherry to seal the victory. It is a good thing he did not black out.

Game 8: Clemson 37, Florida State 34

As Clemson players spoke to the media on the field at Doak Campbell Stadium following the Tigers' dramatic come-from-behind win over Florida State, Jordan Leggett just smiled when he noticed some familiar faces in the stands.

A group of Clemson supporters, and a few FSU fans, waited for the players to get done with their interviews so they could say hello and chat for a little while. As it turned out, the group were mostly Leggett supporters, coming over from his hometown of Navarre, FL—a three-hour drive to Tallahassee from the northwest Florida Panhandle.

"It just felt good to be back so close to home with all my friends in the stadium," Leggett said.

Among those from his hometown was of course Leggett's mother. She had not seen her son play in person all year. It's not like coming to Clemson for a home football game from Navarre is an easy ride.

However, getting to Tallahassee was a little bit easier, and as it turned out, it was well worth the trip. Leggett caught the game-winner, a 34-yard catch-and-run that he capped by diving for the pylon, while using his right hand to keep him off the ground long enough to get the football over the goal line for the touchdown.

"It's just so great because my mom got to see it," Leggett said.

Ten months earlier, no one knew if Leggett would even be at Clemson. At the time, he contemplated leaving school early for a career in the NFL. It made sense. He

was coming off a career year, in which he was a finalist for the John Mackey Award as the nation's best tight end.

But even after the great year he had, Leggett knew he was not ready to play on Sundays, not yet. He still had some work he had to get done. He wanted to graduate from college. He wanted to get better at his craft. He wanted to help Clemson win a national championship.

Hearing and seeing that kind of maturity from the 6-foot-5, 260-pound tight end was a bit surprising. Three years earlier, he openly admitted to the media he was lazy. He did not study film, and he sometimes loafed in practice.

Slowly, but surely, Leggett's maturation and development in Head Coach Dabo Swinney's program took off. By the time of his junior year, he was no longer loafing and being lazy; instead, he had become one of the best tight ends Clemson has ever had, and by the time the Florida State game was over, he could lay claim that he was the best ever.

Like his team, Leggett found out the 2016 season was not going to be a bed of roses. The Tigers' first game at Auburn was perhaps the worst of his career. He did not catch a single pass. He whiffed on a couple of blocks and was penalized on back-to-back plays in a key moment of the game that killed a potential scoring drive and cost Clemson points.

Things did not get better in the following weeks against Troy and S.C. State, as he produced just one catch for nine yards in the two games combined. It left Clemson fans wondering where Jordan Leggett disappeared to. It left Leggett frustrated.

However, Leggett did not panic. He stayed patient. He worked even harder, and then came the trip to Atlanta. He caught four passes for 31 yards, including one touchdown, as he helped Clemson win at Bobby Dodd Stadium for the first time in 13 years.

The next week against Louisville, he hauled in the game-winning touchdown, which allowed him to break the program's all-time touchdown record for a tight end.

"I don't think anything's changed, really. I don't find myself doing anything different," Leggett said. "It's just a matter of different defenses that we face. When we play these bigger teams, they seem to have bigger corners, and whatnot, so it's harder for us to take those easy fade outs. The bigger games, they kind of work out better for me."

It felt good for Leggett to see a familiar face in the stands besides his family after the Florida State game. One of his old high school coaches came down to congratulate his former player.

"That was actually one of our defensive line coaches from my high school. He is a big FSU graduate and fan so we always bumped heads when I committed to Clemson in high school," Leggett said. "He's probably one of my favorite coaches. It's just a face I noticed out of the crowd so it was just good to see somebody I knew."

Leggett also enjoyed seeing Florida State again. The year before in Death Valley, he had six catches for what was then a career-high 101 yards.

This time around he was in Tallahassee, but once again the Seminoles had no answer for Leggett. The senior hauled in five passes for a career-high 122 yards in Clemson's 37-34 victory, the Tigers' second at Doak Campbell Stadium since FSU joined the ACC in 1992.

"It was just like the last time we played them. The middle of the field is always so wide open," he said. "So we were able to hit them on that last year and I guess they didn't change anything this year, so it was just another big game for me."

With his 122 yards, Leggett became the first tight end in Clemson history to record two 100-yard receiving games in a career.

"Two of my biggest games have come against FSU. Especially them not recruiting me is kind of like a 'How do you like me now?' kind of thing," he said.

With 2:17 to play in the game, and trailing 34-29, with the ball resting at the Seminoles' 34-yard line, Clemson cooffensive coordinator Tony Elliott called for wide receiver Hunter Renfrow to run a post, as the second receiver, while Artavis Scott, who was up top, ran a curl route. Jordan Leggett, who was at the bottom of the trips formation, ran a corner.

The goal was to get Leggett locked up in a favorable man-to-man situation. What he got was wide open.

"Basically the safety was over the top of me and basically the nickel was outside of our second receiver (Renfrow). They are supposed to switch it off, but if the second receiver is going vertical after 10 yards, that nickel is supposed to collect him," Leggett said. "We took [the nickel] with Renfrow and took him 10 yards deep with the post and once he did that post, that is threading the safety, and so they both went with him and I just ran a corner and it was wide open."

In other words, there was busted coverage on the play. Leggett was not supposed to be that wide open. But he was. So he caught the ball, turned up field, and then made a spectacular play in getting the ball in the end zone.

The winning-touchdown was Leggett's third catch on the game-winning drive. He also had a 41-yard catch-and-run back in the first quarter to set up Wayne Gallman's first of two touchdowns.

"I just feel like I'm a very trustworthy receiver," he said. "Deshaun knows I'm going to catch the ball whenever he throws it to me and I'm just a big body and he sees me because I'm bigger than anybody else he sees out there."

On the game-winning drive, Watson and Leggett connected for a 25-yard gain on the first play of the possession, 11 yards on a third-and-five from the FSU 45, and then of course the 34-yard touchdown.

The best part about it is he got to do in front of his mom.

Game 9: Clemson 54, Syracuse 0

Earlier in the week, Syracuse Head Coach Dino Babers compared his team's trip to Death Valley against No. 2 Clemson as a David vs. Goliath type matchup, saying, "give us a slingshot and a rock."

Syracuse might have brought the sling shot, but no one loaded the rock, as the Tigers hammered the Orange 54-0. Of course it helped that the Clemson offense had perhaps its best game of the season in totaling 567 yards, which included 370 passing yards from both Deshaun Watson and Nick Schuessler.

Watson completed 13 of 16 passes for 169 yards and two touchdowns, while Schuessler came off the bench and hit 11-of-17 passes for 177 yards and two more scores. It marked the first time in Clemson history that two quarterbacks threw for 169 yards or more in the same game.

Watson left the game late in the second quarter with a bruised shoulder with Clemson driving. He could have returned in the second half, but there was no need with Schuessler playing well. The senior threw a five-yard touchdown pass to Artavis Scott just before halftime and then found Deon Cain in the back of the end zone in the third quarter for his second score.

Watson also threw a touchdown pass to Cain . . . a perfectly thrown 65-yard scoring toss, while also hitting Mike Williams on a 14-yard touchdown. The junior quarterback also ran for a one-yard score.

Running back Wayne Gallman had a five-yard run, and safety Tanner Muse returned a crazy interception that bounced off a cleat of a Syracuse player 64 yards for a touchdown. That gave the Tigers a 54-0 lead, with 7:40 to play in the game.

As good as Clemson was on offense, the defense was just as good. The Tigers held the Orange to 277 total yards for their second shutout of the season. The defense forced three turnovers overall, all interceptions, while sacking 'Cuse twice.

Game 10: Pittsburgh 43, Clemson 42

From the moment they got back from Arizona, following last year's loss to Alabama in the College Football Playoff Championship Game, Clemson head coach Dabo Swinney praised his leaders on the 2016 team.

And despite the stunning loss to an unranked Pittsburgh team at home, the Tigers' first regular-season loss in 24 games, that leadership did not change. In fact, Swinney credited that leadership for the amount of focus and resolve he saw from his team following the 43-42 loss to the Panthers.

"I think the best leadership definitely comes from within and we have that. It is on the coaches, too. We have a job to do, but I have always said the best leadership comes from within. That's what this team is special about. From Day One, the leadership has been awesome. From the time the game was over in Arizona from where we are right now, they have done a great job."

But this was the first time that leadership had been tested. After finding ways to win, when they could have easily lost, against Louisville, N.C. State, and Florida State, the Tigers did not make that one play against Pitt to get them over the top. Instead, they watched someone else go win the game as Pittsburgh's Chris Blewitt hit a 48-yard field goal with six second left.

"The loss could be a blessing in disguise," quarterback Deshaun Watson said. "We are just going to continue to do what we do and focus on what we can control and let everything else take care of itself."

The game seemed like it was in the bag. Despite throwing two interceptions in the first half, Watson had settled down and was having a record-breaking day in Death Valley.

The All-American set ACC and Clemson records for passing yards in a game. Then, with the Tigers clinging to an eight-point lead more than halfway through the fourth quarter, Watson had his team on the doorstep ready to put the game out of reach with a little more than five minutes to play.

But instead of putting the game away, he put it in jeopardy, and it eventually cost Clemson.

On second-and-goal from the Pittsburgh three-yard line, he rolled to his right, where tight end Jordan Leggett and wide receiver Hunter Renfrow were covered by three defenders in the end zone. Instead of throwing the ball away, he tried to fit the football into a small window to Renfrow, where Pitt linebacker Saleem Brightwell intercepted the pass and returned it 70 yards to the Clemson 30-yard line.

A few plays later, Pitt running back James Conner rumbled 20 yards for a touchdown, and all of sudden Pitt was back in the game.

"He came across the middle. The guy made a play," Watson said. "They made a play and went down and scored. They capitalized on it. That's all that matters. They did their part and we did not do ours."

However, Clemson still had a chance to ice the game. Watson led Clemson back down the field, where he connected with Artavis Scott, Hunter Renfrow, and Mike Williams. But with third down-and-one at the Pitt 35, the Tigers failed to get that one yard on two straight plays with 58 seconds to go.

"Fourth-and-one . . . we need one yard. We have to get one yard. Third-and-one . . . third-and-one and fourth-and-one we need one yard and we did not get it. So we had an opportunity to win the game right there and we did not get it and they did. They made the play," Swinney said.

Pitt took over on downs and subsequently went down and won the game on Blewitt's 48-yard field goal.

"It's a game of matchups, and we did not win our matchups," Watson said.

Clemson was winning them early on, especially Watson, who threw a Clemson-record 70 passes, while completing a school record 52 of them for an ACC-record 580 yards and three touchdowns.

"It's all good, but at the end of the day my main focus is trying to get the W. I just wanted to win," Watson said.

"I could have gone 0-for-30 with zero passing yards and if I get the W, that's all that matters.

"We made a lot of plays and did a lot of great things, but at the end of the day, we made a couple of mistakes that kind of kept them in the game. Give credit to Pittsburgh. They came down here and earned it after a tough loss last week down at Miami. They came down here and did not shy away from the challenge. You have to give them credit. They came in and outplayed us and made more plays at the end of the game," said Watson.

Luckily for Clemson, all was not lost. Later in the night, the Tigers learned No. 3 Michigan and No. 4 Washington both went down, keeping the second-ranked Tigers right in the thick of things in the College Football Playoff race. On any other weekend in November, the Pitt loss would have destroyed a season where the goal is to get back to the College Football Playoff.

"We have a tough race that we are in the middle of, and this is definitely a little setback, but again, it is an opportunity for us to grow from it and that is what we are going to do," said Swinney. "We are going to get our mind right and flush it and move on and see if we can find a way to win our division this week. There is a lot out there."

Losing is not something this Clemson program is used to doing. Not only was the Pitt game the first regular-season loss in two years, but it was the first time in 22 games, since 2013, the Tigers lost in Death Valley. It was such an odd feeling, the team did not know how to act.

Only eight players on the entire roster had experienced the feeling of losing at home.

"Everybody on this team hates to lose. We really did not know what to do. I'm glad it is not a habit around here and is not going to become one," Swinney said.

The silver lining?

"The last time we lost a game we had to wait nine months to play again. That's the one thing I remember. We don't have to wait nine months to play, and not only do we get to play, but we get a chance to line up and play for our division title," Swinney said.

"The other thing is we have a good football team. We had a bad day against Pitt, but we have not had a bad year. There are definitely some things we can correct, but we have a really good football team. It's no different than if we are 10-0. Just because we are 9-1 does not change anything about our team."

Game 11: Clemson 35, Wake Forest 13

It's interesting a fourth-and-one play the week before delayed Clemson from clinching a spot in the ACC Championship Game. A week later, another fourth-and-one helped the fourth-ranked Tigers' run to the championship game.

On Clemson's first possession at BB&T Field in Winston-Salem, NC, it moved the football to the Wake Forest 42, where it faced fourth-and-one. A week earlier against Pitt, the Tigers faced a similar situation late in the game. Needing a first down to seal a win and clinch the ACC Atlantic, running back Wayne Gallman was stopped for no gain.

Pitt took over on downs at its own 35 and drove down for the game-winning field goal.

Gallman, and Clemson's maligned offensive line, were not denied on this Saturday in Winston-Salem, NC. Gallman broke through a big hole between the tackles and then bounced it outside for a 42-yard touchdown. Though it was not the winning score nor did it seal the victory, Gallman's run did, however, set the tone for the evening, as the Tigers rushed for 254 yards in a 35-13 victory.

Gallman finished the night with 162 yards on 22 carries, while adding a final touchdown in the fourth quarter, sealing Clemson's win and berth in the ACC Championship Game.

Clemson quarterback Deshaun Watson also rushed for two scores and had 47 yards on seven carries. Watson threw for 202 yards on 22-of-33 passing, which included a 15-yard touchdown pass to Mike Williams.

The Tigers finished the game with 456 yards.

Watson made the score 14-0 with a three-yard touchdown on third-and-goal with 6:22 to go in the first quarter. The touchdown run capped a seven-play, 59-yard drive.

Williams extend the lead to 21-0 with 1:10 to play in the opening quarter with his 15-yard touchdown on a fade to the end zone. Williams finished the game with six catches for 58 yards.

At one point, the Tigers converted on seven straight third-down conversions to extend the lead to 28-0 with 12:44 to play in the half, when Watson ran in from two yards out.

Wake Forest finally got things going when Ray-Ray McCloud muffed a punt at the Clemson 27-yard line. Mike Weaver then nailed a 42-yard field goal four plays later to get on the board with 10:04 to play in the first half.

A 41-yard pass to tight end Cam Serigne set the Demon Deacons up deep in Clemson territory, and running back Cade Carney finished the drive off with a 1-yard touchdown run. That made the score 28-10 with 3:31 to play in the half.

Wake added another Weaver field goal in the third quarter to make the score 28-13, but Gallman's one-yard touchdown with 10:50 to play in the game sealed the deal for the Tigers.

Clemson's defense held the Demon Deacons to 197 total yards. Wake was just 2-for-15 on third downs.

Game 12: Clemson 56, South Carolina 7

Before he came to Clemson, Deshaun Watson told one of his high school coaches, who happened to be a Clemson graduate, he was not ever going to lose to South Carolina.

A year and a half later, while being interviewed for a story in a national magazine, Watson again declared he would not lose to the Tigers' most hated rival. You can call it arrogance, cockiness, or just plain confidence, but whatever it was, Watson was true to his word.

He never lost to the Gamecocks.

In his first year against the Gamecocks, the Gainesville, GA, native forever became a hero in the rivalry after leading Clemson, despite a torn ACL in his left knee, to a 35-17 victory, snapping Carolina's five-game win streak in the series.

The next year in Columbia, he was unstoppable in a 37-32 win. The 2015 Heisman Trophy Finalist completed 20-of-27 passes for 279 yards, while rushing for three scores and throwing a 55-yard touchdown pass to Deon Cain.

He also finished the game with 114 yards rushing on 21 carries. One of his three rushing touchdowns went for 30 yards.

Then there was this year's performance. It was not only the greatest performance by a quarterback in Clemson history, but it was the greatest one in the rivalry's storied history. Watson, in what was to be his last game in Death Valley, threw six touchdown passes, tying his own school and ACC record, while completing 26-of-32 passes for 347 yards in a 56-7 victory over the Gamecocks.

"South Carolina was seventh in the country in pass defense coming into that game—seventh in the country! He goes out and completes 81 percent of his passes, six touchdowns and he should have had eight," said Clemson head coach Dabo Swinney.

Keep in mind, Watson did that to South Carolina in just two-and-a-half quarters.

"His ability to impact the game with his mind, his ability to impact the game with his legs, there is just nobody else out there. This guy is special," Swinney said.

In his three games against the Gamecocks, Watson completed 60-of-78 passes (.769) for 895 yards and nine touchdowns to just one interception. The junior has also rushed for 146 yards and five touchdowns in those three games.

Combined, he was responsible for 1,041 total yards and 14 touchdowns. But more important, he was 3-0, just the fourth quarterback in Clemson history to beat the Gamecocks three times in his career, joining the likes of Clemson legends Steve Fuller, Homer Jordan, and Charlie Whitehurst.

"I know who I am and I stay true to my word. I prepare for moments like this and I know my teammates would do the same thing," said Watson afterward.

In the week leading up to the South Carolina game, the Tigers got word about what was coming out of Columbia. USC players told the local media that they thought Clemson was soft, especially on the offensive line.

They said, despite a two-game losing streak to the Tigers at the time, that Clemson was their little brother in the rivalry and they always will be. Though they may have just been words, they were words, nonetheless, that resonated inside the bellies of guys like defensive end Christian Wilkins, defensive tackle Carlos Watkins, defensive tackle Dexter Lawrence, defensive end Clelin Ferrell, and linebacker Ben Boulware.

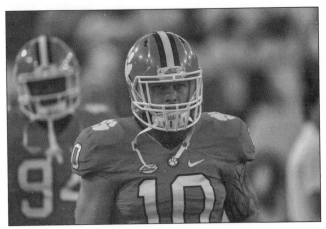

Linebacker Ben Boulware led the Tigers with 131 tackles in 2016.

Boulware, a native of nearby Anderson, SC, was definitely irritated the most. That is why he kind of blacked out when he got in the huddle just after warm-ups prior to the rout.

With his team huddled around him, Boulware appeared to be giving a fiery speech to get his teammates pumped up, and though he does not really remember what he said, it worked.

The Tigers just did not beat South Carolina, they obliterated the Gamecocks. While Watson threw his record-tying six touchdown passes, the offense racked up 622 yards overall. On defense, Boulware and company limited the Gamecocks to a season-low 218 total yards, including just 52 in the first half.

"It was super fun. To kind of go out there and dominate your little brother, like they were saying during the week, to dominate them in all phases for all four quarters was super fun," Boulware said.

South Carolina did not manage a first down until the 12:28 mark of the second quarter, its 17th play of the game. USC had just three first downs in the first half and finished the game with 14.

After the game, Clemson defensive tackle Carlos Watkins said Boulware got the entire team fired up with his speech.

"He was fired up. He was emotional," the senior said. "It's our last game in the Valley. He was talking for the seniors. He was just saying to dominate and give it everything you got. I felt like we did that today. We went out there with a chip on our shoulder.

"They said some stuff in the media that did not sit right with us. We showed them."

South Carolina quarterback Jake Bentley was rattled all night. Coming into the game, Bentley had completed better than 66 percent of his passes. He had thrown six touchdown passes to just one interception in his first five games as the starter.

However, against Clemson, he struggled. He completed just 7-of-17 passes for 41 yards and was intercepted on the second possession of the game. The Tigers sacked him twice and hurried him all night. He was eventually pulled for fellow freshman Brandon McILwain in the third quarter.

"I just knew from watching film throughout the week we were going to dominate them," Boulware said. "We were hearing their quarterback was the savior of the world. They got a Heisman at every position, but that is not what it is.

"I don't have to be nice to them anymore. I don't have to play them again. We knew from Day One we were going to dominate and that is exactly what we did."

Not one to say much, and definitely not one to boast, Watson got out of character for a little while in front of the media after the game. Fueled by the comments coming out of the Gamecocks' camp earlier in the week, Watson did not hold back his thoughts this time.

"In our head it's like the daddy beating the son. The daddy gave the son a whipping," he said. "We run this state. When you look at the longtime record, it speaks for itself."

Game 13: Clemson 42, Virginia Tech 35

All year long, Clemson was a marked team.

As the national runner-up, the defending ACC Champions, and the preseason's second-ranked team, the Tigers were pretty much everyone's "Super Bowl" in 2016.

Being the hunted, as opposed to be the hunter, was a different dynamic for a program that constantly had to prove itself from 2011-'15. There is a different mentality and approach that has to go into it.

"Everyone wants to beat us, and everyone is going to play different and make sure they bring their A-game whenever they step on the field with Clemson," quarterback Deshaun Watson said in the week leading up to the ACC Championship Game against Virginia Tech. "We still have the same mentality, same focus and same preparation. Everyone is going to be focused to the nth degree. We just go out there and compete.

"We understand it's hard to win at this level consistently. . . . It's hard to go out and perform and blow everyone out. It's not always going to happen like that."

For the most part, with the exception of the loss to Pitt on Nov. 12, Clemson handled it well while maneuvering though a season that had its up and downs. The Tigers finished the regular season 11-1 and were ranked No. 3 in both the Associated Press and the Amway Coaches Polls. They won the ACC's Atlantic Division and were playing for a second straight ACC Championship.

The Hokies were all that stood between them and returning to the College Football Playoff for a second straight year.

"This team has been very easy to coach. Very easy to coach," Clemson head coach Dabo Swinney said. "We have unbelievable leadership, and I think, again, it goes back to when we started this spring, a total different mindset just because they had an experience to draw on that no previous team had.

"They'd had a 14-1 season, but we lost the wrong game. Alabama was 14-1, too, but they won the National

Championship. They lost the right game. That was a tough pill for everybody to swallow going back to work in the spring. It's a different mindset, I think, a different understanding of knowing what it takes, not just thinking that you know what it takes, but also knowing that you're good enough.

"The leaders of this team have been incredible, and then our schedule has been good as far as we haven't had to play 10 straight [games]."

Heading into last year's ACC Championship Game against North Carolina, the Tigers were playing their 10th straight game without a bye week. Swinney said his team was exhausted, especially his defense, which lacked depth at key positions. Guys like Ben Boulware, B.J. Goodson, Shaq Lawson, and Kevin Dodd played just about on every down in those 10 games.

"Our open date this year fell at a good time. You know, we've caught some breaks as far as being able to keep some guys healthy, but we're still a very young team, and we're playing two true freshmen at tackle," Swinney said. "This team has had its own challenges, but they've handled it well."

No one handled it as well as Watson. At the beginning of the year, expectations were placed so high on him, he could not possibly reach them. But he came close, especially when it mattered the most.

Down eight points, he threw two touchdown passes in the final eight minutes to rally the Tigers past Louisville in what turned out to be the de facto ACC Atlantic Division Championship. He did the same at Florida State a few weeks later, and then in the ACC Championship Game against Virginia Tech, he was once again magnificent when it mattered the most.

Watson made several what only can be described as "Heisman Moments" as he willed his Clemson team to a second straight ACC Championship, the first for the program since the 1986-88 teams won three straight. The Clemson quarterback not only threw for three touchdowns and rushed for two more, but he made one spectacular play after another in the 42-35 victory over the Hokies.

"We have been saying this ever since he walked onto campus. He is an unbelievable talent football-wise, mentally and physically," Clemson cooffensive coordinator Tony Elliott said, "He never gets rattled in the big moments and he plays his best when the game is on the line and when there is the most pressure."

On the Tigers' final scoring drive of the night, Watson drove his team 75 yards in eight plays, taking 4:07 off the clock. Most important, it came after the Hokies had trimmed what was a 21-point second-half lead to seven points following quarterback Jerod Evans's five-yard touchdown run with 11:35 left in the game.

Watson's fifth touchdown responsibility came on a zone-read concept where he faked like he was about to run and then threw to a wide-open Hunter Renfrow, who walked into the end zone untouched. On that same drive, he stayed in the pocket despite pressure and threw per-

fect passes to both Renfrow for 31 yards and Deon Cain for 30 that moved the Tigers into scoring position.

On that drive, Watson completed 4-of-5 passes for 82 yards.

"He had five touchdowns so he was pretty consistent all night long," Swinney said. "But I tell you what, right there at the end of the game when you've got to have the first down . . . he went and got it to put us in victory formation, that's about as good as it gets right there."

The play Swinney was referring to was Watson's 11-yard run that sealed the Tigers' victory. Following Virginia Tech's next-to-last timeout with 1:04 left in the game, Watson, on a designed quarterback run, ran 11 yards up the middle on second-and-five to ice the win.

Watson finished the game with 85 yards on 17 carries, including touchdown runs of three and two yards.

Swinney said afterward he could not just name one "Heisman Moment" because his quarterback had so many. However, if there was one, it was his 30-yard completion to Cain when Virginia Tech defensive coordinator Bud Foster brought pressure. Watson hung in and delivered a perfectly thrown back-shoulder fade to Cain down the near sideline.

"They brought a split front and they brought the box, and then Deon did a good job of bearing the box up and just slid into the weak side," Watson said. "I knew I had pressure from the field, so I just kind of rode to my left because it was just about time to get Deon Cain off the release, and I just gave him a shot.

"I always tell my receivers, whenever we have man or any situation, I'm going to give you guys a shot. You all are going to be special. You made the play. And that's what type of play it is. We just always say, give him a shot. He's going to go up and get it. And that's all my receivers. So it's a blessing to have those guys on my team. They make me look good."

On the next play, Watson found Renfrow for what turned out to be the eventual game-winning touchdown.

"He made big throws all night long, just critical plays. The throw to Deon is just a tremendous play and great effort by Deon, as well. The play on the last touchdown to Renfrow, zone-read concept and, you know, he read it out and then he felt the defense support from the perimeter so he took the screen and we walk in for a touchdown. I mean, there were a lot of moments," Swinney said. "He rushed for 80 something yards, averaged five yards a carry. He's been unbelievably consistent, you know. This is a guy that since October or November and now in December, there ain't anyone better than this guy right here."

After throwing six touchdown passes in the Tigers' rout of rival South Carolina, Watson followed it with five touchdown responsibilities in the ACC Championship Game, with a College Football Playoff berth on the line.

Watson finished the night completing 23-of-34 passes with touchdown passes to tight end Jordan Leggett for 21 and 10 yards and then the 15-yard toss to Renfrow. He had 373 total yards, including 288 through the air.

For his performance, Watson was voted the ACC Championship Game's Most Valuable Player for a second year in a row.

"I think if there is anything that warrants him being in New York as a Heisman Finalist that is it. He has the heart of a champion," Elliott said. "He embraces the opportunity, where some guys run from the opportunity and do not want to take the last shot. He wants the ball in his hand. He is going to show up and he has proven it time and time again. It is a testament to who he is as a person and as a competitor. That is why we believe he is the best player in the country."

Game 14: Clemson 31, Ohio State 0

It would have been much easier for Jadar Johnson to have kept his opinions to himself, but how much fun would that be?

The Clemson safety is not one to hold back his feelings on something he feels strongly about. So when he was asked about Ohio State quarterback J.T. Barrett and how the Tigers might defend him in the 46th Fiesta Bowl, Johnson expressed his opinion about the Big Ten's Player of the Year.

"We have played better quarterbacks than him," Johnson said during the week leading up to the Fiesta Bowl. "I'm not taking anything away from him. I don't think he is a bad player. He is definitely a good player, but he does not stand out as one of the best quarterbacks that we have played this year as a defense."

Barrett had tallied 3,275 yards of total yards and had accounted for 33 touchdowns in leading the third-ranked Buckeyes to an 11-1 record and a spot in the College Football Playoff Semifinal.

"There are probably some people that feel that way in the media, which is cool, too," said Barrett. "They have a right to their own opinion. It is not for me to really fight my stance. I know how I feel about myself. I'm comfortable in my skills and the guys we have on offense and our team."

Clemson had played some pretty special quarterbacks during the course of the 2016 season. Of course there was Louisville quarterback and Heisman Trophy winner Lamar Jackson, Florida State's Deondre Francois, Syracuse's Eric Dungey, and Virginia Tech's Jerod Evans. All of them ranked ahead of Barrett in terms of yards, and three of them—Jackson, Francois, and Evans—had a higher passing rating.

Barrett had thrown for 2,428 yards and 24 touchdowns that year, while completing 61.8 percent of his passes. He threw just five interceptions in 346 attempts.

However, Johnson still was not impressed. He said it was Barrett's legs and his ability to run the football that made him special and so difficult to stop. The junior rushed for 847 yards and nine touchdowns.

"I feel like he is a great quarterback with his legs. I don't feel real strong about his arm," Johnson said. "I

don't think he is one of the best passers. So I feel like if we can limit him on his legs and limit him in the running game, we will have a pretty good chance going against this offense because they are a run-first offense."

The Buckeyes actually ranked ninth in the country in running the football at 258.3 yards per game.

"They want to run, run and run. Get you to commit to the run and then play-action you and throw on you deep," Johnson said. "As long as we can stop those runs and not give them four or five yards a run. If we can limit them to things like that then I think we will be pretty good."

Johnson insisted he was not trying to be mean or anything toward Barrett and the Buckeyes' offense, but he felt they had not seen a defense like Clemson's.

"I'm just very confident in my team. I just don't think they have played a defense as good as ours," the senior safety said. "Someone came to me and asked what the difference is between us and Michigan? I told them I could not really speak on that because I have not watched Michigan play defense. All I know is that our defense has the best of both worlds.

"I hear a lot of people calling us soft, but I don't really think we are soft at all. I just feel like we have the best of both worlds and we can switch it up when we need to. We can be a finesse defense at times. We have a defensive line that can hit you with the quick moves, the spin moves. We have linebackers, they are not too big, but they can go out and cover. They have good speed. And we can cover in the secondary.

"On the other hand, we have D-linemen that can actually bull-rush you with the power. We have a power side to our D-line. Then with our linebackers, even though they can cover, they can feel the gaps, too. And they are very physical. Even with having the speed in the secondary, we have guys that can come down and tackle, too. We feel like we have the best of both worlds with our defense."

Barrett said Johnson's comments did not give him any extra motivation for the Fiesta Bowl, and the Buckeyes were not hanging the quotes on the bulletin boards in the locker room.

"We are okay. We are good. Somebody in the past said something about our defense. They saw how that went," Barrett said. "That's how we feel about that. If you want to talk, that is okay. We still have to go play the game."

Barrett was talking about when Oklahoma third-string quarterback Austin Kendall called OSU's defense "basic" and added that starting quarterback Baker Mayfield will "light them up." That did not work out too well for the Sooners, as the Buckeyes won the game 45-24.

"I'm not trying to get in any battle with him or nothing. I don't want to really go back and forth," Johnson said. "We will have to play on the 31st and we will see how that goes."

Johnson did admit he let things go a little too far, and he should have kept his comments to himself.

This was not the first time Johnson let his mouth get ahead of his feet. Prior to the Louisville game, he promised he would body-slam quarterback Lamar Jackson if he tried to hurdle him in the game.

Of course, Johnson backed up his words when he had a six-tackle night, an interception, and one pass broken up. However, Clemson Head Coach Dabo Swinney and his teammates rathered he keep his mouth closed in the future.

"[Swinney] talked to me at practice and told me to watch what I say," Johnson said while recalling the conversation. "We don't need to add any more fuel to the fire, and just do all of my talking on the field.

"They know how it goes with the media," he continued. "They know sometimes you might say a little too much and the media just runs with it. But they know I did not mean any harm by it. They definitely told me to watch what I was saying. They had the best interest for me and told me not to say too much and don't let them bait me into saying anything wrong."

It was ironic when Johnson went out to do the coin toss prior to the game that standing directly across from him was Barrett. The two did not speak. They just shook hands and went about their business.

Barrett then called tails during the coin toss for the Buckeyes. But the coin landed on heads, and Clemson won the toss and deferred the football to the second half. The coin toss was a good indicator on how the game was going to go for Barrett and the Buckeyes.

Barrett was harassed by Clemson's defensive line all night. He threw for just 127 yards, despite throwing the ball 33 times. Though he completed 19 passes, Barrett was also picked off twice, sacked three times, and rushed for minus-two yards on 11 carries as the Tigers backed up Johnson's words.

"That's what teammates are for," Clemson linebacker Dorian O'Daniel said after the Tigers' 31-0 victory. "He said what he said, and he felt confident about it when he said it. He could not take it back. He knew he was going to have to back it up. We were not going to leave him out there to dry. We are teammates. We are family and that's what brothers are for."

Johnson finished the game with four tackles from his strong safety position, but his teammates knocked down four of Barrett's passes, while Cordrea Tankersley and Van Smith each grabbed an interception. Clemson's Kendall Joseph also forced a fumble, which was recovered by Christian Wilkins.

"If you are going to talk big, you have to play big," Boulware said. "He did that tonight. Everybody on our backend, the front four guys . . . I think Kendall and I were very consistent just managing and directing everybody in the traffic.

"I think in all three levels, it was a very dominating performance."

It was a dominating performance by the Clemson defense. Ohio State netted a season-low 215 total yards and had just nine first downs the entire game.

The Buckeyes averaged just 3.8 yards per carry and never really got anything going consistently. They never ran a play inside Clemson's 20-yard line, while the two interceptions came at the one-yard line and in the end zone.

How bad was it? It marked the first time an Urban Myer-coached team had been shut out, and the first time since 1993 Ohio State was shut out in a game. It was also the first time the Buckeyes experienced being shut out in a bowl game since the 1920 Rose Bowl.

"We knew we could come out and have an excellent game like that, we just had to do it. We put it all out there on the field tonight and we put a goose egg up," Johnson said. "That's what it is all about. Coach V gave us a great game plan. Ben got us together. He is really the leader of this defense. I give so much credit to Ben. Then, when we came out here, he got us together, made us stay focused, no matter what kind of extracurricular activity that we were doing. We came out here and did our thing."

What they did was back Johnson up.

Game 15: Clemson 35, Alabama 31

When Jalen Hurts raced 30 yards up the middle of the field for a touchdown with 2:07 to play, giving Alabama a three-point lead, Deshaun Watson just smiled.

"They left too much time on the clock," Watson said he thought to himself on the Clemson sideline just before leading the Tigers on a drive for the ages in a 35-31 victory, clinching the program's first national championship since 1981.

ESPN analysts Kirk Herbstreit and Joey Galloway have both said if there was one game they had to win and they had to pick a quarterback who could go win the game for them, they would both choose Deshaun Watson.

Why?

It's Watson's ability to stay calm under pressure. He never gets lost in the moment. No moment is too big for him.

Such was the case earlier in the season, when the Tigers trailed at Florida State by five points with 3:23 left on the clock.

Earlier in the game, Watson had thrown two interceptions and just seemed a little off from his normal self. But when it was crunch time and Clemson needed one last scoring drive, Deshaun was Deshaun. He was not nervous, he was not too high, he was not too low . . . he was just calm. He was ready to lead his team down the field and get the win.

"He handles adversity better than most other people," Clemson tight end Jordan Leggett said. "He just goes out there and moves on to the next play. He just brings a whole different kind of confidence to the offense and helps us play easier, play with calmness. We can just chill and relax and go out there and play.

"It was stressful [being down], but we knew we were going to win no matter what."

Without even blinking, Watson led Clemson on a five-play, 75-yard drive that he capped with a 34-yard touchdown pass to Leggett for the winning score.

"I feel blessed to have the best quarterback in the country. Obviously, the media and other people are going to say certain things. But I believe he is the best player in the country and he has unbelievable poise and unbelievable knowledge," Clemson cooffensive coordinator Tony Elliott said.

The win in Tallahassee on Oct. 29 was the third time this season Watson led the Tigers on a game-winning drive at the end of regulation or overtime. He also threw a winning touchdown pass to Leggett—this time for 31 yards—in Clemson's come-from-behind win over Louisville on Oct. 1 and threw a 10-yard touchdown pass to Artavis Scott to beat N.C. State in overtime on Oct. 15.

"It honestly does not surprise me," said Michael Perry, Watson's quarterbacks coach in high school. "He obviously is very talented. God blessed him tremendously, but when you put his talent with that work ethic, that's what makes him what he is. I guarantee you right now, that kid is in his room looking at film. There is no doubt."

WATSON'S BIGGEST FAN

Watson has hundreds of thousands of fans, but his biggest fan might reside in Tuscaloosa, AL.

Alabama head coach Nick Saban, who recruited Watson when he played at Gainesville High School, said prior to the start of the College Football Playoff that if he had input into the Heisman Trophy process, he would have given his vote to the Tigers' star quarterback.

Saban saw firsthand how good a quarterback Watson is when he is at his best. Watson completed 30 of 47 passes for 405 yards and four touchdowns in the 2016 National Championship Game. He also rushed for 73 yards against the Alabama defense, which came into the contest with the best defense in the country.

"I think he is a fantastic competitor and a great player and played a fantastic game against us. I don't get to see him all that much during the season, but I have a tremendous amount of respect for the guy. He did a fabulous job," Saban said.

Though Saban is a fan, Watson was the last guy he wanted to see with the ball in his hands with the national championship on the line.

"Deshaun Watson, I've said this all week long, is probably the most dynamic player in college football, maybe the best player in college football relative to what he does for his team," Saban said in the week leading up to the championship game. "A combination of his ability to pass the ball accurately, execute their offense in the passing game, as well as his physical ability to run the ball and add quarterback runs to their whole system of very good players, whether it's running backs or wide receivers, and he can utilize all the talent on their team because of his skill set."

Saban could not put his finger on just one thing Watson does well because he does so many things well.

"Sometimes you look at an athletic quarterback, and you think, well, this guy is going to run around and extend plays all the time," the Alabama head coach said. "He does that extremely well when he needs to. But that's not his style of play. He reads the defense. He gets the ball out of his hand quickly. He does a really good job of reading what you're playing on defense and tries to take advantage of it relative to where he needs to go with the ball.

"I think trying to disguise things is important, but I also think not allowing him to extend plays, which is where they made some big plays on us a year ago where the defense breaks down because of his athleticism and then he takes advantage of it."

AN UNCOMMON QUARTERBACK

Perry remembers how calm Watson was the day he and his Gainesville teammates played Sandy Creek High School in the quarterfinal round of the state playoffs in 2011. Sandy Creek had a 41-game winning streak and was the favorite to win another state championship.

Watson was a sophomore, and he did not care.

"He just played phenomenal. It was like he was a man amongst boys and he was just a sophomore going against a state power," Perry said. "They had won 41 games in a row, and he just ends it just like that. He just led us up and down the field."

Watson completed 23-of-32 passes that night for 169 yards and two touchdowns. He also rushed for 129 yards in the 35-21 victory.

"He was not rattled. He never gets rattled," Perry said.

And that is what makes Watson uncommon among a world of common quarterbacks.

"That's why he is such a good quarterback because that's what you have to have. With the quarterback position it can be an up-and-down roller-coaster, but Deshaun is just as steady as he can be," Perry said.

That was never more obvious than in the national championship game. Here Watson was, down three points to an Alabama team that had won 26 straight games, while going against the best defense in the country, 68 yards away from the end zone and with 2:01 showing on the clock.

"We practice two-minute all the time, and we prepare for moments like this all the time," said Watson, who totaled four touchdowns and threw for a championship record 420 yards on 36-of-56 passes. "We had so many situations throughout the season where we did it before halftime and at the end of the game. So it was just another opportunity for us to show what we're about, just on a bigger stage."

THE DRIVE

Ninety-seven times in Nick Saban's career, his teams have entered the fourth quarter with a doubt-digit lead, and all 97 times they walked away with a victory.

That was the case in the 2017 National Championship Game. Thanks to a 68-yard touchdown pass from Hurts to tight end O.J. Howard, the Crimson Tide had a 24-14 lead entering the final quarter.

However, that quickly changed when Watson found Mike Williams in the end zone from four yards out, cutting the lead to three at 24-21 with 14:00 to play.

On Clemson's next possession, it took the lead for the first time, 28-24, as Wayne Gallman went in from a yard out to cap a six-play, 88-yard drive that took 1:55 off the clock with 4:38 left in the game.

The lead was short-lived, as Alabama got a great third-down pass from Hurts to ArDarius Stewart, and then three plays later he sprinted into the end zone from 30 yards out, setting up the greatest drive in Clemson history or possibly in the history of college football.

"God put us there for a reason, and we just went out there, and I told the guys, 'Hey, let's be great, let's be special,'" Watson said. "My offensive line gave me time, the receivers made big, big plays, and I just pretty much had the easy part, just getting the ball in the direction of the receivers and let them go out there and make the plays."

Clemson opened "The Drive" with a five-yard pass to Leggett. On the next play, Watson found Williams, who made a circus-like catch down the left side for 24 yards to the Alabama 39.

On the next play, Clemson used a little trickery as Artavis Scott caught a pass and then flipped it backward to running back Wayne Gallman, moving the football to the 33. After a one-yard run to the 32 by Gallman, Watson hit Hunter Renfrow for a six-yard gain on third-and-three, moving the ball to the Alabama 26.

With 19 seconds to go, Watson fired a pass to Leggett's left shoulder as the senior made a twisting grab to snag the ball for a first down at the 19-yard line with 14 seconds to play. A play later, Williams drew a pass interference penalty in the end zone, placing the ball at the two-yard line with six seconds to play.

"We were not playing for overtime. We were going for the win. That's our mentality," Swinney said.

Swinney said cooffensive coordinator Jeff Scott, who knew Alabama liked to go to man-to-man coverage when backed inside their five-yard line, was adamant Clemson run a rub route, where Artavis Scott cuts inside and tries to get in the way of the defender covering Renfrow, allowing him to break open in the flats.

So as Watson rolled to his right, Renfrow was wide open for the winning touchdown.

"Never in a million years did I think I would catch the game-winning pass," Renfrow said. "It's been such a journey for me. It's like I got knocked out in the third quarter and this was all a dream.

"Credit to—I think my faith in God really got me through it, just passing up the money to go to App State and to come and play for a guy like Coach Swinney, and a quarterback like Deshaun is pretty special."

The whole drive was special. It was just 68 yards, but it meant so much more. Watson said, even before he

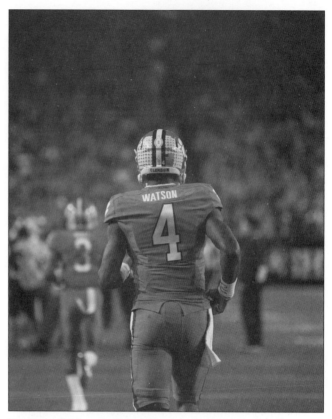

Deshaun Watson led the Tigers to the 2016 National Championship.

threw the game-winner to Renfrow, he just enjoyed the moment and knew what was about to happen. He knew history was being made, and he, along with his Clemson teammates and coaches, was right in the middle of it.

"I just kind of slowed down the moment," Watson said. "I just kind of smiled to myself and just knew because I knew that we were inside the five and I knew they were going to play straight cover zero man, and I knew if (Scott) makes his block and get the little pick, Renfrow was going to get in the end zone.

"I kind of smiled, and I knew before I even snapped the ball it was going to be a touchdown. All I had to do was just get the ball to him. I slowed down the moment, everyone made their blocks and did their part, and I did my part, and we pulled it out."

After coming up short in last year's title game to Alabama, Clemson's players and coaches made a pact at the start of the 2016 season that if they got back to the championship game, they would do all they could to make sure no one left with any regrets.

When Renfrow caught the game-winner from Watson with one second to go, Clemson had accomplished its mission . . . they were National Champions.

"It was an awesome feeling, and it was a great way to finish off the game," Watson said.

THE MAN WHO BELIEVED IN DABO SWINNEY

Dabo Swinney tried to hold back the tears as ESPN's Samantha Ponder interviewed him just moments after Clemson's national championship victory over Alabama.

With his mom, Carol, and wife, Kathleen, hugging him the whole time, Swinney thought about all of those who came before this team, those who were here with him when his dream of bringing Clemson back to national prominence first began.

"It has been an unbelievable eight years. This is for all of our teams because they are all a part of this," Swinney said. "They all get a piece of this trophy. . . . Eight years ago, my goal was to put Clemson back on top, and tonight that is a reality."

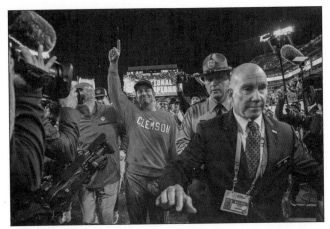

Dabo Swinney has been named National Coach of the Year numerous times.

"This was our night and this was our time," he continued. "This has been a process in the making for us. Hats off to our team, and I'm just so happy for the Clemson Nation. This is unbelievable. I know Terry Don Phillips is sitting at home, and Terry Don, I'm not here without you brother. I appreciate you."

It was Phillips that gave Dabo Swinney a chance when he named him as the interim head coach at Clemson following Tommy Bowden's resignation on October 13, 2008.

Swinney eventually won the job after posting a 4-2 record down the stretch, including a 31-17 victory over Steve Spurrier and rival South Carolina. Phillips, who held a national coaching search the whole time and interviewed some strong candidates, took some heat from alumni, boosters, and fans by hiring a coach who had no previous experience as a coordinator and six years earlier was selling real estate.

"We did as thorough of a search as you could before we selected Dabo," Phillips said. "You want to do your due diligence and ensure that if in fact you are going to go with an individual at that time that did not have the experience as a coordinator and prior to coming to Clemson had been involved in real estate . . . So regardless of how we felt, we needed to do a very thorough search, which we did. We interviewed some very good sitting head coaches and coordinators, and when it was all said and done and visiting with the other coaches, I just

truly believed in my heart of hearts that Dabo had some attributes that would make him successful.

"I really did not have any doubt that he would be successful. Now, I'm not sure that I saw the national championship in the cards. I would like to say that I was that smart, but I can't say that I did. But I thought he was a special young man. He came up the hard way. He has earned everything that he has gotten. No one has given him anything, and what you see is what you get."

What Clemson got was a fiery, passionate football coach who will fight for his players, coaches, Clemson University, and its fan base.

"There is no facade to him," Phillips said.

Even when Clemson struggled in 2010, going 6-7, which included a loss to South Florida, and fans were calling for Swinney's head, Phillips never backed away from his commitment to Swinney. Following a 29-7 loss to South Carolina at home that same year, Phillips met Swinney in his office after the game and told him he was never as sure he was the man for the job then he was that night. The next year, Clemson won its first ACC Championship in 20 years and has been on a roll ever since.

In the last six years, Clemson has won at least 10 games every season, has won 70 games overall, five division titles, three ACC Championships, played for the national championship twice and of course won the football program its second national championship with its 35-31 victory over Alabama.

Along the way, Swinney has beaten national championship coaches such as Les Miles, Urban Meyer (twice), Bob Stoops (twice), Jimbo Fisher, and now Nick Saban.

In the Tigers' playoff run at the end of the 2016 season, they hammered Ohio State 31-0 in the Fiesta Bowl and then beat big, bad Alabama in the national championship game, to snap its 26-game winning streak. Instead of things being said like, "he should not have been a head coach or he was too inexperienced" at the time, Swinney is now considered one of the best coaches in the country, and after winning a national championship, some say he is one of the top three coaches in the country.

"I certainly think he is right at the top. He has proven that," Phillips said. "Back-to-back College Football Playoff appearances and he had a great shot of winning it (in 2015)... Ever since he beat Les with that last-second field goal, his program has been on a very steep climb up. Dabo does not have to back down to anybody these days."

But like Swinney said, none of it, the win over LSU, the two victories over Ohio State and Oklahoma, the 70 victories in the last six years, and the national championship win over Alabama, would not have been possible had it not been for Terry Don Phillips believing in him when no one else did.

"I really appreciated that. It meant a great deal to me. There was no question about it," Phillips said. "Dabo is a special person and so are Kathleen and his family. He is just a tremendous person, and I'm just really happy for him.

"He had to go through some rough times after I named him head coach and just kept his nose to the grindstone and he kept working."

SWINNEY BUILT A CULTURE TO WIN, NOT A WINNING CULTURE

When Dabo Swinney walked into Terry Don Phillips's office for his first interview, he carried with him two binders. One of the binders was Swinney's plan for the football program. The other was a marketing plan.

"That was not normal," Phillips recalled of the interview. "A coach always comes in for an interview with his plan for the program. What coaches he wants on his staff, their recruiting philosophy and all of that, but I had never seen a coach come in and have a marketing plan in place.

"Dabo had all these ideas, and I think it comes from his business background, but he had a plan for everything. And everything was organized."

Swinney's organizational skills was one of the things that separated him from the other candidates who had applied to be Clemson's new head coach after Tommy Bowden stepped down at midseason in 2008.

Of course, Phillips had already seen Swinney's organizational skills several times before in his role as Bowden's recruiting coordinator and wide receivers coach. It's one of the reasons why Phillips offered Swinney the interim job when Bowden stepped down.

"This was an opportunity to see how he would do," Phillips said.

"I walked out of his office walking on the clouds," Swinney said. "I was empowered and energized because of his belief in me."

From the time he was in elementary school, Swinney was organized. In those days, everyone had trapper keepers to keep everything neat and put away. Swinney took full advantage of his. He used his to plan out each day. To put his homework where it was supposed to be and have his notes easily accessible for studying.

"I was always one of those kids that was organized, detailed, and thought things through," Swinney laughed when thinking back to those days. "I wrote things out. To this day, I'm constantly writing things out. I can't stand to be unorganized. I'm always planning and thinking."

These days, Swinney is still the same planner. While everyone else is caught up in the moment of what is happening now, the Clemson coach is already planning for several years to come.

"It is just like a business cycle. You have the birth, you have growth, you have plateau, you have decline, and you have death," he said. "The goal is to never plateau, to always stay in that growth, and that doesn't mean you don't have setbacks, dips, and those things. You want to always kind of be growing.

"The way you do that is that you constantly evaluate, constantly look for ways to improve and then surround yourself with the right people, recruit the right guys, and understand who you are and in this business recruit to that, but you truly have to nurture the culture every day."

Swinney says this is where people generally make mistakes. They get comfortable. They lose sight of what truly got them in that position in the first place. They begin to focus on the outside things more than what is happening on the inside.

Prior to Swinney taking over the program, Clemson had become a program that could not get over the hump. Back when Danny Ford was running things in the 1980s, Clemson had become one the premier programs in the country. Ford's teams owned the ACC and had the fifth-best winning percentage in college football.

But after Ford was forced to step down in January of 1990, Clemson spent the next two decades trying to recapture those glory days. Ken Hatfield was not the answer because he did not fit the Clemson mold. Tommy West was too much of a Clemson guy and did not have the vision to take the program where it needed to be, while Bowden had the right ideas and vision, but he just could not get the program to the next level.

So what made Swinney the guy who put Clemson back on the map?

"To me it is just a constant never-ending process of fighting for and nurturing the culture that we have established," Swinney said. "Those are decisions that are made, it is recruiting, discipline of a player . . . it is whatever. It just has to constantly be out in the forefront."

It was on October 13, 2008, around 11:30 p.m., when Jeff Scott finally sat down on the coach with his wife, Sara. It had been a long day for Scott. In a 16-hour span, his former head coach and boss had stepped down, and he went from being a graduate assistant to the team's wide receivers coach.

Scott was excited because he knew from being around the profession his whole life that this was a great opportunity for him. Right about that same time on ESPN's SportsCenter, the ticker at the bottom of the screen rolls across that Dabo Swinney was named Clemson's interim head coach, and following that it said, "0 of the last 29 interim head coaches went on to to be the full-time head coach."

"My wife looked at me and said, 'those odds aren't very good,'" Scott said laughing.

But something down inside told Scott that Swinney was going to beat those odds.

"It was his optimistic attitude. He really just breathed in some life and really had this attitude of belief," Scott recalled.

"Swinney, like now, just wanted those players to buy into the program, and that is when the 'All In' slogan got going.

"Before that, you did not really hear 'All In' as much as you hear it now with high school and college teams, but that was really what his message was to the players," Scott said.

Swinney's message to the team that day: "I need you to be all in. I only have six weeks at this thing and I'm asking you to be all in and fully committed and if not you don't have to play and you can take the rest of the year off, but if you are going to show up at practice tonight I expect you to be all in and let's go get this thing done."

Clemson has been getting it done ever since. Though there was a little hiccup in 2010, as he continued to build the culture, Swinney has had nothing but success since taking over the program. He finished his interim season with a 4-2 regular season, which included a win over Steve Spurrier and South Carolina, which removed the interim coach tag in front of his name and replaced it with head coach.

In his first full season, Clemson won nine games and advanced to the ACC Championship Game for the first time. In 2011, the Tigers won the first of Swinney's three ACC Championships and began the program's streak of six straight 10-win seasons.

In 2015, the Tigers opened the year with 14 straight wins and played for the national championship, while this past season they won a second straight ACC Championship for the first time in 28 years and were back in the College Football Playoff.

"You have to build a foundation, and then you change the culture and build a culture through graduation, through discipline, through recruiting, and through staffing," Swinney said. "Then through alignment, between the board, the President, the AD, and yourself . . . get everybody on the same page. That is basically what has happened here. Once you get that established, you have to stay on the hunt for what is next. You can't ever feel like you arrived. You never arrive."

Obviously, Swinney did not plan to be an interim coach when he thought about the day he would finally get his opportunity to be a head coach. But that experience allowed him to implement his thoughts and prove they could work.

"It allowed me the chance to share that with Terry Don, the president, and some of the people on the board and so forth, and then it was trying to sell it to them," he recalled. "It was not easy early on because the things I wanted to do were outside the box. It took some guts on their part. They just kind of gave me a little slack. Then I would pull it tight again, and I would need a little more slack.

"I would win some battles along the way, but Terry Don was amazing. He allowed me to grow and he allowed me to be who I am. He allowed me to set the boundaries of the program and then eventually he said, 'Okay! We are on the right path here. You get what you earn.' So I had to go earn some credibility, earn some respect and kind of pay my dues a little bit. One day at a time and one battle at a time. I have such great appreciation for where we are right now because I know where we came from. I have been behind those closed doors fighting for little things that have made a big deal. I have a great appreciation for that and that is why I'm always giving a history lesson to our players because they don't know anything except what they know. I want them to have a great understanding of where we have come from."

Since those humble beginnings, Swinney has built a Clemson program that seems to have the staying power to last.

Since Swinney became the head coach, Clemson finished the WestZone Project, which took the program to another level as far as enhancing the game-day atmosphere, recruiting, and the program's infrastructure. It built a state-of-the art indoor practice facility in 2012, and in January, 2017 the new $55 million football complex opened, which is said to be the best in the nation.

"To go from where we were then to where we are now has been very special to be a part of that," Scott said.

But Scott says those are not the things that make what Swinney has done at Clemson special. He says it's the way Swinney built the program is what needs to be appreciated.

"There are different ways you can try to build a program," he said. "You can sign junior college guys and go take shortcuts, but Coach Swinney would always say, 'We are not trying to build a great team. We are trying to build a great program.'

"A great program is one that wins consistently at a high level year after year after year. That's what I'm really proud about now . . . six years in a row with six-plus seasons. That is very rare in college football, especially in this day and age. That was part of Coach Swinney's vision. He had opportunities early in his coaching career where he could have made decisions that might have been better for the moment but not better for the long term."

Once such incident came in the spring of 2012, when star wide receiver, Sammy Watkins, was arrested and charged with simple possession of marijuana. Swinney

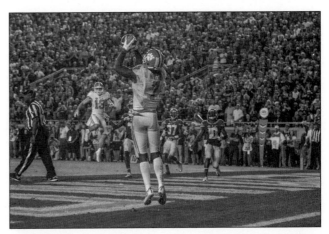

Mike Williams had 1,361 receiving yards and 98 receptions in 2016. He also caught 11 touchdown passes.

could have given the All-American a slap on the wrist, and maybe suspended him for a game where it would not have mattered if he played or not, but instead, he suspended him for the first two games of the season, including the Auburn game, which was played in the Georgia Dome that year as part of the Chick-fil-A Kickoff Classic.

"That was not the best decision for that team and for that game, but it was the best decision for the foundation of the football program," Scott remembers. "For him to be thinking that way when making those kinds of decisions, it says a lot about his vision for the program. It is one reason, I believe, we are where we are today and where we are headed."

Despite all of the success of this year's team and the 2015 season, Swinney still believes the best is yet to come to Clemson.

"I remember vividly after the 2010 season, where we won just six games, but I was more convinced than ever that we were on the right path and the culture was growing and I could see it," Swinney said. "I remember saying at a press conference that we did not have the season that we wanted to have, but it's 2010 and when 2020 gets here we are going to look back and it is going to be the best decade in Clemson history.

"Of course everybody looked at me like I was crazy, but to be here now, and we are in 2016, I think we have the best winning percentage ever right now, but the best is yet to come. We still have work to do. I'm really proud of where we are because we have worked hard and nobody has given us anything. We have worked for it, we earned it, we fought for it and we have done it the right way. Most importantly, we have built men through the process. We have created graduates and champions in life."

NEW FOOTBALL COMPLEX TO SERVE THE HEART, NOT THE TALENT

Before he beat LSU, Ohio State, and Oklahoma, and before he beat Alabama to win Clemson its first national championship since 1981, Dabo Swinney walked up the tower that stands in the middle of the Clemson practice fields and joined longtime friend and colleague Hugh Yaughn.

Yaughn, a longtime former high school football coach who now serves as an equipment manager on Clemson's football team, runs the time of each period during individual workouts for Swinney's youth and high school football camps in the summer. From time to time, Swinney makes his way up the tower to speak with Yaughn and to get a different perspective on how camp is going.

On this particular day, Swinney told Yaughn about his vision to one day bring the entire Clemson football program together in one central area. At the time, there was no indoor practice facility. There were just the two

grass fields and a turf field beside the Jervey Athletic Center.

"I remember him telling me as he pointed to the turf field. He said, 'Coach, that's going to be our indoor practice facility right there,'" Yaughn recalled. "Then he pointed to the soccer fields and the space between us and the indoor track facility and said, 'I see that as a football complex where we will have everything we need and we will not have to ever go across a street or through a parking lot again to get to practice.'

"Then he said, 'We have to win first.'"

Later that fall, Clemson won its first Atlantic Coast Conference Championship in 20 years, and thus began Swinney's vision of what some outsiders are calling, "Dabo's World."

By the end of the 2012 football season, Clemson moved into its 80,000-square foot, $10 million Indoor Football facility just ahead of its victory over LSU in the Chick-fil-A Bowl. The first piece of Swinney's vision was in place; now the Clemson football program had to earn the rest.

Since the Poe Indoor Practice Facility was built, Swinney has taken the Clemson program to the next level. The Tigers have gone 49-7 the last four seasons, which includes back-to-back ACC Championships in 2014 and 2015, wins over Ohio State and Oklahoma in the Orange Bowl, a win over Ohio State in the Fiesta Bowl, two berths in the College Football Playoff, a national runner-up finish, and a national championship victory over Alabama.

In early April of 2013, Swinney journeyed to Tuscaloosa, AL, to give his respects after the passing of former Alabama athletic director Mal Moore. It was during that visit that he got his longtime friend and former Alabama teammate, Thad Turnipseed, to give him a tour of the football operations center he helped build for Nick Saban and the Alabama football program.

"When he came down for the funeral, I took him through everything I built at Alabama. I could tell he had a lot of this already in his mind," Turnipseed recalled.

Swinney did. In fact, Swinney had already spoken with Clemson athletic director Dan Radakovich about his plan and what he ultimately wanted to do.

"When Dan started we had some meetings about what we felt needed to be done to make us a championship program. I applaud Dan for being so willing to listen to what I felt about the subject," Swinney said. "We went back and forth with an exchange of ideas. Finally I drew a diagram on a piece of paper where the new building was connected to the new indoor facility.

"He said, 'Let's do it.'"

But to do it, Swinney needed someone who could take his vision and make it come alive. Turnipseed was that guy.

Soon after Moore's funeral, Swinney persuaded Turnipseed to come to Clemson for a visit. It did not take long for the Clemson head coach to convince his old friend to come on board.

"It felt good and it felt real here," Turnipseed said.

Swinney knew what he wanted Turnipseed to do, but the concept of building a football operations center was still an idea, so he needed to find him a job to do in the meantime.

"I said to him, 'What do you want me to do?' Dabo said, 'Thad, I really don't care if you do something for a year.' He had been telling me things all day, but in the end he said, 'I just want you to find something and make us better,'" Turnipseed said. "The first day he hired me, I was director of high school relations. By day three I became the director of recruiting. On day ten I became the director of recruiting and external affairs."

At Alabama, Turnipseed spent 11 years where he started as the director of capital projects, designing and overseeing over $200 million in athletic projects. Some of those projects included two end zone expansions and a $40 million improvement to the football operations center.

Prior to coming to Alabama, Turnipseed owned his own construction company for six years and was a project manager at another one for two years before that.

"Alabama hired me to build all of their facilities. That was my first seven years at Alabama. I was building facilities," Turnipseed said. "Then during those seven years, I was hired as the director of capital projects. I became the director of management and then event management. I was touching a lot of those departments within those seven years, and then Nick Saban came.

"Within three weeks, Nick Saban started calling me his director of football external affairs and that's what brought me more into the football world. I had a wide view of how the athletic department works."

And that's why Swinney wanted him. He knew Turnipseed had the knowledge to turn his vision into a reality.

"Thad has been invaluable in the process because he went through this with so many facilities at Alabama. He knows all the details that must be addressed," Swinney said.

Ground broke in November of 2015 on the 142,000-square foot, $55 million football complex, and the football program moved in just a couple of weeks after beating Alabama in the national championship game.

"This was Dabo's vision from day one. I had no idea I would be building a football building this quick when I got here, but this is my wheelhouse," Turnipseed said.

Swinney's goal for the Allen Reeves Football Complex is to provide members of the football program and visitors with a unique Clemson experience. In addition to an indoor replica of the Hill and Howard's Rock, the facility includes a career development and leadership center known as Paw Journey, a players' lounge, locker rooms, training/rehab facility, weight room, a nutrition center, dining facility, meeting rooms, coaches' offices, and a first-of-its-kind recruiting war room.

Yes, there are other amenities, such as a bowling alley, a movie theater, a nap room, a nine-hole putt-putt course,

and outdoor seating and grilling areas. But those are just amenities. They're not what the structure is about.

"I have always preferred the situation where you walked from the meeting room to the practice field," Swinney said. "I just think it is a better situation for the coaches and the players to be in the same facility. It was in the planning stage for two years and now it is becoming a reality.

"This will allow us to have a football operations center where it all happens . . . the practice, the indoor facility, the weight room, everything. You name it. It's total operations, right there, so you're with them and interacting with them all the time."

When Swinney envisioned the new football complex, it wasn't just a vision to give Clemson an edge over its competitors or a recruiting advantage. His goal was to have a facility that will bring his entire team together. When he saw offensive tackle Sean Pollard and tight end Cannon Smith carrying their fishing poles and walking back from the moat and into the facility just after they moved in, Swinney knew the building was going to be worth every penny.

"These players don't have a dorm. There is no dorm," Swinney said. "It is not like they live together or anything like that. You get in these positions where guys are with their position group. These guys are going to interact with each other. It is really going to be, I think, a great team-building type of building for us.

"Again, this is a chance to develop these guys and make sure they have an unbelievable experience here."

Swinney said the new building is about building champions on and off the field.

"I'm just so proud of how we have formulated that and what it is going to be able to do for our current players and our former players. It is just amazing," he said. "That is what it is all about. It is about building champions.

"The building just sets the standard. We talk about best is the standard, and I don't think there is anything better."

When it comes to the amenities for the student athletes, there is no one that has it better in the country. There is a basketball court as well, a wiffle ball field, arcade games, a ping-pong table, a pool table, and PlayStation and Xbox games. And let's not forget the slide.

"This building is to serve the heart and not the talent," Turnipseed said. "If you serve the heart and not the talent and you love, serve, and care for one another . . . that is the whole theme of this."

What makes the football complex so special is that so many people have invested a lot of time and resources into building it.

"We had a lot of thoughts from a lot of people, starting with Dabo, on getting this on what it became," Turnipseed said. "We have the land here. We were fortunate enough to have the soccer fields and we were fortunate enough to have a president and a board of trustees that understood the vision and the importance of what we are doing.

"We had to build the soccer fields. That allowed us to have this space. Very few people, and I don't know of anybody, who has the land opportunity to do what we have been able to do and how it allows us to tie this all together."

Swinney has said the new football complex will be the football program's home for generations to come. Turnipseed says it will be the standard in College Football, as well. Others schools who have recently visited Clemson say Clemson is an A-plus when it comes to its new facility, while everyone else is just a C-minus at best. That's the gap between Clemson and everyone else.

"The nap room, the bowling alley, the theater, the outdoor seating area, a lot of people don't do the dining hall. Most people do the dining with the general student body on campus," Turnipseed said. "Dabo has been strong about creating a culture. The more time we eat together and spend time together, the closer we are going to be.

"[The president, the board of trustees and the athletic director] they could have all said they weren't going to do that. The one reason we are successful here is because

Dabo respects the chain of command. He is an ultimate team player. Some coaches have an ego. I think, when a college football program gets in trouble is when you have a coach who does not respect the chain of command or becomes bigger than the president or bigger than the athletic director. Everybody bought into this thing.

"This building here is the standard for college football for many years to come. Most people, no matter what they try to do, they can't come close to it because they don't have the land. It will be economically impossible unless they have some billion dollar T. Boone Pickens to come in and take out half a billion dollars' worth of facilities, which likely is not going to happen. This is the foundation for Clemson football for generations. This is a difference maker."

It's a vision Dabo Swinney started years ago before he even won his first ACC Championship. He wanted to bring Clemson together. He wanted to make it a family once again. And he has.

"Some people might be able to build a building that is close to it, but until they get a Dabo Swinney that believes in that philosophy, their building will never function the way we function here," Turnipseed said.

FOOTBALL HISTORY

September 30, 1896—A small crowd gathered in one of the barracks rooms and discussed the advisability of organizing a football association and to devise some means of getting a coach. The organization, known as the Clemson College Football Association, was perfected and the following officers elected: President Frank Tompkins, Secretary & Treasurer Charlie Gentry, Manager T.R. Vogel, Temporary Captain R.G. Hamilton. A committee of three was appointed to consult Professor Riggs as to management of a football team and to ask his aid as coach.

October 5, 1896—Practice began on campus on a 50' x 200' field in front of the college.

October 31, 1896—Clemson played its first football game, defeating Furman 14-6 in Greenville, SC. It was the first time that many of the Clemson players had seen a full-sized football gridiron. Charlie Gentry was credited with scoring the Tigers' first touchdown.

November 21, 1896—Clemson defeated Wofford 16-0. When the team arrived back on campus that night, the cadet corps, along with faculty members, led the team around in a buggy led by a torchlight procession and proceeded to go all over the campus. With this win, Clemson claimed the state title.

November 10, 1897—Clemson defeated South Carolina for the first time and won the school's second state championship. A total of 2,000 spectators witnessed the 18-6 triumph. Clemson took an early 4-0 lead when South Carolina's Lee Hagood fumbled on the Gamecocks' 31-yard line and Clemson's W.T. Brock caught the fumbled ball in the air and raced 30 yards for a touchdown.

October 20, 1898—The Tigers played their first home game against Bingham. Clemson won 55-0, as W.C. Forsythe kicked every PAT (11). R.T.V. Bowman, the man for whom the field at Clemson is named, was an assistant coach at that time with Clemson and helped referee the game.

November 10, 1899—The football association stood on a very weak financial basis. The organization could not even afford to hire a coach. W.M. Riggs agreed to coach the Tigers for free.

December 8, 1899—John Heisman was hired as head coach.

October 22, 1900—The Tigers defeated Wofford 21-0. Actually, Clemson scored many more points, but a pre-game agreement between the two stated that every point Clemson scored after the first four touchdowns would not count. No one could keep an accurate count after Clemson scored its first 21 points after just six minutes elapsed. All touchdowns Clemson made were called back and the ball given to Wofford deep in Clemson territory on such penalties as running over a Wofford tackler.

November 29, 1900—Clemson's 35-0 win over Alabama allowed John Heisman's team to finish the year undefeated (6-0). It was Clemson's first undefeated team and was the only team to win all of the games in a season until the 1948 squad went 11-0. Clemson won the SIAA Championship, its first conference title.

October 5, 1901—Clemson opened the season with a 122-0 win over Guilford, the most points scored in Tiger history. They averaged 30 yards per play and a touchdown every minute and 26 seconds. The first half lasted 20 minutes, while the second half lasted only 10 minutes. Legend has it that every man on the team scored a touchdown in the game.

October 30, 1902—Col. Charles S. Roller Jr., who was football coach of Furman, was the only referee for the Clemson-South Carolina game. Bronco Armstrong, a famous Yale player and official, was to be the umpire, but there was in a railroad wreck on the way to Clemson, and it was impossible for him to get to the game in time. Not a single penalty was called in the game. A riot between Tiger and Gamecock fans broke out the night after the game. Officials at both colleges called off the football series between the two schools. Clemson and South Carolina did not meet again in football until 1909.

November 27, 1902—Clemson played in the snow for the first time in a game against Tennessee. The Tigers won the game 11-0 and claimed the Southern Intercollegiate Athletic Association crown, their second league title in three years.

October 10, 1903—Clemson beat Georgia 29-0. In the first 10 minutes, Clemson fumbled the ball three times. After the game, the Georgia team made a deal with the Clemson team. They would give the Clemson team a bushel of apples for every point Clemson would defeat Georgia Tech above the score Clemson made against Georgia. The score turned out to be Clemson 73, Georgia Tech 0. Apples were plentiful around Clemson that winter—44 bushels.

October 17, 1903—Clemson defeated Georgia Tech 73-0. Clemson rushed the ball 55 times for 615 yards, still a school record, while Tech ran the ball 35 times and collected 28 yards. The second half was shortened to 15 minutes.

October 28, 1903—The Tigers defeated N.C. State 24-0 in Columbia, SC, at the fairgrounds. One incident that delayed the game's start was the fact that the sideline spectators, in their eagerness to see each play, crowded in front of the grandstand and on the field. They played twenty-minute halves, because the field had to be given to the racing association at 12:45 p.m. Even the short halves could not be played out, and the time limit was up when 16 minutes of the second half had been played. Heisman married Evelyn Barksdale in Columbia after the game.

November 24, 1903—Clemson participated in its "First Bowl Game." The game between Clemson and Cumberland was billed as the game to decide the "Championship of the South," as the winner would be the champion of the SIAA. The game ended in an 11-11 tie.

November 26, 1903—One day after Georgia Tech's deadline for its offer had expired, Heisman wired Georgia Tech President Lyman Hall that he would accept its offer of $2,250 per year plus 30 percent of net receipts to coach its athletic teams.

September 30, 1904—Clemson began practice under new Head Coach Shack Shealy, who was at one time a great football player. He played varsity ball six years, four at Clemson and two at Iowa State. He is still the only Clemson graduate to serve as head coach of the Tiger football team.

November 11, 1905—The Clemson-Auburn game was called on account of darkness. Clemson won 6-0.

November 29, 1906—Clemson's first forward pass occurred in a 10-0 win over Georgia Tech. Powell Lykes dropped back to kick but instead made a forward pass of 30 yards to George Warren. Clemson finished the season 4-0-3 and was cochampion for the SIAA conference crown.

September 28, 1907—The cadets of Clemson College braved wind and rain at Bowman Field to witness the Tigers in their earliest season opener to date. Clemson met Gordon Military Academy on a muddy field. Clemson was playing under new head coach Frank Shaughnessy.

November 4-9, 1907—Clemson played three games within a week's time. Clemson lost to Auburn 12-0 on November 4 and lost to Georgia in Augusta, GA, on November 7. The Tigers barely made it back in time to play Davidson at Clemson on November 9 and lost 10-6.

April 1, 1908—Tiger football hopes of the 1908 season were shattered on this day, not by what happened in spring practice, but what 300 students did as a college prank on April Fool's Day. The cadets were expelled for removing a Civil War cannon from the town square of Pendleton, four miles down the road from campus, and bringing the cannon back to Clemson. Many of the football stars, as well as many future stars, were among those who were expelled.

October 2, 1915—Clemson dedicated Riggs Field prior to a 6-6 tie with Davidson. Clemson would play its football games at the facility through 1941. It is now the home of Clemson's soccer stadium.

October 9, 1915—The Tigers traveled to Knoxville, where they won fame by defeating the defending conference champion Tennessee 3-0. Bill Harris drop-kicked a 20-yard field goal for the only score of the game in the fourth quarter. Tennessee was the defending champion of the SIAA.

October 13, 1917—Clemson downed Furman 38-0, as the Tigers' Stumpy Banks scored five touchdowns, a record that still stands today.

November 16, 1918—The University of South Carolina athletic authorities provided the use of their stadium to Clemson and The Citadel for their annual game. South Carolina was playing at Furman that day, and the field was not going to be used by the Gamecocks. The reason the game was played at Columbia was that the military officials from both schools would not allow players to be absent from any military duties due to athletic events. Since the game was played in Columbia, both schools' cadets and football teams would be able to make the trip to Columbia and return to duty on time. Clemson's John O'Dell scored the game's only touchdown, as the Tigers won 7-0. Both teams made it back to their campuses before their passes expired.

December 27, 1926—Josh Cody was named head football coach at Clemson.

September 19, 1928—Clemson began this season with new uniforms. The Tigers wore a brilliant orange jersey for the first time, with black composition cloth stripes on the front with purple numbers.

December, 1928—O. K. Pressley, a center, was named a third-team All-America honoree by the Newspaper Enterprise Association. He was Clemson's first All-America athlete in any sport.

May 6, 1929—Josh Cody, Clemson head coach, was presented with a new automobile that afternoon as a gift from alumni, faculty, students, and friends of the college. A special collection was taken up to purchase the new Buick. The presentation ceremony was staged in front of Tillman Hall.

October 17, 1930—Maxcey Welch scored five touchdowns (all rushing) in Clemson's 75-0 win over Newberry. Welch and Stumpy Banks are the coholders of that Clemson touchdown scoring record.

March 13, 1930—Josh Cody signed a new contract to stay at Clemson through the 1932 season.

November 26, 1930—Cody announced that the Furman game the next day would be his final as head coach of the Tigers.

November 27, 1930—Clemson defeated Furman 12-7 to conclude the Tigers' third-straight eight-win season, the only eight-win season in Clemson history between 1896-1930. The 1930 Tigers concluded the season with an 8-2 record and posted four shutouts. In fact, only Tennessee and Florida scored over a touchdown against the Tigers in this season.

November 29, 1930—The Tiger student newspaper published an extra edition about Coach Cody, hoping

to convince him to remain as coach. Cody had become a popular mentor because of his 29-11-1 record, including a perfect 4-0 record against South Carolina, the only coach in Clemson history to have a perfect ledger against the Gamecocks.

January 2, 1931—After reconsidering his decision for over a month, Cody made his resignation final.

January 17, 1931—Jess Neely was named head football coach at Clemson. He was the second consecutive Vanderbilt graduate to coach the Tigers. Cody was a 1917 graduate of Vandy and Neely graduated in 1923. In fact, eight of the nine Clemson head football coaches between 1931-98 were graduates of current SEC schools.

October 16, 1931—Clemson suffered a surprising 6-0 loss against The Citadel in a game played in Florence, SC. After the game, Neely, Captain Frank Jervey, and others met in a car outside the stadium to discuss ways Clemson could help its football program get back on track. The meeting started the ball rolling toward the establishment of the IPTAY Foundation. Clemson would score just three touchdowns and win one game during the 1931 season.

October 14, 1933—Clemson played at George Washington in a 0-0 tie. This was the first time Clemson had ever played under the lights. Fans followed the game on a grid graph in Tillman Hall at the Clemson chapel. A grid graph was an electrical machine that was marked off like a football field. Lights were so arranged on the graph that every possible play was flashed on the board. The lineups of both teams were written on the sides, and the man carrying the ball on each play had a light flashed by his name. Another light representing the runner moved along the board in the same direction and for the same distance as the runner.

August 20, 1934—IPTAY, the nation's first scholarship fundraising organization, was founded. Dr. Rupert Fike, a cancer specialist from Atlanta and Clemson class of 1908, wrote Jess Neely a letter documenting the formation of the organization.

"Last night we had a little meeting out at my house and organized the IPTAY Club," Fike wrote. "The purpose [of IPTAY] shall be to provide financial support to the athletic department at Clemson and to assist in every other way possible to regain for Clemson the high athletic standing which rightfully belongs to her."

The organization was first established as a secret organization, and initial membership dues were set at $10 a year. Many had suggested that $50 be the minimum donation, but Fike's foresight thought it would be best to get as many supporters involved as possible, so he established the $10 minimum.

The excitement about the organization carried over into the 1934 season, and the Tigers ran to their first winning season since 1930. Clemson had gone 0-5-1 against Furman and South Carolina in those years, then defeated both teams in 1934.

November 19, 1935—Clemson held its first night football practice. Two powerful floodlights were installed at the practice fields. The Clemson coaches wanted more practice time with the players, and that was the reason the lights were brought in. The extra practice did not pay off however, as Clemson lost its final game that year to Furman 8-6.

November 17, 1937—Clemson defeated Florida in Gainesville by a 10-9 score. Don Willis scored Clemson's only TD of the game on a one-yard run that culminated a 65-yard drive on Clemson's opening possession. Later, Clemson gave up a safety and a touchdown, so Florida led 9-7 heading into the fourth quarter. But the Tigers drove 60 yards late in the game, and Ben Pearson booted a 27-yard field goal to win the game.

At the time, it gave Clemson a 4-4 record in 1937, but it proved to be a program builder, much as Clemson's win over South Carolina in 1980 did. The Tigers posted a 22-2-2 record over a 26-game period that started with that win at Florida. Clemson's only losses in that 26-game period were to Tennessee in 1938 and Tulane in 1939. Tennessee ended the 1938 season with a 10-0 record and ranked second in the nation, while Tulane ended the 1939 season with an 8-0-1 mark and fifth in the country.

November 5, 1938—Clemson scored with big plays in a win over George Washington 27-0. The Tigers scored three touchdowns on plays of at least 65 yards, the first time in history Clemson had scoring plays of that distance in the same game. Banks McFadden ran 70 yards for a score on the first Clemson play from scrimmage. Later, Shad Bryant scored on a 65-yard punt return and on a 65-yard run off a lateral. George Washington actually had more first downs, 15-13, yet lost by 27 points.

September 23, 1939—Banks McFadden ran 90 yards for a touchdown in Clemson's 18-0 win over Presbyterian College. It is still the longest run in Clemson history. McFadden had a career-high 173 yards in 15 attempts on this day.

September 30, 1939—Clemson suffered its only loss of the season to a revenge-minded Tulane eleven. The Tigers had beaten the Green Wave the previous year by a 13-10 score. This season, however, Tulane defeated Clemson 7-6. Despite the loss, it was a game that brought acclaim to Clemson for its ability to play so close with the team that would end the year ranked fifth in the nation. McFadden was all over the field on this day, throwing for Clemson's only touchdown and defending enemy passes from the secondary. His punting kept Tulane bottled up in its own territory. He had 12 punts for 504 yards, including a record six punts of at least 50 yards. Unfortunately, he was involved in what proved to be the

game's deciding moment, as his extra point attempt after Clemson's only touchdown was blocked.

October 19, 1939—Clemson outgained South Carolina 402-90 in a 27-0 thrashing of the Gamecocks. Banks McFadden threw for 85 yards and rushed for 76 in just 14 attempts.

October 26, 1939—Clemson showed it was a deep enough team to win without All-America player Banks McFadden, who missed the Navy game with an injury. Shad Bryant had a 40-yard run for a score in Clemson's 15-7 win at Annapolis.

November 3, 1939—Clemson won in the Washington, D.C., area for the second-straight week, defeating George Washington 13-6. Bryant had 127 yards rushing and scored Clemson's only touchdown. The game was played on a Friday evening.

November 11, 1939—McFadden completed just four passes against Wake Forest, but three were to Joe Blalock for 105 yards, the first 100-yard receiving game in Tiger history. It was the final home game for McFadden and the rest of the Tiger seniors.

November 13, 1939—Clemson was ranked in the AP poll for the first time. The Tigers beat Wake Forest 20-7 to improve to 6-1. Clemson had 33 poll points on that November 13 ranking and one first-place vote out of the 85 votes in the poll that week. Clemson remained in the top 20 over the next three weeks, and each week Clemson had exactly one first-place vote. However, in the final poll, even though Clemson had run the table to finish 8-1 in the regular season, that individual failed to vote Clemson #1, as the Tigers did not have a first-place vote in the December 11 [final] poll.

November 18, 1939—Clemson won away from home for the fourth-straight time, a 21-6 win over Rhodes. Banks McFadden and George Floyd combined for 126 yards rushing.

November 25, 1939—Clemson concluded its 8-1 regular season with a 14-3 victory over Furman. Shad Bryant ran for 94 yards and gained 75 more in punt returns. McFadden scored two touchdowns and had 10 punts for a 42-yard average, intercepted a pass, and completed a pass.

December 8, 1939—Clemson accepted a bid to play in the Cotton Bowl. It was Clemson's first postseason bowl game appearance. Clemson met Cumberland in a postseason "Championship of the South" game in 1903, but it was not considered an established bowl.

December 11, 1939—Clemson ranked 12th in the final poll by the Associated Press, Clemson's first appearance in a final season AP poll. The Tigers had 112 poll points, just behind Boston College, who had 120.5 poll points for 11th place. Clemson would defeat Boston College in the Cotton Bowl, but the AP did not have a poll after the bowls. In fact, for whatever the reason, the AP did not have a final poll after the bowls until after the 1968 season. Thus, Clemson actually would have had a much higher ranking by today's standards if there had been a poll in January of 1940.

December 15, 1939—Banks McFadden was named a first-team All-America honoree by AP and a third-team selection by UPI. He was the first Clemson player honored by the AP. Later that year, he was named the Nation's Most Versatile Athlete for 1939. Earlier in the year, he had led Clemson to the 1939 Southern Conference Championship in basketball, still the only postseason championship in Clemson history.

January 1, 1940—In Clemson's first bowl appearance, it defeated Boston College 6-3. Charlie Timmons scored the game's lone touchdown from two yards out and rushed for 115 yards. McFadden keyed the defense with four pass deflections of Boston College passes, and he also averaged 43 yards per punt. Boston College drove to the Clemson eight with three minutes left, but Shad Bryant and McFadden knocked away third- and fourth-down passes to save the day for the Tigers.

"Clemson is every bit as good as they were cracked up to be," said Boston College Coach Frank Leahy, still the second-winningest coach in college football history on a percentage basis. "We lost to a great team, one of the best I have ever seen. I have the satisfaction of knowing that while we were beaten, the game wasn't lost on a fluke."

January 10, 1940—Jess Neely resigned as athletic director and football coach to accept the head football coaching job at Rice. Neely had inherited a $47,000 deficit when he arrived in 1931 and earned Clemson $100,000 during his tenure, leaving with $57,000 in the treasury. His overall record at Clemson was 43-35-7. He would be inducted into the College Football Hall of Fame in 1971.

January 11, 1940—Frank Howard was named head coach. At the Athletic Council meeting that day, Professor Sam Rhodes, a council member, nominated Howard for the position. When a call for a second was asked, Howard, standing in the back of the room, said: "I second the nomination." It is perhaps the only recorded time in history a coach has seconded his own nomination for head coach.

July 25, 1940—Banks McFadden accepted a bid to play in the College All-Star game against the Green Bay Packers on August 29. He scored one of the two touchdowns for the College All-Stars.

September 1, 1940—McFadden signed a one-year contract to play with the Brooklyn Dodgers professional football team. He led the NFL in yards per carry in 1940 but did not like the bright lights of New York and returned to Clemson.

September 21, 1940—In Frank Howard's first game as head coach, Clemson scored on the first offensive play as George Floyd reversed around left end and raced 18

yards untouched for a touchdown. The Tigers went on to a 38-0 win over Presbyterian College.

October 12, 1940—Clemson shut out Wake Forest 39-0 in Clemson's second game of the season at Riggs Field. It was Clemson's third shutout in the first four games of the Howard era. It was the last home game of the season for the Tigers, who would go on to win the Southern Conference title even though seven of the nine games were on the road.

October 24, 1940—Frank Howard won his first game as head coach in the rivalry with South Carolina. The Tigers were victorious 21-13, thanks to five interceptions by the Tiger defense. Howard coached in 30 Clemson-South Carolina games. Incredible as it may seem, both Clemson and South Carolina scored exactly 411 total points in those 30 games.

October 28, 1940—It didn't take Howard long to get the Tigers into the nation's top 10. With the 5-0 start, the Tigers earned 136 poll points and ranked #10 in the nation, Clemson's first top-10 ranking in the AP poll. Two writers ranked Clemson #1.

November 23, 1940—Clemson won the Southern Conference title with a 13-7 win over Furman. Ed Maness led the way for the Tigers with 136 yards rushing on 18 carries. It was the first of eight conference titles for the Tigers under Frank Howard.

October 6, 1941—Work began on Memorial Stadium. Frank Howard supervised the chore of cleaning, digging, and leveling the site as well as cutting large trees and clearing underbrush. They also installed a pipe for drainage under the field.

October 11, 1941—Clemson defeated Boston College at Fenway Park 26-13. Joe Blalock scored two touchdowns as Clemson overcame a 6-0 deficit after the first quarter. BC outgained Clemson 363-281, but Clemson came away with the victory.

October 23, 1941—Booty Payne became the first Clemson player to pass for over 200 yards in an 18-14 loss to South Carolina. He completed 9-16 passes for 202 yards in the contest. It was one of just three 200-yard passing games by a Tiger in the decade of the 1940s.

November 15, 1941—Clemson defeated Wake Forest 29-0 in the last game at Riggs Field.

November 22, 1941—The Tigers put on the greatest rushing defense exhibition in the first 100 years of Clemson history, holding Furman to -21 yards rushing in a 34-6 win in Greenville. Charlie Timmons scored three touchdowns and added four extra points in his final game as a Tiger. The 22 points scored rank sixth-best in Clemson history for a single game by an individual. But Timmons was not the leading rusher in the game, as teammate Sid Tinsley picked up 127 yards on just seven carries.

September 19, 1942—Memorial Stadium opened, and the Tigers ran down the hill for the first time. Butch Butler gained 192 yards, as the Tigers opened the new stadium in front of 5,500 with a 32-13 win over Presbyterian College. It was the most yards rushing by a Tiger in the decade of the 1940s. High school students were admitted for 25 cents, while servicemen were allowed in for 50 cents.

September 25, 1943—World War II took virtually all of Clemson's veteran players, and the Tigers started nine first-year freshmen at the 11 positions in a 13-12 loss to Presbyterian College. Clemson had just a 2-6 record this season with no one older than a sophomore playing in a game, as the armed services took Clemson's entire junior and senior classes.

October 19, 1944—First rain at a Clemson-South Carolina game since 1896. Despite the conditions, Sid Tinsley rushed for 146 yards in 22 carries to lead the Tigers to a 20-13 victory.

September 22, 1945—Fourteen Clemson backs netted 516 yards in a 76-0 win over Presbyterian College. Freshman Bobby Gage led the Tigers with 144 yards, including 88 on a touchdown run, the longest run from scrimmage by a Tiger in the decade of the 1940s. The Tigers had 11 rushing touchdowns in the game, still a Clemson record.

October 24, 1946—The Clemson vs. South Carolina game was played under unusual circumstances. Counterfeit tickets had been printed, and 10,000 more people than the capacity showed up for the game. Fans stormed the gates and stood on the sidelines, even on the field at the opposite end of the field when the game action was taking place. Coach Howard recalled fans standing next to him on the sideline telling him what plays to run. South Carolina won on this bizarre day 26-14.

September 24, 1947—Clemson flew to Boston College on an Eastern Airline DC-4. It marked the first time that a state football team had flown to a football game. The quicker traveling did not help, however, as Boston College defeated the Tigers 32-22.

November 8, 1947—Clemson began a 15-game winning streak, the longest in school history, with a win over Furman 35-7.

November 22, 1947—Bobby Gage ran for 141 yards and passed for 233 as he led Clemson to a 34-18 win over Auburn. Gage threw four touchdown passes and had 374 yards total offense, records that stood almost 50 years. Hank Walker was Gage's favorite receiver, as he pulled in 10 passes for 148 yards. It is still the second-most receptions in a single game in Clemson history, and the yardage total is the sixth-best. It was the first time in Clemson history that the Tigers had a 100-yard rusher, a 100-yard receiver, and a 200-yard passer in the same game. The Clemson defense was also outstanding, holding Auburn to -9 yards rushing.

June 1, 1948—Frank Gillespie was named the Southern Conference Athlete of the Year. He played football, basketball, and baseball during the academic year and was the first Tiger athlete to be named a conference athlete of the year.

September 25, 1948—Clemson beat Presbyterian College 53-0 in the first night game at Clemson. Clemson also defeated N.C. State 6-0 in a home night game the following week.

October 2, 1948—Gage continued his All-America triple-threat season by returning a punt 90 yards for a touchdown in Clemson's 6-0 win over N.C. State at Death Valley. It was the longest punt return at Memorial Stadium until 2006.

October 21, 1948—A #14 Tiger team beat South Carolina 13-7 in Columbia. Captain Phil Prince was the hero for the Tigers, as he blocked a South Carolina punt with just 4:15 left in the contest. Oscar Thompson recovered it at the 11 and ran it in for a touchdown, giving Clemson the 13-7 lead.

November 6, 1948—Bobby Gage put on the most efficient passing exhibition in Clemson history in a 41-0 win over Furman. He completed 9-11 passes for 245 yards and two touchdowns. His efficiency rating of 310.7 is still a Clemson record for a minimum of 10 attempts. He averaged 22 yards per attempt, a record by far in Clemson history. The defense was just as effective, holding the Paladins to -12 yards in total offense, still the best total defense effort in Clemson history for a single game.

November 22, 1948—The Tigers were ranked #9 in the AP poll, their highest ranking in history. Eight voters ranked Clemson #1 in the nation.

November 27, 1948—Clemson accepted a bid to play in the Gator Bowl after it beat Auburn 7-6 in a hard-fought game played in Mobile, AL. It was Clemson's first bowl bid since the 1939 season. Ray Mathews scored on a one-yard run with just 6:35 left to give Clemson its only lead of the game.

November 29, 1948—Clemson ranked 11th in the final AP poll. Again, Clemson suffered from not having a poll after the bowl games. Clemson won another regular season game, then defeated Missouri in the Gator Bowl to close a perfect season. But these wins were not reflected in the final ranking. The AP did not have a postbowl poll until 1968.

December 4, 1948—Clemson closed out its perfect regular season with a 20-0 win over The Citadel in a game played in Charleston. The December 4 date is the second-latest regular season game in Clemson history. The 10th-ranked Tigers did not allow The Citadel to make a first down in the game, the only recorded time in Clemson history that the Tigers did not allow a first down. The Bulldogs also failed to complete a pass in the contest.

The victory was Clemson's sixth road win of the year, a record that still stands for road wins in a season. Only four Clemson teams have had a perfect road record since 1948, and that was the 1981 National Championship team, the 1995, 2015, and 2016 Tigers.

December 6, 1948—Frank Howard was named Southern Conference Coach of the Year, his first of three Coach of the Year selections in his career.

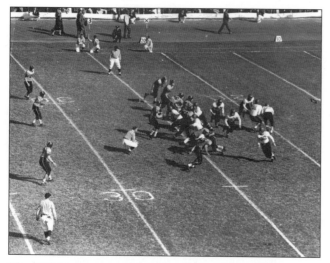

The 1948 team was undefeated with an 11-0 record.

January 1, 1949—The Tigers won the Gator Bowl by a 24-23 score over Missouri. Fred Cone scored two first-quarter touchdowns as Clemson raced to a 14-0 lead. After Missouri tied the game, Gage threw a nine-yard scoring pass to John Poulos, a play that completed a 80-yard drive. Jack Miller's 32-yard field goal in the fourth quarter proved to be the winning margin. Missouri would score a late touchdown to come within 24-23. But that was the final score. You could not go for two points in those days, so Missouri did not have the opportunity to tie the score after their touchdown that took place with less than five minutes left. Both teams had exactly 298 yards of total offense in the game.

Clemson closed the season with a perfect 11-0 record, the only team in college football with 11 wins that year and one of just three with a perfect record. Notre Dame and Michigan were both 9-0-0 that season but did not play in a bowl game.

November 26, 1949—Clemson closed out the decade of the 1940s with a 20-20 tie against Auburn in Mobile, AL. Clemson had just a 4-4-2 record but closed 2-0-1 over the last three games, giving the program momentum heading into the 1950 season.

September 30, 1950—Clemson defeated Missouri 34-0 in the second game of the season. The Tigers of Columbia, MO, had been ranked in the preseason top 20. Three Clemson backs rushed for at least 100 yards, the second straight game Frank Howard had three 100-yard rushers

in the same game. It has happened just four total times in Clemson history.

October 7, 1950—Clemson recorded its third-straight shutout to open the season with a 27-0 win over N.C. State in a home night game. Wyndie Windham again led the Clemson defense in tackles and according to legend knocked out N.C. State players on four consecutive plays in this game.

October 28, 1950—Clemson defeated Wake Forest in Winston-Salem in a battle of top-20 teams, 13-12. Clemson lineman Bob Patton blocked the extra point in the final minute to preserve the victory for Clemson. It is the only time in Clemson history that a Tiger has blocked a kick on the last play of the game to give Clemson a victory.

November 28, 1950—Clemson accepted a bid to play in the Orange Bowl.

January 1, 1951—Clemson appeared in the Orange Bowl for the first time and squeaked out a 15-14 win over Miami (FL) to complete an undefeated season. Sterling Smith's tackle of Frank Smith in the end zone gave Clemson a safety with under six minutes left in the game and gave the Tigers the victory. Don Wade also had two interceptions in the game. It was Clemson's second undefeated season in the last three years for Howard's Tigers.

Sterling Smith tackled the Miami ball carrier behind the goal line for a safety in Clemson's 15-14 victory over the Hurricanes in the 1951 Orange Bowl.

November 27, 1951—Clemson accepted a bid to play in the Gator Bowl. This was done against the wishes of the Southern Conference, who had made a rule its members could not go to a bowl game. Clemson and Maryland, which both accepted bowl bids, were given sanctions. The two teams were told they will not be allowed to play any other conference teams in 1952. This resulted in teams leaving the Southern Conference and forming the ACC.

November 8, 1952—Don King, making his first and only career start as tailback, rushed for 234 yards on 33 carries in Clemson's 12-12 tie at Fordham. The performance is still a record for a Clemson freshman and still stands as the third-highest single-game total in Clemson history. King, who had 240 rushing yards in the first half and -6 in the second half, was substituting for an injured tailback and returned to quarterback the next week. He never played tailback again.

May 8, 1953—Clemson joined the Atlantic Coast Conference.

October 31, 1953—Clemson won its first ACC game in history, 18-0 over Wake Forest in a contest played at Clemson.

September 18, 1954—Clemson Head Cheerleader George Bennett fired a cannon after each Tiger score. The cannon was purchased by Bennett's father, and the tradition is still carried out today.

October 9, 1954—Clemson upset 14th-ranked Florida in Jacksonville 14-7.

November 16, 1956—Vice President Richard Nixon was in attendance at the Clemson-Miami football game on this date. As he was surrounded by security from various agencies, a loud explosion sounded and alarmed the bodyguard along with the vice president. To everyone's relief, it was discovered that it was just the cannon fired off by a Clemson cheerleader when Clemson kicked off. The eighth-ranked Hurricanes defeated the Tigers 21-0 in the game played at Miami, FL.

November 24, 1956—Clemson defeated Virginia 7-0 at Clemson to clinch the Tigers' first-ever ACC Championship.

December 1, 1956—Clemson clinched an Orange Bowl berth with a 28-7 win over Furman at Clemson.

January 1, 1957—Colorado defeated Clemson 27-21 in an exciting Orange Bowl in Miami. Clemson had trailed 20-0 at the half, and Frank Howard threatened to resign at halftime. But, the Tigers came back to take a 21-20 lead in fourth quarter, only to see the Buffalos score late to win the game.

March 25, 1957—It was announced that Clemson and South Carolina would play at Clemson on Saturday, November 12, 1960, ending the 61-year-old state classic, Big Thursday.

September 20, 1958—Clemson ran down the hill on a rug for the first time. The rug was officially given to Clemson on this date before the Clemson-Virginia game by W.W. Pate, Sr., president of Wunda Weave Company. It measured 104 feet long and was 13 feet wide. Also at this game, Clemson's first expansion of Memorial Stadium was used for the first time. Memorial Stadium was expanded from 20,000 to 38,000 seats.

September 27, 1958—Clemson defeated North Carolina 26-21, as Frank Howard picked up his 100th collegiate coaching win. Doug Cline scored on a two-yard run with 2:52 left to give Clemson the win. It was one of four times in 1958 that Clemson scored a touchdown in the last quarter to win the game. Also, the scoreboard at the east of the stadium was used for the first time. The scoreboard had an added feature, as the Tiger above the scoreboard still wags his tail after each Clemson touchdown.

October 6, 1958—Clemson was ranked eighth in the country, the highest ranking in Clemson history, at that time.

October 11, 1958—Clemson kept its top-10 ranking alive with a 12-7 win at Vanderbilt. Harvey White scored the game-winner on a three-yard run with three seconds left to win the game. It is the latest game-winning touchdown in Clemson history.

November 19, 1958—Clemson defeated N.C. State 13-6 and won its second ACC championship in three years.

November 29, 1958—Clemson accepted a Sugar Bowl bid to face top-ranked Louisiana State.

December 24, 1958—It was announced that Clemson would take the rug that the Tigers used to run down the hill to the Sugar Bowl. The rug weighed 527 pounds.

December 27, 1958—Clemson announced it would wear navy blue jerseys with wide numerals front and back. They'd also wear orange helmets with a white stripe from back to front in the center, to give a contrasting color for the nationwide television coverage of the game.

January 1, 1959—Top-ranked Louisiana State, led by Heisman Trophy winner Billy Cannon, beat Clemson 7-0 in the Sugar Bowl. Cannon, a halfback, threw a touchdown pass to give Louisiana State and Paul Dietzel the national championship-clinching victory. It was the first time Clemson had ever played the #1 team.

September 19, 1959—Clemson defeated North Carolina in Chapel Hill 20-18 in a battle of top-20 teams. The Tar Heels were ranked #12 in the preseason poll.

October 22, 1959—Clemson won the last Big Thursday game by defeating South Carolina 27-0. Harvey White was on target all day, hitting 9-10 passes for 162 yards and two scores. Clemson fans tore down the steel goal posts, which were set in concrete, following the game.

November 21, 1959—Clemson defeated Wake Forest 33-31 for Clemson's second ACC title in a row. George Usry scored on a one-yard run with 4:24 to go to give Clemson the triumph.

December 19, 1959—Clemson defeated TCU in the Bluebonnet Bowl 23-7. The Horned Frogs, led by All-America player and future Dallas Cowboy Bob Lilly, were ranked seventh in the nation entering the game. The victory is also the 300th in Clemson history.

October 1, 1960—The west stands were used for the first time, as Clemson beat Virginia Tech 13-7.

October 8, 1960—Clemson defeated Virginia 21-7 and used special pants for rain protection in this game. After the contest, Clemson sent the pants to Greenville and allowed Furman to use the pants for a game that night against William & Mary. Furman Coach Bob King said, "after those big Clemson boys got out of them, some of our guys had a hard time making them stay up and we had to tape the legs of the pants for several players." The pants beat two teams from Virginia on the same day.

November 12, 1960—Clemson defeated South Carolina by the score of 12-2 in the first-ever appearance for South Carolina at Clemson.

November 11, 1961—A team resembling Clemson entered the field prior to the meeting with South Carolina. They did a few serious calisthenics and then started dancing to band music. The team was actually members of the Sigma Nu Fraternity of South Carolina. Clemson students entered the field and worked some of the imposters over. Finally, state police brought order to the field.

October 13, 1962—Hal Davis raced 98 yards with a kickoff return for a touchdown against Georgia, the last time a Tiger would return a kickoff for a score for 25 years.

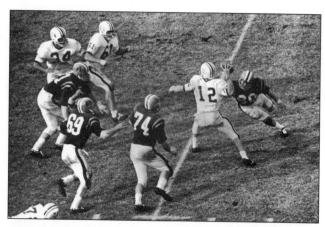

Clemson defeated South Carolina 20-17 in 1962. The Tigers wore blue jerseys left over from the 1959 Sugar Bowl in this game.

November 17, 1962—Clemson upset Maryland as Rodney Rogers kicked a 23-yard field goal with 84 seconds left in the game.

November 24, 1962—Clemson defeated South Carolina, as Rogers kicked a 24-yard field goal with 1:31 left. The Tigers wore blue jerseys in this game, the ones that were used in the Sugar Bowl. Clemson claimed the 20-17 victory when South Carolina quarterback Dan Reeves was

sacked deep in South Carolina territory on the last play of the game.

October 12, 1963—Clemson and Georgia tied 7-7, but the main item of interest was the strange weather. A hail storm hit at 2:50 p.m. and caused temperatures to plummet from 84 degrees to 57 degrees in 45 minutes. Almost an inch of hail poured in a 20-minute period, and the game was delayed. Clemson blocked two field goal attempts to preserve the tie.

November 23, 1963—The South Carolina-Clemson game was postponed due to the death of President John F. Kennedy.

November 28, 1963—Clemson defeated South Carolina on Thanksgiving Day 24-20. It was the fifth win in a row for the Tigers to close the season.

November 6, 1965—Two Clemson single-game records were established in a 17-13 loss at North Carolina. Thomas Ray became the first Tiger to throw for 300 yards in a game when he completed 21-43 passes for 323 yards. His star receiver, Phil Rogers, caught 11 passes for 129 yards to set the single-game reception record.

September 24, 1966—First game in which Howard's Rock was present at Death Valley. Clemson downed Virginia 40-35 in one of the most exciting games in the history of the facility and adding to the legend of Howard's Rock. Clemson trailed 35-17 with just over a quarter remaining in the game but rode the passing of Jimmy Addison to keep its perfect record alive against Virginia. Addison was 12-19 for 283 yards and three touchdowns, including a 74-yarder to Jackie Jackson with 3:49 remaining that proved to be the game-winner.

October 22, 1966—Clemson traveled to Los Angeles to play Southern Cal for the first time. This was the longest trip for a Clemson football team at the time. The Trojans won the Pac-Eight that year, won the Rose Bowl, and defeated Clemson 30-0. Clemson visited Universal Studios prior to the game and had their photos taken with many of the television stars of the era.

November 12, 1966—Frank Howard won his 150th game and clinched at least a tie for the ACC championship with a 14-10 victory over Maryland. Clemson won the ACC outright the next week with a 6-1 record. Clemson was 0-3 outside the league in 1966, and all three of the games were against top-10 teams (Georgia Tech, Alabama, and Southern California).

November 26, 1966—Clemson downed South Carolina to win the ACC 35-10. Tiger offensive lineman Harry Olszewski picked up a midair fumble and ran 12 yards for the key touchdown. No Clemson offensive lineman has scored since.

September 23, 1967—Clemson started the tradition of rubbing Howard's Rock when running down the hill. Clemson responded with a 23-6 win over Wake Forest.

October 28, 1967—Alabama and Bear Bryant came to Clemson to face Frank Howard's Tigers before a sellout crowd at Clemson. Bryant's team won the close game 13-10.

November 18, 1967—Clemson painted its shoes orange for the N.C. State game, and the Tigers upset the 10th-ranked Wolfpack 14-6. Clemson clinched a tie for the ACC championship with the victory, the sixth and final ACC title of Frank Howard's celebrated career. The Tigers had to get the orange paint from eight stores in the area. N.C. State's defense had worn white shoes all season, and that was the reason for the ploy.

November 25, 1967—Clemson beat South Carolina 23-12 to claim the ACC Championship. Buddy Gore broke the ACC single-season rushing record with 1,045 yards and finished the season eighth in the nation in rushing.

September 28, 1968—Richie Luzzi returned a missed field-goal try 108 yards (100 officially) for a touchdown, the longest play in Tiger history.

October 25, 1969—Danny Ford was one of the Alabama captains for the Clemson-Alabama game at Clemson. Bob Hope was in town for a homecoming show that night. Bear Bryant's team defeated Clemson 38-13. Clemson lost by a sizable margin but moved the ball consistently. In fact, Clemson had a 200-yard passer, 100-yard rusher, and 100-yard receiver for just the fourth time.

November 1, 1969—Frank Howard won his last game as a Clemson coach in Death Valley with a 40-0 win over Maryland. It is still Clemson's largest margin of victory against the Terrapins.

December 10, 1969—Frank Howard resigned from football coaching duties but remained in the capacity of athletic director. Howard had first come to Clemson in 1931 as an assistant under Jess Neely.

December 17, 1969—Hootie Ingram was named head football coach.

July 21, 1970—Clemson announced the use of a new logo—the tiger paw. With the aid of Henderson Advertising Agency, the tiger paw became the new trademark of Clemson athletics.

October 31, 1970—Don Kelley had the greatest return game in ACC history when he gained 223 yards on interception and punt returns in a 24-11 win over Maryland. He had a record 167 yards in punt returns, including an 85-yarder for a touchdown, and also had a 56-yard interception return.

October 9, 1971—Hootie Ingram gained his only win over a ranked team as Clemson coach when the Tigers defeated Duke 3-0 in a defensive struggle at the Oyster Bowl in Norfolk, VA. Duke was ranked 14th in the nation entering the contest.

November 27, 1971—Eddie Seigler became the first Clemson kicker in history to boot a field goal of at least 50 yards. His 52-yarder was important in the 17-7 Clemson win over South Carolina.

December 5, 1972—Hootie Ingram resigned as Clemson football coach, and Red Parker was named as his replacement.

September 28, 1974—Georgia Tech made its first appearance in history at Clemson. For years, Clemson had always gone to Atlanta for the series. Clemson won the contest 21-17.

October 5, 1974—Clemson defeated Georgia in Death Valley 28-24, giving Clemson wins over Georgia and Georgia Tech in the same season for the first time since 1914.

November 16, 1974—The playing surface of Memorial Stadium was named Frank Howard Field. This day also featured the longest play in Clemson history, a 97-yard touchdown pass from Mark Fellers to Craig Brantley. Clemson defeated Virginia 28-9.

November 23, 1974—Clemson beat South Carolina 39-21 to close a perfect 6-0 season at home. Ken Callicutt had 197 yards rushing and 55 more receiving to key the attack. It was a Clemson record for all-purpose rushing at the time. South Carolina players wore two different color helmets in the game, as the Gamecock seniors wore black helmets and the rest of the team wore white. Willie Anderson had 21 tackles from his middle guard position, still a Tiger record for an interior lineman. He was named *Sports Illustrated* National Player of the Week.

November 21, 1976—Clemson scrimmaged at an adjacent field and warmed up there until game time before a 28-9 upset of South Carolina.

December 1, 1976—Charley Pell was named head football coach.

September 17, 1977—Clemson defeated Georgia 7-6, and this marked the first time that Clemson had won in Athens since 1914.

November 12, 1977—Fifth-ranked Notre Dame, led by quarterback Joe Montana and 25 other players who would eventually play in the NFL, defeated Clemson in Death Valley 21-17. It was the closest game for the Irish in the last nine games of the season. Notre Dame won the national championship that year. A total of 38 players who participated in this game went on to play in the NFL. The list included both quarterbacks, Montana and Steve Fuller, who both won Super Bowl Championships.

November 19, 1977—A 20-yard pass from Steve Fuller to Jerry Butler with just 49 seconds left enabled Clemson to beat South Carolina 31-27. The Tigers had led 24-0, then South Carolina came back to take a 27-24 lead prior to the final Clemson drive. The win earned the Tigers a trip to the Gator Bowl.

September 16, 1978—Clemson won its 100th game in Death Valley with a 58-3 win over the Citadel. Steve Fuller was a perfect 9-9 passing in the contest, an all-time Clemson record for consecutive completions at the time. Clemson was a record 15-17 passing in the contest and set a school record for team passing efficiency.

November 18, 1978—Clemson clinched the ACC championship with a thrilling victory over Maryland in College Park. Steve Fuller hit touchdown passes of 87 yards to Jerry Butler and 62 yards to Dwight Clark. The game also included a 98-yard run by Maryland's Steve Atkins, the longest run in history against the Tigers.

November 25, 1978—Clemson fans used the south upper deck for the first time in Clemson's 41-23 win over South Carolina. At the time it was the largest crowd ever to see a football game, from Philadelphia to Birmingham. Clemson had three backs gain over 100 yards rushing in the game for the first time since 1950. The victory also clinched Clemson's first 10-win season since 1948.

November 28, 1978—Steve Fuller was tied for sixth place in the Heisman Trophy voting with Ted Brown of N.C. State and received 19 first-place votes.

December 4, 1978—Charley Pell resigned as Clemson's head coach.

December 5, 1978—Danny Ford, offensive line coach for the Tigers, was named as Pell's replacement. He became the head coach at age 30, the youngest Division I head coach in the nation.

December 10, 1978—Danny Ford was announced as the Tigers' coach in the Gator Bowl.

December 29, 1978—Clemson defeated Ohio State 17-15 at the Gator Bowl in Danny Ford's first game as head coach, and Woody Hayes's final game at Ohio State. Freshman Cliff Austin scored the winning touchdown. He would score another important touchdown three years later against Nebraska. Charlie Bauman made the key play with an interception of an Art Schlichter pass with just two minutes left. He ran the return out of bounds on the Ohio State sideline and was punched by Hayes.

May 3, 1979—All-America player Jerry Butler became the fifth pick of the 1979 NFL draft when he was chosen by the Buffalo Bills. This was the highest selection of a Clemson player since the 1939 season, when Banks McFadden was the #4 selection of the Brooklyn Dodgers.

September 22, 1979—Clemson won its 400th game in history, a 12-7 victory over Georgia.

November 16, 1979—Clemson won at Notre Dame 16-10 behind Obed Ariri's three field goals. The Irish had taken a 10-0 lead in the first half, but Ariri's field goals and a 26-yard touchdown run by quarterback Billy Lott proved to be the difference. It was just the third time in the last 40 years that Notre Dame's seniors lost their final home game. The next

day Ariri kicked the only goal for the Clemson soccer team in an NCAA Tournament victory over South Carolina.

October 11, 1980—Obed Ariri booted a 52-yard field goal with six seconds left to give Clemson a 27-24 victory at Virginia. Clemson had trailed by two touchdowns entering the fourth quarter, and this was the greatest fourth quarter comeback in Clemson history. Ariri's boot is also the longest field goal to win a game in Clemson history.

November 8, 1980—Jeff Davis had a then-school record 24 tackles vs. North Carolina in a head-to-head battle with Lawrence Taylor. The Tigers had the ball inside the North Carolina five with a chance to win, but Taylor sacked quarterback Homer Jordan on third down. Obed Ariri, who led the nation in field goals in 1980 with 23, booted a 27-yarder in the first half to become the NCAA's career field goal leader. The Tar Heels were victorious by a score of 24-19, Clemson's last home loss for four seasons.

November 22, 1980—Clemson defeated #14 South Carolina 27-6 in a contest that gave the Tigers momentum heading into 1981. Willie Underwood played the game of his life with two interceptions for 101 yards, including one for a 37-yard touchdown. Underwood entered the game, the 47th of his career, without an interception. He was named *Sports Illustrated* National Defensive Player of the Week. Clemson kept South Carolina Heisman Trophy winner George Rogers out of the end zone.

September 19, 1981—Clemson forced nine Georgia turnovers, most ever by a Clemson opponent, in handing Herschel Walker his only regular-season loss as a Bulldog, 13-3. The Bulldogs were the defending national champions and ranked fourth in the nation entering the contest. It was the highest-ranked win for the Tigers at Death Valley until 2003.

Jeff Davis and the Tigers had a then-school record 24 tackles against North Carolina in 1980.

October 31, 1981—Clemson had 756 total offensive yards against Wake Forest in an 82-24 win. The Tigers set 21 school, stadium, and conference records in the game that remains the highest-scoring game in ACC history. The Tigers scored 49 points in the first half, then scored on the first possession of the second half. Clemson scored its final touchdown on a 72-yard run by Craig Crawford, his first carry as a Tiger and the longest touchdown play in Tiger history for a player on his first play. Clemson was 12-12 on third downs and scored 12 touchdowns on the day. The Tigers had a record 536 yards rushing and averaged 8.7 yards per play.

November 7, 1981—Clemson stopped North Carolina 10-8 in Chapel Hill in the first battle of top-10 teams in ACC football history. Jeff Bryant recovered a fumble in the last two minutes of the game on a North Carolina lateral. Bryant was the only player who realized the play was a lateral.

November 14, 1981—Clemson claimed the ACC title with a 21-7 win over Maryland. Homer Jordan completed 20-29 passes for 270 yards in the contest. At the time, it was the most completions in a game for a Tiger quarterback in a Clemson victory.

November 21,1981—Clemson finished the regular season with a perfect 11-0 record with 29-13 win over South Carolina. It was Clemson's first perfect regular season since 1948.

November 30, 1981—Clemson was ranked #1 by AP, for the first time. Clemson moved to the #1 ranking when Penn State whipped Pittsburgh and quarterback Dan Marino 48-14.

January 1, 1982—Clemson claimed it first National Championship with a 22-15 win over Nebraska in the 48th annual Orange Bowl Classic. Cliff Austin, who had been trapped in an elevator for two hours at the Clemson hotel earlier in the day, scored one of the Clemson touchdowns.

January 4, 1982—The cover of *Sports Illustrated* featured Perry Tuttle celebrating after his touchdown catch in the Orange Bowl. It was the first and only time a Tiger athlete has appeared on the cover of *Sports Illustrated* while a Clemson student.

October 16, 1982—Cliff Austin broke the Clemson record for most rushing yards in a game, with 260 in a rout of Duke.

November 27, 1982—Clemson defeated Wake Forest 21-17 at the Mirage Bowl in Tokyo, Japan, and also sewed up its second-straight ACC title.

January 1, 1983—Terry Kinard was named National Defensive Player of the Year by CBS Sports. CBS announcer Lindsey Nelson presented him the award during halftime of the Cotton Bowl. Kinard had led Clemson to a 9-1-1 record and led the team in tackles and interceptions.

April 26, 1983—A record 10 Clemson players were chosen in the NFL draft. Terry Kinard, who was the #10 pick of the entire draft by the New York Giants, led the group.

September 3, 1983—The north upper deck was used for the first time in a victory over Western Carolina, bringing the capacity to over 80,000.

November 12, 1983—3,000 Clemson students arrived at Death Valley at 7:00 a.m. to blow up 363,729 balloons. The 80,000 fans released the balloons as the team ran down the hill. On the field, Mike Eppley was outstanding with three touchdown passes, and Kevin Mack rushed for 186 yards in his final game in Death Valley. He scored his final touchdown with just one shoe on, as he had lost it during his 56-yard run for a score. Clemson downed the Top-20 Boomer Esiason and Maryland team 52-27.

November 19, 1983—Clemson closed the 1983 season with a 22-13 win at South Carolina. The game gave the Tigers a 30-2-2 record for over the last three years, the top record in college football.

September 8, 1984—Clemson defeated Virginia in Charlottesville 55-0. Virginia ended the season with an 8-4 record and went to a bowl game. At the time, it was the largest margin of victory in Clemson history over a team that went to a bowl game. Mike Eppley led the way, hitting 8-14 passes for 172 yards and a pair of scores. The Tigers advanced to #2 in the nation with the win.

In 1983, a world-record number of balloons were released as the Tigers defeated Maryland.

September 22, 1984—Georgia defeated Clemson in Athens 26-23 on a 60-yard field goal by Kevin Butler with 11 seconds left. Clemson, which had a 20-6 lead at halftime, ran the ensuing kickoff back to Georgia territory, and a personal foul was thrown against the Bulldogs after the tackle. But, after a long debate, officials ruled the game had ended when the foul was committed, and Donald Igwebuike, who led the nation in field goal percentage in 1984 (17-18), was denied an opportunity to tie the game from 42 yards away.

November 10, 1984—Clemson defeated Virginia Tech 17-10 in the greatest matchup of defensive linemen in Death Valley history. Clemson featured All-America star William Perry, and Virginia Tech featured Outland Trophy winner and future All-Pro Bruce Smith. Clemson also had freshman Michael Dean Perry, who went on to earn six Pro Bowl selections.

September 14, 1985—David Treadwell showed a foreshadowing of things to come with a 36-yard field goal on the last play of the game to give Clemson a 20-17 victory at Virginia Tech in the season opener. Perry Williams had a Clemson record five pass deflections in this game.

September 21, 1985—Clemson and Georgia met in the first nationally televised (CBS) football game from Clemson. Georgia won the game 20-13, thanks to a fourth quarter fumble recovery by offensive lineman Peter Anderson. No opposing offensive lineman has scored a touchdown in a game since.

November 23, 1985—Clemson beat South Carolina 24-17 and accepted an Independence Bowl bid.

September 20, 1986—Clemson defeated Georgia 31-28, as David Treadwell kicked a 46-yard field goal with no time left on the clock. Athens, GA, native Norman Haynes led Clemson in tackles with 14, while Terrance Flagler led the offense with nearly 200 all-purpose running yards.

November 1, 1986—Terrance Flagler scored four touchdowns, two receiving and two rushing, and gained 274 all-purpose yards in Clemson's 28-20 win at Wake Forest. He had an 88-yard run in the contest, the longest of his career. The all-purpose yard total is still a Clemson record for an individual.

November 15, 1986—Clemson tied Maryland 17-17 to win the ACC Championship, as Treadwell kicked a 20-yard field goal with two seconds left. Both Clemson coach Danny Ford and Maryland coach Bobby Ross coached the game from the press box due to suspensions imposed by the ACC.

December 27, 1986—Clemson won the Gator Bowl championship with a 27-21 win over Stanford. Clemson scored all 27 points in the first half and then held on as Brad Muster led a furious comeback.

January 3, 1987—Clemson was ranked #17 in the nation in the final AP poll, its first final top-20 ranking since 1983.

September 19, 1987—David Treadwell booted a 21-yard field goal with two seconds left to beat Georgia on national TV 21-20.

September 26, 1987—Clemson had not returned a punt or kickoff for a touchdown in 17 years before having one of each in a 33-12 win over Georgia Tech. Donnell Woolford scored on a 78-yard punt return and Joe Henderson on a 95-yard kickoff return. Clemson had gone 999 punt and kickoff returns without a touchdown prior to Joe Henderson's score.

January 1, 1988—Clemson gained 499 yards in handing Penn State its worst bowl game defeat (35-10) in the Citrus Bowl. Rodney Williams was named the Player of the Game, as he threw for 214 yards. Terry Allen rushed for 105 yards, and Keith Jennings caught seven passes for 110 yards, giving Clemson a 200-yard passer, 100-yard rusher, and 100-yard receiver in the same game for the first time since 1969. Clemson was ranked #10 in the final UPI poll.

September 17, 1988—Florida State defeated Clemson 24-21 in the "Puntrooskie Game" at Death Valley. It was the first battle of top-10 teams in the history of Death Valley. Clemson had Florida State deep in its own territory late in the fourth quarter with the score tied at 21 when Florida State coach Bobby Bowden ran an intricate fake punt play that resulted in Leroy Butler streaking 78 yards to the Clemson three. Florida State booted a field goal to win the game.

November 12, 1988—Clemson clinched an ACC record-tying third-straight ACC title with a 49-25 win at Maryland. Clemson scored 28 points in the fourth quarter on just nine offensive plays.

November 19, 1988—Clemson gained revenge for a loss at South Carolina in 1987 with a 29-10 win over the Gamecocks at Clemson. Rodney Williams was masterful in running the Tiger offense in his final home game. He would end his career with 32 wins, still a record for a Tiger quarterback.

January 2, 1989—Clemson became the first ACC team to defeat Oklahoma in a 13-6 Citrus Bowl victory. Clemson held the Oklahoma offense without a touchdown for just the second time in the decade of the eighties. Clemson closed the season with a #9 ranking and became the only school in the nation to win a conference title, a bowl game, and rank in the final Top 20 for three straight years.

September 9, 1989—Clemson earned a landmark victory at Florida State, 34-23. The Tigers jumped out to a 21-0 lead behind a 73-yard interception return by Wayne Simmons and a 73-yard touchdown run by Terry Allen. The victory moved Clemson to #7 in the AP poll, and it was the last loss of the season for Florida State, who eventually ended the season ranked #3 in the nation by AP and #2 by UPI.

November 18, 1989—Clemson slaughtered South Carolina 45-0, the largest margin of victory for Clemson in the series in 89 years. Clemson outgained the Gamecocks 466-155 and picked up 355 yards rushing. Clemson's fifth-rated defense forced five turnovers. Terry Allen rushed for 89 yards, then suffered a knee injury just before halftime and never carried the ball for the Tigers again.

December 30, 1989—The Tigers defeated West Virginia 27-7 in the Gator Bowl. It was Clemson's fourth-straight bowl victory and the fourth-straight year Clemson concluded the season ranked in the national top 20. The Tigers held West Virginia to just 119 yards passing and forced Heisman Trophy runner-up Major Harris into three fumbles. Chester McGlockton sacked Harris in the end zone and recovered the ball for a touchdown for Clemson's final score.

January 18, 1990—Danny Ford resigned as head coach after 11 full seasons. He finished his career tied for first in ACC history in career victories with 96, and he was second in winning percentage. He had a 96-29-4 overall record and 76-percent winning mark. He was the third-winningest active coach in the nation at the time of his resignation.

January 21, 1990—Ken Hatfield became Clemson's 22nd head coach. Hatfield had been the head coach at Arkansas since 1984 and took his alma mater to bowl games each of his six seasons.

September 1, 1990—Clemson defeated Long Beach State 59-0 in the first game of the Ken Hatfield era. Clemson scored two touchdowns via return, one on an interception return by Arlington Nunn and one on a kickoff return by Doug Thomas. NFL legend George Allen, who was making a comeback as a coach, led the 49ers. Unfortunately, the venerable coach who led that team to a 6-5 record died at the end of the season from pneumonia.

October 13, 1990—Eventual national champion Georgia Tech defeated Clemson 21-19 in Atlanta. Clemson rushed for over 300 yards in the game yet lost to Bobby Ross's team. Chris Gardocki's 60-yard field goal attempt to win the game was just a couple of yards short.

January 1, 1991—Clemson shut out Illinois 30-0 in its first Hall of Fame Bowl appearance. It was Clemson's largest margin of victory in a bowl game. The win elevated Clemson to #9 in the final AP poll and gave the Tigers a Top-10 ranking in Ken Hatfield's first year. He was the first ACC coach ever to take a team to a Top-10 ranking in his first year. It was a record 40th win for Clemson's seniors.

October 26, 1991—Clemson wore purple jerseys for the first time since the 1930s in a 29-19 victory over #10 (*USA Today*) N.C. State. Freshman Nelson Welch, who kicked a Clemson-record five field goals, led the #18 (AP) Tigers. Clemson scored its first touchdown on a fake field goal, as Rudy Harris ran three yards for a score.

November 16, 1991—The Tigers clinched their 13th ACC Championship, first under Ken Hatfield, with a 40-7 win over Maryland at Death Valley. DeChane Cameron was 13-23 for 213 yards in leading Clemson to victory in his final home game.

November 23, 1991—DeChane Cameron gained 322 yards of total offense, 206 passing and 116 rushing, to lead Clemson to a 41-23 win at South Carolina. Clemson also had a 100-yard receiver in the game, giving Clemson a 200-yard passer, 100-yard rusher, and 100-yard receiver (Terry Smith) in the same game for just the fifth time in Clemson history.

November 30, 1991—Clemson ran its overseas record to 2-0 with a 33-21 win over Duke in the Coca Cola Bowl in Tokyo, Japan. Clemson had to score 26 points in the fourth quarter to register the victory. It was Ken Hatfield's 100th win as a college coach.

September 12, 1992—Florida State defeated Clemson 24-20 in the first night game at Clemson since 1956. ESPN televised the contest. Clemson had taken a 20-17 lead in the fourth quarter on a touchdown pass to Terry Smith.

The Seminoles, led by quarterback Charlie Ward, scored the winning TD in the two final minutes.

October 10, 1992—Clemson overcame a 28-0 deficit to defeat Virginia in Charlottesville 29-28. Nelson Welch kicked a 32-yard field goal with 52 seconds left to cap the comeback. Quarterback Louis Solomon came off the bench with the score 28-0 and led the comeback. His 64-yard scoring run just before the half changed the course of the game. The win over the #10 Cavaliers was just the third in Clemson history over a top-10 team on the road.

November 7, 1992—Clemson soundly defeated #18 North Carolina 40-7 at Death Valley, the largest margin of victory for the Tigers over a top-20 team in history. Freshman Patrick Sapp hit 13-23 passes for 205 yards, while Rodney Blunt scored three TDs in leading the Clemson offense. The Tigers controlled the clock for a record 42:58.

November 24, 1993—Ken Hatfield and Clemson University announced a separation, ending Hatfield's four-year career as head coach. Hatfield was 32-13-1 at Clemson, and his .707 winning percentage was third in ACC history when he departed.

November 29, 1993—Tommy West was named Clemson's 23rd head coach and took over the team heading for the Peach Bowl. West, who spent the 1993 regular season as head coach at UT Chattanooga, became the sixth coach in Division I history to make his head coaching debut for a school in a bowl game and the second coach to ever become head coach for a bowl game after not serving as an assistant at that school during the regular season.

December 31, 1993—Clemson scored the latest touchdown to gain victory in a game since 1958, as Patrick Sapp connected with Terry Smith with 0:20 left to defeat Kentucky 14-13 in the Peach Bowl. West experienced his fifth-consecutive bowl victory with Clemson, as the Tigers won four straight bowl games during his years as an assistant (1986-89).

September 3, 1994—For the first time ever, Clemson faced a team coached by a Clemson graduate. Bobby Johnson, an academic All-ACC defensive back for the Tigers and a 1973 graduate, brought his Furman Paladins to Memorial Stadium. Clemson came away with a 27-6 win. Clemson inducted Frank Howard, Steve Fuller, and Banks McFadden into the Ring of Honor prior to the game.

September 17, 1994—Clemson and Virginia met in the 1,000th ACC football game in history. Virginia won 9-6. Andre Carter had three takeaways in the game, just the fourth Tiger in history to do that.

October 15, 1994—Nelson Welch became the ACC's career field goal leader with a 47-yarder in the third quarter at Duke. It gave Welch 61 career field goals, breaking the record of 60 held by Jess Atkinson, Scott Sisson, and Obed Ariri.

November 5, 1994—Nelson Welch became Clemson's career scoring leader with five field goals and a PAT in Clemson's 28-17 upset of 12th-ranked North Carolina in Chapel Hill. Clemson's defense held the Tar Heels to 11 yards rushing. Clemson started an all-first-year freshman backfield.

May 15, 1995—The Banks McFadden building was dedicated. The facility is the home of Clemson football administration and with top-of-the-line facilities for players and coaches.

August 12, 1995—The Carolina Panthers and the Denver Broncos played the first professional game in the history of Memorial Stadium. The Panthers won the exhibition game over the John Elway-led Broncos.

September 17, 1995—The Carolina Panthers met the St. Louis Rams in the first regular season NFL game in Death Valley. It was the first of eight regular season games for the expansion Panthers at Clemson Memorial Stadium.

October 7, 1995—Clemson wore "turn back the clock" uniforms for the Clemson-Georgia game at Death Valley. The uniforms were replicas of those worn by the 1939 Clemson team that went to the Cotton Bowl, the first bowl appearance in Clemson history. Georgia won the thrilling game 19-17, but that would be Clemson's final regular-season loss of 1995. Leomont Evans had 18 tackles in the contest, the most ever by a Clemson defensive back.

November 11, 1995—Two all-time Clemson records were set on the same day in Clemson's 34-17 win over Duke. Raymond Priester gained 263 yards rushing to break Cliff Austin's Clemson single-game mark. All-America player Brian Dawkins had three interceptions in the first quarter to set a quarter record and tie the single-game mark for interceptions. The game was played in a driving rainstorm in the first half and brilliant sunshine in the second.

November 18, 1995—Clemson outscored South Carolina 21-0 in the fourth quarter to defeat the Gamecocks in Columbia 38-17. It was Clemson's fourth-straight win in Columbia. The victory clinched a bid to the Gator Bowl for the Tigers.

December 10, 1995—The defending Super Bowl-champion San Francisco 49ers defeated the Carolina Panthers at Death Valley. Jerry Rice caught one touchdown pass from Steve Young in the contest that attracted over 75,000 fans.

December 15, 1995—Linebacker Anthony Simmons was named UPI National Freshman of the Year, the first defensive player in the history of the award. Simmons led Clemson in tackles (150), 46 more than any other freshman in school history.

January 26, 1996—Clemson legend Frank Howard, the school's head coach from 1940-'69, passed away at his home in Clemson. Howard, who still had come to his office a month prior to his death, died on the same day

as his former teammate and Alabama legend Bear Bryant, 13 years later.

September 7, 1996—Clemson's centennial team was honored at halftime of the Clemson vs. Furman game. The Tigers wore their "Turn back the Clock" uniforms for this game, a 19-3 Clemson victory. Clemson had a school record 12 sacks in the win.

Frank Howard was Clemson's head football coach from 1940-'69.

November 2, 1996—Clemson held Maryland without a touchdown for the fourth-straight year in a 35-3 Tiger victory. Anthony Simmons keyed the Clemson defense that had eight sacks with 15 tackles for loss. Maryland had not scored a touchdown against Clemson since 1992.

November 9, 1996—The Tigers upset 15th-ranked Virginia 24-16 in Charlottesville. Clemson had two players rush for over 120 yards in the contest, as Kelton Dunnican had a career-high 123 yards and Raymond Priester had 122. It was the second time in four years that Clemson had defeated a ranked Virginia team on the road.

December 28, 1996—Raymond Priester became Clemson's career and single-season rushing leader in a 10-7 loss to Louisiana State in the Peach Bowl. Priester gained 151 yards rushing in 25 attempts, giving him 1,345 yards for the season and 3,010 for his career. He broke his own single-season record and broke Kenny Flowers's career record in the game.

September 13, 1997—Matt Padgett kicked a 20-yard field goal with 19 seconds left to give Clemson a 19-17 win at N.C. State. Nealon Greene became the first quarterback in school history to have consecutive 250-yard passing games. The senior also had 76 yards rushing, and the 336 yards total offense were the second most in Clemson history.

September 20, 1997—Tony Horne and Florida State's Peter Warrick put on the greatest individual all-purpose running show in the history of Death Valley. Horne had 10 receptions for 131 yards and had 267 yards of all-purpose running, while Warrick had a 90-yard punt return and an 80-yard touchdown reception in gaining 372 yards of all-purpose running as Florida State defeated Clemson 35-28.

October 4, 1997—Nealon Greene tied a Clemson record for touchdown passes with four in a 39-7 rout of UTEP. He completed three of the scores to Tony Horne, and that also tied a Tiger single-game record.

November 8, 1997—Rahim Abdullah returned an interception 63 yards for a touchdown, clinching a 29-20 Clemson victory in overtime over Duke. It was the first overtime game in Clemson history, the first in ACC history involving two league teams.

November 22, 1997—Clemson earned its third-straight bowl bid with a 47-21 victory over South Carolina in Columbia. It was Clemson's fifth-straight victory in Columbia over the Gamecocks. Antwan Edwards was the star for Clemson with two interceptions, including one that he returned for a touchdown. The 47 points were the most by the Tigers against South Carolina since 1900.

December 8, 1997—Anthony Simmons was named first-team AP All-America, his third straight year on one of the top three teams. He became Clemson's second three-time All-America player in history.

September 19, 1998—Antwan Edwards became the first Clemson player in history to have two runs of at least 80 yards in the same game. The All-America defensive back had a 93-yard fumble return for a touchdown, longest in Clemson history, and an 85-yard kickoff return in a 20-18 loss at Virginia. It was Clemson's first-ever loss on September 19th after eight straight wins.

October 31, 1998—In a 46-39 loss to N.C. State, quarterback Brandon Streeter set the Clemson single-game passing yardage (329) and completion (27) record. He threw three touchdown passes in the fourth quarter. For the first time ever, Clemson had two 100-yard receivers in the same game. Brian Wofford had 9-128 and a touchdown, while classmate Mal Lawyer had 8-100 and two touchdown receptions. Clemson could not overcome the performance of Tory Holt, who had 11-225 and four touchdown catches.

November 12, 1998—Clemson played host to its first-ever ESPN home Thursday night game, a 24-21 loss to a top-25 Georgia Tech team. Georgia Tech scored the winning touchdown with just one minute remaining.

November 18, 1998—It was announced that the South Carolina game of November 21 would be Tommy West's final game as Clemson head coach.

November 21, 1998—Clemson beat South Carolina 28-19 in West's final game as Clemson coach. The victory, played before a crowd of 84,423, ended a seven-game winning streak for the road team in the series, tied for the longest streak of its kind in NCAA history. A highlight of the contest was a 48-yard interception return for a touchdown by Clemson outside linebacker Howard Bartley, who came back to letter as a senior after two torn ACL operations. Tiger fans tore down the goalpost after the game, just the second time in the history of Death Valley that the goalposts came down after a Tiger victory. Coach West, his wife Lindsey, and son Turner were carried off the field at game's end.

December 2, 1998—Tommy Bowden was named head football coach.

December 5, 1998—Former South Carolina Coach Brad Scott was hired as Clemson's assistant head coach under Tommy Bowden. Scott was also hired to coach the tight ends.

September 11, 1999—Bowden recorded his first win as Clemson head coach, a 33-14 victory over 19th-ranked Virginia. Quarterback Brandon Streeter threw for a school record 343 yards and was named National Player of the Week by *USA Today*.

October 16, 1999—Woodrow Dantzler broke a 52-year-old Clemson standard for total offense in Clemson's 42-30 victory at Maryland. Dantzler gained 435 yards of total offense, including 183 yards on the ground, a record for yards rushing by a Tiger signal-caller at the time. Travis Zachery rushed for three touchdowns, as well.

October 23, 1999—In the first meeting of father and son head coaches in Division I college football history, Bobby Bowden and Florida State defeated Tommy Bowden and Clemson 17-14. The game was played before a record crowd of 86,092 and was televised nationally by ESPN. Clemson had a chance to tie the eventual national champs, but Tay Cody tipped Tony Lazzara's 41-yard field goal attempt with 1:57 left.

November 6, 1999—Keith Adams set a school record with four sacks and six total tackles for loss, leading Clemson to a 58-7 win over Duke in the final home game of the season. The Bronko Nagurski Committee named him National Defensive Player of the Week. Brandon Streeter completed 22-30 for 279 yards in his final home game, as well.

November 20, 1999—Clemson defeated South Carolina 31-21 in Columbia to clinch a bid to play Mississippi State in the Peach Bowl in Tommy Bowden's first season. Keith Adams had a school record 27 tackles in the contest. Rod Gardner's 29-yard touchdown reception from Woodrow Dantzler on a fourth-down play iced the game for the Tigers.

December 1, 1999—Tommy Bowden was named ACC Coach of the Year, Clemson's first selection for that honor since 1981.

September 9, 2000—Clemson beat Missouri 62-9 at Death Valley, the school's highest point total since 1981. Brian Mance had three takeaways in just 16 scrimmage plays on defense.

September 23, 2000—Woodrow Dantzler rushed for 220 yards, an ACC record for a quarterback, in Clemson's 31-10 win over Virginia. Dantlzer also passed for 154 yards, bringing Clemson to a 4-0 record and a #7 AP ranking.

September 30, 2000—Bob Bradley worked his 500th consecutive Clemson football game on this day, a 52-22 win at Duke. Bradley served as Clemson SID or SID Emeritus for 45 years.

October 21, 2000—Clemson improved to 8-0 with a 38-24 victory at North Carolina. Reserve quarterback Willie

Simmons threw four touchdown passes, three to Rod Gardner, in the win. Clemson overcame a 17-point deficit, the third-largest deficit overcome to gain victory in Clemson history.

October 22, 2000—Clemson was ranked third in the nation in the *USA Today* poll, Clemson's highest ranking in any poll since the 1984 season.

October 30, 2000—Legendary Clemson sports figure Bob Bradley passed away at the age of 74. He had been presented the Order of the Palmetto by the governor's office two days prior to his passing.

November 18, 2000—Rod Gardner made a spectacular 50-yard catch with 10 seconds remaining to set up Aaron Hunt's 25-yard game winning field goal with just three seconds remaining in Clemson's 16-14 win over South Carolina in Death Valley.

"The Catch II"—Rod Gardner made a spectacular 50-yard catch with 10 seconds remaining to set up an Aaron Hunt 25-yard field goal with just three seconds remaining to give Clemson a 16-14 win over South Carolina in Death Valley.

December 5, 2000—Kyle Young and Chad Carson were both named first-team Academic All-America players, the only year in history Clemson has had two first-team Academic All-America players.

January 5, 2001—Clemson was ranked 16th in the final AP poll and 14th in the final *USA Today* poll. It was Clemson's first final top-25 ranking since 1993, its highest final ranking since 1991.

April 24, 2001—Rod Gardner was selected in the first round, the 15th pick overall, by the Redskins.

September 15, 2001—The Clemson vs. Duke football game scheduled this day was postponed until December 1 due to the terrorist attacks in New York City on September 11, 2001.

September 29, 2001—Clemson defeated Georgia Tech in Atlanta by the score of 47-44 in overtime. Woodrow Dantzler scored on an 11-yard run in the extra period to give Clemson the win. Dantzler rushed for 164 yards and passed for 254 in the all-around performance that

brought him National Player of the Week honors by USAToday.com. Georgia Tech was ranked #9 entering the game. It was the highest-ranked road win for the Tiger program since 1981.

October 13, 2001—Two weeks and one game after gaining 418 yards of total offense at Georgia Tech, Woodrow Dantzler trumped that performance with a 517-yard day at N.C. State. Dantzler broke numerous Clemson records in completing 23-27 passes for 333 yards and four scores. He also rushed 23 times for 184 yards and two scores. The six touchdowns and 517 yards were Clemson single-game marks. Dantzler went over 4,000 yards passing and 2,000 yards rushing in the game, the first player in ACC history to do both.

December 1, 2001—Woodrow Dantzler became the first player in NCAA Division I history to pass for 2,000 yards and rush for 1,000 yards in the same season. Dantzler reached the plateau with an 18-yard run for a touchdown against Duke in Death Valley. Dantzler completed the regular season with 2,360 yards passing and 1,004 yards rushing.

December 11, 2001—Clemson was the only school in the nation with a Hall of Fame inductee and a National Football Foundation scholar at enshrinement ceremonies in New York City. Terry Kinard became just the second Tiger inducted into the College Football Hall of Fame, joining the legendary Banks McFadden. Kyle Young was named a National Football Foundation Scholar-Athlete. Earlier in the week, Young became just the second offensive lineman in college football history to be named a first-team Academic All-America player three times.

December 31, 2001—Clemson gained its first bowl win since 1993 with a 49-24 victory over Louisiana Tech in the Humanitarian Bowl in Boise, ID. Clemson scored 28 points in the third quarter to blow the game open. Woodrow Dantzler, playing in his final game at Clemson, captured game MVP honors by completing 15-23 passes for 218 yards and four touchdowns. Bernard Rambert rushed for 101 yards and had 77 yards receiving to support a Clemson offense that gained 548 yards of total offense. Four different freshmen, Derrick Hamilton, Airese Currie, Roscoe Crosby, and Ben Hall, scored touchdowns for the Tigers.

September 14, 2002—Derrick Hamilton gained 256 all-purpose rushing yards in Clemson's 24-19 win over Georgia Tech in Death Valley. Hamilton gained 97 yards rushing, 97 in punt returns, 41 in kickoff returns, and 22 receiving in accumulating the fifth highest all-purpose running total in a single game in Clemson history. He had a 77-yard scoring run and a 79-yard punt return.

November 2, 2002—Clemson scored 24 points in the fourth quarter and overcame a 14-point fourth quarter deficit for just the second time in Clemson history in a 34-31 win at Duke. Aaron Hunt kicked a 21-yard field goal with eight seconds left to give the Tigers the victory. Freshman Charlie Whitehurst completed a Clemson single-game record 34 passes and threw for a school-record

420 yards in the victory in his first college start. He also tied the Clemson record for touchdown passes in a game with four.

November 9, 2002—For the second straight game, Charlie Whitehurst tied the Clemson single-game touchdown pass record with four at North Carolina in a 42-12 Clemson win in Chapel Hill. His passing efficiency rating of 241 for the game was a Clemson single-game record given a minimum of 20 attempts.

November 23, 2002—Clemson outscored South Carolina 14-0 in the final quarter to defeat its state rival 27-20 at Death Valley in the 100th meeting between the two schools. Charlie Whitehurst completed 27-38 passes for 287 yards in the contest.

September 9, 2003—Jim Phillips, the "Voice of the Tigers" for 36 years, died suddenly in the early morning hours after suffering an aneurysm of the aorta. Phillips had served as Clemson's play-by-play announcer for football and men's basketball since 1968, and he had also done baseball and women's basketball for many years. He worked 401 Clemson football games in his career, as the season opener in 2003 against Georgia was his 400th. His final game was the Clemson-Furman game on September 6, 2003. The following Saturday when the Tigers faced Middle Tennessee, a tribute for Phillips's career was played over the video scoreboard at Death Valley. The band concluded its halftime performance by forming "JIM" as it marched off the field. Sports Information Director Tim Bourret handled the play-by-play duties for the Middle Tennessee game, a 37-14 Tiger win. The following week, Pete Yanity was named as Phillips's interim replacement, a title that was changed to permanent the following spring.

September 20, 2003—Charlie Whitehurst threw for 298 yards and three touchdowns, and the Clemson defense held Georgia Tech to just three points and 45 yards rushing in a 39-3 victory in Atlanta. It was Clemson's largest margin of victory over Georgia Tech since 1903, when John Heisman was the Clemson coach. It was also the largest margin of victory in any ACC road game for the Tigers since 1984.

October 11, 2003—Clemson extended its all-time record in overtime games to 3-0 with a 30-27 victory over Virginia in Death Valley. Kevin Youngblood scored the winning, "walkoff" touchdown on a four-yard touchdown pass from Charlie Whitehurst. Yusef Kelly, in his only healthy game of the 2003 season, rushed for 88 yards to lead the Tiger ground game.

November 8, 2003—Clemson shocked the college football world with a 26-10 victory over #3 Florida State in Death Valley. It was the highest-ranked team Clemson had beaten in its history. The Tigers were coming off a 45-17 loss at Wake Forest the previous week, and Florida State was coming off a 37-0 victory at Notre Dame. It was Clemson's first win over Florida State in 14 years. Aaron Hunt

kicked four field goals and became Clemson's career scoring leader that night. Charlie Whitehurst threw for 272 yards, including 123 to wide receiver Derrick Hamilton. Clemson allowed Florida State only 11 yards rushing, the fewest in the Bobby Bowden coaching era at Florida State. Tye Hill led the secondary with an early interception and was named ACC Defensive Player of the Week.

November 22, 2003—Charlie Whitehurst completed his first 10 passes and threw for three touchdowns passes on Clemson's first three possessions in Clemson's 63-17 victory at South Carolina. It was the most points scored by Clemson against South Carolina in history and the largest margin of victory for Clemson in the series since 1900. It was also the most points scored by Clemson in any game since an 82-24 win over Wake Forest in 1981. Chad Jasmin rushed for four touchdowns, becoming the first Tiger to score four touchdowns against the Gamecocks since 1918. Jamaal Fudge had two interceptions to lead the Clemson secondary.

December 1, 2003—Tommy Bowden was named ACC Coach of the Year, the second time in five years that he won the award.

December 2, 2003—Tommy Bowden and Clemson University agreed to a three-year contract extension.

December 8, 2003—Clemson announced it had received 33,000 applications for tickets to the 2004 Peach Bowl, 13,000 more tickets than its supply. It was the greatest ticket demand for a Clemson bowl game since the 1982 Orange Bowl.

January 2, 2004—Clemson defeated #6 Tennessee 27-14 in front of a record crowd of 75,125 fans at the Chick-fil-A Peach Bowl at the Georgia Dome in Atlanta. It was the highest-ranked team Clemson had defeated in a bowl game since a win over #4 Nebraska in the 1982 Orange Bowl. Chad Jasmin was named the offensive MVP after rushing for a career-high 130 yards in his final game as a Clemson Tiger. Charlie Whitehurst added 246 yards passing and Kyle Browning scored on an eight-yard run on a "Panther" play in the second quarter to help spur the offense. Leroy Hill led the defense with 12 tackles, including two for losses. Combined with the victory over #3 Florida State the previous November, Clemson defeated two top-10 teams in the same season for the first time since 1981. It also gave Tommy Bowden three victories over coaches who had won the National Championship over the last four games of the season.

January 5, 2004—Clemson was ranked #22 in the nation in the final AP and *USA Today* polls and #16 in the final Sagarin computer ranking.

January 9, 2004—Tommy Bowden was named a finalist for the 2003 Bear Bryant Award.

September 25, 2004—Justin Miller set an NCAA record with 282 kickoff return yards at #8 Florida State. He returned two kickoffs for touchdowns of 97 and 86 yards, which set the

Clemson single-game record and tied the NCAA record. The Tigers lost the game to the Seminoles 41-22.

October 16, 2004—Clemson recorded 11 sacks, the most in the Tommy Bowden era, in a 35-6 Homecoming victory over Utah State. The Tigers held the Aggies to -20 rushing yards, the fewest Clemson had ever allowed against a Division 1-A opponent.

November 6, 2004—Clemson scored 21 unanswered points and held #10 Miami (FL) scoreless in the second half to upset the Hurricanes 24-17 in overtime at the Orange Bowl. It was Clemson's third win over a top-10 team over two seasons, and the Tigers' record in overtime improved to 5-0.

November 20, 2004—Clemson scored 14 early points and only allowed South Carolina to snap the ball in Tiger territory four times, as the Tigers defeated the Gamecocks for the seventh time in eight years by a score of 29-7. It was Clemson's 11th win in its last 12 games at Death Valley since 2003. It was also Clemson's 600th all-time win.

June 4, 2005—Banks McFadden, regarded by sports historians as Clemson's greatest all-around athlete in its 109-year intercollegiate sports history, passed away after a lengthy bout with cancer. The native of Great Falls, SC, died at the home of his daughter (Lil Arrants) in Ormond Beach, FL. He was 88 years old. McFadden was buried on Cemetery Hill behind Clemson Memorial Stadium. Flags on the Clemson campus were lowered to half-staff in McFadden's honor. A moment of silence was observed in McFadden's honor prior to Saturday night's NCAA Tournament baseball game against College of Charleston at Kingsmore Stadium. McFadden was a standout at Clemson in football, basketball, and track, earning three letters in each sport from 1936-'40. He earned All-America honors in both basketball (1938-39) and football (1939) and was named the nation's most versatile athlete in 1939.

September 3, 2005—Clemson opened the season with a thrilling 25-24 victory over #17 Texas A&M at Death Valley. Jad Dean kicked a school record six field goals, including a 42-yarder with two seconds left to give Clemson its first season-opening win over a ranked team since 1958.

September 10, 2005—Clemson had its second-straight thrilling victory in a 28-24 win at Maryland. Reggie Merriweather scored on a 38-yard run with 2:58 left to give Clemson the victory. Charlie Whitehurst connected on 18-22 passes for 178 yards in leading Clemson to the victory. The Tigers overcame a 10-point deficit in the fourth quarter to gain the victory. Clemson had a 9:47 drive during the game, the longest in Clemson history in terms of time of possession.

September 17, 2005—Miami (FL) defeated Clemson 36-30 in the longest game in Tiger history, a triple-overtime contest before a sellout crowd at Death Valley. Clemson tied the score with 15 seconds left on a 27-yard field goal by Jad Dean. Clemson tied the score at the end of the first

overtime on a fourth-down touchdown pass from Whitehurst to Curtis Baham (six yards). Tyrone Moss scored what proved to be the game-winner in the third overtime on a 25-yard run. It was the first overtime loss in Clemson history after five consecutive wins.

September 24, 2005—Clemson lost an overtime game for the second-straight week, a 16-13 loss to Boston College in Death Valley.

October 13, 2005—Clemson won its first-ever Thursday night ESPN game in a 31-10 victory at N.C. State. Freshman James Davis ran through a defense that had three starters who would be drafted in the first round by the NFL the following April. Davis had 143 yards and scored two touchdowns on just 12 carries before suffering a broken wrist in the third quarter. Charlie Whitehurst completed 22-31 passes for 246 yards.

November 5, 2005—Charlie Whitehurst's 37-game streak as the starting Tiger quarterback came to an end when he missed the Duke game due to a sore shoulder. Will Proctor took over the reigns and led Clemson to a 49-20 win by completing 13-21 passes for 201 yards and two scores.

November 12, 2005—Clemson handed Florida State a 21-point loss in Bowden Bowl VII at Death Valley. Chansi Stuckey scored two touchdowns, his first two touchdown catches as a Tiger, and Charlie Whitehurst completed 21-32 passes for 269 yards and three scores on Senior Day. Clemson held Florida State to just 124 yards passing and outscored the Seminoles 21-0 in the second half.

November 19, 2005—Clemson defeated a top-20 South Carolina team on the road for the first time in a 13-9 victory. Charlie Whitehurst beat the Gamecocks for the fourth-straight year, the first time in the history of the series a starting quarterback had a perfect 4-0 record in the series.

December 27, 2005—Clemson defeated Colorado in the Champs Sports Bowl 19-10 behind a 150-yard rushing performance by freshman James Davis, who was named MVP. Colorado head coach Gary Barnett had been fired a few days prior to Christmas. Clemson held Colorado to 124 yards total offense and 17 yards rushing, the best defensive effort by in a bowl game by any team in 2005.

September 2, 2006—Clemson opened the season with a 54-6 win over Florida Atlantic, but it was a costly win, as preseason All-America linebacker Anthony Waters was lost for the season with a torn ACL. Waters went on to be drafted by the San Diego Chargers, despite playing just one game. He was voted one of the permanent team captains at the end of the season by his teammates, the only Tiger captain in history to play just one game during that season.

September 16, 2006—James Davis scored on a one-yard touchdown run with eight seconds left to give Clemson a 27-20 victory over #9 Florida State in Tallahassee. It was Clemson's third win over the Seminoles in four years, the first ACC team to defeat the Seminoles three out of four years. Davis had set up the winning score with a 47-yard run earlier in the drive.

October 7, 2006—Gaines Adams returned a botched field-goal attempt 66 yards for a touchdown to lead a fourth quarter comeback in a 27-17 win at Wake Forest. Clemson trailed 17-3 in the fourth quarter before Adams's play, which was one of the top-four game-changing plays in college football in 2006. It marked just the third time in school history that the Tigers overcame a deficit of 14 points or more in the fourth quarter to gain victory. Wake Forest would go on to win the ACC Championship.

October 16, 2006—It was announced that ESPN College GameDay would come to Clemson for the first time in history for an October 21 game between #12 Clemson and #13 Georgia Tech. The crew of Chris Fowler, Kirk Herbstreit, and Lee Corso broadcast from Bowman Field from 10:00 a.m. until 12:00 p.m. in front of a crowd of over 7,000, the largest on-campus GameDay crowd at that point in the program's history.

October 21, 2006—Clemson defeated #13 Georgia Tech 31-7 in Death Valley. Clemson was ranked #12 in the nation entering the game, and it was the first battle of top-25 teams in Death Valley in 14 years. James Davis rushed for 216 yards and C.J. Spiller added 116 yards on the ground to lead Clemson to a 321-yard rushing performance. It was the first time in history that Clemson had a 200-yard rusher and 100-yard rusher in the same game. Spiller scored on a 50-yard run and 50-yard reception, the first player in Tiger history to have one of each in a game.

October 22, 2006—Clemson was ranked #10 in the AP poll and #11 in the *USA Today* poll, the Tigers' highest rankings since the 2000 season.

April 28, 2007—The Tampa Bay Buccaneers took Gaines Adams in the first round of the NFL draft. He was the fourth pick of the entire draft, tied for the highest selection by a Tiger in history. Adams was the first defensive player taken in the draft, as well.

May 9, 2007—The National Football Foundation and College Football Hall of Fame announced that Jeff Davis would be inducted into the College Football Hall of Fame in December of 2007. Davis was the third Clemson player to be inducted, joining Banks McFadden and Terry Kinard. He was the second member of Clemson's 1981 National Championship team inducted, as well.

September 3, 2007—Clemson opened the season with a 24-18 victory over #19 Florida State on Labor Day evening. The nationally televised game on ESPN was the first on Labor Day for the Tiger program in 25 years. Cullen Harper became the first Tiger quarterback in history to beat a ranked team in his first career start. It was Clemson's fourth win in the last five years over Florida State, and it was the fifth-straight win for the Tigers over a top-25 team, tying a school record.

September 22, 2007—Clemson defeated N.C. State on the road by a score of 42-20 behind 608 yards of total offense. Clemson gained 340 rushing yards, behind 166 yards by James Davis and 114 by C.J. Spiller, while quarterback Cullen Harper threw for 268 yards and two touchdowns. The 608 yards were the most in Tiger history in an ACC road game.

October 6, 2007—Virginia Tech defeated Clemson 41-23, thanks to three returns for touchdowns. The #14 Hokies scored on an interception return, punt return, and kickoff return to take a 31-8 lead. Clemson outgained Virginia Tech 380-219, thanks to 372 passing yards by Cullen Harper, but the Tigers still lost the game.

October 20, 2007—Clemson defeated eventual MAC champion Central Michigan 70-14 behind five touchdown passes from Cullen Harper, which tied his own record that he set earlier in the year against Louisiana-Monroe. Harper was 20-22 for 273 yards, as the Tigers scored 56 points in the second and third quarters combined. In fact, Clemson scored all 70 of its points in a 34:04 time period.

November 10, 2007—Clemson defeated defending ACC champion Wake Forest 44-10 at Memorial Stadium. C.J. Spiller became the first Tiger in history to return a kickoff for a touchdown in consecutive games. He had an 84-yard return for a score against Duke the previous week and went 90 yards against the Demon Deacons.

November 17, 2007—The Tigers lost to #18 Boston College for the third year in a row by three points or less. The game decided the champion of the ACC Atlantic Division. Boston College scored on a 43-yard touchdown pass by Matt Ryan with just 1:46 left in the contest.

November 24, 2007—Mark Buchholz booted a 35-yard field goal on the last play of the game to give Clemson a 23-21 win at South Carolina. Cullen Harper connected with Aaron Kelly four times for 70 yards on the final drive to set up the game-winner. Clemson blocked two punts in the game, including one that was returned for a touchdown by La'Donte Harris.

December 31, 2007—C.J. Spiller won offensive MVP honors in the Chick-fil-A Bowl against #21 Auburn even though Clemson lost the game in overtime. Spiller became the first Tiger in history to have at least 100 rushing yards and 100 kickoff return yards in the same game. His performance included an 83-yard run, the longest touchdown play in a bowl game in Clemson history.

October 13, 2008—Head coach Tommy Bowden resigned on this Monday morning after a meeting with Athletic Director Terry Don Phillips. That afternoon, Dabo Swinney was named interim head coach.

October 18, 2008—Dabo Swinney coached his first game as head coach against Georgia Tech, just five days after he took over the program. He instituted the "Tiger Walk" prior to the game. Georgia Tech won the contest 21-17.

November 1, 2008—Clemson defeated Boston College in Chestnut Hill by a score of 27-21 to claim the first O'Rourke-McFadden Trophy, which is given to the winner of this rivalry game each year. It was Clemson's first win over the Eagles in 50 years. C.J. Spiller had 242 all-purpose yards to win the first "Leather Helmet Award." Aaron Kelly became Clemson's career leader in receiving touchdowns when he hauled in his 19th on a four-yard reception from Cullen Harper in the fourth quarter. James Davis became Clemson's career rushing touchdown leader when he ran for his 43rd on a 23-yard carry in the first quarter. It was Dabo Swinney's first win as a head coach, as well.

November 29, 2008—Clemson defeated South Carolina 31-14 to become bowl-eligible for the 10th-straight year. It was Dabo Swinney's first game as a head coach in the rivalry game, and it gave the Tigers four wins in the last five games of the season to finish on a strong note.

December 1, 2008—The interim tag was removed from Dabo Swinney's title, and he was named head coach of the Tigers.

September 5, 2009—C.J. Spiller took the opening kickoff of the season and raced 96 yards for a touchdown in Clemson's 37-14 win over Middle Tennessee. It was the first time a Tiger returned the opening kickoff of a season for a touchdown.

October 24, 2009—Kyle Parker hit Jacoby Ford on a 26-yard touchdown pass on third-and-11 in overtime to lift Clemson to a 40-37 victory at #8 Miami (FL). It tied for the highest-ranked team Clemson defeated on the road in school history. C.J. Spiller, playing in front of his father for the first time as a Tiger, gained 310 all-purpose yards to establish a school record. DeAndre McDaniel was named National Defensive Player of the Week for his two interceptions, including one that he returned 23 yards for a score. There were nine lead changes in the game, as neither team scored twice in a row.

November 7, 2009—Spiller gained a school record 312 all-purpose yards in Clemson's 40-24 victory over Florida State in what proved to be Bobby Bowden's last appearance as Florida State's head coach in Death Valley. Spiller had 165 rushing yards and 67 receiving yards. The victory gave Clemson wins over Florida State and Miami (FL) in the same season for the first time.

November 14, 2009—Spiller threw a touchdown pass, caught a touchdown pass, and rushed for a touchdown in Clemson's 43-23 win at N.C. State. Kyle Parker won the battle of quarterbacks [over Russell Wilson, who would be drafted by the Colorado Rockies the following June] by completing 12-18 passes for 183 yards and two scores.

November 21, 2009—Clemson clinched the ACC Atlantic Division Championship with a 34-21 win over Virginia. The victory was the sixth in a row for the Tigers and moved the team to a #15 ranking in the AP poll.

November 28, 2009—Spiller returned the opening kickoff 88 yards for a touchdown at South Carolina. It was the seventh kickoff return for a score of his career, a new NCAA career mark. It was also the fourth of the season for Spiller, an ACC mark.

December 5, 2009—Spiller rushed for 233 yards and four touchdowns, but it was not enough, as #12 Georgia Tech defeated Clemson 39-34 in the ACC Championship game at Tampa, FL. Clemson averaged 9.5 yards per carry and 8.1 yards per play in the contest, in which neither team punted. Both teams gained at least 300 rushing yards, the only college game in 2009 in which both teams had at least 300 yards on the ground.

December 12, 2009—Spiller finished sixth in the Heisman Trophy balloting announced this day. He had 26 first-place votes and 223 points in the balloting.

September 4, 2010—Dawson Zimmerman booted a 79-yard punt in a victory over North Texas, the second-longest punt in Clemson history at the time. He finished the day with a 51.0-yard net average on six punts, best in Clemson history.

September 18, 2010—Clemson lost a 27-24 overtime contest at Auburn, the closest it came to suffering a loss in the 2010 season. Auburn won the national title with a 14-0 record. Andre Ellington had 140 rushing yards and Kyle Parker passed for 220 yards to lead the Clemson offense, while Da'Quan Bowers had four tackles for loss.

November 13, 2010—Dustin Hopkins kicked a 55-yard field goal on the last play of the game to give Florida State a 16-13 victory over Clemson. Had the Tigers won that game, they would have been ACC Atlantic Division champions. Jamie Harper totaled 143 yards on 27 carries and nine receptions for 54 yards in the best all-around performance of his career. The nine receptions set a Clemson record for a running back.

December 6, 2010—Da'Quan Bowers won the Bronko Nagurski Award as the top defensive player in the nation according to the Football Writers of America. He became the first Tiger to win that award and the first to win any national position award since 1982, when Terry Kinard won the CBS Sports National Defensive Player of the Year award. Bowers was presented the award at a banquet in Charlotte, NC.

September 17, 2011—Clemson defeated defending National Champion Auburn 38-24 in Death Valley. The win elevated Clemson's record against a defending National Champion in games played at Clemson to 3-0, and it ended Auburn's 17-game winning streak, the longest winning streak snapped by a Clemson football team in history. The Tigers gained 624 yards of total offense, their most ever against an SEC team.

September 24, 2011—Tajh Boyd passed for 344 yards and three touchdowns in leading Clemson to a 35-30 victory over #11 Florida State. Freshman Sammy Watkins had seven receptions for 141 yards and two touchdowns. The

Tigers had 443 yards of total offense against a defense that finished the year fifth in the country in total defense.

October 1, 2011—Clemson defeated Virginia Tech for the first time in 22 years with a 23-3 victory in Blacksburg. Clemson held Virginia Tech to 258 yards of total offense. Virginia Tech was ranked #10 entering the game, and the victory gave Clemson three straight wins over top-20 AP-ranked teams, a first for an ACC team.

October 15, 2011—Sammy Watkins set a school record with 345 all-purpose yards in Clemson's 56-45 win at Maryland. He had an 89-yard kickoff return for a score and added two receiving touchdowns. Clemson overcame an 18-point deficit to win the game.

October 22, 2011—Kourtnei Brown had two returns for touchdowns in Clemson 59-38 win over North Carolina. Brown became the first Clemson defensive player to score two touchdowns in one game since 1954. Tajh Boyd tied a Tiger record for passing touchdowns with five. Clemson scored all 59 of its points in the first three quarters.

October 23, 2011—With an 8-0 record, Clemson moved up to #5 in the nation in the BCS standings, its first top-five mark in school history.

November 12, 2011—Chandler Catanzaro booted a 43-yard field goal on the last play of the game to give Clemson a 31-28 victory over Wake Forest and clinch the ACC Atlantic Division title. It was Clemson's first walkoff kick in regulation in Memorial Stadium.

December 3, 2011—Clemson won its first ACC title in 20 years with a 38-10 win over Virginia Tech in Charlotte. Virginia Tech was ranked #3 in the nation in the coaches' poll, and the win tied for the highest-ranked team Clemson beat in its history. Tajh Boyd was named MVP, as he completed 20-29 passes for 240 yards and three scores. The win clinched Clemson's first Orange Bowl berth in 30 years.

December 7, 2011—Dwayne Allen was named winner of the John Mackey Award, as the nation's top tight end. He became the first offensive player in Clemson history to win a national position award.

December 15, 2011—Dwayne Allen and Sammy Watkins were both named AP first-team All-America players. Allen was the first Clemson tight end named to the first-team since Bennie Cunningham in 1975. Watkins became just the fourth first-year freshman in college football history to be named an AP first-team All-America player.

December 31, 2011—Coach Dabo Swinney was named the winner of the Bobby Dodd National Coach of the Year Award. It marked the first time a Clemson head coach won a National Coach of the Year Award since Danny Ford in 1981.

December 31, 2012—Chandler Catanzaro kicked a 37-yard field goal as time expired to give Clemson a 25-24 win over No. 7 Louisiana State in the Chick-fil-A Bowl. The ACC Tigers trailed 24-13 entering the fourth quarter but scored the final 12 points for the dramatic victory. It

was Clemson's 11th win of the season, its highest total since its National Championship season of 1981 (12-0) and gave the Tigers a final *USA Today* ranking of No. 9.

January 25, 2013—The Clemson Indoor Football Practice Facility was dedicated. The structure was built at a cost of $10 million. A full-size regulation 100-yard field is enclosed in the building that consists of 80,000 square feet.

August 31, 2013—Clemson defeated No. 5 Georgia 38-35 in front of 84,350 fans at Death Valley. Clemson was ranked No. 8, and the win gave the Tigers consecutive wins over top-10 SEC teams. Clemson became the first nonconference school to win consecutive games against top-10 SEC teams. Sammy Watkins had a 77-yard receiving touchdown from Tajh Boyd, who threw three passing touchdowns and ran for two others. Danny Ford was inducted into the Clemson Ring of Honor prior to the game. ESPN College GameDay was also in town prior to the game.

November 2, 2013—No. 8 Clemson defeated Virginia 59-10 in Charlottesville, as Tajh Boyd passed for 377 yards and Sammy Watkins had eight receptions for 169 yards. That included a 96-yard receiving touchdown in the second half, one of the longest pass plays in Clemson history.

November 23, 2013—Clemson defeated The Citadel 52-6 on Military Appreciation Day. The highlight came when U.S. Army veteran Daniel Rodriguez had a two-yard receiving touchdown from Cole Stoudt in the fourth quarter, the first score of the Purple Heart recipient's career. It was also the final home game of Tajh Boyd's career, who completed 21-28 passes for 288 yards and five passing touchdowns. Sammy Watkins became Clemson's career leader in receiving yards in the game, breaking the record of 3,020 by his former teammate DeAndre Hopkins.

November 27, 2013—Chad Morris was named National Assistant Coach of the Year by the AFCA.

January 3, 2014—Clemson concluded its 11-win season with 40-35 victory over No. 6 Ohio State. It gave Clemson wins over a top-10 team to end the season in consecutive years, the only FBS team to do that in 2012-13. Sammy Watkins set an Orange Bowl and Clemson record with 16 catches for 227 yards and two scores. Tajh Boyd had 505 yards of total offense and accounted for six touchdowns in his final game. He also had a career-high 127 rushing yards. Vic Beasley had a Clemson bowl game record four tackles for loss. Stanton Seckinger caught what proved to be the winning touchdown on a pass from Boyd in the fourth quarter. It was the 32nd win as a starting quarterback for Boyd, tying the career record held by Rodney Williams (1985-88).

January 7, 2014—Clemson was ranked No. 7 in the final *USA Today* poll and No. 8 in the final AP poll. Both were the best final rankings for the program since the Tigers won the 1981 national title.

September 27, 2014—Making his first start, freshman Deshaun Watson set a Clemson record with six touchdown passes in a 50-35 win over North Carolina. It was the first time in history Clemson has scored exactly 50 points in a game.

October 11, 2014—Vic Beasley became Clemson's all-time sack leader in a 23-17 win over Louisville. He recorded a three-yard sack in the first half, his 29th as a Tiger, one more than Michael Dean Perry and Gaines Adams had accumulated. Clemson scored a touchdown on a 72-yard punt return by Adam Humphries and a fumble recovery by Tavaris Barnes. Deshawn Williams deflected a pass at the goal line on Louisville's last play to preserve the win. Ten defensive players from this game would be drafted the following May.

November 29, 2014—Playing with a torn ACL, Deshaun Watson threw for two scores and ran for two others in Clemson's 35-17 win over South Carolina that ended the Gamecocks' record five-game winning streak in the series. Artavis Scott had seven catches for 185 yards and two scores, the most receiving yards by a Clemson player against South Carolina and the most ever by a Tiger in Death Valley. Wayne Gallman added 191 yards rushing in 27 carries, the second most rushing yards by a Tiger against South Carolina.

December 29, 2014—Clemson concluded the season with its 10th victory, a 40-6 win over 24th-ranked Oklahoma. Cole Stoudt gained MVP honors by throwing for 319 yards and three touchdowns as the Tigers' 34-point win tied a school record for victory margin over a ranked opponent. The win gave Clemson three straight bowl wins over opposing coaches that had won the national championship, a first in college football history.

October 3, 2015—Clemson defeated sixth-ranked Notre Dame in the first meeting between the two teams since 1979. In a torrential downpour, the Tigers jumped out to a big lead and escaped with a 24-22 win in the final seconds as Carlos Watkins led a host of tacklers that stopped the Fighting Irish's two-point try.

October 24, 2015—Clemson tied the program's largest margin of victory against an ACC opponent and gave Miami (FL) its worst defeat in history with a 58-0 rout in Sun Life Stadium. The Tigers rushed for over 400 yards in the victory.

November 3, 2015—The Tigers were ranked No. 1 in the College Football Playoff poll for the first time in history. Clemson would go on to be ranked first in each of the six polls released during the season.

December 5, 2015—The running tandem of Deshaun Watson and Wayne Gallman led Clemson to a thrilling 45-37 win over North Carolina in the ACC Championship Game, cementing Clemson's place as the No. 1 seed for the College Football Playoff.

December 9, 2015—Dabo Swinney was named Home Depot National Coach of the Year, the first of 10 the Tiger

coach would receive from a national standpoint. He was also the ACC Coach of the Year.

December 12, 2015—Deshaun Watson, Clemson's first Heisman Trophy finalist in history, finished third in the voting for the top award in college football. He was the first player in FBS history to pass for over 4,000 yards and rush over 1,000 in the same season.

December 31, 2015—For a second straight bowl game and fourth consecutive year against a coach that had previously won a national championship, Clemson beat Bob Stoops's Oklahoma team in the Orange Bowl 37-17. The win was the 14th of the season, a school record.

January 11, 2016—Clemson played for the National Championship against Alabama. The Crimson Tide won 45-40, but Deshaun Watson set a championship game record with 478 yards of total offense.

August 21, 2016—Clemson was ranked second in the preseason Associated Press poll. Clemson was also second in the Coaches Poll released earlier in the month. This is the highest preseason ranking in Clemson history in either of the major polls. Clemson was fourth in the preseason poll by the Coaches and the Associated Press in 1988, and fourth by Associated Press in 1984. This also marks the fifth straight year Clemson has been ranked in the preseason of both polls.

September 3, 2016—Clemson opened the 2016 season with a 19-13 win over Auburn in front of a sellout Jordan-Hare Stadium. The Tigers batted down a Hail Mary pass attempt on the final play of the game to move to 1-0 on the season.

Deshaun Watson passed for 248 yards and a touchdown, while wide receiver Mike Williams caught nine passes for 174 yards to lead the playmakers. Defensively, Clemson came up with three takeaways and held Auburn to just 262 yards.

October 2, 2016—Marcus Edmond tackled James Quick one yard shy of a first down at the three-yard line on fourth down with :33 seconds left in the game, as fifth-ranked Clemson held on for a thrilling 42-36 win over third-ranked Louisville at Memorial Stadium.

Led by quarterback Deshaun Watson, who was 20-31 passing for 306 yards and five touchdowns, the Tigers came out on top of the back-and-forth matchup featuring electrifying offensive displays from both teams. Clemson also upped its home winning streak to 19.

October 15, 2016—Third-ranked Clemson, specifically backup cornerback Marcus Edmond, did it again. For the second home game in a row, Edmond made the game-saving play, this time with his first career interception in the end zone in the first overtime in Clemson's 24-17 win over NC State at Memorial.

Kyle Bambard's 33-yard field-goal attempt as time expired in regulation sailed wide right, keeping the hopes of Clemson alive. Artavis Scott's 10-yard receiving touchdown in overtime gave the Tigers a 24-17 lead, then on the Wolfpack's first play in overtime, Edmond ended the game with an interception in the end zone.

October 29, 2016—Third-ranked Clemson trailed Florida State 28-20 entering the fourth quarter, but rallied late in a 37-34 come from behind win to stun the Seminoles in Doak Campbell Stadium in Tallahassee, FL. Jordan Leggett provided the go-ahead touchdown with 2:06 remaining, and Clemson pushed its perfect record to 8-0. It was Clemson's first win in Tallahassee since 2006, and only the second win for the Tiger program at Doak Campbell Stadium since the Seminoles joined the ACC in 1992.

Deshaun Watson was masterful in the fourth quarter after a pair of costly turnovers earlier in the game. The signal-caller finished 27-for-43 for 378 yards and two touchdowns, while adding 52 yards on the ground as well. Leggett produced a career-best 122 receiving yards, most in school history by a tight end.

November 1, 2016—Clemson is ranked second in the first 2016 College Football Playoff Poll.

November 19, 2016—Wayne Gallman rushed for a season-high 161 yards and two touchdowns to lead fourth-ranked Clemson to its second straight ACC Atlantic Division title with a 35-13 win over Wake Forest. The Tigers secured the program's sixth consecutive 10-win season.

November 26, 2016—Deshaun Watson passed for six touchdowns, the most ever by a Tiger against South Carolina, in third-ranked Clemson's 56-7 victory over the Gamecocks at Memorial Stadium. Clemson won its third game in a row over the Gamecocks.

Watson finished the game 26-32 passing for 347 yards, as his six touchdown passes tied a career high. Mike Williams was on the receiving end of three of those touchdown passes, ending with 100 yards on six receptions, all in the first half. Wayne Gallman fueled Clemson's rushing game with 112 yards and a touchdown on 19 carries, and the Tigers as a whole outgained the Gamecocks 622-218.

December 3, 2016—Deshaun Watson accounted for five touchdowns and Cordrea Tankersley ended a Virginia Tech threat with his second interception as the No. 3 Clemson Tigers handled the Hokies 42-35 to win the program's 16th ACC Championship at Camping World Stadium in Orlando, FL.

Watson passed for 288 yards and three touchdowns, while adding 85 rushing yards and two more scores to collect Most Valuable Player honors. Tankersley's second interception came with Virginia Tech facing a 4th-and-6 and threatening in Clemson territory with less than 90 seconds to play.

December 4, 2016—The announcement that ACC Champion Clemson would play Ohio State in the College Football Playoff in the PlayStation Fiesta Bowl on December 31 in Glendale, AZ was made.

This was Clemson's second trip to Glendale. In 2015, Clemson's season ended at the facility with a 45-40 loss to Alabama in the National Championship game.

December 10, 2016—Clemson quarterback Deshaun Watson finished second to Louisville quarterback Lamar Jackson in the Heisman Trophy balloting. It marked the second consecutive year the Tiger signal caller finished in the top three of the voting of over 900 media from around the nation.

December 31, 2016—Second-ranked Clemson jumped out to a 17-0 halftime lead and cruised to a 31-0 victory over No. 3 Ohio State in the Fiesta Bowl at University of Phoenix Stadium in Glendale, AZ. The Tigers, who improved to 13-1, handed Buckeye head coach Urban Meyer his first shutout loss. It was also the highest-ranked team Clemson has ever defeated, as Ohio State was ranked second in the AP and coaches polls.

Quarterback Deshaun Watson and defensive end Clelin Ferrell earned MVP honors. Watson, the Offensive MVP, was 23-36 passing for 259 yards and a touchdown. The junior also had 57 yards and two scores on 15 carries. Wayne Gallman added 85 yards and a touchdown on 18 carries. Ferrell ignited a dominant performance by the Tiger defense, who limited Ohio State to just 215 total yards. Ferrell had three tackles for loss and a sack.

January 9, 2017—Deshaun Watson's touchdown pass to Hunter Renfrow with one second left sealed one of the greatest National Championship battles in history, with Clemson winning its second crown ever after a 35-31 defeat of number-one ranked Alabama. It was the first win in program history over the nation's top-ranked team.

"The difference in the game was the love we had for each other," said head coach Dabo Swinney. "This was a blessing, and it's surreal. Eight years ago, Terry Don Phillips gave me a chance to lead this program. We set out to put Clemson back on top. We came up short last year, but tonight the Clemson flag is flying at the top of that mountain."

Watson was responsible for four touchdowns, including two in the fourth quarter as Clemson rallied from an early 14-0 deficit. It was Clemson's first win ever in a bowl when trailing by 14 or more points. Watson, named Most Valuable Player, threw for 420 yards and three touchdowns while adding a score on the ground. Renfrow caught two of the touchdowns, giving him a second straight National Championship game with multiple receiving scores. The former walk-on finished with a game-high 10 catches for 92 yards. Jordan Leggett and Mike Williams added 95 and 94 receiving yards, respectively.

January 10, 2017—Clemson was ranked first in both the final Associated Press and Coaches' poll.

MEN'S
Golf

FROM THE FIRST TEE BOX IN 1930

Clemson University golf dates to 1930. That year, the Tigers posted a 3-3 record, including a victory over Furman and two over Presbyterian, while dropping matches to Georgia, Emory, and Furman. That first edition of the Clemson golf team was coached by the Reverend George Hodges, minister of the Methodist Church in Clemson.

The next 45 years saw many dual match victories, but Clemson golf did not reach regional or national prominence until the 1970s. Clemson won the State Intercollegiate Tournament in 1947, 1950, 1957, 1959, 1960, and 1975. Some early individual medalists included Billy Delk, who won the 1950 and 1951 State Intercollegiate Tournament.

Assistant football coach and head boxing coach Bob Jones coached the golf team in 1931-49, and again in 1970-74. Bob Moorman was the head coach in 1950-61, and head basketball coach Bobby Roberts led the golf team in 1962. Assistant football coach Whitey Jordan took over in 1963-68.

A renewed interest in all of Clemson's Olympic sports, spearheaded by then-Athletic Director Bill McLellan, allowed for increased funding for the golf team.

THE BOBBY ROBINSON COACHING ERA

Former Athletic Director Bobby Robinson can be considered the man responsible for turning the program into a consistent national contender. During his 10-season reign as coach (1974-83), Robinson guided the Tigers to some of their greatest triumphs. His accomplishments include being the first coach to take a Tiger team to the NCAAs and producing a pair of All-America golfers, nine All-ACC selections, and three top-20 teams. Much of Clemson's modern-day success can be attributed to the foundation that Robinson built.

Before Robinson's tenure, no Tiger team had ever won an ACC championship, and no Tiger linkster had ever appeared in the NCAA individual tournament.

LARRY PENLEY LEADS CLEMSON TO NATIONAL PROMINENCE

During Larry Penley's 30+-year career as Clemson's head coach, the Tigers have earned just about every honor possible during his tenure.

That includes Penley's induction into the Collegiate Golf Hall of Fame at the age of 44, winning an NCAA Championship (2003), coaching two Ben Hogan Award winners (D. J. Trahan and Kyle Stanley) and three US Public Links Champions (Kevin Johnson, DJ Trahan, and Corbin Mills), and leading the Tigers to 22 top-20 seasons.

In the summer of 2009, he watched former Tiger Lucas Glover win the United States Open. Then, in August, 2009, it was announced that Penley was selected for the South Carolina Golf Hall of Fame. In December of that year, it was announced Clemson's new golf building would be named in his honor.

The building was dedicated in September of 2011 and is one of the finest golf facilities in the nation.

Penley has been a model of consistency since he became head coach in the fall of 1983. All 33 of his previous Tiger teams have been selected for the NCAA Tournament, including 26 that have advanced within the national tournament.

In his career, Clemson has posted 24 top-25 finishes, 22 top-20 finishes, 18 top-15 finishes, 12 top-10s, and eight top-five finishes at the NCAA Championships. That includes a streak of seven-straight top-10s from 1997-2003.

One of those top-10 finishes came in 2003, when the Tigers won the national championship with a two-stroke victory over Oklahoma State on the Cowboys' home course. It was Clemson's only national championship in golf.

CLEMSON WINS 2003 NATIONAL CHAMPIONSHIP

When you walk into the Larry B. Penley Golf Building, Clemson's 2003 NCAA National Championship Trophy is displayed proudly, as it should be. It was the Tigers' only national championship in men's golf and only the fourth overall for the university.

Jack Ferguson, who had played with a calming demeanor all week long, two-putted for par on the final hole to secure a two-stroke victory over Oklahoma State at the Karsten Creek Golf Course—the Cowboys' home course—in Stillwater, OK.

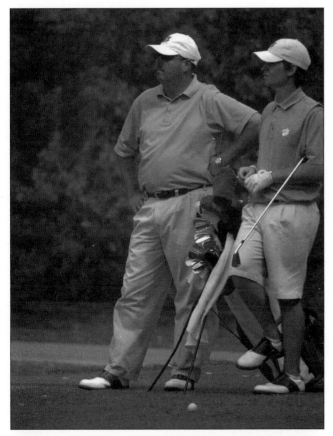

Head Coach Larry Penley has led Clemson to 21 top-20 seasons.

"It was a great feeling," Penley said. "Any championship is special, but to win it at Oklahoma State made it even more special because they had been the program that had the most NCAA Tournament appearances, the most national championships, and the most tradition.

"We have great respect for their program, so to win on their home course was memorable."

But as precious as the 2003 National Championship Trophy is, there is one other trophy in the clubhouse that arguably means a little more or at least as much. This trophy is a little bit harder to find. It sits off to the left in another trophy case and often gets passed by as visitors admire the National Championship Trophy.

But the fact of the matter is, Clemson may not have won the national championship in 2003 if it were not for its wild comeback in the ACC Tournament at the Old North State Club in New London, NC. The Tigers had not won a golf tournament that spring and were down five strokes to first-place Wake Forest and were in third place when the final round began.

As the afternoon wore on, things were not getting any better, as Clemson's first group hit the 16th green down 10 strokes.

"It looked like we were going to lose," Penley recalled. "We were down 10 shots with three holes to play to Wake Forest."

The Demon Deacons were one of the best golf teams in the country at the time. They finished fourth in the nationals that year and were ranked third in the Final *Golfweek*/Sagarin rankings.

"Wake Forest had a great team that included current PGA Tour standout Bill Haas," Penley said. "They were really good, and they had us beat."

But all of sudden, the Tigers started dropping birdies like flies. Penley counted at least 10 birdies hit the cup in the final three holes as the Tigers roared to the front of the leaderboard. Once Wake saw Clemson making a charge, the pressure mounted as the Demon Deacons bogeyed a couple of times to put Clemson in position to win.

When Ferguson dropped a birdie from 10 feet out, the Tigers had come all the way back to win the ACC Championships, and more important to establish much-needed momentum.

"For whatever reason, the confidence just grew for our other guys," Penley said. "From that point, I knew we were going to win it all."

From that point on, Clemson started to dominate. The Tigers' individual record was 183-8-3 in 2003. After the ACC, they moved on to the East Regionals at Auburn and ran away from the field, winning by 14 shots.

"We never had a team that dominated college golf the way they did. I won't say that was the most talented team we ever had—we had some other great teams—but they found a way to get it done all year long.

"No team has ever dominated like that. We had one third-place finish and six wins, and the rest were second-place finishes. No team [in college golf] before or since has won a conference, regional, and National

Championship in the same year. I don't think any team will ever do that."

The reason the Tigers were doing so well had everything to do with who was playing. D. J. Trahan was the 2002 National Player of the Year, while Matt Hendrix, Greg Jones, and Ferguson were All-America golfers at one point in their careers. Though not an All-America golfer, Ben Duncan was the leader of the team. He always played well and gave the Tigers a chance to close out or win tournaments on the last day, rarely putting his team in harm's way.

In fact, Duncan had a great NCAA Tournament, as his score counted in each of the last three rounds.

"There were a lot of reasons for our success," Penley said. "We finished third the year before at Ohio State and actually led after 36 holes. We had all five guys back, and the key piece of that was the NCAA's best player, D. J. Trahan, deciding to return to school.

"He knew there was unfinished business. He had a phenomenal senior year. It was probably the easiest coaching job I ever had. They knew what to do and were focused from day one."

Though Clemson had not won a national championship, everyone was expecting the Tigers to do so when they headed out to Stillwater. So the pressure was mounting, also because Clemson was attempting to do something no one has ever done—win the conference, as well as the regional and the national championship, in the same season. A CBS television crew followed the Tigers and documented all three rounds.

"Postseason means everything in college golf," Hendrix said. "We won conference and played well against some good teams like Georgia Tech and Wake Forest. Then, we played really well at Regionals. The media hype started between there and nationals. No one had ever swept all three tournaments.

"Everything that could be played against us was done. Plus, we faced a lot of media pressure."

The biggest pressure of all was playing in Stillwater. Playing at Karsten Creek gave the Cowboys an edge over everyone in the field, and Clemson knew if it was going to make history it was going to have to beat Oklahoma State.

"That was set up, in my opinion, in the best way it could give their coach an advantage," Hendrix said. "I remember the course being very difficult. Every hole, we were playing for par.

"In the final round, it just became a down-to-the-wire dogfight with Oklahoma State. I remember Jack Ferguson hanging in there playing with Hunter Mahan. It came down to the last two holes. We had a lead, but Jack had to hang onto it, playing against Hunter, and he did that."

The amazing part was how Clemson never cracked under the pressure of the tournament. The Tigers were in or near the lead in each of the first three rounds, never trailing by more than four strokes. Clemson, Oklahoma State, and UCLA were the top three teams in the country

that year, and they were paired up all four days, which added to the intrigue.

"We knew we would have to beat Oklahoma State, and it came down to the two of us," Penley said. "They had Hunter Mahan and Alex Noren, who has won three times on the European Tour. They were really, really good. It became a head-to-head battle, but it worked out for us."

It's amazing that it did, especially with more than 500 Cowboy fans following their home team around the golf course. Add the 90-degree heat to top it off; it's amazing how the Tigers kept their composure.

"It was amazing," Hendrix said. "We did the sweep under all that pressure, and the media pressure, too. It didn't end early . . . but we played some of our best golf in the final tournament."

Especially Ferguson, who had to hold off the charging Mahan. On the last hole, Mahan hit his second shot 15 feet from the cup, setting up an eagle three. The place exploded, as it appeared the Cowboys might steal the title away from the Tigers at the last second.

But Ferguson never panicked. He was in this same position several weeks earlier at the ACC Championships, and he drained a 10-foot birdie for the win. Though he was playing with perhaps the best golfer in the country at the time, and everyone was pulling against him, he was sitting just 15 feet away from the cup and knew he just needed to two-putt to win the National Championships. And he did it.

"It was a big challenge and a lot of pressure, but this team was mature enough and prepared for it," Penley said.

And they are still the only team in the history of men's college golf to win a conference, regional, and national championship in the same year.

"It was a total team effort. We did not have an individual finish in the top 15 of the NCAA Tournament, yet we won the National Championships," Penley said. "That shows you how solid we were as a team."

That is, a team that came together on a day in late April, while realizing its full potential in the ACC Tournament. It's a day that will forever be bookmarked as the beginning of the greatest run in the history of college golf.

OTHER FACTS ABOUT THE 2003 SEASON

Penley's Tigers also won the ACC Championships and the NCAA East Regional title that spring, making Clemson the first program in NCAA history to win its conference, regional, and national championship in the same year. Clemson won a school record six team titles for the academic year and ranked number one in the nation by *Golfweek*/Sagarin and the Golf Coaches Association for the entire season.

As a result of these achievements, Penley was named the National Coach of the Year by *Golfweek* and the Golf Coaches Association for 2003. He also received Coach of the Year honors from the ACC and for the NCAA at the District level.

Three All-America golfers led the team. D. J. Trahan capped his brilliant career with first-team All-America honors. He also was named first-team All-ACC for the fourth consecutive year, joining Jonathan Byrd as the only four-time All-ACC selections in school history. Jack Ferguson was a second-team All-America golfer, after appearing in only a handful of tournaments as a fresh-man in 2001-02. His birdie putt on the last hole won the ACC Championships, and then his par on the 72nd hole clinched the NCAA title. Matt Hendrix was a third-team All-America honoree and Verizon Academic All-District selection. Gregg Jones, another starter for the entire year, was a first-team All-ACC selection. Ben Duncan, the fifth starter on the championship squad, rounded out his Clemson career with a strong showing in the NCAAs.

PENLEY'S EARLY CAREER

Penley has had a high level of success since he first be-came head coach. After serving as an assistant on Clem-son's 1983 team that finished fifth in the nation, then the highest finish in school history, Penley took a young team to a 19th-place finish in his first year. Dillard Pruitt, who earned All-America honors for a second time in his career before going on to a distinguished eight-year run on the PGA Tour, paced the club that year.

Penley brought the Clemson program to another level in 1986-87, as he captured his first ACC title and the pro-gram's second. Overall, Clemson won a then-record five events and finished second in three others behind a team that featured All-America golfers Chris Patton and Kevin Johnson. Clemson finished 11th at the NCAA Tournament that season. Penley was named ACC and NCAA District Coach of the Year for the first time.

Clemson's current mentor had one of the best teams in school history and the nation in 1988. That year, the Tigers won five events for the second-straight season, including four victories in the spring. Clemson won the ACC title for the second-straight year and captured the Chris Schenkel Invitational on the way to 10 top-five finishes.

In the 1988-89 season, Kevin Johnson and Chris Patton received All-America honors again and led the Tigers to a third-place finish at the NCAA Tournament, Clemson's highest ranking ever at the time. In every tournament the Tigers entered, they finished in the top five and the team had a 72.61 stroke average, best in school history at the time. Johnson ended his career as one of Clemson's top golfers in history. He had won the United States Public Links (1987) and earned a spot on the Walker Cup team (1989) during his Clemson career.

In 1989-90, Penley's Tigers won four tournaments, including the ACC title, and finished 12th at the NCAA Tournament. For the second time ever, the team was ranked number one going into the spring season. When Chris Patton won the 1989 US Amateur, the program

received considerable attention. He was the low ama-teur at the 1990 Master's. Three Tigers—Patton, Oswald Drawdy, and Danny Ellis—earned All-America honors in the spring season.

Many thought the program would decline a bit after Patton's graduation, but three freshmen made an impact in 1990 and continued to bring the Tigers to new levels of consistency over the next three years. Danny Ellis, Bobby Doolittle, and Nicky Goetze kept Clemson's NCAA Tournament top-15 streak intact, including a fourth-place finish in 1992-93. The 1993 team actually had five players earn some type of All-America honors, a first in Clemson history. That team also won Penley's first NCAA Regional title.

Despite being a young team, in 1994 Clemson finished ninth in the NCAA Tournament. Mark Swygert, a senior on the Clemson team, finished third and 11-under-par in the tournament. Swygert broke four Clemson individual records in NCAA play with that performance. He had an overall score of 277 (-11), which beat the previous best of Dillard Pruitt by 10 strokes. Swygert's 65 in the third round is still the best ever by a Tiger in the NCAA Tour-nament vs. par (65) (-7).

The 1996-97 academic year brought more nation-al acclaim to the Clemson program, as junior Charles Warren won the NCAA Championships at Conway Farms in Chicago. ESPN captured the thrilling one-shot win in a playoff over Brad Elder. Warren went on to earn first-team All-America honors along with senior Richard Coughlan, who shared ACC Player of the Year honors.

The 1997-98 season was the best on record in many respects. In addition to Clemson's number-two NCAA finish and final ranking, the team set 11 school season records. That team had nine first- or second-place finish-es, also a record for one season. All five starting players averaged under 73.0, also a first for a Clemson team. The squad was 29-under-par for the season, 104 strokes better than the previous school record.

Clemson continued the excellence in 1998-99 with five tournament titles to tie the single season school mark, a number-one national ranking much of the year, and a number-eight finish at the NCAA Tournament. Only four opponents out of the 67 different teams the Tigers faced had a stroke and won-loss advantage against Clemson. Clemson had a 77.3 percent winning mark against those 67 teams, including a 71-37-4 record against the 29 other schools in the NCAA Tournament.

It seemed improbable that the records established by the 1997-98 team could be eclipsed. But that was the case in 1999-2000, as the Tigers established a team stroke aver-age record with a 71.32 mark. The team was 77-under-par for the year. Four Tigers earned All-America honors, in-cluding Lucas Glover, who was a first-team choice after a record-setting 71.24 stroke average for the year. Clemson won the ACC Tournament and the East Regional in the same year for the first time ever, then finished seventh at the NCAAs. Current PGA Tour players Lucas Glover, D. J. Trahan, and Jonathan Byrd all played on that team.

Lucas Glover won the 2009 US Open.

The 2000-01 season marked the end of the Lucas Glover and John Engler era at Clemson. Both were first-team All-America selections in their final seasons and led the Tigers to a second-place NCAA finish, just as they had in their freshman season.

The success of the 2001-02 season was a testimony to Penley's ability to keep the Clemson program at a high level on a consistent basis. Most college golf observers thought Penley's success level would take a step backward in 2001-02. With the loss of first-team All-America golfers Glover and Engler, the Tigers were ranked just ninth in the preseason Precept Coaches poll. But, the Tigers won the Ping Preview in the fall and quickly returned to the top five of the polls.

In addition to the win at the Ping Preview, Penley's Tigers won the NCAA East Regional in a cochampionship with #1 ranked Georgia Tech. The Tigers finished in the top five in 10 of their 12 tournaments that year, including seven top-three finishes. The Tigers concluded the campaign with a number-three finish at the NCAAs at Ohio State.

Trahan furthered Clemson's tradition in 2002 by winning the Ben Hogan Award as the top college golfer

in the nation. He had a 70.33 stroke average, second-best in the nation and eighth-best in NCAA history at the time. Trahan won three tournaments, the first Tiger to do that, and had three other second-place finishes. He then led the Tigers to the national championship in 2003 and finished his career with five tournament victories, tied for the Clemson all-time record.

CONTINUED SUCCESS

In January of 2004, Penley was inducted into the Golf Coaches Association's Hall of Fame, quite an accomplishment for someone just 44 years of age at the time. The victories continued in the spring of 2004, when he led the Tigers to the ACC Tournament and East Regional Championship and finished with another top-20 finish at the NCAA Tournament.

Clemson has had four more top-16 finishes since the 2004 season with a seventh place at Sunriver, OR, in 2006, the fifth place finish in 2008 at Purdue, a 16th-place finish at The Honors Course in 2010, and the 14th-place finish in 2016 at Eugene, Oregon.

Penley has led Clemson to the NCAA East Region title seven times, including a pair of "three-peats." No other college coach has won more than his seven NCAA Regional Championships.

The former All-ACC golfer at Clemson has won 70 tournaments as head coach of the Tigers, fourth in NCAA history for a coach at one school. He is third among active coaches with that total. He has won at least one tournament in 31 of his 34 seasons as Clemson head coach. He also has 74 second-place finishes, giving him 144 first or runner-up finishes in his career at Clemson in 414 tournaments.

CHARLES WARREN WINS 1997 NATIONAL CHAMPIONSHIP

With a brilliant final-round 67 capped by a one-hole sudden death playoff victory, Clemson's Charles Warren charged from six shots behind on the final day, mastered the challenging and temperamental Conway Farms links course, and declared himself heir to Tiger Woods as the 1997 NCAA golf champion.

The ACC Tournament victory in April was the first championship of his college career and marked a dramatic turnaround from what up until then had been a difficult junior season. Warren had finished no higher than 15th in any spring tournament prior to an eight-place finish in the Ping Intercollegiate the week before the ACC Tournament and in the preceding two tournaments had finished 62nd and 42nd.

It was a fast, furious, and finally a nail-biting finish for the Clemson junior—the ACC champion, a two-time All-America golfer, and now the champion of the 100th NCAA Tournament.

The moments following his championship were a blur—congratulations from rival and runner-up Brad

Elder of Texas; celebration with his teammates and coach; signing autographs and then rushing from a national television interview to the awards ceremony and on to the media room for a formal question-and-answer session.

With his "official" obligations behind him, Warren found a phone and called his parents, sharing his jubilation and accepting the congratulations from his father—present at many Clemson golf outings but unable to attend that year's tournament.

"It just tore him up not to be here today," said Warren. "He gets so excited out there on the course—worse than I am. I'm just glad they got to watch it on TV. It was awesome."

Warren paused and shook his head, seemingly in amusement at himself. "I really don't know how I feel—I honestly have no idea," he said. "It's weird. This is going to take a while to sink in."

In winning the NCAA title, Warren became Clemson's first NCAA solo event champion.

"Charles is a tough, tough nut," said Penley. "You can't crack him when he's in position to win a tournament.

"I could tell today on the back side, when I started walking with him on No. 13, that he was just incredibly focused. You could tell that his concentration level was right there."

FORMER PLAYERS HAVE SUCCESS

Clemson players have flourished under Penley's leadership. No fewer than six of his former players participated in various PGA Tour events in 2016.

Lucas Glover won the 2009 United States Open and finished ninth on the PGA Tour money list in 2009.

Clemson had 12 players on the ACC 50-Year Anniversary team in 2002, and 11 of the 12 players were coached by Penley. His former players have combined to win 10 PGA Tour events through the year 2014.

Individually, Clemson has had 17 top-10 NCAA Tournament finishes in Penley's career. That includes the NCAA Championships by Charles Warren in 1997, and his number-two finish in 1998. Kyle Stanley finished second in 2007 and 2009 and won the Ben Hogan Award in 2009. Ben Martin finished ninth in 2010.

Penley has been honored for his success in the ACC, winning the ACC Coach of the Year honors seven times overall. He was the first coach in ACC history to win this award three consecutive years (1996-97-98). He has nine ACC Championships to his credit, third on the all-time list of ACC mentors.

Penley has to rank as the best combination player-coach in Clemson history next to the legendary Banks McFadden. In the 1930s, McFadden was an All-America player in football and basketball and coached the Clemson basketball team for nearly a decade. Penley was chosen All-ACC as a Tiger golfer and has led Clemson to nine ACC titles as a coach. He is one of only two coaches in Clemson sports history to do

this (former women's track coach Wayne Coffman is the other). He has played for and coached Clemson in the NCAA Tournament.

In addition to the success of his former players on the PGA Tour, former Penley players have brought distinction to the school in national amateur tournaments. Chris Patton won the 1989 United States Amateur, while Danny Ellis advanced to the finals in 1993. Johnson won the US Public Links championship in 1987, and Trahan won the same event in 2000. Corbin Mills won the Public Links in 2011. Ben Martin was a finalist at the 2009 US Amateur and played in the 2010 Masters.

Over the years, Penley's program has produced 54 All-America selections, including at least two in nine of the last 20 years.

Penley has coached eight different players who have played in the Walker Cup. That includes Matt Hendrix, who posted a 2-0-1 record in the 2003 event. In 2001, senior Lucas Glover and sophomore D. J. Trahan were both members of the 2001 United States Walker Cup team. Jonathan Byrd was a member of the United States Walker Cup team in 1999 and played on the Palmer Cup team in 1999 and 2000.

Clemson dominated the Palmer Cup teams of 2000 and 2001 with three players each year. John Engler was a three-time selection to the United States Palmer Cup team. Trahan was the captain of the United States team in 2002, leading the US to victory at the event held in Ireland. Penley was honored with his selection as the 2004 Palmer Cup team coach.

In 2012, for the first time in PGA Tour history, college teammates squared off in a sudden-death playoff. Clemson's Jonathan Byrd started the final round three strokes ahead of former Tigers teammate and US Open champion Lucas Glover.

Glover seemed to have it won in regulation only to see Byrd make a dramatic birdie on the closing hole to force a playoff. Glover won the playoff.

US OPEN CHAMPION

It all started innocently enough. Dick Hendley, a former football star at Clemson, loved Clemson so much he wanted to share his passion for the Tigers with his grandson, Lucas Glover.

Hendley was an outstanding blocking back for Frank Howard's teams from 1947-'50. He opened holes for great players like Ray Mathews and Fred Cone. He was so good, in fact, he was awarded the Jacobs Blocking Trophy for the state of South Carolina and the Southern Conference in 1950.

He was a part of two of the greatest Clemson teams of all time, the 1948 squad, which went 11-0 and beat Missouri in the 1949 Gator Bowl, and the 1950 team that went 9-0-1 and beat Miami in the prestigious 1951 Orange Bowl.

Hendley, who also played baseball, was inducted into the Clemson Hall of Fame in 1984, and a year later he was celebrating it with Glover. From that point, the two attended every Clemson home game until 1997.

Hendley's love for Clemson grew on Glover so much there was no other school he wanted to attend. But Clemson football was not the only passion Hendley shared with his grandson. He also shared with Glover his love for golf, and like Clemson football games, Glover latched on to the game and made it his own.

"My grandfather got me my first golf club when I was three years old," Glover said. "One of his friends was a golf rep and he asked him to make a club. I put it in my hands and it was a perfect fit."

And Glover has been a perfect fit for golf.

After a brilliant playing career at Clemson, in which he posted two All-America seasons, Glover earned his card to play on the PGA Tour.

In June of 2009, he brought his playing career to a new level at the Black Course at Bethpage State Park, a par-70 course just 25 miles from New York City. It was the United States Open, and Glover was about to record one of the greatest moments in Clemson sports history.

It was destined to be a special week for Glover and Clemson. The USGA decided to have an all-Clemson pairing for the first two rounds (something they also did with three players from Oklahoma State).

Glover played with D. J. Trahan and Kyle Stanley for the first 36 holes.

Maybe it was because he was playing with his Clemson brothers, but whatever it was, it was working. Glover shot a 69 in the first round and made another strong move with a 64 in the second round. His second-round performance included six birdies and no bogeys.

In the third round, Glover fell behind by six shots as Ricky Barnes reached 11-under-par at one point in the third round. But Barnes came back to the field, and Glover moved back to seven-under-par by the end of the round.

He trailed Barnes by just one shot entering play on Sunday.

In the final round, the former Clemson star made three bogeys on the front nine and made the turn at four-under-par for the tournament. He grabbed the lead, however, as Barnes shot a five-over-par score on the front nine.

Glover made five straight pars from holes 10-14 to remain at four-under-par. Tiger Woods was charging and had it to one-under-par, just three back, while Phil Mickelson made an eagle on the par-five 13th to tie Glover at four-under. But Mickelson gave a stroke back on the difficult 15th hole to go to three-under-par.

The key hole for Glover was the par-four 16th. After making bogey on the 15th to drop into a tie for the lead with Mickelson at three-under, the Greenville, SC, native hit his approach on 16 to within four feet. He made the putt for birdie to go back to four-under.

Mickelson made another bogey on 17, and all of a sudden Glover had a two-shot lead. The former Clemson standout made pars on the last two holes to win by two shots over Mickelson, David Duval, and Barnes.

With the victory came $1.3 million, a 10-year exemption to the US Open, and a five-year exemption to the Masters, the British Open, and any PGA Tour event.

At Clemson, Glover helped guide the Tigers to national runner-up spots in 1998 and 2001 and was a three-time All-ACC first-team performer and a two-time All-America honoree. He was also just the second Clemson golfer to win at least one tournament in three different years.

Like his grandfather did, the US Open Champion says Penley played a big role in his development as a professional golfer.

"Coach Penley has been as important as anyone in my career," Glover said. "He had credibility with us from day one because he had been there and done that. He had been such a good player himself, and it is a lot easier to listen to someone who is doing it himself out on the course."

In 2007, Glover was inducted into the Clemson Athletic Hall of Fame, joining Hendley to become the only grandfather/grandson combination in the Hall's history.

"My grandfather and my uncles all played golf and just loved the game," Glover said. "He had a putting green installed in his backyard at Thornblade so I could have my own practice green. It is still there."

GOLF HISTORY

April 8, 1930—Clemson played its first-ever golf match. The Tigers defeated Presbyterian, 13.5-4.5.

April 12, 1930—Clemson defeated Presbyterian 15.5-2.5 in the Tigers' first home golf match.

1932—Clemson claimed a tie for the state championship, having defeated South Carolina once and Furman once.

March 26, 1937—Clemson defeated Hampden-Sydney 9.5-8.5 to start a five-match winning streak that included wins over Wake Forest, The Citadel, Presbyterian, and South Carolina.

April 12, 1938—The Tigers opened the season with a 9-9 tie with Big-Ten member Michigan. The Tigers also opened the 1939 season with the Wolverines.

April 22, 1939—Clemson finished second in the first-ever state tournament played in Columbia, SC.

April 5, 1946—Clemson started the 1946 season with a 17.5-.5 win over Davidson, which started a 19-match win-streak for the Tigers that lasted over three seasons.

May, 7, 1947—The Tigers defeated Wofford 20.5-6.5 to complete a perfect 8-0 season.

May 9-10, 1947—Clemson finished third at the Southern Conference Tournament, markings the first time that the Tigers had entered the event.

May 20-21, 1947—Clemson won the state tournament that was held in Spartanburg, SC.

April 23, 1948—Clemson defeated Presbyterian 26.5-.5, which was the 18th straight dual match that the Tigers had won spanning over three seasons. The streak ended on May 14, 1948, as South Carolina defeated the Tigers 12-6 in Columbia, SC.

May 10-12, 1950—Clemson won the State of South Carolina Tournament held in Spartanburg, SC.

April 26-27, 1957—Clemson won the State Tournament in Hampton, SC.

May 16-17, 1959—The Tigers won the State Tournament in Hampton, SC.

April 29-30, 1960—For the third time in four years, Clemson won the State Tournament in Hampton, SC.

1974—Clemson won the State of South Carolina Golf Tournament.

April 11-13, 1975—The Tigers won the State of South Carolina Golf Tournament.

June 25-28, 1975—Freshman Jim White became the first Tiger ever to play in the NCAA Tournament. This year's tournament was held in Columbus, OH.

April 15-17, 1976—Senior Parker Moore became the school's first ACC Medalist as he shot a 71-68-68 for a 207 total in the three-day tournament.

May 28-31, 1980—Clemson appeared in its first NCAA Tournament as a team at the Ohio State University Course in Columbus, OH. The team finished in a tie for 12th. Kevin Walsh was the highest finisher for the Tigers as he shot a 299 and finished in 26th place. Clarence Rose was Clemson's first-ever All-America golfer.

April 16-18, 1982—Clemson took home its first ACC Team Championship in 1982 at Northgreen Country Club in Rocky Mount, NC. Sophomore Dillard Pruitt finished second in the tournament to lead the Tigers.

May 26-29, 1982—The Tigers finished 16th at the NCAA Tournament in Pinehurst, NC (No. 2). Tony Nimmer finished 16th as he shot a 289.

May 5, 1983—Bobby Robinson resigned as head coach of the Tiger golf team so he could devote all of his time in administration. Larry Penley, an All-America golfer and All-ACC performer for the Tigers, took over as coach. Penley played on the 1978-81 Clemson golf teams.

June 8-11, 1983—Finding themselves in 22nd place after the first round of the NCAA Tournament, the Tigers, led by Dillard Pruitt and Julian Taylor, pulled off a fantastic finish. They ended up fifth, as the Tigers averaged 290 over the final three days at San Juaquin Country Club in Fresno, CA. Taylor finished the tournament ranked 15th and Charles Raulerson finished 20th. Norman Chapman, Dillard Pruitt, and Tony Nimmer comprised the remainder of Clemson Golf's first-ever top-five finisher.

May 23-26, 1984—Dillard Pruitt finished 13th in leading Clemson to a 19th-place finish in the NCAA Tournament at Bear Creek Golf World in Houston, TX.

May 22-25, 1985—Clemson finished 27th at the NCAA Tournament at the Grenelefe Golf and Tennis Resort in Haines City, FL.

May 28-31, 1986—Clemson finished 21st at the NCAA Tournament at Bermuda Run Country Club in Advance, NC.

April 17-19, 1987—The Tigers won the ACC Championships at Bryan Park in Greensboro, NC. Brad Clark finished second with a three-day total of 211.

June 10-13, 1987—The Tigers finished 11th at the NCAA Golf Tournament in Columbus, OH. Kevin Johnson finished ninth overall in the tournament. Larry Penley was named the 1987 ACC and District III Coach of the Year.

April 15-17, 1988—Clemson won the ACC Golf Championships at Cardinal Golf Club in Greensboro, NC, with a three-day score of 880. The Tigers' Kevin Johnson won the individual championship with a three-day total of 214.

May 25-28, 1988—Clemson finished 17th in the NCAA Tournament at the North Ranch Country Club in Westlake Village, CA. Kevin Johnson was named first-team All-America.

June 7-10, 1989—The Tigers finished third at the NCAA Tournament at the Oak Tree Country Club in Edmond, OK. Kevin Johnson would have won the individual national championship, but a controversy over the signing of his scorecard on the second day of competition resulted in a round of 69 being voided.

Summer, 1989—Individual play brought attention to the Clemson program in the summer of 1989. Chris Patton won the US Amateur Championships at Merion Country Club in Ardmore, PA. Patton won the last of six matches over Danny Green, 3 and 1 in the finals. He became the second Tiger to compete in the Masters (Parker Moore was the other in 1977), finishing as the low amateur and 39th overall in the prestigious event. Patton also competed in the US Open and the British Open.

April 20-22, 1990—Clemson and N.C. State tied for the ACC Championships at Northgreen Country Club in Rocky Mount, NC. Chris Patton led the Tigers as he finished in a tie for third place in the tournament.

June 6-9, 1990—The 1990 linksters became the fourth-straight top-20 Tiger team with a number-12 finish at the Innisbrook Golf and Tennis Club in Tarpon Springs, FL. Danny Ellis finished in a tie for eighth place to lead the Tigers.

June 5-8, 1991—Clemson finished 13th at the NCAA Tournament at the Poppy Hills Country Club in Pebble Beach, CA.

May 15-17, 1992—Danny Ellis won the individual championship as the Tigers finished second at the Atlantic Coast Conference Tournament at the Northgreen Country Club in Rocky Mount, NC. Ellis shot a three-day total of 208.

June 3-6, 1992—The Tigers finished 12th at the NCAA Tournament. Nicky Goetze led Clemson with his 23rd-place finish.

May 19-21, 1993—Clemson won the NCAA's East Region Championship. Bobby Doolittle finished second in leading the Tigers.

June 2-5, 1993—Clemson's incredible depth was highlighted in the 1993 NCAA Tournament at the Champions in Lexington, KY. It was a fourth, lesser-known senior who led the Tigers to the number-four finish at that year's tournament. Thump Delk, who had never broken par in his career and played in only five tournaments all season, fired rounds of 71-71-73-72, totaling 287, one-under-par for the four-round tournament, and finished third overall.

Mark Swygert finished seventh overall and one stroke behind Delk. The duo's performance garnered them

honorable mention All-America awards. Three other Tigers—Nicky Goetz, Danny Ellis, and Booby Doolittle—also earned All-America honors. Therefore, five Clemson golfers earned some type of All-America honors in 1993. This was a first in Clemson history and possibly a first in NCAA Division I golf history.

May 19-21, 1994—The 1994 Tigers won the NCAA Tournament's East Regional at the Grand National Lake Golf Course in Auburn, AL. Mark Swygert fired a third-round 67 to finish the tournament in a tie for first place. Coach Penley also received rounds in the 60s from Richard Coughlan and Tommy Biershenk to lead the Tigers to the championship.

June 1-4, 1994—Mark Swygert tied the Clemson record for low finish in an NCAA Tournament with a third-place 11-under par effort. Clemson finished the event in ninth place, marking the fourth top-10 finish in Clemson history in NCAA play.

Swygert, who finished his career with seven rounds of par or better in NCAA play, was an All-America golfer but oddly enough did not make All-ACC.

May 18-20, 1995—Clemson won the NCAA Tournament's East Regional for the third year in a row. Led by 213 tournament totals from Richard Coughlan and Mike Byce, the Tigers won the regional by 12 strokes over ACC rival North Carolina at the Yale University Golf Course in New Haven, CT.

May 31-June 3, 1995—Clemson finished 21st at the NCAA Golf Tournament at the Ohio State University Course in Columbus, OH.

April 19-21, 1996—At the ACC Tournament at the Old North State Club in New London, NC, head coach Larry Penley was named ACC Coach of the Year for the second time in his career. Richard Coughlan, Joey Maxon, and Charles Warren were tabbed as All-ACC selections.

May 29-June 1, 1996—Clemson finished 14th at the NCAA Tournament at the Honors Course in Chattanooga, TN. Joey Maxon paced the Tigers with his ninth-place finish. Charles Warren finished 15th nationally, and Joey Maxon 19th, as players in the Sagarin Rankings.

April 18-20, 1997—The Tigers won the ACC Tournament at the Whitewater Country Club in Fayetteville, GA. Charles Warren won the individual championship with a three-day total of four-under-par 212. Joey Maxon finished fifth. Byrd became the first freshman in Clemson history to be recognized as first-team All-ACC. Clemson finished third as a team in the final poll. Charles Warren was ranked fifth, and Richard Coughlan was ranked ninth.

May 15-17, 1997—The Tigers finished second at the NCAA East Regional at the Cascades Course at the Homestead in Hot Springs, VA.

May 28-31, 1997—Charles Warren came back from a six-stroke deficit entering the final round and won the NCAA Tournament at Conway Farms in Lake Forest, IL. Warren is the first Clemson golfer in history to win the National Championships. The native of Columbia, SC, fired a 67 on the final day, the lowest final round ever for a Clemson golfer in NCAA Tournament play. He then defeated Brad Elder in a one-hole playoff.

Warren also won the ACC Tournament and thus became the first league player in history to win the ACC and NCAA Tournaments in the same year.

Richard Coughlan joined Warren on the first-team All-America squad, the first time Clemson had two first-team selections. Coughlan finished sixth at the NCAAs and was named ACC Coplayer of the Year in a vote of the coaches.

May 28-31, 1997—Clemson finished third at the 1997 NCAA Golf Tournament. The duo was the prime reason Clemson finished third at the NCAA Tournament, tying for the highest finish in school history. Joey Maxon, Elliot Gealy, and Jonathan Byrd were the other three starters on this team that also won the Ping Intercollegiate and the ACC Championships.

March 14-16, 1998—The Tigers finished second at the NCAA East Regional at the Melrose Course in Daufuskie Island, SC.

April 17-19, 1998—Clemson won the ACC Championships at Uwharrie Point in New London, NC. The Tigers' Charles Warren won the event, as he shot 68-68-69 for an 11-under 205 total.

May 27-30, 1998—The Tigers finished second at the NCAA Golf Tournament at University Course in Albuquerque, NM. Clemson shot a 31-under-par team score for the event, the second-best team score in NCAA National Tournament history. Unfortunately, UNLV shot the lowest tournament score versus par in history, 34-under. Charles Warren finished second in the NCAA Tournament with a 16-under-par 272.

Warren concluded his Clemson career with two ACC championships, an NCAA Title (1997), and the runner-up spot at the NCAA Championships (1998). He finished his career with 17 Clemson school records, including lowest stroke average in a season (71.28) and most rounds under par in a season (23). Warren was named the recipient of the Dave Williams Award, which is given to the top senior golfer in the nation.

Clemson finished second in the nation. Charles Warren finished seventh and Joey Maxon finished 17th nationally.

June 2-5, 1999—Clemson finished eighth in the NCAA Golf Tournament at the Hazeltine National Golf Course in Chaska, MN. Lucas Glover finished eighth in the tournament to lead the Tigers.

The Tigers finished fifth in the final poll. Jonathan Byrd finished sixth, John Engler ninth, and Jonathan Byrd was ranked 14th.

April 21-23, 2000—Clemson won the ACC Championships at the Old North St. Club in New London, NC. John Engler finished second in the tournament.

May 18-20, 2000—The Tigers won the NCAA Regional at the Glenmaura National in Moosci, PA.

May 31-June 3, 2000—Clemson finished seventh in the NCAA Tournament at the Grand National, in Opelika, AL. D. J. Trahan shot a four-day total of six-under 282 for a 15th-place finish.

June 5, 2000—Four Clemson golfers, one at each level of the selection process, earned All-America honors, according to the Golf Coaches Association. The Golf Coaches Association made the announcement. Lucas Glover, who was chosen first-team All-America, set a Clemson record for stroke average in a season with a 71.24 figure that year.

John Engler was named second-team All-America. Senior Jonathan Byrd was named third-team All-America by the Coaches Organization. Freshman D. J. Trahan was chosen to two All-America teams. The native of Inman, SC, was named to the Freshman All-America team and was an honorable mention All-America honoree.

June 7, 2000—Clemson was ranked third in nationally in the final poll.

April 20-22, 2001—John Engler was the ACC Tournament's Individual Medalist at the Magnolia Course in Orlando, FL. Clemson finished second as a team.

May 30-June 2, 2001—The Tigers finished second in the NCAA Tournament at the Duke University Course in Durham, NC. D. J. Trahan finished seventh in the tournament, Lucas Glover finished 11th, and John Engler finished 16th.

June 3, 2001—Clemson seniors John Engler and Lucas Glover were both named first-team All-America by the Golf Coaches Association. Sophomore D. J. Trahan, Clemson's top performer at the NCAA Tournament over the weekend, was named an honorable mention All-America selection.

May 16-18, 2002—Clemson finished first at the NCAA Regional at Settindown Creek in Roswell, GA. D. J. Trahan finished first in this event.

May 29-June 1, 2002—Trahan finished eighth in leading the Tigers to a third-place finish in the NCAA Tournament at the Ohio State University Course in Columbus, OH.

June 3, 2002—Trahan won the Jack Nicklaus Award as the top player in college golf for the 2001-02 academic year. The award is presented by the Golf Coaches Association of America and is voted on by college coaches. Trahan was also named to the Association's Ping

All-America first team. Gregg Jones, a sophomore, earned second-team All-America honors.

June 14, 2002—Clemson golfers D. J. Trahan and Gregg Jones both ranked among the top 12 college players nationally, according to the final *Golfweek*/Sagarin player rankings. Trahan rated second in the nation by the computer rankings, while Jones finished 12th. The Clemson team ranked second in the nation in the final Sagarin poll. The Golf Coaches Association final ranking listed the Tigers third.

April 18-20, 2003—Clemson won the ACC Championships at the Old North St. Club in New London, NC. Jack Ferguson finished third in the event.

May 15-17, 2003—Clemson finished first at the NCAA Regional at Auburn University Course, in Auburn, AL.

May 27-30, 2003—Clemson won the National Championships at Karsten Creek Golf Course in Stillwater, OK. Jack Ferguson finished 19th to lead the Tigers. Trahan finished 22nd.

May 31, 2003—Coach Larry Penley won the Dave Williams Award as the National Coach of the Year, as selected by the Golf Coaches Association. Three of his players—D. J. Trahan, Jack Ferguson and Matt Hendrix—were named first-, second-, and third-team All-America players, respectively, by the same association. Penley led the Tigers to the school's only golf national championship in 2003.

June 2, 2003—Clemson was ranked first in the nation in the final *Golfweek*/Sagarin computer rankings. D. J. Trahan, Jack Ferguson, and Matt Hendrix were all ranked in the top 10 of the final individual rankings. It marked the first time Clemson had three of the top-10 players in the final computer rankings. Trahan finished second in the *Golfweek*/Sagarin computer ranking for the second straight year. Ferguson was ranked fifth in the nation, while Matt Hendrix was ninth.

April 16-18, 2004—Clemson won the ACC Championships at the Old North St. Club in New London, NC. Jack Ferguson finished second in this event.

May 20-22, 2004—Clemson finished first at the NCAA East Regional at the Yale University Course, in New Haven, CT.

June 1-4, 2004—Clemson finished 18th in the NCAA Tournament at the Cascades Course, in Hot Springs, VA.

June 7, 2004—Clemson golfers Matt Hendrix and Jack Ferguson were both named second-team All-America golfers by the Golf Coaches Association of America. It was the second consecutive year that both players were named to an All-America team. Ferguson was a second-team selection in 2003, and Hendrix was a third-team choice. The Tigers finished 18th in the final poll.

May 31-June 3, 2006—Clemson finished seventh as a team at the NCAA Tournament at the Crosswater Golf Club in Sunriver, OR. Brian Duncan was the Tigers' top finisher.

The 2003 Clemson Golf Team won the NCAA National Championship.

June 5, 2006—Clemson golfers Brian Duncan, Stephen Poole, and Vince Hatfield all ranked in the final top 50 of the *Golfweek*/Sagarin Computer rankings.

Brian Duncan was the highest-ranked Clemson player, at #27. Stephen Poole finished 42nd, and Vince Hatfield was ranked 46th.

As a team, Clemson finished seventh in the nation with a 71.13 rating, according to the *Golfweek*/Sagarin poll.

Clemson finished the year with the number-one schedule ranking in the nation (71.82). It marks the second time in four years Clemson had the top schedule ranking. Clemson also held that honor the year the Tigers won the National Championships.

June 12, 2006—Brian Duncan and Stephen Poole were both named honorable mention All-America golfers by the Golf Coaches Association. It was the first selection for both players.

June 6, 2007—Freshman Kyle Stanley was named a first-team Ping All-America by the College Golf Coaches Association. Stanley is the first freshman in Clemson history to be named a first-team All-America golfer.

May 28-31, 2008—Clemson finished fifth in the NCAA Tournament at the Birck Boilermaker Complex, in West Lafayette, IN. Kyle Stanley finished seventh in the tournament to lead the Tigers.

June 6, 2008—Sophomore Kyle Stanley was named honorable mention All-America by the Golf Coaches Association. Stanley led Clemson to a fifth-place finish at the NCAA Golf Championships last weekend. The Tigers finished fifth nationally as a team.

April 17-19, 2009—David May of Clemson tied for first place individual honors with Matt Hill of N.C State at the ACC Tournament that was played at the Old North

The Larry B. Penley Golf Building was completed in 2011.

St. Club in New London, NC. May shot 71-69-66 for a 206 total, 10 shots under par, in leading the Tigers to a second-place finish.

May 22, 2009—Clemson junior Kyle Stanley was awarded the 2009 Ben Hogan Award at Colonial Country Club in Dallas, TX. The honor is given each year to the top collegiate golfer.

June 22, 2009—Former Clemson All-American Lucas Glover won the 2009 United States Open on Monday at the par-70 Black Course at Bethpage Golf Club in Farmingdale, NY, with a final round 73 and 72-hole score of four-under-par 276. Glover finished two shots ahead of Phil Mickelson, David Duval, and Ricky Barnes to become the first former Clemson golfer to win a Major tournament.

The Tigers' young squad that started three freshmen at the NCAA Regional for just the fifth time in history finished with a team score of 19-over-par, 559.

Kennerly finished with a one-under-par 69 on Saturday after an opening round 68 and second round 69 for a 206 total. Combined with his final two rounds at the ACC Tournament, he finishes the year with five consecutive rounds in the 60s, a school record. Many players had scored in the 60s four consecutive rounds, including Corbin Mills last year, but never five in a row.

June 1-3, 2010—Clemson finished 16th at the NCAA Tournament at the Honors Course in Ooltewah, TN. Ben Martin finished ninth in the tournament.

June 10, 2010—Ben Martin was named an honorable mention All-America golfer by the Golf Coaches Association of America.

October 21, 2011—The Larry B. Penley Golf Building—a 7,700-square foot, three-story clubhouse, and home for the Clemson golf team—was dedicated.

June 20, 2012—Corbin Mills was named a third-team All-America honoree.

May 16-18, 2013—Sophomore Billy Kennerly established a significant school record, but the Clemson golf team failed to advance to the NCAA Championship Tournament after a tie for 12th place team finish at the NCAA Regional at Karsten Golf Club in Tempe, AZ.

April 25-27, 2014—Austin Langdale and Stephen Behr both shot rounds of three-under-par 69 to lead Clemson to a third-place finish at the ACC Men's Golf Championships at The Old North State Club in New London, NC

May 15-17, 2014—Clemson finished sixth in the 14-team NCAA regional field at Rich Harvest Farms Golf Club in Sugar Crove, IL. The Tigers did not advance to the National Championship Tournament.

May 14-16, 2015—Clemson finished fifth in the 13-team NCAA Regional at the Finley Golf Course at Chapel Hill, NC. With the fifth-place finish, Clemson advanced to the NCAA Championships. Austin Langdale was Clemson's top finisher, finishing seventh in the tournament.

May 29-31, 2015—Clemson finished 30th at the NCAA Golf Championships at the Concession Golf Club, in Bradenton, FL. Individually, Austin Landale was 59th for the Tigers.

April 20, 2016—Clemson golfer Stephen Behr was the recipient of the 2016 Byron Nelson Award. The announcement was made on the Golf Channel. The honor is presented each year to the graduating senior who excels not only on the course, but in the classroom and in the community. Behr is the first Clemson golfer to win the award, which dates to 2002.

April 22-24, 2016—Carson Young shot a four-under-par 68 on Sunday, and all five Clemson golfers finished in the top 16 for the first time in the history of the school's participation of the event, as Clemson won the ACC Men's Golf Championships at the Old North State Club in New London, NC Clemson finished with a team score of 25-under-par 839 for the 54 holes and three days, the third-best score vs. par in Clemson history at the league championship and the best since 2004, when Clemson shot 27-under in winning the event.

May 16-18, 2016—Graduates Miller Capps and Stephen Behr each shot under-par rounds to lead Clemson to a third-place finish out of 14 teams at the NCAA Regional Golf Tournament in Stillwater, OK. Clemson finished with a team score of 901 for the three-day 54-hole event and qualified for the NCAA National Tournament at Eugene Country Club in Eugene, OR. Behr finished eighth individually at the tournament.

May 27-29, 2016—Austin Langdale had a one-over-par 71 and classmate Carson Young had a two-over-par 72 on Sunday to lead Clemson to a five-way tie for 14th place at the NCAA Men's Golf Championships at Eugene Country Club in Eugene, OR. Clemson finished with a score of 27-over-par 867, tied with Louisville, Oklahoma, TCU, and Georgia.

June 23, 2016—Clemson graduate golfer Stephen Behr was named a second-team All-American by *Golfweek* and a third-team All-American by the Golf Coaches Association of America. Teammate Austin Langdale was named an honorable mention All-American by *Golfweek*.

John Thomas (J.T.) Horton was named the first women's golf coach at Clemson University. Larry Penley, director of golf, made the announcement on August 19, 2011.

Horton came to Clemson after four years (three seasons of competition) as the head coach at Tulane. He restarted the program after Hurricane Katrina halted it from the fall of 2005 until the fall of 2008.

"I would like to personally thank Dr. Terry Don Phillips, Kyle Young, and Coach Larry Penley for this amazing opportunity," said Horton upon accepting the position. "Very few times are coaches fortunate enough to coach at their dream job. Clemson University is my dream job, and I am honored to be a part of such an elite university and athletics program.

"Clemson Golf has a wonderful reputation in the golf community. I am so excited to work with Coach Penley, as he is easily one of the best and most well-respected coaches in the country. There is a great expectation with the golf program. I am looking forward to working extremely hard in putting together a successful women's program that the Clemson family will be proud of!"

In his three seasons at Tulane, Horton was the Conference USA Coach of the Year twice (2009 and 2010) and led the program to the NCAA National Tournament twice and the NCAA regional three times. Tulane won the Conference USA championship twice and won five tournament titles overall.

Clemson started competing in the 2013-14 season.

HESTER TAKES THE REINS

Kelley Hester joined Clemson as its women's golf head coach in 2016, after several years at Furman University and a total of 15 years of head coaching experience.

Director of Athletics Dan Radakovich praised Kelley's abilities to lead student athletes both on the course and in the classroom throughout her career.

From 2005-'08, Hester coached Stacy Lewis at the University of Arkansas, where Lewis was the 2005 SEC Freshman of the Year, 2007 National Champion, and 2008 SEC Championships Individual Medalist and Player of the Year. Lewis, who broke onto the LPGA Tour in 2009, has won 11 LPGA events, two of which were majors.

Hester was named the Southern Conference Coach of the Year in 2015 and 2016. Under her leadership, Furman produced the SoCon Player of the Year those two years as well and the SoCon Freshman of the Year for three years straight.

In 2016, Hester guided Furman to a 20th-place finish at the NCAA Championships after the team placed fourth at the NCAA Bryan Regional. Taylor Totland, whom Hester had recruited early in her Furman tenure, placed 20th among the nation's individuals in 2016 after qualifying for the NCAA Championships in 2015.

In 2015, five of Hester's student-athletes were honored on the All-SoCon Team, while three of her newcomers were named to the SoCon All-Freshman Team. Hester led Furman to consecutive second-place finishes at the SoCon Championships, before the team captured a first-place finish there in 2015.

Before joining Furman, Hester served as the head coach at the University of Georgia (also her alma mater) and Arkansas for five years each and one year at UNLV.

In her time at Georgia, Hester led the Bulldogs to five-straight NCAA Regional appearances and 10th and 15th place at the 2008 and 2009 NCAA Championships, respectively. In 2009, Hester was named the LPGA National Coach of the Year. Another highlight of her Georgia tenure, Hester also recruited, coached, and developed Marta Silva Zamora, who was named National Player of the Year in 2011.

Hester, a four-year letter winner and three-time All-Southeastern Conference selection during her time at Georgia (1993-'96), was a member of Georgia teams that placed fourth at the 1993 NCAAs and captured the 1993 and 1994 SEC Championships. She also tallied 21 top-20 finishes in 40 tournaments during her four-year career there.

WOMEN'S GOLF HISTORY

July 18, 2011—Clemson Athletic Director Terry Don Phillips announced that the school will add women's golf as a varsity sport beginning with the 2013-14 academic year.

Aug. 19, 2011—John Thomas (J.T.) Horton was named the first women's golf coach at Clemson University. Horton came to Clemson after four years (three seasons of competition) as the head coach at Tulane. He restarted the program after Hurricane Katrina halted it from the fall of 2005 until the fall of 2008.

Nov. 16, 2011—Clemson Head Coach J.T. Horton announced the signing of Lauren Salazar of Santa Clara, CA, and Taylor Ramsey of Milledgeville, GA, to national letters of intent. They are the first two signees for the Clemson's women's golf program.

July 15, 2012—Clemson's first women's golf schedule was announced. The schedule called for the Tigers to play

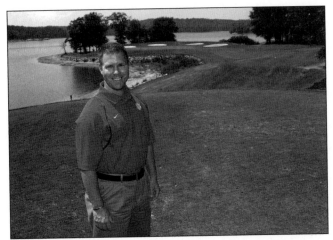

Horton arrived from Tulane as coach of the women's golf team.

nine tournaments against teams from traditional national golf powers. The inaugural season of Clemson women's golf will feature four tournaments in North Carolina, three in South Carolina, one in Louisiana, and one in Florida.

The first tournament in the history of Clemson women's golf was the College of Charleston Cougar Classic at Yeamans Hall Club in Charleston, SC, September 8-10.

August 8, 2013—Clemson freshman Ashlan Ramsey was ranked as the number-one women's amateur golfer in the world according to *Golfweek* rankings.

September 8-10, 2013—The Clemson women's golf team began its inaugural season at the 11th annual Cougar Classic at Yeamans Hall in Hanahan, SC. The three-day, 54-hole tournament included 20 teams.

Ashlan Ramsey and Sloan Shanahan tied for second with four-under-par scores of 212 to lead the Clemson women's golf team to a second-place finish at the 11th annual Cougar Classic.

Clemson finished just one shot behind champion Florida. The 20-team field included five teams that finished in the

top 25 at the NCAA National Tournament the previous season.

February 26, 2014—The Clemson women's golf team was ranked tenth in a poll released by GolfStat.com. It is the first time the inaugural team has been ranked in the top 10 by any poll.

March 13, 2014—Freshman golfer Ashlan Ramsey was named to the 2014 USA Curtis Cup Team. The eight-player team represented the USA in the 2014 Curtis Cup Match, held June 6-8 at St. Louis (MO) Country Club.

April 17-19, 2014—Lauren Salazar shot a final-round 74 to lead Clemson to a tie for ninth place team finish at the 2014 ACC Women's Golf Championships. The 11-team event was held at the par-71 Sedgefield Country Club in Greensboro, the home of the PGA Tour's Wyndham Championship.

It was Clemson's first appearance in the ACC Women's Golf Tournament, as the program is in its first season. Clemson, ranked 12th nationally by Golfstat and 14th by the Golf World Coaches Poll entering the event, was the only team in the field to play an all-freshman lineup on the historic Donald Ross-designed course that opened in 1926.

April 28, 2014—Clemson was selected to the NCAA Women's Golf Tournament and will compete at Tumble Creek at Suncadia Resort in Cle Elum, WA, May 8-10. The top eight schools after 54 holes of play will compete in the NCAA National Championships May 20-23 at Tulsa Country Club in Tulsa, OK.

May 6, 2014—Freshmen Ashlan Ramsey and Sloan Shanahan were both named to the All-ACC Women's Golf Team. The Clemson team is in its first season of varsity competition and will compete in the NCAA West Regional in Cle Elum, WA. starting on Thursday.

May 8-10, 2014—Clemson's all-freshman team failed to advance from the NCAA West Regional in Cle Elum, WA, as the Tigers finished 13th in the field of 24.

April 17-18, 2015—Clemson finished in a tie for eighth place at the ACC Tournament at the Sedgefield Country Club in Greensboro, NC. Marisa Messana finished 21st individually as the top Tiger.

September 13-15, 2015—Freshman Alice Hewson took comedalist honors to lead Clemson to a fifth-place finish out of 20 teams at the College of Charleston Cougar Classic at Yeamans Hall in Hanahan, SC. It was the season opening tournament for the Tigers.

September 14, 2015—Alice Hewson broke the Clemson single-round scoring record by three shots in the second round of the College of Charleston Cougar Classic at Yeamans Hall Golf Club in Charleston, SC. Hewson, playing in just her second round as a college golfer, fired a seven-under-par 65.

September 20-22, 2015—Alice Hewson won her second consecutive tournament to lead Clemson to a tie for fourth place out of 17 teams at the Lady Paladin Invitational at the Furman University Golf Course on Tuesday. Hewson finished with a score of 213, three-under-par on the par-72 course.

October 10-12, 2015—Lauren Stephenson captured co-medalist honors to lead Clemson to a second-place team finish at the Yale Women's Intercollegiate at the Course at Yale in New Haven, CT.

December 6, 2015—Ashlan Ramsey became the first former Clemson women's golfer to qualify for the LPGA Tour on Sunday during the fifth and final round of the LPGA Qualifying Tournament in Daytona Beach, FL. She will be fully exempt for the 2016 season.

April 1-3, 2016—Freshman Alice Hewson fired a two-under-par 70 and classmate Lauren Stephenson added an even-par 72 to lead Clemson to a fifth-place finish out of 14 teams at the first Clemson Invitational at The Reserve at Lake Keowee in Sunset, SC. Clemson fired a three-over-par 291 team score on the final day to improve from seventh to fifth over the final 18 holes. This was the first time that Clemson had played host to a tournament.

April 15-17, 2016—Lauren Stephenson shot an even-par 72 on the last day of the event, while Alice Hewson, Marisa Messana, and Sydney Legacy all finished tied for 19th for the 54-hole tournament, leading Clemson to a sixth-place finish at the 2016 ACC Women's Golf Tournament at Sedgefield Country Club in Greensboro, NC.

April 25, 2016—Clemson's women's golf team receives a bid to the NCAA Tournament. It is the second time the program has received a bid in its three years.

May 4, 2016—Alice Hewson was named first-team All-Conference and the ACC Freshman of the Year. She is the first Clemson women's golfer to be named ACC Freshman of the Year.

May 5-7, 2016—Clemson's women's golf team finished eighth out of 18 teams at the NCAA Shoal Creek Regional at Birmingham, AL. Freshman Lauren Stephenson qualified for the NCAA National Tournament as an individual during the competition. The Tigers needed a top-six finish as a team to advance to the NCAA National Tournament in Eugene, OR.

May 20-22, 2016—Clemson freshman Lauren Stephenson finished 58th after three rounds at the NCAA Women's Golf National Championships at Eugene Country Club in Eugene, OR, on Sunday. She did not make the cut for the fourth and final round of the individual championship. Stephenson had a three-over-par 75 on Sunday and finished with a three-day total of 221, five over par. She needed to shoot 218 to qualify for a playoff for the final spot in the fourth round and is the first Clemson women's golfer to qualify for the NCAA National Tournament.

July 1, 2016—Clemson parted ways with Head Coach J.T. Horton.

July 14, 2016—Following several successful years at Furman University, Kelley Hester joins Clemson as its women's golf head coach. Hester brings 15 years of head coaching experience to the Tiger program.

CLEMSON
Rowing

THE START OF THE PROGRAM

Clemson announced that women's rowing would be added as a varsity sport in 1997, with the first season taking place during the 1998-99 academic year.

Susie Lueck was named the first-ever women's rowing coach in the spring of 1998. On October 1, 1998, Lueck announced the members of Clemson's inaugural team.

The first-team consisted of 46 athletes from 15 states. Twenty student-athletes from South Carolina were on the team. The Clemson oars were also unveiled. The white oars contain an orange Tiger Paw logo on the blade.

Clemson competed in the Head of the Chattahoochee Regatta in Gainesville, GA. The competition was Clemson's first as a varsity team.

LUCY DOOLITTLE AND AIMEE FOX WERE CLEMSON'S FIRST ALL-AMERICANS

Lucy Doolittle was named Clemson's first All-American in rowing in 2001. Doolittle earned three CRCA All-South Region honors, becoming the Tigers' first-ever selection in 2000. She was the first Tiger rower to be inducted into the Clemson Athletic Hall of Fame in 2008.

Aimee Fox was named first-team All-American for the first time in 2002. She also earned two consecutive CRCA All-South Region honors. She was selected twice to the All-ACC team and was a member of the ACC Crew of the Year in 2001.

Clemson's Varsity 8+ was named 2001 ACC Crew of the Year. This boat consisted of Gail Cardorniga (coxswain), Aimee Fox, Katherine Sloan, Farrell Finstad,

Lauren Henne, Megan McGuirt, Lucy Doolittle, Kathy Sickinger, and Lisa Mischley.

Also that season, the Varsity 4+ won the ACC Championships. That boat consisted of Kathryn Barton, Jaimee Kamnik, Nicollette Burgess, Christina Lindsey, and Lisa Christopher (Coxswain). This was Clemson's first-ever ACC Championship boat.

The 2005 Novice 8+ also won the ACC Championships. Members of that boat were Ford Heiner, Sara Kolozaike, Kathryn Clayton, Krista Gregan, Tami Mayer, Emily Lynch, Lindsay Sheppard, Kathryn Wait, and Abbey Fernandez (Coxswain).

SARAH COOPER EARNS VARIOUS HONORS

Sarah Cooper rowed at Clemson in 2004-07. She was named All-American twice, a first-team selection as a junior and second-team choice in 2007 as a senior.

She was also a two-time All-Region performer. Cooper was a three-time All-ACC rower and was the program's first three-time honoree.

RICHARD RUGGIERI LEADS CLEMSON TO NEW HEIGHTS

Richard Ruggieri was the head coach at Clemson from 2007-'10. Under his guidance, the program reached new levels. During his years at Clemson, the Tigers went to the NCAA Tournament and won the ACC Championships.

He was named ACC Coach of the Year in 2009 and was the CRCA South Region Coach of the Year in 2008 and 2009.

FIRST NCAA CHAMPIONSHIPS APPEARANCE FOR THE TIGERS

Clemson went to the NCAA Championships for the first time in 2008. The Varsity 8+ participated for the first time in school history on May 30-June 1, 2008, in Gold River, CA.

Suzanne Van Fleet helped lead the Varsity 8+ crew to the NCAA Rowing Championships that season. She was named first-team All-American by the CRCA. She was also named to the All-ACC team and was a first-team All-Region her senior season. Van Fleet was a team captain for the 2007-08 season and was named Clemson's Rower of the Year as a senior. She was named to the All-ACC Academic Team and was named a National Scholar Athlete three times for her outstanding academic performance during her career.

Clemson's Novice 8+ won the ACC Championship in 2008 at Clemson, SC. The boat consisted of Brittany Robertson, Sarah Daanen, Nicole Bowen, Grace Wolff, Emily Forney, Kelsey Hudome, Corey Geer, Leah Kelly, and Victoria Graham (coxswain).

CLEMSON WINS ACC CHAMPIONSHIP, GOES TO NCAAS WITH FULL SQUAD

Jessica Leidecker was a rower at Clemson in 2006-09. She was a two-time All-America rower. As a junior in 2008, she was named to the second-team and garnered first-team All-America honors as a senior. She was also a first-team All-Region selection twice and a two-time All-ACC honoree.

As a junior, Leidecker was a member of the Varsity 8+ crew that advanced to the NCAA Rowing Champion-

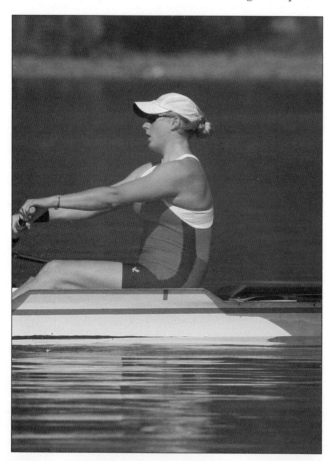

Jessica Leidecker was a member of the Varsity 8+ that was named ACC Crew of the Year.

The 2009 Rowing Team won the ACC Championship.

ships for the first time in school history and earned many accomplishments throughout the season. She helped lead the Varsity 8+ to an ACC Championships and ACC Crew of the Year as a senior. Leidecker was also a member of Clemson's only ACC Championships team in program history.

Later the same year, Clemson advanced to the NCAA Rowing Championships for the first time as a team and finished 12th overall at the regatta in Cherry Hill, NJ. The Varsity 8+ crew finished the season ranked 12th in the US Rowing/CRCA poll. The 12th-place finish is the highest final ranking to date.

Leidecker competed in the U23 World Rowing Championships during her Clemson career. She finished in fourth place with the women's 4- in 2008 and earned a silver medal with the women's 8+ in 2009. She is now an assistant coach for the Tigers.

Members of the 2009 ACC Championships Varsity 8+ boat included Cumbest, Cummings, Wolff, Kozuszek, Nance, Robb, Bendik, Leidecker, and Englund (coxswain).

LEIDECKER WAS KEY IN CLEMSON'S SUCCESS

"Clemson was not on my radar when I first started looking at schools," said Jessica Leidecker.

"I remember Assistant Coach Ferrell Finstad contacted me and I decided to visit Clemson. They rolled out the red carpet for me. We went to a football game and I loved the school spirit. I wanted to go to a school that felt like home to me. I also wanted to go to a school with a small college town atmosphere. Another criterion I wanted was I wanted to go where the team was not already in the top 10. I wanted to join a team that I felt like I could help contribute to the speed. I wanted to be part of a team that would go to the NCAA Championships for the first time and win the conference for the first time. Clemson had my major and everything felt so right."

During her career, Clemson accomplished both of her goals during her junior and senior seasons.

"Winning the ACCs for the first time was awesome. We had confidence that we had the speed. We felt we could race with anyone. I remembered Virginia was ahead at the beginning. We walked back through them and got to open water. About 750 meters to go, we felt that we were going to win—it was a cool feeling—something you can't really describe. There is a bond between all nine of us in that boat. During my junior and senior seasons, we kept improving and gaining speed. We became closer and closer—we had confidence that we were fast. To this day, all nine of us keep in contact with one another. That's a great thing about sports; you develop relationships and build friendships that last a lifetime."

VARSITY 4+ CREW WINS NATIONAL CHAMPIONSHIP

Clemson's Varsity 4+ crew won the National Championships on May 29-31, 2009. The National Champions included Kelly Murphy, Lydia Hassell, Callen Erdeky, Allison Colberg, and Meredith Razzolini (coxswain).

This was the first National Championships won by a Clemson boat. As a team, Clemson finished 12th at the NCAA meet with 43 points.

That season, the Varsity 4+ raced in 21 races and finished first 16 times.

ROBBIE TENENBAUM LEADS PROGRAM

Robbie Tenenbaum became head coach in 2010. During his tenure, he coached the ACC's Crew of the Year in 2011. The Varsity 4+ crew won the ACC Championships in 2012. That crew included McKenzie DuBrul, Rebekah Clogston, Katie Mosier, Taylor Hoynacki, and Carissa Richardson (coxswain). He also coached Clemson to a 15th-place finish at the NCAA Championships in 2011.

"I am real happy with our progress so far and the strides we have made in our program," said Tenenbaum.

"I tell our student-athletes that they are here rowing for the greatest program in the country. I know our bow ball is not ahead of everybody else's in every race. However, 'greatest' is defined by more that just the outcome of an individual race.

"Our kids possess great attitudes, and incredible work ethics, and they are incredible to be around. We are trying to make the program faster and we are taking the necessary steps to be one of the best programs in the country as far as success on the water.

Robbie Tenenbaum coached the ACC's Crew of the Year in 2011.

"The kids are what make our program great," said Tenebaum. "Their unwavering desire to be better every day is tremendous. They know what it takes to make the team faster on the water and they are working hard in helping the team become faster. Our program is very unselfish and mature. The concept of team is very evident in our program. My philosophies on being successful are very simple. First work hard, give 100 percent of yourself all of the time, and be open to change and be willing to do things differently that will help make the program faster.

"We have made it our culture here to strive to be our best. The better we do as a program, the better our recruiting. We have a great school here at Clemson and with the outstanding academics that also helps us in recruiting. We have things at Clemson that will help us become very successful for years to come," said Tenenbaum.

WOMEN'S ROWING HISTORY

July 11, 1997—Clemson officials announced that women's rowing will be added as a varsity sport. Although a new sport to Clemson, collegiate rowing has existed for almost 150 years. Rowing was the first intercollegiate sport in the United States, with the first regatta occurring between Harvard and Yale in 1852.

April 28, 1998—Susie Lueck was named Clemson's first head coach for women's rowing.

October 1, 1998—The members of Clemson's inaugural team was announced by coach Susie Lueck at a press conference, consisting of 46 athletes from 15 states. Twenty athletes from South Carolina were on the team. The Clemson oars were also unveiled at the press conference. The white oars contain an orange Tiger Paw logo on the blade.

November 9, 1998—The Clemson rowing team competed in the Head of the Chattahoochee Regatta in Gainesville, GA. The competition was Clemson's first as a varsity team.

March 13, 1999—Clemson Rowing coach Susie Lueck led the dedication and a ceremonial ribbon cutting at the school's new boathouse at the East Bank on the shores of Lake Hartwell. The day's festivities began with the dedication of the Tigers' six new rowing boats. The rowing team captains, Lauren Henne and Meridith Brand, were announced on this day. The event ended with competition among the classes of the Clemson rowing team.

March 27, 1999—Clemson played host to the Clemson Sprints on Lake Hartwell. Over 20 teams participated in this event. This was the Tigers' first-ever home meet.

April 29, 2000—Clemson finished second in the first-ever ACC Championships. The event took place on Lake Monticello, in Charlottesville, VA. Katherine Sloan was the first Tiger ever to be named All-ACC.

April 11, 2001—The Clemson rowing team was ranked 15th, according to the US Rowing/CRCA NCAA Women's Rowing poll. This was the first time the Tigers had been ranked.

April 28, 2001—Clemson coach Susie Lueck was named ACC Coach of the Year at the ACC Championships at Lake Hartwell. Clemson finished second in the meet. The Tigers' varsity 4+ won the ACC Championships.

May 21, 2001—Four Clemson rowers were named to the All-South Region team. Lucy Doolittle, Aimee Fox, Gail Cadorniga, and Lauren Henne claimed All-Region honors for the Tigers.

May 24, 2001—Clemson rowing head coach Susie Lueck was named the South Region Coach of the Year, as announced by the Collegiate Rowing Coaches Association.

June 13, 2001—Clemson rower Lucy Doolittle was named to the Collegiate Rowing Coaches Association Division I All-America first team. Doolittle, a junior from Mauldin, SC, is Clemson's first All-America rower.

May 22, 2002—The Clemson rowing team completed the season ranked 22nd, according to the 2002 US Rowing/CRCA NCAA Women's Rowing poll.

June 11, 2002—Four members of the Clemson rowing team were named to the Collegiate Rowing Coaches Association All-South Region teams. Lucy Doolittle, Aimee Fox, and Emily Kuivila earned first-team honors, while Sally Kukla was named a member of the second team.

July 31, 2002—The Collegiate Rowing Coaches Association (CRCA) announced the fourth annual All-America first and second teams. Clemson rowing's Aimee Fox and Lucy Doolittle were named to the first and second teams, respectively.

May 28, 2003—Two Tigers were named to the CRCA All-Region rowing team. Senior Emily Kuivila was named first-team All-South, while sophomore teammate Mary Nell Green received second-team All-South honors.

April 17, 2004—Juniors Mary Nell Green and Robin Mescher were named to the All-ACC team. The nine-member team is made up of eight rowers and one coxswain from all four ACC schools. This is the first time they have received this honor.

May 24, 2004—Clemson rowing is well represented in the sixth annual All-Region and National Scholar Athlete awards, announced by the Collegiate Rowing Coaches Association on Monday. Green was selected to the first-team All-South Region as well as National Scholar-Athlete, after compiling a 3.87 GPA in psychology.

April 23, 2005—Clemson finished second overall at the 2005 ACC Rowing Championships held on Lake Hartwell. Clemson claimed the third race of the morning, the Novice 8+.

The Tigers won the Novice 8+ race. Clemson finished second in all other events. The Tigers' Novice 8+ consisted of Abbey Fernandez (coxswain), Sierra Wait, Lindsey Sheppard, Emily Lynch, Tami Mayer, Krista Gregan, Kathryn Clayton, Sara Kolodzaike, and Ford Heiner. Clemson's Novice 8+ is the second crew to earn an ACC Championships for the school.

Ashlee Brown, Sarah Cooper, and Liz Averyt were named All-ACC. Susie Lueck was named ACC Coach of the Year. It marked the second time during her time at Clemson that she has won the award, as she also won it in 2001.

May 20, 2005—The Collegiate Rowing Coaches Association announced that Ashlee Brown was named first-team All-South and Elizabeth Giannini was named second-team All-South.

June 2, 2005—Clemson rower Ashlee Brown was named a second-team All-America rower by the Collegiate Rowing Coaches Association.

June 29, 2005—Clemson rower Ashlee Brown was announced as one of 58 student-athletes to receive an NCAA postgraduate scholarship on Tuesday. The honor is the latest in a long line of accolades this spring for the senior Varsity 8+ rower.

May 22, 2006—Clemson junior Sarah Cooper was named a 2006 All-Region selection by the Collegiate Rowing Coaches Association.

May 31, 2006—Clemson rower Sarah Cooper was named a CRCA All-America rower. Cooper, a native of Westminster, SC, became the fourth CRCA All-America rower in school history.

April 6, 2007—The contract of Clemson women's rowing coach Susie Lueck was terminated. The announcement was made by Athletic Director Dr. Terry Don Phillips. Assistant coach Shaw Tilton assumed the duties of the head coach for the remainder of the season. Lueck had been the coach of the Clemson rowing team since its inaugural season in 1998-99, after serving at Gonzaga in the same capacity for six years.

May 22, 2007—Clemson's Sarah Cooper was named to the Collegiate Rowing Coaches Association All-South Region team for the second-straight season.

June 11, 2007—The Collegiate Rowing Coaches Association released its list of the All-America teams. Clemson senior Sarah Cooper was named second-team All-America, the second consecutive year she was honored by the coaches' organization as an All-America rower. The decorated rower was a first-team All-America pick in 2006.

June 29, 2007—Richard Ruggieri, who had spent the previous seven seasons at the University of Louisville, was named head coach for the Clemson rowing program on June 29. He became just the second head coach in the history of the program, which began during the 1998-99 academic year at Clemson.

April 19, 2008—Clemson finished runner-up at the ninth annual ACC Rowing Championships at Lake Hartwell. The Tigers' Novice 8+ crew came in first in their race, while Clemson finished as the runner-up in each of the other three races. Clemson's Novice 8+ crew consisted of Victoria Graham (coxswain), Corey Geer, Leah Kelly, Kelsey Hudome, Emily Forney, Grace Wolff, Nicole Bowen, Sarah Daanen, and Mitchel Robertson.

Suzanne Van Fleet was named All-ACC for the second consecutive year. Liz Robb and Jessica Leidecker joined her on the All-Conference team. The three Clemson rowers named to the All-ACC team tied the school record for most Tiger rowers honored in a single season. In addition to being named to the All-ACC team, Robb was also named the ACC's Freshman of the Year. This is the first time a Clemson rower has received this honor.

May 20, 2008—For the first time in school history, Clemson was chosen to participate in the NCAA Rowing Championships. After an excellent performance in the Aramark South/Central Sprints, the Varsity 8+ crew was selected for the championship. The crew consisted of Elyse Roenick (coxswain), Jessica Leidecker, Suzanne Van Fleet, Brittany Cummings, Megan Bendik, Liz Robb, Hilary Cumbest, Ford Heiner, and Michelle Nance. The championship was held May 30-June 1 at Sacramento State Aquatic Center in Gold River, CA.

June 4, 2008—Jessica Leidecker and Suzanne Van Fleet were named to the first team, while Megan Bendik, Liz Robb, and Elyse Roenick (coxswain) were second-team selections on the Collegiate Rowing Coaches Association All-South team.

June 10, 2008—The Collegiate Rowing Coaches Association announced that Clemson rowers Suzanne Van Fleet and Jessica Leidecker have been named to the Division I All-America Team. Van Fleet was named to the first team, while Leidecker was a second-team selection. This award recognizes outstanding performances of individual rowers and coxswains at NCAA Division I institutions.

June 20, 2008—The Clemson rowing team was ranked fourteenth in the final US Rowing/Collegiate Rowing Coaches Association NCAA Division I Varsity Eight Coaches Poll. The Tigers Varsity 8+ had one of the most successful seasons on record, competing in the NCAA Rowing Championship for the first time in school history. This marks the highest final ranking in program history.

April 20, 2009—Clemson claimed its first-ever Atlantic Coast Conference Rowing Championships on Lake Melton in Oak Ridge, TN. The Tigers were led by their Varsity 4+ and Varsity 8+ crews and finished with 55 points to capture the conference title.

The 2009 Clemson Varsity 8+ won the ACC Championship and was named ACC Crew of the Year.

Virginia, winners of the previous nine ACC championships, finished just one point behind the Tigers, with 54 total points. Miami placed third with 34 points, followed by Boston College with 23, Duke with 21, and North Carolina with 19.

In addition, Clemson's Varsity 8+ was named the ACC Crew of the Year. The winning crew was composed of Carla Englund (coxswain), Jessica Leidecker, Meg Bendik, Liz Robb, Michelle Nance, Stefanie Kozuszek, Grace Wolff, Brittany Cummings, and Hilary Cumbest.

Clemson's 14th-ranked Varsity 8+ finished first ahead of No. 11 Virginia with a time of 6:38.40, marking the first time in the history of the conference championship that Virginia did not win the Varsity 8+ race. The Tigers' victory was also just the fifth time a non-Virginia crew won an event at the championship regatta. Virginia finished with a time of 6:47.92, followed by Miami, Boston College, Duke, and North Carolina.

Clemson's Varsity 4+ team consisted of Meredith Razzolini (coxswain), Lydia Hassell, Brittany Robinson, Caitlin O'Neill, and Callen Erdeky.

Jessica Leidecker, Carla Englund, Hilary Cumbest, Brittany Cummings, and Michelle Nance were all named All-ACC.

April 24, 2009—After leading Clemson to its first ACC Rowing Championship in school history, Richard Ruggieri was named the ACC Coach of the Year. Ruggieri, in his second year at Clemson, led the Tigers to a variety of accomplishments during his tenure.

May 24, 2009—Jessica Leidecker, Brittany Cummings, Hilary Cumbest, and Stefanie Kozuszek were named to the Collegiate Rowing Coaches Association All-South team. Leidecker and Cummings were named to the first team, while Hilary Cumbest and Stefanie Kozuszek were second-team selections.

May 31, 2009—The Varsity 4+ captured Clemson's first-ever national championship in rowing at the NCAA Rowing Championships in Cherry Hill, NJ.

The Tigers' Varsity 4+ captured the Grand Final by 1.76 seconds over Wisconsin to earn 16 team points. Clemson led by more than two seconds at both the halfway mark and the 1,500-meter mark before holding off the Badgers down the stretch. The winning time for the Tigers was 7:26.78, while Wisconsin crossed the finish line in 7:28.54. Yale (7:30.81), California (7:32.01), Stanford (7:32.29), and Virginia (7:34.26) finished in third through sixth place to complete the championship field.

The Tiger's winning crew consisted of Kelly Murphy, Lydia Hassell, Callen Erdeky, Allison Colberg, and coxswain Meredith Razzolini.

The Varsity 8+ reached the petite finals of the national championship and finished in 12th place, which marks the best finish in Clemson history. The Varsity 8+ also earned a variety of honors from the ACC, most notably being named the ACC Crew of the Year after winning the conference championship. The crew was also named the ACC Crew of the Week twice for its outstanding performances throughout the season.

June 5, 2009—Clemson rowers Hilary Cumbest, Brittany Cummings, and Jessica Leidecker were all named to the Collegiate Rowing Coaches Association All-America Team. Leidecker was named to the first team, while Cumbest and Cummings were second-team selections.

All three rowers were members of the Varsity 8+ boat. The crew finished the season ranked 12th in the nation and competed in the NCAA Championship for just the second time in school history.

May 30, 2010—The Clemson rowing team finished its 2009-10 season with a 15th-place finish as a team at the NCAA Rowing Championships on Lake Natoma in Sacramento, CA.

The Tigers finished with 21 points to finish in 15th place as a team, just one point behind 14th-place Ohio State.

June 4, 2010—Richard Ruggieri, Clemson's Rowing Coach for three seasons, resigned effective immediately as announced by Clemson University Director of Athletics, Dr. Terry Don Phillips.

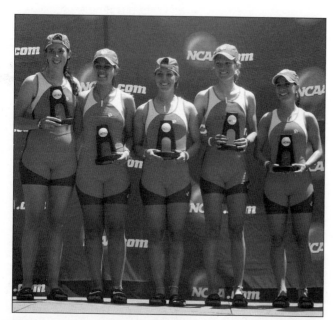

NCAA Varsity 4+ Champions (left to right): Kelly Murphy, Lydia Hassell, Callen Erdeky, Allison Colberg, Meredith Razzolini (cox.)

June 4, 2010—Robbie Tenenbaum, an assistant rowing coach at Clemson, named Interim Head Rowing Coach for the Tigers.

Tenenbaum has just completed his first complete season with the Tigers. He came to Clemson from Coral Gables, FL where he served for two years as the Head Women's Rowing Coach at the University of Miami. Prior to his stint at Miami, he was an assistant coach at the University of Washington for the 2006-07 season, where he helped lead the Washington Huskies to a top-10 finish at the NCAA Championships.

Ruggieri had led Clemson to an ACC Championship and three top 20 finishes since he took over the coaching duties in 2008.

June 10, 2010—Brittany Cummings was named first-team All-America by the Collegiate Rowing Coaches Association.

April 23, 2011—The 14th-ranked Clemson women's rowing team posted a second-place overall finish at the ACC Championships on Lake Hartwell. Clemson's First Varsity 8+ was named ACC Crew of the Year at the conclusion of the Championship. Their impressive finishes throughout the year and victories over multiple top-20 teams helped them win the award. The crew was comprised of Laura D'Urso, Laura Basadonna, Becca Brown, Liz Robb, Sarah Daanen, Heather Cummings, Grace Wolff, Stephanie Cameron, and coxswain Katie Bruggeling. Liz Robb, Laura D'Urso, and Laura Basadonna were named first-team All-ACC.

May 29, 2011—The Clemson women's rowing team completed the final day of the NCAA Championships on Sunday with a 15th place team finish. The Tigers are one of only 13 schools nationally to finish in the Final 16 of the NCAA Rowing Championships in each of the last three years.

June 8, 2011—Clemson freshman Laura D'Urso was named to the 2011 CRCA All-America second-team. The native of Dunross, Culdaff, Ireland was a member of Clemson's Varsity 8+, the 2011 ACC Crew of the Year. D'Urso was also named to the All-South District first-team and was an All-ACC recipient at the 2011 ACC Championships.

April 21, 2012—The Clemson rowing team hosted the 13th Annual ACC Rowing Championships on Lake Hartwell on Saturday morning. The Tigers finished second in team points behind Virginia, who captured its third-straight, and 12th overall, conference crown.

In the first official race of the day, Clemson's Varsity 4+ won the Tigers' first Varsity 4+ title since 2009. The crew of Carissa Richardson (coxswain), Taylor Hoynacki, Katie Mosier, Rebekah Clogston, and Kenzie DuBrul posted a time of 7:37.9 to defeat second-place Duke (7:46.6) and third-place Virginia (7:47.1). The Tigers' victory marked

only the fifth time Virginia has lost an event in the 13-year history of the ACC Championships.

May 22, 2012—Clemson, SC: Five Clemson rowers were named to the South All-Region Teams, announced by the CRCA on Tuesday. Junior Laura D'Urso was named to the South All-Region first team, while senior Kate Biladeau, freshman Giulia Longatti, and junior coxswain Katie Bruggeling were named to the South All-Region second-team.

June 6, 2012—The Clemson rowing team finished 20th in the final Collegiate Rowing Coaches Association/US Rowing Coaches Poll that was announced by the organization. This was the fourth-straight season that the Tigers have finished in the top 20 in the final national poll.

Heather Cummings was also named a second-team All-America honoree.

May 12, 2013—The 16th-ranked Clemson women's rowing team finished second with 43 points at the ACC Championships on Lake Hartwell on Sunday. The Tigers also had three rowers named to the All-ACC team announced by the conference on Sunday: Caroline Hackler, Milena Heuer, and Giulia Longatti.

May 28, 2013—Two Tigers were named All-South Region by the College Rowing Coaches Association. Junior Laura Basadonna was named first-team All-South Region, while senior Heather Cummings earned second-team honors.

June 8, 2013—The Clemson women's rowing team finished the 2013 season ranked 18th in the final College Rowing Coaches Association Coaches Poll. The Tigers were ranked in every poll this season.

The Tigers' final ranking of 18 is the highest final ranking for Clemson since 2011, when they finished the season with a final ranking of 13. Clemson has been ranked in the top 20 in the final poll every season since the CRCA began ranking teams in 2010.

June 11, 2013—Clemson junior Laura Basadonna named a second-team Pocock All-American by the College Rowing Coaches Association. The Torino, Italy, native becomes the 11th CRCA All-American in school history.

The Clemson women's rowing team battled stiff competition in the finals of the ACC Championships to finish fourth overall on Saturday on Lake Hartwell. The Tigers recorded 48 points on the day after finishing fourth in three of four races.

May 16-17, 2014—Following the championship, Samantha Duggan was named first-team All-ACC while Paula Wesselmann was named second-team All-ACC. It was the first time earning All-ACC honors for both.

May 28, 2014—Two Tigers earned All-South Region honors while 11 were named a National Scholar-Athlete by the College Rowing Coaches Association. Clemson's

11 National Scholar-Athletes is tied for the second most in the country.

Sophomore Milena Heuer was named first-team All-South Region with sophomore Paula Wesselmann receiving second-team honors. Both were named All-South Region for the time in their respective careers.

May 28, 2014—Robbie Tenenbaum, Clemson's head rowing coach the last four seasons, will not return for the 2014-15 season, Director of Athletics Dan Radakovich announced Wednesday. Tenenbaum's contract expired June 30, 2014.

June 9, 2014—Sophomore rower Milena Heuer was named a second-team Pocock All-American by the College Rowing Coaches Association. The native of Leer, Germany, is the 12th CRCA All-American in school history.

Heuer is the first freshman or sophomore to earn an All-America honor since 2011, when teammate Laura D'Urso was a second-team All-American as a freshman. The honor comes two weeks after Heuer was named first-team All-South Region, the first such selection of her career. Heuer spent all of 2014 in the First Varsity 8+ after spending the final three regattas of 2013 with that crew.

July 8, 2014—Stephen Frazier Wong was named head coach of the Clemson rowing program.

May 15-16, 2015—The Tigers finished in fifth place at the 2015 ACC Rowing Championships on Saturday at Lake Hartwell. Virginia won the ACC crown for the sixth consecutive year, followed by Notre Dame, Syracuse, and Louisville. Samantha Duggan and Milena Heuer were honored as All-ACC selections following the event. Duggan, a senior, was a first-team performer, her second straight season being honored by the conference. Heuer, a junior, was a second-team choice, giving her a second career all-conference accolade.

May 28, 2015—Seven student-athletes from Clemson were named National Scholar-Athletes by the College Rowing Coaches Association, while Samantha Duggan and Milena Heuer earned All-Region honors, as well. Duggan was named to the first team, while Heuer was named to the second team.

May 13-14, 2016—The Clemson rowing program finished sixth at the ACC Championships on Saturday. Virginia (99 points) won the team title for the 16th time and was followed by Duke and Syracuse in a tie for second place (75). The Second Varsity 4+ posted the top finish of the championships in fourth place. Paula Wesselmann, stroke seat of Clemson's First Varsity 8+, earned second-team All-ACC recognition.

MEN'S
Soccer

EARLY BEGINNINGS IN THE 1930s

Fred Kirchner started the men's soccer program at Clemson in 1934 and coached the team until 1939.

Clemson and Furman played in the very first soccer match in the state of South Carolina on February 14, 1934.

Kirchner graduated from Clemson in 1931 and was the intramural director at Clemson for several years. He had a 9-5-4 record overall, including a 5-1-2 mark in matches played at Clemson.

His brother, Alfred Kirchner, was a goalkeeper on the 1936, 1937, 1938, and 1939 teams.

Coach Fred Kirchner and Alfred Kirchner were brothers from Greenville, SC, who both served in World War II. Alfred later was the principal at Blue Ridge High School and Berea High School in the Greenville, SC, area. After World War II, Fred became a professor at Appalachian State.

EARLY PLAYER LAVERN PYLES LOOKS BACK ON THE EARLY YEARS OF SOCCER

According to LaVern Pyles, the four years he spent at Clemson changed him forever.

When Pyles decided to enroll at Clemson, the country was still in the midst of the Great Depression, and he decided he needed more education after spending some time in the work force.

"We were in the Great Depression. I graduated from high school in 1937 and went to work for AT&T's Western Division for two years. The company was unable to make it and they started laying people off and then I got the word that I was laid off in the summer of 1939. I was in Washington, DC, and I met a friend that went to Clemson. We were working together and he told me all about Clemson. His name was Frank Dellastatious. The more he talked about Clemson, I knew it was the place for me. The discipline and the regimentation sounded just like what I needed in my stage of life. I decided I needed higher education and I applied to Clemson in July of 1939. I was accepted to Clemson in August.

"I met another young man that was going to Clemson and his name was Charlie Carter. I remember in early September heading to Clemson for the first time with Charlie in my 1931 Ford Model A convertible coupe. It took us two days to get there. When I got there, they had very few parking spaces. Freshmen were not allowed to have cars, I found out after I arrived that freshmen were not allowed to have cars, so I got a few demerits with that honest mistake. The upperclassmen in my Company H2 let me keep the car, and we would go to away football games in my car. I lived in what we called 'Barn One'; it was located behind Barracks number two.

"At that time we had 2300 students and 776 freshmen. We had compulsory chapel. I remember Dr. Sikes welcoming us, and I remember him saying, 'Gentlemen four years from now only 50 percent of you will still be here.' He and all of us knew there was a war brewing and also the Great Depression was still in effect for many families. In 1939, the cost was $450 for an out-of-state student; $50 of that went to buy the cadet uniform. I was a waiter in the dining room, and I was responsible for three tables, eight people per table, 24 in all. I got paid around 71 cents per day.

When Pyles got to Clemson, he soon became interested in extracurricular activities, including the pursuit of university athletics.

"I went out for football and I got the uniform, the canvas pants, and the leather helmet, and I practiced with the freshman team. After a few days of this, I finally told the coach that it was too much and I needed to concentrate on my education. I did participate in intramurals for my company team.

"Later on in the semester, I went out for soccer after Dellastatious talked me into it, and I enjoyed it—it was fun. We played and practiced on Bowman Field. We wore our own shorts and shoes. Very few had soccer shoes that should have been worn for soccer. Our coach, Fred Kirchner, was a nice man. He was busy doing a lot of things at Clemson. He worked for the YMCA and he was in charge of the movie house."

Pyles had a very successful military, business, and political career. His desire to live life to the fullest and his interest to help others also made him a successful citizen.

With the arrival of World War II, the soccer program was disbanded, and it wasn't until 1967 that Clemson fielded another men's soccer team under the guidance of Dr. I.M. Ibrahim.

DR. I.M. IBRAHIM COACHED CLEMSON TO TWO NATIONAL CHAMPIONSHIPS

Ibrahim coached Clemson to the NCAA Soccer Championships in 1984 and 1987 and took Clemson to the NCAA Tournament in 17 of his 28 seasons. He led the program to the Final Four of college soccer six times and won 11 ACC Championships, tied for the most league titles by any coach in Clemson sports history.

Born in Haifa, Israel, he entered the United States in 1960 and attended Shorter College in Rome, GA. In his last two years at Shorter, he played and served as the coach of the soccer program. Upon his graduation from Shorter in 1964, he moved to Clemson, where he earned his MS and PhD in chemistry.

In 1967, he approached then-Assistant Athletic Director Bill McLellan about starting a varsity soccer program. McLellan thought the idea was sound and asked Athletic Director Frank Howard to start the program with Ibrahim as head coach.

Ibraham had Clemson in the national top 20 by his sixth year, and the Tigers won the ACC Championships in 1972 with a 13-1-1 record. By 1975, just the ninth year in the program's history, he had Clemson ranked at the top of the national polls. He would bring Clemson to a number-one national ranking at some point in nine different seasons in his Clemson career.

Between 1972 and 1979, Clemson won eight consecutive ACC Championships, the longest run of ACC titles in any sport in Clemson history. During that time, Clemson did not lose a single league match and posted a 38-0-2 record.

Ibrahim finished his career with an overall record of 388-102-31 for his 28 years, for a .774 winning percentage. He had a 32-16 record in NCAA Tournament competition, and the .667 winning percentage is among the top-10 winning percentages in NCAA soccer history.

His 388 wins rank second in ACC men's soccer history, and his .774 winning percentage is also second. He took Clemson to a final top-20 national ranking 19 seasons, a record that stood among all Clemson coaches until 2007, when Larry Penley took the Clemson golf program to a 20th top-20 finish at the NCAA Tournament.

Ibrahim was a master recruiter who coached nine Clemson soccer players who were named to the ACC's 50-year Anniversary men's soccer team in 2002. Eleven times one of his players was named the ACC Player of the Year, and he coached 16 different players who earned All-America honors by the National Soccer Coaches Association.

While he had many outstanding seasons, his two national championship campaigns stand out. His 1984 team posted a 22-4 record, but it had a difficult path to win the title. Along the way, Clemson had to defeat the top four seeds in the tournament, including a victory over two-time defending champion and number-one ranked Indiana in the championship match. Clemson downed the Hoosiers 2-1 in the Kingdome in Seattle, WA, in a match televised nationally on ESPN. It marked the first time in any NCAA Tournament that a team had beaten the top four seeds in the field to win the championship.

In 1987, the Tigers were seeded 23rd but made a miraculous run with victories on the road against 14th-ranked Evansville, top-ranked Indiana, and sixth-ranked Rutgers to reach the Final Four.

Clemson was rewarded for its exceptional play by playing host to the Final Four that year at Historic Riggs Field. The Tigers won the semifinals over eighth-ranked North Carolina and the championship over 20th-ranked San Diego State. Clemson defeated San Diego State by a 2-0 score at Riggs Field, the only time Clemson has won a national championship in any sport on its campus.

"The most memorable game to me was the 1984 national championship game in the Kingdome," said Ibrahim in a 2008 interview. "We had beaten the best teams in the country to get there, including the No. 2, 3, and 4 teams, and then we met the number-one team in the country, Indiana, a two-time defending national champion going for a three-peat.

"Against Indiana, we played to a 0-0 tie in the first half and then scored a go-ahead goal in the second half. Indiana responded with a tying goal with less than 10 minutes remaining. I had been waiting 18 years for this national championship and was hoping the players were still up to the task of scoring a winning goal.

"It was late in the game and the score [was] tied 1-1. I remember us being awarded a corner kick and was signaling to the players for Maxwell Amatasiro to take the kick and they yelled back at me, 'He can't, coach, you have him on the bench.' I quickly put him in the game, and he served a perfect near-post cross, Dick Landgren flicked it, and John Lee headed it in.

"The second-most memorable game in my career has to be the 1987 national championship game. The entire season was quite memorable. The 1987 season was going to be a rebuilding year, but we had some veteran players—Bruce Murray, Paul Rutenis, Tim Genovese, Paul Carollo, John Hummel, and Jamey Rootes—coming back. We also had a great freshmen class coming in, like Andres Alos, Pearse Tormey, Joey Feinberg, John Meek, and Edo Boonstoppel.

"I did not have any expectations that year, and we suffered through a 1-4-1 record in the ACC, and we lost in the first round of the ACC Tournament. It left me with few expectations for an NCAA Tournament bid. However, we were selected to the field of 24 that year as the 23rd team, and we were just happy to be there.

"It was such a thrill to win a national championship for Clemson, with a huge number of Clemson fans witnessing."

Clemson defeated San Diego State 2-0 in the NCAA Championship game at Historic Riggs Field.

Ibrahim finished his career with an overall record of 388-102-31 over his 28-year tenure, for a .774 pct. He had a 32-16 record in NCAA Tournament competition. Between 1972 and 1979, Clemson won eight consecutive ACC Championships. During that time, Clemson posted a 38-0-2 record against ACC competition. Ibrahim also coached Clemson to a final top-20 national ranking in 19 seasons. Under Ibrahim, Clemson won 11 ACC Championships and went to the NCAA Tournament semifinals six times.

Ibrahim coached the Clemson men's soccer program from its rejuvenation in 1967 until his retirement after the 1994 season. After his retirement from coaching, he continued to develop a successful business career that included his ownership of two retail stores in Clemson.

Dr. I.M. Ibrahim died suddenly on July 12, 2008, in Seneca, SC, at the age of 67. Ibrahim collapsed and died of a sudden cardiac arrest while playing golf at Cross Creek Plantation in Seneca, SC, where he was a longtime member and regular weekend golfer.

HENRY ABADI, ONE OF CLEMSON'S EARLY STARS

Dr. I.M. Ibrahim led the Tigers to two National Championships in 1984 and 1987.

Perhaps no one player has had such a great effect on a program as did former Clemson soccer player Henry Abadi.

Abadi played two years at Miami-Dade Junior College in Florida. Before transferring to Clemson, he told Tigers Coach I.M. Ibrahim that he could not play on certain days.

"When Coach Ibrahim talked with me about transferring to Clemson and playing out my two years' eligibility at Clemson, I tried to be completely honest with him," said Abadi in a previous interview. "I told him that, being a Seventh Day Adventist, I would under no circumstances play on Friday nights and Saturdays. He accepted me on that basis, and two other soccer players transferred with me."

Thus, the tradition of playing soccer on Sunday afternoons at 2:00 p.m. was born. Previously, many Clemson soccer matches were played on Saturday before a home football game or on a Saturday afternoon when the football team was playing away. But playing on Sunday caught on not only at Clemson, but among the other ACC and area schools as well, and the crowds and the popularity of soccer flourished.

"I guess we started the tradition of playing on Sundays," said the late Coach Ibrahim in an interview. "Because of Henry, we started playing games on Wednesdays and Sundays, and it really helped our crowds. He could not play on Saturdays, and we respected that."

On the soccer field, Clemson's success reached great heights in 1972. The Tigers finished the 1972 season with a 13-1-1 record overall and the ACC Championship. Clemson advanced to the NCAA Tournament's Final 16, and Abadi finished that year with 27 goals.

Abadi's name is prominent in Clemson's record book, having established records that are still intact today.

In 1973, the Tigers finished the season with a 16-1 record overall and another ACC Championship. The Tigers finished third in the NCAA Tournament and were ranked fourth in the final coaching poll. Abadi scored 32 goals that season, still a Clemson record that was tied by Jimmy Glenn in 1993.

After such a dominating senior performance, Abadi was named first-team All-ACC for the second straight year. He also earned first-team All-America honors, making him Clemson's first first-team All-America player on the pitch.

Abadi helped lay the foundation of success that the Tigers would enjoy in the decades of the 1970s and would carry on into two National Championships in the 1980s.

Ironically, in 1973, the Tigers advanced to the NCAA Semifinals on Wednesday, January 2, and lost to UCLA 2-1 in Miami, FL. If Clemson had won the match, the Tigers would have played St. Louis for the National Championship on Friday evening, January 4. Going into the Final Four, Abadi had already said he would not have played on that Friday after sundown. Former *Greenville News* columnist Dan Foster wrote a column about Abadi and his religious convictions and him not playing if Clemson advanced to the National Championship match. Years later, Foster said that was one of his favorite columns he ever wrote.

Abadi, with his religious convictions, is to be admired. He not only helped start the trend of Clemson playing soccer on Sunday afternoons, but also helped lay the foundation of one of the most successful programs nationally. At the same time, he did not sacrifice his personal and religious convictions and beliefs—quite a career.

THE NWOKOCHA BROTHERS

Christian and Nnamdi Nwokocha were brothers from Onitsha, Nigeria, who added scoring punch to the Clemson attack in the late-'70s and early-'80s. Christian played during the 1975-78 seasons. During that time, he was a 1978 All-America player and was named first-team All-ACC three times. He led the ACC in goal scoring with 20 in 1976 and led the league in 1978 with 18 goals.

In 1978, he helped the Tigers reach the semifinals in the NCAA Tournament. For his career, he scored 59 goals and had 27 assists. He also helped the Tigers win four ACC Championships during his career.

As soon as Christian graduated, Nnamdi arrived at Clemson and was one of Clemson's greatest soccer players of all time.

Nnamdi was a two-time All-America player, in 1979 and 1981, and was a three-time first team All-ACC selection. In 1979, as a freshman, he was the ACC's Player of the Year. That same year he led the Tigers to the NCAA

Nnamdi Nwokocha scored 74 goals and had 23 assists during his career at Clemson.

Championship game. He led the ACC in goal scoring in 1979, 1980, and 1981 and tallied 171 career points, including 74 career goals. Nnamdi set an ACC record, as he scored in 11 consecutive matches in 1980.

One of the most remarkable performances was when he scored an ACC record seven goals in one half against Belmont Abbey on September 9, 1979. Nnamdi was selected as a member of the ACC's 50-Year Anniversary Team.

Nnamdi died of meningitis at the young age of 46 in his native country of Nigeria. He had been working in eastern Nigeria as an advisor to a Governor of the State for Sport Affairs.

BRUCE MURRAY WINS HERMANN AWARD, LEADS CLEMSON TO TWO NCAA TITLES

When a player comes to the end of his career, a crowning moment for that athlete is being remembered and being honored for his past accomplishments.

For former Clemson soccer player Bruce Murray, he feels as if his career has come full circle by being inducted into the National Soccer Hall of Fame in June 2012.

"By being inducted into the National Soccer Hall of Fame, that closed the loop," said Murray. "All of the play and hard work paid off, and I was very happy and touched by that prestigious honor. I joined a lot of prestigious company, and as I entered the Hall of Fame, I took with me several other people, the coaches, and my teammates down through the years on all levels who made this honor possible."

As far as playing, Murray misses some aspects of the game, but not all of them.

"I'm often asked, do I miss playing the game? I don't miss the injuries, the concussions, the hard knocks of traveling; however I do miss the banter and the humor in the locker room and the camaraderie of my teammates. I love the game of soccer, and it has afforded many opportunities.

"I remember my first international goal that I scored. It was against Uruguay. My instructions from Coach Lothar Osiander were to stay back and pass it to teammates John Hakes or Tab Ramos. In one play, I stepped in and won a ball. I looked up and a guy was about to tackle me with both feet up with his spikes coming at me. I avoided him and I went around another defender. I was actually dribbling. I took one more touch and then from 30 yards out I fired a shot and it went in the upper corner of the goal. So much for following instructions!

"I really enjoyed seeing the world. I played against East Germany when they were a separate country. I was there before the collapse of the Berlin Wall and we played the Soviet Union in Moscow a week before that country collapsed and broke into different countries. That was very odd; I saw a lot of history in real time.

"I remember at the World Cup before we played Italy in Rome. We were about to take the field, and we were nervous coming out. I grew up a Washington Redskins fan and have been all of my life. As we were coming out,

I saw Dallas Cowboys longtime Head Coach Tom Landry and his fedora and Pittsburgh's outstanding running back Franco Harris near us. Coach Landry nodded and winked at me, like he was telling me everything was going to be all right. I gained confidence from that. I couldn't believe the Cowboys' coach was at the World Cup match, and me being a Redskins fan, I was getting confidence from him in Italy halfway around the world! I really respected Coach Landry, though. He must have brought us luck, and we played well and lost 1-0 to Italy. We had a chance to tie the match but just missed as Peter Vermise's shot was deflected."

Murray, a US Men's National Team midfielder and forward, tallied 86 games and 21 goals throughout his career for the United States. When Murray retired from the National Team in 1993, he was its all-time leader in both caps and goals. Murray made his first full international appearance against England in 1985 and his last was against Venezuela in 1993.

Murray played in all of the United States' games in the 1990 World Cup, including all 10 qualifiers during 1988 and 1989 and the three games in the finals in Italy in 1990. He scored a goal against Austria in the US's last game of the World Cup finals. He also played in all of the United States' wins in the 1991 CONCACAF Gold Cup and the 1992 US Cup, as well as the 1988 Olympic Games, the 1992 Intercontinental Cup, and the 1993 Copa America.

Murray played several seasons with the Washington Stars and Maryland Bays of the ASL/APSL and one season with the Atlanta Ruckus of the A-League.

As far as some classic moments, Murray has several.

"I think that US soccer started to get on the soccer map when we defeated Trinadad and Tabago. I think this victory set things in motion at the Gold Cup in 1991. We started getting results over Ireland, Italy, and we turned the tide against Mexico. I was glad to be part of this renewal."

At Clemson, Murray won the Hermann Trophy as the top men's soccer player in the country in 1987. He led Clemson to two NCAA Championships in 1984 and 1987.

Bruce Murray won the 1987 Hermann Award. Murray had 20 goals and 11 assists in Clemson's National Championship season in 1987.

He was a two-time All-America player. Murray had the winning goal in three NCAA Tournament games for the Tigers in 1987 on the way to the National Championship.

In the Evansville match, during the 1987 NCAA Tournament, Clemson had a free kick, and Murray was discussing the situation with teammate Paul Rutenis. Murray said, "I'm going to shoot the ball." Murray rifled the ball from 35 yards out in the upper left corner of the goal with 16:18 left in the match to give the Tigers a 2-1 lead and eventually the win. After the match, Murray's game-winner was described by Evansville's Coach Fred Schmalz as "The best free kick I have ever seen in college soccer."

"That was probably my most memorable goal I had at Clemson," said Murray. The next week he scored the game-winning goal with 15:33 left to lead Clemson to a 2-1 victory over number-one-ranked Indiana in Bloomington.

Murray was named first-team All-ACC in 1985 and 1987. He was also the first Clemson player in history in the 40-40 club (over 40 goals and 40 assists in a career). He is sixth in school history in total points, with 142, and seventh in total goals, with 48. Murray is second in school history with 46 career assists.

In the 84 games he played during his career, Murray had either a goal or an assist in 56 games. He played for the US national team and was the United States' all-time leading scorer when he retired from soccer. He is also a member of the ACC 50-Year Anniversary Team and was named one of the top 50 male athletes in ACC history in 2003, the 50th year of the ACC.

Modestly, Murray may feel as though his career has come full circle and his playing days are behind him, but along the way it was a tremendous career full of heroics, firsts, and accolades. As far as Clemson fans and US soccer fans are concerned, he had the kind of career that was well deserving to be enshrined in the Soccer National Hall of Fame.

THE 1984 NATIONAL CHAMPIONSHIP

There was nothing tainted about Clemson's 1984 NCAA Soccer Championship. Clemson faced its toughest regular season schedule in history, as seven teams were ranked in the top 20 and two others were top-10 teams in Division II. Then, Clemson faced the toughest possible draw in the NCAA Tournament and conquered all the odds.

The season opened with a 5-0 win over Connecticut, the nation's number-two ranked team. The Tigers overwhelmed the Huskies, but losses to UCLA (2-1) and Indiana (4-3) at the Indiana Classic, and a 2-0 loss at Duke, left Clemson with a 5-3 record heading into the last week of September. It was time for some lineup changes.

Dr. I.M. Ibrahim moved more of his younger players into the attacking positions on the team, and the results were gratifying. Clemson won its next 10 matches, including an overtime win at South Carolina, 3-2, a contest in which Clemson actually trailed in the extra period. Only a November 2nd loss to Virginia spoiled the rest of the schedule, and Clemson qualified for the NCAA Tournament for the 12th time in 13 years with a 17-4 regular season record.

Clemson had to face 15th-ranked N.C. State in the first round of the NCAA Tournament at Raleigh, NC. This was the team Clemson had beaten in the last week of the regular season, and all the motivational factors were on N.C. State's side. But Clemson got a late goal from Bruce Murray to capture a 2-1 win on the road. In the next contest, Clemson had to face the nation's top-ranked team, Alabama A&M. The Tigers put on a scoring blitz in the first half, with three quick goals in the first 20 minutes on the way to a 3-1 victory.

Clemson's starting goalkeeper, Tim Genovese, was injured in that game, however, and the Tigers would have to go with a walk-on, Shawn Cartmill, the rest of the tournament. The native of Atlanta, GA, responded like a seasoned veteran in the quarterfinal victory at Virginia with a 1-0 shutout.

It was on to UCLA for the semifinals, and this would be the easiest task for Clemson. The Tigers scored four quick goals and coasted to a 4-1 victory. Clemson then met number-two ranked, and two-time defending National Champion Indiana in the National Championship game at the Kingdome in Seattle.

Clemson completed its sweep with a 2-1 victory. John Lee scored on a header in front of the net with 1:42 left to give Clemson its first National Championship in soccer and its second national team title overall.

Clemson had beaten the number one, two, three, and four seeds in the tournament in winning the title, the first time in the history of any NCAA event that a team had beaten the top four teams in gaining its championship.

Maxwell Amatasiro was named the Championship's MVP as he assisted on both Clemson goals. Adubarie Otorubio was named a first-team All-America player and was an All-Conference choice for the fourth straight season. Bruce Murray was named National Rookie of the Year, and captain Charlie Morgan was a first-team All-ACC choice.

Adubarie Otorubio was a three-time All-American in 1982-84.

THE 1987 NATIONAL CHAMPIONSHIP

Going into the 1987 season, Dr. I.M. Ibrahim thought the season could be a major rebuilding year. In fact, in August of that year, he said the National Championship was not a realistic goal. Clemson's head coach had never been more excited about being wrong.

In 1987, after struggling in ACC play with a 1-4-1 record, the unranked Tigers won five straight matches in the NCAA Tournament and became the first sport in Clemson history to claim a second National Championship. The talented 1984 edition also won the national title, but the performance of the 1987 club rivals any miracle in NCAA sports.

On November 5, the Tigers lost in overtime in the first round of the ACC Tournament to North Carolina, and, on bid day, few thought Clemson would be invited to the Big Dance. Nevertheless, the Tigers got the 23rd spot in the 24-team tournament and were shipped out to Evansville, IN, and the Great Lakes regional.

"At the time, we were just happy to get into the tournament," said Ibrahim. "After we had so many frustrating games against teams in our area, it was to our advantage to go to another region."

Clemson downed Evansville 2-1 in a close, physical game on November 15. But most soccer experts, and those who are not experts, in fact, thought Clemson's season would end at Indiana.

The Hoosiers had never lost a home NCAA Tournament game in 18 tries over the years. In addition, Indiana legendary coach Jerry Yeagley, who lost to Clemson in the 1984 championship game and would be looking for revenge, had the number-one ranked team in the nation.

But, for the second straight game, Clemson used a second-half Bruce Murray goal to win the game by a 2-1 margin. The shocking upset threw the NCAA Tournament into a tailspin. Ranked teams from Virginia and South Carolina also lost, and it appeared that "a team of destiny" would capture college soccer's top prize.

For the third straight week, Clemson had to go on the road, this time to Rutgers. In what proved to be Clemson's most trying game of the tournament, Bruce Murray scored two goals, and the Tigers had a 3-1 lead with just a few moments left.

But after a Rutgers goal with just five minutes left, the Scarlet Knights were back in business. With less than two minutes remaining, Rutgers had a penalty kick. However, Clemson goalkeeper Tim Genovese, playing on his birthday, made the save on a shot from one of the leading goal scorers in the nation, Peter Vermese, and Clemson was going to the Final Four.

The Monday after the Rutgers game, the Tigers were awarded the home site for the Final Four. Along with Clemson, North Carolina, making just its second appearance in the NCAA Tournament; undefeated favorite Harvard; and West Coast Cinderella San Diego State made up the Final Four field.

Clemson took on the Tar Heels in the first semifinal in front of 6,500 fans. North Carolina had beaten Clemson twice during the season with physical play, but that would not be the case on Clemson's large field on this day. Freshman Pearse Tormey scored two goals and rookie Dave Veghte added another as Clemson routed the Heels, 4-1, much to the delight of the capacity crowd.

That left Clemson one game away, a date with the number-five-seeded team from the West, San Diego State. It was Cinderella against Cinderella in the finals: the 23rd-ranked team against the 24th-ranked team.

The Tigers dominated play in the first half, and the Aztecs did not get a shot on goal in the first 35 minutes of play. Clemson scored the first goal of the game on a pass by Bruce Murray to Paul Rutenis, who headed the ball into the goal.

San Diego State threatened early in the second half and even hit the post on one occasion, but a Richie Richmond goal with just 41 seconds left gave the Tigers an insurmountable 2-0 triumph and the National Championship.

The 8,332 fans stayed in the stadium for 20 minutes after the game to join in the celebration of one of the top overachievements in Clemson history.

"I was very happy for the way our seniors came through for us . . . that is perhaps my greatest satisfaction," said Ibrahim. "Our seniors led a young group. We started six freshmen in the NCAA Tournament, but Paul Rutenis, Bruce Murray, Tim Genovese, and James Rootes held them together.

"I dreamed about this earlier in the season, but quite honestly I did not think we could win the championship. But our fans and our team believed we could. This championship was a great credit to our fans and their support as well as the players. I think the fan support meant a goal per game during the Final Four."

Murray was the recipient of the Hermann Award, the Heisman Trophy of college soccer, and joined Rutenis on the first-team All-America squad.

GOALKEEPER U

Jaro Zawislan (1990-93) attended Clemson and started every game over his four-year career. He was a three-time All-Atlantic Coast Conference and four-time All-South Region selection, in addition to being named the Most Valuable Player of the 1993 ACC Tournament. He is the only player in the history of the ACC to be named the MVP and not play on the championship team.

He set school records for career saves (446), single-season saves (134), career wins by a goalkeeper (58), and career starts (88). He was also named an Academic All-America player.

Zawislan received a Bachelor of Arts degree in computer science from Clemson and also earned a Bachelor of Education degree from the University of Toronto in 1999. He earned a Master's degree in liberal studies from Creighton in 2001.

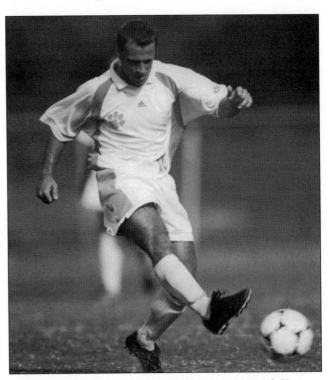

Wojtek Krakowiak won the 1998 Hermann Award. He was the 1998 consensus National Player of the Year.

Jamie Swanner was an All-America player and was the National Goalkeeper of the Year in 1983. He had 15 solo shutouts in 1982 and 14 in 1983. He had a 0.43 goals allowed average for his career.

Other goalkeeping All-American players include Matt Jordan (1997), Doug Warren (2002), Phil Marfuggi (2005), and Josh Campbell (1998).

NATIONAL LEADERS

In 1973, Henry Abadi led the nation in scoring with 32 goals. Wolde Harris and Jimmy Glenn led the nation in scoring in 1993. Glenn scored 32 goals and Harris scored 29 that season. In 1994, Wolde Harris led the nation in scoring, with 26 goals.

Wojtek Krakowiak led the nation in goal scoring, with 31 in 1998. Also that same year, Mark Lisi was the nation's top assist man, with 17. Rivers Guthrie was tied for the nation's lead in assists, with 18, in 1994.

TREVOR ADAIR LEADS CLEMSON TO 6 NCAA QUARTERFINALS AND THE 2005 FINAL FOUR

Trevor Adair reached one of his top professional goals when he led Clemson to the 2005 College Cup Final Four. It was his first appearance at the Final Four and the Tigers' first appearance in 18 years. Adair led the Tigers to a #3 final national ranking in 2005. Adair also led the Tigers to six NCAA Final Eight appearances. In eight of his 14 years at Clemson, the Tigers were ranked in the Top 12 in at least one final poll, including a third-place finish in 2005. Adair coached 14 All-America players and 47 All-ACC selections, and his teams made nine NCAA Tournaments and won two ACC Championships.

In 1998, Adair led the Tigers to the ACC Championship (both regular season and tournament) and to the quarterfinals of the NCAA Tournament for the second consecutive season. He led Clemson to 22 wins, tying the school record and a total that is still among the top-10 victory totals in NCAA history. He also set the school record for most consecutive wins, with 17 straight during the 1998 campaign. Clemson finished the season ranked first in the Soccer America poll and fourth in the NSCAA poll. The 22 wins included seven victories over top-20 teams. Adair was named ACC Coach of the Year, and star forward Wojtek Krakowiak won the Hermann Award.

Trevor Adair, who was the head coach at Clemson from 1995-2008, had a 173-91-27 record in 14 years at Clemson.

WOJTEK KRAKOWIAK WINS PRESTIGIOUS HERMANN AWARD

Wojtek Krakowiak won the 1998 Hermann Award. He was the 1998 consensus National Player of the Year, as he was the *Soccer America*, *Soccer Times*, and *College Soccer Weekly* National Player of the Year.

He was also named the 1998 ACC Player of the Year and was named first-team All-ACC. He scored 31 goals and had eight assists in 1998, as he led Clemson to the NCAA quarterfinals for the second year in a row.

Krakowiak led the ACC in goals scored (31) and points (70). He is third in Clemson history for most goals scored in a single season, with 31 in 1998. Krakowiak left school one year early to turn professional.

FORMER CLEMSON PLAYERS IN THE WORLD CUP

Defender Oguchi Onyewu and midfielder Stuart Holden played for the United States on the 2010 World Cup Team. Holden played at Clemson in 2003 and 2004. He was named second-team All-ACC in 2004.

Onyewu played for Clemson in the 2000 and 2001 seasons and was named to the *Soccer America* MVP team in 2001 and was a NSCAA All-America player in 2001. Onyewu was a Hermann Award Finalist in 2001. During his career at Clemson, Onyewu was named first-team All-ACC in 2000 and 2001.

Bruce Murray and Eric Eichmann both played on the United States national team in 1990.

WOLDE HARRIS, A SCORING GREAT, EARNS HIS CLEMSON DEGREE

No matter where a player may go, there's no better feeling than coming home.

For former Clemson men's soccer star Wolde Harris, it's one of the greatest feelings in the world. In August of 2012, Harris received his degree from Clemson, after some hard work and determination.

Harris last played soccer at Clemson in 1995, some 17 years before he became a Clemson graduate. Since that time, he has played professionally in the MLS and started a business of running

Oguchi Onyewu was a member of the US World Cup team in 2006 and 2010.

soccer camps in his native country of Jamaica. But the idea of finishing his degree has always been on his mind since he made a promise to his parents when he turned professional.

For two years, Harris served as an assistant coach of the Clemson men's soccer team under Coach Mike Noonan and went to school, finishing up where he left off a few years ago and earning a BS in management.

Harris didn't mind "coming home"; it was just a matter of finding the time. Harris doesn't hesitate in stating how much he loves Clemson and has many fond memories of his college days.

"They accepted me and made me feel very comfortable at the start. It felt like a family. We used to eat dinner together and hang out with each other. Coach I.M. Ibrahim did a great job of instilling teamwork and camaraderie," he said. "My teammates made me feel very comfortable and express myself and the love for soccer. Each player sacrificed his personal goals and worked hard for the good of the team. It was a wonderful experience at Clemson and we had a lot of fun."

Harris, a Kingston, Jamaica, native, made the most of his Clemson experience, as he finished his career as one of the best players ever at Tigertown.

Harris played soccer for Clemson from 1993-'95, after spending his freshman season at the University of Connecticut. In only three years at Clemson, he became the Tigers' all-time career goal scorer with 76, second on the Atlantic Coast Conference's career list.

In 1995, he was a finalist for the Hermann Award and received All-America honors that season. He was a three-time All-Atlantic Coast Conference selection that included first-team honors in 1995.

Harris led the nation in goal scoring with 26 goals in 1994 and was second in the nation in 1993 behind teammate Jimmy Glenn (32), with 29. He was tied for fifth for most goals scored nationally in 1995 with 21. Harris also is second on the school's career list for most points, with

170. He is the Tigers' all-time leader for most game-winning goals, with 21. His eight career hat tricks are tied for first on the Clemson career list. He is only the second player in Clemson and ACC history to score 20 or more goals for three consecutive seasons. He was also named a member of the ACC's 50th Anniversary team.

Harris also liked the environment at Clemson and the support shown to the soccer program.

"The facilities and the support at Clemson are unbelievable," said Harris. "As a player from Jamaica, this helped me relax and be comfortable. There's no place like Historic Riggs Field. It would be packed and we have some awesome fans supporting us. There would be fans and supporters from other sports coming to watch us play. It was definitely a family feeling. And, as they say there is nothing like the Clemson family."

Harris played professionally in the MLS. He joined MLS for the first time in 1997, after spending 1996 with the Colorado Foxes, leading the A-League in goals with 17. Harris played three seasons with the Colorado Rapids, scoring 13 goals in 1998. In 2000, he was traded to the New England Revolution for draft picks. Wolde's best season with the Revs was his first, when he scored 15 goals. Harris would spend three-and-a-half seasons in New England, before being traded to the Kansas City Wizards midway through 2003. He spent 2004 with Swedish club Bodens BK before coming back to MLS and Colorado in 2005. In eight years in MLS league play, Harris scored 51 goals and added 31 assists. He signed for Salvadoran outfit Club Deportivo FAS in August 2006.

Harris has also played for the Jamaican national team during his career. He played his last international match in 2002 against Guadeloupe, earning over 28 caps.

After playing professionally, Harris wants to give back. In the past two summers, he worked at Coach Mike Noonan's soccer camp. In Jamaica, he was involved in

Wolde Harris scored 76 goals in only three years.

youth football in the United States and Jamaica. In December 2009, he launched a business called Jamaica Grassroots Football Company with his father and brothers, teaching and coaching youth about the game of soccer.

"I enjoyed working with Coach Noonan's program, when I was finishing my degree. I don't start something and not finish it. I remember when I got drafted in the pros my Dad said you're going back and get your degree. This was the most opportune time to do this. Clemson is my home away from home, and it is where I met a lot of good people. It's always great to come home to Clemson and be part of the Clemson family."

On that August day in 2012, he became an alumnus.

HEAD COACH MIKE NOONAN LOOKS TO CONTINUE WINNING TRADITION

Mike Noonan began coaching at Clemson in January 2010. Since then, he has worked hard to establish a Clemson program that wants to obtain success not only on the playing field, but also in the classroom.

"My 'vision' for the Clemson Men's Soccer program is to fulfill the dream of winning the third NCAA Soccer Championship in school history," Noonan said. "This would add to the legacy that Dr. I. M. Ibrahim established for the program during his 35-year tenure and that Coach Adair upheld. More important, it will solidify the men's soccer program within Clemson Athletics as a leader in a vibrant and successful university that puts educational values and personal development at the core of its mission.

"Our process for fulfilling this dream has centered on a core group of values that encompasses and identifies success in our current environment. Those values are as follows and are the cornerstones of all decisions we make:

- Emphasize Education;
- Pursue Excellence;
- Do Things the Right Way;
- Produce Winners;
- Teamwork—Learn to Be a Part of the Team;
- Nurture Maturity and Responsibility through the Game;
- Respect Tradition; [and]
- Have Fun.

"We have attempted to build a culture that is secure for all of our stakeholders. We attempt to communicate honestly and clearly our objectives and standards. We believe this will ultimately produce an environment of trust that will fulfill our dream. Clemson Soccer is a 'player-centric' team where the players are expected to voice and share their opinions. However, they must also be open to the experience and expertise of the coaching and support staff that strives daily for their consistent development as people first, students second, and players third."

NOONAN LOVED, GROOMED, AND FED THE SOCCER PROGRAM BACK TO ELITE STATUS

Mike Noonan did not say a word. After his Clemson soccer team wrapped up his first practice at Clemson in the spring of 2010, he just sat in the coaches' locker room in silence.

For 30 minutes Noonan just kept to his thoughts.

"This was an ACC program, much less it was Clemson," Noonan said. "In the ACC, soccer has always been dominant and it continues to be. The talent that was on display was significantly less than what we had just left at an Ivy League nonscholarship institution.

"I'm not saying there were not any good players, but the athleticism, the fitness piece, the intangible pieces . . . The best way to describe it is the players looked at me in the first meeting like a stray dog. If you get a stray dog, they need three things. They need to be loved. They need be groomed. And they need to be fed. The Clemson soccer program needed to be loved, it needed to be groomed, and it needed to be fed."

And that's what Noonan and his staff set out to do.

Since those days back in 2010, Noonan has nurtured the men's soccer program through patience, hard work, and dedication and has got the program back among the elite in college soccer. In 2014, he guided the Tigers to their 14th ACC Championship, and in 2015, the program returned to the College Cup Championship Game for the first time since 1987.

In 2016, Clemson advanced to the ACC Championship Game for a second time in three years, and to the Elite 8 Round of the NCAA Tournament.

"The history and the tradition of the program is something that Clemson has always been proud of," Noonan said. "Coach Ibrahim was a cantankerous coach, but he is still the only coach who wore two [national] championship rings and that is part of the Clemson pride and Clemson wanted to get that back.

"So that has been our mission and I think the consistency of doing that is probably the most important thing we will focus on now."

Few teams have been as consistent as Clemson from 2013-'16. The Tigers made the NCAA Tournament all four years, and advanced to the College Cup Final Four and was the national runner-up in 2015. They have also made it to the Sweet 16 and the Elite 8 rounds during that time. Clemson has played for the ACC Championship twice, won it once, while posting an impressive 54-20-15 record during that span, including a 17-3-4 mark in 2015.

"You always want to stay in the moment, but you are always striving to be a better program and be a better team," Noonan said. "It is not necessarily about winning the trophies. That's the end game. That's what comes with it, but I think if you stay in the winning zone, and that is something I have been very proud of.

"We have been in the ACC Tournament every year. We have been in the Final Four of the ACC Tournament every year, but our first year. If you stay in the winning zone, then sooner or later you are going to pop through and win it. So we have to stay in the winning zone of the national picture and see if we can get back to the place where we can win one."

The Tigers came close in 2015. Thales Moreno scored a goal and connected on the winning goal in the penalty kick round as Clemson advanced to the College Cup for the eighth time in school history, and for the first time in 10 years.

Clemson and ACC rival Syracuse battled to a 0-0 draw after two overtimes, but Clemson again won the penalty kick shootout 4-1 to advance to the College Cup's Championship game in Kansas City, MO. Andrew Tarbell was in goal for the Tigers and made eight saves that night.

Clemson ultimately lost to Stanford in the College Cup Finals, but Noonan had got the program back to the level where it belongs. Kyle Fisher was named first-team All-America and teammates Andrew Tarbell (Goalkeeper) and Paul Clowes (Midfielder) were named to the second team, while Tigers' forward T.J. Casner was named to the third-team.

"The people of character, who were on our first team, were the ones who set that foundation for the Keegan Priests, for the Wes Nelsons, for the Tommy Drakes, and for who has come after them," Noonan said. "Each year, it takes another step forward so now the expectation of our incoming players by the current players is significant. It is clear. It is simple because the core values have not changed.

"Now the players, and not that they feel comfortable, but it is comforting to know what those are. When you put people in an environment that they know what to expect and they know they can count on certain things and certain people and there is a level of trust that develops from the minute that you start recruiting someone, then you just have to deal with the soccer pieces and the soccer pieces are the fun pieces. The challenging pieces are always the team's dynamic and getting the right people, as they say, on the bus."

MEN'S SOCCER

February 14, 1934—Clemson played its first-ever soccer match and lost to Furman 1-0 in Greenville, SC. Fred Kirchner was the head coach.

December 9, 1939—The Tigers defeated Duke 1-0 at home for the Tigers' last match before the 1967 season.

Oct. 6, 1967—In the resumption of men's soccer at Clemson, the Tigers claimed a 4-0 win over Furman in Greenville, SC. Frank Schmidt scored the Tigers' first goal in this match with an assist from Gary Fleetwood.

Oct. 10, 1967—The Tigers played their first-ever home match and defeated Erskine, 9-1. Clemson's Leo Serrano registered five goals in this game.

Nov. 11, 1967—The Tigers won their first ACC match with a 4-3 win over N.C. State in Raleigh, NC.

January, 1969—Mark Rubich was named Clemson's first All-America player.

Oct. 10, 1970—Andy Demori scored five goals against Emory.

Sept. 25, 1971—Nabeel Kammoun scored five goals against Jacksonville.

Oct. 10, 1971—Jon Babashak scored five goals against Furman.

Oct. 15, 1972-Sept. 28, 1980—Clemson went unbeaten in ACC play. During this time, the Tigers compiled a record of 40-0-2 against ACC foes, while claiming eight ACC championships.

Duke broke the streak with a 3-1 victory over the Tigers.

October 15, 1972-November 2, 1984—During this time, Clemson went unbeaten against ACC teams at home, compiling a record of 31-0-4. Virginia broke the streak with a 2-0 win over Clemson.

Oct. 17, 1972—Clemson was ranked for the first time ever in the ISAA poll. The Tigers were ranked 20th with a 6-0-1 record.

Nov. 12, 1972—Clemson won its first ACC Championship with a 3-0 win over Maryland.

Nov. 20, 1972—Clemson played in its first NCAA Tournament match and defeated West Virginia 3-2

Sept., 1973—The Tigers were ranked in the top 10 for the first time ever. Clemson was ranked tied for eighth in the ISAA preseason poll.

Sept. 16, 1973—Henry Abadi scored five goals against N.C. State.

Sept. 26, 1973—Henry Abadi scored six goals against Western Carolina.

Nov., 1973—Coach I.M. Ibrahim was named ACC Coach of the Year.

Nov. 4, 1973—Henry Abadi scored his 32nd goal of the season in a match against South Florida. Abadi scored the goal at the 15:36 mark into the game. The 32 goals set a Clemson record for most goals in a season. This was also the first ranked opponent Clemson had ever defeated. The Tigers were ranked sixth and South Florida 11th.

Nov. 11, 1973—Clemson won the ACC Championship with a 3-1 victory over Maryland.

Henry Abadi scored 20 goals in the first five games of the 1973 season.

This is a picture of the 1933-34 Clemson soccer team. Head Coach Fred Kirchner is standing on the far left. The picture was taken on Historic Riggs Field.

Dec. 9, 1973—Clemson defeated Pennsylvania 1-0 in the NCAA Tournament quarterfinals.

Jan. 2, 1974—The Tigers reached the semifinals of the NCAA Tournament and lost to UCLA 2-1 in an overtime game. Clemson finished tied for third in the NCAA Tournament.

Nov. 10, 1974—Clemson won the ACC Championship with a 5-0 triumph over Maryland.

Sept. 12, 1975—For the first time in Clemson history, the Tigers defeated a top-10 team. Second-ranked Clemson defeated third-ranked SIU-Edwardsville 2-1.

Sept. 23, 1975—The Tigers were ranked number one, according to the ISAA poll, for the first time in the school's history.

Oct. 26, 1975—Christian Nwokocha scored five goals against Duke.

Nov., 1975—Clyde Browne was named ACC Player of the Year for the fourth straight year. He is the only four-time league MVP in any sport in ACC history.

Nov. 9, 1975—The Tigers completed an undefeated ACC season with a 5-0 record as Clemson beat Maryland 5-1 in College Park, MD.

Oct. 26, 1976—Coach I.M. Ibrahim won his 100th career game at Clemson with a 3-1 win over St. Louis in St. Louis, MO.

Oct. 31, 1976—Christian Nwokocha scored six goals against Flagler.

Nov. 9, 1976—Clemson won the ACC Championship with an 8-0 win over North Carolina.

Nov. 28, 1976—The Tigers defeated Philadelphia Textile 3-2 in the NCAA Tournament quarterfinals.

Dec. 4, 1976—The Tigers lost to San Francisco 1-0 in the semifinals of the NCAA Tournament in Philadelphia at Franklin Field.

Oct. 23, 1977—Second-ranked Clemson defeated number-one St. Louis 3-1 at Clemson, the Tigers' first win over a number-one-ranked team in soccer.

Nov. 6, 1977—Clemson completed an undefeated regular season with a 2-1 win over Maryland in College Park, MD. Also, the Tigers won the ACC Championship.

Nov. 26, 1977—The Tigers lost to Brown 2-1 in the NCAA quarterfinals.

Nov., 1978—Coach I.M. Ibrahim was named ACC Coach of the Year.

Nov. 5, 1978—Clemson defeated Maryland 3-2 and captured the ACC Championship.

Nov. 25, 1978—The Tigers defeated St. Francis (NY) in the NCAA quarterfinals 4-0 in Tampa, FL.

Dec. 9, 1978—The Tigers lost to San Francisco 2-1 in the semifinals of the NCAA Tournament.

Dec. 10, 1978—Clemson won the consolation game of the NCAA Final Four with a 6-2 win over Philadelphia Textile.

Sept. 19, 1979—Nnamdi Nwokocha scored seven goals against Belmont Abbey, all in the first half.

Dec. 2, 1979—Clemson defeated American in the NCAA quarterfinals 1-0.

Dec. 8, 1979—Clemson defeated Columbia 4-1 in the NCAA semifinals at Tampa, FL.

Dec. 9, 1979—Clemson lost to SIU-Edwardsville 3-2 in the Championship game of the NCAA Tournament at Tampa, FL.

Sept. 21, 1980—Nnamdi Nwokocha scored three goals against N.C. State. This marked the fourth consecutive game that he had scored a hat trick.

Sept. 24, 1980—Clemson played its first home night game ever. The Tigers were 1-0 winners over UNC-Charlotte.

Sept. 19, 1982—Second-ranked Clemson defeated number-one-ranked SIU-Edwardsville 2-1 in Edwardsville, IL.

Oct. 6, 1982—Nnamdi Nwokocha scored his 74th and final goal of his career as he completed a hat trick against Florida International at Clemson in a 5-0 Tiger win. The 74 goals set the school career record.

Oct. 22, 1982—Coach I.M. Ibrahim won his 200th match at Clemson with a 5-0 win over North Carolina.

Nov. 20, 1982—The Tigers were Southern Regional finalists in the NCAA Tournament with a 2-1 overtime, penalty-kick loss to Duke in Durham, NC.

August, 1984—Jamie Swanner played for the United States Olympic team in Los Angeles, CA.

Nov. 18, 1984—Clemson defeated 15th-ranked N.C. State in the first round of the NCAA Tournament in Raleigh.

Nov. 25, 1984—Ninth-ranked Clemson defeated the nation's top-ranked team, Alabama A&M, 3-1 and won the Southern Region of the NCAA playoffs.

Dec. 1, 1984—In the NCAA quarterfinals, the Tigers defeated Virginia 1-0 at Charlottesville, VA.

Dec. 9, 1984—Clemson claimed a 4-1 victory over UCLA in the NCAA semifinals in Los Angeles, CA.

Dec. 16, 1984—Clemson defeated second-ranked Indiana 2-1 in the National Championship game at the Kingdome in Seattle, WA. Maxwell Amatasiro was named the game's MVP, as he assisted on both Clemson goals. John Lee scored the game winner at the 88:18 mark. In doing so, Clemson became the first-team (regardless of sport) in

NCAA history to defeat the top-four seeds in a postseason tournament.

January, 1985—Adubarie Otorubio was named All-America, and he became the first Clemson soccer player to be named All-America for three years.

Nov., 1985—Coach I.M. Ibrahim was named ACC Coach of the Year.

Nov. 24, 1985—Clemson lost to South Carolina in the Southern Regional Finals of the NCAA Tournament in a two-overtime shootout.

Sept. 1, 1987—Clemson unveiled the remodeled Riggs Field. This marked the first time the new 6,500-seat grandstand was used. Clemson was an 8-0 winner over UNC-Asheville.

Nov. 15, 1987—Clemson defeated Evansville 2-1 in the opening round of the NCAA playoffs.

Nov. 22, 1987—The unranked Tigers defeated number-one-ranked Indiana 2-1 in the championship game of the Great Lakes Regionals.

Nov. 29, 1987—Clemson defeated Rutgers 3-2 in Piscataway, NJ, in the NCAA quarterfinal game.

Nov. 30, 1987—It was announced that Clemson would play host to the NCAA Final Four. Harvard, North Carolina, San Diego State, and Clemson made the field. This was the first time in the history of the NCAA Soccer Tournament that the Championships would be contested on the campus of one of the participating schools.

Dec. 5, 1987—The Tigers defeated North Carolina in the semifinal game of the NCAA Tournament, 4-1.

Dec. 6, 1987—Clemson defeated San Diego State 2-0 and won the National Championship, the second in school history. A crowd of 8,332 witnessed the Championship game. The attendance at this game was the largest to see an NCAA Soccer Championship match.

January 14, 1988—Bruce Murray was named the recipient of the Hermann Award, given annually to the nation's top soccer player.

August, 1988—Eric Eichmann and Bruce Murray played for the United States Olympic team in Seoul, South Korea.

Oct. 5, 1988—Coach I.M. Ibrahim won his 300th career match with a 2-0 win over Georgia State in Clemson, SC.

June, 1990—Former Tigers Bruce Murray and Eric Eichmann represented the United States team in the World Cup.

Oct. 28, 1990—Clemson tied Virginia 1-1 and captured the 1990 ACC regular season title.

Nov., 1990—Coach I.M. Ibrahim was named ACC Coach of the Year. Jimmy Glenn was named ACC Rookie of the Year.

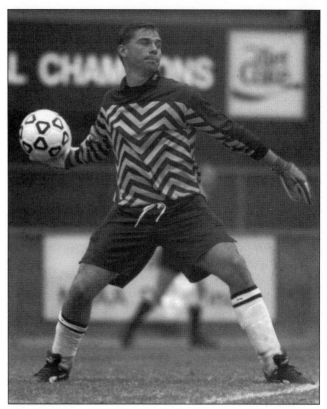

Jaro Zawislan holds the Clemson career record for most saves (446), most minutes played (7,829), most wins (58), and most games started and played (88).

Sept. 23, 1992—Coach I.M. Ibrahim won his 350th career match, a 5-0 win over Presbyterian.

Oct. 4, 1992—Jaro Zawislan broke a 23-year-old school record for most saves in a career. Zawislan had seven saves in the Old Dominion game, which gave him 280 career saves. Zawislan broke the record of Gary Pace (1967-69), who had 276.

Oct. 24, 1993—With a 2-0 win over Wake Forest, Clemson won the ACC regular-season championship.

Nov. 2, 1993—Jimmy Glenn was named ACC Player of the Year, while Dr. I.M. Ibrahim was named ACC Coach of the Year.

Nov. 5, 1993—Jimmy Glenn scored his 32nd goal of the season against North Carolina. This tied the school record for most goals in a season set by Henry Abadi in 1973.

Nov. 14, 1993—Head coach Dr. I.M. Ibrahim won his 375th game of his career with a 2-0 win over UNC-Greensboro.

Nov. 21, 1993—Jaro Zawislan started his 88th career game, setting a new Clemson career record.

April 13, 1994—Jaro Zawislan won the Atlantic Coast Conference's Jim Weaver Award (postgraduate scholarship), which is given annually to the ACC top student-athletes. Zawislan graduated in three and one-half years, earning a BS in computer science.

Sept. 4, 1994—Wolde Harris scored five goals against Vanderbilt in Clemson's 8-0 win.

October 9, 1994—Clemson played Virginia on ESPN-2.

Dec. 7, 1994—Coach Dr. I.M. Ibrahim resigned. Throughout his 28 years as head coach, Ibrahim's teams compiled a 388-102-31 record, won two NCAA National Championships, had six Final Four appearances, and made 17 trips to the NCAA Tournament.

Jan. 25, 1995—Trevor Adair was named head coach. Adair was head coach at Brown University before coming to Clemson. At Brown, he compiled a 34-24-5 record.

Sept. 6, 1995—Clemson defeated Central Florida 3-0 in Trevor Adair's first win as head coach of the Tigers.

Nov. 1, 1995—Wolde Harris set a new Clemson career record for most goals scored in a career, with 76. Also, he became the second ACC and Clemson player to score 20 or more goals in a season for three consecutive years. Clemson defeated Wofford 6-0, the program's 400th all-time victory.

July, 1996—Miles Joseph and Imad Baba both played for the United States Olympic team in the 1996 Games.

April 9, 1997—Craig Wenning won the Atlantic Coast Conference's Weaver-James Award.

May 7, 1997—Craig Wenning won the University's Norris Medal. The Medal is given each year to the graduating student who, on the basis of exceptional scholastic achievement and leadership ability, is judged by the University Scholarships and Awards Committee to be the best all-around student.

Sept. 23-Nov. 29, 1998—Clemson won a school record 17 matches in a row.

Sept. 27, 1998—Clemson won its 100th all-time Atlantic Coast Conference match, a 3-1 win over N.C. State.

Nov. 8, 1998—With a 1-0 win over Wake Forest, Clemson won the ACC Regular Season Championship.

Nov. 15, 1998—Clemson defeated Duke 1-0 in the ACC Championship match. Scott Bower scored the goal, with an assist by Mark Lisi.

Nov. 16, 1998—Clemson finished the regular season ranked first in the Soccer America poll.

Dec. 12, 1998—Wojtek Krakowiak was named the recipient of College Soccer's Hermann Award in Richmond, VA. Krakowiak finished the 1998 season with 31 goals and eight assists, for 70 points. He also scored 10 winning goals.

Dec. 1998—Clemson finished the season ranked fourth in the final NSCAA poll.

Oct 22, 1999—Head Coach Trevor Adair won his 100th career match with a 1-0 victory over South Carolina.

Nov. 19, 2000—Clemson defeated Furman 3-2 in the first round of the NCAA Tournament at Clemson, SC. Clemson was seeded second in the NCAA Tournament.

Nov. 26, 2000—Connecticut defeated Clemson 2-1 in the NCAA Round of 16 in overtime. The Huskies eventually won the National Championship.

June 6, 2001—Clemson players Oguchi Onyewu, Doug Warren, Eric Lewis, and Kenneth Cutler were selected to play for the US Under-20 National Team.

Sept. 7-9, 2001—Clemson defeated Florida International 7-1 and Notre Dame 4-0 to win the Furman Invitational.

Nov. 18, 2001—Clemson defeated Virginia 1-0 in capturing the ACC Championship. Ian Fuller scored the game's lone goal and was named the tournament's MVP.

Nov. 25, 2001—Clemson defeated Kentucky 1-0 in the second round of the NCAA Tournament. Kenneth Cutler scored the winning goal at the 123:13 mark.

Dec. 2, 2001—The Tigers defeated Alabama-Birmingham 3-2 in the NCAA Tournament's Round of 16. OguchiOnyewu scored the game's tying goal (88:22) and the winning goal (106:55).

Dec. 9, 2001—Indiana defeated Clemson 2-0 in Bloomington, IN, in the NCAA Tournament's quarterfinals.

Aug. 31, 2002—Clemson tied number-one-ranked Indiana and won the Indiana Invitational in Bloomington, IN. Clemson had defeated Bulter on the previous day 3-0.

Nov. 10, 2002—The Tigers defeated Western Illinois 3-2 in overtime, as Clemson won its 500th match in the program's history.

Nov. 27, 2002—Clemson tied Coastal Carolina in the second round of the NCAA Tournament. The Tigers advanced to the NCAA Tournament's Round of 16 after winning the penalty kick round.

Nov. 30, 2002—The Tigers upset number-one-ranked Wake Forest 2-1 in overtime in the NCAA Tournament's Round of 16. Brett Branan scored both Clemson goals.

Dec. 7, 2002—Stanford defeated Clemson 2-0 in the NCAA Tournament Round of Eight at Stanford, CA.

Nov. 21, 2003—Clemson and Virginia Tech played to a 3-3 tie in the first round of the NCAA Tournament. Virginia Tech advanced to the second round by winning the penalty kick round.

Sept. 10-12, 2004—Clemson defeated Brown 1-0 on Sept. 10 and defeated Yale 3-2 on Sept. 12, in winning the Brown Invitational.

September 11, 2005—Clemson and Old Dominon tied 0-0, as Clemson won the Old Dominion Invitational. Clemson defeated William and Mary 3-2 on September 9 in the first match of the tournament, on an Alan O'Hara goal in the second overtime.

November 18, 2005—Clemson defeated Coastal Carolina 2-0 in the opening round of the NCAA Tournament.

November 22, 2005—Clemson defeated N.C. State at Raleigh, NC, in the second round of the NCAA Tournament.

November 27, 2005—Clemson defeated Notre Dame 1-0 in the NCAA Tournament to advance to the Final Eight in Clemson, SC.

December 2, 2005—Clemson defeated Creighton 1-0 in the NCAA quarterfinals in front of 6,680 spectators. Charlie Roberts scored the game's only goal with 39 seconds left. This was the second-largest crowd in Riggs Field history. The win sent Clemson to the NCAA Final Four for the first time since 1987.

December 9, 2005—New Mexico defeated Clemson 2-1 in the NCAA Final Four at Cary, NC.

June, 2006—Former Clemson player Oguchi Onyewu was a starter on the United States World Cup Team.

September 1 & 3, 2006—Clemson defeated Memphis 2-0 and Oral Roberts 2-0, as the Tigers won the Memphis Invitational in Memphis, TN.

September 8, 2006—The Tigers defeated number-one-ranked Maryland 2-1 in front of 6,821 fans, the third-largest crowd in Riggs Field history. Danny Poe scored the winning goal at the 73:58 mark.

September 15, 2006—Clemson defeated North Carolina 1-0 in front of 7,012 fans, the second-largest crowd in Riggs Field history. Danny Poe scored the game's lone goal at the 53:44 point in the match.

November 16, 2006—Clemson defeated Gardner-Webb 3-1 in the second round of the NCAA Tournament.

November 19, 2006—UCLA defeated Clemson 3-0 in the NCAA Round of 16 in Los Angeles, CA.

July 12, 2008—Former coach I.M. Ibrahim died of a heart attack.

June 16, 2009—Coach Trevor Adair resigned after 14 years at Clemson. Phil Hindson was named the head coach for the 2009 season.

Adair posted a record of 174-91-26 in his Clemson career that included nine trips to the NCAA Tournament and eight top-12 national poll finishes.

January 5, 2010—Mike Noonan was named coach of the Tigers. He becomes the fourth head coach in the program's history.

June, 2010—Former Clemson player, Oguchi Onyewu was a starter on the United States World Cup team. Former Tiger Stuart Holden was also on the squad.

January 27, 2011—Clemson Head Men's Soccer Coach Mike Noonan was inducted into the Connecticut Soccer Hall of Fame.

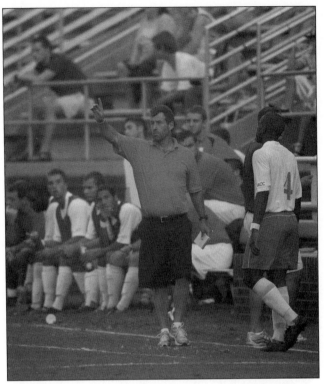

Mike Noonan was named the Tigers' head coach in 2010.

June 4, 2011—Bruce Murray was inducted in the National Soccer Hall of Fame in a ceremony that took place before the US Men's National Team's match against Spain at Gillette Stadium in Foxborough, Mass.

September 2, 2011—The Tigers defeated South Carolina 2-0 in front of 7,423 fans , setting a new regular-season attendance record.

October 14, 2011—Iain Smith scored at the 89:59 mark as Clemson upset #14 Boston College 2-0 in at Historic Riggs Field. This tied the school record for the latest goal scored in regulation.

October 28, 2011—Clemson upset number-one-ranked Maryland at Historic Riggs Field .

December 12, 2013—Thomas McNamara was named an academic All-American and an on-field All-American. He became the 18th Clemson athlete to accomplish this feat and only the second Tiger soccer player.

January 16, 2014—Thomas McNamara was drafted by Chivas USA in the MLS Draft held in Philadelphia, PA. The midfielder was the first pick in the second round, the 20th overall selection. Chivas USA plays in the Los Angeles suburb of Carson, CA.

May 1, 2014—Two Clemson men's soccer players, Thomas McNamara and Alex Stockinger, were honored by the Atlantic Coast Conference by being selected for the Weaver-James-Corrigan Award and the Thacker Award.

The Weaver-James-Corrigan and Jim and Pat Thacker postgraduate scholarships are awarded to selected student-athletes who intend to pursue a graduate degree following completion of their undergraduate requirements.

October 31, 2014—Austen Burnikel scored two goals in leading 19th-ranked Clemson to a 2-0 victory over N.C. State at Clemson. With the victory, Clemson tied for first for the Atlantic Coast Conference's Atlantic Division Title.

November 9, 2014—Fourteenth-ranked Clemson and 18th-ranked Wake Forest played to a 1-1 draw in the quarterfinal of the ACC Tournament at Historic Riggs Field. The Tigers, however, advance to the seminfals by winning the penalty kick round.

November 11, 2014—Bobby Belair scored in the 88th minute to send the game into overtime, and Clemson and second-ranked Notre Dame played to a 1-1 tie in the semifinals of the ACC Tournament at Cary, NC. Paul Clowes sent the ball into the box from a corner kick to Belair. For the second straight match, Tarbell played all 110 minutes in the match, but Glodack was the Tigers' goalkeeper in the penalty kick part of the match. The Tigers won the penalty kick round 5-4.

November 16, 2014—Clemson defeated Louisville 2-1 in overtime to win the ACC Tournament at Cary, NC. This marks the 14th ACC Men's Soccer Championship for Clemson in the program's history. The Cardinals scored early in the first half and maintained the lead until Paul Clowes scored with only three seconds remaining in regulation (89:57) to knot the score. Senior and Clemson native Ara Amirkhanian scored the game-winner for the Tigers in the second overtime period with assists from Diego Campos and Kyle Fisher in the 105th minute of play. Paul Clowes was named the ACC Tournament's MVP.

November 24, 2014—Diego Campos scored one goal and assisted on the other as the seventh-seeded and seventh-ranked Clemson men's soccer team edged No. 25 Coastal Carolina 2-1 Monday night in the second round of the NCAA Tournament at Historic Riggs Field. The Tigers advance to the Round of 16 for the first time since 2006 and for the 23rd time in program history. The victory was the first NCAA Tournament win for Clemson since 2006.

November 30, 2014—North Carolina ended Clemson's season with a 2-1 victory over the Tigers in the NCAA's Round of 16 at Clemson, SC. This also ended a 10-match unbeaten streak for the Tigers.

December 16, 2014—Clemson finished the season ranked 11th in the final NSCAA (National Soccer Coaches Association of America) poll. It was the Tigers' highest ranking in the final NSCAA poll since 2005, when that team was ranked in a tie for third.

October 2, 2015—Clemson celebrated the 100th Anniversary of Historic Riggs Field in grand style with a 2-0 victory over Virginia Tech.

November 8, 2015—Clemson defeated Boston College 3-0 in the ACC Tournament quarterfinals at Historic Riggs Field.

November 11, 2015—Syracuse defeated Clemson 2-0 in the ACC Tournament semifinals at Historic Riggs Field.

November 16, 2015—Clemson was seeded second in the NCAA Tournament. This was the highest seed for Clemson since the 1998 season, when that team was seeded first.

November 22, 2015—Four different players scored five goals to help the No. 2 National Seed Tigers to a 5-2 victory over Elon in the NCAA Second Round on Sunday night at Historic Riggs Field. The five goals were the most scored by Clemson in an NCAA Tournament contest in exactly 17 years, when the Tigers defeated Lafayette 5-0 on Nov. 22, 1998.

November 29, 2015—Redshirt senior Kyle Murphy scored the winning goal in the 79th minute of play as Clemson defeated 15th-seeded UC Santa Barbara 3-2 in the NCAA Round of 16 at Clemson, SC .

December 1, 2015—Kyle Fisher and Paul Clowes were both named as semifinalists for the Mac Hermann Trophy, given to the best player in college soccer.

December 4, 2015—Thales Moreno scored a goal and connected on the winning goal in the penalty kick round as Clemson advanced to the College Cup for the eighth time in school history, the first time in 10 years. After regulation and 20 minutes of overtime, the game remained a 1-1 draw. The Tigers, however, won the penalty kick shootout 3-1.

December 11, 2015—Clemson and Syracuse battled to a 0-0 draw after two overtimes, but Clemson again won the penalty kick shootout 4-1 to advance to the College Cup's Championship game in Kansas City, MO. Andrew Tarbell was in goal for the Tigers and made eight saves.

December 12, 2015—Kyle Fisher was named first-team All-American and teammates Andrew Tarbell (Goalkeeper) Paul Clowes (Midfielder) were named to the second team. The Tigers' forward T.J. Casner was named to the third-team.

December 13, 2015—Stanford's Jordan Morris scored two goals and Corey Baird had two assists, while Eric Verso had one goal and one assist as the Cardinal defeated Clemson in the National Championship match 4-0 at Kansas City, MO.

Clemson finished the season with a 17-3-4 record overall.

December 16, 2015—Clemson Head Men's Soccer Coach Mike Noonan was named National Coach of the Year by the National Soccer Coaches Association of America (NSCAA).

December 17, 2015—Senior Paul Clowes and redshirt junior Andrew Tarbell were recognized for their accomplishments on the field and in the classroom by the NSCAA. Both Tigers were named Scholar All-Americans by the association and earned undergraduate degrees from Clemson University on the same day.

November 6, 2016—Clemson and Syracuse played to a 1-1 tie in regulation, but Clemson advanced to the ACC Tournament semifinals as the Tigers won the penalty kick round 4-2 at Historic Riggs Field in Clemson, SC.

November 9, 2016—Clemson's Alex Happi scored with 1:29 left to go in regulation as Clemson defeated Boston College in the semifinal round of the ACC Tournament at Clemson, SC. Aaron Jones was credited with the assist.

November 13, 2016—Wake Forest defeated Clemson 3-1 in the Championship game of the ACC Tournament at Charleston, SC.

November 20, 2016—Alex Happi scored the game-winning goal in the 93rd minute as Clemson defeated South Carolina 2-1 in the second round of the NCAA Tournament. Clemson received a first-round bye.

November 27, 2016—Austen Burnikel scored two goals and assisted on the third goal in Clemson's 3-1 victory over Albany in the NCAA Tournament's round of 16.

December 2, 2016—Korte Ford scored the match's lone goal in leading Denver to a 1-0 victory over Clemson in the NCAA quarterfinal match at Historic Riggs Field.

WOMEN'S
Soccer

NCAA Final Eight:

1997, 1999, 2000, 2006

NCAA Final 16:

1997, 1998, 1999, 2000, 2001, 2006

ACC Regular–Season Champion:

2000, 2016 (tie)

Top-25 Seasons:
1994 (13th), 1995 (15th), 1996 (11th), 1997 (7th), 1998
(11th), 1999 (6th), 2000 (5th), 2001 (10th), 2002 (14th),
2003 (17th), 2004 (25th), 2006 (T14th), 2014 (20th),
2015 (6th), 2016 (11th)

CLEMSON ADDS WOMEN'S SOCCER IN 1994

Clemson added the popular sport of women's soccer to its list of programs in 1994.

In 1993, Tracey Leone came to Clemson a year early to start the program and the process of recruiting. Having had a successful men's program for several years, it was only logical that Clemson would add women's soccer. But how soon would it become a winning program?

For Clemson, it came immediately. From the start, Clemson began going to the NCAA Tournament in its first year as a varsity program.

TRACEY LEONE IS NAMED FIRST COACH

Along with her husband, Ray—who served as her assistant at Clemson from 1994-'98 and then became co-head coach in 1999 before guiding the program for a year himself when his wife took the job as the US Under-19 National team coach in 2000—Leone quickly built Clemson's new program into a conference and national contender.

"We always love coming back to Clemson, and we always feel like we don't get back enough," said Tracey Leone,

who was Clemson's first head coach in 1994-2000. "Right when you come back, you feel like it's your home, even though you've left it. You'll always consider it your home."

Clemson became a fixture in the nation's top 10, while the combined Leone eras saw the Tigers make seven consecutive NCAA Tournament appearances (including the quarterfinals in '97, '99, and 2000) and produce 20 All-Conference players.

Also, Clemson became the first serious ACC rival to the supremacy of league and national powerhouse North Carolina, where Leone played as a midfielder during her standout college career. Looking back, she credits the early success at Clemson to having time to prepare.

"Well, we were lucky," said Leone. "I think Clemson's commitment right from the start to give us a year before we even played, so that we could put the team together, was a huge advantage. We were hired in June, but we didn't have to play until the following fall. So we had a year to have people visit, and to go out and recruit and try to find the right personnel and the right players that would fit Clemson.

"It was a pretty easy place to sell. All you have to do is get them on campus, and people love this place. They love the football games, and the atmosphere for the soccer. Plus, the campus is beautiful, and the town is charming."

Besides leading the US Under-19 team to a World Championship in 2002, Leone was an assistant coach for the US Women's National Team that won the Gold Medal in the 2004 Olympics in Athens, Greece.

"I've always followed Clemson's program after we left," said Leone. "We look online all the time to see how Clemson does, and I think we always will, because this program was like our baby, and we'll always feel that we're a part of what's happening here."

Leone said that the decision to leave Clemson wasn't planned and was exceedingly difficult.

"It was a really hard decision, probably the hardest decision we've ever had to make," she affirmed. "Because we felt when we're here, that we we're going to retire here. We had no preconceived notion of ever leaving. As long as Clemson wanted us, we felt we were going to be here.

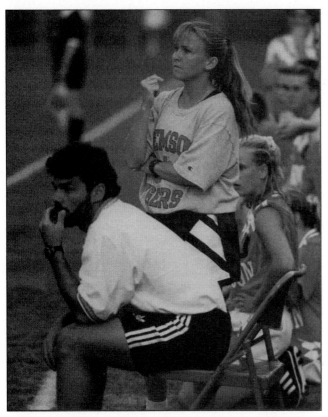

Ray Leone was an assistant to his wife Tracey and was named a co-head coach in 1999. He was the head coach in 2000. Ray had a 33-10-3 record at Clemson.

"I think when the US soccer position opened, and I had that opportunity, my full intention was to come back to Clemson and finish my time here. Then, in the meantime, Ray got a great opportunity at Arizona State, so we had to think long and hard about his profession and his career, and that's why we did what we did."

"We've loved everywhere we've lived, between South Carolina, Arizona, and now Boston. But I think we'll always feel Clemson has a very special place in our heart."

THE LEONE ERA BEGINS AT CLEMSON

Clemson had a successful first season in 1994. Clemson lost to North Carolina in the first-ever match on September 4th. From this point, Clemson won 15 of their next 17 matches in the regular season. Clemson lost to N.C. State in the ACC Tournament in Chapel Hill, NC. The Tigers met N.C. State again in the NCAA Tournament at Historic Riggs Field. The game ended in a 1-1 tie, but N.C. State advanced in sudden-death penalty kicks.

The Tigers were 14-7 in 1995 and played in the NCAA Tournament for the second year in a row. In 1996, the Tigers were 15-7-1 and finished 11th in the final poll. Clemson played host to the ACC Tournament at Historic Riggs Field. The Tigers lost to North Carolina in the Championship game. Clemson again played in the NCAA Tournament.

In 1997, Clemson advanced to the NCAA quarterfinals for the first time ever in school history. The Tigers defeated Georgia and UNC-Greensboro in the first two rounds.

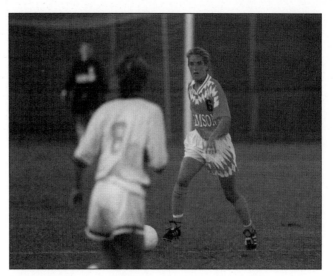

Sara Burkett was an All-America honoree in 1997.

In the quarterfinal round, Santa Clara was victorious over Clemson 3-0. The Tigers finished 10th in the final poll.

For the season, Jennifer Crawford led Clemson in goal scoring, with 17. Sara Burkett was Clemson's assist leader, with 12. Clemson had three wins over top-10 teams—#4 William & Mary, #5 Virginia, and #8 Virginia. Also, Burkett became Clemson's first All-America player in women's soccer and was named first-team All-ACC for the third straight year. Sheri Bueter was also an All-Conference selection, and both she and Burkett were named to the NSCAA All-Southeast Regional Team.

In 1998, Clemson advanced to the ACC Championship game and lost to North Carolina in Orlando, FL. The Tigers advanced to the NCAA Round of 16. Clemson defeated Vanderbilt in the first round and then lost to Penn State. Clemson defeated three top-20 teams during the season.

SHERI BUETER WAS ONE OF CLEMSON'S EARLY STARS

Clemson Athletic Hall of Fame inductee Sheri Bueter describes her excitement for being part of the women's soccer inaugural program.

"I'm glad that I had a part in the beginning of the women's program at Clemson under two of the top coaches in women's soccer—Ray and Tracey Leone. I also am delighted that I was alongside of some of the best recruits in the country that had already committed to Clemson. I knew the struggles academically that could come with being a student-athlete, and Vickery Hall (Clemson's academic support center) gave me the confidence that I would be able to balance athletics and academics successfully.

"Clemson is part of my family. While an athlete at Clemson, I felt like everyone's daughter. They opened their arms and hearts and embraced me as well as our new soccer program like I never could have imagined. Even though I have left campus, that feeling still lives on."

ANOTHER NCAA QUARTERFINAL APPEARANCE

Clemson finished the year with a 14-7-2 record in 1999. The Tigers advanced to the NCAA quarterfinals for the second time in the program's six-year history. After the Tigers received a first-round bye, Julie Augustyniak scored her first goal of the season with only 41 seconds remaining to give Clemson a 1-0 win over Marquette in the second-round match at Clemson, SC on November 13.

The eighth-ranked Tigers went on to battle 11th-ranked Wake Forest to a 0-0 tie at Clemson in the round of 16 on November 20 and advance to the Final Eight by winning the penalty kick round 3-1. Cindy Mullinix scored the winning penalty kick for Clemson. The Tigers lost to North Carolina in the NCAA quarterfinal round.

Clemson also finished sixth in the final poll.

ACC REGULAR-SEASON CHAMPIONS

The 2000 season was a special year, as Clemson won the ACC regular-season championship. The Tigers won 12-straight matches to start the season, including a season-opening win over 14th-ranked UCLA, and another one of the victories came against #1 North Carolina at Historic Riggs Field. The Tigers also defeated 14th-ranked Virginia 2-1 and 11th-ranked Florida. In the NCAA Tournament, Clemson defeated 15th-ranked Duke and 14th-ranked Florida State. Clemson's next opponent was UCLA in the NCAA quarterfinals at Clemson.

The Bruins made their second trip to Clemson, and this time UCLA defeated Clemson 2-1 in a battle of two top-six teams. Clemson was fourth and UCLA was sixth. The Tigers were ranked fifth in the final poll.

This was the last year for Ray Leone at Clemson, as he took the head coaching job at Arizona State.

TODD BRAMBLE LEADS THE TIGERS

Todd Bramble took over the head coach duties in 2001. In his rookie year, Clemson went 15-5-1 and advanced to the NCAA Final 16. Clemson finished 11th in the final poll.

After a 14-8 record in 2002 and a 14th-place finish that year, Bramble and the Tigers were 11-7-2 in 2003 and finished ranked 17th in the final poll.

In 2004, Clemson finished the season ranked 25th. Clemson was 10-8-2 on the year. In 2005, Clemson was 9-9-2 on the season and went to the NCAA Tournament. The Tigers advanced to the NCAA quarterfinals for the third time in school history.

The 2006 season proved to be a successful year for the Tigers, who advanced to the NCAA quarterfinals for the fourth time ever. In the first round of the NCAA Tournament on November 10 at Historic Riggs Field, Clemson and Vanderbilt played to a 1-1 tie, and the Tigers advanced on penalty kicks 4-3. The Lady Tigers then faced #9 Oklahoma State in the second round on November

12. The game was scoreless after two overtime periods, and Clemson went on to win the penalty kick round by a score of 4-2.

In the NCAA Round of 16 in Stanford, CA, on November 17, Clemson faced #23 Stanford, and it marked the third-straight match that advanced to penalty kicks after ending in a 0-0 tie. Clemson won 4-2 in the penalty kick round, marking the third consecutive match in which the Lady Tigers tied and advanced by winning the penalty kick round. Clemson had an NCAA soccer first by becoming the first-team ever to advance three consecutive matches in tournament play by winning penalty kick rounds. Florida State defeated the Tigers in the NCAA quarterfinal round.

In 2007, Clemson went to the NCAA Tournament and the Tigers finished 10-6-2. This was Todd Bramble's last season as head coach of the Tigers.

Todd Bramble coached the Tigers from 2001-'07, and during that time he had a 80-51-17 record at Clemson.

"I have nothing but fond memories of my time spent coaching at Clemson. It is such a tight-knit community with incredible fan support that it was a pleasure to go to work every day and compete at Historic Riggs Field," Bramble said. "Having big shoes to fill, I am pleased we were able to maintain our reputation as one of the elite soccer programs in the country during my time there. We consistently recruited student-athletes

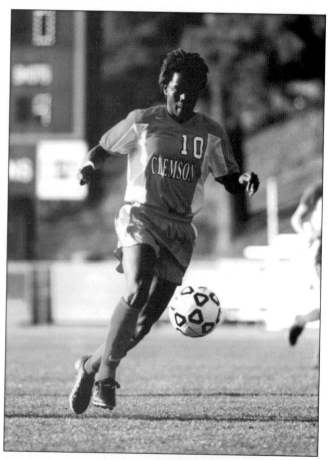

Deliah Arrington holds the Clemson career record for most points (127) and goals (50).

who excelled on and off the soccer field and competed well every year both in the ACC and in our nonconference games."

Bramble took Clemson to the NCAA Tournament every year during his tenure. The Tigers went to the NCAA quarterfinals in 2006.

"Our run to the Elite 8 in 2006 was an unforgettable season, upsetting a couple of tournament favorites along the way and advancing in three games on penalty kicks," said Bramble.

"I was fortunate to coach a tremendous number of players who were extremely talented. Deliah Arrington, Lindsay Browne, Courtney Foster, and Nuria Zufia were some fan favorites on the attacking side of the ball. Allison Mitchell, Paige Ledford, Lydia Vandenbergh, and Elizabeth Jobe were phenomenal two-way midfielders, while Allison Graham was the most sophisticated playmaker I have seen at Clemson.

"Jenny Anderson, Sarah Turner, and Molly Johnson are defenders I would take on my team any day, but I would have to say the biggest difference-maker I coached in my time there was goalkeeper Ashley Phillips," said Bramble.

EDDIE RADWANSKI LOOKS TO LEAD TIGERS BACK TO NATIONAL PROMINENCE

Eddie Radwanski took over the head coaching duties at Clemson in 2011 after a successful stint at UNC-Greensboro.

"We're certainly trying to reconnect with the great history and alumni that Clemson has and reestablish ourselves on the field while adhering to strong academic presence as student-athletes," said Radwanski.

"We are trying to bring back qualities that have always been part of the Clemson women's soccer program—commitment, loyalty, eminence, mentality, sacrifice, playing with one heart, and never giving up. One thing I've always known about Clemson is they never quit battling. We are working on embedding that in our culture [to] reestablish that quality to the Clemson women's soccer program," said Radwanski.

RADWANSKI HAS THE RIGHT FORMULA FOR SUCCESS

When he came to Clemson in 2011, Eddie Radwanski was taking over a Clemson program that had not been very successful in the three years prior to his arrival.

"It seems so long ago when I think about it," Radwanski said when thinking back to December 17, 2010, the day he was hired to lead the women's soccer program at Clemson.

Once a very proud program that competed in 14-straight NCAA Tournaments, the women's soccer program fell from the top of the ACC to the bottom in a very short time.

"We were taking over a program that had not been very successful for whatever the reasons, and I knew I had a job to do," Radwanski said. "From Day 1, I wanted to paint the picture of what we wanted to do and this is how we think we are going to be and come join us. From there, we took the first steps of changing, evolving, and developing the culture for where we are today."

Today, the Tigers are once again ACC Champions.

In his sixth season, Radwanski took Clemson back on top of the ACC, as the program won a share of its second championship in history. However, to get there was not an easy journey.

Radwanski's first three teams at Clemson were not so strong. However, his players competed hard and laid the foundation for the success the program is having today.

After going 6-12 in 2011, the Tigers improved slightly the next year with a 6-10-2 mark. In 2013, they went 7-8-3, and by 2014, they earned a bid to the NCAA Tournament with a 13-3-3 record.

"There were good kids that were in those classes and were good people," Radwanski said. "Really without them, I don't think we will be where we are at this moment. You need people to buy in early on, especially when you evolving, you are changing and you are setting a different type of standard. Some people can stick and do that, and some people have a hard time doing that."

In 2015, Clemson advanced to the second round of the NCAA Tournament and finished with a 13-4-2 mark, while Radwanski was named the NSCAA Southeast Regional Coach of the Year and junior goalkeeper Kailen Sheridan was named a third-team All-American by the NSCAA. Sheridan became just the seventh All-American in Clemson history and first since Ashley Phillips in 2006.

Sheridan also became the third goalkeeper in Clemson history to earn NSCAA All-America honors, as Phillips and Katie Carson received the same honor.

In 2016, Clemson won the ACC regular-season championship for a second time, and for the first time since 2000, thanks to a 14-5-4 record. The Tigers finished 6-1-2 in the ACC and advanced to the ACC Tournament semifinals. In the NCAA Tournament, they made it to the Round of 16 before being eliminated.

Kailen Sheridan made two huge saves and also made her own penalty kick attempt to send the 12th-ranked Tigers to the NCAA's Round of 16 in Chapel Hill, N.C. Clemson and No. 17 Arkansas tied 0-0 in 110 minutes, but the Tigers advanced 4-2 on penalty kicks to make the final 16 of the national tournament for the first time in 10 years.

Number-six North Carolina defeated Clemson 1-0 in the NCAA Round of 16 at Chapel Hill.

"The 2013 freshman class, the [2016 seniors] was the group that started from ground zero," Radwanski said. "That group is one of the big reasons why we were able to change the face of the program back to where we want it to be."

After leading the Tigers to a share of the ACC Regular-Season Championship, Radwanski was named the 2016

ACC Women's Soccer Coach of the Year. Senior midfielder Catrina Atanda was named to the 2016 NSCAA NCAA Division I All-America third team, as announced by the NSCAA.

"I want our kids to have an incredible experience," Radwanski said. "These are some of the best years in their lives. When they leave here, I get excited when I hear those exit interviews that being at Clemson exceed my expectations and that it was everything I dreamed about and more. 'I had a fabulous time.'

"We always preach that they are going to leave with two very valuable things," Radwanski said. "The first thing is their degree which is going to open up the door and is the key to the next phase in their life and then the other one that is equally as important is their memories, and we want them to be spectacular."

The women's soccer team finished 2016 ranked 12th in the nation in the final poll released be the NSCAA (National Soccer Coaches Association of America). It is

the highest final national ranking for the program since the 2001 season, when the Tigers were ranked 11th in the end of the year NSCAA poll.

"From the beginning, it is not about recruiting great soccer players, but it is about recruiting great people, great families and outstanding students," Radwanski said. "Now, I can sit here and say the byproduct of all of that will take care of itself. The wins, getting to the NCAA Tournament, winning the ACC Championship . . . those things are not going to happen if we don't take care of the little things down here.

"I'm proud that in every year that I have been a college coach, my team has been an NSCAA All-American Academic team. Here at Clemson, close to 80 percent of my team is on the honor roll list. We had the highest GPA in the FBS one year and the highest GPA at Clemson for two years. I'm pleased with the fact we are recruiting the right people. The formula is working."

WOMEN'S SOCCER HISTORY

April 3, 1993—Clemson announced that it would field a women's soccer team for the 1994 season.

June 30, 1993—Tracey Leone was named Clemson's first-ever women's soccer coach.

September 4, 1994—Clemson played its first-ever women's soccer match against North Carolina at Chapel Hill. The top-ranked Tar Heels defeated the Tigers 7-0.

September 9, 1994—The Tigers played their first home match against Loyola (MD). Keri Nelson recorded the Tigers' first-ever goal at the 28:09 mark in the game. Nikki Tompkins was credited with the first assist in program history. Clemson earned its first-ever women's soccer victory by a score of 5-1.

September 18, 1994—Clemson upset #15 Vanderbilt 2-1 in overtime in Nashville. It was the program's first win over a ranked team. The Commodores were ranked 15th in the ISAA poll and 16th by *Soccer America*.

September 26, 1994—Clemson entered the national rankings for the first time in program history. The Tigers were ranked 17th by the ISAA and 19th by *Soccer America*.

October 15, 1994—Clemson won its first Atlantic Coast Conference match with a 4-2 victory over N.C. State at home. Ironically, the Tigers' men's team won their first conference match over N.C. State on November 11, 1967.

November 2, 1994—The Tigers' Carmie Landeen and Sheri Bueter were named second-team All-ACC, as an-

Sheri Bueter holds the Clemson record for most assists in a career with 40.

nounced by the league's office. Landeen was also named ACC Rookie of the Year.

November 3, 1994—Clemson lost to N.C. State in overtime in the first round of the ACC Tournament in Chapel Hill, NC. It was the first-ever match played in the conference tournament for the Tigers.

November 6, 1994—Clemson received its first-ever bid to the NCAA Women's Soccer Tournament. The Tigers were the only first-year team in the nation to earn a bid.

November 9, 1994—Clemson played N.C. State to a 1-1 tie after 150 minutes of the Tigers' first-ever NCAA Tournament match, but the Wolfpack advanced to the next round by winning penalty kicks, 5-4.

September 29-30, 1995—The Tigers won the Clemson Tournament with a 6-0 victory over Florida State and a 7-0 defeat of South Carolina.

October 17, 1995—Clemson claimed its 25th all-time victory in a 4-0 win over UNC-Asheville.

November 1, 1995—Meredith McCullen and Sara Burkett were named first-team All-ACC, and Carmie Landeen earned second-team All-Conference honors.

November 6, 1995—Clemson finished the season ranked 16th in the ISAA poll and 15th according to the *Soccer America* listing.

November 12, 1995—The Tigers lost to Texas A&M by a score of 4-1 in the first round of the 1995 NCAA Tournament in College Station, TX.

September 13-14, 1996—Clemson defeated Virginia 2-1 on September 13 and Georgia Washington 2-0 on September 14 en route to winning the Virginia Invitational.

November 1, 1996—The Tigers defeated eighth-ranked Maryland by a score of 2-0 at Historic Riggs Field, recording the program's first-ever win over a top-10 team.

November 6, 1996—Sara Burkett was named to the All-ACC first team, and Beth Keller was a member of the conference's second-team.

November 7-10, 1996—The Tigers played host to the ACC Tournament on Historic Riggs Field. Clemson lost to North Carolina in the Championship game by a score of 4-1. The Tigers appeared on television in the semifinal and Championship games, marking the first time that the team had ever been on television.

November 11, 1996—Clemson finished 11th in the final *Soccer America* poll.

November 17, 1996—The Tigers lost to Wake Forest, 2-1, in the first round of the NCAA Women's Soccer Tournament, held in Clemson, SC.

December 12, 1996—Clemson was ranked 18th in the final NSCAA poll.

September 23, 1997—Clemson recorded its 50th all-time win in history with a 2-1 victory at N.C. State.

October 24, 1997—Clemson defeated Virginia 2-0 at Historic Riggs Field. The Cavaliers were ranked fifth in the nation entering the contest, making it the program's first-ever win over a top-five team.

November 6, 1997—Sara Burkett was named first-team All-ACC, while Sheri Bueter and Meredith McCullen were both named second-team All-Conference.

November 17, 1997—Clemson defeated Georgia 1-0 in the first round of the NCAA Women's Soccer Tournament.

November 22, 1997—The Tigers defeated UNC-Greensboro in the Final 16 of the NCAA Women's Soccer Tournament at Historic Riggs Field.

November 29, 1997—Clemson fell to Santa Clara 3-0 in the NCAA Women's Soccer Tournament quarterfinals in Santa Clara, CA.

December 6, 1997—Sara Burkett was named to the NSCAA All-America second-team, becoming the first women's soccer All-America player in Clemson history.

October 2-3, 1998—Clemson defeated LSU 7-0 on October 2, and Kentucky 3-2 on October 3, to win the ACC-SEC Challenge.

November 4, 1998—Sara Burkett and Sheri Bueter were named first-team All-ACC, and Beth Keller was named to the conference's second-team. It was Burkett's fourth nomination to the All-ACC first team, and she was just the 13th athlete in Clemson history to be a four-time member of the team.

November 5, 1998—Beth Keller scored a hat trick to lead Clemson to a 4-1 ACC Tournament win over N.C. State. It remains the only postseason hat trick in program history.

November 6, 1998—Keller netted two goals in the Tigers' ACC Tournament semifinal win over Virginia, who was ranked 13th in the nation entering the contest.

November 8, 1998—North Carolina defeated Clemson in the ACC Championship game at Orlando, FL. The game was televised live.

November 11, 1998—Clemson finished 11th in the final *Soccer America* poll.

November 15, 1998—The Tigers defeated 11th-ranked Vanderbilt in the Round of 32 at the NCAA Women's Soccer Tournament. The win was Clemson's 16th of the season.

November 21, 1998—Penn State defeated Clemson 1-0 in the NCAA Tournament Round of 16 at State College, PA.

December 9, 1998—Clemson finished 11th in the final NSCAA poll.

November 13, 1999—Clemson's Julie Augustyniak scored with 41 seconds left in regulation as the Tigers defeated Marquette 1-0 in the second round of the NCAA Women's Soccer Tournament. Clemson had received a first-round bye.

November 20, 1999—Clemson and Wake Forest tied 0-0 in the NCAA Tournament Round of 16 at Historic Riggs Field, and the Tigers advanced to the quarterfinals via penalty kicks.

November 27, 1999—North Carolina defeated Clemson 3-0 in the NCAA quarterfinals in Chapel Hill. This was the second Final Eight appearance for the Tigers in two years.

December 8, 1999—Clemson finished the NSCAA poll ranked sixth in the nation.

August 25-October 1, 2000—The Tigers won 12 straight matches to start the season, setting a school record for most consecutive wins.

August 25-27, 2000—Clemson defeated UCLA and Old Dominion to win the Clemson/Nike Kickoff Classic.

September 1-3, 2000—The Tigers defeated Dayton 2-1 on September 1, and were victorious over Charlotte 1-0 on September 3 en route to the Clemson/Nike Invitational title.

September 13, 2000—Clemson upset number-one-ranked North Carolina 2-1 in the Tigers' first-ever upset over a top-ranked team. Deliah Arrington scored the winning goal at the 74:31 mark in the match.

September 22-23, 2000—The Tigers won the Clemson University Invitational with a 5-0 defeat of UNC-Asheville and a 1-0 victory over Furman.

September 29, 2000—Clemson defeated 14th-ranked Virginia in overtime in Charlottesville to record the program's 100th all-time victory.

November 5, 2000—ACC regular-season champion Clemson led the 2000 All-ACC women's soccer team with a school record four first-team selections, as voted upon by the league's eight head coaches. Deliah Arrington, Nancy Augustyniak, Lindsay Browne, and Katie Carson were the Tigers' four honorees.

Ray Leone won the ACC Coach of the Year award after leading the Tigers to the school's first ACC regular-season title. The 2000 Clemson squad compiled a record of 16-1-1 in the regular season and earned the number-one seed in the ACC Championship. Lindsay Browne was named ACC Freshman of the Year and was a member of the All-ACC Freshman Team.

November 6, 2000—Clemson finished seventh in the final *Soccer America* poll.

November 11, 2000—The Tigers defeated Duke 2-1 in the second round of the NCAA Tournament at Historic Riggs Field after receiving a first-round bye.

November 17, 2000—Clemson defeated Florida State 2-0 in the NCAA Tournament Round of 16.

November 25, 2000—Clemson lost to UCLA by a score of 2-1 in the NCAA Tournament quarterfinals.

December 7, 2000—Four Clemson women's soccer players were named to the NSCAA All-Southeast Region Team. Deliah Arrington, Nancy Augustyniak, and Lindsay Browne were named to the first team, while Julie Augustyniak was a second-team honoree. Coach Ray Leone was named the Southeast Region Coach of the Year.

December 11, 2000—The Tigers were ranked fifth in the final NSCAA poll. Nancy Augustyniak was named a second-team All-America selection by the Association.

Nancy Augustyniak was an All-America player in 2000.

On the same day, five Clemson women's soccer players were drafted by the Women's United Soccer Association (WUSA), which was a women's professional soccer league started in the spring of 2001 consisting of eight teams: Atlanta, Boston, New York, Philadelphia, Orlando-Tampa, San Diego, San Francisco, and Washington, D.C. Defender Nancy Augustyniak was the 33rd overall pick and defender Julie Augustyniak was the 64th overall pick, as the twins were both drafted by the Atlanta Beat. Midfielder Amy Gray was the 90th pick overall by the Washington Freedom, and forward Beth Keller was selected 98th overall by the Philadelphia Charge. Lindsay

The 2000 team reached the quarterfinal round of the NCAA Tournament.

Massengale, a defender, was taken as the 108th overall pick by the Boston Breakers.

December 30, 2000—Ray Leone resigned as the head coach of the Tigers to become the head coach at Arizona State.

January 30, 2001—Lindsay Browne was named National Freshman of the Year by Soccer America.

Deliah Arrington, Julie and Nancy Augustyniak, and Lindsay Browne were named All-America players by *Soccer Times*. Nancy Augustyniak was named to the first team. Arrington and Julie Augustyniak were named to the second team. Lindsay Browne was an honorable mention honoree.

February 10, 2001—Todd Bramble was named the head women's soccer coach at Clemson.

September 2, 2001—Bramble coached his first game as the Tigers' head coach, a 4-0 victory over Richmond in Clemson.

November 16, 2001—Clemson defeated Kentucky 1-0 in overtime in the first round of the NCAA Tournament in Clemson, SC. Cindy Mullinix scored the game's only goal.

November 18, 2001—The Tigers defeated Florida State 1-0 in the NCAA Tournament Second Round in Clemson, SC, with Paige Ledford netting the winning goal.

November 25, 2001—Clemson fell to Florida by a score of 3-1 in the NCAA Tournament's Round of 16 in Gainesville, FL.

December 9, 2001—Goalkeeper Katie Carson was named a third-team All-America selection by the NSCAA.

January 9, 2002—Two Clemson women's soccer players, Katie Carson and Leigh Clark, were named Academic All-Americans by the NSCAA. Clark was named to the first team, while Carson was a member of the third-team.

February 11, 2002—Katie Carson was selected in the third round (21st overall pick) of the WUSA draft by the Philadelphia Charge.

November 8, 2002—Clemson defeated Duke 2-0 in the semifinals of the ACC Tournament. Deliah Arrington netted one goal in the match, becoming the first Tiger to score 50 goals in a career.

November 10, 2002—Clemson fell to North Carolina in the championship game of the ACC Tournament in Orlando, FL. The Tigers defeated N.C. State and Duke en route to the championship match.

November 15, 2002—The Tigers lost to Richmond in the first round of the NCAA Tournament in Charlotte, NC.

February 3, 2003—Two Tigers were chosen in the WUSA draft held at league headquarters in Atlanta, GA. Deliah Arrington was selected in the first round as the sixth

overall pick of the draft by the Philadelphia Charge. Heather Beem was the 25th overall pick, the first pick of the fourth round, by the New York Power.

September 12-14, 2003—Clemson defeated Dayton 2-0 and Rhode Island 2-0 as the Tigers won the Furman Invitational.

November 3, 2003—Courtney Foster was named ACC Player of the Week for the second consecutive week, becoming the first Tiger in history to garner the conference honor in consecutive weeks.

November 14, 2003—Clemson advanced to the NCAA Tournament for the 10th consecutive season. Georgia defeated the Tigers in the first round in Knoxville, TN.

August 27, 2004—The Tigers defeated fourth-ranked Texas 1-0 in Austin, TX. This was the highest-ranked team that the team had ever defeated on the road.

August 29, 2004—Clemson upset fifth-ranked Texas A&M 4-1 in College Station, TX. It marked the first time in 30 years that a Clemson sports team had defeated two different top-five teams in consecutive road contests.

November 12, 2004—The Tigers reached the NCAA Tournament for the 11th straight season. Clemson fell to Auburn, 2-0, in the first round of the tournament.

October 20, 2005—Clemson upset eighth-ranked Duke 1-0 at Riggs Field. Courtney Foster scored the match's lone goal.

November 1, 2005—Courtney Foster, Allison Graham, and Ashley Phillips were named to the All-ACC second-team.

November 11, 2005—Clemson fell to Virginia Commonwealth in the first round of the NCAA Tournament. It was the 12th consecutive season that the Tigers received a bid to the national tournament.

December 14, 2005—Goalkeeper Ashley Phillips was named to the NSCAA All-Southeast Region first team.

September 9-11, 2006—Clemson defeated Furman 4-0 and Charlotte 3-0 to win the Carolina's Cup tournament in Greenville, SC.

October 15, 2006—The Tigers upset ninth-ranked Wake Forest 2-1 at Historic Riggs Field.

October 31, 2006—Julie Bolt, Elizabeth Jobe, and Ashley Phillips were named to the All-ACC second-team, and Katie Vogel was named to the All-ACC Freshman Team.

November 10, 2006—Clemson tied Vanderbilt 1-1 after two overtime periods in the first round of the NCAA Tournament in Clemson, SC. The Tigers advanced to the tournament's second round by winning penalty kicks 4-3.

November 12, 2006—Clemson and Oklahoma State played to a 0-0 draw in the NCAA Tournament's second round at Historic Riggs Field. Clemson won the penalty kick round 4-2 to reach the NCAA Final 16.

November 17, 2006—The Tigers achieved an NCAA Tournament first by advancing three consecutive matches in tournament play by winning penalty kicks. Previously tying Vanderbilt and Oklahoma State and advancing by way of penalty kicks, on this date, Clemson tied Stanford 0- 0 in Stanford, CA, and won the penalty kick round 4-2 to reach the NCAA Tournament quarterfinals.

November 24, 2006—Clemson fell to Florida State in the NCAA Tournament quarterfinals. It was the Tigers' fourth trip to the national quarterfinals in the program's 13-year history.

December 6, 2006—Ashley Phillips was named a third-team All-America by the NSCAA. Phillips (first team) and Elizabeth Jobe (third-team) were named to the NSCAA All-Southeast Region team. Phillips was also a third-team All-America, according to *Soccer Buzz*.

November 7, 2007—Ashley Phillips was named first-team All-ACC, and Julie Bolt and Elizabeth Jobe earned second team honors. The three players combined have amassed eight career All-Conference honors.

November 16, 2007—The Tigers were selected to the NCAA Tournament for the 14th consecutive season. Clemson came back from a two-goal deficit to defeat Charlotte 4-2 in the first round before falling to #15 Tennessee 1-0 in double overtime in the second round of the tournament.

November 30, 2007—Todd Bramble resigned as the coach of Clemson to become the head coach at Alabama.

January 14, 2008—Hershey Strosberg was named the fourth head coach in Clemson women's soccer program history.

October 6, 2008—Former Tiger All-America player Nancy Augustyniak Goffi was the 11th overall pick in the Women's Professional Soccer League draft by the Boston Breakers. Another former star, Jenny Anderson-Hammond, was the 22nd overall pick in the draft, by the NJ/NY Sky Blue FC.

Dec. 17, 2010—Eddie Radwanski was named the Tigers' head coach at Clemson. Radwanski spent 10 years as the head coach at the University of North Carolina at Greensboro before his arrival at Clemson.

September 9, 2014—Clemson was ranked 17th by the NSCAA. This marked the first time since October 27, 2007, that the Tigers were ranked nationally.

November 10, 2014—Clemson received a bid to the NCAA Tournament, the first for the Tigers since the 2007 season.

November 14, 2014—The 22nd-ranked Clemson women's soccer team played 18th-ranked and third-seeded South Carolina Gamecocks to a scoreless double-overtime tie in the first round of the NCAA Tournament at Stone Stadium in Columbia, S.C. The Gamecocks advanced after winning the penalty kick round by a score of 4-3.

December 9, 2014—The Clemson women's soccer team was ranked 21st in the nation according to the final poll released by the NSCAA. It is the first time the Tigers have been ranked in the final national poll since 2006, when Clemson finished tied for 14th.

August 3, 2015—The Clemson women's soccer team is ranked No. 22 in the National Soccer Coaches Association of America (NSCAA) preseason poll. This is Clemson's first appearance in the preseason poll since 2007, when the Tigers were ranked 19th.

September 19, 2015—Clair Wagner scored the game's lone goal in the 102nd minute as #10 Clemson defeated fifth-ranked Notre Dame 1-0 at Historic Riggs Field.

October 2, 2015—The sixth-ranked Clemson women's soccer team capped off a special night of celebration of the 100th anniversary of Historic Riggs Field with a 2-0 victory over Wake Forest. Catrina Atanda and Jenna Weston both scored goals for the Tigers.

November 9, 2015—The sixth-ranked Clemson women's soccer team was one of the top eight overall seeds for the 2015 NCAA Tournament, and the number-two seed in its region, as announced by the NCAA. The Tigers' first round opponent was Furman.

November 14, 2015—Clemson defeated Furman 3-0 in the first round of the NCAA Tournament at Clemson's Historic Riggs Field.

November 20, 2015—The Clemson women's soccer team tied its second round NCAA game 1-1 with Mississippi but failed to advance as the Tigers lost in the penalty kicks round 5-4, at Historic Riggs Field. Clemson finished the season with a 14-4-2 record overall.

November 30, 2015—Head coach Eddie Radwanski was named the NSCAA Southeast Regional Coach of the Year. Radwanski's team finished the 2015 season with a 14-4-2 record and qualified for both the ACC and NCAA Tournaments.

December 9, 2015—Junior goalkeeper Kailen Sheridan was named a third-team All-American by the NSCAA. Sheridan became just the seventh All-American in Clemson history and the first since Ashley Phillips in 2006. Sheridan also becomes the third goalkeeper in Clemson history to earn NSCAA All-American honors, as Phillips and Katie Carson received the same honor.

October 27, 2016—For only the second time in program history, and the first time since 2000, the 14th-ranked Clemson women's soccer team claimed the Atlantic Coast Conference regular-season title. The 14th-ranked Tigers did so with a 1-0 upset victory over sixth-ranked Duke in Durham, NC, winning a share of the conference regular-season crown.

November 3, 2016—After leading the Tigers to a share of the ACC Regular-Season Championship, Head Coach Eddie Radwanski was named the 2016 Atlantic Coast Conference Women's Soccer Coach of the Year.

November 13, 2016—Shannon Horgan scored the game's lone goal in leading 12th-ranked Clemson to a 1-0 victory over Northeastern in the NCAA Tournament's First Round at Historic Riggs Field.

November 18, 2016—Kailen Sheridan made two huge saves and also made her own penalty kick attempt to send the 12th-ranked Tigers to the NCAA's Round of 16 in Chapel Hill, NC Clemson and No. 17 Arkansas tied 0-0 in 110 minutes, and the Tigers then advanced 4-2 on penalty kicks to make the final 16 of the national tournament for the first time in 10 years.

November 20, 2016—Number-six North Carolina defeated Clemson 1-0 in the NCAA Round of 16 at Chapel Hill, NC. The 12th-ranked Tigers finished the season with a 14-5-4 record.

December 2, 2016—Senior midfielder Catrina Atanda was named to the 2016 NSCAA NCAA Division I All-America third-team. This is Atanda's first career NSCAA All-America honor.

December 6, 2016—The Clemson women's soccer team was ranked 12th in the nation in the final poll released by the NSCAA (National Soccer Coaches Association of America). It is the highest final national ranking for the program since the 2001 season, when the Tigers were ranked 11th in the end-of-the-year NSCAA poll.

MEN'S
Swimming and Diving

Clemson started the swimming and diving program on March 29, 1919, when the Tigers swam against Georgia Tech in the basement of the Holtzendorff YMCA Building. Clemson was the first college to field swimming and diving in the state of South Carolina. This pool would serve as home of the Tigers until the 1975 season.

PRESTON BROOKS HOLTZENDORFF, JR. BEGINS THE SWIMMING & DIVING PROGRAM

Preston Brooks Holtzendorff, Jr. was born on Nov. 4, 1894, in or near Atlanta, GA. Earlier that same year, on the campus of Clemson Agricultural College, the Young Men's Christian Association (YMCA) started a new chapter at Clemson College. Little did anyone know at the time that the stories of these two infants would someday be inextricably linked.

Holtzendorff grew up in Atlanta and followed in the footsteps of his three older brothers by graduating from law school at the University of Georgia in 1916. Instead of joining his brothers in their law practice, however, he accepted a position as assistant general secretary of the YMCA at Clemson College, with an office in a brand-new building that had just been completed with a large gift from the Rockefeller Foundation.

Not long after Holtzendorff began his tenure at Clemson, Roy John, the man who had hired him, retired from his post as general secretary. Holtzendorff was soon named as his successor, but before he could settle into the new post, he joined the US Army Air Corps to do his part in World War I. By the spring of 1918, he had earned his wings and a commission as a 2nd lieutenant.

The end of the war brought him home again in the fall of that year. For a brief time, Holtzendorff joined his brothers in their Tulsa, OK, law practice, and it was there that he married Anne Linton of Georgia on April 10, 1919. The newlyweds soon moved back East to South Carolina, and Holtzendorff returned to his post as general secretary of "the Y" at Clemson.

For the next 40 years, "Mr. Holtzy," as students affectionately called him, left a huge mark on the religious, social, and recreational experiences of nearly every cadet on Clemson's campus. During that era, the YMCA was the undisputed center for the social and religious life of the students, and Holtzendorff took full advantage of his opportunity to have a positive impact.

Under his direction, the Y thrived with an array of programs. In 1931, Holtzendorff established the intramural sports program, and by 1937, 80 percent of the student body participated. By the late 1940s, as many as 130 organizations and 2,000 people from the campus and community used the Y facilities every day.

In addition to his daily responsibilities, Holtzendorff found time to coach freshman football for five years, men's tennis for one year, and the swimming team for 27 years. He also served three terms on the National YMCA Board and helped establish the S.C. State Conference of YMCAs. He was a devoted elder of Fort Hill Presbyterian Church, president of the Men of the Church and the Rotary Club, and a charter member of the Clemson Fellowship Club.

But it was more than these activities that made Mr. Holtzy so special; it was his abiding love for and service to Clemson students. For example, with America's entry into World War II in 1941, he began sending newsletters to all the Clemson men serving in the nation's armed forces to keep them abreast of news from the home front and from their comrades. Not only were these newsletters treasured among Clemson alumni, but servicemen from other colleges also subscribed.

The sentiments regarding Holtzendorff's service were captured in the program for the 1957 rededication of the YMCA building, which would later be named for him: "Perhaps no one at Clemson College has been more closely associated with more students and has meant so much to them as Mr. Holtzy." The building was later named for him. In 1959, when he retired, *The Tiger* provided another fitting tribute, describing him as "someone who was more interested in others than himself."

Holtzendorff passed away in 1971.

P. B. HOLTZENDORF III WAS A SWIMMING AND TENNIS STANDOUT

The younger Holtzendorff lettered in tennis in 1939, 1940, and 1941 and was the team captain his senior season. He served as the team cocaptain in 1941 in swimming, and in 1939 he led the Tigers to both the state and Southern Conference titles.

The Clemson basketball and swimming teams won Southern Conference titles the same day, and Holtzendorff played a big part in the tankers' victory.

In the 1930s, Clemson enjoyed success in this new sport. Clemson finished the 1934-35 season with a 6-2 mark overall and a third-place finish in the Southern Conference meet. The Tigers also had an 11-5 record overall in the 1933-34 and 1934-35 seasons.

On March 3-4, 1939, Clemson won the Southern Conference Men's Swimming Championship. P. B. Holtzendorff coached the Tigers, and his son, P. B. Holzendorff III, was the star at the meet. The Tigers finished last in the meet the previous season.

Clemson won six events in the Southern Conference Championships from 1933-'53.

In 1975, Clemson defeated Furman in the first meet at Fike Natatorium in the remodeled Fike Field House. In 1984, it was named the Carl McHugh Natatorium in honor of former Clemson swimmer and longtime coach, Carl McHugh.

The 1939 men's swimming team won the Southern Conference Championship.

In 1986, Clemson won its only Atlantic Coast Conference Championship in men's swimming. In 1989, Clemson won its 11th dual meet of the season, a school record for most wins.

STACHELEK HELPS LEAD THE TIGERS TO SUCCESS

In the mid-1980s, Jeff Stachelek helped lead the Tigers to an ACC Championship in 1986.

When asked about what brought him to Clemson, Stachelek noted that it was the notoriety of the athletic and academic programs that made Clemson so appealing.

"I grew up outside of Chicago, IL, and was familiar with Clemson because of their National Championship football team [1981]. Being recruited during the championship run to a school with an awesome fan base, nice facilities, incredible weight room, awesome weather, and beautiful girls made it an easy decision to become a Tiger. Another plus is that Clemson had the degree I was after and that was financial management."

Stachelek has many memorable moments at Clemson, memories that will last a lifetime.

"I treasure three awesome moments in my swimming career. It was 1982 and it was my freshman season. We came to school early to begin training for the season and get to know our teammates. This was the season after our National Championship football season. Our first game was against Georgia. Most of us had never been to a Clemson football game live and after one practice the guys' team was wearing our 'orange blobs'[sweat suits], when we decided to head over to the 'Pep Rally.' The crowd was crazy. The amphitheater was packed. The band and cheerleaders were on stage, the crowd was spelling out the T-I-G-E-R-S cheer, and we decided we needed to be on the stage. At least 20 of us headed through the crowd and jumped on stage! We gathered in the middle of the stage and started another Clemson cheer. Looking out to the crowd, full of passion and energy, instantly instills a level of pride.

"During my sophomore season during our ACC Championship meet, after Day One, we took the lead in the overall team score. Coach Boettner gathered the team around and said, in his affectionate way, 'All right piss ants, the keys are in the car, the windows down, [and] all we have to do is get in and drive away.' This pumped me up so much I had all best times and made the finals in all three of my events. However, we came up just short of the title.

"It was during my junior year [that] we had really turned into a very strong team, we were getting better every dual meet and winning tough races. With some really great seniors [Coy Cobb, Dick Mercer, and Jay Hebert], we could see ourselves winning the ACC championship. During the ACC Championship meet [at Clemson]—it was back and forth between us and NC State—I think we won 15 of the 20 events in a dominant performance.

However, it came down to the last event of the meet, and NC State beat us to win the title by a point. This was a crushing loss, as we were so close; this instilled a will to win like no other event in my life. We won the title my senior year,"Stachelek recounted.

"My senior year in 1986 did not look like a championship season. We had lost so much talent from the previous year, the opportunity to win a championship seemed slim. However, we had huge performances from fellow seniors [Tim Welting, who won the 200 fly in one of the most exciting races ever watched; Tim Hausmann, who stepped up big in the breaststroke and our relays; Steve Rogers, who battled in his sprint and relay events; and Lee DiPrizito and Jeff Poland, who fought for points in distance events and backstroke]—these guys battled every year for four years—and together we delivered big points that allowed us to win and become the first ACC champions that Clemson ever had in swimming. It was such an uplifting/energizing experience that I am able to remember that night, like it was last week. I still love seeing my teammates—and seeing that look in their eyes—such pride of our accomplishments—plus the great Championship ring."

The sport of swimming and the demands of being a college student take their toll. Learning how to deal with the pressures is a challenge within itself.

"When you are in the middle of your college career it doesn't jump out at you . . . all the 6 a.m. morning workouts, weightlifting, dry lands, wheelies, and the miles of swimming every day," said Stachelek. "You just set the picture in your mind; if you want to be the best you have to work harder than the other guy—that is what we did!"

Stachelek describes how this approach has helped in his professional life as well as his interactions with his own kids.

"In my working career, my common theme is to work harder than the competition. I have learned how to be

better prepared, by putting in the time to know my role in my company and how I can offer more of myself to my job. I enjoy working hard as much as I love spending time with my family.

"I have shared my lessons with my kids, as well. I have been coaching my children's sports teams, where I am able to bring my own energy and passion to them and hope they will learn some of the Tiger passion through me."

Stachelek also described his experience meeting his wife through his participation on the swim team.

"I met my wife-to-be at Clemson—Pam Hayden, who was a member of the women's swimming team. From helping to recruit her to the school, to building a relationship that has lasted a lifetime, our time together at Clemson has provided us a list of stories we are proud to tell our kids about—and [help us] turn them into future Tigers!"

COY COBB WAS ALSO A STANDOUT TIGER

Another standout in men's swimming and diving was Coy Cobb. He won four ACC titles in one season. He was a five-time All-America athlete from 1982 through 1985. He died of cancer at an early age, right out of college. Stachelek was a teammate of his at Clemson.

"[Coy]brought a competitive edge to Clemson Swimming and almost single-handedly made us tougher and learn how to win! Except for a freak accident playing ping-pong [in which he broke his ankle], he was a tough guy. He always had a smile on his face and always attracted a crowd. I always enjoyed being in his crowd. He was a great friend and teammate."

A TENURE COMES TO AN END

Prior to the program's official termination, the Tigers experienced a great amount of success.

In 1989, Clemson won its 11th dual meet of the season. The Tigers were 11-4 overall that season.

In the 2004 season, Clemson won 13 dual meets to set the school record for most victories in a season.

The 2011-12 season would be the Tigers' last season as a varsity sport. The Clemson men's swimming and diving program closed out its storied history on March 22-24, 2012, when a pair of swimmers competed in the 2012 NCAA Championships at the Weyerhaeuser King County Aquatic Center in Seattle, WA.

The Tigers, who were represented by senior Chris Dart and junior Eric Bruck at the meet, finished with 12.5 points.

"Both Chris and Eric completed their Clemson swimming careers at NCAAs," said coach Chris Ip. "We were off of our team goals, but I am proud of their efforts throughout the season. Our swim program is nationally and internationally recognized."

Dart began Clemson swimming's final day by competing in the 200 backstroke. He finished in 23rd place,

Jeff Stachelek helped lead the Tigers to the 1986 ACC Championship.

with a time of 1:44.07, only a second and a half away from a spot in the finals.

Immediately following Dart's swim, Bruck competed in the 100 freestyle. The junior came in 30th place with a time of 43.68 seconds, less than half a second away from a berth in the finals of the event.

Overall, the pair of Clemson swimmers competed in four events at the national championships.

Clemson's meet highlight came on the first day of the meet, when Bruck finished sixth in the 50 freestyle with a time of 19.61 seconds. He qualified for the finals by swimming a time of 19.39 in the preliminaries.

"It was a great swim for Eric," said Clemson coach Chris Ip. "The sixth-best finish in the nation is great for this program. We only have two swimmers here, but we are determined to close out Clemson Swimming in style."

MEN'S SWIMMING AND DIVING HISTORY

March 29, 1919—Georgia Tech defeated the Tigers 45-19 at Clemson. This was the first-ever swimming and diving meet for the Tigers.

1934-35—Clemson finished the season with a 6-2 record overall and a third-place finish in the Southern Conference meet.

March 3-4, 1939—Clemson won the Southern Conference men's swimming Championship. P. B. Holtzendorff III was the star at the meet, setting records in the 100- and 50-yard dashes. Clemson also won the 300-yard medley, with a strong team that included Benton Young, John McKnight, and Ben McKnight. Benton Young was the captain of the team and was undefeated in his last two years of competition, setting a new record at the 1939 Southern Conference meet in the 150-yard backstroke. This was a significant improvement, as Clemson had finished last in the Southern Conference meet in 1938.

December 4, 1975—Clemson defeated Furman 72-41 in the first meet at Fike Natatorium in the remodeled Fike Field House.

1975-76—This was the final season for longtime coach Carl McHugh. McHugh served as the swimming coach of the Tigers from 1947-'76.

March 1, 1976—Bob Boettner was named the men's and women's swimming coach.

January 14, 1984—Clemson's Fike Natatorium was dedicated and renamed the Carl McHugh Natatorium, in honor of the former Clemson swimmer and longtime coach who was on the swimming team in 1933-36 and was the head swimming coach from 1947-'76.

February 21-23, 1985—Clemson won a school record 11 individual championships and finished second in the ACC meet, as Jeff Stachelek and Coy Cobb teamed up to win six ACC individual titles in 1985. Stachelek won three events—the 50-, 100-, and 200-yard freestyle. Cobb won the 100- and 200-yard backstroke and the 100-yard butterfly. Chuck Wade won both the one- and three-meter

Coy Cobb was a five-time All-American from 1982-'85.

diving events and was named the ACC's Most Valuable Diver. Bob Boettner was named ACC Coach of the Year, while Cobb was named the meet's MVP.

February 27-28 & March 1, 1986—Clemson won its only Atlantic Coast Conference Championship. Rick Aronberg won the 500-yard freestyle and the 1650-yard Freestyle. He went on to win the 1650 freestyle for four seasons during his career. Bob Boettner was named ACC Coach of the Year, and Chuck Wade, who won the one-meter diving event, was named the ACC Meet's Most Valuable Diver for the second season in a row.

The 1986 team won the ACC Championship.

February 25-27, 1988—Dave Hrovat won the one-meter and three-meter diving events and was named the ACC meet's Most Valuable Diver.

January 21, 1989—Clemson defeated N.C. State 150-93 for its 11th dual meet win of the season. This is the school record for most wins in a season.

March 6, 1991—Jim Sheridan was named head coach of the Clemson men's and women's swimming teams.

June 25, 1994—Bruce Marchionda was named head coach of the Clemson men's and women's swimming and diving teams.

February 8-10, 1996—Brian Haecker won the one-meter diving contest and was named the ACC meet's Most Valuable Diver.

February 25-28, 1998—Razvan Petcu was named the ACC Rookie of the Year after winning the 100-yard freestyle at the ACC Championships in Charlottesville, VA.

July 17, 2002—Chris Ip was named the head coach of the Clemson men's and women's swimming and diving teams.

May 2003—Eric Shulick was named to the Academic All-America team by CSCAA for the first time. He was named again in the 2004-05 season.

January 4, 2004—The Tigers won a school record 12th meet of the season against Georgia Tech. Seven days later, they won their 13th against N.C. State, the current school record.

May 2004—Tigers set men's swimming and diving team record for highest GPA, with a 3.26 team mark.

November 19, 2005—The Tigers won the Nike Cup Invitational, with 1053 points, in Chapel Hill, NC.

April 30, 2010—Clemson began a two-year phaseout of its men's swimming and diving and women's swimming programs, to be completed by the end of the 2011-12 academic year. Athletic Director Terry Don Phillips made the announcement. Phillips said the women's diving program would continue.

March 24-26, 2011—Clemson finished 25th at the NCAA Meet in Minneapolis, MN. Seth Broster, Eric Bruck, Chris Reinke, and Chris Dart were honorable mention All-Americans in the 200-meter freestyle relay. Bruck was an honorable mention All-American in the 50-meter freestyle.

Feb. 4, 2012—The men's and women's swimming and diving teams hosted their last-ever home meet. The women's team defeated Emory 180-116, and the men's team picked up a 174-121 win.

March 22-24, 2012—Two Tiger swimmers competed in the 2012 NCAA Championships at the Weyerhaeuser King County Aquatic Center in Seattle, WA.

The Tigers finished with 12.5 points, good for 30th place.

WOMEN'S
Swimming

On September 7, 1975, Clemson announced that the school would field women's swimming and diving and that Coke Ellington would be the team's first coach. The sport was a club-level sport the previous year in 1974-75.

Ellington was a native of Moultrie, GA, and he attended Emory before transferring to the University of Georgia. He swam for the Bulldogs in 1963, 1964, and 1965 and won the award for best scholar-athlete on the Georgia swimming team. He also worked as a city editor of newspapers in Rock Hill; Anniston, AL; and Athens, GA, before coming to Clemson. Besides working with the Tiger swimmers, he also worked in the Clemson University Public Relations office. Although he worked with newspapers in various cities, he was quite active in swimming, as he also coached in YMCA swimming programs.

Ellington led the program for one year before Bob Boettner took over the next season in 1976-77.

BOETTNER COMES TO TIGERTOWN

Bob Boettner, previously an assistant at North Carolina State, was named an assistant swimming coach on the men's side for one year in 1975-76 and was hired to assume the head duties of both the men's and women's programs the following year and replace veteran coach Carl McHugh, who coached the men's program for 28 years.

Boettner, a native of Paterson, NJ, played football at East Carolina, where he earned both his undergraduate and graduate degrees in education. A knee injury ended his career on the gridiron and caused him to switch his focus to swimming. Boettner began his coaching career with a two-year stint at J.J. Rose High School in Greenville, NC,

in 1965. Boettner went to N.C. State University in 1967 as a full-time assistant under legendary coach Willis Casey. He also served under Don Easterling at N.C. State. Under his eight seasons at N.C. State, the Wolfpack captured the ACC crown seven times and was a consistent finisher in the nation's top 20.

After coming to Clemson, Boettner was the coach of the men's and women's program for 15 years, from the 1976-77 season through the 1990-91 season. His years at Clemson marked the second-longest men's tenure and the longest women's tenure.

"I have many fond memories of Clemson," said Boettner. "As you may know, I coached both the men's and women's programs. The fact [that] we helped start the women's program and finished in the top 10 on a regular basis was a major accomplishment. On the men's side, we finished in the top three in the ACC for many years and kept getting stronger. I thought we helped develop the men's program and were successful on a consistent basis.

"We had a lot of individual ACC champions, and 67 people won over 200 All-America honors. I thought we made great strides in the swimming and diving program at Clemson. I think a lot of credit needs to go to my assistant coaches. Over the years we had many good assistant coaches, and that helped make things great.

"We also had really great kids. Mitzi Kremer was a two-time national champion. We had Pam Hayden, Coy Cobb, Jeff Stachelek, Richard Bader, and I could go on and on. We had several to make the Olympic Trials. Another thing I am very proud of is that every swimmer that swam for me that stayed at Clemson for four years graduated, except for one student-athlete and he was just one class short," said Boettner.

Although very proud of the swimming accomplishments, he is even more proud of the swimmers' academic standing.

"All of our swimmers were hard-working people. They were also very studious. We would always be one of the top academic sports on campus and I was very proud of that fact. We would recruit good swimmers and made great swimmers out of them. We had a hard time

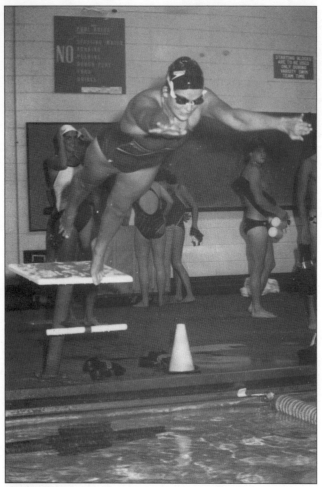

Mitzi Kremer won four NCAA titles during her career. She was the NCAA Champion in the 200- and 500-meter freestyle events in 1987 and again in 1989.

with the 25-yard pool with recruiting, but I think we did well. We could develop swimmers and we had success at it. A lot of times we took chances on kids and they turned out and reached their potential, not only in the pool but also in the classroom as we really emphasized academics.

"My feeling was if I could get a potential swimmer on campus for a visit I would sign them. Clemson is a very special place with a great deal to offer."

Boettner finished his career at Clemson, having led the men's team to an ACC Championship and the women's team to three conference titles. The women's team also had seven top-25 finishes under Boettner.

PAM HAYDEN

One of the greatest women's swimmers at Clemson was Pam Hayden-Stachelek. She was named to the ACC's 50th Anniversary team and was ACC Swimmer of the Year in 1986. She was a 21-time All-America swimmer, which is tops among Clemson swimmers. She entered in five events at the 1988 Olympic trials and was a 10-time ACC Champion. She also became a Clemson Hall of Fame member in 1995.

When asked what brought her to Clemson, the challenges in both academics and athletics were the main reasons.

"The great combination of the athletics and academics was the main draw," said Hayden-Stachelek. "I wanted to go and be part of a good swim team where the women worked out with the men's team, providing better practice competition. It was a team on the rise in the ACC and nationally. Academically, the overall school aligned with my interest of science/microbiology."

Hayden-Stachelek also recalled many memorable moments in the swimming pool.

"Winning the ACC was a huge team accomplishment in 1987, as it was our first. We went to Chapel Hill and saw North Carolina's new pool and they were the team to beat. However, we were up to the challenge, and we had best time after best time. It began to snowball. . . . The Clemson fans came to Chapel Hill with painted chests, faces, hair— it was lots of fun. After we won the title, Coach Boettner jumped off the high dive in his clothes as we celebrated the win. On the way back driving into Clemson, I remember a big sign off the highway congratulating us on our victory, and that's something I won't ever forget.

"I also remember Christmas breaks when we trained on campus when the entire student body was gone," Hayden-Stachelek added. "The school had such a different feel. This really connected you to the campus, the facilities. It made us felt like caretakers of the campus until everyone else came back.

Clemson means a lot to Hayden-Stachelek, and she is very supportive of the school and follows the Tigers faithfully.

"Clemson means everything to us, as we follow Clemson regularly—even living in California, we stay close. We can see the impact we have had as our neighbors' and friends' kids are now going to Clemson because we have had such a positive impact on them," said Hayden-Stachelek.

Mitzi Kremer (L) won a Bronze Medal at the 1988 Olympics (4x100-meter freestyle relay), and Michele Richardson won a Silver Medal (800 freestyle) at the 1984 Olympics.

OTHER CLEMSON GREATS

Mitzi Kremer was another Clemson great who swam for the Tigers. She was a NCAA Champion in the 200-and 400-meter freestyle in 1987 and 1989. She was a 1988 Olympic Bronze medalist in the 4x100-meter freestyle relay.

At Clemson, Kremer was a 16-time All-America swimmer. She helped lead Clemson to three-straight ACC Championships and won five individual ACC Championships from 1987-'89. She was named the ACC Championship MVP in 1987 and 1989.

Another star was Michele Richardson, the 1984 Olympic Silver Medalist in the 800 freestyle and a four-time ACC champion.

Jill Bakehorn was a 15-time All-America swimmer during her career in 1986-89. She was a four-time All-ACC selection and won five ACC championships.

WOMEN'S SWIMMING HISTORY

Sept. 7, 1975—Clemson officials announced that the school would elevate women's swimming to varsity status. Coke Ellington was announced as the team's first coach.

Nov. 11, 1975—Clemson defeated Appalachian State and lost to Brenau in the first-ever women's swimming meet for the Lady Tigers.

March 1, 1976—Bob Boettner was named the men's and women's swimming coach.

March 17-19, 1977—Chris Daggitt became Clemson's first female All-American regardless of sport as she finished 10th in the 400 individual medley at the AIAW National Championship in Providence, RI. Daggitt was a freshman that season and was a native of Dayton, OH.

March 18-20, 1982—Clemson finished 18th at the first NCAA Women's Swimming Meet in Gainesville, FL. Senior diver Cappy Craig finished fourth in the one-meter and seventh in the three-meter diving event. She became the first woman in Clemson history to be named NCAA All-America. This was also Clemson's first-ever top-20 finish in NCAA competition.

February 14-16, 1985—Carolyn Hodge was named ACC Diver of the Year at the ACC Swimming and Diving Meet at Clemson, SC.

March 21-23, 1985—Clemson finished 19th in the NCAA Women's Swimming Meet in Tuscaloosa, AL.

January 25, 1986-November 11, 1989—Clemson had a winning streak of 16 consecutive Atlantic Coast Conference meets.

February 20-22, 1986—Bob Boettner was named ACC Coach of the Year, and Pam Hayden was named the ACC Meet's MVP.

Head coach Bob Boettner led the women's swimming team to three straight ACC Championships in 1987, 1988, and 1989.

March 20-22, 1986—The Lady Tigers finished seventh in the NCAA Women's Swimming Meet in Fayetteville, AK.

February 19-21, 1987—Clemson won the ACC Championships for the first time in program history at the Koury Natatorium in Chapel Hill, NC. The Lady Tigers ended North Carolina's six-year run of ACC Championships. Mitzi Kremer was named the Meet's MVP, and the Lady Tigers' Bob Boettner was named ACC Coach of the Year.

March 19-21, 1987—Clemson finished fifth in the NCAA Women's Swimming and Diving Meet in Bloomington, IN. Clemson's Mitzi Kremer won the National Championship in the 500-yard freestyle, with a time of 4:41.13. She also was the National Champion in the 200-yard freestyle, with a time of 1:45.99.

February 6, 1988—The Lady Tigers defeated Georgia 175-93. This gave Clemson a 9-0 record for the season, the first undefeated season for the Lady Tigers in their history.

February 18-20, 1988—Clemson won the ACC Championships for the second season in a row. Coach Bob Boettner was named ACC Coach of the Year. Pam Hayden won the 500-yard freestyle and the 200-meter butterfly and was on the 400-meter Medley Relay team to help lead the Lady Tigers to the championship.

March 17-19, 1988—The Lady Tigers finished fifth in the NCAA meet at Austin, TX.

February 16-18, 1989—The Lady Tigers won the ACC Championships in Chapel Hill, NC, for the third season in a row. Kremer won the 100, 200, and 500 freestyle events and was a member of the 400 medley relay, the 400 freestyle relay, and the 800 freestyle relay. Clemson won 16 events at the meet. Kremer was named the meet's MVP, while Bob Boettner was named ACC Coach of the Year. Diver Jennie Graviss was named ACC Diver of the Year.

March 16-18, 1989—Clemson finished ninth at the NCAA Championships in Indianapolis, IN. Kremer was the leading point scorer in the NCAA Meet and was responsible for 56 of Clemson's 142 points. Kremer won the National Championship in the 500 freestyle, with a time of 4:39.18. She also won the National Championship in the 200 freestyle, with a NCAA record time of 1:44.78.

February 15-17, 1990—Mandy Meek was named ACC Diver of the Year at the ACC Women's Swimming and Diving Championships in Raleigh, NC.

March 15-17, 1990—Clemson finished 24th at the NCAA Meet in Austin, TX.

March 6, 1991—Jim Sheridan was named head coach of the Clemson men's and women's swimming teams.

March 19-21, 1992—The Lady Tigers finished 20th at the NCAA Meet in Austin, TX.

June 25, 1994—Bruce Marchionda was named head coach of the men's and women's swimming teams.

February 1-3, 1996—Wendy Henson was named ACC Rookie of the Year at the ACC women's meet.

February 20-22, 1997—Clemson won the ACC Championships in Chapel Hill, NC. Bruce Marchionda was named ACC Coach of the Year, and Erin Schatz won the 100- yard and 200-yard backstroke events to lead the Lady Tigers.

July 17, 2002—Chris Ip was named the head coach of the men's and women's swimming and diving teams.

February 20-23, 2008—Junior Michelle Parkhurst was named ACC Most Valuable Swimmer after winning the 100 back, 200 back, 200 free, and 200 free relay. She set ACC records in each of the latter three events.

April 30, 2010—Clemson began a two-year phaseout of its men's swimming and diving and women's swimming programs by the end of the 2011-12 academic year. Athletic Director Terry Don Phillips made the announcement. Phillips said the women's diving program would continue.

Feb. 4, 2012—The men's and women's swimming and diving teams played host to their last-ever home meet. The women's team defeated Emory 180-116, while the men's team picked up a 174-121 win.

MEN'S
Tennis

ONE OF THE EARLY SPORTS AT CLEMSON

The Clemson men's tennis program started in 1907 at Clemson. This was the first year that the then-Clemson Athletic Association paid for the participation of student athletes to represent Clemson in the annual State Tennis Tournament. Clemson did not participate in the first state tournament that was held in Greenville in 1906, but better preparations were made for Clemson's entering in the 1907 tournament.

Clemson held a tournament to see which singles player and which doubles team would represent Clemson in the state tournament. Schools from all over the state participated. Spratt and Riser first represented Clemson.

In 1911, James Erwin represented Clemson, and in 1912 he won the state singles tournament. In 1913, during his

senior season, Erwin again won the state singles championship. James won the Southern Intercollegiate Athletic Association (SIAA) singles title in 1913, and he and his brother John won the SIAA doubles title that same season.

Allen Haskell and Julian Robertson were the 1917 & 1918 State Doubles Champions.

THE ERWINS WERE EARLY TENNIS STARS

The Erwin brothers, James and John, were natives of Spartanburg, SC. They were stalwarts in basketball and tennis.

In tennis, James won the state championship in singles, defeating Grier of Erskine on November 11, 1911, at the Spartanburg Country Club. He won the State Singles Championship again, as he defeated Wingate Waring of the University of South Carolina in straight sets—6-0, 6-1, 6-2—on October 18, 1912, at the Sans Souci Club in Greenville, SC.

James, along with his brother John, defeated Oates and Chambers of North Carolina in straight sets (best three of five)—7-5, 6-4, 6-4—to win the Southern Intercollegiate Athletic Association (SIAA, an early conference composed of ACC and SEC schools) Championship in Columbia, SC, on May 7, 1913. After receiving a first-round bye, the Erwin brothers defeated Goodwin and Brand of Georgia—6-4, 4-6, 6-1—in the semifinals, setting up the appearance in the championship match.

James defeated Malcolm N. Oates of North Carolina in straight sets—6-4, 7-5, 6-2—to capture the SIAA Singles title on May 7, 1913, in Columbia, SC.

On the basketball court, James played in the 1911-12 and 1912-13 seasons. In the first games in Clemson history on February 9, 1912, the Tigers defeated Furman 46-12 and the Butler Guards 78-6 in Greenville. In the Furman game, he scored 22 points and in the Butler Guards game he scored 58 points, still a Clemson single-game record. The next day against Wofford in Spartanburg, he scored 18 points in the Tigers' 34-23 win. Erwin scored 98 points in three days of play.

James graduated from Clemson in textiles in 1913. He was a charter member of Spartanburg Country Club. He was married to Jean Shepherd Erwin, and they had a daughter, Jean.

Erwin enjoyed much success in amateur tennis, winning state amateur championships in 1913, 1916, and 1919, and doubles in 1912, 1913, and 1915. He also played on the champion mixed doubles teams and won the Vanderbilt Cup at Asheville in 1915 for singles. He won several other amateur titles around the state and locally in various cities. He had little if any coaching in tennis as he grew up. He also became an avid golfer as he grew older.

James died on February 6, 1978, in Spartanburg, SC.

John graduated from Clemson in 1914, the same year that Frank Johnstone Jervey (the man after whom the Jervey Athletic Center is named) graduated. He majored in textiles and put together a very impressive athletic résumé.

He was on the Clemson tennis team in 1912, 1913, and 1914. He served as the president of the State Intercollegiate Tennis Association his senior year in 1914. This position was in charge of running the annual state college tennis tournament.

He was also on the first basketball squad that Clemson fielded and was on the Tiger cager squad in 1912, 1913, and 1914 as a forward. He holds the distinction of being the only player-coach in Clemson basketball history, a capacity that he held in 1914.

The 1913 Taps called him "a fine point-getter and very aggressive in every play."

Both brothers ran a grocery wholesaler in Spartanburg, SC. John was a veteran of World War I, where he served as a Navy Ensign. He had a son whom he named after his brother, James Overton.

John died on Friday, March 3, 1972, in Spartanburg, SC.

FIRST DUAL MATCH

Clemson won their first dual competition on April 28, 1921, when Bill Hines and St. John's traveled to Wofford and beat the Terriers 2-0. This was the first dual match that Clemson had ever participated in involving team vs. team.

During the 1920s Clemson played more dual matches and participated in state tournaments. The first men's tennis coach Clemson had was during the 1927 season—Preston Holtzendorff, also the swimming coach for the Tigers. Clemson finished 2-2-1 that year but did not have a team in 1928. In 1929, Hoke Sloan started his 30-year career.

HOKE SLOAN—THE FATHER OF CLEMSON TENNIS

The one man who could truly be called the Father of Clemson Tennis is Hoke Sloan, after whom the varsity tennis center is named. Sloan donated the money that made the facility where the Tigers play today.

Sloan added stability to the program with more organized practices and advice on how to improve in the game of tennis.

Sloan did not receive a salary for coaching tennis at Clemson until the end of his career. Many times he would use his personal automobile and carry the Tigers to their respective matches during the course of a season. He would take the Tigers to Florida and other southeastern states for tougher competition during the spring break week. Due to the arrival of the Great Depression, Clemson did not field tennis teams in 1932, 1933, and 1936 and during the war years of 1944 and 1945. Nevertheless, Sloan was always there coaching the game he loved so much and sharing his knowledge with others.

Sloan was born in nearby Pendleton, SC, in 1896. He grew up in Clemson, attended Clemson College, and played tennis for the Tigers in 1915. He subsequently transferred to and graduated from Auburn in 1917. His tennis days started at the city courts in and around Clemson while he was a teenager and would continue through his entire life. Sloan served in the Navy during WWI and then returned to Clemson after the war. During his lifetime, aside from coaching Clemson tennis, he was a successful businessman who ran a men's store and was a realtor in the area.

During his tenure, the program was completely non-scholarship, and most of his tennis players were playing others sports, as well. In 1957, he coached the team to a 10-3 record and a third-place finish in the Atlantic Coast Conference. After this season, he retired from coaching, but he continued to teach the game as the director of tennis at Camp Carolina in Brevard, NC. Also during his career, he was a tireless worker for IPTAY, going around the state and surrounding areas enlisting people to join and help Clemson.

Sloan had a 158-121-4 record during his 30-year Clemson tenure. He passed away on December 22, 1979.

DUANE BRULEY LEADS TIGERS TO FIRST ACC CHAMPIONSHIP AND UNDEFEATED SEASON

Duane Bruley was the head coach of the Tigers from 1963-'73. He led the Tigers to their first Atlantic Coast

The 1969 team won the school's first ACC Championship.

Conference Championship in 1969 with a 16-0 mark. He served as the head coach for 11 seasons and also as professor of chemical engineering at Clemson. Bruley had a 150-42 record and is the winningest coach at Clemson as far as winning pct. for coaches with ten or more years experience, regardless of sport.

"I got my doctorate at the University of Tennessee and I coached tennis there. I had won the Knoxville city championship and I had been giving lessons and this is how General Neyland heard about me and gave me the job of head tennis coach at the University of Tennessee."

Bruley's decision to continue coaching at Clemson happened by chance.

"I had a job offer at Clemson teaching in their chemical engineering department, and I was really excited about it. I had no idea about the tennis coaching job being open at Clemson. In fact, I didn't think I would coach anymore.

"It so happens that Coach Frank Howard contacted me once I accepted the teaching job at Clemson. He told me they were losing their coach this season and he needed a tennis coach. Again, I hadn't planned on coaching tennis anymore, but it was so tempting that I took the offer. I really appreciate Coach Howard helping me and giving me the opportunity to be the head tennis coach at Clemson.

"I remember one day that Coach Howard wanted to see me. I nervously went to his office; I had no idea what he wanted. He told me in his gruff voice, 'You know Bruley, I always thought tennis was a sissy sport. But I just want to shake your hand and congratulate you. Anyone that beats Georgia Tech is all right with me.' I will never forget that. We had beaten Georgia Tech earlier in the week. He told me I was doing a great job, so I felt really great about what we were doing.

"I also officiated junior tournaments and I got to meet some wonderful people, and this helped in our recruiting, as well."

Bruley described why his first match at Clemson was so memorable, and it was not necessarily because it was his first match.

"I never will forget my first match as head coach at Clemson. We were playing our rival, South Carolina, in a conference match on March 23, 1963. We defeated the Gamecocks 9-0. What made this match so unbelievable is that we did not lose a game in the entire match! We won every set 6-0. All six singles and all three doubles matches were 6-0, 6-0. I never heard of a match being won like that before or since. It was a great way to start my career at Clemson."

STORIES FROM 1969 TENNIS TEAM, BY PLAYERS JIM POLING AND DAVID COOPER

THREE FLORIDA BOYS FROM WINTER PARK ANCHOR THE 1969 TEAM

It was fall of 1968 and the start of another school year at Clemson. Fall at Clemson was always about football, but there was excitement in the air for tennis, as well. It

was the culminating and very last year that David Cooper, Jim Poling, and Ed Shelton would play together on the same team. The three players each had been recruited by Coach Duane Bruley from Winter Park, FL. All three had been on the same Winter Park High School team, and all three were coached by legendary Rollins coach Norm Copeland. Now, all three would play their last year for Clemson. They would all play key roles in 1969, as Clemson would claim the school's first Atlantic Coast Conference Championship.

David Cooper played number-one singles and number-one doubles with Jim Poling that year. Jim played number-five singles, and Ed Shelton played number-six singles and number-three doubles. They were the cornerstones, but for sure, the '69 team had a lot of diversity and talented players.

Nicky Kelaidis, who played number-two singles, was from Greece. He went on to play professionally for several years before he went to teach for the French Tennis Federation at Roland Garros. The number-three player was Suppi Rahim, who was from Pakistan and the brother of former Clemson #1 player Zulfi Rahim.

Gordon Herbert, who played fourth, was probably the most unusual of all.

COACH FRANK HOWARD DISCIPLINES A TENNIS TEAM MEMBER

Gordon Herbert was a former United States Marine and had survived the famous Hill 81 Battle in Vietnam. After those experiences, he surely had the right to be a free spirit. During his Clemson days, he was one of the first really long-haired hippies any of us had seen; however, he could sure play tennis! One day after Herbert had finished getting taped up in the training room, he ran into Athletic Director and Head Football Coach Frank Howard. The two got into a heated discussion about the length of his hair. It ended with Coach Howard chasing Gordon out to the courts with a pair of scissors. About 50 people enjoyed the spectacle with the rotund Howard running after Herbert. Coach Howard was only wearing his boxer shorts!

THE EXPERIENCES THAT BOND A TEAM

It's funny the kind of things that you remember when you share so much with a group of guys. It is the emotional attachment that comes from sharing the same hopes, dreams, and beliefs at this special time of your life.

Trips to play other schools were always fun. Most of the trips were less than 150 miles, so we could make it there and back on the same day. We always took two state cars. Coach Bruley would drive one and most of the guys would try their best to get in the other car to not have to listen to tennis-talk for the whole trip.

One evening on the trip back, in the noncoach car, the driver was kind of stuck in traffic, so he turned on his flashers. Since we had a state license tag, people thought we were a police car, and they all pulled over to let us go through. We laughed all the way home never thinking of the consequences had a real police car seen us pull this stunt!

CHAMPIONSHIP SEASON

In the Spring of 1969, the team won match after match, beating both archrival South Carolina and perennial tennis powerhouse North Carolina in the regular season. In the ACC Tournament that was held at N.C. State that season, David Cooper won the singles title, while Jim Poling and Cooper won the doubles title to lead the Tigers to their first-ever ACC team title.

Eddie Shelton, Jim, and all the other members of the team contributed important wins during the tournament, as well. After the tournament, back at the motel, all the team players joined forces to throw Coach Duane Bruley into the swimming pool in celebration.

Looking back to those very special times, and to those very special guys on the team, it is quite profound that you remember so many simple things that were shared. The bigger events that became our proud memories were spawned under great emotion from a group effort given by the bond of "Team." The unique way that players held up under the pressures of many individual challenges was best experienced when we stood side by side with a teammate who shared the same dreams, goals and beliefs.

THE KRIESE YEARS 1975-2008 (AS TOLD BY COAUTHOR CHUCK KRIESE)

COACH KRIESE: CLEMSON TENNIS WILL ALWAYS BE SOMETHING MUCH DEEPER THAN WINS AND LOSSES

Clemson Tennis has enjoyed a worldwide reputation for quality player development, deep integrity, and the toughest training program in tennis. The young men that played on any of the Clemson tennis teams understood what it meant to play with pride for their school, be strong teammates to each other, and how to honor the sport with their best efforts. They also knew what it was to compete. Not only did they know how to compete against their rival opponents, they learned to look deep within themselves and to stretch the limits of their bodies, mind, and their souls. The lessons learned by the experience of Clemson Tennis would be lessons learned for life. The bond of brotherhood between the men on the team was for life, as well.

When I look back at my more than 12,000 days of coaching and the time spent working with young people at Clemson University, I do so with great humility and pride.

For some time, I didn't have any idea of how I got the job at a major university like Clemson at age 25. I did not know why then-Athletic Director Bill McLellan and his assistant, Bobby Robinson, would believe that I could

do the job at that young age. McLellan would later say that he just trusted Don Wade. Don Wade told him that I could coach. Don Wade said that I would get the job done. Don Wade was a Clemson man and then the athletic director at my alma mater, Tennessee Tech.

I got to Clemson by the grace of God and with some help from Coach Don Wade.

Clemson hired me at 25, and I owe my coaching life to Bill McLellan for taking a chance on me. I found out after 10 years or so at Clemson that Coach Don Wade had a lot to do with my getting to coach at Clemson. He recommended me to Bill McLellan, and I'm forever grateful. It had originally been a longtime goal of mine to be the tennis coach at my alma mater, Tennessee Tech. I had already figured that if I couldn't coach at Tech, I would go back to Indiana and coach high school basketball.

I would not be selected as the tennis coach at Tennessee Tech. I was extremely disappointed, but at the same time quite grateful for my six years of study there, getting my undergraduate and graduate work under my belt. It was in the middle of the Vietnam War, and I would have been drafted for sure without being able to play tennis at Tech. I have often stopped by the piece of sidewalk next to the administration building at Tech to show my children where I made one of the greatest momentum-changing decisions of my life.

As I walked from my final exam of my Master's degree work at Tech that day in '74, I stopped to think about the six wonderful years of education that I had received and the way my life would have been different if Tech had not given me the scholarship to play tennis. The Vietnam War was on, and I most certainly would have been drafted had it not been for Tech. God tugged at my coat that day, and instead of heading back home, I chose to walk back across campus to thank Coach Don Wade, who was the athletic director.

I remember telling Coach Wade that it would remain my lifelong dream to coach at Tech, and if the job ever opened up, even if it were 1999, to please consider me once more for the job. He said he would.

Coach Wade said that he appreciated my coming by to see him. I thought that my college coaching chances were gone for good. I did not know that Coach Wade had been a football teammate and a classmate of Bill McLellan, the athletic director at Clemson. The two would meet at an AD's meeting a few weeks after my short meeting with Coach Wade, and it came up that McLellan was looking for a tennis coach at Clemson. Two months later, I was busy in a tennis teaching position in Montgomery, AL, when I got a call from Clemson. It was a strange call and from a school that I had never been to in my life.

We often have experiences in life where we just feel comfortable and know that we had been there before.

From the moment that I saw Clemson, I felt that I had already been there before. Maybe it was my youthful lack of understanding how hiring processes worked, but I knew in my heart as I left campus that this is where I was meant to be. I would spend the next 33 years or 12,000 days of my life at Clemson. God absolutely does work in mysterious ways. I thank Him always for guiding me and helping me to have a humble heart when I didn't get the job at Tech, and I thank these wonderful men at Clemson for giving me that chance as a young man.

The noncompromising daily work, the traditions, the many youngsters that became men on our teams, and the great seasons as well as the bad, are all irreplaceable. They came and went so quickly, and all were packed to the brim with deep emotion, powerful meaning, and unforgettable memories. Our players came in as freshmen and left four years later as strong men willing to take on leadership roles in the world. I am very proud of every relationship that I had with these young men during those years. Many of the friendships have grown stronger over the years. The sharing of each and every experience during this critical time of their lives left irreplaceable marks on all of us.

The bonding of each team, and the unity developed between players as they struggled and worked together for a noble cause, are among the best memories of my life. What we accomplished was done so with great pride for our school, with great honor of the process of how we went about doing it, and was done so with great love for each other. Few can ever really know the power and magnitude of watching a group of men as they work, sweat, and suffer together for the same goals. It was unique and it was good. There were no shortcuts taken. There was

Chuck Kriese was a three-time National Coach of the Year.

not a stone left unturned in the pursuit of excellence. That special pride that was Clemson Tennis will last for generations to come. I will remember always those great "Men of Morning Madness."

MORNING MADNESS TRAINING

I tried many times to call it something like "Tiger-Pride Training," but the players always liked to call it "Morning Madness." Morning Madness was a tradition like no other. It gained recognition around the country as the way that all Clemson tennis players had to earn their starting place on the team. There was no other way to make the team—two to three tough weeks of 5:44 a.m. running at the track and no balls and no rackets used until the base work was done. There were some great stories of heroics during those early autumn mornings.

I never cut a player for my first 18 years as the Clemson coach. If a young man was committed enough to stay out and go through what he had to do at the track, he got a spot at least on the "Work Team" or the "White Team." Of course, the "Orange Team members" were the starting lineup players and the returnees from the previous year. They knew they had to show up for the fall season in good shape or it was a torturous period of training alongside of so many who wanted their spots. It was a great system, as those guys who weren't on the top team at the start would train hard for a year, and I always felt that one or two would get good enough to make the varsity the next year. I needed that extra base of players, as Clemson was so far from any metropolitan area of tennis players, and this enabled me to have a couple of guys ready for each year other than a top recruit who I would bring to the team.

Cris Robinson did not want to quit. Whenever I think of him, I think of this Bible verse:

"Consider it all joy my brothers, whenever you face trials of many kinds, because you know that the testing of your faith develops perseverance. Perseverance must finish its work so that you may mature and be complete, not lacking in anything." James 1: 1-4

I call it Tiger Pride, my athletes call it Morning Madness; two weeks of 6:00 a.m. running with time trials including a 5:15 mile required to make the team.

At the end of the trials in '91, only one player remained. Cris was smaller than the others at 5'7", and a diabetic. Although he tried valiantly—eight times—his personal best, 5:23, fell short. I was bombarded by the urge to make an exception. If any kid ever deserved it, he did. But on the court and in the world, Cris would not just be competing against small diabetics. I reaffirmed to him the reality that the 5:15 mile was the only way to make the team. He agreed without reservation. I think we both knew this would be the last attempt. With two upperclassmen and a ball of kite string, we made one more try. I tied fifteen feet of string around the waist of each pacer and told Cris, "When you're at the end of your rope, tie a knot and hang on." As they ran, if the string broke, he lost; if he dropped it, he quit. Each pacer would run two laps each, with Cris following close behind.

The pacers did their job. The half-mile time was 2:31. The handoff was made to the second pacer. Lap three was always the backbreaker. This time the string got taut down the backstretch, as Cris's pace slowed. "No!" I yelled. "One more tough minute. There's a chance," I yelled inside. As he rounded the final backstretch on lap four, I knew he would make it. The stopwatch read 5:11 as he fell across the finish line.

My emotions were high as I coyote-howled and laughed outrageously and ran with Cris on his Victory Lap with the string in hand.

A strong-minded kid, his coach, his supportive friends, and thirty feet of kite string had overcome this barrier and stumbling block. God is the greatest coach. He allows trials, but he gives us whatever we need to get the job done.

After a very rough start, Cris showed tremendous perseverance many more times, as he went on to win six US Amateur titles in the two-year period of 1994 and 1995. He was also The MVP on the Tigers' 1995 team.

KRIESE AND SOME OF HIS HEADLINE PLAYERS

The following biographical stories describe many of the men and the coaches that built the heritage of Clemson tennis excellence, which became known around the world. The accomplishments and leadership training that has been Clemson tennis will be remembered for years to come. It helped to change the scope of college tennis from West Coast Dominance. It also changed the way that players trained for tennis in the USA and also had impact around the world. The following stories describe many of: "The Men of Morning Madness."

MIKE GANDOLFO—"CLEMSON'S FIRST MEN'S TENNIS ALL-AMERICAN"

Mike Gandolfo was Clemson's first All-American. He was named the ACC's Tournament MVP two straight years in 1979 and 1980 and was the National Collegiate Senior Player of the Year, as well. He was a great worker and developed into a great player.

Without a doubt, Mike Gandolfo had the best serve that I have ever witnessed in tennis! Mike had a great left-handed baseball pitching motion, but his use of his legs and his racket speed were not to be compared with any player that I have coached or seen at any level. It was so good that between Mike's sophomore and junior seasons, he played a full tournament schedule and never lost his serve in doubles for the whole summer.

We once packed the stands in the late-'70s with people (mainly fraternity boys), with the promise that anyone returning a "Gandolfo Serve" would win a case of beer (drinking age was 18 back then). Posters were up all over campus saying, "Are you faster than a speeding bullet?" A hundred or more students came out to try that day. They all lined up and one after another failed to get a racquet on the ball. Needless to say, there was a great crowd that day for the match. However, the spectators won no beer.

Yet it was much more than a great serve that Gandolfo brought to that foundation of excellence at Clemson. Mike was a late bloomer for sure. I saw something special about him, as his junior ranking coming into Clemson was only #23 in the state of Florida. Mike lived off of his serve, while he worked tirelessly to develop the rest of his game. His freshman and sophomore years were good as he worked and moved up the lineup, but by his junior year, he had secured his top spot on the first of many championship Clemson teams. He led the Clemson team to an undefeated ACC run in 1979 and the ACC Tournament Championship in 1980. That team reached the NCAA Final Eight, and Mike led the way, receiving many accolades.

Mike Gandolfo was the most timely "difference-maker" in Clemson tennis history. He and the group of guys he played with changed the paradigm. That first recruiting class was quite special. They set the standard for years to come. Mike turned out to be one of the best competitors in the ACC and in the nation.

Mike won 89 singles and 113 doubles matches in his career. He was an All-America player in 1980.

KRIESE'S FAVORITE TEAM EVER?

That team of 1979 and 1980 was made up of very special guys with big hearts and big hunger to be great. They set the standard and the work ethic for years to come, as they refused to ever be mediocre in anything that they did on the court. They understood how to compete, and they believed in each other. They changed the whole paradigm and set the bar for what the standard would be for Clemson tennis for the next 13 years. Their reputation for toughness and playing hard-nosed tennis will be remembered for a long time.

Clemson only lost two ACC matches during those 13 years (from 1979 to 1991) and set a precedent of high achievement by great commitment and work ethic that many teams would try to copy around the United States. Clemson tennis was even mentioned in random *USA Today* articles about some of the great athletic traditions around the country. One of the directors of tennis who I worked with after retirement in Maryland stated, "As a youngster growing up in Finland and then training in Germany, we knew well of the tough training that went on at an American college named Clemson." After those special teams of '79 and '80, it was the norm for Clemson tennis to be the hardest-working team and the toughest competitors in college tennis. Witnessing the dramatic growth by Gandolfo and the others on that first recruiting class, the focus on recruiting the right type of player to fit that mold was the norm. The traditions of hard work,

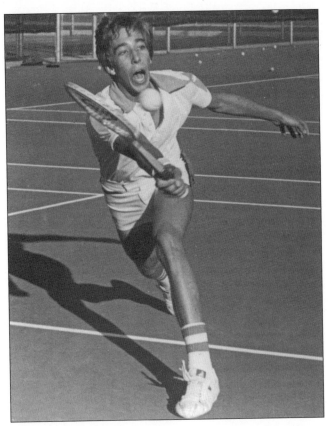

Mark Dickson was the 1982 ITA Senior Player of the Year.

integrity, and teamwork became the model for many, and Clemson tennis became known and respected worldwide.

MARK DICKSON

Mark Dickson was another one of our first recruits. Mark was tall, lanky, and quite skinny. Although he had shown some good promise in the junior ranks, he was behind most of the other top US boys in his development at age 18. All of the guys on that early team had great work ethics and were ambitious, but Mark had a belief system that was second to none. I really didn't know if Dickson had the necessary strength and fitness to be a top pro, but I learned early in my coaching career that one person with great belief can be a majority, and it is better to let youngsters have impossible big dreams than no dreams. Mark got to #12 in the world as a professional, but you would never have guessed that he could have accomplished so much if you had seen him as a freshman. He was a man of deep conviction, and from day one, he knew what he was trying to accomplish.

Dickson had a great love of the game, and he took in every lesson provided by wins and losses alike. Once, after a very devastating loss, he told me, "I realize that it is part of the process of getting me ready for pro tennis." As many players would wait to see what developed in their collegiate careers to be professional, Mark had a mindset that everything that he experienced was just part of his training for something that was already going to take place. Being a pro player was what he did every day

already. He also was a late bloomer and used his college experience as his launching pad.

Dickson was a three-time All-America player at Clemson and went on to an eleven-year career on the ATP tour. He had wins over players such as Ivan Lendl, Yannick Noah, and many more. He reached a career-high of #12 in the world in singles and #7 in the world in doubles. He is a member of the Clemson Athletic Hall of Fame and became a college coach after his excellent professional career.

Dickson won 128 singles matches and 101 doubles matches in his Clemson career.

PENDER MURPHY

Murphy started winning matches that no one thought possible, and he became almost legendary, as his match win streak went to 31 straight in the season of 1980. Interestingly, teammate Jean Desdunes had a 29-match win streak at the same time. The interteam rivalry worked out quite well to help the team to its first top-10 ranking and a 34-2 record that year. Murphy's streak was only broken by a freak accident at the NCAA team event in Athens, GA, that year.

In a match against Steve Feinberg of Princeton, Murphy ran his head into a backstop while diving for his opponent's shot. Murphy jumped up, only to sit down quickly again with blood flowing out of his head. The match had to be defaulted, Murphy had eight stitches sewn into his head, and the nation's longest win streak had been broken. Murphy was to Clemson tennis what John Havlicek had been to the Celtics or Jim Taylor had been to the Packers. If you were ever to beat Clemson, you had to beat Murphy, but also you had to beat the work ethic that he passed on to each and every member of those special teams of which he was a member. Murphy was clutch over and over again.

Pender ended up being a two-time All-America player and rose as high as #102 on the ATP professional

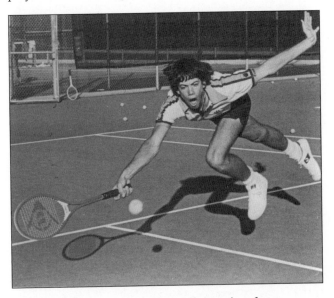

Pender Murphy was a two-time All-America player.

tour. He defied all odds, as his less-than-flashy game won, and won, and won. I refer to Pender as one of my favorite players of all time, as he was blue collar through and through. He really was the glue for that great team that we had; Pender had a very special mind for the game of tennis. He always knew what he had in the tank that day and always played within his limitations of each and every situation. He was one of the best that I have ever seen in taking away his opponents' legs, beating his opponents mentally, and breaking their hearts. I saw many a great player fall to Murphy's inner strength. Pender is a member of Clemson's Athletic Hall of Fame.

Murphy won 120 singles matches and 119 doubles matches during his career.

JEAN DESDUNES

Jean used to sleep in my top bunk in Port Washington, NY, when he was only an 11-year-old. I was there getting my start in tennis under "The Great Harry Hopman," and Jean would ride in on a train from Brooklyn and train each weekend.

Jean Desdunes never met a stranger. He was one of the friendliest and kindest people you could ever meet. He was so fast! It was so much fun to watch him play an opponent who was a big hitter and slow.

Learning how to play in public parks of Brooklyn and Miami, Jean was somewhat unconventional. He would go to the net virtually on every point and would frustrate opponents with his touch. During his freshman year, Jean scored wins over the number-one ranked junior singles player in the world and also the number-one doubles team in the world with fellow Clemson Floridian Orestes Baez. Jean ended his career by winning over 150 singles and 150 doubles matches and was a 2010 inductee into the Clemson Hall of Fame.

Jean also went on to be head coach at Georgia Tech. (His team was one of only two ACC teams in the 1980s to beat the Tigers. That tough loss was somewhat endurable, as a Clemson man's team had beaten us.) Just like Kinnear and Berger, Desdunes went on to work as a United States National coach. You always knew that Jean was destined for great things. He understands people, and his ability to be concerned with others has allowed him to do many great things.

RICK RUDEEN

It is said that "Dependability and Reliability are the best abilities." Rick Rudeen was Clemson's steadiest player of all time in winning 172 singles matches during his collegiate career. This is an NCAA record for the most singles record in a career by a player, to the best of my knowledge. A late bloomer also, he was from the same era of tennis in West Florida that produced Mark Dickson, Mike Gandolfo, Craig Boynton, and many others. Rick played two years of professional tennis. Rick and Kent Kinnear get my vote as being the two best clutch

players that I ever coached at Clemson. He won a lot of great matches for us. He always played with great balance and precision. Rick also won the Rafael Osuna Award his senior year, which was the National Intercollegiate Sportsmanship Award.

Rudeen won 172 singles matches and 123 doubles matches in his Clemson career.

LAWSON DUNCAN

A player who was virtually unheard of until late in his junior career, Lawson Duncan came to Clemson from the hills of western North Carolina and went on to win 70 matches in his freshman year. He also played his way to the finals of the NCAA Tournament as a freshman. Many said that he learned how to play tennis by himself on a backboard in Cullowhee, NC. With some help from his father, Duncan honed his skills in that mountain town. He is the best athlete for sure that I have ever coached. Duncan won the National Intercollegiate Rookie of the Year Award in 1984, as well.

Duncan set all of the records in my training programs at the track by running a 400-meter run in 50 seconds flat and the mile run in 4:41. Actually, Frank Salazar ran a 4:24 ten years later, but both times were phenomenal for tennis players. He was a relentless worker. I remember Lawson would practice four hours with the team, and then after dinner, you could hear the thump, thump, thump of the backboard as he would hit another hour or two into the night. Can you believe that Lawson won 70 matches his freshman year and played over 80 matches during that year? Lawson used every opportunity possible to become great, and that is why he became a top-50 player in the world. Duncan went on to become the NCAA finalist in 1984 and led the team to another top-10 finish. He was named National Freshman Player of the Year and went on to have wonderful career in the pro ranks.

RICHARD MATUSZEWSKI

When I'm asked who is my favorite player of all time, I've often pointed to Richard Matuszewski. If anyone ever epitomized the Clemson program and what it stood for throughout my career, Richard was it. Matuszewski was the type of player that we always looked for in a recruit. He had lots of talent that had not been developed. He was humble and hard-working, and most of his tennis instruction had been done by his own father at their home in upstate New York.

Matuszewski started out on the team as the number-14 player on our roster as a freshman. A short 30 months later, he had qualified for the US Open Men's Singles and won his first round beating #11 in the world, Steve Denton. Matuszewski went on to be a singles and doubles All-America player (the tennis program's only four-time All-America player) his junior and senior years.

He also won the 1986 National Indoor Title with Brandon Walters. His #49 in the world ranking as a professional lists him as one of the eight players whom I coached to top-100 ATP rankings. He also made the Final 16 at Wimbledon in 1996. His growth was incredible, and extremely uncommon in such a short period of time. He also won the Van Nostrand Intercollegiate National Award. His deep integrity, a tireless work ethic, and strong character allowed Matuszewski to accomplish great things in a short period of time.

The recruitment of Matuszewski was an interesting situation. I was walking behind some courts at the National Indoor Event in Dallas, en route to see another player who had a high ranking. I saw this slender young man with long and flowing strokes that were absolutely beautiful to watch. He was losing the match, but he played with such ease and grace that I stayed at his match instead of proceeding over to watch the high-ranked player. By the end of the match, I said to myself that I wanted to coach that young man. Within a week, I had talked Richard and his father into visiting Clemson, and he decided to come.

I thought to myself many times after, that if I had not seen him playing out of the corner of my eye, I would have missed one of the greatest coaching adventures of my life. Richard was surely the most natural tennis player that I ever coached. All who watched him saw his gifts. On that particular recruiting trip, I am so glad that I saw him first.

I should surely mention Brandon Walters, as well. He was one of the best doubles players that we had for that decade of the '80s.

Matuszewski won 166 singles matches and 125 doubles matches. Walters won 142 singles matches and 147 doubles contests.

KENT KINNEAR

Kinnear played in 35 Grand Slam doubles events over his 12-year professional career. Following the most common profile of "Clemson Greats," he was also a late bloomer for tennis. Kinnear was a gifted basketball player in high school and a fundamentally solid tennis player. His coach, Steve Behrman, was a college teammate of mine. Kinnear's most unique qualities were his inner strengths of mind and heart. Coach Dennis Emery of Kentucky once described what it was like to compete against Kinnear by saying, "You may be able to beat Kinnear's tennis game, but you really never have a chance to beat Kinnear."

Kinnear was never out of a match. Coach Peter Smith of Southern Cal always reminds me of his match against Kinnear when he played at Long Beach State. He led Kinnear in the third-set tiebreaker 6-0 and had six consecutive match points. Kinnear prevailed that day, as he usually would in clutch situations. Kent was once also down 6-0, 3-0 against a player from the University of Tennessee and ended up winning the match. He and Vince Van Gelderen were also down 6-2, 3-1 to the number-two seeds Cannon and Talbot of Tennessee at the NCAA Tournament and came from behind to win, as well. He was best when it was

all on the line and definitely one of the best clutch players of all time at Clemson. He did the right thing under pressure over and over and never flinched.

He never went backward after he went forward. His jumps in playing levels never came dramatically, but he never went backward. His was excellent because he would get just a bit better each and every day while growing in confidence with every win and never allowed setbacks to keep him from seeing his finish line.

Kent's long professional career was followed by a job as a national coach for the United States Tennis Association. He also coached at the University of Illinois. His successes were a tribute to the Clemson developmental program, as he started as a lower ranked junior player and was only a starter in doubles during his freshman year. He ended his career, however, as an All-America player and one of Clemson's all-time greatest players.

Kinnear won 124 singles matches and 111 doubles matches.

JAY BERGER

"Jay Berger became the most famous of all Clemson players after he graduated. Jay was not only a top professional, reaching #7 in the world on the ATP circuit, but he coached at the University of Miami, coached the 2010 United States Olympic Team in Beijing, China, and went on to become the Director of Men's Tennis for the United States, as well. Jay also played and coached Davis Cup for the United States.

It was always obvious that Jay knew instinctively how to compete.

He was as special in that regard as any athlete that I have ever seen. He gained energy and focus from pressure. He understood it and loved to be in the heat of the moment, no matter how tough it was. He surely had the "X" factor when it came to competition.

Berger was small of stature but had the heart of a gladiator. He recorded the second-most wins in a season (57) behind Duncan in 1985. I often tell the story about Jay's going back to play junior events after his freshman year at Clemson. He surely wanted to skip them and only play entry professional events. I was insistent that he use his last year of eligibility and do the dirty work of playing where the pressure was. He did not like it at all until he won three events, including the National Clay Court Championship and the Boys-18 Championships at Kalamazoo, MI.

Winning that tournament got him a wild-card entry into the men's US Open at Flushing Meadow for 1985. Jay shocked the tennis world by making the Round of 16 and losing in four tough sets to Yannich Noah. He actually turned down a pro contract to come back to Clemson for a 65 percent scholarship. It is unheard of today for a player to not jump ship early when such a thing happens. Jay and his father were quite smart in that way, in that they planned for the long run; and therefore, they built a good base for a long career in professional tennis. Jay has served the United States very well over the years as a great coach and mentor to hundreds of young people. He is one of Clemson's greatest sports stars of all time.

JOHN SULLIVAN—ALL-AMERICA ATHLETE AND ACC PLAYER OF THE YEAR WHO NEVER LOST AN ACC MATCH

John Sullivan never lost an ACC Match. He was 28-0 in the ACC during his career at Clemson and was an athlete through and through. Sullivan and Lawson Duncan were the best pure athletes that I've ever coached. I saw this tall, lanky, basketball-looking kid playing at the National Championships at Kalamazoo in the summer of 1985.

John Sullivan was a great athlete and competitor. He was also a top basketball player in New York, and I knew then that I had to get this young man on our team. Sullivan showed his toughness during his career with his undefeated ACC record and going on to be a two-time All-America player. He was also named ACC Player of the Year and made it to the top 150 in ATP doubles. Every team on which he played won the ACC Championships.

VINCE VAN GELDEREN

Vince was voted as one of the top 50 all-time players in the history of the ACC. Vince came to Clemson as a walk-on and earned a scholarship after his first season. He was number-seven on the team for most of his freshman year and worked tirelessly to improve all aspects of his game.

Vince went on to be a two-time All-America player. He and Kent Kinnear also reached the Final Four in doubles at the 1988 NCAA doubles tournament. They did so with a stunning come-from-behind win over the number-two-seeded team in the tournament, Cannon and Talbot from Tennessee. Vince played on the pro tour for three years before returning to the Netherlands, where he owns a tennis training center. Like many of his teammates on the Clemson teams, he reached the top 200 on the ATP tour. Vince was ACC Tournament Player of the Year in 1989, as well.

Van Gelderen won 107 singles and 100 doubles matches in his Clemson career.

MITCH SPRENGELMEYER

My recruitment of Mitch Sprengelmeyer sparked the momentum, producing many good teams of the 1990s. I noticed Sprengelmeyer for the first time at age eight when his father, Mike, brought him to a clinic put on by The South Carolina Tennis Association at Clemson. I'll never forget the smooth ball-striking and the excellent hand-eye coordination that I saw that day in the young lad. Mitch grew into his body late and was a bit slow of foot until he got to be 17. I recruited him anyway, as I saw the inner qualities that I had always liked about late bloomer players. Mitch's tennis fundamentals were

honed well from an early age, as his father, Mike, was one of the best teaching pros in the South and in the country.

Mitch's maturity, work ethic, and ability to learn quickly were unique. Much like Kinnear, Sprengelmeyer had a knack for learning from his losses while gaining confidence from his wins. Just like Kinnear, Mitch never went backward. His self-esteem was intact from an early age, and you just didn't ever have to worry about the emotional issues that usually accompany college-aged players. He would grow from whatever experience was put in front of him. That sure makes it easy on a coach.

Mitch would go on to be the only player in NCAA history to win the National Senior Player of the Year award and to be named the Van Nostrand Award winner for the top American professional prospect of the year. He played pro tennis for four years and reached #92 in the world in the ATP doubles tour. He and his doubles partners had three wins over the famous Bryan Brothers, who have gone down in history as the greatest doubles team of all time.

I shunned the advice from some that Sprengelmeyer was too small and would not be able to have impact at the collegiate level. I believed in the Florence, SC, native. My hunch paid off, as Sprengelmeyer became one of the greatest college players of the '90s and one of the all-time best players in ACC history. Mitch would lead his Clemson Tigers to their 11th ACC title in 1997 and was the top US-born player in college tennis that year.

Sprengelmeyer finished his career with 115 singles wins and 112 doubles victories.

A CHAMPIONSHIP OF FAITH IN 1997

The question that I was most often asked when our team won the ACC Championship on April 20, 1997, was, "Which championship of the 11 that your teams have won feels the best and is the most gratifying?"

Of course, what are you supposed to say? Number 6 or 7, because of this or that?

No, definitely not! Of course, the coach is supposed to tell everyone that this one feels the best because of this reason and that reason, and that is the story all expect to hear. Well, I did answer the correct way, saying, "this one is definitely the best," but I quickly added that the 1980 championship finishes in a tie or a very close second. I am extremely sincere and honest in saying so because it's true.

After our teams had so much success between 1978 and 1991, I truly found out what perseverance really means, and since then, my spirit has been tested from the depths. When you're winning, you can't do much wrong. All players, parents, fellow coaches, and others feel you have some special magic.

But when you're going through rough times, doubt, and just plain lack of faith, permeates everywhere. Many quit, most don't give their whole heart, and some project negative emotions when there are tough times. I believe we won this year because this group simply believed and kept the faith, hanging in there and not quitting out of personal pride more than anything else.

During those locust years when we didn't win championships, I maintained that this job is my teaching vocation and nothing more. Our destiny was in God's hands, and I would do His will in teaching my boys, regardless of material reward. I did not think that we would win the ACC title this year. I felt that we were still a year or two away. Fortunately for all of us, my timing was not God's timing. His timing allowed it now. I don't mean the trophy, either; that was nice, but the real championship was the team's opportunity to realize the fruits of its labor. There is a saying, "Dare things so great that without the intervention of God, they are destined to fail." The team and I have no choice except to give God the credit on this one.

Why then was this championship the best? Well, first of all only this team and the 1980 team had no team members on the roster who had been on a championship team before. Every player had to believe and trust from the bottom of his heart and keep the faith in something that they had not seen before. The other teams always had older members who had won championships by teaching the others what to do.

The number-two reason is that as a coach, I truly realize the importance of getting up off of the mat when you're knocked down, and oh how sweet it is when the extra perseverance produces a championship.

What lessons we all learned that year! I think 1997 will be remembered by all involved with Clemson tennis as a tremendous year, a year when all learned the importance of Faith.

THE THOMPSON BROTHERS: NATHAN, MICAH, AND JAMIN

The three Thompson Brothers of Baltimore were known as good tennis players but were more so superior athletes. The combination of athleticism and work ethic is what Kriese loved in tennis players and what had been the foundation for years in the Clemson tennis program. Micah Thompson was the first of the three to join the Tigers in 2000.

Shortly after, his brother Jamin joined the Tigers as a transfer from the University of Miami. The finishing touch of the Thompsons came with Nathan joining the team in 2002. He would go on to become an All-America player and the ACC Player of the Year in 2005.

Nathan was a raw athlete who excelled in basketball more than tennis in his later high school days. His freshman year would delegate him to a lower position on the team for a lot of on-court learning and development. As he was nominated for the National Senior Player of the Year in 2005, it was the completion of three great years of leading the Tigers as their number-one player. Nathan would go on to a professional career, where he won 15 Futures events on the professional tour and became one of Clemson's greatest ever. He became the 23rd-ranked professional player in the United States in 2009.

The Thompsons were critical to the success of the Clemson program. The Thompsons were superior athletes and were able to thankfully continue Clemson's winning tradition, garnering the seventh Elite Eight finish at the NCAAs. They had a high ranking of number-five in the nation after achieving one of the greatest road wins in history by beating the mighty Southern Cal Trojans at their home courts in Los Angeles.

ACC'S 50TH ANNIVERSARY TEAM

Clemson Men's Tennis had 15 of the 50 total players represented on the 50th Anniversary Atlantic Coast Conference Team. This was the greatest number of players on the team from one school, regardless of sport.

The players who were on the 50th ACC anniversary team were Jay Berger, Owen Casey, Jean Desdunes, Mark Dickson, Lawson Duncan, Mike Gandolfo, Kent Kinnear, Richard Matuszewski, Pender Murphy, Miguel Nido, Rick Rudeen, Mitch Sprengelmeyer, John Sullivan, Vince Van Gelderen, and Brandon Walters.

NATIONAL PLAYERS OF THE YEAR

Clemson has had four National Players of the Year— Mike Gandolfo (1980), Mark Dickson (1982), Jean Desduens (1983), and Mitch Sprengelmeyer (1997) have all been honored.

In 1984, Lawson Duncan was named the National Rookie of the Year, and Rick Rudeen won the Osuna Award (National Sportsmanship Award). Richard Matuszewski (1986) and Mitch Sprengelmeyer (1997) won the Van Nostrand Memorial Award, given annually to an outstanding senior who is the top American professional prospect.

Chuck Kriese was named National Coach of the Year in 1981 and 1986. He retired after the 2008 season.

CHUCK MCCUEN BECOMES EIGHTH HEAD COACH OF THE TIGER PROGRAM

Chuck McCuen was an assistant under Kriese for seven years before taking over as the head coach in 2009. McCuen was the tennis director at Georgia State for 19 years prior to coming to Clemson. He was named Conference Coach of the Year five times and propelled Georgia State into a top-70 nationally ranked tennis program.

McCuen had a positive impact on the Clemson program in 2003, when he helped the Tigers to 25 wins, including a 6-2 record in the ACC. It was Clemson's highest win total since 1989. The success continued in 2004, when Clemson advanced to the Final Eight of the NCAA Tournament and posted a record of 26-12. The Tigers also finished the 2005 campaign with a 26-12 record. Clemson won at least 23 matches five consecutive years (2003-07) for the first time since the 1979-86 era. The streak coincided with McCuen's arrival at Clemson. Overall, Clemson had a 145-79 record for the six years during which time he was Kriese's top assistant.

While attending Gainesville Junior College, he reached the semifinals of the NJCAA National Championships in singles. He became an NAIA All-America player after transferring to Flagler College in St. Augustine, FL, and went on to earn a double degree in recreation management and history in 1983.

McCuen helped create the first collegiate wheelchair team in the United States. There are now seven schools that award scholarships in wheelchair tennis.

McCuen has Clemson roots, as former tennis coach Hoke Sloan is a cousin and former Swimming and Diving Coach Carl McHugh is a great-uncle. McCuen's grandfather, Matthew Lee McHugh, graduated from Clemson in

1904 and was awarded the Clemson Meritorious Service Award in 1981.

While at Georgia State, he was active in the community, contributing his time to Atlanta's youth tennis programs as a tennis instructor.

In the Spring of 2010, he was inducted into the Flagler Athletic Hall of Fame. He is married to Dr. Linda McCuen, and they have one daughter, Lauren, who is a special education teacher in Anderson, SC.

On June 7, 2016, Chuck McCuen announced his retirement as head coach of the Clemson men's tennis team. John Boetsch, an assistant coach and associate head coach of the Tigers for the previous eight seasons, was named the ninth head coach in Clemson men's tennis program history.

MEN'S TENNIS HISTORY

November 13-14, 1907—Clemson first participated in the State of South Carolina Tennis Tournament at the Furman Athletic Club in Greenville, SC.

November 11, 1911—James Erwin defeated Grier of Erskine, three sets to one, in claiming the State Intercollegiate Tournament held at Spartanburg, SC.

The Erwin brothers were also star basketball players and were members of the school's first basketball team.

October 16-18, 1912—Erwin defeated Wingate Waring of South Carolina 6-0, 6-1, 6-2 to claim the State Intercollegiate Tournament.

May, 1913—Erwin won the Southern Intercollegiate Athletic Association (SIAA) Singles Tournament. He, along with his brother, John Erwin, won the Southern Intercollegiate Athletic Association (SIAA) Doubles Tournament.

October 21, 1916—Julian Robertson and Allen Haskell won the State Intercollegiate Tournament in doubles.

October 19, 1917—Robertson and Haskell won the State Intercollegiate Tournament in doubles for the second year in a row.

April 28, 1921—Clemson defeated Wofford 2-0 in the first dual match ever for the Tigers.

May, 7 1921—The Tigers' Bill Hines defeated W.M. Holcombe of Wofford in the finals en route to winning the State Intercollegiate Tournament in singles held at Spartanburg, SC.

April 29, 1922—Wofford defeated Clemson 2-1 in the first-ever home dual meet for the Tigers.

May 6, 1922—Clemson's Jim Grey won the State Intercollegiate Tournament in singles.

May 5, 1923—The Tigers' Jim Grey won the State Intercollegiate Tournament in singles. Grey and Fitzgerald won the State Intercollegiate Tournament in doubles.

May 10, 1923—Clemson defeated Oglethorpe in Atlanta, GA 4-1 to wrap up the season and finish the year with a 4-1 record.

April 1, 1929—Hoke Sloan coached his first match as the Clemson head coach in a 6-0 loss to Davidson.

April 8, 1930—Sloan won his first match as head coach of the Tigers with an 8-1 win over Erskine in Due West, SC.

May 5, 1930—Clemson defeated The Citadel 5-2 to win the final five matches of the season, and the Tigers finished the year with a 7-4-1 record overall.

May 11, 1934—The Tigers defeated the College of Charleston 8-1 in Charleston, SC. The Tigers finished the year with a 9-1 record.

May 18, 1934—Tate Horton won the State Intercollegiate Tournament in singles in Greenville, SC.

April 6, 1935—Clemson defeated Mississippi State in the season opener and went on to win nine matches against three losses that season.

May 18, 1935—Tate Horton and Henry Woodward won the State Intercollegiate Doubles Tournament.

May 6, 1940—The Tigers defeated Mercer 4-3. This was the 14th victory for the Tigers that season, and it set the record for the most wins in a season. The Tigers would not win this many matches in a season until the 1962 campaign.

April 30, 1951—Clemson defeated Furman 8-1 and finished the year with a 7-1 record.

May 8, 1952—The Tigers defeated Wofford 5-4 at Spartanburg to finish the year with a 10-1 record. Including the 1951 season, Clemson had a 17-2 record over the course of the two years. Including the last two matches of the 1951 season, and the first eight matches of the 1952 season, the Tigers had a 10-match winning streak.

April 1, 1954—Clemson played its first Atlantic Coast Conference match and lost to South Carolina 5-4 in Columbia.

April 20, 1954—The Tigers lost to Maryland 6-3 in its first Atlantic Coast Conference match played in Clemson, SC.

April 26, 1954—Clemson won its first-ever Atlantic Coast Conference match with a 5-4 win over South Carolina.

April 27, 1954—The Tigers won their first Atlantic Coast Conference road match with a 6-3 win over Wake Forest.

May 4, 1958—Hoke Sloan coached his last match at Clemson in a 5-4 loss to South Carolina in Columbia, SC. His coaching career spanned over a 29-year period.

May 5, 1962—Clemson defeated Virginia 8-1 at Clemson, SC, to finish the season with a 14-1 record and a 5-1 mark in the ACC.

April 27, 1963—The Tigers lost to North Carolina 8-1 but finished the year with an 11-2 record and a 6-1 record in league play. In 1962 and 1963, Clemson had a 25-3 record in the two seasons. Clemson was 11-2 in the ACC during that time.

April 27, 1965—Clemson defeated Duke 9-0, its 14th victory of the season. Clemson finished the year with a 14-4 record and a 5-2 mark in the ACC.

June 12-17, 1967—Clemson finished tied for 26th in the NCAA Tennis Championships held in Carbondale, IL.

April 19, 1969—Clemson defeated N.C. State 9-0, as the Tigers completed an undefeated season, 16-0.

May 8-10, 1969—Clemson won the ACC Championship for the first time in history. The Tigers won the tournament with 65 points, three ahead of North Carolina's 62.

May 12,1971—Clemson defeated Duke 6-0 in the last regular season and ACC match for the Tigers this season. With the victory, Clemson won the ACC regular-season championship.

June 18-23, 1973—The Tigers placed 22nd in the 1973 NCAA Tennis Championships held in Princeton, NJ.

June 17-22, 1974—Clemson finished tied for 35th in the NCAA Championships.

August 10, 1975—Chuck Kriese was named head coach.

April 13-15, 1979—Clemson's Mike Gandolfo was named ACC Player of the Year at the ACC Tournament.

May 25, 1979—The Tigers reached the Final 16 in the NCAA Tournament team championships. Clemson lost

Mike Gandolfo was the 1980 ITA Senior Player of the Year.

to Southern Methodist 5-0 and finished the season ranked 15th in the country.

Feb. 16-Apr. 23, 1980—Pender Murphy won a Clemson-record 29 consecutive singles matches, a record that still stands today. He won 26 of the 29 matches in straight sets. The streak stopped in the first round of the NCAA Tournament in Athens, GA, when he ran into a pole in the University of Georgia indoor facility and had to retire.

April 18-20, 1980—Clemson won the ACC Championship. The Tigers' Mike Gandolfo was named ACC Player of the Year for the second season in a row. Chuck Kriese was named ACC Coach of the Year.

May 19-26, 1980—The Tigers reached the Final Eight in the NCAA Tournament Team Championships. Clemson defeated Princeton 5-4 on May 19 and lost to Stanford 7-2 on May 20. Mike Gandolfo and Mark Dickson were named All-America singles players, while Pender Murphy was named an All-America player in singles and doubles. Mark Dickson reached the Final Eight in the NCAA Singles Individual Tournament. Gandolfo was named the ITCA Senior Player of the Year. Clemson finished the season ranked eighth in the country.

April 17-19, 1981—Clemson won the ACC Championships at Clemson, SC.

May 16-24, 1981—The Tigers reached the Final Eight in the NCAA Tournament in the team championships. Clemson defeated Miami (FL) 6-3 on May 16 and lost to Southern Cal on May 17. Mark Dickson and Pender Murphy were named All-America honorees in both singles and doubles. Dickson finished the season ranked tied for third in the country in singles play. Clemson finished the season ranked seventh in the country.

May 20, 1981—Chuck Kriese was named 1981 ITCA National Coach of the Year. Kriese earned Coach of the Year honors following a vote of the NCAA tennis coaches throughout the nation. He was the first Clemson coach in any sport to be named National Coach of the Year.

September 9, 1981—Kriese was named 1981 United States Tennis Association National Coach of the Year.

February 6, 1982—Clemson defeated the nation's top team for the first time ever in men's tennis in a 5-4 win over UCLA. Clemson was ranked #6 heading into the match that was played in Los Angeles, CA.

May 15-23, 1982—The Tigers reached the Final Eight in the NCAA Tournament in the team championships. Clemson defeated Arkansas 5-4 on May 15 and lost to Southern Methodist 5-4 on May 16. In Clemson's 5-4 win over Arkansas, the Tigers swept the doubles play. Mark Dickson and Jean Desdunes were named All-America singles players. Dickson finished the season ranked 13th in the country in singles play and was named the ITCA Senior Player of the Year. Clemson finished the season ranked seventh in the country.

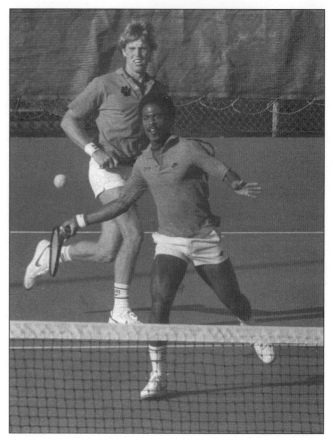

Jean Desdunes holds the Clemson career record for most doubles victories with 153.

April 15-17, 1983—Clemson won the ACC Championships, in Atlanta, GA.

May 14-22, 1983—The Tigers reached the Final Eight in the NCAA Tournament Team Championships. Clemson defeated Cal Irvine 7-2 on May 14 but lost to Southern Methodist 5-4 on May 15. Rick Rudeen and Jean Desdunes were named All-America singles players.

The doubles team of Richard Akel and Craig Cooper finished the season ranked 11th in the country. Desdunes was named ITCA Senior Player of the Year. Clemson finished the season ranked ninth in the country.

April 20-22, 1984—Clemson won the ACC Championships in College Park, MD.

May 12-20, 1984—The Tigers reached the Final 16 in the 100th annual NCAA Tournament Team Championships. Clemson lost to Stanford 5-4 on May 12. Individually, Lawson Duncan was a NCAA Singles Tournament finalist. Duncan lost to Georgia's Michael Pernfors 6-1, 6-4 in the Championship match on May 20, a one-hour-and-25-minute match played in front of 4,017 spectators. Lawson Duncan was named All-America in singles play and finished the season ranked fourth in the country in singles. He was also named the ITCA Rookie of the Year. Clemson finished the season ranked 10th in the country.

February 10, 1985—Clemson's Brandon Walters and Richard Matuszewski won the ITCA National Indoor Intercollegiate Doubles Championships. This was the first National Championship victory in Clemson Tennis history. The Tigers defeated Steve Couch and Gerald Marzenell of Houston 7-6, 6-3.

May 18-20, 1985—Clemson won the ACC Championships in Chapel, Hill, NC.

May 18-26, 1985—The Tigers reached the Final Eight in the NCAA Tournament Team Championships. Clemson defeated Louisiana State 5-1 on May 18 but lost to UCLA 5-3 on May 19. Miguel Nido was named All-America in singles, while Richard Matuszewski was named All-America in both singles and doubles. Brandon Walters was named All-America in doubles. The doubles team of Matuszewski and Walters finished the season ranked fourth in the country. Clemson finished the season ranked eighth in the country.

February 20, 1986—Clemson reached an all-time best #2 ranking in the ITA poll for the first time ever.

March 22, 1986—Clemson defeated #1 Pepperdine by an incredible 8-1 score in a match played in Malibu, CA.

April 17-19, 1986—Clemson won the ACC Championships and Chuck Kriese was named ACC Coach of the Year.

May 17-25, 1986—The Tigers reached the Final Eight in the NCAA Tournament in the team championships. Clemson defeated Oklahoma State 5-0 on May 17 but lost to Stanford 5-3 on May 18. Richard Matuszewski reached the Final Eight in the NCAA Singles Individual Tournament. Jay Berger was named All-America in singles and Matuszewski was named All-America in singles and doubles. Matuszewski finished the season ranked 12th while Berger finished 13th in the country in singles play. The doubles team of Matuszewski and Walters finished the season ranked eighth in the country. Chuck Kriese was named USTA National Coach of the Year. Clemson finished the season ranked fifth in the country.

April, 1987—Clemson won the ACC Championships. The tournament was cancelled due to rain. The Tigers were declared champions by virtue of the regular season.

May 15-23, 1987—The Tigers reached the Final 16 in the NCAA Tournament Team Championships. Clemson defeated Kansas 5-0 on May 15 and lost to Georgia 5-2 on May 16. The doubles team of Vince Van Gelderen and Kent Kinnear reached the Final Four in the NCAA Doubles individual tournament. Craig Boynton, Kent Kinnear, John Sullivan, and Vince Van Gelderen were named All-America in doubles. The doubles team of Kinnear and Van Gelderen finished the season ranked seventh in the country. Clemson finished the season ranked 14th in the country.

April 21-23, 1988—Clemson won the ACC Championships in Winston-Salem, NC. Kent Kinnear was named the ACC Player of the Year. Chuck Kriese was named ACC Coach of the Year.

May 20-28, 1988—The Tigers reached the Final 16 in the NCAA Tournament Team Championships. Clemson lost to Kentucky 5-2 on May 21. Clemson finished the season ranked 10th in the country.

April 21-23, 1989—Clemson won the ACC Championships. The Tigers defeated North Carolina in the Championship match on April 23, 8-1. Clemson clinched the match in only 63 minutes. John Sullivan was named the ACC Player of the Year. Chuck Kriese was named ACC Coach of the Year.

May 19-28,1989—The Tigers reached the Final 16 in the NCAA Tournament Team Championships. The Tigers lost to LSU 5-2 on May 20. Todd Watkins and Vince Van Gelderen were named All-America doubles players. John Sullivan finished the season ranked 12th in the country in singles play. Clemson finished the season ranked 13th in the country.

May 15 and 17, 1991—Clemson defeated Duke on March 15 and Cal-Irvine on March 17 by the identical score of 5-4 in consecutive matches. In each match, the Tigers were behind 4-2, and Clemson had to win all three doubles matches to claim the victory.

May 15, 1992—Mississippi defeated Clemson in the first round of the NCAA Tournament.

May 27, 1992—Clemson finished 20th in the final ITA poll.

Feb. 12, 1994—Chuck Kriese won his 400th career match, a 4-3 win over Indiana.

May 13, 1994—North Carolina defeated Clemson 4-2 in the NCAA Region II Tournament in Columbia, SC.

May 5, 1995—Clemson defeated North Carolina 4-3 in the first round of the NCAA Region II Tournament in Norfolk, VA.

May 6, 1995—Duke defeated Clemson in the semifinals of the NCAA Region II Tournament in Norfolk, VA.

May 10, 1996—Duke defeated Clemson in the semifinals of the NCAA Region II Tournament.

April 18-20, 1997—Clemson defeated Wake Forest (4-0), Florida State (4-2), and Duke 4-3 in winning the 1997 Atlantic Coast Conference Men's Tennis Championships in Norcross, GA. The victory over 12th-ranked Duke was Chuck Kriese's 100th career win over a top-20 team.

April 20, 1997—Bruce Li won the clinching match at number-two singles over Duke's Alberto Brause in leading Clemson to the 1997 Atlantic Coast Conference Men's Championships. Li was named the ACC Tournament's MVP.

April 23, 1997—Mitch Sprengelmeyer was named the 1997 Atlantic Coast Conference Men's Tennis Player of the Year. Chuck Kriese was named the ACC Coach of the Year.

May 9-10, 1997—Clemson defeated North Carolina but lost to Duke in the NCAA Region II Tennis Tournament.

May 22, 1997—Mitch Sprengelmeyer won the ITA Senior Player of the Year and the John Van Nostrand Memorial Award (senior having the most potential for a professional tennis career). He is the first player in history to win both awards in the same year. Sprengelmeyer was named a All-America singles player by the Intercollegiate Tennis Association and finished the season ranked 19th by the ITA.

May 28, 1997—Clemson finished the season ranked 19th as a team. In singles, Mitch Sprengelmeyer finished 19th. The doubles team of Sprengelmeyer and Li finished the season ranked 23rd.

May 5, 1998—South Carolina defeated Clemson in the first round of the NCAA Region II Tournament in Richmond, VA.

April 10, 1999—Chuck Kriese won his 500th career match, a 5-2 victory over North Carolina.

May 13, 2000—Clemson began play in the NCAA Tournament for the 19th time in the past 21 seasons. On that day, the Tigers defeated a top-25 Miami, FL, team 4-3.

April 19-22, 2001—Clemson made a run in the ACC Championships. The Tigers downed N.C. State, North Carolina, and Virginia before losing to third-ranked Duke in the finals.

September 2, 2002—The ACC 50th-Anniversary Team was announced. Clemson led the way with 15 selections, the most in the conference and the most selections for Clemson in any sport.

January 26, 2003—Clemson defeated sixth-ranked Georgia by a count of 4-3 at home. The Tigers improved to 4-0 against 6th-ranked teams at home.

May 15, 2004—The Tigers defeated Minnesota 4-0 in the first round of the NCAA Tournament.

May 15, 2004—Clemson upset sixth-ranked Duke 4-3 in the second round of the NCAA Tournament.

May 22, 2004—Clemson defeated TCU 4-2 in the NCAA Round of 16.

May 24, 2004—UCLA defeated the Tigers 4-0 in the NCAA Round of Eight at Tulsa, OK.

Feb. 18, 2005—Clemson defeated Tennessee Tech 7-0. This was Chuck Kriese's 600th career win, which came against his alma mater.

March 19, 2005—Clemson defeated ninth-ranked Southern Cal by a 4-3 score. It was Clemson's first win at

Southern Cal and Clemson's first top-10 road win since a victory at eighth-ranked Miami (FL) in 1992.

April 21, 2005—Nathan Thompson was named the Atlantic Coast Conference Men's Tennis Player of the Year.

May 10, 2005—Thompson was named the Intercollegiate Tennis Association's (ITA) Ted Farnsworth Senior Player of the Year for the Mideast Region.

May 14, 2005—Clemson defeated Northwestern 4-0 in the first round of the NCAA Tournament.

May 15, 2005—Georgia defeated Clemson 4-0 in Athens, GA, in the second round of the NCAA Tournament.

March 13, 2006—Clemson defeated Arizona State 5-2 for the program's 1,000th all-time victory.

May 13, 2006—Clemson defeated South Carolina 4-1 in the first round of the NCAA Tournament in Chapel Hill, NC.

May 14, 2006—North Carolina defeated the Tigers 4-1 in the second round of the NCAA Tournament in Chapel Hill, NC.

May 11, 2007—Clemson defeated Elon 4-0 in the first round of the NCAA Tournament in Winston-Salem, NC.

May 12, 2007—Wake Forest defeated Clemson 4-3 at Winston-Salem, NC in the second round of the NCAA Tournament.

November 2, 2007—Chuck Kriese announced that the 2008 season would be his final year leading the Tiger program. He retired from the position in August of 2008 after 33 seasons as head coach.

April 9, 2008—Kriese coached his last home match of his 33-year career.

July 7, 2008—Chuck McCuen, who has served as an assistant men's tennis coach at Clemson for six seasons, was named head tennis coach.

Jan. 24, 2009—McCuen won his first match as head coach, a 7-0 victory over The Citadel.

Jan. 16-March 19, 2010—Clemson won the first 15 matches of the season. This was the second-best start in school history.

May 10, 2013—Clemson's Dominique Maden defeated Filipp Pogostkin at number-four singles in clinching the match and leading the 23rd-ranked Tigers to a 4-3 victory over #42 Boise State in the first round of the NCAA Men's Tennis Tournament at Knoxville, TN.

This is the first NCAA appearance as a team for Clemson since the 2007 season. It also marks the 25th time that the Tigers have played in the NCAA Tournament since the event went to a team dual match format in 1977.

May 11, 2013—Brandon Fickey defeated Gerardo Meza at number-three singles in clinching the match and giving sixth-ranked Tennessee a 4-3 victory over 23rd-ranked Clemson in the second round of the NCAA Men's Tennis Tournament at Knoxville, TN.

Clemson finished the season with a 19-8 record. The match lasted five hours and 12 minutes. The match was moved indoors toward the end of doubles because of thunderstorms.

May 28, 2013—Clemson men's tennis team finished 21st in the final Intercollegiate Tennis Association (ITA) Poll. This is the first time since the 2007 season that the Tigers have finished in the top 25 in the final ITA poll. It is also the highest that the Tigers have been ranked in the final ITA poll since the Tigers were ranked 19th in the final listing in 1997.

May 9, 2014—The 21st-ranked Tigers opened the 2014 NCAA Championships with a 4-1 win over Purdue in Lexington, KY. With the win, Clemson advanced to the second round of the NCAA Tournament.

May 10, 2014—The 21st-ranked Tigers suffered a 4-3 loss to 13th-ranked Kentucky, the tournament's 15th national seed in Lexington, KY. With the loss, Clemson concluded the season in the NCAA Championships, second round at 21-9, recording the program's first 20-win season since 2007.

May 25, 2014—Hunter Harrington and Dominique Maden's impressive run in the NCAA Doubles Championships came to an end in the NCAA semifinals. The Tigers' ninth-ranked duo fell to the number-two national seed, Mikelis Libietis and Hunter Reese of Tennessee, 6-4, 6-2, at the Dan Magill Tennis Complex in Athens, GA.

Harrington and Maden's tournament run included wins over the fourth- and fifth-ranked doubles teams in the nation and saw them earn ITA All-America honors for 2014 by virtue of their berth in the NCAA quarterfinals. They became just the third doubles team in Clemson history to reach the semifinals of the NCAA Doubles Championships, as two Tiger teams had done so previously, in 1987 and 2004.

May 27, 2014—The Clemson men's tennis team was ranked 22nd in the final national poll released by the Intercollegiate Tennis Association. The Tigers finished the 2014 season with a 21-9 overall record, posting the program's first 20-win season since 2007, and advanced to the second round of the NCAA Championships for the second-straight year.

The Tigers have finished in the top 25 of the final national poll two consecutive seasons, as they were 21st in the final team rankings in 2013. It is the highest finish for the program in two consecutive final polls in 25 years, since the 1988 and 1989 seasons, when the team was ranked 10th and 13th, respectively.

June 4, 2014—The duo of Hunter Harrington and Dominique Maden was ranked fifth in the final doubles poll released by the ITA. It is the best final national ranking for a Clemson doubles team since 1985, and the second-best finish in program history. Harrington finished 46th nationally in singles, and Maden finished 78th.

June 7, 2016—Chuck McCuen announced his retirement as head coach of the Clemson men's tennis team. John Boetsch, an assistant coach and associate head coach of the Tigers for the past eight seasons, was named the ninth head coach in Clemson men's tennis program history.

WOMEN'S
Tennis

NCAA Tournament Final 16:

1983, 1993, 1996, 2005, 2007, 2008, 2009, 2010, 2011

NCAA Tournament Final Eight:

1983, 2004, 2005

NCAA Tournament Final Four:

2004, 2005

ACC Champions:

1982, 1983, 1984, 1985, 1986, 1987, 2004, 2008

ACC Regular-Season Champions:

1978, 1979, 1980, 1982, 1983, 1985, 1986, 2004, 2007

Top-25 Seasons:

1977 (9th), 1978 (13th), 1980 (12th), 1981 (9th), 1982 (18th), 1983 (7th), 1984 (15th), 1985 (19th), 1986 (8th), 1987 (20th), 1990 (21st), 1991 (25th), 1992 (23rd), 1993 (12th), 1994 (18th), 1996 (20th), 2003 (19th), 2004 (5th), 2005 (10th), 2006 (18th), 2007 (11th), 2008 (13th), 2009 (11th), 2010 (11th), 2011 (14th), 2012 (25th), 2013 (13th), 2014 (13th), 2015 (18th)

MARY KING WAS FIRST WOMEN'S COACH

Clemson women's tennis program has been a very competitive force on the national scene since its inception in 1975.

Mary Kinnerty King was not only the first women's tennis coach, but she was also the first women's basketball coach at Clemson. Her first year as the women's basketball coach equated to a 14-11 record.

After the inaugural year of women's basketball, she coached the women's tennis team for the next seven years and compiled a 133-47 record, for a 739 pct. During that time, the Tigers were ranked in the top 20 in the final poll four times under King. In 1978, the Tigers finished 13th in the final poll. In 1980, the Tigers finished 12th, and in 1981,

Clemson finished ninth. In 1982, King led the Tigers to its first ACC Championship and an 18th-place finish. The Atlantic Coast Conference title was Clemson's first of any kind for the Tigers in the school's athletic history.

SUSAN HILL—THREE-TIME ALL-AMERICA PLAYER

The Clemson women's tennis team got off to a very successful start, and a large part of this success is due to Susan Hill. Hill, a freshman from Signal Mountain, TN, was successful from day one, when she arrived on the Clemson campus.

During her freshman year in 1978, when she played number-one singles, Hill won the state AIAW Tournament and the AIAW Regional Tournament. She advanced to the AIAW National Tournament as a freshman. She finished the year with a 29-4 record and was named an All-America athlete. The Lady Tigers finished 13th in the final poll.

Her sophomore season was also a banner year. She advanced to the second round of the AIAW National Tournament and teamed with her sister Carolyn to capture the consolation doubles championship in the individual doubles tournament. For her performance, she was again named All-America.

In 1980, Hill was the main reason the Lady Tiers concluded the season ranked 12th in the nation. Hill had a 40-3 ledger in singles play. She won the state and regional tournaments and advanced to the AIAW National Tournament's second round. Hill was named All-America.

In 1981, Clemson advanced to the AIAW Final Eight with a win over San Diego State. The Tigers lost in the quarterfinals to eventual champions UCLA 5-4. Hill qualified for the AIAW National Singles tournament but lost in the first round. She was named an AIAW All-America for the fourth year in a row. The Tigers finished ninth in the final poll.

Susan said she learned tennis from playing with her father and his friends when she started player at the age of 13.

"I never took lessons from a pro," she said. "I learned rather quickly.

"My family is from South Carolina—my father was from Newberry and Mom from Prosperity—so Clemson fit me perfectly." Hill's sister joined her sophomore year, and the pair played doubles for three years. She was recruited by North Carolina, Tennessee, and Pepperdine but chose Clemson.

Hill says that winning the ACC number-one singles position for four times, her unbeaten singles record in the national team tournament, and her induction into the Clemson Athletic Hall of Fame and Ring of Honor were her most memorable moments of he athletic career.

"When I took my first trip to visit and fell in love with [Clemson]. When I think of Clemson, I don't automatically think of tennis. I met my husband at Clemson, and that makes it even more special to me. Clemson is a wonderful place. It's beautiful—the surroundings and atmosphere are so special. Clemson also has big-time sports. It's a great place to be student. As each year passes, I love it even more," said Hill.

FRESHMAN GIGI FERNANDEZ ADVANCED TO THE NCAA FINALS

In 1983, Clemson freshman Gigi Fernandez advanced to the NCAA Finals. She had to win a play-in match to qualify for a spot in the round of 64.

In that match, she defeated Suzanne Khulman of Georgetown. In the first round, she defeated Gen Greiwe of Texas—6-1, 7-6. Fernandez defeated fifth-seeded Gretchen Rush of Trinity—3-6, 6-3, 7-5—in the second round.

In the round of 16, Fernandez defeated Nina Voydat of Southern Cal in three sets—6-1, 1-6, 6-1. Fernandez defeated fourth-seeded Mickie Schillig of San Diego State—6-4, 5-7, 6-4—in the quarterfinals. The semifinal round featured two tiebreakers, before Fernandez defeated eighth-seeded Heather Ludloff of UCLA—7-6, 7-6.

Fernandez met Beth Herr of Southern Cal in the finals. Fernandez served for match point and apparently had the match won, but a controversial line call forced the match to a third-set tiebreaker, and Herr went on to win the National Title—3-6, 6-2, 7-6.

DOMINATING THE ATLANTIC COAST CONFERENCE

Clemson dominated the Atlantic Coast Conference in the decade of the 1980s. The Tigers won the ACC Championship from 1982-'87. From 1975 until 2008, individual flight champions were decided in a tournament format, and some years a combination of regular season play and the tournament were used to decide the ACC flight titles.

In 1983, Clemson won all nine championship flights that year. It was the only year that an ACC school won all nine championships in league history, men or women. Johnson was awarded ACC Coach of the Year honors as a result of this accomplishment.

A total of 10 Tigers were named ACC Player of the Year in the first 11 years the award was given (it was not presented in the 1985 season). Clemson's Susan Hill was named ACC Player of the Year four straight times in 1977-80. Jane Forman won the honor twice, in 1981 and 1984. Ingelise Driehuis was named the ACC Player of the Year in 1986 and 1987 and was also the ACC Tournament's MVP both of those years.

One Clemson player who enjoyed success in the early '80s included three-time singles All-America athlete Jane Forman. Forman won 137 singles matches during her career against only 39 setbacks in 1981-84.

Nicole Stafford was a standout in 1985-88. Stafford won 101 singles matches and was a two-time All-America player, in 1985 and 1987.

Susan Hill was a three-time All-American 1978-80.

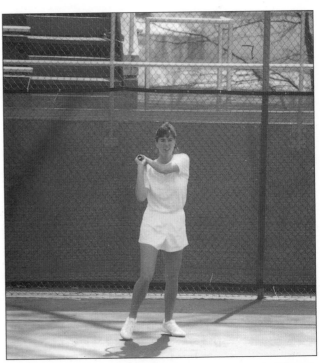

Nicole Stafford was an All-America player in 1985 and 1987.

Cathy Hofer played at Clemson in 1985-88 and was 102-51 in singles. She was a 1986 singles All-America player. She was also named the ACC Player of the Year in 1988.

ANDY JOHNSTON LEADS TIGERS TO SUCCESS

Andy Johnston has been at Clemson since he was 18 years of age. During that time he has played many roles. He's been an athlete, an assistant coach, a head coach, and an administrator.

Johnston was Clemson's women's tennis coach for 15 years, from 1983 to 1997. His career record was 254-160. He also guided the Tigers to five consecutive ACC titles in 1983-1987. Clemson also had 12 top-25 finishes and six NCAA Tournament appearances with Johnston at the helm.

Johnston had an impressive 84-25 record against Atlantic Coast Conference competition, for a 77% winning pct. Included in this record against ACC competition are three undefeated ACC slates. Johnston led his teams to either first or second place in the ACC standing 10 times in his 15-year career.

He also coached the Tigers to 51 All-ACC honors and 13 All-America selections. Johnston led the Tigers to 15 or more victories 12 times.

"I have a lot of great memories at Clemson as the women's head coach," he said. "I would say winning all nine ACC Championship flights in one year is a special memory. Winning five straight ACC Championships; winning the Regional in Columbia, SC in 1996 was another. At that Regional we were down 4-2 after singles and we swept the doubles and beat Georgia 5-4 to advance to the NCAA Final 16. We use to go to the NCAA Tournament as a team, and those were always special. When I first started, they only took 16 and later 20 teams, and that made the invitation to the NCAA Tournament very special.

"We went to the NCAA Final Eight twice, and that was a lot of fun. It was also very special winning five straight ACC Tournament Titles. Obviously when we won all nine ACC Tournament flights, that was a very special time for us.

"Individually, seeing kids advance to the NCAA singles and doubles tournaments was very rewarding. I will never forget GiGi Fernandez having to win a play-in match before she reached the round of 64. She not only won that match, but advanced all the ways to the finals and served for match point and the National Singles Championship in a 12-point tiebreaker. She was up 6-5 in the tiebreaker and she hit a ball down the line and her opponent called the ball out. The call stood and Gigi was so upset and she ended up losing 8-6 in the third-set tiebreaker.

"Gigi got better and better as the year progressed. She got in shape that fall, and she only had a slice backhand. I taught her a topspin backhand and she started to improve and the talent started to show. She told me once

that during her junior career, she only played tennis four months out of the year because she was also on on the national volleyball team. She improved more in one year than anybody I have ever coached. In her professional career she won 17 doubles Grand Slams titles and two gold medals.

"Sophie Woorans advanced to the NCAA Tournament's semifinals, and that was also a memorable moment. Jane Forman was a three time All-American and a two-time ACC Player of the Year, and that was another big moment for us."

One of Johnston's trademarks was always playing a tough schedule. He always wanted to challenge his team and have them grow as the season progressed.

"My philosophy was we wanted to play a tough schedule as often as we could," he explained. "When we started conference play, we would be that much better. Of course, winning the ACC was one of our goals. We wanted to make it to the NCAA Tournament and have one or two All-Americans each season.

"Tennis doesn't solve the world's problems," he continued. "What tennis teaches you is important life lessons. It prepares you for life. Dependability, reliability, and accountability are the three abilities you want. I tried to instill toughness in my athletes. Be a warrior first then a tennis player second. Always play fair, don't take short cuts. Be respectful, be humble and learn how to handle adversity."

COACH ANDY JOHNSTON, ACCORDING TO KRIESE

Andy Johnston and Coach Chuck Kriese arrived in Clemson the same week in the fall of 1975—Kriese as a young coach and Johsnton as a rookie freshman who was set on trying to walk on to the tennis team. The two would serve the Tiger Nation for more than 65 years combined. Kriese states, "Actually, Andy was the first year's lone survivor of morning madness. We had about 50 boys or so trying out as walk-ons that year. When I announced the first night that there would be three weeks of 5:45 a.m. running and that no rackets would be used, many boys just quit on the spot.

"Johnston stayed with the training and won a playoff event to become the lone walk-on that year," said Kriese. "I also remember Andy having to be rushed to the hospital one morning that fall with an appendicitis attack. He bounced back from that and many other adversities. He ended up being a very good tennis player, but that would not be his best contribution to Clemson by any means. Andy Johnston's real gift was that he was a great teacher, an excellent coach, and went on to be a great administrator as well. I really can't think of many things at Clemson that Andy didn't do for Clemson. He has always just been one of those people that got things done when no one else can get them done. What a good man and leader."

SOPHIE WOORONS ADVANCES TO NCAA SINGLES SEMIFINALS

Sophie Woorons had a banner year in 1996. She was a singles and doubles All-America player that season and was named the ACC Player of the Year. She was ranked eighth in the final poll in both singles and doubles and was an All-America honoree in both singles and doubles.

Boba Tzvekovo was an All-America athlete for Johnston in 1994 in singles play. That same season, Janice Durden and Shannon King were all-America doubles players.

Jan Barret was a doubles All-America player and Wooran's partner in doubles in 1996. The 1996 squad advanced to the NCAA Tournament's Final Eight.

THE HEART OF A CHAMPION

There's not a day that goes by that Nancy Harris doesn't smile. Even when she is engaged in a serious discussion with one of her players or an assistant coach, she still has that warm, inviting glow that seems to make the day better.

"Nancy is always like that," said former player and Clemson All-America athlete Keri Wong.

"She doesn't stay down long. She is always there encouraging us, pushing us, saying, 'Let's go Tigers!'"

Harris' uplifting personality and charisma is one of the reasons so many of her former players, coaches, and managers come back each summer to help with her weeklong tennis camps, which run in four sessions every June.

"I really take things day-to-day," Harris said. "I don't know how other coaches do it, but I really do the best I can every day. If I take care of today, then all the tomorrows will be taken care of."

Harris' office inside the Hoke Sloan Tennis Center reflects her philosophy. Her office isn't filled with trophies and things of that nature. Instead, it is filled with the things that are dear to her heart, like family photos, team pictures, and two additional very special items.

Behind her desks on the wall hangs a big ACC logo, signed by the entire 2004 team. From the right of her desk, looking from her seat, is another ACC logo on the wall, and this one is signed by the entire 2008 team.

The significance of both is that they represent Harris' two ACC Tournament Championships, both of which she is very proud of, but for different reasons.

Harris' 2004 team is arguably the best in the program's history. The Tigers, led by one of the nation's best players in Julie Coin, advanced to the NCAA Final Four. They were the first Tigers' women's program in any sport to advance to the national semifinals of the NCAA Tournament.

"It was such a great group of women, and it was so neat to see them rewarded," Harris said. "They were just a fun group of kids. They are our 'Legacy Team.'

"They laughed when I told them that, but I told them, 'You have to understand. You have gone where no other group of women at Clemson have ever gone. You are a Legacy because every team after you will aspire to do better.'"

Clemson has not had a team do any better, though the next year—with four of the same players—it returned to the Final Four. But the 2004 team was statistically the better of the two.

That year, the Tigers finished the year 26-4, the best in school history in terms of win percentage. Coin was ACC Player of the Year and an All-America athlete. The team finished ranked No. 5 in the country at year's end and cruised through the ACC regular season with a perfect 8-0 record, while staying perfect with a sweep in the ACC Tournament as well.

But before all of that, Harris was skeptical of how good her team could be after what she called a disappointing show in Salt Lake City, Utah.

"It was just horrible," Harris recalled. "We went out there with that high altitude they have and none of our girls could find the court. The whole team was sort of just patched together. At that point, I never would have thought that team would go all the way to the Final Four."

The 4-3 loss to BYU was the Tigers' last defeat until eighth-ranked UCLA ended the magical season in the Final Four in Athens, GA.

"They just got better with every match. It was amazing," Harris said. "Sometimes in life and sport, when you are faced with adversity, it brings out the best in you. It helps you show what you are made of."

In between Salt Lake City and Athens, Clemson won 15 straight matches, including a win over No. 5 Duke to clinch the ACC Championship, a win over archrival South Carolina in the second round of the NCAA Tournament, a win over No. 13 Texas A&M in the Round of Sixteen, and then a stunning 4-3 victory over No. 10 Washington in the quarterfinals.

"That was a big upset," Harris said. "Everyone expected Washington to beat us. That was a memorable moment because of Ioana Paun. She was the first woman to put Clemson in the Final Four.

"I called her 'Big I' because she could see the court so well. She was very tactically smart. She figured out she was mentally stronger than her opponent and had the game style to break her opponent down. She could thread the needle and put the tennis ball anywhere she wanted it. Her opponent was very aggressive and she kept the kid deep in the court and let her go for everything.

"When she would try to come in, Big I would thread the needle and pass her. She had her opponent totally frustrated. When Big I won, she turned to her teammates and pumped her fist hard. It was an amazing moment."

Coin, along with Alix Lacelarie, earned All-America status again in 2005, and though the road wasn't as easy the second time around, the Tigers stayed the course and returned to the Final Four by winning eight of their last 10 matches to close the year.

Inside that stretch were two wins over No. 13 North Carolina—including one in the national quarterfinals—a win over No. 16 Duke, and a win in the Round of 16 over No. 6 Northwestern. Before its magical run through the NCAA Tournament, the Tigers advanced to the ACC Finals for a second-straight year and were 8-2 inside conference play.

Clemson finished the season with a 22-9 record and 10th in the final rankings.

The 2008 team had the ingredients and the potential to possibly be as good as the 2004 and '05 teams. The Tigers were blessed with players like Ani Mijacika and Ina Hadziselimovic. Both were All-America players, and Mijacika became the first player in Clemson history—male or female—to be ranked No. 1 in the country in 2008. She subsequently earned ACC Player of the Year honors following the 2009 season.

But before the 2008 season could get started, injuries plagued the squad—senior Carol Salge suffered a chest injury early in the season that held her out for six weeks, while Federica Van Adrichem and Alexandra Luc were hampered with nagging injuries.

The injuries started to mount following three straight wins to start the season. After that, the Tigers started a six-game skid that took a while to recover from. At 5-9 overall and 1-2 in the ACC, they slowly started to get healthy, and that is when potential turned into production.

With No.1-ranked Mijacika cruising to a 30-8 record, the rest of the Clemson team started to follow suit, as the Tigers rolled off 12 victories in a row, including wins over No. 2 Georgia Tech, No. 9 Duke (2), No. 13 North Carolina, and No. 19 Michigan.

"Ani Mijacika was one of the greatest talents I have ever seen in the world," Harris said. "Of all the professionals I have seen play and compete, she really had the talent to be like Julie [Coin] and be up there in the top 60 in the world.

But the moment of the season occurred in the ACC Championship match against ninth-ranked Duke in Altamonte Springs, FL. Clemson's win streak, which at this point was at nine, had started with a stunning 6-1 victory over the Blue Devils earlier in the season.

This time around, Duke was motivated by the regular-season loss to the Tigers and rallied from a 3-1 deficit to tie the match at 3-3 after Hadziselimovic, who had been solid all year, lost at No. 4 singles. Clemson was in trouble.

Salge's match was the last match and it wasn't looking good for the Tigers. Down 5-2 in the third set, she had already fallen behind 30-0 as she set to receive.

"Carol heard the roar of the crowd, so she knew Ina had lost," Harris said. "You could see the look on her face, it was like, 'Oh no! It's all on me now.'"

To make matters worse, she was cramping.

"I was already up there and Carol was cramping, she was going down," Harris said. "So we went to the back fence and sat her down and put a cold towel on her. Ani

comes around to the back of the fence and is talking to Carol through the fence as we are attending to Carol.

"Ani's telling her, 'Carol you can do this. I know you can. You can do this.' Carol was about to pass out. It was at least 100 degrees. But then Carol sees the entire team come up and all of sudden she gets up. I walk back over to the team and stand next to them and she looks over at her teammates and says, 'I got it! Don't worry, I got it.'

"I was thinking, 'Boy, she is down 30-love and she is receiving at 5-2 down.' But she comes back," Harris continued. "All of sudden she starts playing phenomenal and she comes back and wins the match. What was so amazing was how the television people had all the cameras on Duke's team and was just waiting for Duke to win it. They weren't even looking at our girls and then slowly at five-all, they start to pan over and show the girls at Clemson.

"It was really amazing. It was a real testament to how the chemistry and the care for each other helped them and guided them. That's what won the match. It wasn't anything more than that. Carol looked into the eyes of her teammates and said, 'I will not lose this match.'"

Clemson carried the momentum from the Duke victory into the NCAA Regionals, where it knocked off Winthrop and 19th-ranked Michigan to advance to the Sweet 16 for the second straight season.

In all, Harris has won a school record 268 matches at Clemson heading into the 2013 NCAA Tournament, her 12th consecutive trip and 14th overall. She has had two Final Four teams and reached the Sweet 16 seven times, but when she walks into her office, she is instantly reminded of her 2004 and 2008 ACC Championships and automatically they bring a smile to her face.

FRENCH 'COIN' COMES UP HEADS

When Harris first met Julie Coin, she had not seen the native of France hit a tennis ball. It was the freshman's first week at Clemson and she was out on the court warming up. Harris wanted to evaluate the young international player and see how she really played the game.

"You oftentimes don't get to see international players play, so you study the results and hope that they are the player you hope they are going to be," Harris said. "My assistant had seen her play and had told me that I was going to love her because she played the game with the same style that I like, which is an all-court player that plays with a very aggressive style."

So Harris hit around 20 balls with Coin and suddenly stopped.

"I brought her up to the net and asked her, 'Do you have any idea of how good you are?'" Harris recalled.

The Clemson coach told her right there that if she ever wanted to be a top 60 player in the world, "You can be in the top 60. There is no doubt in my mind if you are willing to work for it."

And that's what she became. After she led Clemson to back-to-back Final Fours in 2004 and '05, Coin turned professional, and three years later she defeated Eva Hrdinova, in straight sets—6-3, 6-3—in the first round of the 2009 US Open.

"The thing about Julie is that you always felt that she was on top of you," Harris said.

"You were overwhelmed with her sense of presence and how she pressured you. She was constantly moving forward and through the ball.

"That's what the best players in the world do."

When she was at Clemson, Coin reached the semifinals of the NCAA Singles Championships in 2004. She was also ranked as high as No. 2 in the ITA Tennis poll during the 2005 season and earned All-America status three times over her career.

She also helped the Tigers claim the 2004 ACC Championship and was named the conference's Player of the Year that season.

"It never entered her mind that she could be that, though it was very evident to me," Harris said. "When she came here, she had never played on a tight court. There were things she had never been exposed to. She is what you would call a 'Raw Talent.' She was a junior French player, but she had never been picked to be a superstar. She was a diamond in the rough."

WONG AND BEK

It was kind of a tense moment when Josipa Bek and Keri Wong huddled on the sideline during a doubles match against Dartmouth. The two, usually smooth and eloquent in their style of play, were out of sync somewhat in a match they should have easily been in control of.

"We weren't that focused," Wong recalled. "Jo and I talked about how we needed to concentrate more so we could grab control of the match."

So with a new sense of purpose, Clemson's best doubles tandem in history got back on the court with a look

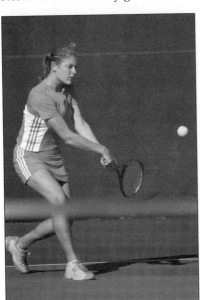

that can only come from the eye of a tiger. But, that sense of concentration, power, and will took a backseat for a little while longer.

On the very next point coming out of the break, Wong decided she had enough and she was no longer going to mess around.

"I told Jo I was going to smack this next serve as hard as I could," she said.

And that's exactly what happened. However, Wong

All-America player Julie Coin was a top-60 player in the world.

was so intent on blasting the serve, she forgot the most important part when it comes to playing tennis—she did not hit the ball cleanly. Instead of hitting an ace, the junior hit the ball with the frame of her racket, causing it to shoot straight up into the air and into the spectators' seats above the court.

"It was so funny because we were acting like we were going to be so focused on the match and everything, and then she frames it and hits the ball right into the crowd. It was really funny," Bek said laughing. "We just started laughing. I mean hard. We tried to keep going, but we laughed for a while."

Actually they laughed for several more games before finally turning their sole attention to Dartmouth in what turned out to be an easy 8-4 victory.

"Jo was sitting at the net looking forward, ready to smack the ball if they made a return. But, she just sat there for a second and then realized the ball was not coming back," Wong said. "We both just looked at each other and died laughing after that.

"It was a pretty funny moment."

Though they can laugh at themselves, no one can laugh at the results Bek and Wong produced during the 2010-2011 tennis season. The two Tigers produced a 34-11 record when playing together, which concluded in the final match at the NCAA Championships.

Bek and Wong advanced to the championship match in all three major collegiate championships—the ITA All-American Championships that fall, the ITA Indoor Championships in the winter, and the NCAA Championships. They were the first Tigers to accomplish such a feat, and just the second to reach the NCAA Finals since Gigi Fernandez did the same in the 1983 NCAA Individual Championships.

"We went into the Nationals feeling like we can play with the best teams in the country," Bek said. "We had all the belief and confidence that we could do well. Once you play in the finals at All-America and then in the finals at National Indoors, you know you can play against any team."

That's what the two did.

The Tigers' season was the best in Clemson history. Bek and Wong, at one point in the year, held the nation's top ranking for more than a month, the first such Clemson duo to hold that distinction. They also defeated two different No. 1 doubles teams.

The 34 wins were the most by a doubles team for one season in the program's history, easily passing the old mark of 29, which was set in several different seasons.

When Harris recruited Bek from Osijek, Croatia and Wong from Jackson, Mississippi, she saw the potential the two had then. So when she got them on campus in the fall of 2008, she figured she would pair them up at that time just to see what happened.

"It did not work out too well," the Clemson coach said. "At that time, they were not right for each other. They were too different. It was not a good match."

That's true, they weren't. That fall, they struggled when they played together in practice. First of all, they did not understand each other, with Wong being a Southern girl from Mississippi and Bek's English still raw.

They also did not play the same game. Bek is an emotional player, who plays every point as if it is the last. She wears her emotions on her sleeve and can be loud with her celebration after a forehand winner or show her disdain for a bad shot.

Wong, on the other hand, is quiet and reserved, rarely showing any emotion at all.

"They are just two different players," Harris said.

They also possess different styles of play.

"Keri is like a surgeon," says Harris. "She places the ball so beautifully and effortlessly, it's unreal sometimes. She can just wear an opponent out. When she knows she has them on the run, then she will go in and finish them off.

"Jo is like a grasshopper. She is all over the court. But, she has so much energy and is so athletic. She can make the most unbelievable shots you have ever seen."

Knowing she still needed to get these two together at some point, Harris allowed their skills to grow a little more as individuals before pairing them back up again.

In a little experiment during Bek's and Wong's sophomore year, the two paired up again in practice. Harris wanted to see how much they improved over time while playing doubles with other people. It left Bek and Wong scratching their head at the time, as they again struggled for consistency.

"We were coming from different cultures and everything, so it took us some time to understand each other," Bek said. "Coach tried to put us together again in our sophomore year and we did not do so well, but then after a while, we started to realize how good we can be together."

When the 2010-'11 season began, it did not take Clemson long to see its future with Bek and Wong as a duo. The two began the year by ripping through the All-American Championships, which included wins over doubles teams from Florida, Mississippi, and Duke.

From there, the momentum carried through the indoor season, where they again advanced to the championship match of a major tournament. This time the Tigers beat Southern Cal and California to reach the finals of the ITA Indoor National Championships.

"Though they are both different in their styles, they are still the same when it comes to being aggressive," Harris said. "That's why they play so well together. They both have that killer instinct, and they know when they have their opponents on the ropes.

"So the style in which they get there may be different, but once they get there, the result is the same."

Wong admits that they have something in common.

"We move well on the court together," says Wong. "There are not many teams that play two-up. I think that is a big difference, that we both play up at the net."

Bek and Wong finished their careers ranked first and second all-time in overall victories, while earning multi-

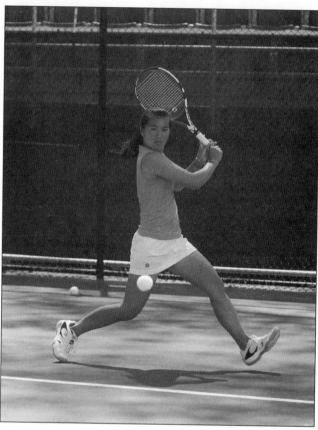

Keri Wong has teamed up with Josipa Bek to become a successful doubles tandem, despite their different styles.

ple All-America honors. Bek won 118 doubles matches, while Wong won 117. They also ended their careers ranked first and second all-time in combined singles and doubles. Bek had 224 career wins in her four seasons, while Wong won 220 matches.

You can only wonder what they could have accomplished if they just learned how to play together a little bit earlier in the careers. But maybe that's what made them so great together in the first place.

WOMEN'S TENNIS HISTORY

September 7, 1975—Clemson athletic officials announced that Clemson would field women's tennis for the first time in the spring of 1976.

March 10, 1976—Clemson played its first dual match and defeated Georgia State, 9-0, in Atlanta, GA.

March 28, 1976—The Tigers played their first ACC opponent and were victorious over N.C. State, 7-2, in Charlotte, NC.

April 22-24, 1977—Clemson won the AIAW State of South Carolina Collegiate Tournament.

October 6-8, 1977—Clemson finished second in the inaugural ACC Women's Tennis Tournament in Winston-Salem, NC. Susan Hill won at number-one singles and the doubles team of Carol Fullerton and Colette Bennett won at number-two doubles.

April 20-22, 1978—The Tigers won the AIAW State of South Carolina Collegiate Tournament at Furman University in Greenville, SC. Clemson won five of the six singles flights. Hill won the number-one singles flight, while Carol Fullerton won the number-two doubles flight. Bennett won at number-four singles, and Libby Cooper won at number-five singles, while Vicki Eynon won at number-six singles. In doubles, Hill and Vicki Eynon won at number-three doubles.

May 11-14, 1978—Clemson won the AIAW Southern Regional II Tennis Tournament in Memphis, TN. Bennett and Fullerton won the doubles tournament with a 7-5, 6-2 victory over Beth Bondurant and Barbara Goldman from Virginia. Hill won the singles title with a 6-1, 6-3 victory over Cindy Brinkler of Virginia.

June 5, 1978—Clemson defeated Ohio State in the first round of the AIAW National Tournament, consisting of 24 teams at Salisbury State College in Salisbury, MD. The next day, in the second round, LSU defeated Clemson 6-3.

June 8, 1978—The Lady Tigers finished 13th in the final poll. Hill was named an All-America player and ACC Player of the Year, as a freshman.

June 9-14, 1978—Hill and Bennett played in the 64-player draw at the AIAW National Tournament. Hill lost to fourth-seed Barbara Jordon of Stanford 6-2, 6-2. Bennett lost to Anne Broyles of SMU—6-2, 6-0. In doubles, Bennett and Fullerton won their first-round match over Wheaton and Horan of Minnesota—6-3, 6-4. In second round doubles, seventh-seeded Lea Antonoplis and Susie Brown of Southern Cal defeated the Clemson duo—6-2, 6-2. In consolation singles, Hill advanced to the quarterfinal round and lost to Fekucua Hutnick of Rollins—6-4, 6-3. Bennett advanced to the finals of the consolation bracket and lost to Hutnick—6-3, 6-2.

October 13-15, 1978—Susan Hill was named the MVP of the ACC Tournament.

May 9-12, 1979—Susan Hill qualified for the National AIAW Singles Tournament and Hill and her sister Carolyn Hill qualified for the doubles tournament at the Southern Region II Tournament.

June, 1979—Susan Hill was named ACC Player of the Year.

June 9, 1979—Susan Hill defeated Karen Kettenacker of Iowa—6-1, 6-2—in the first round of the 64-player AIAW Singles Tournament at Iowa City, IA. Kim Jones of San Diego State defeated Hill in the second round later in the day. In doubles, the team of Hill and her sister Carolyn Hill lost to Snelson and Price in the first round—6-3, 6-0. The Hill sisters won the consolation doubles tournament, as they defeated Kelly and Kelly of Tennessee—6-4, 6-1.

October 19-21, 1979—Susan Hill was named the MVP of the ACC Tournament.

May 8-10, 1980—Clemson qualified as a team at the AIAW Region II Tournament at Johnson City, TN. Susan Hill qualified for the singles competition.

June 3, 1980—Clemson lost to California 5-4 in the first round of the AIAW National Tournament in Baton Rouge, LA, in a 24-team draw.

June, 1980—Clemson finished 12th in the final poll. Susan Hill was named an All-America honoree and ACC Player of the Year.

June 5-7, 1980—Clemson advanced to the semifinal round of the team consolation draw at the AIAW National Tournament in Baton Rouge, LA. The Tigers defeated North East Louisiana 7-2, Texas Christian 5-4, and South Carolina 5-4. The Tigers lost to UCLA 8-1 in the semifinal round.

June 8, 1980—The Tigers' Susan Hill defeated Diane Wortman of Montana—6-0, 6-1—in the first round but fell to fourth-seeded Sandy Collins of Texas at Permian-Basin in the second round of the 64-player draw at the AIAW National Singles Tournament in Baton Rouge, LA. Hill finished with a 40-3 record in singles.

October 17-19, 1980—Susan Hill was named the MVP of the ACC Tournament and finished second in the ACC Tournament. Hill won the number-one singles flight. Jane Forman won the number-three singles flight. Forman and Jody Trucks won the ACC number-two doubles flight.

May 6-8, 1981—Clemson defeated Vanderbilt 7-2, South Carolina 5-4, and North Carolina 5-4, as the Tigers won the AIAW Region II Tournament in Lexington, KY. Susan Hill was named the Most Valuable Player of the Regional. Clemson qualified for the AIAW National Tournament in Tempe Arizona. Susan Hill won the individual singles championship of the AIAW Region II Tournament.

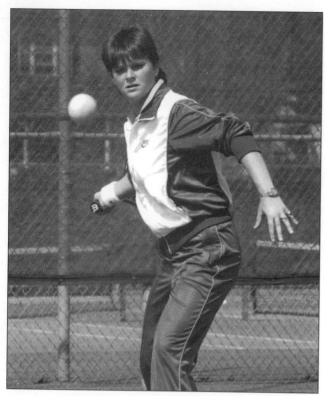

Jane Forman had a 137-39 career record in 1981-84. She is the all-time winningest player in Tiger history.

June 3, 1981—Clemson participated in its third AIAW National Tournament. The Tigers upset sixth-seeded San Diego State, 5-4 in the 16-team tournament. The next day, UCLA defeated Clemson 7-2 in the Quarterfinal Round.

June, 1981—Clemson finished ninth in the final poll. Susan Hill was named an All-America player and ACC Player of the Year, the fourth straight year she was named ACC MVP.

October 23-25, 1981—Clemson won the ACC Championship in Durham, NC, the first in the school's history. Forman was the ACC Champion at number-one singles. Clemson also won three other conference singles flights. The Tigers' Jody Trucks won at number-two singles, Melissa Seigler won at number-four singles, and Lori Miller was the AC Champion at number-five.

May 16, 1982—Clemson played in the inaugural NCAA women's tennis tournament. The Lady Tigers lost to number-one seed and eventual National Champion Stanford 9-0, in Salt Lake City, UT. Forman participated in the NCAA singles tournament. She advanced to the second round and was named an All-America player.

May, 1982—Clemson finished 18th in the final poll.

August 5, 1982—Andy Johnston was named head coach of the Lady Tigers.

October 3, 1982-March 3, 1983—Clemson won 16 straight matches during this period. It started with a win over Florida State and ended with a lost to Trinity.

April 15-17, 1983—The Lady Tigers won the ACC Championship in Chapel Hill, NC. Clemson won all six singles and all three doubles championships, a first for any conference team—men or women. Jody Trucks was named ACC Player of the Year and MVP of the ACC Tournament. Andy Johnston was named ACC Coach of the Year. This was the first season that the tournament was held in the spring.

May 14, 1983—Clemson defeated Oklahoma State 5-4 in the second annual NCAA Women's Tennis Tournament in Albuquerque, NM. The Lady Tigers won their 30th match of the season, the most ever by a Lady Tiger team.

May 15, 1983—The Lady Tigers lost to eventual tournament finalist Trinity, 8-1 in the quarterfinal round of the NCAA Tournament.

May 19-22, 1983—Gigi Fernandez was a finalist at the NCAA individual singles tournament. Fernandez played in a prequalifying match and won six straight matches to reach the finals. She lost to Beth Herr of Southern California in the finals—3-6, 6-2, 7-6.

May, 1983—Clemson finished seventh in the final poll. Forman and Fernandez were named All-America players. Fernandez finished the season ranked fifth in the country in singles play.

April 7, 1984-April 4, 1987—Clemson won 28 consecutive matches against Atlantic Coast Conference teams.

April 13-15, 1984—The Lady Tigers won the ACC Championship. Forman was named ACC Player of the Year and MVP of the ACC Tournament.

May 12, 1984—Clemson lost to second-seeded Stanford, 9-0 at the 16-team NCAA Tournament in Los Angeles, CA.

May, 1984—The Lady Tigers finished 15th in the final poll. Forman was named All-America for the third time of her career. Forman also finished 10th in the final singles poll.

April 12-14, 1985—The Lady Tigers won the ACC Championship. Johnston was named ACC Coach of the Year.

May, 1985—Clemson finished ranked 19th in the final poll. Nicole Stafford was named All-America.

April 11-13, 1986—The Lady Tigers won the ACC Championship. Ingelise Driehuis was named ACC Player of the Year and MVP of the ACC Tournament. Andy Johnston was named ACC Coach of the Year.

May 15, 1986—Arizona State defeated Clemson 5-4 in the 16-team NCAA Tournament.

May 21, 1986—Cathy Hofer advanced to the NCAA round of 16 at the NCAA singles tournament, where she lost to fifth-seeded Beverly Bowes of Texas—6-2, 6-4.

May, 1986—The Lady Tigers finished eighth in the final poll. Hofer and Driehuis were named All-America players. Hofer finished the season ranked 10th in the final singles poll. The Tigers were 26-3.

April 10-12, 1987—Clemson won its sixth-straight ACC title, and Ingelise Driehuis was named ACC Player of the Year and MVP of the ACC Tournament.

May, 1987—The Lady Tigers finished 20th in the final poll, and Driehuis was named an Academic All-America player. Driehuis was also named an All-America honoree in both singles and doubles. Her doubles partner Nicole Stafford was also named All-America. Driehuis finished 10th in the final singles poll.

April, 1988—Hofer was named ACC Player of the Year and MVP of the ACC Tournament. Hofer finished the year with a 30-12 record in singles.

May, 1988—The Lady Tigers finished the season ranked 22nd in the final poll. Clemson was 18-10 and 5-2 in the ACC.

May, 1990—Clemson finished the year ranked 21st in the final poll. Clemson finished the season with a 15-9 record overall.

May, 1991—The Lady Tigers finished the season ranked 25th in the final poll. Clemson was 15-1 overall and 6-1 in the ACC.

May, 1992—Clemson finished the season ranked 23rd in the final poll. Clemson was 15-8 overall.

February 14-April 25, 1993—Freshman Emma Peetz won 25 straight singles matches during this span to set a new school record.

February 24, 1993—Andy Johnston won his 200th career match with a 9-0 win over Georgia Tech.

April 29, 1993—Johnston was named ACC Coach of the Year.

May, 1993—Johnston was named Southeast Coach of the Year.

May 12, 1993—Clemson defeated Kansas 5-3 in the first round of the NCAA Tournament in Gainesville, FL.

May 13, 1993—Third-seeded Duke defeated Clemson 5-0 in the round of 16 at the NCAA Tournament in Gainesville, FL.

May, 1993—Clemson finished 12th in the final ITA poll. The Tigers were 20-6 overall.

May 13, 1994—Southern Cal defeated Clemson 6-0 in the first round of the NCAA Tournament in Athens, GA.

May 19, 1994—Boba Tzvetkova advanced to the round of 16 in the NCAA singles tournament in Athens, GA. She lost in the round of 16 to Paloma Collantes of Mississippi—7-6, 6-2.

May, 1994—Clemson finished 18th in the final ITA poll. Boba Tzvetkova, Shannon King, and Janice Durden were all named All-America players.

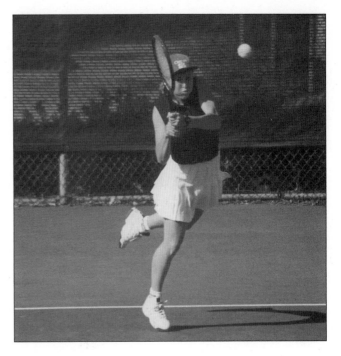

Sophie Woorons advanced to the NCAA Tournament's Final Four in the singles tournament in 1996.

April 21, 1996—Sophie Woorons was named ACC Player of the Year.

May 3-5, 1996—Clemson won the NCAA Southeast Regional Tournament. The Lady Tigers defeated South Alabama, South Carolina, and Georgia as Clemson advanced to the NCAA Final 16.

May 18, 1996—The Lady Tigers lost to second-seeded Stanford in the NCAA Tournament's Round of 16 in Tallahassee, FL. Stanford was the tournament's finalist.

May 25, 1996—Sophie Woorons advanced to the NCAA Tournament's Final Four in the singles competition. She lost to number-one seed Kelly Hunt of Kansas—7-5, 6-4. Woorons finished the season with a 31-11 record.

May, 1996—Clemson finished 19th in the final ITA poll. Woorons was named All-America in singles and doubles. Jan Barrett was named an All-America honoree in doubles.

June 20, 1997—Coach Andy Johnston resigned and was named the Assistant Athletic Director for Football Management.

August 1, 1997—Clemson hired Nancy Harris as coach of the Lady Tigers. She became only the third women's tennis coach in Clemson history.

May 15, 1998—Clemson advanced to NCAA Tournament play in Nancy Harris's first season as head coach. The Tigers lost to Tennessee 5-0 in the first round.

April 15, 2000—The Tigers defeated Georgia Tech 6-3 to close the regular season with a 14-5 record, giving Clemson its first Top-25 ranking in three years and a bid to the NCAA Tournament.

May 11-12, 2002—Clemson upset 16th-ranked William & Mary 4-3 in the first round of the NCAA Tournament before falling to Wake Forest 4-1 in the second round.

October 28, 2002—Julie Coin won the ITA Southeast Regional Championship, becoming only the third Tiger to earn that honor.

April 13, 2003—Clemson upset 12th-ranked North Carolina 4-3 to finish the regular season with a 7-1 record in the ACC and a second-place regular season finish.

May 10-11, 2003—The Tigers defeated #36 Baylor 4-1 in the first round of the NCAA Regional Championships before falling to #11 North Carolina 4-1 in the second round. Clemson finished the season ranked 19th, which was the highest final national ranking for the Tigers since the 1996 season. Clemson finished with a 19-6 record overall.

October 27, 2003—Clemson's Maria Brito and Julie Coin won the ITA Southeast Regional Doubles Championship, becoming the first doubles team in program history to claim that title.

March 17-May 22, 2004—The Tigers won 15 consecutive matches. In this streak, Clemson defeated six top-15 teams.

April 16-18, 2004—Clemson won the ACC Championship held in Raleigh, NC, after winning the regular season crown with a 7-0 record. Coin was named the ACC Player of the Year and Alix Lacelarie earned tournament MVP honors.

May, 2004—Coach Nancy Harris was named the 2004 Wilson/ITA Southeast Region Coach of the Year. Assistant coach Sylvain Malroux was selected as the 2004 Wilson/ITA Assistant Coach of the Year. The committee also named Coin the 2004 Southeast Region Player to Watch.

May 15-16, 2004—The Tigers won the NCAA regional tournament. They defeated Troy State 4-0 and #33 South Carolina 4-1 to advance to the NCAA Round of 16.

May 20-22, 2004—Clemson defeated #13 Texas A&M 4-1 in the NCAA Final 16 and #10 Washington 4-3 in the Round of Eight before falling to #8 UCLA 4-0 in the NCAA Tournament's Final Four. The team finished the season ranked #5, the highest final ranking to date in program history. Clemson finished the year with a 26-4 record.

May 24-28, 2004—Coin reached the semifinals of the NCAA singles tournament. She was named an All-America athlete and was a finalist for the 2004 Collegiate Women Sports Award for tennis. In the NCAA doubles competition, Coin and Maria Brito advanced to the second round before falling.

January 11, 2005—Clemson was ranked third in the first ITA poll of the season, the highest national team ranking in the program's history.

April 17, 2005—The Tigers claimed their 500th total victory with a 5-2 win over #16 Duke at the Hoke Sloan Tennis Center in the final regular season match of the season.

May 13-14, 2005—Clemson won its second consecutive NCAA Regional title by defeating #58 Furman 4-0 in the opening round and #20 William & Mary 4-0 in the second round.

May 19-21, 2005—In the NCAA Championships, the Tigers reached the semifinals for the second straight year. They edged sixth-ranked Northwestern 4-3 in the Round of 16 and defeated #13 North Carolina 4-1 in the Elite Eight before falling to #1 Stanford 4-2 in the Final Four. The team was ranked #10 in the final ITA poll and finished the year with a 22-9 record.

May 24-26, 2005—Coin became the first Clemson women's tennis player to reach the Round of 16 in the NCAA singles competition twice in her career, as she advanced to the Round of Eight. She earned her second All-America honor in singles and was also named an All-America honoree in doubles with Alix Lacelarie. Coin and Lacelarie reached the second round in the NCAA doubles tournament and were ranked 10th in the final ITA doubles poll. Coin was ranked second in the final singles poll, the highest for a Clemson women's tennis player in history.

October 17, 2005—Freshman Federica Van Adrichem won the ITA Southeast Regional Championship, becoming just the fourth Tiger to make that claim.

April 21-22, 2006—Clemson earned a bye for the first round of the 2006 ACC Tournament and then defeated #7 North Carolina 4-1 in the quarterfinals. The Tigers fell to 10th-ranked Georgia Tech 4-1 in the semifinals.

May 12-13, 2006—The Tigers won a 4-0 decision over Siena in the first round of the NCAA Regionals. The Tigers then fell to 20th-ranked Kentucky in the second round at Clemson, SC. The team finished with a 17-8 record.

April 15, 2007—With a 6-1 victory over Virginia Tech, the Tigers concluded their ACC schedule with a 10-1 record to earn a share of the conference regular season title. It marked the ninth time Clemson had finished first in program history and the second time under Coach Nancy Harris.

April 19, 2007—Ani Mijacika was named the 2007 ACC Freshman of the Year, becoming the first Clemson player in history to garner the honor.

May 11 & 12, 2007—Clemson defeated

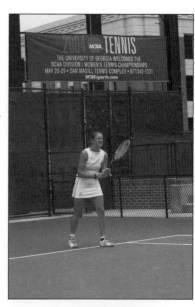

Julie Coin reached the Round of 16 in the NCAA singles tournament twice in her career.

Coastal Carolina 4-0 in the first round of the NCAA Tournament. The Tigers also defeated Virginia in the second round.

May 14, 2007—Ani Mijacika added another accolade to her list after being named the ITA Southeast Region Rookie Player of the Year. She is the first Tiger player to win this award.

May 18 2007—Clemson lost to 10th-ranked California in the Round of 16 at the NCAA Tournament in Athens, GA. The Tigers finished the season with a 22-5 record overall.

May 22-27, 2007—Mijacika and sophomore Federica Van Adrichem completed a historic run at the NCAA Doubles Championships. The duo became the first Tiger team to advance past the quarterfinals round of the tournament, falling to William & Mary's top-seeded team in the semifinals after posting wins over teams from Notre Dame, UCLA, and Stanford.

June 1, 2007—The doubles team of Mijacika and Van Adrichem earned the highest ranking in program history at #4 in the final ITA doubles poll.

October—November, 2007—Mijacika completed one of the most impressive falls in history, as she reached the finals of the season's top two tournaments in the Riviera/ITA All-American Championships in October and the ITA National Indoors in November.

February 22, 2008—Mijacika earned the #1 singles ranking in the ITA Tennis poll. In doing so, she became the first player in Clemson tennis history to be ranked as the best in the nation.

April 18-20, 2008—The Tigers won the ACC Championship, held in Altamonte Springs, FL, defeating the top and second-seeded teams en route to the title. Clemson was victorious over North Carolina, 4-2, in the second round before knocking off #1-seed Georgia Tech, 4-1, in the semifinals. The Tigers then defeated second-seeded Duke, 4-3, in the finals for the program's eighth conference championship. The Tigers' Carol Salge was named the tournament MVP.

May 9-10, 2008—Clemson defeated Winthrop 4-0 in the first round of the NCAA Tournament. The Tigers advanced to the Final 16 when Clemson defeated 19th-ranked Michigan 4-1.

May 15, 2008—The Tigers lost to fourth-ranked Stanford 4-0 in the NCAA Tournament's Round of 16. Clemson finished the year with a 17-1-0 record.

September 19, 2008—Former player Gigi Fernandez was inducted into the ITA Women's Hall of Fame, which is held on the campus of the College of William and Mary.

March 3, 2009—Clemson moved to ninth in the ITA poll. Mijacika was ranked number one in singles and Josipa Bek number four in singles.

April 16, 2009—Ani Mijacika was named the 2009 ACC Women's Tennis Player of the Year

May 8-9, 2009—The Tigers defeated Winthrop 4-0 in the first round of the NCAA Tournament. Clemson advanced to the Sweet 16 for this third consecutive year, defeating 20th-ranked North Carolina in the second round of the NCAA Tournament.

May 15, 2009—Fifth-ranked Notre Dame defeated Clemson 4-0 in the NCAA Tournament's Round of 16. Clemson concluded the year with a 19-8 record.

May 22, 2009—Josipa Bek and Ina Hadziselimovic reached the Final Eight of the NCAA Doubles Championships, giving Clemson five All-America honors in a single season for the first time in school history. Mijacika and Bek were named All-America double players. Mijacika was also named an All-America singles player.

October 26, 2009—Bek won the ITA Carolina Regional Singles Championship and advanced to the finals in the Doubles Championship with Hadziselimovic

May 14-15, 2010—Clemson hosted the NCAA Tournament opening rounds for the fifth consecutive season and earned the number-nine overall seed in the tournament. Clemson defeated the College of Charleston, 4-0, and capped a dramatic 4-2 win over #19 Georgia in the second round to advance to the NCAA Tournament's Final 16.

May 20, 2010—The Tigers lost to the eventual National Champion Stanford in the NCAA Round of 16. Clemson finished the season with a 24-6 record.

October 10, 2010—Juniors Josipa Bek and Keri Wong advanced to the finals and finished as runners-up in the ITA All-American Championships in Pacific Palisades, CA.

November 7, 2010—Bek and Wong again advanced to the finals of a major tournament, this time knocking off the nation's #1 on the way to a runner-up finish at the USTA/ITA Indoor National Championships.

May 11-12, 2011—Clemson defeated Wichita State 4-0 in the first round of the NCAA Tournament. Clemson also defeated 21st-ranked Arkansas 4-2 in the second round.

May 19, 2011—Florida, ranked number one in the country, defeated Clemson 4-1 in the NCAA Tournament's Round of 16. Clemson ended its season with a 21-11 record.

May 11-12, 2012—The Tigers defeated Arizona Sate in the first round of the NCAA Tournament before losing to sixth-ranked Georgia 4-3 in the second round of the tournament. Clemson finished the season ranked 25th with a 16-10 record.

May 10, 2013—The 13th-seeded Clemson women's tennis team took down Ohio Valley Conference Champion Eastern Kentucky, 5-0, in the first round of the 2013 NCAA Women's Tennis Team Championships at the Hoke Sloan Tennis Center on the Clemson campus.

May 11, 2013—The 13th-seeded Clemson women's tennis team overcame a 2-0 Vanderbilt lead and a bout of rain in defeating the 19th-ranked Commodores, 4-2, in the NCAA Women's Tennis Team Championships at the Hoke Sloan Tennis Center. With the victory, Clemson advanced to the NCAA Round of 16, held at the Kahn Tennis Center in Urbana, IL, and hosted by the University of Illinois.

May 17, 2013—The Clemson women's tennis team took the doubles point and the first singles decision, but fourth-seeded Georgia rallied to beat the 13th-seeded Tigers, 4-2, in the NCAA Tournament's Round of 16 in Urbana, IL. Clemson finished the season with a 16-8 mark.

May 22, 2013—Clemson's Beatrice Gumulya and Yana Koroleva each advanced to the second round of the NCAA Singles Championships in Urbana, IL on Wednesday. With Gumulya and Koroleva advancing, it marked just the fourth time in school history that two or more Tigers have won a match at the NCAA Singles Championships in the same season.

Gumulya won a 6-3, 7-5 decision over No. 61 Dominique Harmath of Rice and Koroleva, a national 9-16 seed, defeated 23rd-ranked Jenny Jullien of St. Mary's, 3-6, 6-3, 6-4 in a rain-interrupted match.

A third Tiger, freshman Liz Jeukeng, suffered a 0-6, 7-5, 6-7, to 76th-ranked Cindy Chala of Virginia Commonwealth in a match that took nearly four hours due to rain stoppages and being forced indoors.

May 23, 2013—Sophomore Yana Koroleva defeated North Carolina's Zoe De Bruycker, 3-6, 6-2, 6-2, in the second round of the NCAA Women's Tennis Singles Championship at the Khan Outdoor Tennis Complex in Urbana, IL. Koroleva becomes the first Clemson player to advance to the NCAA Round of 16 since 2009, when Josipa Bek accomplished the feat. In doing so, Koroleva earns her first All-America honor.

Fellow sophomore and teammate Beatrice Gumulya fell short in her upset bid of seventh-seeded Gina Suarez-Malaguti of North Carolina. Gumulya won the first set, 6-2, reeling off the final five games, but Suarez-Malaguti surrendered just two games the rest of the way en route to the 3-6, 6-0, 6-2 victory. Gumulya's breakout season ends with a sparkling 26-6 overall record.

May 24, 2013—Clemson Sophomore Yana Koroleva kept her National Championship hopes alive with a 7-5, 7-6 win over No. 5 Zsofi Susanyi of California in the Round of 16 at the Khan Outdoor Tennis Complex in Urbana, IL.

Koroleva becomes just the fourth player in Clemson history to advance to the quarterfinals of the Singles Championships, joining Gigi Fernandez (1983), Sophie Woorons (1996), and Julie Coin (2004, 2005).

May 25, 2013—Clemson sophomore Yana Koroleva fell to defending NCAA Singles Champion Nicole Gibbs of Stanford, 6-1, 6-1, in the quarterfinals of the 2013 NCAA Singles Championships in Urbana, IL. Koroleva ends the season at 28-8, and became just the fourth player in school history to reach the round of eight in the 64-player field.

May 28, 2013—The Clemson women's tennis team finished the season ranked 13th in the nation by the Intercollegiate Tennis Association. The Tigers finished the year 16-8, and advanced to the NCAA Round of 16. It is the 11th straight season that the women's tennis program finished among the top-25 teams in the nation.

Overall, the women's tennis program has finished among the top-25 in the nation 27 times in 38 seasons. Additionally, the program has finished inside the top-15 in eight of the last ten seasons, and 15 times all-time.

June 5, 2013—Three Clemson women's tennis players were listed among the top 45 in the final national singles poll, released by the Intercollegiate Tennis Association. All-American Yana Koroleva closed the season ranked 13th to lead the Tigers, while freshman Liz Jeukeng finished 42nd, and Beatrice Gumulya came in 45th. Gumulya and Koroleva also entered the final rankings at No. 34 in doubles.

April 20, 2014—With two wins over top-ten league opponents in the final week of the regular season, Clemson finished tied atop the ACC regular season standings with Virginia, Miami and North Carolina at 12-2, claiming a part of the ACC regular season championship

May 9, 2014—Despite an hour-and-a-half rain delay forcing the match indoors, the 13th-seeded Clemson women's tennis team downed UNC-Wilmington, 4-0, in the NCAA Team Championship First Round at the Hoke Sloan Tennis Center in Clemson, SC. The win marks the 13th consecutive season that Clemson has advanced past the first round.

May 10, 2014—The Clemson women's team advanced to the NCAA Round of 16 for the seventh time in the last eight seasons with a 5-0 win over Auburn at the Hoke Sloan Tennis Center.

May 15, 2014—Clemson fell to fourth-seeded Duke, 4-1, in an NCAA Team Championship Round of 16 contest that finished after midnight on Friday morning on the Feild Courts at the Dan Magill Tennis Complex. Clemson closes the season at 22-7 overall, and advanced to the Round of 16 for the ninth time in 11 seasons.

May 21, 2014—Junior Romy Koelzer and senior Yana Koroleva each earned victories in the First Round of the

2014 NCAA Singles Championships on at the Dan Magill Tennis Complex in Athens, Ga. Koelzer won her NCAA debut over Nadia Ravita of Kentucky, 6-3, 3-6, 6-3, and Koroleva defeated Baylor's Kiah Generette, 6-3, 6-3.

May 22, 2014—Jessy Rompies and Beatrice Gumulya were the beneficiaries of a stunning development at the NCAA Doubles Championships, as the nation's number-one doubles team and top seed retired due to injury in their head-to-head match. UCLA's Robin Anderson and Jennifer Brady, ranked No. 1 in the nation, forfeited early in the first set, leading 3-0, sending Clemson's duo on to the Round of 16 at the 32-team Doubles field. In singles play for the Tigers, Yana Koroleva suffered a three-set defeat to 9-16 seed Chanelle Van Nguyen of UCLA, 3-6, 7-5, 6-3, and Romy Koelzer lost in straight sets to Lynn Chi of California, 7-5, 6-1, ending their respective seasons.

May 23, 2014—Clemson's doubles team of Jessy Rompies and Beatrice Gumulya was eliminated from the Round of 16 at the NCAA Doubles Championships at the Dan Magill Tennis Complex. The Clemson duo mounted an incredible comeback in the match against the nation's 13th-ranked tandem, Caroline Price and Whitney Kay of UNC, but fell 6-3, 2-6, 7-6(5), in the contest.

May 27, 2014—For the eleventh time in the past 12 seasons, the Clemson women's tennis team finished the season ranked among the top-20 teams nationally in the final Intercollegiate Tennis Association poll. The 2014 squad, which went 22-7 and earned a share of the ACC Regular Season championship with a 12-2 record, closes the year ranked 13th.

It's the 28th time in school history that the team has finished in the top-25, which includes every season since 2002, all under 2014 ACC Coach of the Year, Nancy Harris.

June 4, 2014—The Intercollegiate Tennis Association unveiled the final 2014 individual rankings on Wednesday, which includes five members of Clemson's 13th-ranked squad in singles and doubles. The ITA ranks 125 players in singles and 80 doubles teams via computer formula. Junior Romy Koelzer was the highest-ranked player in singles, coming in at 33rd. She advanced to the Second Round of the NCAA Singles Championships, falling to eventual finalist Lynn Chi. Yana Koroleva came in at 34th, after playing at the top position for most of the season. She also advanced to the Second Round individually. Beatrice Gumulya also worked her way into the rankings at 89th after going 23-13 this season.

In doubles, the tandem of Koroleva and Gumulya finished 15th, the highest-ranked duo at Clemson since Keri Wong and Josipa Bek finished 2011 ranked 3rd. Gumulya also teamed with Jessy Rompies to finish 26th, which includes their default win over the number-one tandem in the nation in the Round of 32 at the NCAA Championships. Koroleva and Tristen Dewar came in at 72nd.

May 8, 2015—The 21st-ranked Clemson women's tennis team improved to 14-0 in NCAA First Round matches over the last 14 years with a 4-0 win over South Alabama on Friday afternoon in Tuscaloosa, Ala.

May 9, 2015—For the 10th time in the last 12 seasons, the 21st-ranked Clemson women's tennis team secured a spot in the NCAA Sweet 16, following a 4-2 upset over No. 13 Alabama in the NCAA Second Round in Tuscaloosa Ala.

May 15, 2015—The fourth-seeded Vanderbilt Commodores defeated 21st ranked Clemson 4-0 in the NCAA Tournament's round of 16 at Waco, Texas.

May 20, 2015—Joana Eidukonyte and Beatrice Gumulya won their first round matches in the NCAA Singles Championships in Waco, Texas on the campus of Baylor University. With the wins, both players advance to the second round of the national singles tournament on Thursday.

Eidukonyte, a 9-16 national seed in the tournament and the nation's 12th-ranked singles player, defeated No. 29 Joana Vale Costa of LSU in straight sets, 6-2, 6-1. The 36 wins place Eidukonyte in a tie for seventh in Clemson history in terms of singles victories in a single season. Gumulya, ranked 60th nationally, defeated 95th-ranked Cindy Nguyen of Hawaii in her first round match by a score of 6-1, 6-4. With the win, the senior from Jakarta, Indonesia improved to 29-9 on the season. Senior Romy Koelzer's Clemson career ended on Wednesday with a three-set loss (7-5, 2-6, 6-4) to 85th-ranked Sophie Watts of Fresno State.

May 21, 2015—Singles player Joana Eidukonyte and the doubles team of Beatrice Gumulya and Jessy Rompies clinched spots in the Sweet 16 at the NCAA Singles & Doubles Championships held on the Baylor University campus.

Eidukonyte, a 9-16 national seed in the tournament, defeated No. 33 Catherine Harrison of UCLA in Thursday's second round 6-2, 6-3.

Clemson's duo of Rompies and Gumulya, ranked and seeded No. 4, defeated Vanderbilt's Colton and Campbell.

Also in singles action Gumulya's fell 6-2, 6-4 to No. 11 and 9-16 seed Stephanie Wagner of Miami.

May 22, 2015—The women's tennis doubles team of Beatrice Gumulya and Jessy Rompies won its Sweet 16 match at the NCAA Doubles Championships With the win, the duo improves to 29-5 overall and advances to the Elite Eight of the tournament.

Gumulya and Rompies, ranked No. 4 in the country and seeded fourth in the tournament, defeated No. 19 Guiliana Olmos and Zoe Scandalis of Southern Cal in straight sets, 6-4, 6-3, and advanced to the quarterfinal round.

In singles, Jamie Loeb of North Carolina defeated Clemson's Joana Eidukonyte 6-3, 6-1. She finished with a 37-7 record overall and tied for sixth in Clemson history for most singles wins in a season.

May 23, 2015—Caroline Doyle and Ellen Tsay defeated Clemson's Beatrice Gumulya and Jessy Rompies 4-6, 6-4, 6-4 in the quarterfinals of the NCAA Doubles Championships in Waco, Texas. The pair, which is one of the more decorated doubles teams in Clemson history, The Tiger duo compiled a 29-6 record, ranked in a tie for second in Clemson history in terms of doubles victories in a single season.

May 26, 2015—For the 12th time in the past 13 seasons, the Clemson women's tennis team finished the season ranked among the top-20 nationally in the final Intercollegiate Tennis Association poll as announced by the association. The Tigers finished 18th in the final poll of 2015.

June 3, 2015—The Intercollegiate Tennis Association released the final 2015 individual rankings on Wednesday afternoon, which included four members of Clemson's team. Joana Eidukonyte was Clemson's highest ranked singles player at No. 16. Senior Romy Koelzer was ranked 44th and played number one singles for the Tigers most of the season. Beatrice Gumulya, finished the year ranked 57th.

Gumulya and partner Jessy Rompies, both All-American selections after reaching the NCAA Quarterfinals, finished the season ranked fourth nationally in doubles. Thanks to a 29-6 overall record, the duo earned the

highest final season ranking by a Clemson doubles team since Keri Wong and Josipa Bek were ranked No. 3 at the conclusion of the 2011 season.

June 4, 2015—For just the third time in program history, and the first in six years, three members of the Clemson women's tennis team earned All-America honors, as announced by the Intercollegiate Tennis Association. Seniors Beatrice Gumulya and Jessy Rompies were named Doubles All-Americans, while junior Joana Eidukonyte earned the national honor in singles for the 2015 season.

May 13, 2016—The Clemson women's tennis team fell to Rice in the first round of the NCAA Tournament by a score of 4-1 in Nashville, Tenn. The loss brings Clemson's season to an end and their overall record to 10-11 for the 2016 season.

May 25, 2016—Joana Eidukonyte won her first round match in the NCAA Singles Championship in Tulsa, Okla. Eidukonyte, ranked 26th in the nation in singles, defeated 107th-ranked Alexandria Stiteler of South Alabama, 6-2, 7-5. Clemson freshman Ayan Broomfield, lost to Tennessee's Sadie Hammond 6-2, 5-7, 7-5.

May 26, 2016—In the second round of the NCAA Singles Tournament Breaunna Addison of Texas defeated Joana Eidukonyte 6-3, 6-2.

June 1, 2016—Joana Eidukonyte was 30th and Ayan Broomfield was 66th in the final Intercollegiate Tennis Association singles poll. In doubles, Eidukonyte and Fernanda Navarro was ranked 46th as a doubles team.

MEN'S
Track & Field

Men's Outdoor Track & Field

Conference Championships
Southern Intercollegiate Athletic Association—1909, 1910, 1911
Atlantic Coast Conference Outdoor Champions—1980, 1982, 1989, 1990, 1991, 1993, 1997, 1998, 2000, 2001, 2004

Top 25 NCAA Finishes:

1982 (19th), 1988 (T15th), 1989 (T23rd), 1991 (T13th), 1992 (12th), 1993 (T10th), 1994 (11th), 1995 (T10th), 1996 (17th), 1997 (T17th), 1998 (T11th), 1999 (19th), 2000 (10th), 2002 (T4th), 2007 (24th), 2008 (T21st)

Men's Indoor Track & Field

Atlantic Coast Conference Indoor Champions—1987, 1989, 1990, 1981, 1992, 1993, 1997, 1998, 1999, 2000, 2001, 2002

Top 25 NCAA Finishes:

1987 (T18th), 1989 (8th), 1990 (22nd), 1992 (2nd), 1993 (2nd), 1994 (24th), 1995 (11th) 1997 (T25th), 1998 (3rd), 1999 (3rd), 2000 (T10th), 2001 (T20th), 2002 (7th), 2007 (15th), 2008 (12th), 2009 (T23rd), 2011 (T22nd)

Clemson first started track and field in 1905. The new coach was Dr. F. H. H. "Rock" Calhoun. Calhoun was a graduate of the University of Chicago and was hired by the Clemson Board of Trustees to be a Geology Professor, a position he would hold for several years. He consented to organize the first track and field team at Clemson in the spring of 1905.

EARLY SUCCESS

Clemson began to have early success in this new sport at Tigertown in 1908, as the Tigers finished sec-ond in the Southern Intercollegiate Athletic Association (SIAA). The SIAA was an early conference consisting of many SEC and ACC teams, as well as Texas and North Carolina.

In 1909, 1910, and 1911, the Tigers won the SIAA Championship. Norman Byrd led the Tigers to the first of these two championships. In his senior year (1910), Byrd finished first in the 100-yard and 440-yard dashes and the running broad jump.

In 1911, Fritz Furtick was the leading Tiger point-winner, having gained first place in the running broad jump and finishing second in the pole vault for a total of 17 points.

NORMAN BYRD, EARLY CLEMSON TRACK STAR

Norman Byrd was one of the early track stars who ran for Clemson.

Byrd came to Clemson in 1906 from the small town of Branchville, SC. He was born on August 10, 1888 to parents J.N. and Alice Byrd.

While at Clemson, he majored in civil engineering and ran track for four years and was captain of the team in 1910. The Clemson yearbook, Taps, humorously stated: "He made himself famous as the only original human airplane in existence. He can run the hundred yards in 10 seconds flat when not frightened. When afraid, he breaks all records."

While at Clemson, Byrd was on the *Clemson Chronicle* staff, the *Tiger* staff, and the Taps yearbook staff. He served as Editor-in-Chief of Taps his senior year.

In 1908, as a sophomore, Byrd finished second in the 220-yard dash and the 440-yard dash at the SIAA meet. He also won the running broad jump with a distance of 20'9 ½". His efforts helped Clemson to a second-place finish behind the meet champion, Vanderbilt. During the spring of 1908, Clemson defeated both Georgia and Georgia Tech in dual meets.

During his junior year (1909), he won the 100-yard dash in 10 $\frac{1}{5}$ seconds; the 220 yard-dash in 23 seconds; the

440-yard dash in 52 ¾ seconds; and the running broad jump at 21' 5 ¼". Because of his effort, the Tigers won the SIAA meet in Nashville, TN on May 15. That year, Clemson finished 4-0 in dual meets, having claimed victories over Georgia Tech, Georgia, North Carolina, and Gordon Institute.

During Byrd's senior season, Clemson played host to the SIAA meet on Bowman Field. Much excitement was in the air, as this was a way to showcase the Clemson campus. Byrd again won the 100-yard dash, with a time of 9 4/5 seconds; the 440 yard dash in 52 seconds; and the running broad jump at 20'6".

The Tigers ran away with the meet and finished first with 70 points, while Vanderbilt and Georgia were tied at a distant second-place with 15 points. Georgia Tech was fourth with eight points.

During his career, Byrd won eight first-place finishes and accumulated 46 points in three SIAA meets for the Tigers, a school career record in this category. He set school and conference records in the 100-yard dash and also set school records in both the 220-yard dash and the broad jump.

After he graduated, Byrd returned to his hometown of Branchville, SC and was a farmer, school teacher, and a merchant. He died on January 6, 1955 of heart disease.

FIRST ALL-AMERICA

Perhaps one of the most well-known Clemson track and field athletes in the early 1900s was Ross O'Dell.

O'Dell gained his fame as one of the best pole vaulters in the nation, having gone to the 1928 Olympic Trials and participating in the Penn Relays in Philadelphia, PA.

O'Dell grew up in Liberty, SC, and set various records at that time at Liberty High School. He went to Clemson, where his father had graduated (T. Ross O'Dell).

Ross made a name for himself early at Clemson by winning championships at the state and the Southern Conference meets. He won the pole vault event three times and set school, state, and conference records at both the state and the Southern Conference meets in the pole vault.

Ross graduated in 1928 with a degree in Agriculture. He served as county agent in Elljay, Ga and Newman, Ga. He was a teacher at Elljay High School and also coached track there.

During his sophomore year (1926), he won the pole vault and high jump competitions twice in three dual meets. He also finished in the top three in the high hurdles, broad jump, and shot put at each meet. At the Georgia Tech relays, he set a record in the pole vault at 12 feet and four inches and placed second in the high jump. At the state meet, he set a record in both the pole vault and the broad jump.

He won the Southern Conference meet in the pole vault and set a new conference record. At the NCAA meet

on June 12, 1926, in Chicago, IL, he finished second with a vault of 13 feet.

During the 1927 season as a junior, O'Dell won the pole vault in six competitions. He was the high scorer in points for Clemson in all of the dual meets that season. In the state meet, he again won the pole vault and set a new record. He tied for first in the high jump and finished second in the broad jump.

At the Southern Conference meet, he set a new pole vault record and finished fourth in the broad jump. At the NCAA meet on June 11, 1927, in Chicago, IL, he finished tied for second in the pole vault.

In 1928, he was Clemson's leading point man in all of the dual meets and won the pole vault at six different meets. At the state meet, he set records in the high jump and the pole vault. He jumped so high in the pole vault that sideline benches from the football field had to be placed under the standards so the bar could be raised. He also won the shot put competition.

At the Southern Conference meet, he broke the conference record in the pole vault for the third consecutive year, with a mark of 13'3". This record would stand until the 1958 track season, 30 years later, when his son was a senior football player at Clemson. At the 1928 Penn Relays, he finished second in the pole vault.

At the 1928 NCAA meet, he tied for fourth, with a vault of 12'6".

At the Southeast Olympic Trials in Atlanta, GA on June 3, 1928, he finished first in the pole vault. In the Olympic Trial Finals at Harvard Stadium in Cambridge, MA, he was a sixth-place finisher. After the Olympic Trial Finals, O'Dell was very optimistic.

"They started the bar at 11'6"," he said. "The first man dropped out at this height, and then several were eliminated at 12'6". I was the first man over, at 13 feet. I was feeling good and thought I had a chance, but others cleared 13 feet as well. They raised the bar to 13'6" and everyone knocked the bar over on their first two tries. I have never before come so close to clearing a height and not make it. At each attempt at 13'6", I got my entire body over, but the other fellows told me I was turning my left shoulder into the bar on my release from the pole. It was a great experience, and I did my best. I hope to clear 14 feet one day."

According to today's standards, O'Dell would be a three-time All-America athlete. O'Dell is one of three Clemson Track and Field athletes in history to finish in the top four at the NCAA Outdoor meet. Of these three athletes, he is the only one to have two second-place finishes.

His son Bill O'Dell, who played football at Clemson,, was quick to describe how his father loved Clemson: "Dad really loved Clemson and going to school there. When it came my time to choose schools, I liked Clemson and I also was interested in Auburn. Both schools were interested in me in playing football. Dad had a talk with me and he said, 'Auburn is a nice school, but you're going to Clemson.' I'm glad he did, as I played football and enjoyed my days at Clemson too."

COACH HOWARD COACHES TRACK

Coach Frank Howard not only was the head football coach for 30 years at Clemson, but he was also the head track coach from 1931-'40.

On one occasion at the Presbyterian Track in Clinton, SC, one of Howard's track stars, Banks McFadden (also a Clemson football and basketball great), was participating in the long jump. University of South Carolina's Dick Little had defeated McFadden in the previous two years, and McFadden wanted badly to avoid a similar fate. Nevertheless, Little broke the state record on his first jump, and McFadden wasn't close on his first attempt. McFadden got closer on his second attempt, but he felt something was still wrong and had serious doubts about beating Little's leap at this meet. Walking away from the pit, McFadden told Howard about his problem.

"I told him I didn't know if I was over-striding or under-striding, or what was wrong, but I just didn't feel confortable," McFadden said. Coach told me 'boy, come on down here with me.'" They walked back to the pit and Howard took out a tape measure and set one end at the takeoff board and stretched the tape into the landing area. Howard told him, "'Here's 22-feet. So that you will have a target, I will put this towel right here. What I want you to do is just clear this towel and you'll be all right.' I said, 'Thanks coach, I appreciate that.'"

When McFadden turned his back to go back up the runway, Howard took the opportunity and moved the towel further down the pit another foot.

"I was in the right frame of mind," said McFadden. "I reared back and took off. I aimed for the towel and I missed it, I was just short. I was disappointed. I saw Coach Howard there and he saw that I was disappointed. I said, 'Coach, what did I do wrong?' About that time, they announced that I had broken the state record and beat Little's mark. Coach Howard looked at me and said, 'You didn't think I was going to leave that towel at 22 feet, did you?'"

Coach Howard was later quoted after telling this story, "Now that's great coaching!"

Howard also introduced McFadden to the track events that consisted of hurdles. "I had never run the hurdles before and knew nothing about it," said McFadden. Coach Howard threw me the book on hurdling techniques and said 'Read it, I'm just the football line coach.'

"Coach Howard was a man who really knew how to handle people," McFadden said. I had never jumped that far in my life. I have to believe he thought I was a pretty good athlete, and he tried to get something out [of] me that I wasn't getting out of myself."

ROCK NORMAN

Rock Norman came to Clemson in 1940. During an 18-year period, he was the cross country and track and field coach, varsity and freshman basketball coach, and assistant football coach. He won seven state track and field titles at Clemson, and at one time his team won 17 consecutive dual meets.

Overall, he spent 51 years in the coaching profession, 34 of them coaching track, basketball, and football at Clemson, The Citadel, Furman, and the University of South Carolina. He spent five years as a coach of football, basketball and track at Furman. He then spent eight years at the University of South Carolina where he was the varsity basketball coach for two years. In 1936, he arrived at The Citadel, and his 1938-39 basketball team won the state championship.

He was inducted into the State of South Carolina Athletic Hall of Fame, the Clemson University Athletic Hall of Fame, and the Roanoke College Athletic Hall of Fame. The outdoor track and field that the Tigers use today is named in his honor.

P. WEE GREENFIELD ELEVATES TRACK AND FIELD AT CLEMSON

During the decades of the 1960s and early '70s, the track and field team started sending members to the NCAA track and field meet on a regular basis, and Clemson started to become a threat to win the ACC Championship. During this era, P. Wee Greenfield led the program.

Greenfield made an immediate impact to Clemson's fortunes in track and field. In his first six years on the job, the Tigers had a dozen individual champions. Altogether, he had 33 individual winners in his 14 years as Clemson coach in both ACC indoor and outdoor meets. He also coached Avery Nelson, Clemson's first All-America (Triple Jump). He also coached three-time All-America athlete Roger Collins (Javelin).

According to longtime Sports Information Director Bob Bradley, he instilled in his players things other than track skills. "He wanted each one of his athletes to be an ambassador for Clemson. He wanted all of them to be gentlemen at all times and he wanted them to get their college degree. He kept up with his former athletes after they went into the working world and stayed interested in them."

The native of Ranger, TX led the Tigers to a second-place finish in the ACC outdoor meet in both 1964 and 1965 and had third-place finishes two other times.

He was always in great demand as a starter at major track meets throughout the nation, especially the internationally-known Penn Relays in Philadelphia.

Before Greenfield retired, he and his Tigers got to enjoy a new track and field facility in 1974 at what is now the Rock Norman Track and Field complex.

Dr. I.M. Ibrahim, previously the soccer coach, took over the track and field program after Greenfield retired for two seasons.

CLEMSON WINS FIRST ACC CHAMPIONSHIP

In 1980, Clemson won its first Atlantic Coast Conference Championship under coach Sam Colson. Julius Ogaro won three events at the meet—the 5,000 meters, 10,000 meters, and the 3,000-meter steeple chase, a unique combination that was very challenging. For his efforts, he was named the meet's most valuable performer.

Clemson won another Atlantic Coast Conference Championship outdoors in 1982. That team also finished ninth at the NCAA meet.

Clemson won its first-ever Atlantic Coast Conference Indoor Track and Field meet in 1987. Wade Williams led the Tigers to the first-place finish and subsequently an 18th-place finish at the NCAA Indoor Track and Field meet. In 1988, the Tigers finished tied for 15th place at the Outdoor Track and Field meet.

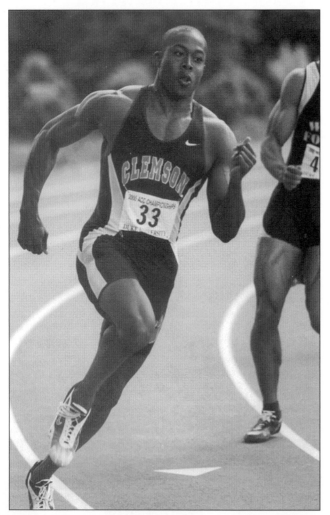

Shawn Crawford won a gold medal in the 200 meter dash as the 2004 Olympics.

BOB POLLOCK ERA: ATLANTIC COAST CONFERENCE DOMINATION, NATIONAL RECOGNITION

Clemson hired Bob Pollock on July 25, 1988, starting a new era in Clemson Men's Track and Field. In his first season as coach of the cross country and track teams, he won the triple crown as he led his team to the ACC Championship in Cross Country, Indoor Track, and Outdoor Track—all in the same academic year.

This set the tone for what was in store for Clemson track and field for the next 20 years. During this time, Pollock won 21 Atlantic Coast Conference Championships, (11 Indoor, Nine Outdoor and one Cross Country). He was also named the ACC Coach of the Year a total of 19 times in indoor and outdoor track and field.

In 1992, he was named the National Coach of the Year after leading Clemson to a runner-up finish at the NCAA Indoor Track and Field meet.

He coached the Tigers to 29 top-25 finishes in cross country, indoor track and field, and outdoor track and field at the NCAA Meet. He coached almost 200 All-America athletes at Clemson and 18 athletes who advanced to the Olympic Games. He also coached 13 NCAA National Champions, including three who won multiple titles. Two of his Clemson athletes, Shawn Crawford and Carlton Chambers, won Olympic gold medals.

"I have enjoyed continuing the success and rich tradition of Clemson track and field and cross country during my tenure," said Pollock before he retired. "Our program is nationally recognized due to the commitment, dedication, talent, and desire to excel by our student-athletes and assistant coaches.

"I have been proud to be associated with these people at Clemson. Athletics is an exciting and challenging part of my life. I am grateful to have had the opportunity to work with so many wonderful people."

Pollock was inducted posthumously into the Clemson Athletic Hall of Fame in 2010 and into the National Collegiate Track and Field Coaches Hall of Fame in 2012. In 1996, he was inducted into the Appalachian State Athletic Hall of Fame.

Pollock passed away on February 20, 2010 from cancer.

Bob Pollock led Clemson to 21 ACC Championships (indoors and outdoors) during his 20 years as head coach of the Clemson Track and Field team.

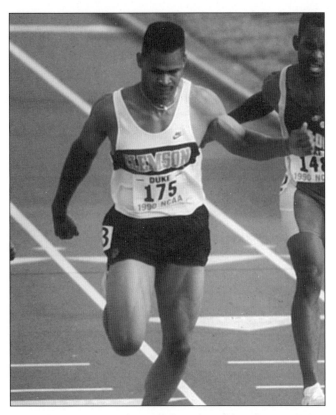

James Trapp was a 10-time All-America athlete from 1990-'92.

MOST DECORATED ATHLETES

Clemson had numerous All-America athletes during the Bob Pollock era. One of the standouts included Shawn Crawford (1997-2000), who was an 11-time All-America runner. He was a four-time All-America in indoor track and was honored seven times in outdoor track and field. Crawford won a total of 11 ACC Championships, nine of which were at the ACC Indoor Championships.

Crawford won three National Championships during his career. He won the 200-meter dash at the 1998 NCAA Indoor Championships. He also won the 200-meters in both the indoor and outdoor NCAA Championships in 2000. Crawford won two gold medals in the 2004 Olympics in the 200-meter dash and the 4x400-meter relay.

James Trapp (1990-1992) earned 10 All-America honors, four for indoor track and six for outdoor. Trapp won a total of 12 ACC Championships as a sprinter—six outdoor and six indoor.

Michael Green subsequently won three National Championships as a sprinter in 1992 and 1993. He won the NCAA Indoor 55-meter dash in 1992 and 1993, along with as the NCAA Outdoor 100-meter dash in 1993.

Tony Wheeler (1994-97) was an eight-time All-America runner, while Jeremichael Williams (1996-98) and Duane Ross (1992-95) were both seven-time All-Americas.

Ato Modibo won 15 ACC Championships in his career in 1999-2000, 12 of which were indoors.

JAMES TRAPP—A TRUE CLEMSON CHAMPION

Olympian James Trapp was a two-sport athlete at Clemson in 1990-92. In those three years, he was a 14-time ACC Champion and a 10-time All-America sprinter. He also played football and eventually played in the NFL for 11 years, winning one Super Bowl. Nevertheless, he says track is what kept him a Tiger.

"Track is what got me to stay at Clemson," Trapp said. "After my freshman football season, I was going to transfer to Oklahoma, but I wanted to stay because of track and field and Coach Pollock."

Trapp vividly remembers many moments from his career at Clemson.

"I remember at the ACC Meet my freshman year we had run the 4x100 meters and won that. After the race, I noticed my spikes were worn out and coming apart. Teammates and myself told Coach Pollock that Trapp needed new shoes. Coach Pollock simply said, 'We'll put some tape on the shoe and they will be all right.' So what I did, I borrowed my roommate Larry Ryan's shoes and luckily his events were opposite of mine so we shared the same shoes and made it through the meet. Later on, I received a new pair of spikes and had everything I needed throughout my career. I guess it was because I was a freshman or something that I couldn't get another pair of shoes at that meet. Coach Pollock was a great man, and he always was trying to watch the school's budget."

"Another moment that I will never forget is going to the NCAA Indoor meet and our team finished second in the nation. Green won the 55 meters and I won the 200 meters. That was an awesome experience."

MEN'S OUTDOOR TRACK AND FIELD HISTORY

April 17, 1905—Georgia defeated Clemson in Athens, GA in the very first track meet for the Tigers. Fred "Rock" Calhoun, a geology professor, was the first track and field coach.

May 12, 1906—In the Tigers' first-ever home track meet, Clemson defeated Georgia 59-49 on Bowman Field. The meet came down to the last even, the Mile Run. Bleachers were emptied as the crowd lined the circuit. Clemson won the mile run and the contest by 10 points. Of the 12 events contested, Clemson won eight.

1907—Clemson ran in four dual matches, winning two and losing two. The Tigers defeated Georgia Tech and South Carolina and lost to North Carolina and Georgia. Fritz Furtick was accountable for 72 points for the Tigers during this season, or more than a fourth of the total (263) that Clemson scored that season.

May 23, 1908—The Southern Intercollegiate Track Meet was held in Atlanta, GA. Vanderbilt came in first, with 42 ½ points, followed by Clemson, with 27. Warren won the 220-yard low hurdles with a time of 28 and ⅕ seconds, and Norman Byrd won the running broad jump with a distance of 20 feet and, 9 ½ inches. F. Fleming won the shot put competition. They were Clemson's first-ever conference champions.

1909—Clemson defeated Gordon Institute 94.5-13.5, Georgia 83.5-24.5, Georgia Tech 80-28, and North Carolina 62-46 in dual meet competition during the season giving the Tigers a 4-0 record.

May 15, 1909—An enthusiastic rally welcomed home the victorious Clemson track team from Nashville, TN after Clemson won the Southern Intercollegiate Athletic Association Track and Field meet. Earlier in the 1909 season, Clemson went 4-0 in dual meets. At the conference meet, Byrd won four events, and the Tigers won eight of the 12 events that day. The Tigers won the meet with 60 points, followed by Vanderbilt with 39 and Georgia Tech with nine points.

May 14, 1910—Clemson won the Southern Intercollegiate Athletic Association (SIAA) Track and Field Meet on Bowman Field at Clemson, SC. Byrd won three events in leading the Tigers. The Branchville, SC native won the 100-yard dash, the 440-yard dash, and the running broad jump. Barnett won the one-mile run. Stevens won the 120-yard high hurdles and the 220-yard low hurdles. White won the high jump. The Tigers won the meet with 70 points. Vanderbilt and Georgia finished in a tie with 15 and Georgia Tech was fourth with eight points. The Tigers won eight of the 12 events contested that day.

1911—Clemson defeated Georgia Tech on April 24, and South Carolina on May 1. This gave the Tigers a perfect 7-0 record in dual meets dating back to the 1909 season.

May 6, 1911—For the third year in a row, Clemson won the Southern Intercollegiate Athletic Association Track and Field meet. The AAU meet was held simultaneously and the Tigers were declared champions in that meet as well making the Tigers the champions of the South. The Tigers claimed seven first-place finishes.

May 11, 1912—The Tigers won the May Day Event of the Birmingham Athletic Club in Birmingham, AL. The Tigers defeated Georgia Tech and Auburn at this meet.

May 18, 1912—Clemson finished third in the SIAA meet at New Orleans, LA. A. C. Tuberville won the shot put and finished third in the discus and the hammer throw to lead the Tigers.

1913—Clemson defeated Georgia Tech in the last meet on Bowman Field.

1916—The Tigers did not have a track and field team in 1914 and 1915. However, a rejuvenated effort allowed for the Tigers to field a track team once again. The team's head coach was Professor A. H. Ward, a former Clemson track performer. Clemson defeated Newberry on April 14 before losing to Davidson by two points on May 13. This broke Clemson's string of consecutive victorious dual meets at 10, dating back to the 1909 season. Ironically, Davidson was Clemson's first football opponent on Riggs Field.

1917—Davidson defeated the Tigers 60-54 in the only meet for the Tigers (because of World War I, many teams disbanded, and the lack of funds also caused hardships for many schools). This was also the first track and field meet at Riggs Field. Alex Lewis served as Head Coach.

1919—The Tigers did not have a track team in 1918 due to World War I but returned the following year. Clemson defeated South Carolina 71-28 on May 17. The Tigers finished fifth with nine points in the Georgia Tech Meet that featured 15 collegiate teams at Grant Field in Atlanta, GA.

1921—Clemson went 4-0 in dual meets, amassing 335 5/6 points compared to the opposition's 104 1/6. Clemson defeated Georgia, Davidson, South Carolina, and Wofford.

May 7, 1921—Clemson won the inaugural State Track and Field meet in Columbia, SC. Clemson finished first The Tigers scored more than seven points more than all the other teams combined.

April 29, 1922—The Tigers won the state track and field meet in Columbia, SC for the second year in a row. Walter Redfern of Clemson was the highest point winner, with 16.

May 5, 1923—Clemson won the state track and field meet in Clemson, SC for the third year in a row, dominating the event with 108 points and taking first place in all the events except one.

May 18-19, 1923—Jack Chandler was Clemson's first Southern Conference track champion, as he won the 100-

yard dash in a time of:10.1/5. This was also the inaugural Southern Conference track and field meet.

May 2, 1925—The Tigers once again won the State Track and Field meet in Clinton, SC. Wallace Roy of Clemson established a new record when he ran the 440-yard dash in 51 seconds at the state track and field meet.

June 12 & 13, 1925—Carter Newman and Wallace Roy entered the fourth annual NCAA outdoor track and field meet. The duo was the first Clemson athletes to enter any event in the NCAA Tournament.

1926-28—Ross O'Dell was Clemson's first field event champion at the Southern Conference Track Championships, as he won the pole vault for three consecutive seasons. His best vault was 13'3".

May 14-15, 1926—Clemson's three-man team captured three first places and set two conference records in the Southern Conference meet, held at Chapel Hill, NC. Roy set a new conference record and won the 440 run, and Newman won the 880 with a new conference record.

June 11-12, 1926—O'Dell vaulted 13 feet, good for second in the pole vault at the NCAA Outdoor Track and Field meet at Stagg Field in Chicago. O'Dell is the first Tiger to score and place at the NCAA outdoor track and field meet.

June 10-11, 1927—O'Dell finished in a tie for second with a vault of 12'6" at the NCAA outdoor track and field meet in Chicago, IL. Carter Newman, a half-miler, also ran in the meet but did not pace.

April 28, 1928—O'Dell was the first Clemson athlete to participate in the prestigious Penn Relays, finishing in a tie for second in the pole vault.

May 5, 1928—Clemson won the State Track and Field meet. O'Dell took three firsts in the meet—the pole vault, high jump, and the shot put—and was the leading point scorer in the meet, with 18 points.

June 3, 1928—Clemson's Ross O'Dell finished first in the pole vault with a 13' effort at the Southern Olympic Trials in Atlanta, GA. He qualified for the National Olympic Trials in Cambridge, MA.

June 8-9, 1928—Ross O'Dell tied for fourth in the pole vault at the NCAA Outdoor Track and Field Championship.

May 4, 1929—The Tigers won the State Track and Field meet in Clinton, SC. J.M. Lineberger of Clemson set a new state record in the mile run (4:38.8). A. T. Andrews set a new state record in the two-mile run, 10:13.

1932-34—Gordon Lynn participated in the NCAA track and field meet in 1933. Lynn won the Southern Conference Championship in the 100-yard dash in 1932 and 1933 and also won the 220-yard dash in 1934.

April 29, 1933—Gordon Lynn finished third in the Penn Relays in Philadelphia in the 100-yard dash.

May 5, 1934—Clemson and South Carolina tied for first at the State Track and Field meet at Clinton, SC.

May 16, 1934—Clemson finished sixth at the Southern Conference track and field meet in Durham, NC. Lynn finished first in the 220.

May 4, 1935—The Tigers won the state track and field meet with 71 5/6 points. Carter set a new state record in 120 high hurdles. Blackwell set a new state record in the javelin.

May 1- 2, 1936—Clemson won the state track and field meet. J.H. Green set a new state record in the mile, and Mac Folger set a new state record in the 120 high hurdles.

May 16, 1936—Folger won the Southern Conference Championship by winning the 220 low hurdles. Carter finished tied for first in the high jump. The Tigers finished fourth in the Southern Conference Track and field meet with 22.5 points.

May 1, 1937—Bob Carter won the 120 high hurdles and the high jump in leading Clemson to the state track and field championship. The Tigers won the State Track and Field meet with a one-point victory over South Carolina. Clemson finished the event with 46 points followed by South Carolina with 45. The Citadel scored 21 followed by PC with 19, Furman 18, Wofford 12, Erskine 2, and Newberry 0.

May 6, 1939—The Tigers won the State Track and Field meet for the fifth time in the decades of the 1930s. McFadden placed in four events, winning the 120 high hurdles and finished second in the 220 low hurdles and the broad jump. He finished third in the javelin.

May 4, 1940—The Tigers won the State Track and Field meet in Clinton, SC. Banks McFadden placed first in three events: the 120 high hurdles, the 220 low hurdles and the broad jump. He also finished third in the shot and scored 18.1/4 points for the Tigers.

May 3, 1941—Clemson won the State Track and Field meet for the third year in a row. Walker finished first in the mile and two-mile runs. Clemson won the state meet with 56.5 points. South Carolina was runner-up with 44 points, followed by PC, Furman, and Newberry.

May 1, 1943—The Tigers won the state track and field meet for the 10th time since 1928.

****The Tigers did not field a track team during 1944 and 1945.

1949—Clemson had a 4-0 record in dual meets. The Tigers scored 100 points for the first time ever in a meet against Wofford.

May 14, 1949—The Tigers won the State Track meet in Clinton, SC.

May 12, 1951—Clemson won the State Track and Field meet with 74 2/5 points. PC was the runner up followed by the Citadel and Wofford.

May 11-12, 1956—John Steedley was Clemson's first ACC champion in outdoor track, as he won the 120-yard high hurdles.

May 7, 1957—Clemson won the State Track and Field meet in Clinton, SC, where Paul Snyder and Wilbur Simmons were high scorers for Clemson, as each athlete scored eight points.

June 17-18, 1960—John Dunkelberg participated in the NCAA track and field meet at the University of California.

May 3-4, 1964—Clemson won the State Track and Field meet.

May 8-9, 1964—Avery Nelson was the ACC outdoor track meet's Most Outstanding Performer, as he set a new conference record in the triple jump. Clemson finished second in the meet.

June 18-20, 1964—The mile relay team of Jimmy Wynn, Douglas Adams, Hayes Cone, and Cecil Huey finished sixth in the one-mile relay at the NCAA outdoor track and field meet in Eugene, Oregon. The Tigers tied for 53rd in the meet as a team.

June 13-15, 1968—Roger Collins finished fourth in the javelin throw at the NCAA outdoor meet in Berkeley, CA. The Tigers finished tied for 38th in the meet.

May 9-10, 1969—Roger Collins was the ACC outdoor meet's Most Outstanding Performer, as he set a new ACC record in the javelin.

June 19-21, 1969—Roger Collins finished sixth in the javelin throw at the NCAA outdoor meet, where Clemson finished tied for 48th as a team.

June 18-20, 1970—Roger Collins finished fourth in the javelin throw at the NCAA outdoor meet at Drake University in Des Moines, Iowa. Clemson finished in a tie for 39th place.

1977—Clemson tied for 26th at the NCAA outdoor track and field meet in Champaign, IL. Mike Columbus finished sixth in the discus throw and earned All-America honors. Stuart Ralph finished third in the javelin.

June 1-3, 1978—Clemson finished 23rd at the NCAA outdoor track and field meet behind the performance Ralph, who finished second in the javelin. Ralph participated in four NCAA meets for his career.

April 17-19, 1980—Clemson won the Atlantic Coast Conference Championship in outdoor track for the first time in history. Desai Williams won the 100- and 200-meter runs. Also, Julius Ogaro won the 5,000- and 10,000-meter run along with the 3000-meter steeplechase. He was named the meet's Most Valuable Performer.

The 1980 Clemson Track and Field team won the school's first ACC Championship.

June 2-6, 1981—The Tigers tied for 31st nationally at the NCAA Outdoor Track and Field Championship in Baton Rouge, LA. Ogaro finished fifth in the 3000-meter steeplechase, while Hans Koeleman finished sixth, and both earned All-America honors. Mike Hartle finished fifth in the javelin to earn All-America honors.

April 15-17, 1982—The Tigers and N.C. State tied for the ACC Outdoor Track Championship with 144 points each. The Tigers' Hans Koeleman was named the meet's Most Valuable Performer, as he won the 3000-meter steeplechase.

June 2-5, 1982—Clemson finished 19th at the NCAA outdoor track and field meet. Jack Harkness finished second in the discus, earning All-America honors. This was Clemson's first outdoor track & field top-20 team in history. Mike Hartle finished seventh in the javelin, and Jim Haughey finished 10th in the 5,000-meter run.

April 21-23, 1983—Clemson finished second in the ACC Outdoor Track Championship, where Hans Koeleman was named the meet's Most Valuable Performer, winning the 5,000-meter run and the 3,000-meter steeplechase.

May 30-June 4, 1983—The Tigers finished tied for 40th at the NCAA outdoor track and field meet. Jim Haughesy finished ninth in the 5,000 meters and Wybo Lelieveld finished fourth in the 1500-meter run.

April 19-20, 1985—Greg Moses was named the Most Valuable Performer at the Atlantic Coast Conference outdoor track and field meet, as he won both the 100- and 200-meter dashes in Raleigh, NC.

May 27-June 1, 1985—Victor Smalls finished fourth nationally at the NCAA outdoor track and field meet. Clemson finished in a tie for 36th place.

June 4-7, 1986—Mike Spirtioso finished second in the shot put and Victor Smalls finished sixth in the high jump at the NCAA outdoor track and field meet in

Indianapolis, IN. Spiritoso's second-place finish was the highest for a Clemson field event athlete since Ross O'Dell finished tied for second in 1927. Clemson finished 30th as a team.

June 3-6, 1987—Mike Spiritoso finished eighth in the shot put and Terrance Herrington finished third in the 1500-meter run as the Tigers finished tied for 41st as a team in the NCAA Outdoor Track and Field Championship.

June 1-4, 1988—Clemson finished 15th at the NCAA outdoor track and field meet. Dov Kremer finished second in the 5000-meter run to pace the Tigers. Terrance Herrington finished fourth in the 800-meter run and Yehezkel Halifa finished fifth in the 10,000-meter run.

April 22-24, 1989—Clemson won the ACC Outdoor Track and Field Championship, and Bob Pollock was named ACC Coach of the Year. Terrance Herrington won the 1500-meter run for the second time in his career to lead the Tigers to the championship.

May 29-June 3, 1989—Clemson finished 23rd at the NCAA Outdoor Track and Field Championships in Provo, UT. Terrance Herrington led the way with his third-place finish in the 1500-meter run.

April 20-21, 1990—James Trapp was named the Most Valuable Performer as he led Clemson to the championship at the ACC outdoor track and field meet. Trapp won the 100- and 200-meter dashes, and he was also a member of the league-winning 4x100- and 4x400- meter relay teams. Coach Bob Pollock was named ACC Outdoor Track Coach of the Year.

April 19-20, 1991—Clemson won the ACC Outdoor Track and Field Championships in Chapel Hill, NC. The Tigers' Michael Green won the 100-meter dash and ran on the championship 4x100-meter relay team. Dave Wittman won the 3000-meter steeplechase and the 1500-meter run, and Coach Pollock was once again named ACC Outdoor Track Coach of the Year.

May 29-June 1, 1991—The Tigers finished 13th as a team at the NCAA Outdoor Track and Field Championships behind the 4x100-meter relay's second-place finish. The team consisted of Doug Thomas, Green, Larry Ryans, and Trapp. Trapp also finished fourth in the 100-meter dash, while Green finished fifth in the same race.

April 17-18, 1992—Trapp won the 100- and 200-meter dashes and was named the Atlantic Coast Conference's Most Valuable Performer at the ACC Track and Field meet in Tallahassee, FL. Pollock was again named ACC Outdoor Track Coach of the Year.

June 3-6, 1992—Clemson finished 12th at the NCAA Outdoor Track and Field Championships. Trapp was a three-time All-America, finishing third in the 100-meter race and fourth in the 200-meter dash. He was also on the 4x100-meter relay team that finished sixth nationally.

April 15-16, 1993—Clemson won the ACC Outdoor Track and Field Championships in Chapel Hill, NC. Green won the 100- and 200-meter dashes and was on the 4x100-meter relay championship team, as he won the meet's Most Valuable Performer trophy. Pollock earned yet another ACC Outdoor Track Coach of the Year honor.

June 2-5, 1993—The Tigers finished tied for 10th in the NCAA Outdoor Track and Field Championships. Green won the National Championship in the 100-meter dash.

June 1-4, 1994—The Tigers finished 11th in the NCAA Outdoor Track and Field Championships. Mitchel Francis finished second in the 400-meter intermediate hurdles.

October 29, 1994—Kevin Hogan won the individual championship at the ACC Cross Country Meet in Atlanta, GA.

May 31-June 3, 1995—Clemson finished 10th at the NCAA Outdoor Track and Field Championships in Knoxville, TN, as Duane Ross won the National Championship in the 110-Meter high hurdles.

May 29-June 1, 1996—Clemson finished 17th at the NCAA Outdoor Track and Field Championships in Eugene, OR. Carlton Chambers finished sixth in the 200-meter dash and fourth in the 100-meter dash.

April 18-19, 1997—The Tigers won the ACC Track and Field Championships in Atlanta, GA. Jeremichael Williams won the 110-meter high hurdles and was a member of the championship 4x100-meter relay team. Tony Wheeler won the 200 meters and was a member of the 4x100-meter relay team as well. Pollock also received ACC Outdoor Track Coach of the Year accolades.

June 4-7, 1997—Clemson finished 17th at the NCAA Outdoor Track and Field Championships in Bloomington, IN. Jeremichael Williams finished seventh in the 110-meter high hurdles and was a member of the 4x100-meter relay team that finished second. Besides Williams, Chambers, Wheeler, and Kenny Franklin were members of the 4x100-meter relay team.

April 17-18, 1998—Clemson won the ACC Outdoor Track and Field Championship in Orlando, FL. Shawn Crawford won the meet's Most Valuable Performer trophy, as he won the 100-meter and 200-meter dashes and was a member of the ACC's championship 4x100-meter relay team. Pollock was named ACC Outdoor Track Coach of the Year.

June 3-6, 1998—Clemson finished 11th at the NCAA Outdoor Track and Field Championship in Buffalo, NY. Crawford received All-America honors in the 100- and 200-meter dashes and as a member of the 4x100-meter relay team.

June 2-5, 1999—The Tigers finished 19th at the NCAA Outdoor Track and Field Championship in Boise, ID. Crawford finished sixth in the 200-meter dash and was on the 4x100-meter relay team that finished fifth. Other members of the 4x100-meter relay team included Charles Allen, Kenny Franklin, and Anthony Moorman. Ato Modibo finished fifth in the 400-meter dash.

April 21-22, 2000—Clemson won the ACC Outdoor Track and Field Championship. Shawn Crawford was named the meet MVP at the Atlantic Coast Conference Outdoor Track Championships at Duke's Wallace Wade Stadium in Durham, NC, as he won both the 100- and 200-meter dashes. He was also on the winning 4x100-meter relay team, along with Jacey Harper, Allen, and Moorman. Todd Matthews won the 110-meter high hurdles, and Fred Sharpe won the 400-meter intermediate hurdles. Ryan Lewis won the pole vault, Malcolm Reynolds won the high jump, and Andy Giesler won the decathlon, as the Tigers won eight individual titles. This was the third Atlantic Coast Conference Outdoor Championship for the Tigers in the last four years.

Another highlight in the meet was Clemson's sweep of the top three spots in the 100-meter high hurdles, as Todd Matthews finished first, Sultan Tucker second, and Allen third.

With the win, Clemson won seven of the last eight indoor and outdoor ACC Championships, sending the senior class of Allen, Crawford, Williams, and Steve Alexander out with the most ACC championships won by a Clemson senior class. The Tigers have won 16 of a possible 24 conference championships since 1989.

May 31-June 3, 2000—The Clemson men's track team finished 10th at the NCAA men's outdoor track and field meet held in Durham, NC. Crawford won the National Championship in the 200-meter race, with a time of 20.09, and finished sixth in the 100-meters to lead the Tigers. Matthews finished third in the 110 meter high hurdles, and Sharpe finished seventh in the 400-meter intermediate hurdles.

Clemson finished the meet with 21 points, the best of ACC teams. Clemson finished one point ahead of South Carolina who had an 11th place finish. The 10th-place finish tied a school record for the best finish at the NCAA outdoor track and field meet. The 1993 and the 1995 Tigers both finished in 10th place at the NCAA outdoor track and field meet.

April 20-21, 2001—The men's track and field team won its tenth overall and second consecutive ACC title at Disney's Wide World of Sports Complex in Orlando, FL. This was the eighth championship under current head coach Bob Pollock and fourth in the last five years. The Tigers swept the top four spots in the 100-meter dash. Jacey Harper won the event with a time of 10.25, while Larry Griffin finished second, Sultan Tucker posted a third-place finish, and David Collins was fourth. Harper also won the 200-meter dash and was a member of the 4x100-meter relay that claimed the ACC Championship.

Andy Giesler won the decathlon and Jason Meany won the 5000 meters.

May 30-June 2, 2001—Clemson finished tied for 57th at the NCAA Outdoor Track and Field Championship at Hayward Field in Eugene, Oregon. Giesler finished seventh in the decathlon and Todd Mathes finished ninth in the 110-meter high hurdles. Modibo finished eighth in the 400-meters.

April 19-20, 2002—The Clemson men's track and field team finished second at the 2002 ACC Outdoor Track and Field Championships held at the University of Virginia in Charlottesville, VA. Dwight Thomas claimed three event titles, as he won the 100-meter dash, 200-meter dash and 110-meter hurdles.

The 4x100-meter relay team of Larry Griffin, Otto Spain, Harper, and Airese Currie won the ACC Championship.

May 29-June 1, 2002—The Clemson men's track and field team earned its highest finish in the history of the program, as the Tigers tied for fourth with 32 points at the NCAA Track and Field Championships in Baton Rouge, LA.

Previously, the Tigers had finished as high as 10th (1993, 1995, 2000). It was the 13th time that Clemson had finished in the top 25 under Coach Pollock, and the ninth top-15 finish in the last 15 years.

Redshirt freshman Dwight Thomas and senior Todd Matthews led the Tigers. Thomas claimed two second-place finishes, one in the 100-meter dash and one in the 200-meter dash. He recorded a time of 10.29 in the 100-meter dash, only .07 seconds off the pace of Justin Gatlin, the event winner. Thomas posted a time of 20.60 in the 200-meter dash, good for another second-place finish. In the 110-meter hurdles, Matthews recorded another second-place finish for the Tigers. He broke the tape in 13.53, a personal-best time.

Thomas completed his rookie campaign with four All-America honors. Indoor, he was an All-American in the 60-meter dash and followed that with three honors outdoors as a member of the 4x100 meter relay, as well as honors in the 100-meter and 200-meter dashes.

Thomas, along with juniors Otto Spain, Harper, and freshman Airese Currie, earned All-America honors as members of the Tigers' 4x100-meter relay team that finished second in that event, with a school record time of 38.82.

April 19, 2003—The men's track and field team finished second at the 2003 ACC Outdoor Championships held at NC State's Paul Derr Track in Raleigh, NC.

The Tigers won four events, while 14 Clemson athletes earned all-conference honors. Clemson's 4x100-meter relay team of Larry Griffin, Spain, Currie, and Tye Hill claimed the title with a time of 40.20. This is the fourth consecutive 400-meter relay title for the Tigers. Freshman Roy Cheney won the 110-meter hurdles, and Spain claimed the 400-meter dash with his time of 46.30, a regional qualifying mark. Hill won the decathlon with 7,068 points.

June 11-14, 2003—Itay Magidi finished eighth in the 3000-meter steeplechase and teammate George Kitchens earned All-America honors in the long jump as he finished 10th at the NCAA Outdoor Track and Field Championship. Magidi and sophomore George Kitchens each garnered the accolade for the first time in their careers. Clemson finished tied for 70th at the meet.

April 16-17, 2004—The Clemson men's track and field team claimed its 11th Atlantic Coast Conference Outdoor Track and Field Championship on Belk Track at Fetzer Field in Chapel Hill, NC. The Tigers tallied 224 points to win the 2004 title, capturing their first-team title since 2001 and setting the all-time ACC record for points scored at a conference meet. The Tigers won six events in this meet. Tye Hill won the 100-meter dash. Michael Bolling won the 400-meter intermediate hurdles. Adam Linkenauger won the high jump, Kitchens won the long jump, and Rick Hill won the decathlon. Larry Griffin, Tye Hill, Ronald Richards, and Currie won the 4x100-meter relay.

Clemson swept the top three spots in the decathlon, as Rick Hill captured his second ACC decathlon title with 7300 points. Brent Hobbs took second place with 7180 points and Ryan Hunter was third with 6626 points.

June 9-12, 2004—Kitchens earned All-America honors at the 2004 NCAA Outdoor Track and Field Championships in the long jump in Austin, TX. With this year's honor, he became the first Tiger to earn the distinction twice in the long jump. Kitchens also tied the Clemson record for the highest finish in the long jump at the NCAA Championships, joining former All-America athlete Kai Maull, who also placed eighth in 1999. The Tigers tied for 68th as a team in the meet.

April 21-23, 2005—Clemson finished second in the ACC Outdoor Track and Field Championship in Tallahassee, FL. Linkenauger won the high jump and Kitchens won the long jump competition.

June 8-11, 2005—Three Tigers were named to the All-America team at the NCAA Outdoor Track and Field Championships in Sacramento, CA. Ronald Richards finished fifth in the 100 meters, while Scott Kautz finished ninth in the 400-m IH. Magidi finished seventh in the 3000-meter steeple chase. Clemson finished tied for 37th as a team.

April 20-22, 2006—The track & field team finished in the runner-up spot at the ACC Outdoor Championships held at Kentner Stadium on the Wake Forest campus in Win-

ston-Salem, NC. The Tigers tallied 119 points overall. It marked the fourth runner-up team finish for Clemson in the last five years at the conference outdoor competition. Travis Padgett, a freshman, won the 100-meter dash in his first-ever ACC outdoor meet. Linkenauger won the high jump and Ryan Koontz won the Decathlon.

June 7-10, 2006—Clemson finished in a tie for 26th place at the NCAA Championships in Sacramento, CA after tallying 10 points. Travis Padgett finished fourth in the 100-meters and Jason Bell finished sixth in the triple jump. Koontz finished seventh in the decathlon. Padgett, Bell and Koontz were named All-Americans.

April 19-21, 2007—Padgett successfully defended his crown in the 100-meter dash to lead Clemson to a second-place showing at the ACC Outdoor Track & Field Championships in College Park, MD. He was the first Tiger to claim back-to-back 100-meter titles at the outdoor conference meet since Greg Moses achieved the feat in 1985 and 1986.

Linkenauger won the high jump for the third straight time. The group of Cowin Mills, Andrew Porter, Travis Swaggard, and Corey Brown won the 4x400-meter relay for the Tigers. Matt Clark won the 10,000-meter run.

June 6-9, 2007—Clemson finished 24th in the NCAA track and field outdoor meet at Sacramento, CA. Padgett finished third in the 100-meter dash and Mitch Greeley finished tied for fourth in the pole vault. Padgett, Corey Brown, Cowin Mills, and C.J. Spiller finished seventh in the 4x100-meter relay.

The Tigers finished 15th at the NCAA Indoor Championships in March, giving Pollock's program a top-25 team finish in both settings this season. The last time that occurred at Clemson was in 2002, when the Tigers were seventh indoors and tied for fourth at the outdoor meet. Pollock had, at this point, guided the Tigers' track & field program to top-25 indoor and outdoor finishes in the same season a total of 11 times in his coaching career.

April 17-19, 2008—The Tigers finished second at the Atlantic Coast Conference outdoor track and field meet in Atlanta, GA. Padgett won the 100-meter dash. The Tigers also won the 4x100-meter relay. Mitch Greeley won the pole vault championship.

April 24, 2008—Pollock was named outdoor ACC Coach of the Year for the ninth time, while junior Travis Padgett was honored as Most Valuable Track Performer, giving him a clean sweep of MVP honors in both indoor and outdoor track in 2008. Both honors were determined by a vote of the league's head coaches.

Padgett won the 100-meter race for the third consecutive year. He was also on the 4x100-meter relay team along with Guy, Corey Brown, and Cowin Mills. Mitch Greeley won the pole vault competition.

June 11-14, 2008 NCAA—Padgett finished second and teammate Jacoby finished fifth in the 100-meter dash at the NCAA Track and Field Meet in Des Moines, IA. As a team, the Tigers finished tied for 21st.

Clemson had at least one All-America athlete in each of Bob Pollock's 20 seasons with the men's track & field program. Matt Clark was also an All-America runner in the 10,000-meters race.

June 17, 2008—Pollock announced his retirement as coach, effective the end of the United States Olympic Trials in early July. Pollock served as the head coach of the men's program for 20 years and led the cross country, indoor track, and outdoor track programs to a combined 21 ACC Championships.

April 16-18, 2009—Jacoby Ford led a 1-2-3 sweep of the men's 100-meter dash on the last day of the ACC Outdoor Championships in Coral Gables, FL. It marked the first sweep of the three spots in that event since Clemson

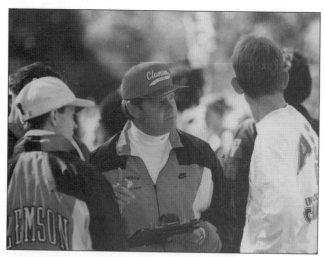

Bob Pollock was the Head Track and Field Coach at Clemson from 1988-2008.

did it in 2001 with Jacey Harper, Larry Griffin, and Sultan Tucker.

Ford became the sixth different Clemson sprinter to win both the indoor 60-meter dash and outdoor 100-meter dash in the ACC in the same season. Shawn Crawford (1998) was the first to accomplish the feat. The double was also previously accomplished by Jacey Harper (2001), Dwight Thomas (2002), Tye Hill (2004), and Travis Padgett (2008).

It marked the fourth straight year a Clemson athlete has claimed the 100-meter dash, and ninth time in the last 12 years of the event. Padgett won the crown each of the last three seasons, prior to Ford's triumph.

June 10-13, 2009—Ford finished ninth in the 100-meter race and Murdock, Spiller, Guy, and Ford finished third

in the 4x100-meter relay at the NCAA outdoor track and field meet in Fayetteville, AR. As a team, Clemson finished in a tie for 40th place.

Ford earned All-America status in both the 100-meter dash and 4x100-meter relay. He finished ninth in the former race, but pulled up midway through the race due to a hamstring injury. It was Ford's second straight All-America honor in the 100-meter dash.

For his career, Ford was now a five-time USTFCCCA All-America athlete. Included among the honors was his national championship performance indoors in the 60-meter dash.

The relay group of Justin Murdock, C.J. Spiller, Trenton Guy, and Ford finished in third place Friday. It marked the third career All-America honor in track for Spiller, a standout on the football field for the Tigers. Spiller previously earned All-America status with the 4x100-meter relay team in 2007.

April 18-20, 2013—The Clemson men's track and field team finished third at the ACC Track and Field Championships held at Raleigh, NC . Spencer Adams won the 110 Meter Hurdles at the meet.

June 5-8, 2013—Spencer Adams earned his third consecutive third-place finish in the 110 high hurdles in Eugene, Oregon. Clemson finished in a tie for 35th place in the meet. Adams was named an All-American in the 110 meter hurdles as was Reggie Lewis for his eighth-place finish.

April 17-19, 2014—The Clemson men's team finished 11th at the Atlantic Coast Conference Track and Field Meet at Chapel Hill, NC. Torian Ware was an All-ACC performer in the high jump and so was Marcus Brown in the shot put.

June 11-14, 2014—Torian Ware finished 11th in the high jump competition at the NCAA Track and Field meet in Eugene, Oregon. Ware was named a second-team All-American in the event. Reggie Lewis was named a second-team All-American in the 100 meter dash as he was 14th.

May 14-16, 2015—Tevin Hester won the 100 and 200 meter dashes in leading Clemson to a fourth place finish at the Atlantic Coast Conference Track and Field Championships. Justin Johnson won the 110 meter hurdles, and Torian Ware finished first in the high jump. Hester was named the meet's MVP for track events.

June 10-13, 2015—Tevin Hester finished sixth in both the 100 meter and 200 meter dashes at the NCAA Track and Field meet at Eugene, Oregon. Hester was named a first-team All-American in both events. Clemson finished 31st as a team, the highest finish for the Tigers in the NCAA Outdoor event since 2008. Justin Johnson finished seventh in the 110 meter hurdles and earned first-team

All-American honors. Torian Ware finished 10th in the high jump and was a second-team All-American in the event.

May 13-15, 2016—For the second year in a row, Tevin Hester won the 100 and 200 meter dashes at the Atlantic Coast Conference Track and Field Championships in Tallahassee, FL . The Clemson men finished seventh as a team in the meet. For the second year in a row, Hester was named the meet's MVP for track events.

June 8-11, 2016—The Tigers finished 33rd as a team at the NCAA Track and Field meet at Eugene, OR. Tevin Hester finished sixth in the 200 meter dash and 10th in the 100 meter dash. Hester was named a first-team All-American in both events for the second year in a row. In the 4x400 relay, Cordell Lamb, Michael Cheeks, Jorel Bellafonte, and Jeffrey Green earned All-America honors as they finished fifth.

MEN'S INDOOR TRACK HISTORY

March 8, 1931—Clemson finished 12th in the second annual Southern Conference indoor track meet, the first-ever indoor track and field meet for the Tigers. J.M. Lineberger finished second in the mile event to be the first Tiger to ever score in an indoor event.

February 27, 1937—Bob Carter finished first in the high jump at the Southern Conference indoor meet in Chapel Hill, NC. Carter's winning height was 6' 3/8".

February 22, 1941—Ralph Fennell finished in a tie for first in the pole vault at the Southern Conference indoor meet. The Tigers finished tied for seventh place in the meet.

February 28, 1942—Fennell won the Southern Conference pole vault event for the second year in a row. Fennell won with a vault of 12'10". The Tigers finished seventh in the meet.

February 26, 1955—Alston Mitchell was Clemson's first ACC champion in indoor track, as he won the high jump competition in Chapel Hill, NC.

February 23, 1980—Hans Koeleman was named the meet's Most Valuable Athlete at the ACC indoor meet in Greensboro, NC. Teammate Desai Williams was a close second in the vote. Koeleman broke the school record in the mile run and the two-mile run. Williams set the ACC and school record in the 60-yard dash and the 440-yard dash, as he won both events, and he was also a member of the mile relay team that finished first. The Tigers finished second in the meet, the best effort by a Tiger team in the history of the indoor meet.

March 14-15, 1980—Hans Koeleman earned All-America honors in the mile run, as he finished fourth at the NCAA Indoor Track and Field Meet in Detroit, MI. Koeleman is the first Clemson male student-athlete to score at a NCAA indoor track and field meet. Clemson finished in a tie for 37th place.

March 13-14, 1981—Koeleman earned All-America honors in the two-mile run, finishing fourth at the NCAA

Indoor Track and Field Meet in Detroit, MI. Clemson finished in a tie for 48th at the meet.

March 12-13, 1982—Wybo Lelieveld finished second in the 1000-yard run at the NCAA indoor track and field meet. Clemson finished in a tie for 37th in the meet.

March 11-12, 1983—Lelieveld finished fourth in the mile rule at the NCAA indoor track and field meet. The Tigers finished in a tie for 40th place.

March 8-9, 1985—Victor Smalls finished in a tie for sixth place in the high jump at the NCAA indoor track and field meet in Syracuse, NY. The Tigers finished in 54th place at the meet.

March 14-15, 1986—Greg Moses finished seventh in the 55-meters at the NCAA indoor track and field meet in Oklahoma City, OK.

February 20-21, 1987—Clemson won the ACC Indoor track and field meet for the first time ever, scoring 103 points, six ahead of N.C. State, at East Tennessee State's Memorial Center in Johnson City, TN. The Tigers had seven athletes named to the All-ACC team, andcoach Wade Williams was named ACC Indoor Coach of the Year. Mike Spiritoso won the shot put and the 35-pound weight throw to lead the Tigers, whobroke Maryland's 25-year streak of consecutive ACC Titles. Clemson also became only the third school to win the ACC indoor title.

March 13-14, 1987—Clemson finished 18th at the NCAA indoor track and field meet behind shot putter, Mike Spiritoso's second-place finish. This was Clemson's first top-20 national team finish in men's indoor track.

March 11-12, 1988—Yehezkel Halifa finished sixth in the 3000-meters at the NCAA indoor track and field meet. The Tigers finished tied for 51st at the meet in Oklahoma City, OK.

February 17-18, 1989—Clemson won the ACC Indoor Track Championship. Philip Greyling won both the mile run and the 3000-meter run to lead the Tigers. Clemson's Bob Pollock was named the ACC Indoor Track and Field Coach of the Year.

March 10-11, 1989—Clemson finished eighth at the NCAA Meet in Indianapolis, IN. The 4x800-meter relay team ran a World Record Time of 7:17.45. The time could not stand as a world record because the team did not consist of four athletes from the same country. Seven Tigers were named All-Americas at the meet. Mike Radziwinski, Dave Wittman, Phil Greyling, and Terrance Herrington were named All-Americans for their first-place, world-record time of 7:17.45 in the 3,200 meter relay. Yehezkel Hallifa finished fourth in the 5000 meters, and Dov Kremer finished sixth in the same race. Greg Moses finished fourth in the 55-meters.

February 9-10, 1990—Clemson finished first at the ACC Indoor Track and Field Championships in Johnson City, TN. Greyling was named the meet's Most Valuable Performer, as he won the 3000-meter run and the mile run. At this meet, Clemson won nine events. Pollock was named the ACC Indoor Track and Field Coach of the Year.

March 9-10, 1990—The Tigers finished 23rd in the NCAA Indoor Championships in Indianapolis, IN behind the 4x800-meter relay's third-place finish. Dennis Hines, David Wittman, Greyling, and Andrew Beecher comprised this team. James Trapp finished sixth in the 55-meter race.

February 22-23, 1991—Clemson finished first at the ACC Indoor Track and Field Championships in Johnson City, TN. Trapp was Clemson's only individual champion, as he won the 55-meter dash.

March 8-9, 1991—Trapp finished fifth in the 55-meter dash, and Larry Ryans finished 11th in the 55-meter high hurdles in Indianapolis, IN.

February 14-15, 1992—Clemson won the ACC Indoor Track and Field Championship. Cormac Finnerty won the mile and 3000-meter runs. Pollock was once again named the ACC Indoor Track and Field Coach of the Year.

March 13-14, 1992—The Tigers finished second in the NCAA Indoor Track and Field Championships. Michael Green won the 55 meters and James Trapp won the National Championship in the 200 meters. Clemson Head Coach Bob Pollock was named the National Indoor Track and Field Coach of the Year. Trapp also finished fourth in the 55 meters. Anthony Knight finished third and Larry Ryans finished fifth in the 55 meter high hurdles. Wesley Russell finished third in the 400 meters Andrew Beehere finished fifth in the 800 meters. And Cormac Finnerty finished third in the 3000 meters.

February 19-20, 1993—The Tigers finished first in the ACC Championships in Johnson City, TN. Michael Green was named the meet's Most Valuable Performer, having won the 55-meter and 200-meter dashes. Pollock received ACC Indoor Track and Field Coach of the Year recognition.

March 12-13, 1993—Clemson finished second in the NCAA Indoor Track and Field Championships in Indianapolis, IN. Green won the 55-meter dash, while Wesley Russell won the 400 meter dash. Cormac Finnerty finished third in the 3000 meters, and Duane Ross finished fourth in the 55-meter high hurdles.

March 11-12, 1994—Clemson finished tied for 24th in the NCAA Indoor Track and Field Championships, as Ross helped the Tigers' cause with a third-place finish in the 55-meter high hurdles. Kendrick Roach finished ninth in the 800-meter run, and Mitchel Francis, Enayat Oliver, Gill Richards, and Roach finished seventh in the 4x400-meter dash.

March 10-11, 1995—Clemson finished in 11th place at the NCAA Indoor Track Championships in Indianapolis, IN behind Tony Wheeler's third-place finish in the 200 meters. Duane Ross finished fifth in the 55-meter high hurdles. Clarence Richards finished sixth in the 400 meters and John Thorp finished seventh in the high jump. Gill Richards, Francis, Oliver, and Wheeler comprised a 4x400-meter team that finished fifth.

February 21-22, 1997—The Tigers won the ACC Men's Indoor Track and Field Championship in Greensboro, NC. Greg Hines won the 55-meter high hurdles, and David Hartzler won the pole vault competition Pollock was named the ACC Indoor Track and Field Coach of the Year.

March 7-8, 1997—Clemson finished 25th at the NCAA indoor track and field meet in Indianapolis, Indiana, as Jeremichael Williams finished second in the 55-meter high hurdles.

February 22-23, 1998—The Tigers won the ACC Indoor Track and Field Championship in Blacksburg, VA. Pollock was named the ACC Indoor Track and Field Coach of the Year.

March 13-14, 1998—Clemson finished third at the NCAA Indoor Track and Field Championship, and Shawn Crawford won the 200-meter National Championship in Indianapolis, IN. Jeremichael Williams finished second, and Greg Hines finished seventh in the 55-meter high hurdles. Charles Allen, Davidson Gill, Aaron Haynes, Kenny Franklin finished third in the 4x400-meter relay.

February 19-20, 1999—The Tigers won the ACC Indoor Track and Field Championship at Blacksburg, VA. Crawford was named the meet's Most Valuable Performer, as he won the 60-meter dash and the 200-meter dash. Coach Pollock was named the ACC Indoor Coach of the Year.

March 5-6, 1999—Clemson finished third at the NCAA Indoor Track and Field Championship at Indianapolis, IN. Ato Modibo won the 400-meter event, and Modibo, along with Allen, Franklin, and Davidson Gill, won the National Championship in the 4x400-meter relay. Sulton Tucker was sixth in the 60-meter hurdles, and Crawford finished fourth in the 200-meter dash.

February 18-19, 2000—The team captured the Tigers' fourth consecutive ACC Indoor Championship title and ninth overall in the past twelve years. Clemson finished the meet scoring 168 points, a new school record.

The Tigers were lead by All-America Crawford, who set a new American collegiate record in the 200-meter dash with a winning performance of 20.43 seconds. Crawford's outstanding time ranked #1 in the country, and set a new ACC record and new school record. Crawford returned to the track with another blazing performance in the 60-meter dash, running the fastest time in the country at 6.56 seconds. He established a new ACC record and ranks second on Clemson's all-time list to former Tiger and two-time Olympian Michael Green, who ran 6.55 seconds in 1993. Sultan Tucker won the 60-meter high hurdles, and Fred Sharpe won the 800 meters.

March 7, 2000—Crawford was chosen as the Southeast Region Athlete of the Year, as announced by the United States Track Coaches Association. Crawford, a senior from Van Wyck, SC, was also chosen as the ACC Indoor Track & Field MVP after winning the 60-meter and 200-meter at the ACC Championships. His time in the 200-meter, 20.43, set a new American collegiate record, plus a Clemson and ACC record, and is the fastest time in the world this year. Pollock was honored as the Southeast Region Coach of the Year.

March 10-11, 2000—The Tigers finished in a tie for 10th place at the NCAA Indoor Track and Field Championship in Fayetteville, AR. Crawford broke the American record and won the national championship in the 200-meter dash. Crawford's winning performance of 20.26 was the third-fastest time ever in the world and the fastest in the world at that time. The time broke the American record of 20.32 held by Rohsaan Griffin and Kevin Little, set in 1996. Crawford won his second national indoor title of his career, as he won the 200-meter title. Crawford set the American record, ACC, Collegiate record, NCAA record, the Tyson Track Center record, and Clemson school record in the 200-meter dash. In the finals of the 60-meter dash, Crawford placed fourth, in a time of 6.67 seconds. Crawford earned two All-America honors (60 meters and 200 meters). Sulton Tucker finished eighth in the 60-meter high hurdles.

February 16-17, 2001—The Tigers won the team title, with 181 points, at the 2001 ACC Indoor Track and Field Championships. This was the fifth consecutive ACC title and 11th overall championship for Clemson in indoor track. The Tigers have won ten of their 11 indoor championships under Pollock.

Clemson swept the top three spots in the 60-meter dash, 200-meter dash, and 400-meter dash. Jacey Harper won the 60-meter dash and the 200-meter dash and was named the meet's MVP. Ato Modibo won the 400 meters and Todd Matthews won the 60-meter high hurdles. Dough Ameigh won the high jump, and Spain, Harper, Copes, and Modibo won the 4x400-meter relay.

March 10, 2001—Former Clemson men's track and field standout Crawford won the World Championship in the 200-meter dash Saturday in Lisbon, Portugal. Crawford, who ran for Team USA and the Mizuno Track Club, became Clemson's second world champion in the 200-meter

dash, as he claimed the indoor title with a time of 20.61. Trapp, a member of the 2001 Super Bowl Champion Baltimore Ravens football team, claimed the 200-meter indoor world championship in 1993.

March 9-10, 2001—The Clemson men's track and field team finished tied for 20th with 10 points at the NCAA Indoor Track and Field Championships in Fayetteville, AS. Tucker finished third in the 60-meter high hurdles, and Todd Matthews finished fifth.

February 15-16, 2002—The team claimed its sixth consecutive ACC Indoor Track and Field Championship at the Dick Taylor Track in Eddie Smith Field House in Chapel Hill, NC. Clemson scored 132 points, outdistancing Florida State, who had 95 points. The Tigers were led by freshman Dwight Thomas, who led the Tigers, claiming the 60-meter dash and 60-meter hurdle races. Jacey Harper won the 200 meters, and Ato Modibo won the 400 meters.

With this ACC title, the Tigers gave coach Pollock his 20th conference championship. Under Pollock, Clemson had won 11 indoor titles, 10 outdoor championships, and the 1989 cross country title.

March 7, 2002—Clemson swept the Southeast Region honors, as Pollock was named region Coach of the Year, and redshirt freshman Dwight Thomas earned region male Athlete of the Year accolades. This year's honor was Pollock's 13th region or district Coach of the Year title. Thomas (Burtonsville, MD) earned region male athlete of the year honors after winning the 60-meter dash and 60-meter hurdles at the 2002 ACC Indoor Championships. Thomas was also the only athlete in the nation to qualify for this year's NCAA Championships in four events (60-meter dash, 60-meter hurdles, 200-meter dash, 1600-meter relay).

March 8-9, 2002—Clemson finished seventh, with 17 points, at the NCAA Indoor Track and Field Championship. Modibo and Thomas each earned All-America honors in the 400-meter dash and 60-meter dash, respectively. Modibo finished fifth in the 400-meter dash with a time of 46.44, earning his seventh All-America accolade. Thomas recorded a time of 6.70 in the 60-meter dash, posting a sixth-place finish and also earning All-America status. Dough Ameigh finished fourth in the high jump, and Todd Matthews finished fourth in the 60-meter high hurdles.

February 21-22, 2003—The Clemson men's track and field team finished second, with 111.5 points, at the ACC Indoor Track and Field Championships held in the Eddie Smith Fieldhouse in Chapel Hill, NC. Jacey Harper won the meet MVP, after capturing the 200 meters. Larry Griffin won the 60-meters dash. Otto Spain won the 400-meter run and Jason Meany won the 3000-meter run.

March 14-15, 2003—Clemson finished in a tie for 28th place at the NCAA Indoor Track and Field Championship. Six student-athletes earned All-America honors at the meet. That was the highest All-America total for Clemson at the Championships since 1999, when seven Tigers earned the accolade. Larry Griffin finished eighth in the 60-meter dash, and Terrance McDaniel finished sixth in the high jump. The 4x400-meter relay of Harper, Michael Bolling, Roy Cheney, and Spain finished seventh.

February 20-21, 2004—The team finished second at the 2004 ACC Indoor Track and Field Championships held at the Clemson Indoor Track and Field Facility. Tye Hill won the 60-meter dash, Derek Gilson won the shot put, Adam Linkenauger won the high jump, and Rick Hill won the heptathlon.

March 12-13, 2004—Clemson finished in a tie for 56th at the NCAA Indoor Track and Field Championship. Roy Cheney was ninth in the 60-meter high hurdles, while George Kitchens finished seventh in the long jump. Kitchens was the Tigers' first All-America in the long jump.

February 17-19, 2005—The Tigers finished second at the ACC Indoor Championships in Chapel Hill, NC. The Tigers tallied 160 points, just 2.5 points shy of Florida State's winning total. It was the closest finish to a men's ACC Indoor Championship since 1996, when North Carolina edged NC State by one point (148.5 to 147.5). Adam Linkenauger captured the high jump competition, while Itay Magidi won the 5000-meter run, and Kitchens won the long jump.

March 11-12, 2005—Clemson finished in a tie for 48th at the NCAA Indoor Track and Field Championship. Linkenauger and Jason Bell competed in the high jump and triple jump, respectively. Linkenauger, who had battled an ankle injury all season, cleared 6'10.25" to finish 13th in the high jump. Bell also placed 13th in the triple jump with his mark of 49'11.25". Kitchens finished seventh in the long jump with a mark of 25'3" to earn his second consecutive All-America honor in this event.

February 23-25, 2006—Clemson finished second at the ACC Indoor Track & Field Championships at Chapel Hill, NC. Mitch Greeley won the Pole Vault, Ryan Koontz won the Heptathlon and Adam Linkenauger won the high jump.

March 10-11, 2006—Clemson finished in a tie for 65th at the NCAA Indoor Track and Field Championship. Brent Hobbs finished 10th and Ryan Koontz was 14th in the heptathlon standings, while Linkenauger was 14th in the high jump. By virtue of being one of the top-eight American finishers, Hobbs became the first Tiger ever to receive All-America honors in the heptathlon.

Mitch Greeley became the first Tiger ever to earn All-America honors in the pole vault, as he finished in a tie for eighth on the first day of the NCAA Indoor Championships. He was the first Clemson athlete ever to compete in the indoor pole vault, and he won the All-America honor in his first attempt.

February 22-24, 2007—Jacoby Ford's spectacular effort in the 60-meter dash highlighted Clemson's efforts at the ACC Indoor Track & Field Championships. Ford led the Tigers by finishing first in the 60 meters and taking a third-place finish in the 200 meters. George Fields finished first in the long jump.

March 9-10, 2007—Clemson sprinter Travis Padgett won the national title in the 60-meter dash to lead the Tigers to a 15th-place finish at the NCAA Indoor Track & Field Championships in Fayetteville, AR. He is the first student-athlete from Clemson to claim a national title since Shawn Crawford won the outdoor 200-meter dash in 2000. He is the first Tiger sprinter to capture the 60-meter dash crown.

Ford finished third in the 60-meter dash with a time of 6.60. Jason Bell finished 10th in the triple jump with an effort of 49'9". Ryan Koontz finished seventh in the heptathlon with 5,569 points. Padgett, Ford, Bell, and Koontz were all named All-America runners.

Clemson finished 15th in the team standings, the program's best effort since the 2002 team placed seventh. Clemson earned 18 points and was just three points shy of tying for 10th place.

March 14-15, 2008—Clemson finished 12th at the NCAA Indoor Track and Field Championship. Sophomore C.J. Spiller was named indoor track & field All-America on Sunday by the US Track & Field and Cross Country Coaches' Association (USTFCCCA). By virtue of his 10th-place finish, he did not make the finals of the event on Saturday. However, he was one of the top eight American finishers and thus earned his first-ever indoor All-America certificate.

Spiller posted a time of 6.67 in the prelims Friday evening, but was beaten out by literally thousandths of a second for the final spot in the finals.

Spiller's All-America effort gave the Tiger program three honorees for the 2008 indoor season. Mitch Greeley was runner-up in the pole vault, with a height of 17' 8 ½", while Travis Padgett placed third in Saturday's 60-meter final, with a time of 6.60.

March 13-14, 2009—The Tigers finished in a tie for 23rd at the NCAA Indoor Track and Field Championship Ford earned his first national championship in track & field, claiming the 60-meter dash to lead Clemson on the final day of competition. His crown is Clemson's second in the event in the last three years, as former teammate Travis Padgett won the NCAA title in 2007. Ford was the ninth individual NCAA indoor champion in men's track & field history at Clemson.

March 12-13, 2010—Clemson finished in a tie for 53rd at the NCAA Indoor Track and Field Championship. Spencer Adams finished eighth in the 60-meter high hurdles, and Miller Moss finished eighth in the heptathlon.

July 24, 2012—The U.S. Track & Field and Cross Country Coaches Association (USTFCCCA) announced the inductees for the 2012 USTFCCCA Hall of Fame. One of the inductees was former Clemson Head Track and Cross Country Coach, Bob Pollock. Pollock led Clemson to 21 ACC Championships in his 20 years as head coach of the school's men's track & field program. Pollock passed away on February 18, 2010 at the age of 60. He was inducted posthumously into the Clemson Athletics Hall of Fame in 2010.

February 21-23, 2013—The Clemson men finished third at the ACC Indoor Championships at Virginia Tech's Rector Field House in Blacksburg, VA. In the men's 400 meter run, senior Brunson Miller became the first Tiger gold medalist in this event since Otto Spain in 2003. The 4x400 relay team of Miller, La'Mont Jackson, Spencer Adams and Ryan Mangone finished first in the event. Adams finished first in the 60 meter hurdles for a second straight year. He is the first Tiger to win the event back-to-back since Sultan Tucker did in 1999 and 2000.

March 8-9, 2013—Spencer Adams finished third in the 60 hurdles and Tevin Hester took seventh in the 60 dash final to lead the Tigers to 25th place at the NCAA Indoor Track and Field Meet at the Tyson Track Center in Fayetteville, AR. The men's top-25 finish was the second in the last three indoor seasons, and the 18th in Clemson history. Both Adams and Hester were named first-team All-Americans in their respective events.

March 15, 2013—Tevin Hester was named ACC Indoor Freshman of the Year as announced by the league's office.

July 9, 2013—Mark Elliott was named the new Track and Field/Cross Country Coach at Clemson.

February 27-March 1, 2014—The Tigers finished 11th in the ACC Indoor Track and Field meet held at Clemson, SC.

March 14-15, 2014—Tevin Hester finished seventh in the men's 60 meters for the second year in a row at the NCAA Indoor Track and Field meet at the Albuquerque Convention Center. In Albuquerque, N.M. Hester was also named an All-American in the 60 meters.

Hester is only the third Tiger to earn multiple first-team All-America honors in the 60 dash, joining Travis Padgett (2007, 2008) and Jacoby Ford (2007, 2009). He took sev-

enth place in the event for a second straight season, clocking a 6.64 in the final on Saturday in Albuquerque, N.M.

February 26-28, 2015—The Tiger men finished fifth at the ACC Indoor Track and Field meet in Blacksburg, VA, an improvement of six positions over its 11th-place showing a year. Tevin Hester won the ACC Most Valuable Track Athlete honors with his first league title in the 200, and a runner-up finish in the 60. The men closed out the meet with a victory in the 4x400 relay. Jeffrey Green passed North Carolina's anchor on the final leg to claim the victory in a time of 3:10.00. He was joined on the gold medal unit by Cordell Lamb, Michael Cheeks and Jorel Bellafonte.

March 13-14, 2015—Tevin Hester finished seventh overall in the 60 meter dash for the third time in a row at the NCAA Indoor Track and Field Meet at Fayetteville, AK. He also finished sixth in the 200 meter dash.

Shai Carpenter took 11th in the men's triple jump in his first trip to an NCAA Championships meet. The Clemson met finished in a tied for 38th place at the meet.

For the third season in a row, Hester was named an All-American in the 60 meter dash. He also was named an All-American in the 200 meter dash.

March 20, 2015—Tevin Hester was named the Atlantic Coast Conference's Men's Track Athlete of the Year as voted on by the league's head coaches.

February 25-27, 2016—Tevin Hester won the 60 meter dash and the 200 meter dash in leading Clemson to a second place finish at the Atlantic Coast Conference Championships in Boston, Mass. For his efforts, he was named the meet's track athlete MVP for the second year in a row. Teammate Jeffrey Green won the 400 meter dash. Green, John Lewis, Cordell Lamb, and Michael Cheeks won the 4x400 meter relay. This was the best finish for the Tigers since the 2007 season. Hester's sweep in the 60 and 200 meter dashes is the first for a Clemson sprinter since the 201 season.

March 11-12, 2016—Senior Tevin Hester finished his indoor collegiate career as one-of-three short-sprinters in Clemson history to earn first-team All-American honors in the 60 meter dash and 200 meter dash. He finished sixth in the 60 meter dash and followed up with a fifth place finish in the 200 meter dash at the NCAA Indoor Track and Field meet in Birmingham, AL. Hester finished his Clemson Indoor career with four first-team All-America honors.

WOMEN'S
Track & Field

AT THE STARTING LINE

Clemson women's track and field started during the 1981-82 season as a distance-only program and remained this way through the 1984-85 season. A complete program was started in 1985-86. Jeannie Burris was the first field event signee.

TINA KREBS WINS THREE NATIONAL CHAMPIONSHIPS IN THREE DIFFERENT EVENTS

In the second year of the program, the Tigers finished in a tie for tenth at the NCAA indoor meet and tied for 20th in the outdoor NCAA meet in 1983 under head coach Sam Colson. That season, Tina Krebs finished first in the 1,000-yard run indoors. At the NCAA outdoor meet, Krebs finished second and Judith Shephard finished fifth.

In 1984-85, Wayne Coffman was named the head coach. Krebs won the National Championship in the 1500-meter run, and Kirsti Voldness finished third in the same race at the NCAA indoor meet, where Clemson finished in a tie for 12th.

The next year, Krebs won her third national championship in a different event—this time the mile run—as she led Clemson to a tie for 12th at the NCAA indoor meet. The 1985-86 season was the first time the Tigers competed in other events besides distance races.

FIELD EVENTS, JUMPS, AND SPRINTS COME TO TIGERTOWN

Jeannie Burris was the first field event conference champion for the Tigers, as she won the shot put at the ACC Indoor Meet in Johnson City, TN in 1987, and the discus in the ACC outdoor meet in 1987 in Atlanta, GA.

Lisa Dillard was the first sprinter to win an ACC championship, as she won the 55 meters indoors in 1989. She also won the 100- and 200- meter dashes at the outdoor meet that Spring in Charlottesville, VA

In the 1989-90 season, Lisa Dillard became Clemson's first sprinter to become an All-American as she finished fifth at the NCAA Indoor Meet and fourth in the 100 meters outdoors in Durham, NC. She also finished seventh in the 200 meters. Also at the same meet Angela Dolby became Clemson's first field event All-American as she finished 11th in the shot put. Dillard earned four All-America honors in her career.

OLYMPIAN KIM GRAHAM LEADS TIGERS TO FIRST ACC CHAMPIONSHIP AND TOP-25 FINISHES

In 1990-91, Clemson finished first at the ACC outdoor meet for its first-ever ACC Championship. At this event, Kim Graham won three titles, as she won the 200 and was the anchor on the 4x100 meter and the 4x400 meter championship relay teams. Her performance earned her MVP of the meet, which Clemson won by three points over the Tar Heels.

Clemson finished in a tie for 12th at the 1991 NCAA outdoor meet.

In 1992, Graham was named the MVP of the 1992 indoor meet, as she won the 55-meter and 200-meter dashes in leading Clemson to its first ACC indoor championship. Clemson finished 22nd at the NCAA Indoor meet. At the outdoor meet the same year, she won the 100- and 200-meter dashes as well as the anchor on the 4x100 meter relay. Graham won 15 ACC Championships during her career (10 indoor). The Tigers finished 17th at the NCAA outdoor meet.

Graham was a member of the Gold Medal winning 4x100-meter relay team in the 1996 Olympics in Atlanta, GA.

"I came to Clemson basically because I fell in love with the school on my first visit. The coaches were nice and we were trying to build a good program, and I liked the idea of being a part of something special. The team had a family atmosphere and that is what I was really looking for. I felt like I was getting the best of both worlds, a good school academically and a good track program."

Graham has many memorable moments in her career, but winning the first ACC Championship was special. "I would have to say winning the ACC title for the first time. It was a close meet and we won the relay and that won the meet for us."

"I will always be a Tiger!" said Graham. "I basically went from a little girl to a woman during the time I spent there. I will never forget the great experiences that I had while being there. I made a great choice."

SHEKERA WESTON WINS 10 ALL-AMERICA HONORS

Shekera Weston ran for the Tigers in 1997-2001 and was a 10-time All-America honoree.

She was a member of the 4x400-meter relay team that finished sixth at the 1998 NCAA indoor meet. She was also an All-America runner in the 400 meters indoors, as she finished ninth in 1999. She was a member of the 4x400-meter relay that finished third indoors in 2001.

In the NCAA outdoor meet, Weston was a member of the 4x400-meter relay that finished fourth in 1997. She finished seventh in the 200 meter-dash in 1999 and was a member of the 4 x100- meter relay squad that finished seventh at the same meet.

She was a four-time All-America selection in the 2001 outdoor NCAA meet, finishing fourth in the 200 meters, 10th in the 400 meters, and was a member of the 4x100 meter relay team that finished fourth. She was also a member of the 4x400-meter relay team that won the National Championship.

Because of Weston's efforts, the Tigers finished third at the NCAA indoor meet in 2001 and in a tie for seventh at the NCAA Outdoor meet that same year. This was Marcia Noad's first year as head coach, and she would serve in that role through the 2007-08 season.

MOTON AND MOTHERSILL WIN NATIONAL CHAMPIONSHIPS

Jamine Moton won the hammer throw in 2002 at the NCAA meet in Baton Rouge, LA.

She had previously finished second in the shot put at the 2001 NCAA outdoor meet. That same year, she finished second in the shot put and third in the weight throw in 2001 in the indoors meet. In 2002 she was eighth

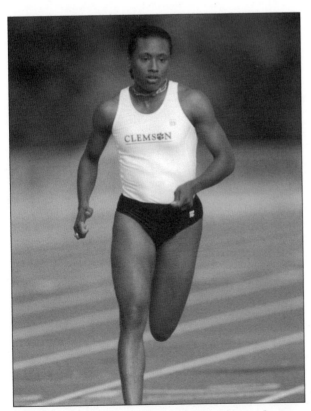

Shekera Weston was a 10-time All-America track star during her Clemson career, from 1997- 2001.

Jamine Moton won the National Championship in the hammer throw in 2002.

in the shot put and second in the weight throw. For her career, she was a six-time All-America athlete.

Moton was named the Atlantic Coast Conference indoor meet MVP, as she won the shot put and the weight throw. In 2002 she was named the Atlantic Coast Conference outdoor meet MVP, as she won the hammer throw and the shot put. For her career, she won 13 total ACC Championships.

In 2001, Cydonie Mothersill won the indoor National Championship in the 200-meter dash. She also was a member of the 4x400-meter outdoor national championship team later that Spring. For her career, she was a four-time All-America athlete.

To add to her resume, Mothersill won a total of six ACC Championships. In the 2001 ACC meet, she was named the meet's Most Valuable Performer. At this meet, she also won the 100- and 200-meter dashes and was on the winning relays teams in the 4x100- and 4x400-meter relay teams.

OLIVEIRA DOMINATES THE TRIPLE JUMP COMPETITION IN 2002-05

Gisele Oliveira won the National Championship in the triple jump at the NCAA indoor meet in 2005. Over her Clemson career, she earned six All-America honors. At the NCAA Outdoor Meet, she was a triple jump All-America honoree for four straight seasons, with two third-place finishes and a second-place mark. In confer-

ence competition, she won seven Atlantic Coast Conference titles, four of which were outdoor events. She won two triple jump indoor titles and one long jump event. Outdoors, she won three triple jump titles and one long jump event.

CLEMSON, A TOP-20 NCAA FINISHER INDOORS AND OUTDOORS FOR THREE CONSECUTIVE YEARS

In 2010, The Lady Tigers finished tied for seventh place at the NCAA indoor meet and later that Spring finished 18th at the NCAA outdoor event. During the 2011 season, Clemson finished 11th indoors and seventh outdoors at NCAAs.

At the 2012 NCAA indoors meet, the Tigers finished tied for fifth, and at the outdoors meet the Tigers finished in a tie for fourth.

PATRICIA MAMONA WINS TWO NATIONAL CHAMPIONSHIPS IN THE TRIPLE JUMP

Patricia Mamona won two national championships in the triple jump at the NCAA outdoor track and field meet. She finished first in the triple jump in both 2010 and 2011.

Mamona earned another All-America honor when she finished second in the triple jump at the 2010 indoors NCAA meet.

Yet Mamona wasn't the only one to succeed on a national level. Brianna Rollins won the National Championship in the 60 meter hurdles at the 2011 NCAA indoor meet. She finished second in the same event in 2012. In the NCAA outdoor meet, Rollins finished second in the 100-meter hurdles. In fact, Clemson had four athletes to finish in the top 12 of this event. Rollins was second, Bridgette Owens was third, Monique Gracia was ninth, and Keni Harrison was 11th.

Rollins was named the Atlantic Coast Conference's Indoor Track Athlete of the Year.

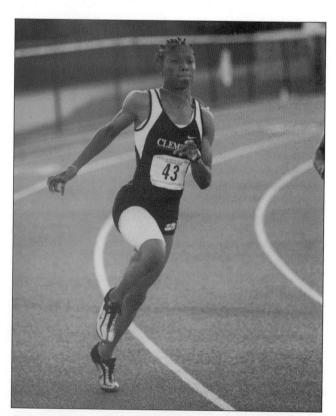

Cydonie Mothersill was a National Champion in the Indoor 200-meter dash and was a member of the National Champion 4x400m relay team in 2001.

Patricia Mamona was a two-time National Champion in the triple jump in 2010 and 2011.

ATLANTIC COAST CONFERENCE SUCCESS

At the 2009 Atlantic Coast Conference Indoor meet, April Sinkler won the high jump and the long jump as she was named the field events MVP of the meet. In 2010, she won the field events MVP at both the indoor and outdoor ACC meets, as she won both the high jump and long jump events. She also won the honor at the 2012 outdoor meet, where she was conference champion in the high jump.

Sinkler finished her career having won eight Atlantic Coast Conference Championships.

Stormy Kendrick was the indoor and outdoor ACC Track Event MVP in 2011. Indoors, she won the 60-meter dash and was on the 4x400-meter relay team at the conference meet. In the ACC outdoor meet, she won the 100- and 200-meter dashes and was a member of the championship-winning 4x100-meter relay team.

Dezerea Bryant was named the Atlantic Coast Conference track event MVP, as she won the 60-meter and the 200-meter dashes at the conference's indoor meet.

Marlena Wesh was named the ACC Outdoor Most Valuable Track Performer at the 2012 conference meet. At that meet, she won the 400-meter dash and was a member of the championship 4x100- and 4x400-meter relay teams. Wesh was a two-time All-America athlete at the NCAA Outdoor Track and Field Championships, finishing sixth in the 400-meter dash, and was a member of the 4x100-relay team that finished third. Wesh was named the 2012 ACC Outdoor Track Athlete of the Year.

As a team, Clemson won both the ACC Indoor & Outdoor Track and Field Championship meets four straight years in 2010, 2011, 2012, and 2013 (eight meets). Clemson also won the conference at the 2015 indoor and outdoor meets.

ROLLINS BRINGS HOME THE GOLD FOR USA, CLEMSON

Losing is not always a bad thing. Without it Clemson might not have an Olympic Champion.

In 2012, Brianna Rollins finished sixth in the U.S. Olympic Trials. At the time, she was still a student at Clemson were she was earning ACC and National Championships, but it was her sixth place finish in the 100-meter hurdles that let her know one day she could be an Olympic Champion.

"I realized I could compete on the professional level," Rollins said to *Clemson World Magazine*. "I had the second fastest time coming back in the finals at the trials. I finished sixth in the finals but seeing that I was competing with the professional and running so close gave me the hope I needed."

That hope became a reality at the 2016 Summer Olympic Games in Rio de Janeiro, Brazil when she crossed the finish line as a Gold Medalist in the 100-meter hurdles.

"Training as an elite-level athlete is a blessing; it comes with a lot of hard work, sacrifices, commitment, and focus, but it is all worth it when the reward is being an Olympic champion and an inspiration to those who look up to me," Rollins said.

Rollins is the first female athlete at Clemson to ever earn Olympic Gold in an individual event, and just the second all-time. To make it even more special, she was a part of the first ever USA sweep in any event in Olympic history.

Rollins won gold after crossing the line in 12.48. Nia Ali's 12.59 was good enough for silver, while Kristi Castlin hit the line in 12.61. Rollins had control of the race and won in near perfect fashion.

"I'm just so excited. We came out here and did our best," Rollins said on NBC afterward. "We came out and got a sweep so I'm grateful to God."

Brianna Rollins won three National Championships, twice in the 60 meter hurdles and once in the 100 meter hurdles.

The Olympics was not the first time Rollins stood on top of the podium. At Clemson she was the NCAA indoor champion in the 60-meter hurdles in 2011 and 2013. In 2014 she won the NCAA outdoor championship in the 100-meter hurdles and at the 2013 IAAF world championships, she won the 100-meter hurdles.

Rollins didn't begin competing in the sport until she was a freshman in high school in her hometown of Miami, Fla. Five years later as a sophomore at Clemson, she qualified for the Olympic Trials.

Rollins told *The Miami Herald* it took her a year to master the three-step footwork between the 33-inch hurdles. Now she's known as a technician, skimming over the sticks with what her personal coach, former Clemson track head coach Lawrence Johnson calls "an unusual combination of pure speed and coordination."

Rollins is the second female from Clemson to win gold in track and field and the first Clemson athlete to win an individual Olympic gold medal since 2004. Kim Graham won a medal as a member of the 4×100- meter relay team in 1996 and Shaw Crawford won the 200-meter dash in 2004. Nine athletes from Clemson have gone on to win Olympic gold.

WOMEN'S OUTDOOR TRACK & FIELD HISTORY

May 28-30, 1981—Cindy Duarte finished fourth in the 3,000-meter run at the AIAW outdoor track and field meet to become the Tigers' first All-America honoreein women's track.

May 31-June 5, 1982—Stephanie Weikert finished fifth in the 3,000-meter run in the first-ever NCAA outdoor track meet in Provo, UT. The Tigers finished tied for 32nd at the meet.

May 30-June 4, 1983—Clemson finished 20th at the NCAA outdoor track and field meet in Houston, TX. Tina Krebs finished second in the 800-meter run, and Judith Shephard finished fifth in the 3000-meter run as both earned All-America honors.

May 27-June 1, 1985—Clemson tied for 35th nationally at the NCAA outdoortrack and field meetin Austin, TX. Krebs earned All-America honors, as she finished fourth in the 1500-meter run.

June 4-7, 1986—Clemson tied for 23rd at the NCAA Outdoor Championships in Bloomington, IN. Krebs finished third in the 1500 meters and Ute Jamrozy finished fourth in the 10,000-meter run.

May 30-June 2, 1990—Lisa Dillard became the first Clemson sprinter to be named All-America, as she finished fifth in the 100-meter dash at the NCAAs. The Tigers finished 33rd as a team.

April 19-20, 1991—Clemson won its first ACC Outdoor Championship in women's track and field Sophomore-sprinter Kim Graham won the 200 meters and was on two victorious relays to lead the Tigers past three-time defending champion UNC 178-175. Clemson trailed the Tar Heels by one team point after 18 events and needed to place ahead of the Tar Heels in the 4x400 relay to win the meet. Graham anchored the relay, which not only finished ahead of the Tar Heels, but finished first in an ACC Meet record time of 3:34.50. Georgia Tech was second in the relay and North Carolina was third. The Tar Heels led the relay after 800 meters, but Clemson's Ane Skak took over the lead after the third leg. The Tar Heels' Kendra Mackey, who had won the 100 meters earlier in the day, caught Graham in the backstretch and held the lead until Graham passed her between the third and fourth turn. Graham was named the ACC meet's MVP, and Coach Wayne Coffman was named ACC Outdoor Track Coach of the Year.

May 29-June 1, 1991—Clemson tied for 12th at the Outdoor Track and Field Championships. Graham finished fourth in the 200-meter dash and the 4x100-meter relay team of Lisa Dillard, Angel Fleetwood, Tara Henderson and Graham finished fifth. Mareike Ressing finished fourth in the 3000 meters and Skak finished sixth in the

800 meters. A total of seven Tigers finished the meet with All-America honors.

April 17-18, 1992—Graham won the ACC outdoor meet MVP. Graham won the 100- and 200-meter dashes and was on the winning 4x100-meter relay team.

Tina Krebs was a three-time National Champion in indoor track.

June 3-6, 1992—Clemson finished 17th at the NCAA Outdoor Track and Field Championship, where Kim Graham finished second in the 200-meter run. Angela Dolby was named All-America for the second time in her career as she finished eighth in the shot put. Karen Hartmann finished sixth in the 1500-meter run, and Angel Fleetwood finished ninth. Nanette Holloway finished sixth in the triple jump.

April 16-17, 1993—Graham was named the Atlantic Coast Conference Outdoor Track and Field meet's MVP Trophy. She won the 100- and 200-meter dashes and was on the winning 4x100-meter relay team.

June 2-5, 1993—Clemson tied for 26th in the NCAA outdoor track and field meet. Graham finished fourth in the 200 meters, and Mareike Ressing finished sixth in the 300 meters. Tonya McKelvey finished 11th in the long jump.

April 21-22, 1995—Nikki Sims was named the co-MVP at the Atlantic Coast Conference Outdoor Track and Field Meet. Sims won the shot put competition at the meet.

May 29-June 1, 1996—Clemson finished in a tie for 49th at the NCAA Outdoor Track and Field meet, where Treshell Mayo finished sixth in the 200 meters.

April 16-17, 1999—Clemson won the ACC Outdoor Championship for the second time in history. Jamine Moton won the shot put and the discus events in leading the Lady Tigers to the conference crown. Coach Ron Garner was named ACC Outdoor Track Coach of the Year.

April 20-21, 2001—Clemson finished second in the ACC Outdoor Track and Field meet.

April 26, 2001—Cydonie Mothersill was named the ACC Outdoor Track and Field Championships Performer of the Year. She was the ACC Champion in the 100- and 200-meter dashes and ran on the 4x100-meter relay and 4x400-meter relay teams that also won their events.

May 30-June 2, 2001—Clemson finished in a tie for seventh at the NCAA Outdoor Track and Field meet at Hayward Field on the campus of the University of Oregon. The 4x400-meter relay team of Michelle Burgher, Cydonie Mothersill, Marcia Smith, and Shekera Weston finished in first place. Jamine Moton finished second in the shot put.

Gisele Oliveira was a National Champion in the indoor triple jump in 2005.

The 4x100-meter relay team of Shannon Murray, Shekera Weston, Michelle Burgher, and CydonieMothersill finished in fourth place. ShekeraWesteron finished fourth in the 200-meter dash.

May 29-June 1, 2002—The Tigers finished tied for 20th at the NCAA Outdoor Track and Field meet. Jamine won the National Championship in the hammer throw. She set an NCAA meet and college record with a toss of 220'6". She also finished 15th in the shot put. Gisele Oliveira finished seventh in the triple jump and teammate Sheri Smith finished ninth.

June 11-14, 2003—Clemson finished in a tie for 36th at the NCAA Outdoor Track and Field meet at Sacramento State University. Oliveira finished third in the triple jump to earn All-America honors. She also finished eighth in the long jump.

April 24, 2004—Oliveira finished third in both the long jump and triple jump events at the Penn Relays in Philadelphia, PA.

June 9-12, 2004—Clemson finished in a tie for 34th at the NCAA Outdoor Track and Field meet at the University of Texas. Oliveira finished third in the triple jump, and Silja Ulfarsdottir finished ninth in the 400-meter hurdles.

April 30, 2005—Oliveira finished second in the triple jump at the Penn Relays in Philadelphia, PA.

June 8-11, 2005—The Tigers finished in a tie for 32nd at the NCAA Outdoor Track and Field meet on the campus of Sacramento State University. Gisele Oliveira finished second in the triple jump. The senior from Porto Alegre, Brazil recorded her third consecutive top-three finish in the event at the national meet. She had also placed third in 2003 and 2004 and fourth her freshman year, in 2002.

April 15-17, 2010—Clemson won the ACC Championship, marking the first time in school history that the Tigers won both the Indoor and Outdoor meet in the same academic year.

June 9-12, 2010—Patricia Mamona finished first in the triple jump in leading Clemson to an 18th place finish at the NCAA Outdoor Track and Field meet. The 4-x100-meter relay team of Michaylin Golladay, Stormy Kendrick, Kristine Scott, and Jasmine Edgerson finished fourth to earn All-America honors. April Sinkler finished 10th in the long jump and 15th in the ripple jump. She also earned All-America honors.

June 22, 2010—Clemson's Patricia Mamona was voted the ACC Field Performer of the Year and Stormy Kendrick was voted Freshman of the Year. Coach of the Year honors went to Lawrence Johnson of Clemson.

April 21-23, 2011—The Tigers won the ACC Track and Field Championship in Durham, NC. Stormy Kendrick won both the 100- and 200-meter dashes to lead Clemson. She was also a member of the 4x100-meter relay championship team. For her outstanding performance, she was named the meet's MVP for track events. Clemson's April Sinkler won the high jump and was named MVP for field events.

June 8-11, 2011—Clemson finished seventh at the NCAA Outdoor Track and Field Championships. Patricia Mamona won the national championship in the triple jump for the second year in a row.

June 17, 2011—Lawrence Johnson earned ACC Women's Outdoor Track & Field Coach of the Year accolades.

April 19-21, 2012—Clemson won its third consecutive ACC Outdoor Track and Field Championship, where Sinkler won the high jump and was named MVP for field events for the second consecutive year. Marlena Wesh was named the MVP for track events, as she won the 400-meter dash and was a member of both of the winning 4x100 and 4x400 relay teams.

June 6-9, 2012—Clemson's Brianna Rollins and Bridgette Owens took second and third, respectively, in the high hurdles in leading Clemson to a tie for fourth place at the NCAA Track and Field meetThis was the highest finish for Clemson at the NCAA Outdoor Championships.

June 15, 2012—Marlena Wesh and April Sinkler were selected as Performers of the Year, as announced by the Atlantic Coast Conference. Wesh was named the Track Performer of the Year, while Sinkler was named the ACC Field Event Performer of the Year. Lawrence Johnson earned ACC Women's Outdoor Track & Field Coach of the Year accolades.

April 18-20, 2013—Clemson won the final event of the meet, the 4x400 meter relay, on its way to a fourth straight ACC women's outdoor track & field title. This was the Tigers' eighth straight league crown overall. The Tigers won in a head-to-head showdown against Florida State to claim the trophy.

The Tiger women finished the meet with 151 points to Florida State's 146.

After Natalie Anthony earned two crucial points in the 5K two days after a grueling 10K, the stage was set with the Tigers and Seminoles tied for the top position. But there was little doubt once the 4x4 began who was going to be champion. Keni Harrison had a great lead leg, and Keisha Richburg, Brittany Pringley and Nia Fluker followed suit to propel Clemson to a win with a time of 3:34.87.

Harrison was named the ACC Most Valuable Track Performer. Harrison scored 38 out of a possible 40 points, winning two relays and an individual event. Brianna Rollins supported with wins in the 100 hurdles and 200 dash.

Rollins and Harrison finished 1-2 in the 100 hurdles. Rollins was the first ACC female to win both the 100 hurdles and 200 dash at the same meet since 1997

Harrison earned a repeat gold medal performance in the 400 hurdles. The sophomore turned in a personal best 56.58, breaking the school record for the event.

Dezerea Bryant won the 100 dash with a time of 11.42, her second straight victory in the event at the ACC Championships.

The women's 4x100 claimed its fourth straight ACC crown in the event, and was just off the meet record with a time of 43.59. The group was composed of Harrison, Rollins, Stormy Kendrick and Bryant. Whitney Fountain won the Heptathlon event with 5,094 points. Brittney Waller was named the MVP in the field events as she was All-ACC in the discus and hammer.

Brianna Rollins was named the ACC Outdoor Track Athlete of the Year.

June 5-8, 2013—Clemson's red-shirt junior Brianna Rollins dazzled the Historic Hayward Field crowd for a second time this week as she ran to another collegiate record in the 100 hurdles at the NCAA Outdoor Championships. She blew away the field to a time of 12.39, one of the top times in history by an American athlete, to lead Clemson's women to a ninth-place team finish. It was the program's third straight top-10 finish at the NCAA Outdoor Championships.

Keni Harrison took fifth place in the same final as Rollins. She ran to a time of 12.87, tying a personal best set earlier this season. It was the first time in history Clemson had two NCAA finalists in the 100 hurdles.

The women's 4x100 relay finished third for the second straight year at the NCAA Championships. The team of Harrison, Rollins, Stormy Kendrick and Dezerea Bryant combined to a time of 43.76. Bryant took the baton in at least fourth place, but charged to push the Tigers past Oregon for third in the final meters.

Bryant followed about 40 minutes later with a fifth-place effort in the 200 dash final. She capped her season with three top-five finishes in the short sprints at the NCAA Indoor and Outdoor Championships, with a bronze medal in the 4x100 as well. Her fifth-place finish was the best for a Tiger female since 2001, when Shekera Weston took fourth.

June 10, 2013—The Clemson women's team, which finished in ninth place, had eight first-team All-America honors. Brianna Rollins led the way, earning a pair of accolades including a National Championship in the 100 hurdles. She was also an All-American with the 4x100 relay.

Keni Harrison collected three first-team honors, most in one season for a Tiger female since Shekera Weston also earned three in 2001. She was fourth place in the 400

hurdles and fifth in the 100 hurdles. Harrison was lead leg for the relay team.

Dezerea Bryant was fifth place in the 200 dash, earning her sixth career first-team All-America accolade. The Wisconsin native also finished 10th in the 100 dash, earning the women's team's lone second-team accolade. Bryant and fellow sprinter Stormy Kendrick composed the final two legs of the bronze medal relay

June 12, 2013—Clemson's Brianna Rollins was been named National Women's Track Athlete of the Year, the U.S. Track & Field and Cross Country Coaches Association (USTFCCCA) announced. She captured her third NCAA National Championship in the 100 hurdles, her first outdoor crown.

December 2, 2013—Former Clemson star Brianna Rollins, the American record-holder and IAAF World Champion in the 100 hurdles, was named the 2013 Jackie Joyner-Kersee Athlete of the Year, USA Track & Field announced. The three-time National Champion and NCAA record-holder in the 60 hurdles and 100 hurdles will received the award at the annual USATF meeting in Indianapolis, IN on Dec. 7.

December 18, 2013—Former Clemson hurdler Brianna Rollins culminated an outstanding 2013 season by collecting The Bowerman—the highest honor awarded in collegiate track & field—on Wednesday at the JW Marriott Grande Lakes in conjunction with the annual coaches' association convention. Rollins was voted the female winner by a combined vote of former winners of the award, selected media and track & field statisticians, coaches and fans.

April 17-19, 2014—The Clemson women's track and field team finished ninth at the Atlantic Coast Conference Track and Field meet at Chapel Hill, NC. Mimi Land and Marlena Wesh collected three all-conference honors for the Tigers. Land was named the ACC's Most Valuable Field Performer. Land earned her honors in the high jump and triple jump. Whitney Fountain was honored in the long jump.

June 11-14, 2014—Whitney Fountain was named a second-team All-American as she finished 12th in the long jump at the NCAA Track and Field meet in Eugene, Oregon.

May 14-16, 2015—Sabria Hadley won the 100 meter dash and was a member of the first place 4x100 meter relay team as Clemson captured first place at the ACC Track and Field Meet in Tallahassee, FL. Natoya Goule won the 800 meters . The 4x100 meter relay team composted of Hadley, Fountain, Parrish and Jacobs. Iana Amsterdam was the Triple jump.

June 10-13, 2015—Natoya Goule finished sixth in the 800 meter run in leading Clemson in a tie for 51st place at the NCAA Track and Field meet in Eugene, Oregon.

May 13-15, 2016—Clemson finished third as a team at the Atlantic Coast Conference Track and Field Meet in Tallahassee, FL. The Tigers' Mimi Land was the champion in the high jump.

June 8-11, 2016—Mimi Land was a second-team All-American as she was 14th in the long jump.

WOMEN'S INDOOR TRACK & FIELD

March 13-14, 1981—Cindy Duarte was Clemson's first female All-America track honoree, as she finished fourth indoors in the 3000-meter run at the AIAW meet in Pocatello, Idaho.

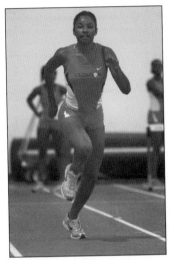

April Sinkler was a seven-time All-America athlete in 2008-12.

March 11-12, 1983—Tina Krebs won the National Championship in the 1000-meter run at the Silverdome in Pontiac, MI at the NCAA Women's Indoor Track Championship. Krebs became Clemson's first woman national champion, regardless of sport. The Lady Tigers finished 10th as a team.

March 8-9, 1985—Krebs won the 1500-meter run, and the team finished 12th at the NCAA Indoor Track and Field meet in Syracuse, NY. Kirsti Voldness also finished third in the same event and earned All-America honors.

March 14-15, 1986—Krebs won the mile at the NCAA Indoor Championship. The team finished 12th at the meet.

February 17-18, 1989—Coach Wayne Coffman was named ACC Indoor Track Coach of the Year.

March 9-10, 1990—Clemson finished 41st at the NCAA Indoor Track and Field meet. Lisa Dillard finished fifth in the 55-meter dash at the Indiana Hoosier Dome in Indianapolis, IN.

March 8-9, 1991—The Tigers finished 35th at the NCAA Indoor Track and Field meet at the Hoosier Dome in Indianapolis, IN. Marcia Fletcher finished ninth in the long jump and Ane Skak finished sixth in the 800-meter run.

February 14-15, 1992—The Lady Tigers won its first ACC Indoor Championship at Johnson City, TN. Kim Graham won the 55-meter and 200-meter dashes in leading the Lady Tigers to the championship. She was named the meet's MVP. Coach Wayne Coffman was named ACC Indoor Track Coach of the Year.

March 13-14, 1992—Clemson finished 22nd at the NCAA Indoor Track and Field Championships, where Karen Hartmann finished third in the 800-meter run.

February 19-20, 1993—Karen Hartmann was named the ACC Indoor Meet's MVP. She won the mile and 800-meter runs.

March 12-13, 1993—Clemson finished 33rd at the NCAA Indoor Track and Field Championships at the Hoosier Dome in Indianapolis, IN. Kim Graham finished eighth in the 200-meter run. Monyetta Haynesworth finished fifth in the long jump and teammate Tonya McKelvey finished sixth.

March 11-12, 1994—The Lady Tigers finished 29th at the NCAA Indoor Track and Field Championships. Mareike Ressing finished third in the 3000 meters and Tonya McKelvey finished 14th in the long jump.

February 23-24, 1996—Coach Wayne Coffman was named ACC Indoor Track Coach of the Year.

March 8-9, 1996—Clemson finished tied for 33rd at the NCAA Indoor Track and Field Championships. Treshell Mayo finished fifth in the 200-meter run.

Kim Graham won an Olympic Gold Medal as a member of the 4x100-meter relay team at the 1996 Olympics in Atlanta, GA.

March 7-8, 1997—Clemson finished 50th at the NCAA Indoor Track and Field Championships in Indianapolis, IN.

January 9, 1998—Ron Garner was named the Women's Track and Field head coach.

March 13-14, 1998—Finished 33rd at the NCAA Indoor Track and Field Championships in Indianapolis, IN. Nikkie Bouyer finished sixth in the 55-meter high hurdles. LaShonda Cutchin, Samantha Watt, Nikkie Bouyer, and Shekera Weston finished sixth in the 4x400-meter relay. Nikkie Bouyer, LaShonda Cutchin, Samantha Watt, and Shekera Weston were all named All-Americas.

March 9-10, 2001—Clemson finished third at the NCAA Indoor Track and Field meet behind Cydonie Mothersill's national championship in the 200 meters. Jamine Moton finished second in the shot put and third in the weight throw. Michelle Burgher, Cydonie Mothersill, Marcia Smith, and Shekera Weston finished third in the 4x400-meter relay.

March 8-9, 2002—Clemson finished 21st at the NCAA Indoor Track and Field meet at Fayetteville, AR. Jamine Moton finished second in the weight throw, and eighth in the shot put. Sheri Smith finished seventh in the triple jump.

March 12-13, 2004—Finished tied for 52nd at the NCAA Indoor Track and Field meet. The Tiger 4x400-meter relay team of Silja Ulfarsdottir, Shakirah Rutherford, Christina Smith, and Randi Hinton placed eighth and all the members of the relay team earned All-America honors.

March 11-12, 2005—Clemson finished tied for 21st at the NCAA Track and Field meet at the Randal Tyson Track Complex on the campus of the University of Arkansas. Senior Gisele Oliviera won the National Championship in the triple jump.

March 2, 2007—Liane Weber was named ACC Indoor Freshman of the Year after claiming the 2007 pentathlon title.

March 9-10, 2007—The Tigers tied for 34th at the NCAA Indoor Track and Field meet at Fayetteville, AR. Della Clark finished third in the weight throw to earn All-America honors.

March 6, 2009—April Sinkler was named the ACC's Most Valuable Women's Field Event Athlete as determined by a vote of the league's head coaches. Sinkler won two events and set personal bests in three at the ACC Indoor Track and Field Championship at Blacksburg, VA. She won the high jump and long jump competitions, setting indoor school records in both events.

March 13-14, 2009—Clemson finished tied for 51st place at the NCAA Indoor Track and Field meet in College Station, TX. Liane Weber finished sixth in the pentathlon to earn All-America honors. She became the first female in Clemson history to earn All-America status in the multi events.

March 12-13, 2010—Clemson finished in a tie for seventh place at the NCAA Indoor Track and Field meet in Fayetteville, AR. Kimberly Ruck finished seventh in the 5000-meter run. The 4x400-meter relay team composed of Brittany Pringley, Brianna Rollins, Sonni Austin, and Jasmine Edgerson, were all named All-America runners for their fifth-place finish in this event. The relay team was composed of all freshmen. Patricia Mamona finished second and earned All-America honors in the triple jump and Liane Weber finished fifth in the pentathlon, earning her second All-America honor in this event.

March 19, 2010—Clemson's Lawrence Johnson was named the ACC Women's Indoor Track & Field Coach of the Year.

February 24-26, 2011—Clemson won the ACC Indoor Track and Field Championship for the second consecutive year at Rector Field House in Blacksburg, VA. Stormy Kendrick won the 60-meter dash and was a member of the championship 4x400-meter relay team.

March 11-12, 2011—Brianna Rollins won the National Championship in the 60-meter high hurdles at the NCAA Track and Field Indoor meet at College Station, TX. The Tigers' April Sinkler finished second in the triple jump

and Marlena Wesh finished eighth in the 400 meters to earn All-America honors.

March 21, 2011—Clemson's Lawrence Johnson was named the ACC Women's Indoor Track & Field Coach of the Year.

February 23-25, 2012—Clemson won the ACC Track and Field Indoor meet for the third straight time at the Reggie Lewis Center in Boston, MA. Dezerea Bryant won the 60- and 200-meter dashes to lead the Tigers to the championship. Marlena Wesh won the 400-meter dash and was also on the championship 4x400-meter relay team. Bryant was named the MVP for the track events.

March 9-10, 2012—Brianna Rollins and Bridgette Owens finished second and third, respectively, in the 60 hurdles to lead the women's team to a fifth-place tie at the NCAA Indoor Track & Field Championships at the Idaho Center Arena. It was Clemson's best NCAA indoor finish since a third-place effort in 2001.

March 16, 2012—Brianna Rollins was named the ACC Indoor Performer of the Year for track events. Lawrence Johnson was named the ACC Women's Indoor Track & Field Coach of the Year.

February 21-23, 2013—Clemson won its fourth consecutive ACC Indoor Championship defeating runner-up Florida State by a 41.5-point margin at Virginia Tech's Rector Field House in Blacksburg, VA. The Tigers' Dezerea Bryant won the 60 Meter Dash and the 200 Meter Dash. She was named the Most Valuable Performer of the meet for the second consecutive year. Bryant is the first female in ACC history to win both the 60 and 200 dashes in consecutive seasons. Marlena Wesh won the 400 meter dash and Brianna Rollins won the 60 meter hurdles. The 4x400 meter relay team of Keni Harrison, Mariena Wesh, Sabria Hadley, and Nia Fluker were champions at the meet. Brittney Waller was the ACC Champion in the weight throw.

February 26, 2013—Clemson Interim Director of Track & Field Shawn Cobey was named ACC Women's Indoor Coach of the Year. It is the first honor for Cobey, who took over on an interim basis on January 8, 2013.

March 8-9, 2013—Brianna Rollins established another NCAA Championships record in the 60 hurdles and claimed her second national title in the event in the NCAA Indoor Track and Field Meet at the Tyson Track Center in Fayetteville, AR. She led Clemson's women to a sixth place finish at the event.

In the 60 meter hurdles, she set the meet record with a time of 7.82 in the prelims, but she went three hundredths faster to cruise to victory in the final. Rollins is the first Clemson female since Patricia Mamona with multiple national titles and only the fourth in school history to accomplish the feat.

Along with Rollins, Dezerea Bryant and Stormy Kendrick earned All-American honors in the 60 meter dash. Bryant finished fourth and Kendrick finished sixth in the 60 meter finals. Bryant also finished fifth in the 200 meters and Brittney Waller finished third in the 20-pound weight throw as they were named All-American in those events.

March 15, 2013—Rollins was named the ACC Women's Indoor Track Athlete-of-the-Year for a second straight season. Brittney Waller was named the ACC Field Athlete-of-the-Year as she won the 20-pound weight event for the third consecutive year. The Freshman of the Year was won by Clemson's Mimi Land.

The jumper out of Albany, GA scored in three different events at the ACC Indoor Championships from Feb. 21-23.

February 27-March 1, 2014—Clemson's women placed 11th at the ACC Indoor Track and Field Meet at Clemson, SC.

March 14-15, 2014—Mimi Land earned All-America honors at the NCAA Indoor Track and Field Championships in Albuquerque, NM. Land became the first Tiger female to earn All-America honors in the high jump competition as she tied for fifth in the event. As a team Clemson finished in a tie for 45th. Land, a sophomore, earned second-team All-America honors in the triple jump as she finished 13th in the event.

February 26-28, 2015—Mimi Land was named the Most Valuable Field Athlete as the Tigers won the ACC Indoor Track and Field Championship in Blacksburg, VA.

Samantha Elliott won the 60 meter hurdles and finished third in the 60 meter dash and Iana Amsterdam won the triple jump. Land earn All ACC honors in the high jump and triple jump as she finished second in both events. She also finished sixth in the long jump. Clemson finished first way ahead of second place Florida State by 21 points. The women's 4x400 composed of Olivia James, Nia Fluker, Deja Parrish and Natoya Goule won the ACC Championship.

March 13-14, 2015—Natoya Goule finished first in the women's 800 after posting a record-breaking time at the NCAA Indoor Track & Field Championships at Fayetteville, AR. The women's 4x400 relay team posted a record-breaking performance to cap off the meet. The Clemson women tied for 12th overall in the team race with 15 points. Goule's 2:01.64 time set a new meet record and topped her previous ACC record of 2:02.77, set in the prelims. Her first-place 800-meter finish was also the first by a Clemson female at the NCAA Indoor meet.

The women's 4x400 composed of Olivia James, Nia Fluker, Deja Parrish and Goule finished fourth overall in the finals.

March 20, 2015—Mark Elliott was named ACC Indoor Track & Field Women's Coach of the Year while Natoya Goule was named the ACC Women's Track Athlete of the Year. The award were voted on by the ACC's head coaches.

February 25-27, 2016—Clemson finished second at the ACC Indoor Track and Field Championships at the Reggie Lewis Center in Boston, MA. Miami claimed the ACC title in the final event of the meet, winning the women's 4x400 meter relay to deny Clemson its third-straight ACC title overall and edged the Tigers 85-83 in the team scoring.

Clemson's Myasia Jacobs led the way for the Tigers with her gold medal in the 60-meter dash. Clemson's distance medley relay team of Grace Barnett, Kaley Ciluffo, Olivia James and Ersula Farrow finished first in the meet.

March 11-12, 2016—Clemson's distance medley relay team of Kaley Ciluffo, Deja Parrish, Ersula Farrow and Grace Barnett finished eighth in the meet and all earned All-America honors. Grace Barnett finished 10th in the mile run and teammate Anasterasia Terrell finished 16th in the triple jump as both athletes earned second-team All-America honors. As a team, Clemson finished 45th.

CLEMSON
Volleyball

NCAA Tournaments:

1993, 1994, 1997, 1998, 1999, 2007, 2008, 2009

ACC Champions:

1997, 1999, 2007

Final Top–25 Rankings:

1999 (22nd), 2007 (22nd)

THE EARLY YEARS

Clemson first started an intercollegiate volleyball program in 1977. During the first five years of the program, Clemson played in Fike Recreation Center. This inaugural year of volleyball produced a winning season upon which a solid foundation was built to promote future growth. Debbie Hammond won her first All-State honor and gave the club a nucleus upon which to build. Hammond led the 1978 team to a 19-10 record before receiving her second All-State award.

The 1979 volleyball team consisted of 11 freshmen, who four years later would comprise one of Clemson's early winningest classes. The Tigers fared well with a 43-13 mark, two tournament championships, and an AIAW Regional appearance. Five freshmen—Cyndi Graf, Lisa Harbison, Kim Johnson, Judy Sackfield, and Elizabeth Latto—garnered All-State honors in 1979.

The 1980 season was the first year volleyball was recognized in the ACC, and a double-elimination tournament was held at the end of the regular season. Clemson finished third in that tournament and turned in a 21-22 overall record. Sackfield and Harbison represented the Tigers on the first-ever All-ACC team.

1981 was a successful year for the Lady Tigers, who finished 34-16 with a pair of tournament champions hips. Again, Clemson finished third in the ACC Tournament.

The 19-15 record ensured the Tigers of another winning season in 1982, which saw Clemson playing its most difficult schedule Sackfield, Harbison, and Cindi Graf

captured All-ACC honors that year. Harbison was a three-time All-ACC selection during her career. This was the first year that the Tigers played in Jervey Gymnasium.

The 1983 club went against nationally ranked teams and played in numerous tournaments. Although the Tigers finished 15-33, Clemson continued the tradition of playing hard in their matches. Tris Miketa was named to the All-ACC team for her outstanding play. In 1984, Deanne Browning starred for the Tigers in the middle hitter position and gained All-ACC honors.

LINDA WHITE LEADS CLEMSON TO WINNING SEASONS

The 1986 team created a great deal of excitement by accomplishing feats that had not been obtainable in recent years. Besides winning a tournament, the Lady Tigers enjoyed their first winning season since 1982 and set a new single-match attendance record in Jervey Gym. All this was accomplished under new coach Linda White. The 1986 season, which was deemed a "New Beginning," definitely lived up to that theme, as a new era was launched for the Tigers volleyball program.

In 1987, the Tigers won 21 matches for the second year in a row, which is the first time in six years that the Tigers had won 20 contests in back to back seasons. Many of the Tigers' records were broken during the course of the season. Wendy Anderson starred for the Tigers and was named first-team All-ACC, as well as being named to three all-tournament teams during the season.

Clemson won 21 matches in 1988 for the third consecutive season. In 1989, Clemson finished the year with a 30-7 record. The 30 victories were the most since the 1981 season. Clemson also finished tied for second in the ACC that season. After the 1991 season, White joined the administration in the Athletic Department. Ernie Arill, a long-time assistant, was the head coach in 1992 and led the Tigers to a 24-9 record.

THE JOLENE HOOVER ERA—NCAA TOURNAMENTS, ACC CHAMPIONSHIPS

Jolene Hoover came to coach the team in 1993. That season was the first time that ACC teams started playing one another on a home-and-home basis. This season was a special one for Clemson, as it was the first time that the Tigers advanced to the NCAA Tournament, where they subseqeuntly lost to Houston in the first round.

"I think being able to have success that first season was huge," said Hoover. "I got the position in December of 1992 and we had seven scholarships available. I think sometimes that players enjoy playing for coaches that recruited them. That year we had a good mix of incoming players and returning players. Two of the returning players were Heather Kahl and Robin Kibben. Robin was one of the finest players to play in the program. Kahl was an unbelievable leader and catalyst on the team. She was a ball girl and knew me when I played in a pro league in Chicago a few years earlier. I think that the success that we have enjoyed goes back to the success we had that first year. We got to the NCAAs when the tournament bracket was only 32 teams. I think that first-team set the tone where the program wants to be and needs to be. That first year we were able to sign Julie Rodriguez out of the Chicago area."

In 1994, Clemson again went to the NCAA Tournament, where they defeated Stephen F. Austin in five games and lost to Houston in the second round. This was also Kibben's senior season. She was named first-team All-ACC in 1992, 1993, and 1994. She was a two-time AVCA All-Region team member.

In Hoover's first three years, the Tigers were 31-11 vs. ACC competition and had two second-place finishes and one third-place finish in the league. In the first three years of her career at Clemson, Hoover led the Tigers to 78 victories. In 1996, Clemson went 17-15 for the year. Rodriguez finished her career as a three-time All-ACC selection.

Head Coach Jolene Hoover has led Clemson to three ACC Championships.

In 1997, Clemson won the Atlantic Coast Conference Championship for the first time in history at Raleigh, NC. Clemson defeated Duke in the quarterfinals, #15 Maryland in the semifinals, and Georgia Tech in the finals. Cindy Stern was named first-team All-ACC in her sophomore season. Clemson won three regular season tournaments that year—Clemson's Big Orange Bash, the Auburn Invitational, and the SMU Invitational. Michelle Thieke, a setter, was named the ACC Tournament's MVP.

When asked about special moments in her career, Hoover doesn't hesitate to mention that winning the first ACC Tournament was special.

"Winning the first ACC Tournament in 1997 was special," said Hoover, who has won well over 400 matches in her Clemson career. Our setter, Michelle Thieke, was playing with a knee injury and we had to adjust defensively so she could be close to the net during the year. She had to play through pain, and she helped lead us to the championship. I remember we had a terrific weekend at the ACC Tournament. Cindy Stern had a big weekend. Also Alison Coday was a great player on that team. It was our first-ever ACC Tournament Championship."

During the 1998 season, Hoover became the winningest volleyball coach in Clemson history. The Tigers again participated in the NCAA Tournament.

Clemson finished the 1999 season ranked 22nd in the final poll. This was the first-ever season-ending national ranking in the history of the program. Clemson finished the year with a 31-3 record, the best in terms of winning percentage in Clemson volleyball history, and won the ACC Championship. Stern was a second team All-America player. The Tigers won three regular season tournaments—the Michigan State Classic, the Big Orange Bash, and the Clemson Invitational.

Jodi Steffes finished her career in 2001 as a four-time AVCA All-District selection. She was also a three-time All-ACC member. In 1998 she was named ACC Rookie of the Year.

CINDY STERN, ALL-AMERICA

"Volleyball is what initially brought me to Clemson," said Cindy Stern, a native of Cincinnati. "But the welcoming, supportive atmosphere is what made me fall in love with it. From the tiger paws painted on the roads that lead you into town, to the southern hospitality, to the enthusiastic fans covered in orange and purple, I was quickly reassured that Clemson was the perfect place for me from the first day of my freshman year.

The 1997 Clemson Volleyball team won the school's first ACC Championship.

"Another deciding factor for me was Coach Hoover. From my first dinner with her on my recruiting trip, I knew that she would not only be the best volleyball coach I would have, but would be an extension of my family. Her family had joined mine for dinner. I remember Carley Hoover was maybe only 8 months old and still in a car seat. It was such a feeling of calm knowing that when I left my family in Cincinnati, I would have a Clemson family. I still keep in touch with Coach Hoover."

When asked about special moments at Clemson, Stern has several.

"My sophomore year when we won the ACC Tournament has to be one of the most memorable moments of my time at Clemson. We went from losing in the first round of the tournament my freshman year to winning the next. It was then that I knew we had the potential to be a great volleyball team.

"I was also especially honored to be selected to train with the National program the summer before my junior year.

"My favorite memory would have to be every Monday of my senior year. Mondays was when the national rankings would come out. I can remember checking the Internet several times before our afternoon practices to see where we were ranked that week. I will never forget the Monday towards the end of the season when we were ranked 13th. It was such an overwhelming sense of pride.

"It was such an honor to be named All-American my senior year. It felt like a validation that all the hard work and dedication over the past four years had paid off," said Stern.

ANOTHER ATLANTIC COAST CONFERENCE CHAMPIONSHIP

In 2007, Clemson won a school record 17 matches in a row before capturing the Atlantic Conference Champi-onship. The Tigers finished the season with a 29-4 record, and Hoover was named ACC Coach of the Year. Clemson also finished ranked 22nd in the final poll and had six players named All-ACC. Clemson advanced to the second round of the NCAA Tournament.

In 2008, Clemson was 23-10 and advanced to the NCAA Tournament's second round. Danielle Hepburn was named ACC Player of the Year.

Clemson went to the NCAA Tournament in 2009 and finished the year 23-10 overall and 13-7 in the ACC. Kelsey Murphy, Lia Proctor, and Didem Ege were all senior leaders that season. Murphy was a three-time All-ACC selection and a three-time All-Region honoree. Proctor finished her career being named All-ACC and a two-time honorable mention All-America player. Ege was a two-time honorable mention All-America player and a two-time All-ACC selection.

Danielle Hepburn was named ACC Player of the Year in 2008.

VOLLEYBALL HISTORY

May 31, 1977—Clemson athletic officials announced the university would field women's volleyball for the first time in the fall of 1977. Grace Lyles was named the Tigers' first coach.

September 28, 1977—Clemson played its first volleyball match and was victorious over USC-Spartanburg, 15-9, 13-15, 16-14 in three sets.

September 28-29, 1977—Clemson won the Mars Hill Invitational—the school's first tournament championship.

November 10, 1979—Clemson won its 43rd match of the year with a win over South Carolina. The 43 wins set the school's record for most victories in a single season.

October 31-November 1, 1980—Clemson participated in the first ACC Volleyball Tournament. The Tigers finished third in the inaugural affair.

November 1, 1980—Judy Sackfield and Lisa Harbison were Clemson's first All-ACC players.

January 21, 1986—Denise Murphy was named to the GTE/CoSIDA Academic All-America second team.

December, 1986—Denise Murphy was named to the NCAA Southeast all-region team, Clemson's first all-district player.

January 26, 1987—Denise Murphy was named to the GTE/CoSIDA Academic All-America second team. Chris Sherman was named to the third-team. This was the first time in Clemson history that a team had two Academic All-Americas in the same year.

November 20–22, 1987—Clemson played host to the eighth annual ACC Volleyball Tournament.

January, 1988—Chris Sherman was named to the GTE/CoSIDA Academic All-American second team, becoming Clemson's first two-time Academic All-America player.

September 15-16, 1989—Clemson won the Big Orange Classic. This was the first regular season tournament to which Clemson had ever played host on campus.

November, 1989—The Tigers finished the season with a 30-7 overall record and a .811 winning percentage, the best in Tiger history.

September 25, 1992—With a five-game victory over Auburn, the Tigers set a school record for the best undefeated start in Clemson volleyball history at 15-0. It was also the longest winning streak in Clemson history.

December 2, 1992—Jolene Jordan Hoover was named head coach of the Tigers.

September 27, 1993—For the first time in the history of the Clemson volleyball program, the team received a regional ranking in the NCAA polls. The Tigers made their debut at the 13th position in the South.

November 6, 1993—Clemson's win over 23rd-ranked Florida State was the Tigers' first-ever victory over a nationally ranked team.

November 18, 1993—Julie Rodriguez was named ACC Rookie of the Year.

December 1, 1993—Clemson played in its first-ever NCAA Tournament match versus Houston.

November 5, 1994—Clemson upset 17th-ranked Duke in three games at home for the 400th victory in the history of the program. It marked the second season in a row that the Tigers defeated a nationallyranked team and the first time Clemson had beaten Duke since 1981.

November 17, 1994—Jolene Jordan Hoover became the first Clemson volleyball coach to be named ACC Coach of the Year. Robin Kibben was named to the All-ACC first-team for the third straight year.

November 20, 1994—The Tigers competed in the championship match of the ACC Tournament, held in Chapel Hill, NC, for the first time in school history. Duke defeated the Tigers in three games, 15-6, 15-9, 15-7. Robin Kibben and Heather Kahl were named to the ACC All-Tournament team.

November 30, 1994—Clemson played host to its second-straight NCAA first-round tournament and posted its first win ever in an NCAA Tournament. The Tigers defeated Stephen F. Austin in five games for the win.

December 3, 1994—For the first time in the history of the program, the Tigers participated in the second round of the NCAA Volleyball Tournament, playing Houston. The Tigers fell to the Cougars, 15-1, 15-13, 15-12.

November 15, 1995—Stephanie Schulz was named ACC Rookie of the Year.

November 21-23, 1997—The Tigers won the Atlantic Coast Conference title for the first time in the program's history. Clemson defeated Duke, 15-11, 16-14, 14-10, in the first round and upset 15th-ranked Maryland in the semifinals, 7-15, 15-10, 15-8, 15-10, at the ACC Tournament in Raleigh, NC. In the championship match, Clemson defeated Georgia Tech, 8-15, 15-3, 15-9, 15-13, for its first ACC title in school history. Michelle Thieke was named the ACC Tournament's Most Valuable Player.

December 6, 1997—Central Florida defeated Clemson, 15-7, 15-13, 15-1, in the first round of the NCAA Tournament in Madison, WI.

November 23, 1998—Jodi Steffes was named the 1998 ACC Rookie of the Year.

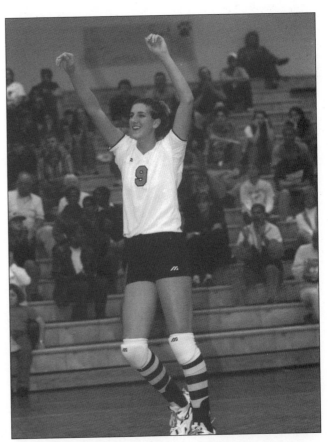

Cindy Stern was not only Clemson's first All-American volleyball player, but she was also the first player in ACC history to be named an All-America player.

December 4, 1998—Clemson defeated Fairfield, 15-9, 15-9, 15-5, in the first round of the NCAA Tournament.

December 5, 1998—Penn State defeated Clemson in University Park, PA, 15-2, 15-11, 15-5, in NCAA Tournament second-round action.

September 3, 1999—October 9, 1999—Clemson won 16 straight matches to begin the 1999 season, the longest winning streak to date in history. The Tigers defeated Texas A&M on Sept. 3 and won their next 15 matches before falling to North Carolina on Oct. 9.

September 7, 1999—The Clemson volleyball program recorded its 500th win with a 15-2, 15-9, 15-5 victory over Winthrop at home.

November 13, 1999—Clemson clinched its first ACC regular season title, going 15-1 in conference matches.

November 15, 1999—The Tigers achieved their highest national ranking in program history when they were listed 13th in the AVCA poll.

November 18, 1999—Cindy Stern was selected as the ACC Player of the Year, Clemson's first in history. Jessi Betcher also earned ACC Rookie of the Year honors.

December 2, 1999—The Tigers played host to the first round of the NCAA Tournament. Clemson fell to Indiana in four games, 9-15, 15-11, 5-15, 12-15. The Tigers concluded what was arguably the best season in program history, posting a 31-3 overall record that included four wins over ranked opponents and set the school record with a .912 winning percentage. The team put together 16- and 15-match winning streaks during the year and also claimed Clemson's lone ACC regular season title with a 15-1 record in league matches. The Tigers also earned their first final top-25 ranking in history, finishing 22nd in the AVCA poll.

December 9, 1999—Jolene Jordan Hoover was named the District III Coach of the Year.

December 16, 1999—Cindy Stern was named second team All-America, the first All-America player in ACC history.

August 1, 2002—The ACC announced its 50th Anniversary Volleyball Team, with seven Clemson players making the list—Alison Coday, Heather Kahl, Robin Kibben, Julie Rodriguez, Jodi Steffes, Cindy Stern, and Michelle Thieke.

January 22, 2003—Cindy Stern was named one of 50 ACC 50th Anniversary Top Female Athletes.

September 24, 2004—Tiger volleyball head coach Jolene Jordan Hoover recorded her 100th ACC victory when Clemson defeated NC State, 30-22, 30-17, 30-24.

November 18-20, 2004—Clemson reached the semifinals of the ACC Tournament in thrilling fashion, as the Tigers entered the event as the ninth seed among the 11 teams. Clemson edged Virginia Tech in five sets in the first

round, 30-19, 36-34, 28-30, 28-30, 15-8. The Tigers then upset #1-seeded Georgia Tech, who had gone 16-0 in the ACC regular season, in the second round, 31-29, 27-30, 30-28, 30-25, before falling to North Carolina in the semifinals, 19-30, 29-31, 23-30.

December 15, 2004—Leslie Finn became Clemson's second volleyball All-America player, earning an honorable mention selection.

September 15, 2005—Cindy Stern was inducted into the Clemson Athletic Hall of Fame.

November 29, 2005—Jeannette Abbott became the fifth Tiger volleyball player to be named the ACC Rookie of the Year.

December 13, 2006—Jeannette Abbott and Danielle Hepburn were named honorable mention All-Americas by the American Volleyball Coaches Association. With the honor, the then-sophomores became just the third and fourth players in Tiger history to earn the accolade and gave Clemson multiple honorees for the first-time ever.

February 2, 2007—Danielle Hepburn was named to the CVU.com Stellar Spikers First Team.

September 14, 2007–October 30, 2007—The Tigers won a school record 17 matches in a row, including a program-best 14 consecutive conference contests. The streak

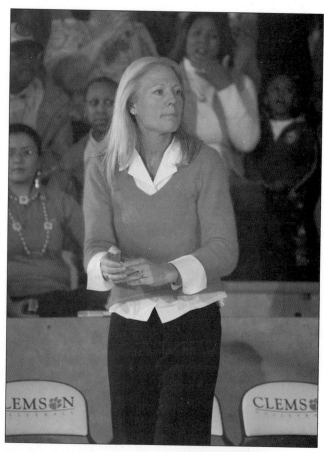

Head Coach Jolene Hoover led the Tigers to eight NCAA appearances.

began with a 3-0 sweep of Kent State in the Clemson Classic and lasted until they suffered a 3-0 loss at Virginia on Nov. 2. The Tigers navigated through the first half of the ACC season with an undefeated record.

October 13, 2007—Clemson upset 13th-ranked Duke in a five-game battle in Durham, NC. It was the highest-ranked opponent that the Tigers had defeated in the history of their program. The victory was also Coach Jolene Jordan Hoover's 300th at the helm of the Tiger program.

November 3, 2007—Jolene Jordan Hoover recorded her 400th collegiate career coaching victory as the Tigers defeated Virginia Tech, 3-1, in Blacksburg, VA.

November 16, 2007—The Tigers clinched their first ACC Championship since 1999 with a 3-0 win over Florida State. Clemson finished the conference season with a 21-1 record to claim the title.

November 27, 2007—Jolene Jordan Hoover was voted as the ACC Coach of the Year for the second time in her career, and a school record six Tigers were named to the all-conference team. Dide Ege, Danielle Hepburn, and Kelsey Murphy were first-team selections, while Jeannette Abbott, Leslie Mansfield, and Meghan Steiner earned second-team honors.

November 30, 2007–December 1, 2007—The Tigers earned a bid to the 2007 NCAA Championships and played host to the first and second rounds. Clemson defeated Alabama by a 3-1 margin in its opening match before falling to eighth-seeded UCLA, 3-1, in the second round.

December 3, 2007—Clemson was ranked 22nd in the final CSTV/AVCA Volleyball poll. It was just the second time in program history that the team was listed in the final rankings.

December 12, 2007—Four Tiger players were named honorable mention AVCA All-America players. Danielle Hepburn became the first player in school history to earn the accolade for multiple seasons, while Didem Ege, Kelsey Murphy, and Meghan Steiner were also honored.

December 2, 2008—Danielle Hepburn was named the ACC Player of the Year, just the second Clemson player to earn the accolade. Kelsey Murphy (1st) and Lia Proctor (2nd) were also named to all-conference teams.

December 5-6, 2008—Clemson played host to NCAA Tournament first and second round action for the second straight year. The Tigers won a five-set thriller over Tennessee to advance to the second round in back-to-back seasons for the first time in program history. Clemson then fell to 12th-seeded Utah.

December 17, 2008—Danielle Hepburn was named to the AVCA All-America third-team.

January 16, 2009—Danielle Hepburn was one of four players nationally recognized as CVU.com honorable mention Blocker of the Year.

February 5, 2009—Danielle Hepburn was named to the CVU.com Stellar Spikers First Team.

December 3, 2009—Kelsey Murphy, Lia Proctor, Didem Ege, and Sandra Adeleye were named All-ACC. Adeleye also joined teammate Alexa Rand in being named to the ACC All-Freshman team.

December 4, 2009—The Tigers played in their third consecutive NCAA Tournament, this time at the University of Kentucky. Clemson lost its first-round matchup to the #17 Oregon Ducks, 3-0.

December 9, 2009—Four Tigers were named to the AVCA all-region team for the East Region. Freshman Sandra Adeleye was named the East Region Freshman of the Year and joined Kelsey Murphy, Lia Proctor, and Didem Ege with all-region honors.

December 7, 2010—Sandra Adaleye was named to the All-ACC team for the second straight season, and Mo Simmons and Hannah Brenner were selected to the All-ACC freshman team.

November 19, 2011—Clemson defeated #22 Miami in five sets in Jervey Gym on senior day.

November 23, 2011—The Tigers' Serenat Yaz, Sandra Adeleye, and Alexa Rand were each voted to the All-ACC team by league coaches.

November 21, 2012—Sandra Adeleye was named first-team All-ACC. Adeleye is the first Clemson volleyball player ever to be named All-ACC for four seasons.

September 6-7, 2013—The Clemson volleyball team defeated Winthrop (25-21, 19-25, 25-22, 25-18) and Furman (23-25, 27-25, 25-17, 25-19) on Saturday to claim the 2013 Big Orange Bash Championship. Senior setter Hannah Brenner was named the Most Valuable Player of the Tournament as the Tigers (4-2) went 3-0, including their 22-25,25-20,25-21,20-25,15-9 win over South Carolina (3-3) on Friday.

December 4, 2013—Senior outside hitter Mo Simmons was named first-team All-ACC and Leah Perri was named to the All-Freshman team. It was the first career honor for both players.

August 29-30, 2014—After dropping a close first set, the Clemson volleyball team fought back and won the next three to defeat Troy 3-1 (24-26, 25-19, 26-24, 25-19) and claim the Big Orange Bash tournament title. Kristin Faust was named MVP of the Tournament. Leah Perry and Karis Watson were also named to the All-Tournament Team.

September 12-13, 2014—The Clemson volleyball team took the Clemson Classic title after winning a battle against Tennessee State in five games (25-15, 23-25, 25-11, 21-25, 15-5) at Jervey Gym. Kate Federico was named MVP of the Tournament. Kristin Faust and Leah Perry were named to the All-Tournament team.

October 17, 2014—The Clemson volleyball team took down Notre Dame 3-0 (25-10, 25-19, 28-26) on Friday night at the Joyce Center on Notre Dame's campus. With the win, the Tigers improved to a 14-5 overall record and 3-3 in the ACC.

The Tigers' win over the Irish was the 800th win in program history,

February 3, 2015—Jolene Jordan Hoover announced her resignation as the head coach of the Clemson volleyball program. Hoover led the Tigers to a 452-259 record in 22 seasons. She is the all-time winningest coach in Clemson volleyball history.

All eight of the Clemson volleyball program's NCAA Tournament appearances were under Hoover's watch. In addition, she coached the Tigers to the program's two ACC Championships, in 1997 and 2007, as well as the ACC regular season title in 1999. During her tenure at Clemson, Hoover coached AVCA All-Americans Cindy Stern and Danielle Hepburn, as well as 17 other Tigers that earned honorable mention All-America honors. She also coached 44 All-ACC performers and 19 ACC All-Freshman Team selections. Stern and Hepburn also earned ACC Player of the Year honors under Hoover,

while Didem Ege was named the conference's Defensive Player of the Year and five Tigers were named ACC Rookie of the Year in her 22 seasons.

March 5, 2015—Hugh Hernesman, who won a conference title and advanced to the NCAA Tournament at Northwestern State in 2014, was named the ninth head coach in Clemson volleyball program history. Hernesman spent the last five seasons at Northwestern State University in Natchitoches, La.

September 11-12, 2015—Clemson recorded its fourth consecutive win, and won the Clemson Classic by defeating USC Upstate in three sets (25-11, 25-21, 25-21). Leah Perri was the MVP of the tournament and was joined by Kate Federico and Kailey Harvell on the All-Tournament Team.

August 26-27, 2016—On the final day of the Big Orange Bash, Clemson defeated High Point and Wofford to win the season opening tournament on its home court in Jervey Gym. The Tigers' Leah Perri, Kailey Harvell and Megan McGinley were the three all-tournament selections with Perri being the MVP.

CLEMSON
Wrestling

The Clemson wrestling program started during the 1975-76 campaign and ended after the 1994-95 season.

During the 20 years as a varsity sport, the program proved to be very successful and produced two national champions.

THE EARLY YEARS

Hewitt Adams was Clemson's first Wrestling coach. He guided the program for two years before Wade Schalles took over before the 1977-78 season. After two sixth-place finishes in the ACC Tournament in the first two years of the program, Schalles led the Tigers to a third-place finish and a 15-3 dual meet record that proved to be the best winning percentage in school history. That season was the first of 17 straight winning seasons for the Tigers.

Schalles came to Clemson after a successful undergraduate career at Clarion State. He was a two-time NCAA Champion and won the gold medal in the 163-pound class at the World Games. He was also named the Outstanding Wrestler at the NCAA Championships on two different occasions. Schalles was also inducted into the National Wrestling Hall of Fame.

At the 1976 Olympics, one month prior to the games, he was favored to win a gold medal but was sidelined with a broken back that occurred during training camp. He was an assistant coach at Arizona State and South Dakota State before coming to Clemson. He set the NCAA record for most wins (153) and most pins (106). Schalles had a career record of 81-27-1 at Clemson in six years of coaching.

Clemson had its first ACC Individual Champions in the 1977-78 season. Larry Cohen won the 118 class, and Rick Drury was the conference's 177 champion. Cohen and Drury were also Clemson's first NCAA meet participants.

In 1979, Noel Loban led the Tigers to a second-place ACC finish in a meet held in Littlejohn Coliseum. He was named the Outstanding Wrestler of the 1979 conference meet.

NOEL LOBAN: 1980 NATIONAL CHAMPION

Noel Loban won the program's first national championship in the 190-pound weight class at the NCAA Championships in 1980. In fact, Loban became the first individual national champion in any sport at Clemson. In 1984, he went on to become Clemson's first alumnus to win an Olympic medal in an individual sport, as he took the bronze medal in the 90Kg class at Los Angeles.

Representing England, Loban defeated Clark Davis of Canada 4-2 to capture the third-place award. Loban set many records at Clemson and had an 86-14 career record.

HEAD COACH EDDIE GRIFFIN LEADS TIGERS

Coach Eddie Griffin arrived in Tigertown for the 1983-84 season and his impact was felt immediately. Despite losing most of the wrestlers who had led Clemson to

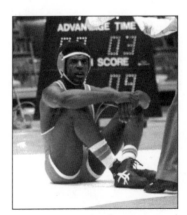

Noel Loban won the National Championship in the 190-pound weight class at the 1980 NCAA Tournament.

a 15-4 record and a NCAA-high 86 pins the previous year, Griffin took Clemson to a second-place ACC finish and a 9-6 dual meet record against one of the toughest schedules in Clemson history.

"Clemson is a great place," said Griffin. It's a great university with a great location and more importantly, it has wonderful people. I remember looking forward to taking the job at Clemson. It was a chance to compete in the ACC and at that time the ACC was very competitive nationally. Clemson was also a good place to raise a family."

Griffin had a unique philosophy of coaching; he used the three R's. "I used to tell my teams over and over, 'Always do the right thing at the right time for the right reasons.' I wanted them to always be on time and do what it takes to be successful."

Included amongst the team's victories during Griffin's inaugural season were triumphs over Oregon State and Brigham Young. In Griffin's first dual match at Clemson, the Beavers came into the Thanksgiving evening match ranked eighth in the nation. By the end of that season, Clemson had sent five wrestlers to the NCAA Tournament, more than any other ACC school that season.

In 1984-85, Griffin led Clemson to a dual meet ranking of number 11 in the nation. This team had a 14-5 ledger and two more Tigers captured ACC titles as Florida native Joey McKenna won his second ACC title and Mark Litts took first-place honors in his weight class.

In 1985-86, the Tigers were ranked 19th in the final dual meet poll and placed 20th at the NCAA meet. McKenna became Clemson's second All-America wrestler with a fourth-place finish at 150 pounds.

The Tigers, hampered with injuries, managed an 8-7 record in 1986-98. Doug Stalnaker won the ACC Championship in the 190-pound classification and represented Clemson, along with heavyweight Brian Raber, at the NCAA meet.

The Tigers finished with an 11-5 mark in the 1987-88 season and sent three wrestlers to the NCAAs. The most successful freshman that year was Donnie Heckel, who captured the ACC crown at 118.

In 1988-89, the Tigers set a school record, placing six wrestlers (Donnie Heckel, Kurt Howell, Mike Bodily, Bill Orr, Kurt Rosenerger, and Bryan Bittle) in the NCAA Tournament. Clemson finished 19-9 overall and 3-2 in the ACC regular season.

The following season in 1989-90, Clemson once again sent six wrestlers to the NCAA meet in College Park, MD. (Donnie Heckel, Kurt Howell, Mike Bodily, Bill Domasky, Dave Miller, and Scott Williams.) Clemson finished the year with a 10-6 record overall, and a 3-2 slate in conference action.

In 1990-91, Clemson's Donnie Heckel was named the 1991 ACC Wrestler of the Year, while Coach Griffin was named the Co-Coach of the Year by the coaches in the Atlantic Coast Conference. It also marked the first time in Clemson wrestling history that the Tigers came away with both awards. Griffin guided the Tigers to a 10-2-1

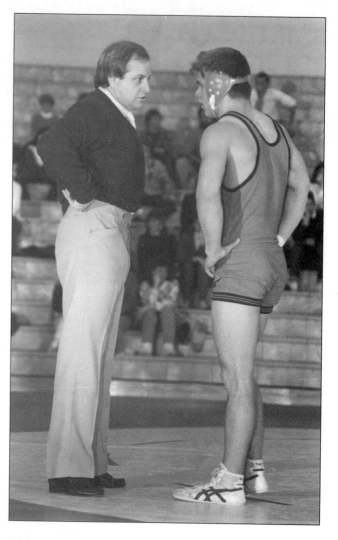

Eddie Griffin led the Tigers to the 1991 ACC regular season championship.

dual meet mark, including a perfect 5-0 mark in the ACC, as Clemson won its first-ever regular season conference title. Kurt Howell (126) and Donnie Heckel (118) came away with All-America honors.

Troy Bouzakis opened the 1991-92 season with a 19-match winning streak. The Tigers finished with a 10-6 record in 1991-92. Mike Miller, John Gardner, Keith Turner, and Scott Williams went to the NCAA meet.

Griffin left Clemson after the 1992 season. He had a record of 101-52-1 during his nine-year tenure.

SAM HENSON WINS TWO NATIONAL CHAMPIONSHIPS

After serving as an assistant coach for one season, Gil Sanchez was named head coach in the summer of 1992. He enjoyed a great season in his first year as the head coach, when the team went 19-9, including a 13th-place finish at the NCAA Tournament. Sam Henson, who captured the 118-pound national championship, led the Tigers. Henson became the first Tiger to go undefeated during a season, with an incredible 34-0 record.

Also during this season, the Tigers had three ACC champions for the first time in the history of the program. Sam Henson won the 118-pound crown, Troy Bouzakis captured the 126-pound title, and Tim Morrissey earned the 177-pound championship. For all three wrestlers, it was their first trip to the ACC Tournament.

In 1993-94, Clemson had its highest finish ever at the 1994 NCAA Tournament, with a seventh-place showing. Henson led the way again, as he won the 118-pound National Championship. For the second year in a row, Henson went undefeated and finished with an impressive 37-0 record. During his two-year Clemson career, he was 71-0. Tim Morrissey also had a strong performance at the NCAAs, earning All-America honors with a third-place finish in the 190-pound weight class. Morrissey had a 31-5 record for the season.

In the second-to-last season of Clemson Wrestling, the Tigers finished second in the 1994 ACC Tournament, with three individual champions—Sam Henson (118), Mike Mammon (150), and Tim Morrissey (190). Following the tournament, Henson was named ACC Wrestler of the Year. Clemson was 14-6 and 3-2 in the ACC that season, for a second-place tie in the ACC standings.

Henson recalls his Clemson career and his second home.

"As soon as I flew in and took my first visit to Clemson, I fell in love with the place," he said. "Clemson had great facilities and the environment was unbelievable! I was a transfer from Missouri and as soon as I saw Clemson, I knew it was the place for me."

As for most memorable experiences, Henson has plenty of them.

"Winning the two national championships was of course the most memorable in my college career. Later on in my career I won the World Title in Iran and was a Silver Medalist in the 2000 Olympics. At the age of 36, I competed at the 2006 World Championships in China and won the bronze medal.

"I had a chance to travel to a lot of places, but I consider Clemson as home. I love the place and it will always mean a lot of me. I'm glad to be a member of the Clemson family."

WRESTLING HISTORY

November 10, 1975—Clemson participated in its first wrestling dual meet. The Tigers lost to Southern Tech 36-10 in Marietta, GA. Chris Carter, a sophomore from Columbia, SC, won at the 167-pound class for the Tigers' first-ever win.

January 23, 1976—Clemson posted its first win in school history as the Tigers defeated the College of Charleston, 30-28, in Charleston, SC.

December 3, 1977—The Tigers won its first wrestling tournament—the Washington and Lee Invitational.

January 21, 1978—Clemson won the Citadel Bulldog Invitational.

March 4-5, 1978—Larry Cohen was the ACC's 118-poundchampion, and Rick Drury was the 177-pound champion at Reynolds Coliseum in Raleigh, NC. On the season, Clemson finished 15-3 in dual meets.

November 10, 1978—Clemson won the Old Dominion Monarch Classic in Norfolk, VA.

December 9, 1978—Clemson won the Tiger Eight-Team Tournament at Clemson, SC.

November 10, 1978—Clemson finished first in the Monarch Classic in Norfolk, VA.

December 9, 1978—The Tigers won the Tiger Eight-Team Tournament.

January 13, 1979—Clemson began a nine-match winning streak that lasted until February 14, 1979. The streak included wins over Georgia, Virginia, and Kentucky.

February 23, 1979—Clemson finished second in the ACC Tournament at Littlejohn Coliseum in Clemson, SC. ACC champions that year included Noel Loban at the 177-pound class and Alan Tanner at heavyweight.

February 29-March 1, 1980—The Tigers' Noel Loban won the 190 weight class, and teammate Bob Isola won the heavyweight division at the ACC Championships at Cameron Indoor Stadium in Durham, NC. Loban was named an All-America wrestler.

March 15, 1980—Noel Loban won the 190-pound weight class at the 50th Annual NCAA Championships in Corvallis, Oregon. Loban defeated Dan Severn of Arizona State in overtime. Clemson finished 14th nationally in the NCAA Tournament as a team.

December 6, 1980—The Tigers won the Tiger Eight-Team.

March 12-14, 1981—The Tigers tied for 58th at the NCAA Tournament at Jadwin Gymnasium on the campus of Princeton University. John Warlick was the Tigers' lone representative, competing in the 126 class.

December 5, 1981—Clemson won the Tiger Eight-Team Tournament.

February 19, 1982—Clemson won their 18th match of the season, a 25-16 victory over Appalachian State in Boone, NC. Clemson finished the season with an 18-6 record overall; the 18 wins were the most in a single season by a Tiger Wrestling team.

February 27-28, 1982—Todd Steer won the ACC Championship at the 118 class. He was also named ACC Wrestler of the Year at Carmichael Auditorium in Chapel Hill, NC.

March 11-13, 1982—Clemson finished 46th in the NCAA Tournament at Hilton Coliseum on the Iowa State campus in Ames, IA.

November 12, 1982—Clemson won the Monarch Open in Norfolk, VA.

December 4, 1982—The Tigers won the Tiger Eight-Team Tournament in Clemson, SC.

1983—Clemson finished 15-4 and led the NCAA with 86 pins. Joey McKenna won the 150-pound weight class, and Gary Nivens won the 177-pound division at the ACC Championships.

March 10-12, 1983—Clemson was 41st at the NCAA Championships at the Myriad Convention Center in Oklahoma City, OK.

July 5, 1983—Clemson named Eddie Griffin as head coach of the Tigers.

November 24, 1983—Clemson upset #8 Oregon State, 23-18, on Thanksgiving Day. This was the first dual match for new coach Eddie Griffin.

February 25, 1984—Clemson finished second in the ACC Tournament in Clemson, SC. Jody Taylor won the conference's 134-pound class.

March 9-11, 1984—Clemson finished in a tie for 52nd place at the NCAA Championships at the Meadowlands Arena in East Rutherford, NJ.

August 9, 1984—Noel Loban won the Bronze Medal representing England in the 1984 Olympic Games. Loban defeated Clarke Davis of Canada, 4-2, to capture the third-place award.

March 1-2, 1985—Clemson achieved a ranking of number 11 nationally during the season. The 1985 team finished with a 14-5 record overall. Clemson's Mark Litts won the conference championship at 158, and Joey McKenna was the conference title in the 142-pound class.

March 14-16, 1985—Clemson was 41st at the NCAA Championships at the Myriad Convention Center in Oklahoma City, OK.

December 30, 1985—Clemson finished first in the Sunshine Open in Orlando, FL.

February 28-March 1, 1986—Joey McKenna won the conference championship at the 150-pound class. He was the only Tiger to win three conference championships.

March 13-15, 1986—The Tigers were ranked 19th in the final dual meet poll and placed 20th in the NCAA meet in Iowa City, IA. McKenna became Clemson's second All-America wrestler with a fourth-place finish in the 150 class.

March 6-7, 1987—Brian Stalnaker won the ACC's 190-pound title at Cameron Indoor Stadium in Durham, NC.

March 4-5, 1988—Donnie Heckel won the 118-pound class and Jim Meetze won the 167-pound title at the ACC Championships at Memorial Gym on the University of Virginia campus in Charlottesville, VA.

March 17, 1988—Clemson finished tied for 46th in the NCAA Tournament at Ames, IA.

March 16-18, 1989—Clemson set a school record, placing six wrestlers—Donnie Heckel, Kurt Howell, Mike Bodily, Bill Orr, Kurt Rosenberger, and Bryan Bittle—in the NCAA Tournament. The Tigers finished 30th in the NCAA Tournament in Oklahoma City, OK. Donnie Heckel was named an All-America wrestler, reaching the final eight in the 118-pound class.

1990—Kurt Howell won the ACC Championship at 126, and Bill Domasky won the league title in the 142-pound class.

March 22-24, 1990—Clemson sent another six wrestlers to the NCAA meet as Donnie Heckel, Kurt Howell, Mike Bodily, Bill Domasky, Dave Miller, and Scott Williams all qualified. Clemson finished 29th nationally at the NCAA Tournament in College Park, MD.

March 1-2, 1991—Donnie Heckel, the conference's 118-pound champion, was named the 1991 ACC Wrestler of the Year, and Eddie Griffin was named the Co-Coach of the Year by the coaches in the ACC. The Tigers finished

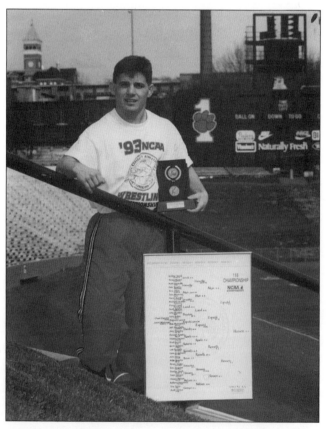

Sam Henson finished his two-year career at Clemson with a 71-0 record.

10-2-1 overall and had a perfect 5-0 mark in winning the ACC regular season conference title.

March 15, 1991—Clemson finished 27th nationally at the NCAA Tournament. Donnie Heckel (118) and Kurt Howell (126) were both named All-America wrestlers.

1991-92—Tory Bouzakis opened the 1991-92 season with a 19-match winning streak.

February 22, 1992—Head Coach Eddie Griffin won his 100th match at Clemson with a 28-9 victory over ACC foe Virginia. Griffin ended his Clemson career with a 101-52-1 record.

March 6-7, 1992—Mike Miller was the conference champion in the 158-pound class, and Scott Williams won the 190-pound class at the ACC Championship.

March 18-20, 1992—The Tigers finished 52nd at the NCAA Meet in Norman, OK. Clemson, however,finished 23rd in the final *Amateur Wrestling News* dual match poll.

1992, Summer—Gil Sanchez was named head coach of the Tigers.

March 5-6, 1993—For the first time ever, Clemson had three conference champions in the same season.Sam Henson (118), Troy Bouzakis (126) and Tim Morrissey (177) all won their respective weight classifications.

March 18-20, 1993—Clemson finished in 13th place at the NCAA Tournamentin Ames, Iowa. Sam Henson captured the 118-pound national championship. He was undefeated with a 34-0 record during for the season. Henson was named an All-America wrestler.

March 4-5, 1994—Clemson finished second at the ACC Championships at University Hall, in Charlottesville, VA. Sam Henson (118), Mike Mammon (150), and Tim Morrissey (190) were ACC Champions. Henson was named ACC Wrestler of the year.

March 17-19, 1994—Henson captured the 118-pound weight class ational Championship for the second year in a row. The Tigers finished seventh as a team at the NCAA Championships and Henson was named an All-America wrestler. Henson was 37-0 during the 1994 season and finished his career with a 71-0 record. Tim Morrissey also received All-America accolades.

February 18, 1995—Clemson wrestled its last dual matches in history as Virginia defeated Clemson 26-11 in ACC action. Later in the day, VMI defeated the Tigers 24-12. Matt Kim won the last bout at heavyweight for the Tigers against both Virginia and VMI.

March 16-18, 1995—Clemson finished tied for 59th at the NCAA Championships in Iowa City, IA.

PART II

ADDITIONAL CLEMSON ATHLETIC STORIES

TRADITIONS, LEGENDS, AND
Special Places

SPECIAL PLACES

Howard's Rock

An iconic symbol of Memorial Stadium is Howard's Rock, a rock from Death Valley, CA that had been a gift from S.C. Jones to Coach Frank Howard. The 20-pound rock was mounted on a pedestal at the top of the Hill on the east side of the stadium. According to legend, it gives Clemson players mythical powers prior to its contest with the day's opposition.

Before each game, Clemson players run down the hill and rub this rock at the top of the hill before making the perilous trip to the stadium floor. The tradition began in 1966 when Clemson alum Samuel C. Jones, Sr., a 1919 Clemson grad, picked up the rock in Death Valley, CA. Since Clemson's football stadium is known as Death Valley, he felt his alma mater should have something in its stadium from the other "Death Valley."

He brought the rock back to football coach Frank Howard and it sat in the Clemson mentor's office for a few months. Finally, Howard asked Executive Secretary Gene Willimon to do something with the rock that was sitting in his office. Willimon went overboard, and thank goodness that he did!

Howard's Rock first made its appearance in Death Valley in 1966.

He brought the rock to the stadium, had it mounted, and affixed a plaque to it. It was unveiled on September 24, 1966, the Saturday when Clemson played Virginia. The Tigers were down 18 points with 17 minutes left and came back to win 40-35 on a 75-yard pass from Jimmy Addison to Jacky Jackson in the fourth quarter. What a debut for the Rock! Addison was named National Player of the Week.

The team members started rubbing the Rock prior to running down the hill on September 23, 1967, a day when Clemson defeated Wake Forest by a score of 23-6. Prior to running down the Hill that day, Howard told his players, "If you're going to give me 110 percent, you can rub that Rock. If you're not, keep your filthy hands off it." And another nationally known tradition was born at Clemson.

Running down the hill

Touching Howard's Rock is just part of Clemson's celebrated stadium entrance.

Described as "the most exciting 25 seconds in college football," it is easily one of the most unique, original, and indescribable arrival of a team to its sideline. The ritual awakens the home crowd and puts fear and awe in the opponents as everyone stares at the top of the hill. It's a common bond of excitement that is shared by Clemson faithful, from the youngest children to the oldest of alumni in attendance—the Tigers are here!

After Clemson's last warm-up, the team retreats to the home dressing room under the West Stands. At about 12:50 p.m. (for a normal 1:00 p.m. game), the team boards charter buses and makes a 90-second drive around the periphery of the stadium to the east side of the field. After everyone is collected at the top of the hill, the cannon sounds, "Tiger Rag" is played, and Clemson charges down the hill and onto the field.

The tradition started innocently enough; it was the quickest way to the stadium from the dressing room when Death Valley was built. When the stadium was constructed in 1942, the locker rooms were in Fike Field House, an athletic facility just up the road. The team used to walk down the street to the hill.

Clemson Football Players Running Down the Hill—This was a tradition started in 1942 when the Tigers used to dress in Fike Field House. The shortest distance to the field was coming down the hill.

When the team reached the top of the hill, the cadets (Clemson was a military school until 1955) formed a tunnel for the team to run through and the crowd really got into it. The tradition continued even when the new locker rooms were built and thus the necessity for the buses.

"Believe me, by the time you get to the bottom of that hill you are ready to play!" said former All-America player and 1981 captain Jeff Davis.

The hill, where the Tigers run down, is covered with a 40-yard rug that the Tigers use to run on when they make their entrance. It is not an easy task, as the first 25 yards of the journey are at a 45-degree angle. It levels off for about 10 yards, and then returns to a 40-degree slope.

The origin of the name "Death Valley" at Clemson

Running down the hill, and touching Howard's Rock are stalwart traditions that allow Clemson to be unique in the college football world.

Another original, but imitated lore, is the nickname of Memorial Stadium, "Death Valley." This nickname has been proven to have origins at Clemson just after World War II before the stadium was even five years old in the mid 1940s, many years before LSU claimed to have used the moniker.

The origin of the name Death Valley originated in the 1940s and it stemmed from the Clemson-Presbyterian College series. For 28 years (1930-1958), Clemson opened the season with the Blue Hose. All of these games were played in Clemson but one, and ironically it was in Coach Howard's first season as head coach of the Tigers (1940). In 1943, with many college players away in World War II, there was naturally a scarcity of players. Many who played in 1943 were freshmen and in that season, Presbyterian surprised the Tigers with a 13-12 victory over Clemson in Tigertown.

In 1944, the Tigers had revenge over the Blue Hose and won 34-0, and in 1945 the Tigers must have still been angry about losing in 1943, and defeated Presbyterian 76-0.

In the spring of 1946, and in the preseason practices before the season began, Presbyterian was preparing to play the Tigers. According to former Presbyterian player and later coach, Cally Gault, the trip to Clemson was very special.

"We talked about the upcoming Clemson game quite often when I was a player as it was a tradition to open the season with them," said Gault.

"After we were beaten so badly in 1945, Presbyterian Coach Lonnie McMillian and us players referred to the Clemson trip as going 'to Death Valley'," recalled Gault. I'm not sure when the press picked up on it, but I'm sure it was real soon.

"I remember both the 1945 and 1946 PC-Clemson games. I was 16 years old as a freshman, and playing in Death Valley was special. I do remember this more than anything—it was hot, and I mean real hot at Clemson! You haven't felt hot until you played in Death Valley in early September!

"Coach Howard picked up on the new nickname of his stadium and he started using it in the media and it became really popular when he started using it," added Gault. Also McMillan used the now famous term in the media to describe the newly built stadium.

To say that Death Valley hasn't been good to the Clemson football fortunes is an understatement. Clemson has won over 72% of its games in one of the epitaphs of college football.

Memorial Stadium

When the stadium was first laid out, a site on the western part of the campus was selected. It was in a natural valley, just perfect for a stadium. Because of the era in which it was built, and with the shortage of material such as iron, the stadium was built out of concrete.

It was announced on September 17, 1941 that the $104,000 stadium construction would soon begin. Clemson civil engineering students surveyed the land and drew up plans for the grandstands, which were built in concrete along the red clay walls of the natural bowl. Credit for the design of the stadium goes to Carl Lee of Charlotte, NC, a Clemson graduate of 1908, and Professor H.E Glenn of the Clemson engineering faculty.

Actual construction began on October 6, 1941. Scholarship athletes, including many football players, did much of the hard work. Two members of the football team, A.N. Cameron and Hugh Webb, did the first staking out of the stadium. Webb returned to Clemson years later to be an architecture professor, and Cameron went on to become a civil engineer in Louisiana.

The crews went to work: clearing, cutting, pouring, and forming. Finally, on September 19, 1942, Clemson Memorial Stadium opened with the Tiger Football team thrashing Presbyterian College, 32-13.Those 20,000 seats installed for Opening Day would grow, and grow, and grow to the 80,000-plus seats that fans use and enjoy today.

Memorial Stadium opened in the 1942 season.

Clemson's legendary coach Frank Howard said that on the day of the first game in the new stadium, "the gates were hung at 1:00 p.m. and we played at 2:00 p.m."

Clemson is lucky to have such a shrine as Memorial Stadium grace its campus. Although named Memorial Stadium to honor those Clemson students who have lost their lives in the nation's wars, the nickname Death Valley is a helpful reminder and serves as a warning to the Tigers' opponents that it's a difficult place to play.

Bowman Field

Also known as the front lawn of Clemson University, the first field for the early football, baseball, track, and even basketball teams was named in honor of Randolph T. V. Bowman (August 1, 1875—April 14, 1899). He was an instructor in forge and foundry at Clemson from February 1895 to April 1899, just after the college opened in 1889. Bowman was best known for his association with college athletics, serving as the first baseball coach and one of the first assistant football coaches. He coached the very first intercollegiate contest played at Clemson, a baseball game with Furman University on April 24, 1896, which the Tigers lost 13–20.

Bowman was credited with clearing parts of the area in front of the "Main Building" (Tillman Hall) and making it suitable to play baseball and other sports. Bowman, who served as the first baseball coach, died at the young age of 23 in 1899. It was decided shortly after his death to name the area in front of Tillman Hall Bowman Field in 1899. In a resolution, signed by Walter Merritt Riggs, Shack Shealy, and J. F. Sullivan dated April 20, 1899, representing the Football Association of Clemson College, it petitioned the President of Clemson College Henry Hartzog to bestow, officially upon the new drill and athletic field, the name of Bowman Field. Apparently he agreed, and it has been known as Bowman Field ever since.

Historic Riggs Field

With the overuse of Bowman Field and the need for a seated stadium, Clemson embarked on building its first athletic facility—Riggs Field.

Perhaps one of the first big "stepping stones" in helping make Clemson successful in athletics today was the construction of Riggs Field. Named after one of the most beloved leaders of the early years at Clemson. Riggs Field is one of the oldest continuously used Athletics Field on a college campus.

What made Riggs Field so significant to the school at the time it was first built in 1915? It was the first major facility on the campus dedicated to intercollegiate athletics.

Riggs Field gave the football team a place to play and practice on its adjunct fields. The baseball field was constructed where the tennis courts are now and the track encircled the football field.

Construction of Riggs Field started in the early summer of 1914. Approximately $10,000 was appropriated for the construction of the facility, which covered almost nine acres. Before its completion, the Clemson Board of Trustees unanimously agreed to name the new athletic complex Riggs Field in honor of Clemson's first football coach and originator of the Clemson Athletic Association, Dr. Walter M. Riggs.

Riggs was the first football coach at Clemson in 1896. He stepped down as head coach in 1897 to devote full time to academics, as he was an engineering professor. He also coached the team in 1899 because the athletic association was low on funds. However, in 1900, the search for a new coach must have been serious, as Riggs hired John Heisman to coach the Tigers. Although no longer the head coach, Clemson athletics and Riggs could not be split. Although not given the title, Riggs also was the equivalent of an athletic director, managing the money and making contracts with other teams. The well-respected Riggs also held many positions over the years in the Southern Intercollegiate Athletic Association (SIAA), an early conference preceding the Southern Conference. Riggs later became president of Clemson on March 7, 1911. He served in this capacity until his death in 1924.

Riggs Field was dedicated in grand fashion on October 6, 1915. The band, corps of cadets, along with faculty and alumni, marched from Tillman Hall to the new field. According to *The Tiger*, the group formed a "C" formation on the field and poured forth a thrilling volume of patriotic Tiger yells and songs. Professor J.W. Gantt, President of the Athletic Association, introduced Dr. Riggs as "the man who has done more for the athletics at Clemson and probably more for southern athletics than any other man."

In presenting the field to the corps of cadets, Dr. Riggs said, "This magnificent field is a token of recognition by the Trustees of Clemson College of the importance of military and athletic training for the cadets. It is to be a place for the teaching of the principles of teamwork and fair play. This large and beautiful athletic field is to stand for the development of the physical man and whether in real work or in play, it is hoped that this field will be used as an agency in the development of high and honorable men. Whether victorious or defeated, may the men of this field always be gentlemen of the highest type." A few minutes later, Dr. Riggs made the initial kickoff in the first football game played on the new field. While on the field, he wore a new orange and blue sweater he had just received from Auburn, his alma mater, as they too wanted to congratulate Clemson and Dr. Riggs for their accomplishments. Clemson and Davidson played to a 6-6 tie that day.

Clemson' football teams compiled a 57-16-6 record during their 27 years at Riggs Field. The baseball team won over 70 percent of its games there when the diamond was part of the complex. Riggs Field today is considered to be one of the top, if not the top, soccer facility in the nation. Clemson started playing soccer at Riggs in 1980. The 1987 NCAA Men's Soccer Final Four was contested there and Clemson won the National Championship before a record crowd of 8,332. As one looks from Historic Riggs Field and sees the grand clock tower of Tillman Hall guarding that part of campus, it is only appropriate that these two symbols of the university are so close in proximity, as both have played such a significant role in Clemson history.

The original configuration of the track and former football stadium and bleachers, were featured in many scenes in the 1974 Burt Lancaster movie *The Midnight Man*, filmed in part at Clemson University in 1973.

Historic Riggs Field is the fifth-oldest continuously used college athletic facility in the nation.

Holtzendorff YMCA

This building overlooking Historic Riggs Field was built in 1915 with a gift from the Rockefeller Foundation. It was built for a total of $75,000. This housed the Clemson Swimming teams that started competing in 1919 and the men's basketball team from the 1916 to the 1922 season. In 1922, a building was built south of Riggs Field where the Fraternity Quad is located today. This building was built by the Clemson students and was home to the men's basketball teams during the 1922 through the 1929 seasons.

On February 1, 1916, Clemson began playing its games in the newly completed YMCA. Clemson played its first game at the YMCA (currently the Holtzendorff YMCA Building) a 39-39 tie to Presbyterian on February 1. Before this time, the Tigers played on Riggs Field or in the basement of Sikes Hall.

Clemson lost to Georgia 24-16 in the first game of a new basketball arena in 1922. During the fall of 1921, the Clemson student body had helped level the ground for the new facility. The building provided Clemson a larger regulation indoor basketball court.

It was named for Preston B. Holtzendorff, the school's first swimming coach who started the program in 1919. He also was the school's first tennis coach in 1927. He died on January 28, 1971.

Fike Field House

Josh Cody was the head coach of both the football and basketball teams in 1927-31, the last coach in Clemson history to coach the two revenue-producing sports. Cody, along with Athletic Director Mutt Gee, were instrumental in the building of the Clemson Field House (Fike), which gave Clemson a state of the art basketball arena during that day.

The gymnasium was built at a cost of $60,000 and was the first stage of Fike Field House to be built. The rest of Fike was built from the receipts of the 1940 Cotton Bowl, the first national bowl game that a Clemson football team attended.

On January 7, 1930, in the dedication game, Furman defeated Clemson 34-28 in the first game played at Fike Field House. It also gave other sports a place to practice in inclement weather, such as track, baseball, and football.

The Clemson Board of Trustees renamed Clemson Field House to Fike Field House on November 25, 1966, in honor of Rube Fike, who was instrumental in starting IPTAY.

The last basketball game played at Fike Field House was February 28, 1968. Fike Field House is now used for intramurals.

Perhaps one of the most difficult places for an opposing team to play a college basketball game during the 1930-1960 era was in Clemson's Fike Field House, located northeast of Memorial Stadium.

Fike Field House was the "crown jewel" in Clemson's campaign to improve its intercollegiate athletic facilities in the earlier years. After Riggs Field was dedicated on October 6, 1915, attention was turned to a new field house and basketball arena.

The Tigers needed a place to dress and train indoors during inclement weather and more than anything a better basketball arena was needed. However, it would be some time before the first ball was shot in the building. A lot of this was due to the poor economic conditions at the time.

Ultimately, the day came for play to take place in the new arena. Furman defeated Clemson 34-28, on January 7, 1930 in the dedication game of Clemson's new field house. A dream had come true with the opening of the new facility.

"It was a "pleasing building of multi-colored brick which made it more attractive to an onlooker's aesthetic sense," according to the 1930 Clemson University yearbook, Taps. But to opponents it was feared and a place where they did not want to play—a real home court advantage for the Tigers.

On April 11, 1941, Clemson dedicated the front segment of Fike Field House. The $75,000 unit housed Athletic Offices, dressing rooms, 23 dormitory rooms and a memorial hall. This wing is the front entrance that is used today in the newly refurbished recreation center.

This facility is where the football players dressed before football games, practices, etc., and it was necessary that the Tigers use the hill to enter Memorial Stadium, simply because it was the shortest route to the south sidelines. Thus the famous "running down the hill" was born. The Tiger football team once practiced on the large field behind the north stands that is used for intramural activities today. Fike became the hub of the Clemson Athletic Department.

This front segment of Fike was built with monies received from the Tigers 6-3 win over Boston College in the 1940 Cotton Bowl Classic in Dallas, TX.

"There wasn't any place I dreaded playing more than at Fike Field House at Clemson said Former Wake Forest Head Coach Horace "Bones" McKinney in an earlier interview. "You could never run away from the crowd there," he added.

"In some places you could get way ahead and put the crowd to sleep. Never in Fike, though, no matter how far down Clemson was, all they had to do was make a couple of quick baskets and the whole place would start shaking again."

Another characteristic of the building that everyone who ever played or coached in Fike recalled would be the darkness. "The bricks were dark, the wood floor was dark, the lights were poor," McFadden said.

"That place was so dark," said McKinney. "The referees had to come in wearing coal miners' helmets. It was dark brown everywhere, and when they started playing things were pitch black. People's feet were the out-of-bounds marks and they'd sit there and pluck the hair on our players' legs when they tried to throw the ball in."

The thing opponents remembered the most about Fike was what Former Clemson football and basketball All-American and former Clemson Head Basketball Coach Banks McFadden called "the biggest advantage—the crowd."

"There wasn't anything else-for the students to do," McFadden remembered. 'There weren't so many cars, and a lot of the underclassmen had to stay on campus anyway. So they came to the game. We had seats for the students and faculty and a few people from Greenville or Anderson. "Nobody drove down from Charlotte or up from Atlanta like they do today. Even if they did, we didn't have anywhere to put them.

There just wasn't enough room. We could put 4,000 or so people in there, including some who had to sit around a live steam pipe that ran around the top of the seats. And the team had to sit on the first row of bleachers."

"That place earned every name that it was called," McKinney said. "It was called the Snake Pit, the Sweat Box, the Cow Palace, and it could be a real hell-hole. There was nothing but dark, and all you could hear was the crowd roaring —louder and louder.

"I'd call a timeout to change strategy, and there'd be 30-40 young men looking over my shoulder as I wrote on the sideline in chalk. They kept hollering, 'No, Bones, that'll never work', 'You better get back on the bus', 'That plan wouldn't win in Peewee League', things like that. They wouldn't stop!"

"It was a different time back then," McFadden said. "The game and conditions have improved 20, 30, maybe 10,000 times since then. But relations were different then, too. It's a pleasant time to look back on."

It's not fun to look back on if you were the visiting team in Fike.

"There was one Clemson-Wake Forest game at Clemson," McKinney recalled. "I had just finished having a heated discussion with the referees and was heading back to the bench. Out of the corner of my eye I saw this thing sailing toward me. I spun around and caught this chunk of ice. It must have been bigger than three baseballs wide.

"I yelled, what idiot threw this thing? And this huge, I'm talking like 300-pounds huge –Clemson football player stood up and said, 'I did.' "I just grinned and said, how do you like the game so far?"

"Banks, when he was coaching at Clemson, would either have some of his football players or the band sitting behind my bench," said McKinney. "I can still see a big tuba right behind me blasting out Tiger Rag several times during a game. I got real familiar with that fight song, Tiger Rag."

Fike served Clemson as the campus gymnasium, dance hall, and boxing ring. Since the 1975-76 season, the Clemson men's and women's varsity swim teams staged their meets in the McHugh Natatorium until the programs were dropped in 2012. On December 4, 1975, the first swimming meet was held at Fike as the Tigers defeated Furman 72-41. The women's diving team used the facility for home meets and practice.

Boxing was a varsity sport at Clemson in 1928 through the 1948 seasons. There were many nights when there was a basketball-boxing double header. They would play the basketball game first and then would start the boxing afterward. Crowds would cram into Fike Field House and have an exciting Saturday night.

Clemson spent 39 basketball seasons at Fike and finished with 200 victories in the building. The boxing team had an incredible record of 33-4-4 in the building for a .854 winning percentage during its years of existence (1928-1948).

It's only appropriate that Fike Field House and Recreation Center is still serving Clemson University and its family. Very similar to Historic Riggs Field, it's a cornerstone in Clemson's athletic history.

Many strange stories have formed from the days of Fike Field House (1929-1968) that bare repeating.

Clemson and Florida State Head Coaches Sit at Midcourt During the Game

In the January 8, 1962 Clemson-Florida State basketball game, the two head coaches did not sit with their respective teams, they sat at mid court together.

They were best of friends. The night before the game long time Clemson Sports Information Director Bob Bradley and his wife Louise had Clemson's Head Coach Press Mavarich and the Seminole Head Coach Bud Kennedy over at their house for dinner.

It wasn't uncommon for the Bradleys to have the home and visiting basketball coaches over for dinner at their house the night before and the evening after the basketball game for meals. Sometimes the referees would be guests of the Bradleys and enjoyed their hospitality.

On this particular night, Mavarich and Kennedy decided they would sit together at center court at the basketball game the following night.

When a time out was called, each coach would go to his bench, hand out some coaching talk, and then back to center court they would go. They sat together side-by-side the entire game. The coaches were asked what they talked about during the game and one of them said, "Your man walked, but they didn't call it," or "He's over my guy's back, I didn't think they were going to call it." "That was a bad call," or "You got by with one then," and so forth.

Clemson won the game, 75-69 with Jim Brennan leading the way with 26 points.

Noise Was Deafening

Fike Field House was known not only as a loud place but a very loud place! The place was packed and the noise would reverberate throughout the building. Bill Currie was the voice of the North Carolina Tar Heels before Woody Durham and he would always come prepared.

Currie was well aware of the noise at Fike Field House, so when he would broadcast a game at Clemson, he would bring a large drink cup with him. He would jam a hole in the bottom of the cup and stick his microphone up through it, and he would talk in the cup. The reason he would do this is so the radio audience could hear him better over the crowd noise.

Dark Arena

Fike was also known as a dark arena that was in need of more light fixtures. The walls were dark, the floor was dark, but it made for an intimate setting for the home team.

Joe Belmont a player at Duke (1953-56) came into Fike Field House at Clemson during warm-ups wearing a miner's helmet with the lamp lit.

One opposing coach even said "that they should have played the game outside in the parking lot if it wasn't so cold. There would be more light under the street lamps than in Fike."

Last Season at Fike

Vic Bubas, a former head coach at Duke, brought his Blue Devils into Fike during the 1967-68 season, the last year in Fike. Bubas said that when the game was over, he was going to come out and kiss the Tiger that was painted on the floor at midcourt goodbye.

True to his word, after he talked to his team and the media after the game, Bubas got down on his all fours and kissed the Tiger.

Television Camera in the Locker Room

One of the earliest telecast games in the ACC came out of Clemson in January of 1958 against The Citadel. Press Maravich was the Tigers' coach.

Just like today, television producers were looking for innovative things, a lot of them being trial and error. One of the things they wanted to do at this particular game was to come into the Clemson dressing room live at half-time and Maravich agreed.

The Tigers led 28-21 at the half. Bob Blackledge, center for the Cadets, was not a factor in the first 20 minutes and Press Maravich told his team while the television camera was on was for his team not to worry about Blackledge. "He's playing outside and he doesn't like to go to the basket." He only had two points at the half and had two fouls.

Coach Maravich always thought that the Bulldogs must had a television or a monitor in their locker room and heard his halftime talk, because Blackledge came out and lit up the scoreboard. He scored 13 of his 15 points in the second half by driving to the basket and The Citadel won the game, 60-57. Needless to say, live television cameras never got close to the Clemson dressing room again as long as Maravich was around.

Dr. Rube Fike

The Clemson Board of Trustees renamed Clemson Field House to Fike Field House on November 25, 1966 in honor of Rube Fike, who was instrumental in starting IPTAY. Fike was a cancer doctor in Atlanta and was a physician to the famous and prize-winning author Margaret Mitchell. He once did not cash a check she had written to him and she was angered. He instead wanted to keep it as a souvenir of her signature. Fike was a 1908 graduate of Clemson and was from Spartanburg, SC.

Other Events at Fike Field House

Many dances and other social events were held at Fike Field House. It was the home of the Clemson Boxing team when it was a varsity sport. Clemson spent 39 basketball seasons at Fike and finished with 200 victories in the building. The boxing team had an incredible record of 33-4-4 in the building for a .854 winning percentage during its years of existence (1928-1948).

Many celebrities and entertainers in their day made appearances at Fike Field House. Probably the most well-known international celebrity to appear at Fike was Evangelist Billy Graham who spoke to the Clemson Cadets on March 21, 1950.

Fike Field House was well-known in its day, and served the university well as Clemson's home basketball and boxing arena and center for Clemson's social events. Today it's still a big part of Clemson as it's the home and the hub of the Clemson Intramural Department.

CLEMSON SCHOOL SPIRIT AND TRADITIONS

Tigerama

The Friday night before Homecoming, an event that is a combination of a pep rally, fireworks display, and skit presentations comprise Tigerama.

Tigerama began in 1956 and was the brain-child of the late Joe Sherman. Sherman, a 1934 graduate of Clemson, started the Clemson News Bureau, the Clemson Communications Center, and the Sports Information Department.

The first Tigerama was planned for the amphitheater, but this never came off because of heavy rains the afternoon and night of its introduction to the fans.

The first Tigerama was held in the ballroom of the Clemson House, with 200 people in attendance.

Homecoming Displays

Every Football Homecoming, there are architectural wonders on Bowman Field. Every year the Clemson fraternities play one-upmanship with the construction of Homecoming floats and displays. There is a central theme surrounding the Tigers and their opponent on Homecoming Saturdays, and innovative displays that take months of planning. It's unlike anything anywhere else in the country.

First Friday Parade

Clemson fans celebrate the first home football game with the First Friday Parade. Fraternities and sororities march along with the Clemson band, cheerleaders, and dignitaries the Friday evening before the first home game. The parade goes down Old Greenville Highway, so it can be enjoyed by everyone on campus and in town.

Senior Platoon

The Senior Platoon was one of the most renowned groups representing Clemson University when the college was a military school. The Senior Platoon gained favorable publicity for Clemson with its precision routine

The Senior Platoon was a precision routine drill team that represented Clemson at pro football games, parades, and other important events. This picture was taken at Boston's Fenway Park.

during its existence in 1930-60. Each year in the spring, approximately 100-150 Clemson cadets would try out for the prestigious drill team. After several weeks of training and initiations, the group was narrowed to 50.

The Senior Platoon practiced for weeks during every spare hour to prepare for their busy schedule of halftime performances not only at Clemson football games (home and away), but at professional football games, Christmas Parades, bowl games, and even the Mardi Gras. Some noteworthy appearances included Yankee Stadium and Fenway Park for halftime performances at professional and collegiate football games.

The fast-stepping (double cadence) drill unit performed intricate maneuvers during its routine and always ended its show with the Queen Ann salute. Part of the routine included the drill team shouting "Beat Car-o-lina, Beat Car-o-lina," encouraging the athletic teams to defeat rival South Carolina in the various athletic contests.

The Senior Platoon was formed in 1929. F.B. "Gator" Farr '30 and his brother, who was a student at The Citadel, would get in discussions as to which school was better. The Citadel had a drill team that traditionally won the summer ROTC drill competition. They decided that the only way to settle the argument was for Clemson to have a drill team and enter the completion. Farr went back to Clemson and organized a drill platoon to enter the competition at the ROTC summer encampment in 1929. Clemson won the competition.

The drill platoon continued and was call "The Fancy Drill Platoon," or Junior Platoon. In 1934, the name was changed to The Senior Platoon, as its members were all seniors or rising seniors.

The group was well known up and down the east coast and represented Clemson with class and dignity.

Clemson Becomes Large City on Football Saturdays

The city of Clemson has a population of about 11,000 fulltime residents. But, on Saturday afternoons in the fall, when over 80,000 fans are in the stands, that population increases significantly. In fact, Clemson moves all the way to the fourth-largest city in the state on home football Saturdays, when over 80,000 fans are in the stands.

Tiger Mascot

Since 1954, a Clemson student has adorned the mascot suit to entertain the Clemson faithful. Joined in 1993 by the Tiger Cub, these furry creatures can be seen wandering through the crowds, signing autographs, having their pictures taken with dignitaries like Presidents Ronald Reagan and George W. Bush, shooting the cannon, or doing pushups each time Clemson scores.

Nickname

The derivation of Clemson's nickname goes back to the turn of the century. In those days, many of the players wore long hair due to lack of helmet strength for more head protection. These long manes might have gained Clemson the name "Lions" had it not been for the orange and purple striped jerseys and stockings the players wore. The stripes resembled Tigers. John Heisman's 1900 team was called the Tigers, and Clemson used an insignia of a Tiger's head with bared fangs with the motto "Eat 'Em Up Clemson."

It also has been proposed that the football players wanted to pay tribute to Walter Merritt Riggs by calling the athletic teams Tigers just like his alma mater Auburn.

Still another theory came from the president of Clemson, Dr. Sikes. He addressed the cadets in 1928 and said Thomas G. Clemson used to carry a cane, which had a large tiger head as its hand rest.

Firing the Cannon at Football Games

There have been several people who have been responsible for the growth of IPTAY through the years, and George Bennett is one of them. Bennett served as the Executive Director of IPTAY for 22 years.

Bennett is also responsible for the cannon being fired when Clemson arrives down the hill and when the Tigers score.

"My uncle played for South Carolina and my father went to West Point in 1954 to see his brother play against Army. Army shot a cannon after each score, and my dad told me Clemson should do the same thing. I was the head cheerleader and I told him, 'Why don't you buy us a cannon?' And he did. George Bennett then went to talk to Coach Howard to seek permission to use the cannon. 'What makes you think we'll score a touchdown this season?' Howard asked. And he finally agreed.

The Clemson cannon was first used on September 17, 1955 in a game against Presbyterian. The first cannon firer was Orlando Perez. "After the first game I got a hand truck and took the cannon and truck over to the physical plant and they fixed it up like it is today," added Bennett.

Homecoming

The first Homecoming football game played at Clemson took place on September 30, 1922, when Centre defeated the Tigers at Riggs Field, 21-0. Clemson has celebrated Homecoming every year since 1922 with the exception of the 1930 and 1938 seasons.

Country Gentleman

Clemson used to have two mascots. In addition to the Tiger, the school used to have the Country Gentleman, a student dressed in purple tails and top hat, carrying a cane. The Country Gentleman concept came about as a result of references to Clemson made by *Greenville News* sportswriter Carter "Scoop" Latimer as the Country Gentlemen. Clemson had the two-mascot system between 1954 and 1972. One reason the Country Gentleman disappeared was that the university wanted to emphasize the Tiger.

Colors

Clemson's official colors are orange and purple. Clemson used to have purple and gold as the official colors, but former football coach and Athletic Director Jess Neely (1931-1939) changed that because he wanted uniforms that were more colorfast. It seems that the weather and constant washings were causing the uniforms to fade. So Neely worked with the Clemson school of textiles and developed deeper colors for uniforms, colors that held up under the rays of the sun and the workings of the washing machines. Because of this, Clemson started using orange and purple in the uniforms.

Tiger Paw

The Tiger Paw has been Clemson's logo since 1970. The Tiger Paw might be the most widely recognized school symbol in the nation. It is something unique to Clemson and Tiger fans are proud of it.

Dr. Robert C. Edwards, then Clemson president, decided in 1969 that he would like "to upgrade the image of the university" and hired Henderson Advertising Co. in Greenville, SC to work on this idea. Company President Jimmy Henderson, a Clemson graduate in 1944, had an idea of what Edwards was thinking.

Among the possible changes being discussed were new uniforms and a new logo that would not replace the Tiger, but complement it.

After about six weeks of thinking out loud on several angles, Henderson presented what was first called a "tiger track" as the new logo. Henderson's people wrote to every school in the nation that had Tigers as its nickname, asking for a picture of its mascot. After most of them had responded, the conclusion was reached that a Tiger is a Tiger, regardless if it was a Persian, Bengal, or Sumatra.

Several other ideas were kicked around, one being the impression of a Tiger's foot or paw. In order to get the real thing, Henderson wrote the Museum of Natural History in Chicago asking for a plaster of Paris cast of the imprint of the tiger's paw.

The imprint was changed to a print, tilted about 10 degrees to the right and presented to the Clemson committee working with Henderson. John Antonio is given credit of coming up with the idea. Antonio was an innovative account executive with Henderson Advertising.

Now the news had to be spread. Football coach Hootie Ingram, basketball coach Tates Locke, All-Conference tailback Ray Yauger, and Wright Bryan, the university's Vice President for Development, made a one-day whirlwind trip to six cities—Florence, Columbia, Charleston, Greenville, Charlotte, and Atlanta. At each stop, they held a press conference. Bryan told the gatherings: "At any university, from time to time there needs to be some symbol which keeps the whole thing together, and the university hierarchy believed that the paw is the answer.

"Symbols like the tiger paw won't help us win football games," Ingram said at one of the stops, "but we hope they will retain the enthusiasm Clemson people are known for around the country."

Today, Tigers Paws are everywhere in Clemson and around the country. They are even on the roads leading to Clemson.

"Tiger Rag" and Tiger Band

Clemson College Band began playing "Tiger Rag" in 1942 after student band director Dean Ross found the sheet music in an Atlanta music store and brought it back to campus for football games. Dean was honored by the Tiger Band in 2002 for the 60th Anniversary of "Tiger Rag."

Hugh H. McGarity became the first official band director in 1947, taking over both the Clemson College Band and Glee Club. He was the first paid professor of music at Clemson. McGarity was director from 1947-'54. Bruce F. Cook was another noted Clemson Band Director (1966-67, 1970, 1973-1981).

Clemson Alma Mater

The Clemson Alma Mater came as a result of an embarrassing situation. A group of Clemson cadets were at an ROTC camp in Plattsburg, New York in May, 1918. Students representing colleges and universities from all over the country were there at the encampment. At an assembly of everyone who was there, each school group was invited to sing its Alma Mater. Clemson did not have one.

The Clemson cadets did yells and chants that they used at football games. They were embarrassed, and in this group was Clemson cadet Albert C. Cocoran, a member of the class of 1919. The Charleston, SC native subsequently worked at composing the words for an Alma Mater for Clemson, which he submitted to the Tiger. At first the music to Cornell's "Above Cayuga's Waters" was used. The Glee Club sang Clemson's new Alma Mater for the first time at a chapel exercise on Monday, February 17, 1919.

A new tune and arrangement for Clemson's Alma Mater was first used in the fall of 1950. Robert E. Farmer and Hugh McGarity are given credit for the music, according to Mark Spede, who has worked as Director of Bands at Clemson.

Tiger Walk

Coach Dabo Sweeney started Tiger Walk on October 18, 2008. This was Sweeney's first game as the Tigers' head coach. The players exit buses on Perimeter Road and walk through fans, cheerleaders, and Tiger band at lot #5 on their way to the locker room. Both the players and the Tiger faithful love it, and it is sure to be a tradition for many years to come.

Alma Mater Salute

During Clemson's military days (1896-1955) cadets were required to wear military uniforms, including their caps, and they would wave them during the game. The Alma Mater salute has continued this tradition by waving the right hand in the air with the thumb folded underneath so the hand appears to be holding a cap at the end of the singing of the Alma Mater. This is also a salute to the Clemson cadets from years past.

SPORTSMANSHIP

Crossing the Finish Line

A few weeks ago at the 2016 Atlantic Coast Conference Championships a shining example of sportsmanship was displayed involving a Clemson women's runner and her counterpart at Boston College.

After covering the grueling course, the Eagles' Madeline Adams fell to the ground with exhaustion as she approached the finish line.

It was evident she wouldn't have the strength to finish the race. Clemson's Evie Tate, with no regard about other runners passing her on the way to the finish line, stopped and helped Adams up and assisted her toward the finish line. Rachel Pearse of Louisville saw that Tate could use some help, so she got on the other side of Adams and the trio crossed the finish line together. Those that were there witnessed something you don't see every day.

Clemson Head Track and Cross Country Coach, Mark Elliott, was moved by the event and wasn't surprised. "It's very commendable what Evie Tate did. She's a team person and I am very proud of her. It's not surprising to me that she helped an opponent cross the finish line when she saw that she was having trouble. What she did is her personality. To me, what she did is the height of sportsmanship."

King Wins Award

Over 60 years ago Clemson running back Don King brought notoriety to Clemson by winning the nationally renowned and prestigious Swede Nelson Award by a simple act of kindness and respect for an injured opponent.

At the time, this was a coveted award that was presented by the Boston Touchdown Club and was given to the college football player who demonstrated sportsmanship during the year. To this day, it remains as one of the oldest awards in the nation given to a collegiate player.

After Wake Forest's Kenny Duckett won the award in 1981, it became a regional award and is only presented to players from the New England area.

In 1953, winning this award was big news for the Clemson football program.

On October 31, 1953, Clemson was playing Wake Forest in Tigertown.

In the third quarter, Wake Forest had the ball at midfield trailing Clemson 12-0 when Demon Deacon quarterback Sonny George failed to get up after being tackled.

Coaches, trainers and teammates surrounded George for at least 15 minutes. Ultimately, King left his Clemson teammates, who were waiting for action to resume, and went over to talk to the Wake Forest players and officials; then, George got up and resumed play. At the time, rules stated that if a player left the field because of injury he would have to sit out the remainder of the quarter, and Wake simply did not have a reliable substitution.

"It was not until Monday morning when Tiger starting linemen Mark Kane and Clyde White stopped by my office that I found out what happened," said Brent Breedin, Clemson's Sports Information Director at the time.

Kane and White explained that Don learned that George would be playing with an injured knee, so he told the rest of the team "when you tackle their quarterback Sonny George--tackle him high and not low, reminding us of his situation. King had knee injuries himself in several games the past two years.

Kane and White went on to say that King explained to his teammates that he is the only quarterback that Wake Forest had and that we didn't want him to have a permanent injury. He had already missed the Miami game and much of the South Carolina game because of the same injured knee. So Don told us again, "if you tackle him the rest of the game hit him high."

"I decided to share this incident with the Boston Gridiron Club," said Breedin. "They obviously liked it, coupled with the good relationship Clemson and Coach Howard had with many of the people in Boston via the Boston College rivalry that began in the 1940 Cotton Bowl, and King was their choice for the award."

In addition to King demonstrating class and sportsmanship he was an outstanding football player. Don King established a Clemson freshman single game rushing record in 1952 that still stands today.

The native of Anderson, SC played for the Tigers and Head Coach Frank Howard from 1952-'55 as a quarterback, and safety. On November 4, 1952 he rushed for 234 yards in a tie game at Fordham, the last time Clemson has played a football game in New York City.

Fordham entered the game leading the nation in rushing defense. King played the tailback position in this game because of injuries to Clemson's regular running backs. It was the only game King played tailback in his Clemson career. It is still the third most rushing yards in a single game by any Clemson back and a record for a Clemson player in a road game.

King led the Tigers in passing for four straight years and in rushing in 1953. He was the first Clemson player to lead the Tigers in passing four consecutive years. It is an accomplishment that has been equaled only by Nealon Greene (1994-97) and Charlie Whitehurst (2002-05) since.

King passed away on February 14, 2013 at the age of 79.

The 1992 Clemson Hall of Fame inductee was a second-team All-ACC quarterback in 1953 and 1954, his sophomore and junior seasons, respectively.

This act of sportsmanship in the Wake Forest game that Halloween afternoon not only won King a prestigious, national award, but he also won the respect of his teammates, coaches, and foes and apparently the admiration of countless others.

THE TWO-DOLLAR BILL TRADITION

It hadn't been too many years ago when the Clemson-Georgia Tech football series was cancelled. From this sad ending a new and longstanding Tiger Tradition was born.

In 1977, the two ancient foes were to go their separate ways. Clemson wanted a home and home series with the Yellow Jackets. But the Georgia Tech administration would not hear of it. Even the two presidents of both schools got involved in the situation and common ground could not be reached.

Clemson played Georgia Tech in Atlanta every year the two schools met except for three games prior to the Yellow Jackets joining the Atlantic Coast Conference. In 1898, the first game in the series, the two teams played on Thanksgiving Day in Augusta, GA. In 1899, the two rivals met in Greenville, SC, also on Thanksgiving Day. The Tigers were victorious in those two games. In the first and only visit to Clemson prior to Georgia Tech joining the ACC, the Tigers defeated the Yellow Jackets 21-17 on September 28, 1974.

In the IPTAY Report dated on September 20, 1977, then IPTAY Executive Secretary George Bennett asked that the Tiger faithful making the trip to Atlanta use $2 dollar bills to show merchants at hotels and restaurants, etc. what an impact the Clemson nation had on the local economy. According to Bennett this was a good way to prove a point—Clemson fans do have an impact on a local economy. "We want to make a big impact on Atlanta this weekend. I would like to ask that every Clemson fan take as many two dollar bills as possible and use these rare bills for every expenditure."

It's really not known exactly how much impact the Clemson fans made on the economy in Atlanta that weekend in 1977, but anytime Tiger fans come to town, restaurants and hotels are full and local businesses not only love the color of green in their tills but all of the orange that fill their establishments.

Clemson defeated Georgia Tech in Atlanta 31-14, on September 24, 1977, in what was to be the last game in the series. The Tigers scored on its first three offensive possessions and built up a 24-7 halftime lead in front of 50,116 fans. The Tigers' Lester Brown rushed for 134 yards on the afternoon.

On April 1, 1978, Georgia Tech joined the Atlantic Coast Conference and this forced the Yellow Jackets to play the Tigers on a home and home basis—the series was resumed without a long interruption in 1983.

The reason Clemson played at Georgia Tech for so many years and participated in the series was because of money. Long time Clemson Head Coach Frank Howard explained that it was a necessary to go to Atlanta every year. "A few years back we needed the money. Going to play in Atlanta with the large population and the big stadium, it was like going to a bowl game. It really paid dividends and helped us during the years," said Howard.

To this day, Clemson fans will spend $2 dollar bills when making a road trip in the opponent's territory.

ONE FOR THE BOOKS

In 1945, the country was recovering from World War II, the troops were returning and many of them going back to college to resume their academic career that was interrupted by serving Uncle Sam in the armed forces.

In 1944 Clemson suffered its worst loss in the series to Georgia Tech, a 51-0 loss in Atlanta. But the 1945 season was to be different.

Coach Howard and Clemson kept things going on campus the best they could. Many schools dropped football, but Clemson managed to always field a team and because of this, Howard said that is why Clemson enjoyed success in the late 40s and 1950s.

"We kept the football team going, and we didn't drop football like many schools did. And because of this, we were ahead and didn't have to play catch up. I feel it helped the morale of the students at Clemson and those abroad. I would write the players serving our country and tell them about what's happening at Clemson and plans for the team when they came back from service," said Howard.

Prior to Clemson playing Georgia Tech on November 24, 1945, Yellow Jacket Head Coach Bobby Dodd, in his first year, announced that his second string would start against Clemson. He wanted to rest his first string players and have them ready for the Georgia game the following week.

"We saw what Dodd said in the newspaper," said Howard. We also knew they didn't scout us any that season. We knew we had a point to make."

Clemson's Butch Butler, who was on a 45-day leave from the Army, scored two touchdowns for Clemson before 20,000 people in Atlanta. Frank Howard said he asked the general for a 45-day leave for Butler because he had the days numbered that he needed him during the football season.

At the start of the game, Clemson proved they were for real and Georgia Tech's first string soon got in the game. The Tigers, led by Butler, upset Georgia Tech, 21-7.

"I think my boys played a whale of a game against Tech," said Howard following the game. "I think everyone will agree they were the class of the ball game from start to finish," said Howard.

A feature of the game at halftime was the appearance of Clemson's famous Senior Platoon. This drill team gained national prominence around the country and brought fame and prestige to Clemson.

The series with Georgia Tech is a very intriguing one and is filled with many colorful characters. It's fortunate for fans that both teams are in the same conference and they continue to play each other year after year.

LEGENDARY PEOPLE

Behind every great program there are outstanding people, and Clemson is not without its share down through the years.

The list of early legends such as Riggs, Heisman, Cody, Neeley, and Howard has been discussed. But a few others who could be called legends are sometimes the people who aren't in the headlines or in front of the cameras.

Medical and athletic training staff

The first doctor known to have worked for Clemson Athletics was Doctor Lee Milford, a 1917 graduate of Emory. He was Clemson College's physician for 30 years and eight months. Milford came to Clemson on Jan. 1, 1926 and retired in the summer of 1956. He served as chairman of the athletic council at Clemson and was a faculty representative to the Southern Conference for 26 years. He was also a leader in the organization of the Atlantic Coast Conference and was one of four people to write the conference constitution and by-laws. He served three terms as president of the Southern Conference and was instrumental in organizing a booking office of conference officials. Frank Howard credits him with countless game-winning decisions made over injured players.

Dr. Jud Hair and Dr. Byron Harder are two other doctors or physicians who have been instrumental in Clemson athletics. Hair was a team physician during the years of 1957-1985, while Harder was a Clemson team doctor for 33 years in 1972-2005.

The Clemson Tiger training room has had many legends. Some of the early trainers were Chappie Johnson, who worked with the Tigers during the decades of the 1930s and 1940s before his death in 1949. Herman McGee, in his 46 years at Clemson, was the head trainer, equipment manager, and assistant trainer between 1936 and 1980. McGee started helping Johnson in March, 1936.

Fred Hoover served as Clemson's Head Athletic Trainer for 40 years (1959-99).

In June 1999, Danny Poole was named to replace Hoover after being an assistant since 1984.

Professionally, Hoover has held just about every administrative post with the National Athletic Trainers Association, including Chairman of the Board. In 1981, he was enshrined in the Citizens Savings-Helms Athletic Foundation Hall of Fame for his work in his chosen field. In 1982, Hoover was inducted into the Clemson Athletic Hall of Fame.

In 1983, Hoover was the recipient of the Distinguished Service to Sports Medicine Award given by the American Orthopedic Society for Sports Medicine. In 1987, he was awarded the South Carolina Hall of Fame Distinguished Service to Sports Award. He was made an honorary member of the Clemson Alumni Physicians Society in 1990. In 1994, the South Carolina Trainers Association created the Fred Hoover Award for Excellence in Athletic Training.

Academic and Administrative Leaders

Dr. R. C. Edwards graduated from Clemson in 1933 and rose through the ranks to become a top executive in the textile field. However, he always wanted to come back to Clemson.

In 1956, Clemson created the office of Vice President for Development, and Edwards got the job of VP. A year later, the then-Clemson president Dr. Robert F. Poole suffered a sudden fatal heart attack and Edwards was appointed acting president in 1958. On April 9, 1959, Edwards became the college's full-time top administrator.

The native of Fountain Inn, SC loved Clemson sports. He was a regular spectator to many athletic events and would be there to see the women's basketball teams off as they left campus for an out-of-town game.

He led Clemson through many changes and monumental events that changed the university forever. Under his leadership, the school's name changed from Clemson College to Clemson University. The first black students enrolled and graduated at Clemson while Edwards was the President. Also, the first female students received their diplomas during his tenure.

Edwards was always ready to serve. When Clemson went to play Virginia in Charlottesville, VA for a football game, Edwards wandered over to ask Bob Bradley, then Clemson's Sports Information Director, if there was anything that he could do at the game to bring the Tigers a victory. Jestingly, Bradley told Edwards that he needed a spotter for the Clemson Football Radio Network. Edwards sprang at the opportunity, apparently not being influenced by the fact that the job paid only five dollars.

He died at the age of 94 on December 4, 2008.

Kenneth Vickery, who graduated from Clemson in the spring of 1938 and went to work as the assistant to the school registrar, was another administrative leader. After a stint in the service, he served as Director of Admissions in 1949, Registrar (1955-70), and was the Dean of Admissions and the Registrar (1970-82).

Vickery served the University from an athletics standpoint from 1971-'82, when he was the NCAA Faculty Representative. During his final academic year at Clemson, the school won the National Championship in football. He was also the President of the Atlantic Coast Conference during the 1976-77 academic year.

Vickery was the recipient of the Clemson Alumni Association's Distinguished Service Award in 1977. Clemson's Academic Learning Center for Athletes, Vickery Hall, was dedicated in his honor in 1991.

He was also a member of Phi Kappa Phi, Tiger Brotherhood, and the Clemson Athletic Hall of Fame. He received the prestigious Algernon Sidney Sullivan Award for his leadership and devotion to the community and Clemson's Alumni Distinguished Service Award. Ken Vickery passed away in October 2006.

Red Ritchie gave 45 years of his life as a professor at Clemson University.

And as most good professors—of which he was one—he taught many other meaningful things in the classroom which can't be found in the textbook.

He started out as an instructor at Clemson in 1926 and rose to be full professor in animal science before his retirement in May, 1971.

While teaching and watching over his Angus cattle were his first loves, Red Ritchie also overlapped in another capacity for the last 18 years before his retirement.

He became the Clemson Faculty Chairman of Athletics in 1955. But even before that, he was getting his feet wet in a field that was to take much of his time and energy.

In 1953, Clemson and six other schools decided to leave the Southern Conference and form the Atlantic Coast Conference.

Dr. Lee W. Milford was Faculty Chairman at the time, but Ritchie attended the first meetings during the formation of the ACC.

He succeeded Milford in 1955 and he kept the post of Faculty Chairman for 16 years.

Ritchie was one of the granite pillars during the early years when the ACC was struggling to attain national prominence. He watched and worked and listened and was one of the ones instrumental in bringing the ACC to the stature it carries today.

He was first chosen as President of the Atlantic Coast Conference in the spring of 1958 for a year in the top seat. He was also president in 1964-65 and again in 1970-71.

But before there was any talk about an ACC, Ritchie had his hand in sports. When IPTAY was formed in 1934, Ritchie and Hoke Sloan, a long-time tennis coach, used to go out and beat the bushes getting memberships. There were some that doubted that IPTAY would be successful, but Ritchie, Sloan, and some others kept plugging away, and they played a big part in helping make IPTAY what it is today.

Rick Robbins, known as "The Colonel" was a colorful man and was very productive in his job. Robbins served as the head academic advisor for all of the athletes from 1967-'80. He had the growl of a Bengal Tiger and the compassion and the heart of a teacher, and there was no big lineman alive who did not both fear and respect him.

Robbins came to Clemson in 1960 as a professor of military science and served as an assistant track coach and became the full-time athletic advisor until his death in 1980. He will always be remembered for his passion, his compassion, and his plain old getting-the-job-done method when working with the student athlete.

Frank Jervey was known to many as "Mr. Clemson" because of his many contributions to the university. He was also called Clemson's Ambassador of Good Will.

Born in Summerville, SC, Jervey served with the Army in World War I after his graduation from Clemson. He was wounded in 1918 during the Battle of France and decorated for extraordinary heroism.

Jervey later served in the Ordnance Corps and became one of the world's foremost authorities on incendiary and small arms ammunition. For his contributions to the nation's war effort in World War I, he was awarded the Expedition Civilian Service Emblem at the Pentagon. He received an honorary Doctor of Science degree from Clemson in 1953 and served as Clemson's Vice

President for Development from 1959-'63. He received the Alumni's Distinguished Service Award the first year they were given in 1960 and was greatly instrumental in obtaining two grants totaling nearly $2 million from the Olin Foundation for Construction and equipping of the ceramic and chemical engineering buildings on the campus.

The Jervey Athletic Center was named in his honor as "a tribute to an alumnus whose life personifies the true meaning of service and loyalty to an institution," said Dr. Robert C. Edwards at the dedication ceremony. He went on to describe Jervey as a man "whose intense interest in and great loyalty to Clemson has never wavered for the slightest moment. The dedication took place on November 19, 1973.

Athletic Administration

Clemson has had a long list of quality leaders in his athletic history. Walter Merritt Riggs comes to mind, as he not only started the Clemson football program, but he was also Clemson's first Athletic Director. After he became President of Clemson College, many of the football coaches took that role.

James G. "Mutt" Gee held the title of Athletic Director in 1927-30. Gee was instrumental in the building of Fike, along with Josh Cody, who was also serving as the head football and basketball coach.

Gee was All-State in football in both 1916 and 1917 and All-Southern in 1917 and was called by his coach, Jiggs Donahue, as "one of the best men I have ever seen at center." Gee was a veteran of both World Wars and spent most of his life in the education field and served as president of East Texas State University in Commerce, TX from 1947 until 1966.

Jess Neeley held both roles during his tenure in 1932-39. During his administration, he continued to try and add sports to Clemson's program. Gee, who started boxing in the late 1920s, had a good idea, as boxing was very popular with the students and local fans alike.

Neely also discussed the possibility of adding sports like lacrosse and wrestling back in the 1930s, but the lack of money and the economic times of the day soon thwarted these efforts. Men's Soccer appeared on the scene in the spring of 1934, but it ended due to the war and the economic times of the day.

Frank Howard took over the Athletic Director/football coach role for Neeley in 1940. Bill McLellan became his assistant in 1954.

McLellan was the main driving force behind Clemson's rise to national prominence in the 1970s and 1980s with the growth of IPTAY.

His theory for success was simply "the Clemson family comes first. They want and deserve the best, and with it comes the facilities to train and to play." Without his vision of where Clemson athletics needed to go, Clemson may never have made the giant leap to national prominence that it did in all sports in the 1980s and 1990s.

The great business sense that he possessed brought a whole new dimension to Clemson and was exactly what it needed during its very rapid period of growth. He was also known as a great leader, and all sports prospered during his tenure. McLellan believed alumni, friends, business, and industry, could accomplish any task and meet any goal as long as they pulled together in the best interest of Clemson.

He led the way and set a standard of excellence for all to follow. In 1971, IPTAY was providing $400,000 annually for scholarships. When McLellan left in 1985, IPTAY had reached $5 million a year for athletic and academic enrichment and it was ranked number one in the nation for fundraising.

During his tenure, all of Clemson athletic facilities either underwent new construction or major renovations. In 1973, Jervey Athletic Center was built. In 1978, the South Upper Deck was completed and the North Upper Deck was finished in 1983. Fike Field House was renovated in the mid 1970s to allow for a new swimming pool and other areas for the intramural department.

Bill McLellan came to Clemson as a football player and earned two letters. He was a member of the 1952 Gator Bowl team. He graduated in 1954 and received a Masters' degree in 1956. He went on to be an assistant football coach, the ticket manager, and assistant athletic director. He became the Athletic Director in 1971 and served in that position until 1985. He is a member of the Clemson and State of South Carolina Athletic Halls of Fame.

Bobby Robinson also had a very successful tenure as Athletic Director.

Robinson served as Clemson's Athletic Director from March of 1985 until June 30, 2002. His service to Clemson, including his work in the housing office, spanned 30 years. In Robinson's 17 years as Athletic Director, Clemson won 56 ACC Championships and had 151 top-25 seasons. A total of 16 of the 19 programs had at least one final top-10 national ranking.

In terms of academics, he designed the concept and building of Vickery Hall, Clemson's student-athlete learning center, a concept that has been copied nationwide.

Robinson put the Clemson golf program on solid footing when he was head coach between 1974-83. He led the Clemson team to its first NCAA team tournament appearance in 1980, its first ACC championship in 1982, and its first top-five national finish (1983). He left the coaching ranks to concentrate on athletic administration. The golf practice facility was named in his honor.

Terry Don Phillips also served as Clemson's Athletic Director, from 2002-'12. During his tenure, he oversaw the building of the West Zone at Memorial Stadium, the Indoor Football Practice Facility, and the Larry Penley Golf Building. Notable hiring under Phillips included basketball coaches Oliver Purnell in 2003 and Brad Brownell in 2010. He also elevated Dabo Swinney from assistant football coach to head football coach in 2008.

Dan Radakovich was named the Athletic Director on October 29, 2012. Clemson President James F. Barker described Radakovich as the right person to build on the strong foundation created under the leadership of Terry Don Phillips, who announced that he was retiring in August of 2012.

Publicizing the Tigers

On the publicity end, there have been many giants in the field. Joe Sherman started the office when he was at Clemson in the 1930s.

Bob Bradley, who is a co-author of this book, served as Sports Information Director from 1956-'89. He continued to assist in the office until his death in 2000. Bradley was one of the stalwarts in the field. His charm and gentleman traits made him one of the best.

Tim Bourret came to Clemson in 1978 and has had a long and faithful career in the Clemson Sports Information office.

Jerry Arp, who was at Clemson in the 1970s working in the sports information office and promotions, was instrumental in urging everyone to wear orange.

Earle "Pepper" Martin, who wore many hats in the Athletic Department during his career, was so faithful to share with the Athletic Department the pictures he took with his array of cameras at sporting events.

Al Adams was also a stalwart in athletic publicity at Clemson and started the popular *Orange and White* newspaper in 1978.

Jim Phillips, "Voice of the Tigers," was the legendary voice of the Clemson Tigers for 36 years. Phillips came to Clemson in 1968 and broadcasted his first Tiger football game on September 21, 1968, a 20-20 tie between Clemson and Wake Forest. Phillips broadcasted his 400th Clemson football game on August 20, 2003 against Georgia, just over a week before his death. He was the only ACC play-by-play announcer to broadcast his school's football, basketball, baseball, and women's basketball games. Over his career, he broadcast over 2,000 Clemson sporting events.

Phillips also served as host of the Clemson football and basketball coach's shows for many years. He broadcasted his 1000th Clemson men's basketball game at the 2002 ACC Tournament in Charlotte. He missed only one broadcast of a Clemson men's basketball game in Littlejohn Coliseum during his time at Clemson, a period of almost 35 years.

Phillips was one of the most honored broadcasters in his field. He was a five-time recipient of the South Carolina Broadcaster of the Year Award. In 1992, he was presented the Master Broadcaster Award by the South Carolina Association of Broadcasters, the highest honor presented by that organization. In 1998, he received the Skeeter Francis Award from the Atlantic Coast Conference Sportwriters Association for his contributions to ACC athletics. He was the first radio personality to receive the award.

Phillips was inducted into the Clemson Hall of Fame in 1992. He passed away in September 9, 2003, just days after calling the Clemson vs. Furman football game.

Jimmy Coggins handled the play-by-play duties of the Clemson games during the 1936-38 seasons. He did it again in 1947-49 as well.

Coggins, along with Coach Frank Howard, started the first Clemson Football Radio Network in 1953. Coggins was the Clemson play-by play man for a total of 18 years, announcing the games through the 1964 season.

Bill Goodrich was the "Voice of the Tigers" during the 1965-67 seasons. Phillips took over in 1968.

Ed Osborne, Monty DuPuy, Pat Williams (NBA executive), Jim Kingman, Bruce Buchanan, Jeff Odenwald, Scott Shannon, Ken Allison, Tim Bourret, Clyde Wren, Mike Eppley, Rodney Williams, Will Merritt, and Pete Yanity have been handling the color and assisting the play-by-play men since 1954. Yanity later became "Voice of the Tigers." Don Munson became the play-by-play man for the Tigers in 2014. He called Clemson's 2016 National Football Championship season.

Handling the tickets for Clemson has been a growing job over the years. Earle Ambrose was the head ticket manager from 1973-'79. Van Hilderbrand, his assistant for three years, ran the ticket office in 1979-2003. Ambrose continued his duties as assistant athletic director and department pilot until his retirement in 1990. Hilderbrand has served as director of events since 2003.

CLEMSON'S FIRST OLYMPIAN

During an Olympic year, the question of who was Clemson's first Olympian and what sport did they participate in comes to mind.

The first Clemson alumnus to represent the United States in the Olympics was John Wofford from Laurens, S.C. He was on the U.S. Equestrian Team in the 1932 Olympics, held at Los Angeles, Calif. He was born on Jan. 1, 1898 in High Point, N.C. The family moved to Laurens, S.C., while he was a youth. He enrolled at Clemson in the fall of 1914 and earned academic acclaim. He graduated from Clemson in 1918 with a degree in botany. Clemson's yearbook, Taps, described him in the 1918 edition as a "fine fellow."

"He has the quality of perseverance along with the determination to succeed."

While a student at Clemson, he was a member of the Calhoun Literary Society and served as president his senior year. He served on The Tiger staff, the student newspaper, and was a member of the Taps staff. He was also a member of the South Carolina College Press Association.

After he graduated from Clemson in 1918, he enrolled at West Point and earned another degree in 1920. At West Point, he participated on the swimming team and also participated in intramural boxing.

He became a career officer, and this is the time his interest in equestrian began. He served with the Army equestrian teams as a member of the cavalry out of Fort Riley, Kan.

In the 1932 Olympics, the United States won five medals, and this would be the best performance for a United States Equestrian Team until the 1984 Olympic Games in Los Angeles, 52 years later. Some of the equestrian events were held in the Los Angeles Coliseum in front of over 100,000 spectators.

John Wofford became the head of a well-known U.S. equestrian family. One of his sons, John E.B. Wofford, was an Olympic medalist. He won a bronze medal in eventing at the 1952 Summer Olympics in Helsinki, Finland. He competed on his father's horse, Benny Grimes. Another son, James Wofford, was in Kansas. He was a silver medal winner in the 1968 and 1972 Olympics in the team three-day event.

"My father rode on the 1932 Olympic show-jumping team in Los Angeles and was a reserve on the team in 1936," said James Wofford. "The first Olympics I remember were in London in 1948. The U.S. Army was still in charge of all three Olympic equestrian disciplines, so the riders were all officers, the horses were for the most part owned by the Army and the grooms and farriers were all enlisted men."

A third son, Warren Wofford, remains the only U.S. team rider to qualify in both show jumping and eventing. He chose show jumping, but only went as an alternate to the 1956 Stockholm Olympic Games. However, Warren did meet his future wife, Dawn Penelope Wofford, who competed on the British Show Jumping Team in the 1956 and 1960 Olympic Games.

John served with the Army equestrian teams as a member of the cavalry out of Fort Riley, Kan. In 1941, then a major, he was named the first U.S. military attaché to Ireland. He retired from the Army as a Colonel in 1943 and owned and operated Rimrock Farm, a horse farm in Milford, Kan., adjacent to Fort Riley.

The U.S. Army had mechanized in 1949, which meant the cavalry was disbanded. In 1951, the U.S. Equestrian Team was formed "to train and field teams for international equestrian competition." Colonel Wofford helped the U.S. Equestrian Team transform from military to civilian status.

Colonel James Wofford was a national leader in the world of equestrian, and as the 2016 Olympics continue, the Clemson nation can be proud of him and his accomplishments and the contributions he made on behalf of the United States.

PLAYERS OF THE YEAR

With the outstanding news that Clemson freshman baseball player, Seth Beer was named the winner of the Dick Howser award as the National Player of the Year, it brings to mind other Clemson athletes who have been named National Players of the Year in their respective sports.

Winning the "Heisman" in any sport shows determination, talent, and a large contribution to a team's success.

In men's soccer, the Hermann Trophy is looked upon as the top award going to the Player of the Year.

In 1987, Bruce Murray was Clemson's first Hermann Trophy winner. The two-time All-American led Clemson to the National Championship that season. Murray had 20 goals and 11 assists in Clemson's National Championship season in 1987. He was named the NSCAA National Player of the Year, and he led the ACC in goals, points, and was second in assists in 1987.

He had the winning goal in three NCAA Tournament games for the Tigers in 1987 against Evansville, Indiana and Rutgers, respectively. He was the first player in Clemson's 40-40 club (over 40 goals and 40 assists in a career). Murray went on to set a record for most appearances for the United States National Team.

Wojtek Krakowiak won the 1998 Hermann Trophy. He was the 1998 consensus National Player of the Year, as he was the *Soccer America*, *Soccer Times* and the *College Soccer Weekly* National Player of the Year. He was also named the 1998 ACC Player of the Year and was named first-team All-ACC.

He scored 31 goals and had eight assists in 1998, as he led Clemson to the NCAA quarterfinals for the second year in a row. He led the ACC in goal scoring (31) and points (70). He is third in Clemson history for most goals scored in a single season with 31 in 1998. Krakowiak left school one year early to turn professional. In 1998, he led the ACC in goals (31) and points (70).

Chuck Kriese, who was the Tigers' Head Men's Tennis Coach in 1976-2004, coached four players who were named ITA National Player of the Year—the equivalent of winning the Heisman in men's tennis.

In 1980, Clemson's first All-American, Mike Gandolfo was named the ITA National Player of the Year. In 1982 Mark Dickson won the award. The next season, Jean Desdunes became the third Clemson player to win the award in a four-year span. The fourth Tiger honored was in 1997 as Mitch Sprengelmeyer won the award as he led the Tigers to the ACC Championship. All four of the players were also named to the ACC's 50th Anniversary Men's Tennis Team.

In men's golf, Clemson's D.J. Trahan won the Ben Hogan Award as National Player of the Year in 2002. Trahan was named first-team All-ACC four times. He was a four-time All-American.

In 2009, the Tigers' Kyle Stanley was the recipient of the Ben Hogan Award. He was National runner up at the NCAA Tournament in 2007 and 2009. He was a three-time All-American selection.

Clemson pitcher Kris Benson was named National Player of the Year in 1996, by *Baseball America* and *Colle-giate Baseball*. He was also the Dick Howser Trophy and Rotary Smith Award winner. He was the number-one overall pick of the 1996 major league baseball draft and a 1996 Olympian.

The Tigers' shortstop Khalil Greene was honored in 2002. *ABCA*, *Baseball America* and *Collegiate Baseball* named him National Player of the Year. He won the Dick Howser Trophy, Golden Spikes Award and Rotary Smith Award in 2002.

In women's track, Brianna Rollins was named the National Track and Field Athlete of the Year in 2013. She also won the USTFCCCA National Track Athlete of the Year in 2013. She was an eight-time All-American and an eight-time ACC Champion in various events at Clemson during her career in indoor and outdoor track in 2009-13.

CLEMSON'S NATIONAL PLAYERS AND ATHLETES OF THE YEAR

Men's Soccer
Hermann Award
1987 Bruce Murray
1998 Wojtek Krakroviak

Men's Tennis
ITA Player of the Year
1980 Mike Gandolfo
1982 Mark Dickson
1983 Jean Desdunes
1987 Mitch Sprengelmeyer

Men's Golf
Ben Hogan Award
2002 D.J. Trahan
2009 Kyle Stanley

Baseball
Dick Howser Trophy
1996 Kris Benson
2002 Khalil Greene
2016 Seth Beer

Women's Track
The Bowerman Award
USTFCCCA National Track Athlete of the Year
2013 Brianna Rollins

IPTAY—LIFE BLOOD OF
Clemson Athletics

IPTAY could be described as a mysterious-sounding name that has become synonymous with Clemson athletics since 1934.

The name IPTAY was picked from the phrase, which stood for "I Pay Ten aYear." Now there are different levels of contributions that are used to fund scholarships for Clemson's student-athletes.

There were apparently several forerunners to IPTAY at Clemson, but IPTAY is the one that finally clicked and has paid off wonderful dividends.

The first known aid to Clemson athletics came just before the turn of the century. The Tigers had just closed, according to one article, "the most brilliant football season in the history of athletics at Clemson," trouncing Georgia Tech, 41-5, in Greenville on Thanksgiving Day in 1899.

Professor W. M. Riggs, who was later to become Clemson president, hadcoached this team just as he had the first-team in 1896, but only this latter time, it was without remuneration. Students decided that the manwho brought football to Clemson from Auburn should be able to devote his full duties to the academic side and that a full-time, employed person should be brought in to coach football.

Thus, a mass meeting was held December 7, 1899, and the Football Aid Society was formed. At this meeting, the conditions and possibilities ofthe season of 1900 were thoroughly discussed and as a result, the society became a permanent organization with the avowed purpose to render all possible assistance to the football association, a forerunner to the Clemson University Athletic Department.

B. H. Rawl was elected president and W. G. Hill secretary-treasurer of the society. A second meeting was held later and it was unanimously agreed that a coach—the best that could be obtained—should be engaged, and the society asked its members for subscriptions payable in September, 1900.

A total of 132 names appeared on the roll of members, and $372.50 was pledged in an hour's time. A ways and means committee was appointed and the object of this committee was to devise means for raising money. This was done and money was raised by various endeavors.

Professor Riggs aided the society in bringing in Auburn Coach John W. Heisman and during the next four years of the Heisman era, Clemson teams had a 19-3-2 record and became one of the South's great football powers.The 1900 team was Clemson's first undefeated squad (6-0).

Although it is not known how long the Football Aid Society stayed in existence, one point seemed to be proved—monetary aid established Clemsonas a football giant to be reckoned with—not for scholarships, as IPTAY now does, but in securing a capable coach who put the Tigers on the gridiron map.

As far as can be determined, no organized effort was made to assist athletic teams at Clemson for the next three decades, although there were individual gifts here and there, usually collected at Clemson meetings.

Josh Cody came along in 1927 and had four highly successful seasons (29-11-1) before Jess Neely arrived on the scene in 1931. That season started what has become known as the "Seven Lean Years," and it was during this time that IPTAY was born.

Neely's first season ended with a record of 1-6-2. Following The Citadel game in Florence on October 13, 1931, Captain Frank J. Jervey recalls that he, Neely, Joe Davis (former Clemson and Rice coach), and Captain Pete Heffner (boxing coach) were sitting in a car outside the stadium talking, following the 6-0 loss at the Cadets' hands. Captain Heffner was a member of the military staff at Clemson, vitally interested in athletics, and assisted with the coaching in his spare time.

Jervey recalls that it was a downcast group in the car. Heffner said in so many words, "What we ought to do is to get the alumni to give Jess some money and help him with the football team."

"How much do you think we should ask from each person?" Jervey inquired.

Jervey remembers picking the figure of $50.00 as the amount of the contribution and to form a "50 Club." Neely believed if he could get $10,000 a year, he could give the Clemson fans a winning football team.

The group talked some more on the subject on the way back to Clemson and then went their separate ways upon arrival at Clemson. The Tigers finished out the season with a 21-0 loss to South Carolina, a tie with Furman, and losses to Oglethorpe, Virginia Military, and Alabama.

Jervey, who was working in Washington at the time, began corresponding with some of his Clemson friends concerning the "50 Club," and one of those friendswas Dr. Rupert H. (Rube) Fike, an Atlanta cancer specialist.

After approximately a year of writing back and forth, about a dozen of Jervey's friends decided to have a meeting in Columbia on the eve of the South Carolina game, on October 19, 1932 at the Jefferson Hotel. Clemson had beaten Presbyterian 13-0, and Erskine 19-0, and lost 13-0 to N.C. State and 32-14 to Georgia Tech, prior to this gathering.

Some of the group, including Fike, thought maybe the $50 figure was a little too high, but nonetheless, some of those present went about starting the "50 Club."

Early records at the athletic department in Clemson show that there were a few contributions of $50, but the total sum came nowhere close to matching the $10,000 Neely had indicated he would need for a winning ball club.

Fike's idea was that if a smaller amount was requested, there would be more money and more members and he went back to Atlanta with the idea in the back of his mind. The Tigers went on to lose to South Carolina, Georgia, and Furman, getting a win off The Citadel and a 7-7 tie with Davidson to finish 3-5-1.

Dr. Fike, determined to find a way to strengthen Clemson's athletic program, which was as dark as the Depression the nation was in, stuck to his guns for the "smaller amount-more members" idea. And to put across his idea, he enlisted the aid of two other Clemson men living in Atlanta, J.E.M. Mitchell, Class of 1912, and Milton Berry, Class of 1913. Fike himself was a member of '08.

Apparently, over a year passed before the first concrete steps were taken and IPTAY was formed. Meanwhile, the 1933 season had come and gone, giving Neely three straight losing campaigns. The Tigers of that year were 3-6-2, losing to Georgia Tech, South Carolina, Ole Miss, Wofford, Mercer, and Furman; while defeating N.C. State, Wake Forest, and The Citadel; and tying Presbyterian and George Washington. The Tigers had won only seven games in three years under Neely.

Although there are several versions as to just how IPTAY started, a letter written by Dr. Fike to Coach Neely, dated August 21, 1934, seems to pretty well pinpoint the exact date of formation. Dr. Fike said in his opening statement of the letter:

"Last night we had a little meeting out at my house and organized the IPTAY Club." He went on to say that those attending the meeting were George Suggs, Gene Cox, E.L. Hutchins, Bill Dukes, J. R. Pennell, George Klugh, Milton Berry, Jack Mitchell, and himself.

The club was to be a secret order, according to an early copy of the constitution, which stated that "anyone who has matriculated at Clemson, has been employed by the college, or is a friend of the college, who can and will subscribe to the purpose of the order by taking the oath of secrecy and paying the initiation and yearly fees, when invited for membership is eligible."

The purpose of the Clemson Order of IPTAY, stated the constitution, "shall be to provide annual financial support to the athletic department at Clemson and to assist in every other way possible to regain for Clemson the high athletic standing which rightfully belongs to her."

Dr. Fike entwined the language of his ritual around the tiger. The Bengal tiger, the Perisa tiger, and Sumatra tiger would be the president, vice president, and secretary respectively. The Exalted Iryaas would be the head coach at Clemson, with "Iryaas" meaning "I receive yours and acknowledge same."

A "lair" would mean a unit body of the order and "region" designated a state, province, or foreign country.

Neely recalled in later years that Fike, Mitchell, and Berry approached him sometime before their August meeting at the Fike home and said:

"What do you think about this IPTAY?"

"About what?" Neely asked with an amazed look.

Then the enthused Fike, Mitchell, and Berry explained their plan of IPTAY to Neely. The distressed coach was for trying anything that would bring the Tigers out of their gridiron doldrums.

Dr. Fike mentioned their visit to Clemson in his letter to Neely. Neely's initiation into the order was arranged to be held at Clemson September 22,1934, "either before or after the Presbyterian game."

The late Leonard R. Booker once recalled that first initiation. It was held in the office of the late J.H. "Uncle Jake" Woodard, long-time alumni secretary at Clemson. In addition to the three Atlanta stem-winders, Booker, Woodard, Neely, and the late J. C. Littlejohn, Clemson business manager, were also present.

The meeting is believed to be the first initiation of new members into IPTAY. The organizers and these new members then began to preach IPTAY to anyone and everyone and money began to come in for Neely and his Tigers.

As close as can be determined, there were 185 people who were members of IPTAY during that first year of 1934-35.

Probably none of these people except Berry, Fike, and Mitchell ever envisioned what IPTAY would do for athletics at Clemson. Neely recalled on one of his visits back to Clemson after going to Rice that they met a lot of skeptical people while making their rounds asking for money "and it took about three or four years before we could start helping a lot of boys." The former Rice head coach and athletic director remembered that most of the 1939 Cotton Bowl team was on scholarship, "but some of them had never played high school ball and just came out for football after coming to Clemson."

Frank Howard, who was on the Clemson staff 44 years, 30 as head coach, was in on the same conversation with Neely, and Howard remembers vividly that there were eight players on the 1950 team, which played in the '51 Orange Bowl, who came to Clemson without a scholarship.

Although bringing Clemson from its lowest ebb into the Cotton Bowl was one of Neely's highlights, he feels that one even more important was getting the athletic department on a sound financial footing. "When we came to Clemson in 1931," Neely recalled, "there wasn't hardly twenty cents in the treasury and when I left here (1940), there was over $20,000."

The Tigers had their first winning season with IPTAY in 1934 (5-4-0), the year IPTAY was formed, but it was probably the 1938 season when the net results really began to pay off. That year Clemson waltzed over Presbyterian, Tulane, South Carolina, Wake Forest, George Washington, Kentucky, and Furman, while losing to Tennessee and tying Virginia Military.

Following the VMI tie, the Tigers won 19 of their next 20 games, with 13 straight being reeled off from the 7-6 loss to Tulane in '39 to the 13-0 defeat to the same Greenies in 1940. The 1939 team was 8-1-0 in regular season play and went on to defeat Frank Leahy's Boston College team, 6-3, in the '40 Cotton Bowl.

The men who were out beating the bushes for IPTAY encountered rough going in those early days. On many occasions, a person was interested in giving, but lacked funds. Harper Gault, a former president of IPTAY, recalls members giving $10-worth of milk, potatoes, or turnips in exchange for membership.

IPTAY was born for just one purpose—to finance athletic scholarships at Clemson. That is still the way IPTAY is run today.

About four or five years after its formation, IPTAY dropped its secret ritual and invited everyone to join in support of Clemson athletics. Then in 1954, Dr. Fike asked to be relieved as president after serving 20 years, and a complete revamping of the club took place.

Donors have contributed millions of dollars to the cause of IPTAY since that meeting in August of 1934 in the quiet surroundings of the Fike home in Atlanta. With these monies thousands of athletes have received an education that might not have otherwise been possible.

Dr. Robert C. Edwards, president of Clemson and the man who succeeded Dr. Fike and became the second president of IPTAY, views athletics as a vital segment of campus life.

"Athletic teams in all sports, both intercollegiate and intramural," he states, "are an essential and integral part of Clemson's total educational program. Clemson University has developed a national reputation in athletic competitions. The support of Clemson athletics year after year by IPTAY members has made this achievement possible.

"More recently," Dr. Edwards continues, "Clemson's reputation as an outstanding scientific and technological educational institution is growing at a remarkable pace.

IPTAY is contributing to this achievement. Student-athletes at Clemson are currently compiling better academic records than the student body as a whole. We are seeking to develop the same competitive spirit in the classroom that prevails in athletic competition."

At first, only dyed-in-the-wool Clemson fans took an interest and joined IPTAY. But in recent years parents of students and athletics, as well as people who never attended Clemson, have become a part of IPTAY.

Just what has IPTAY meant to Clemson, to the State of South Carolina and the many individuals it has helped since 1934?

That would be difficult to put into words. But maybe, Dr. Riggs had the right idea when he spoke these words on football, and athletics in general, in 1899:

"So long as the game of football helps to make better men of our students, stronger in body, more active in mind; men full of energy, enthusiasm, and an indomitable personal courage; men not easily daunted by obstacles or opposition; who control their tempers and restrain their appetites, who can deal honorably with a vanquished adversary, and can take victory moderately and defeat without bitterness.

"And as long as football, properly controlled and regulated, helps the student in his college duties, instead of hindering him; gives zest and pleasure to college life, makes name and fame for the college on account of victories won, not only by skill and prowess of the team on the gridiron, but by their gentlemanly conduct in the streets of the town they play, in the hotels where they quarter, and on the trains.

"So long as it helps to bring about a closer bond of sympathy between students and members of the faculty by creating a common interest apart from the routine duties, so long as in all these ways the best interests of his and other colleges are advanced, and the course of education aided in its highest mission, which is to make the best men out of the material at hand, so long we will say for the game of football, long may it live and prosper."

Although these words were spoken some 35 years before the formation of IPTAY, the ideas expressed by Dr. Riggs are exemplified today in the total education program at Clemson, which Dr. Edwards spoke of.

Dr. Edwards believed "it is utterly impossible to measure in a material sense all that IPTAY has meant to Clemson in the past years. It would be equally difficult to predict all that IPTAY can and will contribute to Clemson in the years that lie ahead."

RUBE FIKE

The number of lives Rube Fike touched hasn't been counted yet. They'll still be added on as long as there is a Clemson.

While he touched thousands, he saved many more, first as a radiologist and physician, and second as an educator. Not an educator as we view one today, but as one who would provide a foundation where worthy athletes

Dr. R. H. Fike is credited as the originator of Clemson's IPTAY organization, which provides scholarships in Clemson men's and women's sports.

would have money available to could continue their education.

Dr. Fike is credited with being the originator of Clemson's world-renowned IPTAY organization, which now provides scholarships in Clemson men's and women's sports.

"I never worked with a person more professional, and one more energetic in wanting to help Clemson than Dr. Fike was," Neely once told George Bennett, who served as Executive Director of IPTAY.

"[Fike's] idea about this whole thing was what started all of the

fundraising [at Clemson]," Bennett continued. "It all goes back to him. He's the grand-daddy, the patriarch, of it all."

IPTAY's main target in the beginning was to improve the football team. And in its first year the Tigers had their first winning season in four years. In the sixth season after formation, Clemson was on the way to its first post-season bowl, the 1940 Cotton Bowl.

From the time IPTAY was formed until his death in 1956, Dr. Fike gave of himself freely to both Clemson and IPTAY, but mainly IPTAY. He served as its first president in a term that ran 20 years. He not only raised money, but he helped shape the future of Clemson University.

A little over $1,600 came into the coffers the first year of IPTAY in 1934, and even less the next year. The year Fike retired as president, the contributions jumped to over $68,000, and it was over $82,000 the year he died. Wonder what he would think of the millions raised now?

In 1966, the Clemson Field House was named Fike Field House in honor of Dr. Fike.

Dr. Fike could be described as a "Benefactor" because he had a knack of doing things that benefitted people.

CLEMSON
Special Heroes

"Freedom is not free"is a very powerful and meaningful statement.

The price of this freedom is paid by the sacrifice, and sometimes, lives of brave men and women.

Clemson's football stadium was named Memorial Stadium as a tribute to the Clemson students who made the ultimate sacrifice in service to the United States. An additional memorial named the Scroll of Honor, completed in 2010, is located just across the street, on the east side of the stadium. It stands as a reminder of why the stadium was named Memorial Stadium and is a permanent epitaph to those who have laid down their lives to preserve the freedom we enjoy today.

A famous United States General once wrote to his wife: "What a cruel thing is war: to separate and destroy families and friends, and mar the purest joys and happiness God has granted us in this world; to fill our hearts with hatred instead of love for our neighbors, and to devastate the fair face of this beautiful world."

War, no matter how fought, or when fought, always has devastating circumstances. At Clemson, almost 500 students and graduates have been killed in this nation's wars and in peacetime operations. All the way back to the First World War until the present, the Clemson family has lost members that served so bravely and courageously.

Clemson has had a long, rich military tradition by answering the call when needed by the military. In the early years, the Clemson Board of Trustees decided that Clemson would use a system of military discipline modeled after Mississippi State students were required to wear uniforms that they had to buy. The Board of Trustees asked the War Department for the detail of an officer to act as Commandant, responsible for life of cadets outside of the classroom.

There have been many proud moments in Clemson's military history. In 1917, the entire senior class sent President Woodrow Wilson a telegram, volunteering its services to the United States' World War I effort. During World War II, Clemson supplied more Army officers than any other institution except West Point and Texas A&M; Clemson also had the largest infantry ROTC in the country.

In 1955, the Corps of Cadets was officially abolished and the student body became civilian. ROTC was compulsory for the freshman and sophomore years until 1969-70, when it became voluntary.

The Clemson students and graduates who lost their lives during their duty of serving our country are listed at the Scroll of Honor, as their names are etched in stone and laid respectively and neatly at the foot of a mound.

A closer look at the ones who served and lost their lives in the line of duty would find many former Tiger athletes.

One such brave soldier was Jimmie Dyess. Dyess was on the Clemson football team in the late 1920s. Dyessholds

Former Clemson football player Jimmie Dyess won the Congressional Medal of Honor and the Carnegie Medal.

the distinction of being the only person in the United Stats ever to have won the Congressional Medal of Honor and the Carnegie Medal.

Jimmy Dyess was the third of four children, and was born on January 11, 1909 in Augusta, GA. Dyess played football at Clemson and at 6-1, 190 pounds he was the starting end on the freshman football team in 1927, and made the varsity squad as a lineman during his sophomore and junior years.

He was a letterman on Clemson's 1929 team that finished with an 8-3 record. But toward the end of that year, his junior season, Dyess suffered a serious knee injury that would prevent him from playing his senior season, so he shifted his focus to the rifle team, where he was the captain and an accomplished marksman.

On July 13, 1928, in the summer between his freshman and sophomore years, Dyess was vacationing with his family at a beach just north of Charleston on Sullivan's Island when a storm rolled in, bringing high winds and waves. He came upon a group of onlookers, as apparently one woman, Miss Barbara Muller, was attempting to rescue another, Mrs. Roscoe Holley, who had been swept out to sea.

Several other unsuccessful attempts had been made by some of the onlookers on the beach. Miss Muller made one last effort to save Mrs. Holley. Upon realizing the situation, Dyess immediately went into the sea after the two women, who had been carried out as far as 200 yards.Dyess was not an experienced swimmer,and nor was he used to such rough currents. After several minutes of near doom, Dyess helped the two women to shore, after which he gave further assistance in aiding the resuscitation.

An article in the Augusta newspaper chronicled the incident, citing that "on-lookers give high praise to Miss Muller for a display of bravery and self-sacrifice seldom equaled and never surpassed, and added that but for the strength and cool-headedness of Jimmie Dyess, both girls would undoubtedly have been lost."

Dyess received the Carnegie Medal for his heroism on that day, an award that is given to heroic Americans and Canadians who, at risk to their own lives, save or attempt to save the life of another. It is "America's highest award for heroism by civilians," and it was presented to Dyess in 1929. Dyess always gave credit to Miss Muller, who also earned the Carnegie Medal, for diving in first after Mrs. Holley.

The Augusta native, nicknamed "Big Red," was a Marine Corps reservist called to active duty in 1940. On Feb. 1, 1944, he led his men in the 4th Marine Division during battle at Green Beach on Roi-Namur Island—one of the Marshall Islands.

At the end of the first day of combat, he found out that there were Marines caught beyond enemy lines and were facing heavy pressure. It was almost dark, but Dyess organized a small rescue force and they broke through enemy lines and braved heavy gunfire to rescue the stranded men.

Closing in on the remaining Japanese military on the second day, Dyess maneuvered troops and tanks inland. Around 10:45 p.m. on February 2, Dyess was struck by a bullet in the head, killing him instantly as he was leading his men. Dyess left behind a 32-year-old wife and eight-year-old daughter.

Because of his bravery and his service beyond the call of duty, Dyess was awarded the Medal of Honor posthumously.

The sad tragedy of losing a set of brothers struck the Clemson family, as Ben McKnight and John McKnight of Kannapolis, NC were killed in World War II shortly after graduating from Clemson.

The McKnight brothers were also stalwart members of the Clemson Swimming team that captured the 1939 Southern Conference Championships. Thebrothers were only 10 months apart in age, with John being the oldest.

They were the sons of Mr. and Mrs. T. C. McKnight, who were living in Elkin, NC. Mr. McKnight, the father, was an administrator at the YMCA in Kannapolis. Both Ben and John practically grew up in the Cannon Memorial Y and Ben wanted to work at a YMCA when he returned home. Both boys graduated from Cannon High School before enrolling at Clemson.

Ben McKnight majored in general science. He was cocaptain of the swimming team and graduated from Clemson in 1941.

As a first lieutenant in the Army, he was in the 128th Infantry Regiment, 32nd Infantry the "Red Arrow" Division.

Ben participated in the Papua Campaign. Initially, his unit blocked the Japanese advance down the Kokoda Trail. He led in the Battle of the Buna-Gona Beachhead beginning November 19, 1942. Ben was killed in action on December 26, 1942 during the Battle for Buna Mission. He was awarded the Combat Infantry Badge, Bronze Star Medal, Purple Heart, American Campaign Medal, Asiatic-Pacific Campaign Medal with Bronze Service Star, and the WWII Victory Medal. His parents had just received a letter from Ben before receiving the news of his death.

John McKnight graduated in 1940 with a degree in general science. As a captain, he was in the transportation corps. He was killed in non-battle injuries on May 28, 1945, in Germany.

Both Ben and John were buried in Columbia, SC, at a double funeral service on December 11, 1948.

Another Clemson hero, Aubrey Rion, was a three-sport athlete at Clemson and served in World War II. He majored in general science and was a member of Tiger Brotherhood and Sigma Tau Epsilon.

He ran track and was a member of the boxing and football teams. He was a reserve tailback behind Banks McFadden on the 1939 team that went on to defeat Boston College in the 1940 Cotton Bowl. In boxing, he was the middleweight for the Tigers that won the 1940 Southern Conference title, as he compiled a 7-1 record that season.

The Columbia, SC native was killed in action at Bastogne, Belgium during the Battle of the Bulge on December 20, 1944. His unit was the 501st Parachute Infantry Regt, 101st Airborne Division.

Gary Pace was a member of the Clemson soccer team in 1967, 1968, and 1969. He was second-team All-ACC and had 234 career saves.

At Clemson he was in the Army ROTC, the Society of American Engineers, and American Society of Civil Engineers. He graduated with a degree in Civil Engineering.

The Easley, SC native served in Vietnam in Unit: B Company, 31st Engineer Battalion, 159th Engineer Group, 20th Engineer Brigade, US Army Vietnam as a Lieutenant.

Pace was killed in action against a hostile force on March 30, 1971, when enemy snipers attacked a fire support base named Lanyard, west of TayNinh City, TayNinh Province, South Vietnam near the Cambodian border. About nine engineers were wounded and three of them were on the ground, helpless and out in the open.

"Fearing that his men were open targets, Gary Pace put his dedication to his men above his own safety and went to their aid," said Tom Colaiezzi, a fellow soldier.

"In the process, Gary was hit with small arms fire from the snipers and was killed instantly. By firing at Gary, the snipers gave away their position and the engineers quickly eliminated them before they could do further damage. Gary was the only American soldier killed in that attack on Lanyard. If not for his efforts, the three wounded engineers and many others would surely have died."

For his heroism, Pace was awarded the Silver Star, Bronze Star, Purple Heart, National Defense Service Medal, Vietnam Service Medal, Republic of Vietnam Gallantry Cross Unit Citation with Palm, and Republic of Vietnam Campaign Medal.

He left behind a wife, Patricia Keller Pace of Lancaster, PA.

Coach Ibrahim, Pace's former soccer coach at Clemson, once recalled Pace and his sacrifice, "Gary was my first goal keeper," said Ibrahim, who coached the Tigers in 1967-94. "He was brave, and I was so sad to hear of his death. It was so sad; Gary was a good man."

In the April 7, 1944, edition of *The Tiger*, then-student Roy Pearce wrote, "It made me sad to read the honor roll. . . . All were great men and we'll never let them down, never!"

As evident from the Scroll of Honor Memorial adjacent to Memorial Stadium, we will never forget the supreme sacrifice those brave soldiers made so that we may enjoy the precious gifts of freedom and liberty that we enjoy today.

AUBREY RION

Aubrey Rion had an early connection to Clemson even before the school was founded.

Aubrey's great-grandfather, Colonel James H. Rion, went to school with John C. Calhoun's children in Pendleton, S.C. at the Pendleton Male Academy. The Colonel's mother was the housekeeper at Fort Hill, the home of John C. Calhoun. He developed a close relationship with the Calhoun family, including Calhoun's daughter Anna Maria Calhoun Clemson and her husband, Thomas Green Clemson. The town of Rion, SC is named for Colonel Rion who became a prominent lawyer.

Aubrey's great-grandfather was Thomas Green Clemson's lawyer, financial advisor and close friend. Rion was a lawyer and the author of Clemson's first will that gave the Fort Hill estate and money to start the school that is Clemson University today. Rion passed away in 1886 of a heart attack. Colonel Richard W. Simpson became Clemson's lawyer, and the pair later made a few changes to the will.

Colonel Rion's wife, Catherine, is said to have advised Clemson on the estate's usage and helped plan some of the early buildings and their location on the Clemson College campus. It is believed that she was an architect and also enjoyed gardening and designing gardens and had a lot of experience in this area.

Aubrey Rion was an all-star athlete at Columbia High School in Columbia, SC.

He and his cousin Holbrook Rion won the state championship in the 220 yard low hurdles five times. Aubrey was also a star football player for his high school team. His cousin Holbrook went to the University of South Carolina and Aubrey chose Clemson.

"My father Holbrook thought the world of Aubrey," said Tuck Rion, a second cousin to Aubrey. "Aubrey had and still has a lot of influence on our family. We talk about him and his accomplishments quite often. He was someone you can look up too and respect. We are very proud of him. I even named my son after Aubrey."

"He was a wonderful brother," said Martha Alvey, Aubrey Rion's sister. "He was an excellent student and athlete growing up. Our other brother Wallace was an excellent student as well. Aubrey loved athletics and excelled at them. You couldn't have asked for two better brothers. I was very close to Aubrey and was very proud of him."

"There is no doubt about it, Aubrey loved Clemson," said Alvey. "When he first started at Clemson he wanted to be a doctor. He was preparing for that field and was going to medical school after Clemson, but World War II changed all that. He used to take me to the Clemson dances, and I would meet his friends and they would be in their Clemson uniforms. He met his wife Janette at one of the dances they used to have. He was a good dancer and was very popular with the ladies," said Alvey.

"He was very special."

"He was the best brother, friend, son, and husband there was," said Rion's sister, Mary Wittenberg. Anyone that knew him always considered him their favorite. He was good to everyone. His death devastated our family."

One of the football teams that helped put Clemson on the national radar was the 1939 team, of which Rion was a part.

At that time the Tigers were experiencing a special year. The school won the Southern Conference basketball and swimming championships on the same day on March 4th. Both events were unexpected as both teams were not favored. It was one of the greatest days in Clemson athletic history.

During that time World War II was starting. The Clemson cadets probably had in their minds that they may have to serve later. But at that time, they were focused on school and working hard to obtain a degree. It was a special time at Clemson as the athletic teams were doing so well. It was toward the end of the Great Depression and the Clemson campus was growing. It was an exciting time, but still an anxious time as the events of the world were so uncertain.

In the fall, it was the football team's time to grab the headlines. The 1939 team was a bright spot for the student body and alumni as Clemson went through the season with an 8-1 record. The Cotton Bowl issued a bid to the Tigers and was gladly accepted. This was a bigtime bowl inviting Clemson to the limelight of the New Year. It was a first for Clemson and the state.

Many of the Clemson players were from the state of South Carolina including Rion. He was a junior that season and was a backup tailback to the legendary Banks McFadden. He was in great company as stars like Joe Blalock, Bob Sharpe, Walter Cox, Shad Bryant, and Charlie Timmons and Joe Payne.

Rion averaged 4.0 yards per carry and scored two touchdowns that season, one against South Carolina and the other against Southwestern.

In his senior season, Frank Howard became the coach of the Tigers. In that season, the Tigers won the Southern Conference Championship with an undefeated league record.

In probably the best game of his career, Rion scored two touchdowns in the N.C. State game in 1940 at Memorial Stadium in Charlotte, NC. He led the team in scoring that year with 28 points and averaged 3.5 yards a carry. Rion scored the winning touchdown against Furman on November 23, 1940 (74 years ago this Sunday) that gave Clemson the Southern Conference title with the 13-7 victory.

Rion was a three-sport athlete at Clemson. He was a boxer for the Tigers and a member of the 1940 Southern Conference Championship team. He was also a member of the Tiger track team running the 100 and 220 yard dashes.

On February 15, 1941 Rion graduated early from Clemson with a degree in general science. He is a member of the prestigious Tiger Brotherhood (an honorary fraternity that is unique only to Clemson) the Columbia-Clemson Club, Block C Club, and the Sigma Tau Epsilon fraternity.

Like many others, Rion was living the American Dream. He graduated from Clemson, been a star athlete, and met his future wife at a dance that was held at Clemson. Everything was looking up for Rion and his future seemed bright. He got a job at Bennettsville (SC) High School as a teacher and coach.

He married Janette Stevenson on July 16, 1941 in Georgetown, SC.

On December 7, 1941, the Japanese bombed Pearl Harbor and the United States was drawn into the Second World War. Rion volunteered for service on June 30, 1942, less than two years after his final appearance on the Clemson gridiron and only six months after Pearl Harbor.

Rion was stationed at Fort Benning, GA for infantry training. He was an instructor at the Infantry School for one year and was transferred to the Parachute Infantry in 1944.

He volunteered to go overseas in October, 1944 because many of his men that he taught were going overseas. As a member of the 501st Airborne of the 101st Division, he saw action in Holland in November of that year.

On June 6, 1944 the Allies landed on the beaches of Normandy, beginning the offensive to push the Germans out of Western Europe and put an end to World War II. Another big event for Rion was the birth of his son Aubrey, Jr. on June 17.

Early on the morning of December 16, the Germans launched their last major offensive as an attempt to reach the American and the Allies' supply depots and ports. It would become known as the infamous Battle of the Bulge.

The next day, the 101st Airborne Division and Rion's Regiment were ordered to the Belgian cross roads of Bastogne, a key road junction in the path of the Germans' attack. The Allies refused to surrender to the Germans and held off Gerd Von Rundstedt's attack until help came. Rion's 501st regiment was the first to come in contact with the Germans. The 501st regiment fought bravely and did not lose any ground. By Christmas the weather had cleared and it allowed air strikes and General George Patton's Third Army reached the tired and embattled 101st Air Borne Division.

Rion did not live to see the victory as he was killed by a sniper's bullet on December 20. He was one of 580 paratroopers killed, wounded, or captured from Rion's Regiment. Rion saw one of his men wounded, and went to his aid. He picked up the wounded soldier and tried to carry him to safety, and that is when he was shot by the German sniper.

Winning this battle was the beginning of the end for the Germans.

Aubrey Rion, a first lieutenant, was awarded the Purple Heart. He was survived by his wife Janette and son Aubrey and is buried at the Luxembourg American Cemetery not far from General George Patton's grave.

Rion is one of almost 500 Clemson Alumni who made the ultimate sacrifice for their country. Their service and sacrifice should always be remembered.

THERE'S SOMETHING IN
These Hills

BY JOE SHERMAN, CLASS OF 1934

Times when so many things seem to be coming unglued are disquieting times. These are disquieting times.

It always intrigues me how nearly any specific condition of nearly any specific time can find some application in a Book that, essentially, was handed down to us by word of mouth century after century.

I believe it says somewhere, "I will lift up mine eyes unto the hills from whence cometh my help."

My thoughts are wandering through these upper South Carolina hills that shelter the University that forms common bonds for many thousands of people whom have studied here, or taught here, or worked here.

There's something in these hills that has touched every one of them, something that has rubbed off on them in varying degrees, something that has built within the breasts of all Clemson men and women an endearing spark akin to an eternal pride.

There's something in these hills. It was here when a handful of fledging faculty members greeted a relatively small band of 446 students more than 100 years ago. That was shortly after convict labor had competed an administration building and clock tower that still dominate these Blue Ridge foothills with a timelessness and serenity that impart inspiration and strength anew each time they are looked upon.

There's something in these hills that has endeared itself to an endless procession of administrators, teachers, students, secretaries, and workmen. Hundreds of names pass through my consciousness, names of people who gave selflessly of themselves to build the institution nestled here and who at one and the same time mined the priceless something the hills contain and returned to them still more of it.

I have my names and I see once more the faces and feel again the beloved personalities that go with them. If you will but close your eyes and drift awhile, you too will recall the names and faces and personalities of those who meant the most to you while the privilege of being among them was yours.

There's something in these hills and from them we have drawn the power to transcend the stresses and strains that tug away, that make things come unglued in these disquieting times, the power to cut through such modern concepts—and such modern facts—as generation gaps, communication gaps, and ideological gaps.

Where is the generation gap when an alumnus who spent four years in these hills before the turn of the century says, "Next to my church and my home, I love Clemson University beyond all other institutions this side of Heaven" and when a graduate-to-be says, "Excepting only my parents, Clemson has meant more to me and done more for me than anything that has touched my life"?

There's something in these hills that has bound together a man over ninety and a boy under twenty; something has given them common ground on which to stand and a start toward bridging, and eliminating, any gap or any stresses or any strain that might try to make unglued whatever they seek for themselves as they move out of these hills into the mountains, the plains, the oceans, the forests, the skies, and the storms of life.

We have all drawn from these hills something to suggest to youth that those over thirty can be trusted and to indicate to those over thirty that the qualities of youth are as sound today as they ever were.

There's something in these hills that brings together and binds together and holds together men and women of all persuasions, of all heights, sizes, weights, and cultural backgrounds—something that cuts across every difference, spans every gap, penetrates every wall—something that makes a man or a woman stand taller, feel better, and say with high pride to all within earshot, "I went to Clemson."

There's something in these hills and I suspect that's what it is—the ability of an institution through the unending dedication and greatness of its people—its administration, its faculty, its staff, its students, and its alumni—to impart to all it touches a respect, and admiration, an affection that stands firm in disquieting times when things around it give impressions of coming unglued.

Yes, there's something in these hills where the Blue Ridge yawns its greatness.

PART III

APPENDIX

CLEMSON
Baseball

BASEBALL COACHES

R. T. V. Bowman 1896-1898
Unknown 1899
John Heisman 1901-03
John McMakin 1904-06
Frank Shaughnessy 1907
Robert Lynch 1908
Jesse Reynolds 1909
Joe Holland 1910
Frank Dobson 1911-13
Thomas Robertson 1914
Vet Sitton 1915
Country Morris 1917
Edward Donahue 1918
Larry Conover 1921
L. V. H. Durfee 1922-24
Thomas May 1925
Cul Richards 1926
Tink Gillam 1927
Joe Guyon 1928-31
Jess Neely 1932-38
Randy Hinson 1939
Tom Rogers 1941
Frank Howard 1943
Walter Cox 1945
Bob Smith 1952-57
Bill Wilhelm 1958-93
Jack Leggett 1994-2015
Monte Lee 2016-Present

WILHELM MILESTONE VICTORIES

Win Date Opponent Score
1 3-24-1958 Michigan State 7-5
100 4-2-1960 Georgia 11-10
200 4-16-1968 South Carolina 6-5
300 3-17-1972 Georgia Southern 2-1
400 3-11-1976 Maryland 6-0
500 4-12-1978 Newberry 6-1
600 3-14-1981 Winthrop 9-5

700 3-12-1984 Marshall 8-1
800 5-5-1986 South Carolina 7-6
900 4-21-1988 Georgia Tech 7-4
1000 4-29-1990 Georgia Tech 17-10
1100 4-8-1992 South Carolina 5-3
1161 5-29-1993 Fresno State 10-3
Note: Home games in **bold**.

BASEBALL ALL-AMERICANS

Rusty Adkins 1965, 1966, 1967
Jason Angel 1991
Jeff Baker-2001, 2002
Chuck Baldwin 1986
Brian Barnes 1988, 1989
Kris Benson 1996
Patrick Boyd 1999
Kurt Bultmann 1999
Gary Burnham 1995
Dave Caldwell 1977
Scott Clackum 1998
Ty Cline 1960
Tyler Colvin 2006
Josh Cribb 2006
Jim Crowley 1991
Matthew Crownover 2015
Andy D'Alessio 2006
Jason Dawsey 1995
Rusty Gerhardt 1971
Nick Glaser 2000
Daniel Gossett 2014
Khalil Greene 2002
Mike Hampton 1994
Taylor Harbin 2005
Kris Harvey 2005
Bert Herffernan 1988
Matt Henrie 2002
Doug Hoffman 1959
Michael Johnson 2002
Billy Koch 1996
Brian Kowitz 1990

Joe Landrum 1947
Matthew LeCroy 1996, 1997
Dave Lynn 1960
Eric Macrina 1991
Brad McCann 2004
Jim McCollom 1985
Billy McMillon 1993
Brad Miller 2011
David Miller 1995
Shane Monahan 1994, 1995
Ryan Mottl 1998
Kevin Northrup 1992
Billy O'Dell 1954
Chris Okey 2015
Kyle Parker 2010
Chad Phillips 1993
Steve Reba 2001, 2002
Reid Rohlman 2015
Kurt Seibert 1976
Richie Shaffer 2012
Bill Spiers 1987
Casey Stone 2001
Tim Teufel 1980
Ken Vining 1996
Denny Walling 1975
Scott Winchester 1995

LONGEST HITTING STREAKS

1. Rusty Adkins 41
3. Brian Kowitz 37
4. Khalil Greene 34
5. Tyler Colvin 26
7. Will Lamb 25

MOST HOME RUNS IN A CAREER

Rk Player Year(s) HR
1. Jeff Baker 2000-02, 59
   Andy D'Alessio 2004-07, 59
2. Michael Johnson 2000-03, 58
3. Matthew LeCroy 1995-97, 53
4. Jim McCollom 1982-85, 52
   Khalil Greene 1999-02, 52
5. Eric Macrina 1988-91, 51

ACC ATHLETE-OF-THE-YEAR

1996 Kris Benson, P

NATIONAL PLAYER OF THE YEAR

1996 Kris Benson, P
2002 Khalil Greene, SS
2011 Brad Miller
(Nation's Best Shortstop)
2016 Seth Beer, OF

NATIONAL FRESHMAN OF THE YEAR

2016 Seth Beer

ALL-COLLEGE WORLD SERIES

1959 Harold Stowe, P
1959 Bailey Hendley, P/OF
1959 Doug Hoffman, OF
1977 Dave Caldwell, OF
2002 Michael Johnson, 1B
2010 John Hinson, 3B

ACC COACH OF THE YEAR

1954 Bob Smith
1988 Bill Wilhelm
1991 Bill Wilhelm
1994 Jack Leggett
1995 Jack Leggett
2006 Jack Leggett

ACC PLAYER OF THE YEAR

1973 Craig White, OF
1974 Steve Cline, P
1975 Denny Walling, OF
1976 Chuck Porter, P
1985 Jim McCollom, 1B
1986 Chuck Baldwin, 1B
1989 Brian Barnes, P
1990 Brian Kowitz, OF
1995 Shane Monahan, OF
1996 Kris Benson, P
2002 Khalil Greene, SS
2011 Brad Miller, SS
2016 Seth Beer, OF

ACC ROOKIE OF THE YEAR

1995 Matthew LeCroy, C
1998 Patrick Boyd, OF
2016 Seth Beer, OF

ACC TOURNAMENT MVP

1989 Brian Barnes, P
1991 Michael Spiers, OF
1993 Jeff Morris, 2B
1994 Shane Monahan, OF
2006 Tyler Colvin, OF
2016 Mike Triller, OF

MOST PITCHING WINS IN A CAREER

Rk Player Year(s) Wins
1. Brian Barnes 1986-89, *44
2. Rusty Gerhardt 1969-72, 34

3. Ryan Mottl 1997-00, 33
Steve Reba 1999-02, 33

CLEMSON'S NO HITTERS

Date Pitcher(s) Opponent Score
4-15-1913 Doc Ezell, Erskine 5-0
4-29-1916 Elmer Long, Virginia Military 2-0
4-17-1924 Lefty Smith, South Carolina 6-0
3-29-1946 Joe Landrum, Erskine 6-0
5-8-1953 Billy O'Dell, South Carolina 2-0
5-6-1967 Nelson Gibson, Georgia Tech 3-0
          Charlie Watson
4-17-1971 Dave Van Volkenburg, # Florida State 11-0
3-16-1973 Lindsay Graham, ^ Maryland 3-0
4-17-1976 Ron Musselman, Virginia 9-0
3-17-1977 Brian Snyder, North Carolina-Wilmington
          8-0
3-10-1980 Mike Brown, *# North Carolina-Wilmington
          2-0
3-5-1982 Jeff Gilbert, Western Carolina 5-0
3-6-1984 Scott Parrish, # The Citadel(2) 6-0
3-18-2009 Justin Sarratt, Scott Weismann, Kyle Deese,
          Tomas Cruz, Matt Vaughn, South Carolina-Upstate
          14-0
*—perfect game; #—seven-inning game; ^—eight-in-
   ning game

HITTING FOR CYCLE

Fred Knoebel at South Carolina on May 5, 1950. Walk in 1st, triple in 2nd, single in 4th, home run in 5th, double in 7th, hit by-pitch in 8th. Clemson won 14-5.

Steve Tucker at Georgia Tech on Apr. 22, 1975. Double in 1st, on by error in 2nd, triple in 4th, home run in 6th, single in 7th, single in 9th. Clemson won 18-3.

Keith Williams at Furman on Apr. 20, 1993. Home run in 1st, double in 3rd, single in 6th, triple in 9th. Clemson won 17-2.

Shane Monahan at Hawaii-Hilo on Mar. 19, 1994. Triple in 1st, single in 2nd, home run in 6th, double in 8th, single in 9th. Clemson won 13-5.

Gary Burnham at Texas-Arlington on Feb. 18, 1995. Double in 1st, triple in 3rd, walk in 5th, strikeout in 6th, homer in 7th, single in 9th. Clemson won 18-0.

MEN'S
Basketball

MEN'S BASKETBALL ALL-AMERICANS

1939 Banks McFadden
1977 Tree Rollins
1980 Billy Williams
1987 Horace Grant
1990 Elden Campbell
1990 Dale Davis
1994 Sharone Wright

RETIRED NUMBERS

#23 Banks McFadden
#30 Tree Rollins
#34 Dale Davis

ALL-SOUTHERN CONFERENCE

1952 Johnny Snee

ALL-SOUTHERN CONFERENCE TOURNAMENT TEAM

1935 Alex Swails
1936 Tom Brown
1938 Banks McFadden
     Ed Kitchens
1939 Banks McFadden
     Jack Bryce
1940 Banks McFadden
1952 Johnny Snee

ALL-ATLANTIC COAST CONFERENCE TOURNAMENT TEAM

1955 Bill Yarborough
1961 Choppy Patterson
1962 Jim Brennan
1964 Nick Milasnovich
1967 Randy Manhaffey
1975 Skip Wise

1976 Stan Rome
1980 Billy Williams
1981 Larry Nance
1984 Murray Jarman
1990 Dale Davis
1993 Sharone Wright
     Chris Whitney
1996 Greg Buckner
1998 Terrell McIntyre
2005 Shawan Robinson
2008 Trevor Booker
     K.C. Rivers
     Cliff Hammonds
     James Mays
2011 Demontez Stitt

ACC PLAYER OF THE YEAR

1987 Horace Grant

ACC ROOKIE OF THE YEAR

1995 Greg Buckner

ACC COACH OF THE YEAR

1987 Cliff Ellis
1990 Cliff Ellis

ALL-ACC

1955 Bill Yarborough
1956 Bill Yarborough
     Vince Yokel
1958 Vince Yockel
1960 Choppy Patterson
1961 Choppy Patterson
1963 Jim Brennan
1964 Jim Brennan
1965 Randy MaHaffey
1965 Jim Sutherland

1967 Randy Mahaffey
1967 Jim Sutherland
1968 Butch Zatezalo
1970 Butch Zatezalo
1975 Skip Wise
1975 Tree Rollins
1976 Tree Rollins
1977 Tree Rollins
Stan Rome
1980 Billy Williams
1981 Larry Nance
1982 Vincent Hamilton
1986 Horace Grant
1987 Horace Grant
1988 Elden Campbell
1989 Elden Campbell
1989 Dale Davis
1990 Elden Campbell
1990 Dale Davis
1991 Dale Davis
1993 Sharone Wright
1993 Chris Whitney
1994 Sharone Wright
1994 Devin Gray
1997 Greg Buckner
1997 Terrell McIntyre
1998 Greg Buckner
1998 Terrell McIntyre
1999 Terrell McIntyre
2000 Will Solomon
2001 Will Solomon
2002 Edward Scott
2003 Edward Scott
2005 Sharrod Ford

2008 K. C. Rivers
2008 Cliff Hammonds
2009 Trevor Booker
2010 Trevor Booker
2011 Demontez Stitt
2013 Devon Booker
2014 K.J. McDaniels
2016 Jaron Blossomgame

COACHES

1911-13 Frank Dobson
1913-15 John Erwin
1915-16 A. H. Ward
1916-17 Country Morris
1919-20 Country Morris
1917-19 Jiggs Donahue
1920-21 Larry Conover
1921-23 E. J. Stewart
1923-25 Bud Saunders
1925-26 A. A. Gilliam
1927-31 Josh Cody
1931-40 Joe Davis
1940-46 Rock Norman
1946-56 Banks McFadden
1956-62 Press Maravich
1963-70 Bobby Roberts
1970-75 Tates Locke
1975-84 Bill Foster
1984-94 Cliff Ellis
1994-98 Rick Barnes
1998-03 Larry Shyatt
2003-10 Oliver Purnell
2010-Present Brad Brownell

WOMEN'S
Basketball

NCAA TOURNAMENT ALL-REGION TEAM

1991 East Regional All-Tournament
Cheron Wells

ATLANTIC COAST CONFERENCE TOURNAMENT MVP

1981 Barbara Kennedy
1982 Barbara Kennedy
1996 Laura Cottrell
1999 Itoro Umoh

ATLANTIC COAST CONFERENCE PLAYER OF THE YEAR

1994 Jessica Barr

ATLANTIC COAST CONFERENCE COACH OF THE YEAR

1990 Jim Davis
1994 Jim Davis

ALL-AMERICAN PLAYERS

1981 Barbara Kennedy
1982 Barbara Kennedy
1985 Janet Knight (3rd)
1989 Michelle Bryant (4th)
1991 Jackie Farmer (4th)
1992 Cheron Wells (3rd)
1993 Shandy Bryan (2nd)
1994 Jessica Barr

REGION ALL-AMERICA PLAYERS

1981 Barbara Kennedy
1982 Barbara Kennedy

1993 Shandy Bryan
1994 Jessica Barr
1996 Stephanie Ridgeway
1999 Itoro Umoh
2001 Chrissy Floyd
2002 Chrissy Floyd
2003 Chrissy Floyd
2004 Lakeia Stokes

FIRST TEAM ALL-ATLANTIC COAST CONFERENCE

Donna Forester 1978
Cissy Bristol 1979
Barbara Kennedy 1980, 1981, 1982
Mary Ann Cubelic 1982, 1983
Janet Knight 1985
Shandy Bryan 1993
Jessica Barr 1994
Tara Saunooke 1995
Stephanie Ridgeway 1996
Amy Geren 1998, 1999
Itoro Umoh 1999
Chrissy Floyd 2002

COACHES

1975-76 Mary King
1976-87 Annie Tribble
1987-05 Jim Davis
2005-10 Cristy McKinney
2010-13 Itoro Coleman
2013-Present Audra Smith

CLEMSON
Boxing

BOXING COACHES

1928 Dizzy McLeod
1929-31 Joe Guyon
1932-33 Capt. Pete Heffner
1934-1941 Bob Jones
1942 Walter Cox
1947-48 Bob Jones

CLEMSON'S CAREER LIST FOR MOST WINS

1. 16-4, Bill Cason, 1937-39
2. 15-1, Russell Dorn, 1937-38
3. 14-4-1, Warren Wilson, 1939-1941

CLEMSON CAREER LIST FOR MOST KNOCKOUTS

4, Bob Jones, 1936-38
3, Warren Wilson, 1939-41
3, Cliff Henley, 1934-36
3, Russell Dorn, 1937-38
3, Bill Cason 1937-39

NCAA TOURNAMENT FINALIST

1938 John Murray

CLEMSON LIST FOR MOST WINS IN A SINGLE SEASON

8, Russell Dorn, 1937
7, Russell Dorn, 1938
7, Bill Cason, 1938

CLEMSON LIST FOR MOST KOS IN SINGLE SEASON

3, Clifford Henley, 1936
2, Rueben Seigel, 1930
2, Bob Jones, 1936 & 1937
2, Russell Dorn, 1938
2, Bill Cason, 1938
2, Henry Covington, 1939
2, Warren Wilson, 1940

SOUTHERN CONFERENCE CHAMPIONS

1937 Russell Dorn, Junior Middleweight
1938 Russell Dorn, Junior Middleweight
    Harvey Ferguson, Light Heavyweight
1940 Harvey Ferguson, Light Heavyweight
    Warren Wilson, Heavyweight
1941 Warren Wilson, Heavyweight
1947 Jerry Orr, Featherweight
    Carl Pulkinen, Lightweight

MEN'S
Cross Country

ALL-AMERICA RUNNERS

(NCAA Finishes)
1980
  Hans Koeleman, 11th
  Terry Goodenough, 24th
1981
  Jim Haughey, 32nd
1982
  Hans Koeleman, 3rd
  Jim Haughey, 34th
1983
  Hans Koeleman, 7th
  Stijn Jaspers, 16th
1987
  Dov Kremer, 22nd
1988
  Yehezkel Halifa, 2nd
  Dov Kremer, 6th
2003
  Scott Shaw, 34th

COACHES

1915-20 No Coach
1920 Roy Ellison
1921 D.K. Summers
1922-24 W.D. Reed

1925-26 Tommy Hart
1927-30 Jules Carson
1931-54 No Teams
1955-56 Rock Norman
1957-59 Banks McFadden
1960-73 H.C. (Pee Wee) Greenfield
1974-75 Jim Moorhead
1976-82 Sam Colson
1983-84 Stan Narewski
1985-87 Wade Williams
1988-07 Bob Pollock
2008-12 Lawrence Johnson
2013-Present Mark Elliott

ACC INDIVIDUAL CHAMPIONS

1976 Dean Matthews
1980 Hans Koeleman
1981 Julius Ogaro
1982 Hans Koeleman
1983 Hans Koeleman
1984 Robert deBrouwer
1986 Martin Flynn
1988 Dov Kremer
1991 Cormac Finnerty
1994 Kevin Hogan
2006 Itay Magidi

WOMEN'S
Cross Country

ALL-AMERICA RUNNERS

(NCAA Finishes)
1981
    Kerry Robinson 25th
    Cindy Duarte 30th
1982
    Stephanie Weikert 16th
1983
    Tina Krebs 7th
1984
    Tina Krebs 5th
1986
    Ute Jamrozy 4th
1989
    Anne Evans 19th
1990
    Anne Evans 7th
    Mareike Ressing 15th
2016
    Grace Barnett 9th

ACC INDIVIDUAL CHAMPIONS

1986 Ute Jamrozy
1990 Anne Evans

COACHES

1977-84 Sam Colson
1985-97 Wayne Coffman
1998 Ron Garner
1999 Ralph White
2000-07 Marcia Noad
2008-13 Lawrence Johnson
2013-Present Mark Elliott

MEN'S
Fencing

ALL-AMERICA FENCERS

1977 Steve Renshaw, Sabre (First)
1978 Steve Renshaw, Sabre (Second)
1979 Steve Renshaw, Sabre (Second)
     Jay Thomas, Épée (Second)
1980 Jay Thomas, Épée (Second)
     Steve Renshaw, Sabre (HM)
1981 Mark Wasserman, Sabre (Second)
     Craig Vecchione, Foil (HM)
     Jay Thomas, Épée (HM)
1982 Jay Thomas, Épée (First)
     Mark Wasserman, Sabre (HM)
     Guy Johnson, Foil (HM)

NCAA FINALISTS

1971
     Wayne Baker, Sabre 9th
     Tom Gambill Épée, 22nd
     Paul Ferry, Foil, 23rd
1976
     Jim Walters, Épée, T15th
     Jim Heck, Sabre, T15th
1977
     Steve Renshaw, Sabre, 5th
     George Podgorski, Épée, 19th

1978
     Steve Renshaw, Sabre, 3rd
     Frank Ceva, Foil, 8th
     Don Fletcher, Épée, 20th
1979
     Steve Renshaw, Sabre, 4th
     Jay Thomas, Épée, 5th
1980
     Steve Renshaw, Sabre, 7th
     Jay Thomas, Épée, 5th
     Craig Vecchione, Foil, 11th
1981
     Mark Wasserman, Sabre, 6th
     Jay Thomas, Épée, 8th
     Craig Vecchione, Foil, 10th
1982
     Guy Johnson, Foil, 9th
     Mark Wasserman, Sabre, 10th
     Jay Thomas, Épée, 4th

ATLANTIC COAST CONFERENCE CHAMPIONS

1980 Steve Renshaw, Sabre
1977 George Podgorski, Épée
1980 Jay Thomas, Épée

FIELD
Hockey

YEARLY GOAL SCORING LEADERS

1977 Not Available
1978, Mary Pat Curley, 11
1979, Susan Alton, 13
1980, Barbie Johnson, 22
1981, Barbie Johnson, 24

YEARLY ASSIST LEADERS

1978 Carol Luce 3
1979 Carol Luce 3
      Melanie Padovano 3
      Sarah Richmond 3
1980 Carol Luce 15
1981 Carol Luce 8
      Lynne Cannon 8

CAREER LEADERS

Goals-Barbie Johnson 54
Assists-Carol Luce 29

YEAR-BY-YEAR FIELD HOCKEY RESULTS

1977 1-11-1
1978 11-5-3
1979 14-2
1980 12-5-2
1981 14-4
Totals 52-27-6

CLEMSON
Football

NATIONAL PLAYERS OF THE YEAR

CBS/Chevrolet Defensive Player of the Year
   Terry Kinard (1982)
John Mackey Award
   Dwayne Allen (2011)
Ted Hendricks Award
   Da'Quan Bowers (2010)
Bronko Nagurski Trophy
   Da'Quan Bowers (2010)
Archie Griffin Award
   Deshaun Watson (2015)
Davey O'Brien Award
   Deshaun Watson (2015, 2016)
Manning Award
   Deshaun Watson (2015, 2016)
Chic Harley Award
   Deshaun Watson (2016)
Johnny Unitas Award
   Deshaun Watson (2016)
Bobby Bowden Award
   Deshaun Watson (2016)
Jack Lambert Award
   Ben Boulware (2016)

NATIONAL COACHES OF THE YEAR

AFCA Coach of the Year
   Danny Ford (1981)
Bobby Dodd Coach of the Year
   Dabo Swinney (2011)
Woody Hayes Trophy
   Danny Ford (1981)
Eddie Robinson Coach of the Year
   Danny Ford (1981)
   Dabo Swinney (2015)
Walter Camp Coach of the Year
   Dabo Swinney (2015)
George Munger Coach of the Year
   Dabo Swinney (2015)
AFCA Coach of the Year
   Dabo Swinney (2015)

Associated Press Coach of the Year
   Dabo Swinney (2015)
CBS Sports Coach of the Year
   Dabo Swinney (2015)
Bear Bryant Award
   Dabo Swinney (2015 & 2016)

NATIONAL FRESHMAN OF THE YEAR

Anthony Simmons 1995
Sammy Watkins 2011

ACC PLAYER OF THE YEAR

Buddy Gore 1967
Steve Fuller 1977, 1978
Jeff Davis 1981
William Perry 1984
Michael Dean Perry 1987
CJ Spiller 2009
Tajh Boyd 2012
Deshaun Watson, 2015

ACC COACH OF THE YEAR

Frank Howard 1958, 1966
Red Parker 1974
Charley Pell 1977, 1978
Danny Ford 1981
Tommy Bowden 1999, 2003
Dabo Swinney 2015

ACC OFFENSIVE PLAYER OF THE YEAR

CJ Spiller 2009
Tajh Boyd 2012

ACC DEFENSIVE PLAYER OF THE YEAR

Keith Adams 1999
Leroy Hill 2004
Gaines Adams 2006

Da'Quan Bowers 2010

ACC ROOKIE OF THE YEAR

Chuck McSwain 1979
Terry Allen 1987
Ronald Williams 1990
Anthony Simmons 1995
James Davis 2005
Sammy Watkins 2011

EARLY STARS FOR THE TIGERS

The following players made All South prior to the
Southern Conference
1900 Norman Walker (T) Buster Hunter (B)
1902 Vet Sitton (E) Jock Hanvey (B), John Maxwell (B)
Hope Sadler (E)
1903 John Maxwell (B), Jock Hanvey (B), O.L.
Derrick (G)
1905 Gus Keasler (C)
1906 Mac McLaurin (T) Fritz Furtick (B)
1913 Shorty Schilletter (G)
1917 Mutt Gee (C)
1919 L.M. Bull Lightsey (G) R.C. Potts (G) Stumpy
Banks (B)
1920 L.M. Bull Lightsey (G)
1922 L.M. Bull Lightsey (T)

ALL AMERICA PLAYERS

O. K. Pressley, Center, 1928
Banks McFadden, Back, 1939
Joe Blalock, End, 1940, 1941
Ralph Jenkins, Center, 1945
Bobby Gage, Tailback, 1948
Jackie Calvert, Safety, 1950
Tom Barton, Guard, 1952
Joel Wells, Back, 1955
Lou Cordileone, Tackle, 1959
Wayne Mass, Offensive Tackle, 1966
Harry Olszewski, Offensive Guard, 1967
Dave Thompson, Offensive Guard, 1970
Bennie Cunningham, Tight End, 1974, 1975
Joe Bostic, Offensive Guard, 1977, 1978
Jerry Butler, Split End, 1978
Steve Fuller, Quarterback, 1978
Jim Stuckey, Defensive Tackle, 1979
Obed Ariri, Placekicker, 1980
Jeff Davis, Linebacker, 1981
Perry Tuttle, Wide Receiver, 1981
Jeff Bryant, Defensive Tackle, 1981
Lee Nanney, Offensive Tackle, 1981
Terry Kinard, Free Safety, 1981, 1982
Johnny Rembert, Linebacker, 1982
James Robinson, Defensive Tackle, 1983
James Farr, Offensive Guard, 1983
William Perry, Middle Guard, 1982, 1983, 1984

Donald Igwebuike, Placekicker, 1984
Dale Hatcher, Punter, 1984
Steve Reese, Offensive Guard, 1985
Terrence Flagler, Tailback, 1986
John Phillips, Offensive Guard, 1986, 1987
David Treadwell, Placekicker, 1987
Michael Dean Perry, Defensive Tackle, 1987
Donnell Woolford, Cornerback, 1987, 1988
Stacy Long, Offensive Tackle, 1989, 1990
Chris Gardocki, Placekicker, 1989, 1990
Rob Bodine, Middle Guard, 1991
Jeb Flesch, Offensive Guard, 1991
Levon Kirkland, Outside Linebacker, 1990, 1991
Ed McDaniel, Linebacker, 1991
Nelson Welch, Placekicker, 1992
Stacy Seegars, Offensive Guard, 1992, 1993
Brian Dawkins, Strong Safety, 1995
Anthony Simmons, Inside Linebacker, 1995, 1996,
1997
Jim Bundren, Offensive Tackle, 1997
Antwan Edwards, Defensive Back, 1998
Keith Adams, Linebacker, 1999, 2000
Rod Gardner, Wide Receiver, 2000
Robert Carswell, Free Safety, 2000
Kyle Young, Center, 2000
Brian Mance, Cornerback, 2002
Leroy Hill, Linebacker, 2004
Justin Miller, Kick Returner, 2004
Tye Hill, Cornerback, 2005
Gaines Adams, Defensive End, 2006
Nathan Bennett, Offensive Guard, 2006
Chris McDuffie, Offensive Guard, 2007
Barry Richardson, Offensive Tackle, 2007
C.J. Spiller, Running Back, 2009
Thomas Austin, Offensive Guard, 2009
DeAndre McDaniel, Safety, 2009, 2010
Da'Quan Bowers, Defensive End, 2010
Dwayne Allen, Tight End, 2011
Andre Branch, Defensive End, 2011
Sammy Watkins, Wide Receiver, 2011, 2012, 2013
Tajh Boyd, Quarterback, 2012
Dalton Freeman, Center, 2012
DeAndre Hopkins, Wide Receiver, 2012
Vic Beasley, Defensive End, 2013, 2014
Grady Jarrett, Defensive Tackle, 2014
MacKensie Alexander, Cornerback, 2015
Greg Huegel, Placekicker, 2015
Jayron Kearse, Strong Safety, 2015
Shaq Lawson, Defensive End, 2015
Jordan Leggett, Tight End, 2015, 2016
Deshaun Watson, Quarterback, 2015, 2016
Ben Boulware, Linebacker, 2016
Condrea Tankersley, Cornerback, 2016
Carlos Watkins, Defensive Tackle, 2016
Christian Wilkins, Defensive Tackle, 2016

MEN'S
Golf

HEAD COACHES

George Hodges 1930
Bob Jones 1931-1939, 1947-1949, 1970-1974
Bob Moorman 1950-1961
Bobby Roberts 1962
Whitey Jordan 1963-1968
Claire Caskey 1969
Bobby Robinson 1975-1983
Larry Penley 1984-Present

NCAA CHAMPION

1997 Charles Warren, Jr.

DAVE WILLIAMS AWARD

(National Senior Player of the
Year)
1998 Charles Warren, Sr.

ARNOLD PALMER AWARD

1997 Charles Warren, Jr.

BEN HOGAN AWARD

2002 D. J. Trahan, Jr.
2009 Kyle Stanley, Jr.

JACK NICKLAUS AWARD

2002 D. J. Trahan, Jr.

BYRON NELSON AWARD

2016 Stephen Behr

ALL-AMERICAS

1980 Clarence Rose (2nd)
1983 Dillard Pruitt (2nd)

1984 Dillard Pruitt (2nd)
1987 Kevin Johnson (3rd)
    Jason Griffith (HM)
1988 Kevin Johnson (1st)
    Chris Patton (2nd)
    Oswald Drawdy (HM)
1989 Chris Patton (lst)
    Kevin Johnson (2nd)
    Oswald Drawdy (HM)
1990 Chris Patton (1st)
    Oswald Drawdy (3rd)
    Danny Ellis (HM)
1991 Nicky Goetze (3rd)
    Bo Beard (HM)
1992 Nicky Goetze (HM)
    Danny Ellis (HM)
1993 Nicky Goetze (2nd)
    Danny Ellis (HM)
    Bobby Doolittle (HM)
    Thump Delk (HM)
    Mark Swygert (HM)
1994 Mark Swygert (HM)
1996 Charles Warren (3rd)
    Richard Coughlan (HM)
    Joey Maxon (HM)
1997 Charles Warren (1st)
    Richard Coughlan (1st)
1998 Charles Warren (1st)
    Joey Maxon (HM)
    Jonathan Byrd (HM)
1999 Jonathan Byrd (1st)
    John Engler (1st)
    Lucas Glover (HM)
2000 Lucas Glover (1st)
    John Engler (2nd)
    Jonathan Byrd (3rd)
    D. J. Trahan (HM)
2001 Lucas Glover (1st)
    John Engler (1st)
    D. J. Trahan (HM)
2002 D. J. Trahan (1st)

Gregg Jones (2nd)
2003 D. J. Trahan (1st)
Jack Ferguson (2nd)
Matt Hendrix (3rd)
2004 Jack Ferguson (2nd)
Matt Hendrix (2nd)
2006 Brian Duncan (3rd)
Stephen Poole (HM)
2007 Kyle Stanley (1st)
2008 Kyle Stanley (HM)
2009 Kyle Stanley (1st)
2010 Ben Martin (HM)
2012 Corbin Mills (3rd)
2016 Stephen Behr (2nd)
Austin Langdale (HM)

NATIONAL COACH OF THE YEAR

2003 Larry Penley

ACC COACH OF THE YEAR

1983 Bobby Robinson
1987 Larry Penley
1996 Larry Penley
1997 Larry Penley

1998 Larry Penley
2003 Larry Penley
2004 Larry Penley
2007 Larry Penley
2016 Larry Penley

ACC MVP

1997 Richard Coughlan
2002 D. J. Trahan
2007 Kyle Stanley

ACC ROOKIE OF THE YEAR

2000 D. J. Trahan
2007 Kyle Stanley
2016 Bryson Nimmer

ACC CHAMPION

1976 Parker Moore
1988 Kevin Johnson
1992 Danny Ellis
1997 Charles Warren
1998 Charles Warren
2001 John Engler
2009 David May (co-champion)

CLEMSON
Rowing

CLEMSON ACC CHAMPIONSHIP CREWS

Year Crew Rowers Time

2001 Varsity 4+ Barton, Kamnik, Burgess, Lindsey,
Christopher (cox.) 7:27.7

2005 Novice 8+ Heiner, Kolodaike, Clayton, Gregan,
Mayer, Lynch, Sheppard, Wait,
Fernandez (cox., 7:20.2)

2008 Novice 8+ Geer, Kelly, Hudome,
Forney, Wolff, Bowen, Daanen,
Robertson, Graham (cox.), 6:46.3

2009 Varsity 8+ Cumbest, Cummings, Wolff,
Kozuszek, Nance, Robb,
Bendik, Leidecker, Englund (cox.), 6:38.4

2009 Varsity 4+ Erdeky, O'Neill, Robinson,
Hassell, Razzolini (cox.), 7:43.1

2012 Varsity 4+ DuBrul, Clogston, Mosier, Hoynacki,
Richardson (cox.) 7:37.9

CRCA ALL-AMERICA ROWERS

2001 Lucy Doolittle (1st)
2002 Aimee Fox (1st)
      Lucy Doolittle (2nd)

2005 Ashlee Brown (2nd)
2006 Sarah Cooper (1st)
2007 Sarah Cooper (2nd)
2008 Suzanne Van Fleet (1st)
      Jessica Leidecker (2nd)
2009 Jessica Leidecker (1st)
      Hilary Cumbest (2nd)
      Brittany Cummings (2nd)
2010 Brittany Cummings (1st)
2011 Laura D'Urso (2nd)
2012 Heather Cummings (2nd)
2013 Laura Basadonna (2nd)
2014 Milena Heuer (2nd)

ACC COACH OF THE YEAR

2001 Susie Lueck
2005 Susie Lueck
2009 Richard Ruggieri

ACC FRESHMAN OF THE YEAR

2008 Liz Robb

MEN'S
Soccer

SOCCER AMERICA MVPS (ALL AMERICA PLAYERS)

1978 Damian Ogunsuyi
1981 Nnamdi Nwokocha
1983 Adubarie Otorubio
    Jamie Swanner
1985 Eric Eichmann
    Bruce Murray
1987 Bruce Murray
1993 Jimmy Glenn
1998 Wojtek Krakowiak
2000 Mark Lisi
2001 Oguchi Onyewu
2005 Nathan Sturgis
    Phil Marfuggi

NSCAA ALL AMERICA PLAYERS

1968 Mark Rubich (HM)
1972 Nabeel Kammoun (HM)
1973 Henry Abadi (1st)
1973 Clyde Browne (3rd)
1974 Clyde Browne (HM)
1978 Christian Nwokocha (HM)
1979 Nnamdi Nwokocha (1st)
1981 Nnamdi Nwokocha (3rd)
1982 Mo Tinsley (3rd)
    Adubarie Otorubio (1st)
1983 Adubarie Otorubio (2nd)
    Jamie Swanner (1st)
1984 Adubarie Otorubio (1st)
1985 Bruce Murray (1st)
    Eric Eichmann (1st)
    Gary Conner (2nd)
1986 Eric Eichmann (3rd)
1987 Bruce Murray (1st)
    Paul Rutenis (1st)
1989 Pearse Tormey (2nd)
1990 Pearse Tormey (3rd)
    Jimmy Glenn (2nd)

1991 Andy Pujats (2nd)
1993 Jimmy Glenn (1st)
1995 Wolde Harris (2nd)
    Dana Quick (2nd)
1996 Danny Care (3rd)
1997 Matt Jordan (1st)
1998 Wojtek Krakowiak (1st)
2000 Mark Lisi (1st)
    Mike Potempa (2nd)
2001 Oguchi Onyewu (2nd)
2002 Doug Warren (1st)
    Dimelon Westfield (2nd)
2005 Phil Marfuggi (2nd)
    Nathan Sturgis (3rd)
2006 Dane Richards (2nd)
2013 Thomas McNamara (2nd)
2015 Kyle Fisher (1st)
    Andrew Tarbell (2nd)
    T.J. Casner (3rd)

ACC PLAYER OF THE YEAR

1972 Clyde Browne
1973 Clyde Browne
1974 Clyde Browne
1975 Clyde Browne,
    Godwin Ogbueze
1976 Godwin Ogbueze
1977 Benedict Popoola
1978 Damian Ogunsuyi
1979 Nnamdi Nwokocha
1983 Adubarie Otorubio
1985 Gary Conner
1993 Jimmy Glenn
1998 Wojtek Krakowiak
2005 Nathan Sturgis (Defensive)
2015 Kyle Fisher (Defensive)
    Paul Clowes (Midfield)

ACC COACH OF THE YEAR

Dr. I. M. Ibrahim 1973, 1978, 1985, 1990, 1993
Trevor Adair 1998

ACC ROOKIE OF THE YEAR

Jimmy Glenn 1990
Paul Stalteri 1996

MVP ACC TOURNAMENT

1993 Jaro Zawislan
1998 Josh Campbell
2001 Ian Fuller
2014 Paul Clowes

NATIONAL COACH OF THE YEAR

2015 Mike Noonan

CLEMSON'S NATIONAL GOAL-SCORING LEADERS

Year	Rk	Player	Goals
1972	1st	Henry Abadi	32
1993	1st	Jimmy Glenn	32
	2nd	Wolde Harris	29
1994	1st	Wolde Harris	26
1995	T5th	Wolde Harris	21
1998	1st	Wojtek Krakowiak	31
2002	T6th	Dimelon Westfield	20

WOMEN'S
Soccer

NSCAA ALL-AMERICA SELECTIONS

1995 Carmie Landeen (3rd)
1997 Sara Burkett (2nd)
2000 Nancy Augustyniak (2nd)
2001 Katie Carson (3rd)
2002 Deliah Arrington (2nd)
2006 Ashley Phillips (3rd)
2015 Kailen Sheridan (3rd)

NSCAA SOUTHEAST REGIONAL COACH OF THE YEAR

2015 Eddie Radwanski

SOCCER BUZZ ALL-AMERICA HONOREES

1997 Sara Burkett, MF (2nd)
1998 Sara Burkett, MF (2nd)
1999 Beth Keller, F (3rd)
2000 Nancy Augustyniak, D (1st)
   Lindsay Browne, F (3rd)

2002 Deliah Arrington, F (3rd)
2006 Ashley Phillips, GK (3rd)

ACC PLAYER OF THE YEAR

2002 Deliah Arrington

ACC ROOKIE OF THE YEAR

1994 Carmie Landeen
2000 Lindsay Browne

WOMEN'S SOCCER COACHES

Tracey Leone 1994-1999
Ray Leone 1999-2000
Todd Bramble 2001-2007
Hershey Strosberg 2008-2010
Eddie Radwanski 2011-Present

MEN'S
Swimming and Diving

CLEMSON HEAD MEN'S SWIMMING AND DIVING COACHES

P. B. Holtzendorff 1927 1948
Carl McHugh 1948 1976
Bob Boettner 1976 1991
Jim Sheridan 1991 1994
Bruce Marchionda 1994 2002
Chris Ip 2002 2012

ATLANTIC COAST CONFERENCE DIVER OF THE YEAR

1985 Chuck Wade
1986 Chuck Wade
1988 Dave Hrovat
1996 Brian Haecker

ATLANTIC COAST CONFERENCE COACH OF THE YEAR

1985 Bob Boettner
1986 Bob Boettner

CLEMSON MEN'S SWIMMING AND DIVING ALL-AMERICA ATHLETES

Rick Aronberg 1986 HM 1650 Freestyle
1987 HM 1650 Freestyle
1989 HM 500 & 1650 Freestyle

Richard Bader 1978 100 Breaststroke
Peter Barkas 1978 400 Individual
Medley Mark Bertz 1982 800 Freestyle Relay
Mark Bridgers 1989 HM 200 Freestyle Relay
Neil Brophy 1982 800 Freestyle Relay
Seth Broster 2011 HM 200 Freestyle Relay
Eric Bruck 2011 HM 50 Freestyle, 200 Freestyle Relay
Coy Cobb 1982 100 Backstroke
1984 100 Backstroke & 100 Butterfly
1985 100 Backstroke & 100 Butterfly
Chris Dart 2011 HM 200 Freestyle Relay
Keith Emery 1982 800 Freestyle Relay
Mark Henly 2004 HM 200m Backstroke
Dave Hoydic 1989 HM 200 Freestyle Relay
Steve Hoydic 1989 HM 500 & 1650 Freestyle
MacElhatten 1982 800 Freestyle Relay
Dave Hrovat 1987 HM 1 Meter Diving Chip
Chris Reinke 2011 HM 200 Freestyle Relay
Mark Weber 1989 HM 200 Freestyle Relay

WOMEN'S
Swimming and Diving

SWIMMING AND DIVING COACHES

Coke Ellington 1975-1976
Bob Boettner 1976-1991
Jim Sheridan 1991-1994
Bruce Marchionda 1994-2002
Chris Ip 2002-2012

DIVING COACH

Leslie Hasselbach Adams, 2012-2016

ATLANTIC COAST CONFERENCE MEET MVP

Pam Hayden (1986)
Mitzi Kremer (1987)
Mitzi Kremer (1989)
Michelle Parkhurst (2008)

ATLANTIC COAST CONFERENCE DIVER OF THE YEAR

Carolyn Hodge (1985)
Jennie Graviss (1989)
Mandy Meek (1990)

ATLANTIC COAST CONFERENCE COACH OF THE YEAR

Bob Boettner (1986)*
Bob Boettner (1987)
Bob Boettner (1988)
Bob Boettner (1989)
Bruce Marchionda (1997)
*Co-Coach of the Year

ATLANTIC COAST CONFERENCE ROOKIE OF THE YEAR

Wendy Henson (1996)

CLEMSON WOMEN'S SWIMMING & DIVING ALL AMERICA ATHLETES

Alexandra Allen 2009 HM 200 Freesyle Relay
Jill Bakehorn 1987 HM 200 Backstroke
           1988 100 & 200 Backstroke, 400 MR, 400 FR, 200 MR, HM 200 IM, 200 FR
           1989 100 & 200 Backstroke, 200 MR, HM 400 MR, 200 IM, 400 FR
           1990 HM 100 Backstroke
Dianne Bravis 1988 400 FR, 200 MR, 800 FR, HM 50 Freestyle, 100 & 200 Freestyle
           1989 200 Freestyle, HM 400 FR, 800 FR
Jenna Burtch 2002 HM 400 MR
Kitty Christian 1986 400 MR, HM 200 MR
           1987 200 FR, HM 200 MR
Cappy Craig 1982 1 & 3 Meter Diving
Mandy Commons 2001 HM 200 MR, HM 100 Breaststroke 2002 HM 400 Medley Relay
Chris Daggit 1977 400 Individual Medley
Liz Dolan 1989 200 FR, HM 800 FR
           1992 HM 100 Backstroke, 800 FR
Janet Ellison 1978 50, 100, 200 Breaststroke, 100 IM, 200 MR
           1980 50 Breaststroke
Callie Emery 1985 800 Freestyle Relay
Coleen Falbo 1978 1650 Freestyle
Sue Flynn   1981 50 Backstroke
Jennie Graviss 1990 HM 1 & 3 Meter Diving
Ruth Grodsky 1987 400 MR, HM 200 MR
           1988 200 MR, HM 200 Breaststroke
           1989 200 MR, HM 400 MR
Shannon Halverstadt 1989 HM 800 Freestyle Relay
Pam Hayden 1985 200 & 500 Freestyle, 800 FR
           1987 500 Freestyle, 200 Butterfly, 800 FR, 200 FR, 400 FR, HM 200 Freestyle
           1988 200 & 500 Freestyle, 200 Butterfly, 400 MR, 400 FR, 800 FR, HM 200 FR
Wendy Henson 1996 HM 200 Freestyle
Patty Hider 2001 HM 200 Medley Relay
Cindy Holmes 1978 200 Medley Relay

Lynda Beth Hughes 1986 HM 200 Medley Relay
  1987 200 FR, 400 FR, 400 MR, HM 200 MR
  1988 200 MR, HM 200 FR
  1989 200 FR, 200 MR, HM 400 FR, 400 MR
Jan Kemmerling 1986 800 FR, HM 200 MR
  1987 200 IM, 400 & 800 FR, HM 400 IM
  1988 400 & 800 Freestyle Relay
Ginny Kirouac 2000 HM 400 Individual Medley
Mitzi Kremer 1987 100, 200, 500 Freestyle, 200, 400,
  800 FR, 400 MR
  1988 800 FR
  1989 100, 200, 500 Freestyle, 200
  MR, 200 Fr, HM 400 & 800 FR, 400 MR
Lindsey Kroeger 2001 HM 200 Medley Relay
  2002 HM 400 Medley Relay
Molly Kueny 1985 800 Freestyle Relay
  1986 1650 Freestyle, 800 FR
  1987 800 Freestyle Relay
Sharon Mecklenberg 1978 200 Medley Relay
Mandy Meek 1990 1 & 3 Meter Diving
Jennifer Mihalik 1998 HM 200 Backstroke
Michelle Parkhurst 2008 HM 200 Freestyle
  2009 HM 200 Freestyle Relay

Lindley Peterson 1978 200 MR, 50 Backstroke
Rachel Regone 2009 HM 200 Freestyle Relay
Julie Reid 1988 200 Butterfly, 400 MR
Michele Richardson 1992 1650 Freestyle, HM 800 FR
Kim Routh 2004 HM 1500m Freestyle
  2005 HM 1650 Freestyle, HM 500 Freestyle
  2006 1650 Freestyle, HM 500 Freestyle
Paulette Russell 1992 500 Freestyle, HM 400 IM, 800 FR
Linda Rutter 1985 200 Butterfly, 800 FR
  1986 400 MR, 800 FR, HM 500 Freestyle, 200
  Butterfly
Erin Schatz 1998 HM 1650 Freestyle
Nadra Simmons 1985 100 Backstroke
  1986 400 MR, HM 100 Backstroke, 200 MR
  1987 100 Backstroke, 400 MR, HM 200 MR
Lauren Sindall 2009 HM 200 Freestyle Relay
Cami Sink 1999 HM 400 Individual Medley
Terry Traynor 1978 1650 Freestyle
Elise Thieler 2001 HM 200 Medley Relay
2002 HM 400 Medley Relay
Susan Weiss 1988 400 Medley Relay
Lara Yaroszewski 1992 HM 800 Freestyle Relay

MEN'S
Tennis

MEN'S TENNIS COACHES

P. B. Holzendorff 1927
Hoke Sloan 1929-1957
Bill Seigler 1958
Les Longshore 1959-1962
Duane Bruley 1963-1973
Bill Beckwith 1974-1975
Chuck Kriese 1976-2008
Chuck McCuen 2009-2016
John Boetsch 2017-Present

ITA NATIONAL SENIOR PLAYER OF THE YEAR

1980 Mike Gandolfo
1982 Mark Dickson
1983 Jean Desdunes
1997 Mitch Sprengelmeyer

ITA NATIONAL ROOKIE OF THE YEAR

1984 Lawson Duncan

USPTA NATIONAL COACH OF THE YEAR

1981 & 1986 Chuck Kriese

ITA NATIONAL COACH OF THE YEAR

1986 Chuck Kriese

ACC TOURNAMENT MVP

1969 David Cooper
1979 Mike Gandolfo
1980 Mike Gandolfo
1988 Kent Kinnear
1989 John Sullivan
1997 Bruce Li

ACC COACH OF THE YEAR

1980 Chuck Kriese

1985 Chuck Kriese
1986 Chuck Kriese
1988 Chuck Kriese
1989 Chuck Kriese
1997 Chuck Kriese

ITA NATIONAL INDOOR DOUBLES TOURNAMENT

1980 Murphy-Dickson (Finalists)
1985 Matuszewski-Walters (Champions)
1986 Matuszewski-Walters (Finalists)

FINAL TOP-25 RANKED PLAYERS

Singles

1981 Mark Dickson T3
1984 Lawson Duncan 4
1985 Miguel Nido 19
1986 Richard Matuszewski 12
1986 Jay Berger 13
1987 Craig Boynton 25
1989 John Sullivan 12
1997 Mitch Sprengelmeyer 19
2006 Clement Reix 23

Doubles Teams

1983 Richard Akel/Craig Cooper 11
1983 Jean Desdunes/Rick Rudeen 18
1984 Andy Krantz/Rick Rudeen 17
1985 Richard Matuszewski/Brandon Walters 4
1985 Jay Berger/Miguel Nido 17
1986 Richard Matuszewski/Brandon Walters 8
1986 Jay Berger/Kent Kinnear 20
1986 Matt Frooman/Brian Page 24
1987 Kent Kinnear/Vince Van Gelderen 7
1987 Craig Boynton/John Sullivan 22
1988 Kent Kinnear/Vince Van Gelderen 19
1989 Vince Van Gelderen/Todd Watkins 21
1992 Greg Seilkop/George Lampert 22
1995 Frank Salazar/Mitch Sprengelmeyer 17

1996 Bruce Li/Mitch Sprengelmeyer 10
1997 Bruce Li/Mitch Sprengelmeyer 23
2000 Darren Knight/Josh Goffi 21
2003 Nathan Thompson/Jarmaine Jenkins 25
2004 Nathan Thompson/Jarmaine Jenkins 23
2006 Jarmaine Jenkins/Clement Reix 24
2013 Dominique Maden/Yannick Maden 8
2014 Dominique Maden/Hunter Harrington 5

CLEMSON ALL-AMERICA PLAYERS

1980 Mike Gandolfo, Singles
    Mark Dickson, Singles
    Pender Murphy, Singles & Doubles
1981 Mark Dickson, Singles & Doubles
    Pender Murphy, Singles & Doubles
1982 Mark Dickson, Singles
    Jean Desdunes, Singles
1983 Rick Rudeen, Singles
    Jean Desdunes, Singles
1984 Lawson Duncan, Singles
1985 Miguel Nido, Singles
    Richard Matuszewski, Singles & Doubles
    Brandon Walters, Doubles
1986 Jay Berger, Singles
    Richard Matuszewski, Singles & Doubles

    Brandon Walters, Doubles
1987 Craig Boynton, Doubles
    Kent Kinnear, Doubles
    John Sullivan, Doubles
    Vince Van Gelderen, Doubles
1989 John Sullivan, Singles
    Todd Watkins, Doubles
    Vince VanGelderen, Doubles
1996 Bruce Li, Doubles
    Mitch Sprengelmeyer, Doubles
1997 Mitch Sprengelmeyer, Singles
2004 Nathan Thompson, Doubles
    Jarmaine Jenkins, Doubles
2006 Clement Reix, Singles
2013 Dominique Maden, Doubles
    Yannick Maden, Doubles
2014 Dominique Maden, Doubles
    Hunter Harrington, Doubles

INTERCOLLEGIATE TENNIS ASSOCIATION (ITA) HALL OF FAME

2012 Chuck Kriese

WOMEN'S
Tennis

WOMEN'S TENNIS COACHES

Mary Kennerty King 1976-1982
Andy Johnston 1983-1997
Nancy Harris 1998-Present

OLYMPIC GOLD MEDALIST

1992
Gigi Fernandez (Doubles)
Barcelona, Spain
1996
Gigi Fernandez (Doubles)
Atlanta, Georgia

NCAA ALL-AMERICA HONOREES

1978 Susan Hill (singles)
1979 Susan Hill (singles)
1980 Susan Hill (singles)
1982 Jane Forman (singles)
1983 Jane Forman (singles)
      Gigi Fernandez (singles)
1984 Jane Forman (singles)
1985 Nicole Stafford (singles)
1986 Cathy Hofer (singles)
      Ingelise Driehuis (singles)
1987 Nicole Stafford (doubles)
      Ingelise Driehuis (doubles)
1994 Boba Tzvetkova (singles)
      Janice Durden (doubles)
      Shannon King (doubles)
1996 Sophie Woorons (singles/doubles)
      Jan Barrett (doubles)
2004 Julie Coin (singles)
2005 Julie Coin (singles/doubles)
      Alix Lacelarie (doubles)
2007 Ani Mijacika (doubles)
      Federica Van Adrichem (doubles)
2008 Ani Mijacika (singles/doubles)
2009 Josipa Bek (singles/doubles)

Ina Hadziselimovic (doubles)
Ani Mijacika (singles/doubles)
Keri Wong (doubles)
2010 Josipa Bek (singles/doubles)
      Ina Hadziselimovic (doubles)
2011 Josipa Bek (singles/doubles)
      Keri Wong (doubles)
2013 Yana Koroleva (singles)
2015 Joana Eidukonyte (singles)
      Beatrice Gumulya (doubles)
      Jessy Rompies (doubles)

NCAA CHAMPIONSHIPS

2011 Doubles Runners-up Josipa Bek, Keri Wong

ITA HALL OF FAME

2008 Gigi Fernandez

ACC PLAYER OF THE YEAR

1977 Susan Hill
1978 Susan Hill
1979 Susan Hill
1980 Susan Hill
1981 Jane Forman
1983 Jody Trucks
1984 Jane Forman
1986 Ingelise Driehuis
1987 Ingelise Driehuis
1988 Cathy Hofer
1996 Sophie Woorons
2004 Julie Coin
2009 Ani Mijacika

ACC FRESHMAN OF THE YEAR

2007 Ani Mijacika
2016 Ayan Broomfield

ACC TOURNAMENT MVP

1980 Susan Hill
1981 Jane Forman
1983 Jody Trucks
1984 Jane Forman
1986 Ingelise Driehus
1987 Ingelise Driehus
1988 Cathy Hofer
2004 Alix Lacelarie
2008 Carol Salge

ACC COACH OF THE YEAR

1983 Andy Johnston
1985 Andy Johnston
1986 Andy Johnston
1993 Andy Johnston
2014 Nancy Harris

FINAL TOP 25 ITA RANKINGS: SINGLES

1982
  16th Jane Forman
1983
  5th Gigi Fernandez
  22nd Jane Forman
1984
  10th Jane Forman
1986
  10th Cathy Hofer
  19th Ingelise Driehuis
1987
  10th Ingelise Driehuis
  22nd Cathy Hofer
1994
  17th Boba Tzvetkova
1996
  8th Sophie Woorons
2003
  18th Julie Coin
2004
  8th Julie Coin
2005
  2nd Julie Coin
2008
  2nd Ani Mijacika
2009
  4th Ani Mijacika
  13th Josipa Bek

2010
  20th Josipa Bek
2011
  13th Josipa Bek
2013
  13th Yana Koroleva
2015
  16th Joana Eidukonyte

FINAL ITA RANKINGS: DOUBLES

1986
  13th Lisa Bobby & Simone Schilder
  20th Ingelise Driehuis & Marianne Groat
1987
  15th Ingelise Driehuis & Nicole Stafford
1993
  18th Shannon King & Janice Durden
1994
  10th Shannon King & Janice Durden
1996
  8th Sophie Woorons & Jan Barrett
2004
  17th Maria Brito & Julie Coin
2005
  10th Julie Coin & Alix Lacelarie
2006
  21st Carol Salge & Federica Van Adrichem
2007
  4th Ani Mijacika & Federica Van Adrichem
2008
  5th Ani Mijacika & Carol Salge
2009
  11th Ani Mijacika & Keri Wong
  24th Ina Hadziselimovic & Josipa Bek
2010
  8th Josipa Bek & Ina Hadziselimovic
2011
  3rd Josipa Bek & Keri Wong
2012
  24th Josipa Bek & Keri Wong
2014
  15th Beatrice Gumulya & Yana Koroleva
2015
  4th Beatrice Gumulya & Jessy Rompies

MEN'S
Track and Field

COACHES

1905-1913 Fred Calhoun
1914-1915 No Team
1916 A.H. Ward
1917 Alex Lewis
1918 No Team
1919 Jiggs Donahue
1920 Lawrence Fox
1921-1923 E.J. Stewart
1924-1925 W.D. Reed
1926-1927 Bud Saunders
1927 Cul Richards
1928-1931 Jules Carson
1932-1939 Frank Howard
1940-1957 Rock Norman
1958-1959 Banks McFadden
1960-1974 H.C. (Pee Wee) Greenfield
1975-77 I.M. Ibrahim
1978-1983 Sam Colson
1984-1985 Stan Narewski
1985-1988 Wade Williams
1989-2008 Bob Pollock
2008-2012 Lawrence Johnson
2013-Present Mark Elliott

ALL-AMERICA LEADERS

Name	Years	Ind	Out	Total
Shawn Crawford	1997-2000	4	7	11
James Trapp	1990-92	4	6	10
Tevin Hester	2013-16	6	3	9
Tony Wheeler	1994-97	2	6	8
Jeremichael Williams	1996-98	2	5	7
Duane Ross	1992-95	3	4	7
Travis Padgett	2006-08	2	4	6
Ato Modibo	1999-2002	3	3	6
Carlton Chambers	1995-98	0	6	6
Michael Green	1990-93	2	4	6
Spencer Adams	2008-13	3	2	5
Jacoby Ford	2007-09	2	3	5
Todd Matthews	1999-2002	2	3	5
Charles Allen	1997-2000	2	3	5
Kenny Franklin	1996-99	2	3	5
Davidson Gill	1995-96, 1998-99	3	2	5
Larry Ryans	1990-92, 1994	3	2	5
George Kitchens	2002-05	2	2	4
Dwight Thomas	2002	1	3	4
Greg Hines	1995-98	1	3	4
Mitchel Francis	1994-95	2	2	4
Enayat Oliver	1992-95	2	2	4
Cormac Finnerty	1991-93	2	2	4
Terrance Herrington	1985, 1987-89	1	3	4

Note: first-team All-Americans only.

COACH BOB POLLOCK

- 2012 USTFCCCA Hall of Fame Inductee
- Coached the Clemson men's track & field program from 1988-2008
- Led the Tigers to 21 ACC Championships (11 indoor, nine outdoor and one cross country); total is still second-most in ACC men's track & field history
- 1992 National Coach of the Year after leading Clemson to runner-up indoor finish
- Mentored nearly 200 All-American players, including 13 National Champions
- Coached 18 Olympians
- Posthumously inducted into the Clemson Hall of Fame in 2010

MOST ACC CHAMPIONS IN A CAREER

(Indoor and Outdoor Combined)

Name	Total	Indiv	Years
James Trapp	12	6	1990-92
Shawn Crawford	11	9	1997-00
Jacey Harper	10	6	2000-03
Michael Green	9	6	1990-93
Tony Wheeler	9	4	1994-97
Jimmy Wynn	9	4	1962-64
Ato Modibo	8	4	1999-02

Hans Koeleman	7	7	1980-83
Andrew Beecher	7	2	1990-93
Adam Linkenauger	7	7	2003-07
Tevin Hester	7	7	2013-16
Dave Wittman	6	5	1988-91
Larry Ryans	6	3	1990-92, 94
Ed Fern	5	5	1973-76
Dwight Thomas	5	5	2002
Terrance Herrington	5	4	1985, 87-89
Desai Williams	5	4	1979-80
Philip Greyling	5	4	1989-91
Duane Ross	5	4	1992-95
Eric Lander	5	5	1993-96
Davidson Gill	5	1	1995-96, 99
Larry Griffin	5	1	2001-04
Travis Padgett	5	4	2006-08
Mike Columbus	4	4	1975-78
Martin Flynn	4	4	1984-87
Mike Spiritoso	4	4	1983-84, 86-87
Cormac Finnerty	4	4	1990-93
Sultan Tucker	4	3	1998-01
Spencer Adams	4	3	2009-13
Wesley Russell	4	2	1992-93
Shawn Thomas	4	2	1994-96
Otto Spain	4	2	2000-03
Tye Hill	4	2	2003-05
Charles Allen	4	0	1997-00

Note: Total includes individual championships plus relay crowns.

INDOOR ALL-AMERICANS

Year	Name	Event	Place	Mark
1980	Hans Koeleman	Mile	4th	4:04.04
1981	Hans Koeleman	2 Mile	4th	8:37.41
1982	Wybo Lelieveld	1000 yd	2nd	2:08.06
1983	Wybo Lelieveld	Mile	4th	4:02.58
1985	Victor Smalls	High Jump	T-6th	7-1
1986	Greg Moses	55 Dash	5th	6.25
1987	Mike Spiritoso	Shot Put	2nd	60-11.25
1988	Yehezkel Halifa	3000 Meters	6th	8:03.35
1989	Wittman, Greyling, Radziwinski, Herrington	4x800 Relay	1st	7:17.45
	Yehezkel Halifa	5000 Meters	4th	14:20.39
	Dov Kremer	5000 Meters	6th	14:23.35
	Greg Moses	55 Dash	4th	6.17
1990	James Trapp	55 Dash	6th	6.20
	Greyling, Hines, Wittman, Beecher	4x800 Relay	3rd	7:20.65
1991	James Trapp	55 Dash	5th	6.21
	Larry Ryans	55 Hurdles	11th	7.42
1992	Michael Green	55 Dash	1st	6.08
	James Trapp	55 Dash	4th	6.22
	James Trapp	200 Dash	1st	20.66

	Anthony Knight	55 Hurdles	3rd	7.21
	Larry Ryans	55 Hurdles	5th	7.26
	Wesley Russell	400 Dash	3rd	46.43
	Andrew Beecher	800 Meters	5th	1:49.40
	Cormac Finnerty	3000 Meters	3rd	8:00.96
1993	Michael Green	55 Dash	1st	6.15
	Wesley Russell	400 Dash	1st	45.92
	Cormac Finnerty	3000 Meters	3rd	8:04.88
	Duane Ross	55 Hurdles	4th	7.26
1994	Francis, Oliver, Richards, Roach	4x400 Relay	7th	3:08.98
	Kendrick Roach	800 Meters	9th	1:50.09
	Duane Ross	55 Hurdles	3rd	7.22
1995	Duane Ross	55 Hurdles	5th	7.25
	Tony Wheeler	200 Dash	3rd	20.90
	Clarence Richards	400 Dash	6th	46.92
	Gill, Richards, Francis, Oliver, Wheeler	4x400 Relay	5th	3:07.34
	John Thorp	High Jump	7th	7-1.75
1997	Jeremichael Willliams	55 Hurdles	2nd	7.24
1998	Shawn Crawford	200 Dash	1st	20.69
	Jeremichael Willliams	55 Hurdles	2nd	7.18
	Greg Hines	55 Hurdles	7th	7.34
	Allen, Gill, Haynes, Franklin	4x400 Relay	3rd	3:09.00
1999	Ato Modibo	400 Dash	1st	46.11
	Sultan Tucker	60 Hurdles	6th	7.86
	Shawn Crawford	200 Dash	4th	20.85
	Allen, Franklin, Gill, Modibo	4x400 Relay	1st	3:07.80
2000	Shawn Crawford	60 Dash	4th	6.67
	Shawn Crawford	200 Dash	1st	20.26
	Sultan Tucker	60 Hurdles	8th	7.97
2001	Sultan Tucker	60 Hurdles	3rd	7.69
	Todd Matthews	60 Hurdles	5th	7.77
2002	Doug Ameigh	High Jump	4th	7-2.5
	Todd Matthews	60 Hurdles	4th	7.79
	Ato Modibo	400 Dash	5th	46.44
	Dwight Thomas	60 Dash	6th	6.70
2003	Bolling, Cheney, Harper, Spain	4x400 Relay	7th	3:08.92
	Larry Griffin	60 Dash	7th	6.73
	Terrance McDaniel	High Jump	5th	6-11.75
2004	Roy Cheney	60 Hurdles	9th	7.77
	George Kitchens	Long Jump	7th	25-4
2005	George Kitchens	Long Jump	7th	25-3
2006	Mitch Greeley	Pole Vault	T-8th	17-6.5
	Brent Hobbs	Heptathlon	10th	5,361
2007	Travis Padgett	60 Dash	1st	6.56
	Jacoby Ford	60 Dash	3rd	6.60

	Name	Event	Place	Mark
	Jason Bell	Triple Jump	10th	49-9
	Ryan Koontz	Heptathlon	7th	5,569
2008	Travis Padgett	60 Dash	3rd	6.60
	C.J. Spiller	60 Dash	10th	6.67
	Mitch Greeley	Pole Vault	2nd	17-8.5
2009	Jacoby Ford	60 Dash	1st	6.52
2010	Spencer Adams	60 Hurdles	8th	7.90
	Miller Moss	Heptathlon	8th	5,638
2011	Miller Moss	Heptathlon	1st	5,986
	Justin Murdock (2nd)	60 Dash	14th	6.73
	Spencer Adams (2nd)	60 Hurdles	15th	7.89
2012	Spencer Adams	60 Hurdles	5th	7.60
2013	Spencer Adams	60 Hurdles	3rd	7.60
	Tevin Hester	60 Dash	7th	6.70
	Brunson Miller (2nd)	400 Dash	12th	46.51
	Marcus Maxey (2nd)	60 Hurdles	12th	7.78
	Torian Ware (2nd)	High Jump	14th	7-0.5
2014	Tevin Hester	60 Dash	7th	6.64
2015	Tevin Hester	60 Dash	7th	6.63
	Tevin Hester	200 Dash	6th	20.86
	Shai Carpenter (2nd)	Triple Jump	11th	51-6.5
2016	Tevin Hester	60 Dash	6th	6.64
	Tevin Hester	200 Dash	5th	21.02

OUTDOOR ALL-AMERICANS

Year	Name	Event	Place	Mark
1965	Avery Nelson	Triple Jump	5th	49-0.25
1968	Roger Collins	Javelin	4th	240-3
1969	Roger Collins	Javelin	6th	239-7
1970	Roger Collins	Javelin	4th	254-5
1976	Ed Fern (USTFF)	High Jump	5th	7-0
	Mike Columbus (USTFF)	Discus	5th	181-2
	Stewart Ralph (USTFF)	Javelin	3rd	241-6
1977	Mike Columbus	Discus	6th	189-6
	Stewart Ralph	Javelin	3rd	257-0
1978	Stewart Ralph	Javelin	2nd	263-4
1980	Terrence Toatley (USTFF)	100 Dash	2nd	10.35w
	Mike Hartle (USTFF)	Javelin	2nd	251-4
	Desai Williams	200 Dash	4th	20.45w
	Williams, Toatley, Sharpe, Davis	4x100 Relay	5th	40.01
1981	Julius Ogaro	Steeplechase	5th	8:32.75
	Hans Koeleman	Steeplechase	6th	8:33.20
	Mike Hartle	Javelin	5th	251-4
1982	Jack Harkness	Discus	2nd	203-4
	Mike Hartle	Javelin	7th	253-0
	Jim Haughey	5000 Meters	10th	14:17.59
1983	Jim Haughey	5000 Meters	9th	14:08.08
	Wybo Lelieveld	1500 Meters	4th	3:41.68
1985	Victor Smalls	High Jump	4th	7-5
1986	Mike Spiritoso	Shot Put	2nd	68-3.25
	Victor Smalls	High Jump	6th	7-1
1987	Mike Spiritoso	Shot Put	8th	58-9.25
	Terrance Herrington	1500 Meters	3rd	3:38.57
1988	Yehezkel Halifa	10,000 Meters	5th	28:58.76
	Terrance Herrington	800 Meters	4th	1:47.58
	Dov Kremer	5000 Meters	2nd	13:56.63
1989	Terrance Herrington	1500 Meters	3rd	3:45.05
	Philip Greyling	1500 Meters	8th	3:46.58
	Dov Kremer	5000 Meters	5th	14:14.28
1990	James Trapp	100 Dash	5th	10.23
	Philip Greyling	1500 Meters	6th	3:41.91
	Larry Ryans	110 Hurdles	9th	13.83
1991	Thomas, Green, Ryans, Trapp	4x100 Relay	2nd	39.24
	James Trapp	100 Dash	4th	10.05
	Michael Green	100 Dash	5th	10.13
1992	James Trapp	100 Dash	3rd	10.25
	James Trapp	200 Dash	4th	20.49
	Wheatley, Russell, Gilbert, Trapp	4x100 Relay	6th	39.25
	Cormac Finnerty	5000 Meters	4th	14:05.09
1993	Michael Green	100 Dash	1st	10.09
	Cormac Finnerty	5000 Meters	7th	14:08.60
	Anthony Knight	110 Hurdles	4th	13.89
	Duane Ross	110 Hurdles	7th	14.08
	Wheatley, Oliver, Gilbert, Green	4x100 Relay	5th	39.35
1994	Mitchel Francis	400 Hurdles	2nd	49.86
	Tony Wheeler	200 Dash	3rd	20.30
	Larry Ryans	110 Hurdles	6th	13.91
	Duane Ross	110 Hurdles	7th	14.11
1995	Duane Ross	110 Hurdles	1st	13.32
	Tony Wheeler	200 Dash	6th	20.64
	John Thorp	High Jump	5th	7-2.25
	Mitchel Francis	400 Hurdles	5th	49.99
	Ross, Wheeler, Chambers, Oliver	4x100 Relay	5th	39.28
1996	Tony Wheeler	200 Dash	3rd	20.60
	Carlton Chambers	200 Dash	6th	20.66
	Carlton Chambers	100 Dash	4th	10.19
	Jeremichael Williams	110 Hurdles	7th	13.71
	Hines, Thomas, Wheeler, Haynes	4x400 Relay	8th	3:09.49
1997	Wheeler, Williams, Chambers, Allen, Franklin	4x100 Relay	2nd	38.92
	Carlton Chambers	100 Dash	4th	10.40

	Jeremichael Williams	110 Hurdles	7th	13.81
1998	Chambers, Crawford, Williams, Franklin	4x100 Relay	5th	39.07
	Greg Hines	400 Hurdles	5th	50.46
	Aaron Haynes	400 Hurdles	13th	51.72
	Shawn Crawford	100 Dash	8th	10.56
	Shawn Crawford	200 Dash	3rd	20.74
	Jeremichael Williams	110 Hurdles	4th	13.76
	Greg Hines	110 Hurdles	7th	13.80
1999	Shawn Crawford	200 Dash	6th	20.75
	Davidson Gill	800 Meters	8th	1:49.95
	Kai Maull	Long Jump	8th	25-7.25
	Ato Modibo	400 Dash	5th	45.37
	Allen, Franklin, Moorman, Crawford	4x100 Relay	5th	39.63
	Allen, Moorman, Gill, Modibo	4x400 Relay	8th	3:05.05
2000	Shawn Crawford	100 Dash	6th	10.26
	Shawn Crawford	200 Dash	1st	20.09
	Todd Matthews	110 Hurdles	3rd	13.57
	Fred Sharpe	400 Hurdles	7th	51.06
2001	Andy Giesler	Decathlon	7th	7,498
	Todd Matthews	110 Hurdles	9th	13.83
	Ato Modibo	400 Dash	8th	46.82
2002	Todd Matthews	110 Hurdles	2nd	13.53
	Dwight Thomas	100 Dash	2nd	10.29
	Dwight Thomas	200 Dash	2nd	20.60
	Currie, Harper, Spain, Thomas	4x100 Relay	2nd	38.82
2003	Itay Magidi	Steeplechase	8th	8:36.92
	George Kitchens	Long Jump	10th	24-9.75
2004	George Kitchens	Long Jump	8th	25-4.5
2005	Ronald Richards	100 Dash	5th	10.38
	Scott Kautz	400 Hurdles	9th	50.24
	Itay Magidi	Steeplechase	7th	8:34.12
2006	Travis Padgett	100 Dash	4th	10.24
	Jason Bell	Triple Jump	6th	51-11.75
	Ryan Koontz	Decathlon	7th	7,284

2007	Travis Padgett	100 Dash	3rd	10.09
	Padgett, Brown, Mills, Spiller	4x100 Relay	7th	40.07
	Mitch Greeley	Pole Vault	4th	17-6.5
2008	Travis Padgett	100 Dash	2nd	10.16
	Jacoby Ford	100 Dash	5th	10.33
	Matt Clark	10,000 Meters	16th	29:50.51
2009	Jacoby Ford	100 Dash	9th	14.34
	Murdock, Spiller, Guy, Ford	4x100 Relay	3rd	38.77
2011	Miller Moss	Decathlon	3rd	7,996
	Justin Murdock (2nd)	100 Dash	12th	10.38
	Spencer Adams (2nd)	110 Hurdles	10th	13.62
	Fraser, Murdock, (2nd) Jackson, Adams	4x100 Relay	12th	39.50
2012	Spencer Adams	110 Hurdles	3rd	13.73
	Warren Fraser (2nd)	100 Dash	13th	10.18
2013	Spencer Adams	110 Hurdles	3rd	13.34
	Reggie Lewis	100 Dash	8th	10.24
	Tevin Hester (2nd)	100 Dash	14th	10.24
	Lewis, Fraser, (2nd) Miller, Hester	4x100 Relay	10th	39.46
	Marcus Maxey (2nd)	110 Hurdles	10th	13.75
	Jameel Abdul-Mateen (2nd)	Long Jump	11th	25-6
2014	Reggie Lewis (2nd)	100 Dash	14th	10.23
	Torian Ware (2nd)	High Jump	11th	7-0.5
2015	Tevin Hester	100 Dash	6th	10.03(w)
	Tevin Hester	200 Dash	6th	20.29(w)
	Justin Johnson	110 Hurdles	7th	13.56(w)
	Torian Ware (2nd)	High Jump	10th	7-1
2016	Tevin Hester	200 Dash	6th	20.68
	Tevin Hester (2nd)	100 Dash	10th	10.22
	Lamb, Cheeks, Bellafonte, Green	4x400 Relay	5th	3:04.75

NATIONAL CHAMPIONS

Charles Allen
    1999 Indoor 4x400 Relay 3:07.80
Shawn Crawford
    1998 Indoor 200 Dash 20.69
    2000 Indoor 200 Dash 20.26
    Outdoor 200 Dash 20.09
Jacoby Ford
    2009 Indoor 60 Dash 6.52
Kenny Franklin
    1999 Indoor 4x400 Relay 3:07.80
Davidson Gill
    1999 Indoor 4x400 Relay 3:07.80
Philip Greyling
    1989 Indoor 4x800 Relay 7:17.45
Michael Green
    1992 Indoor 55 Dash 6:08
    1993 Indoor 55 Dash 6.15
    Outdoor 100 Dash 10.08

Terrance Herrington
    1989 Indoor 4x800 Relay 7:17.45
Miller Moss
    2011 Indoor Heptathlon 5,986 pts.
Ato Modibo
    1999 Indoor 400 Dash 46.11
    Indoor 4x400 Relay 3:07.80
Travis Padgett
    2007 Indoor 60 Dash 6.56
Mike Radziwinski
    1989 Indoor 4x800 Relay 7:17.45
Duane Ross
    1995 Outdoor 110 Hurdles 13.32
Wesley Russell
    1993 Indoor 400 Dash 45.92
James Trapp
    1992 Indoor 200 Dash 20.66
Dave Wittman
    1989 Indoor 4x800 Relay 7:17.45

NATIONAL CHAMPIONS

Michelle Burgher
    2001 Outdoor 4x400 Relay 3:29.97

LaShonda Cutchin
    2001 Outdoor 4x400 Relay (alternate) 3:29.97

Natoya Goule
    2015 Indoor 800 Meters 2:01.64

Tina Krebs
    1983 Indoor 1000 Yard Run 2:28.58
    1985 Indoor 1500 Meters 4:17.45
    1986 Indoor Mile 4:40.82

Patricia Mamona
    2010 Outdoor Triple Jump 45'11.75"/14.01m
    2011 Outdoor Triple Jump 46'1.25"/14.05m

Cydonie Mothersill
    2001 Indoor 200 Dash 22.89
    Outdoor 4x400 Relay 3:29.97

Jamine Moton
    2002 Hammer Throw 220'6"/67.20m

Gisele Oliveira
    2005 Indoor Triple Jump 45'1.75"/13.76m

Brianna Rollins
    2011 Indoor 60 Hurdles 7.96
    2013 Indoor 60 Hurdles 7.79
    Outdoor 100 Hurdles 12.39

Marcia Smith
    2001 Outdoor 4x400 Relay 3:29.97

Shekera Weston
    2001 Outdoor 4x400 Relay 3:29.97

ALL-AMERICA LEADERS

Name	Years	Ind	Out	Total
Shekera Weston	1997-99, 2001	3	7	10
Brianna Rollins	2009-13	5	3	8
April Sinkler	2008-12	3	4	7
Dezerea Bryant	2011-13	4	3	7
Gisele Oliveira	2002-05	1	5	6
Jamine Moton	1998-99, 2001-02	4	2	6
Tina Krebs	1983, 1985-87	3	3	6
Nikkie Bouyer	1996, 1998-99	3	2	5
Kim Graham	1991-93	1	4	5
Marlena Wesh	2010-14	2	2	4
Jasmine Edgerson	2009-13	1	3	4
Stormy Kendrick	2009-13	1	3	4
Cydonie Mothersill	2001	2	2	4
Lisa Dillard	1989-91	1	3	4
Natoya Goule	2015	2	1	3
Michaylin Golladay	2007-11	0	3	3
Patricia Mamona	2007-11	1	2	3
Liane Weber	2007-11	2	1	3
Michelle Burgher	2001	1	2	3
Mareike Ressing	1991-93, 1995	1	2	3
Tonya McKelvey	1991-93	2	1	3

Note: first-team All-Americans only.

ACC CHAMPION LEADERS

(Indoor and Outdoor Combined)

Name	Total	Ind	Years
Kim Graham	15	10	1991-93
Jamine Moton	13	13	1998-99, 2001-02
Marlena Wesh	10	5	2010-14
Dezerea Bryant	9	7	2011-13
April Sinkler	8	8	2008-12
Lisa Dillard	8	6	1989-91
Brianna Rollins	8	5	2009-13
Stormy Kendrick	8	3	2009-13
Gisele Oliveira	7	7	2002-05
Shekera Weston	7	3	1997-99, 2001
Keni Harrison	7	2	2011-13
Jeannie Burris	6	6	1987-90
Cydonie Mothersill	6	3	2001
Liane Weber	5	5	2007-11
Jasmine Edgerson	5	1	2009-13
Angel Fleetwood	5	1	1989-92
Karen Hartmann	4	4	1992-95
Tina Krebs	4	4	1983,1985-87
Lisa Parak	4	4	1989-91
Nikki Sims	4	4	1994-97
Simone Tomlinson	4	4	1995-98

Name			
Michelle Burgher	4	1	2001
Silja Ulfarsdottir	4	1	2002-05
Nia Fluker	5	0	2011-15

INDOOR TRACK AND FIELD ALL-AMERICANS

Year	Name	Event	PL	Mark
1981	Cindy Duarte	3000 (AIAW)	4th	N/A
1983	Tina Krebs	1000 yd	1st	2:28.58
1985	Tina Krebs	1500 Meters	1st	4:17.45
	Kirsti Voldness	1500 Meters	3rd	4:21.85
1986	Tina Krebs	Mile	1st	4:40.82
1990	Lisa Dillard	55 Dash	5th	6.86
1991	Marcia Fletcher	Long Jump	9th	19-8.25
	Ane Skak	800 Meters	6th	2:08.84
1992	Karen Hartmann	800 Meters	3rd	2:04.55
	Nanette Holloway	Triple Jump	5th	42-3.5
1993	Kim Graham	200 Dash	8th	24.43
	Monyetta Haynesworth	Long Jump	5th	20-3
	Tonya McKelvey	Long Jump	6th	19-10.25
1994	Mareike Ressing	3000 Meters	3rd	9:26.10
	Tonya McKelvey	Long Jump	14th	19-.25
1996	Treshell Mayo	200 Dash	5th	23.50
1998	Nikkie Bouyer	55 Hurdles	6th	7.62
	Cutchin, Watt, Bouyer, Weston	4x400 Relay	6th	3:37.34
1999	Nikkie Bouyer	60 Hurdles	9th	8.30
	Shekera Weston	400 Dash	9th	54.23
2001	Cydonie Mothersill	200 Dash	1st	22.89
	Jamine Moton	Shot Put	2nd	53-8.5
	Jamine Moton	Weight Throw	3rd	66-11.5
	Burgher, Mothersill, Smith, Weston	4x400 Relay	3rd	3:34.83
2002	Jamine Moton	Shot Put	8th	53-8.26
	Jamine Moton	Weight Throw	2nd	73-10
	Sheri Smith	Triple Jump	7th	42-5.5
2004	Ulfarsdottir, Rutherford, Smith, Hinton	4x400 Relay	8th	3:34.94
2005	Gisele Oliveira	Triple Jump	1st	45-1.75
2007	Della Clark	Weight Throw	3rd	68-5
2009	Liane Weber	Pentathlon	6th	4,235
2010	Kim Ruck	5000 Meters	7th	16:01.24
	Brianna Rollins	60 Hurdles	9th	8.22
	Pringley, Rollins, Austin, Edgerson	4x400 Relay	5th	3:33.93
	April Sinkler	Long Jump	11th	20-7.25
	Patricia Mamona	Triple Jump	2nd	45-5.25
	April Sinkler	Triple Jump	7th	43-7.25
	Liane Weber	Pentathlon	5th	4,113
2011	Brianna Rollins	60 Hurdles	1st	7.96
	Marlena Wesh	400 Dash	8th	1:07.89
	April Sinkler	Triple Jump	2nd	44-2
	Jasmine Edgerson (2nd)	60 Hurdles	16th	8.65
	Stormy Kendrick (2nd)	60 Dash	13th	7.30
	Stormy Kendrick (2nd)	200 Dash	11th	23.43
	April Sinkler (2nd)	Long Jump	10th	20-1.75
	Brittney Waller (2nd)	Weight Throw	12th	62-10.75
2012	Brianna Rollins	60 Hurdles	2nd	7.93
	Bridgette Owens	60 Hurdles	3rd	8.03
	Marlena Wesh	400 Dash	5th	53.17
	Dezerea Bryant	60 Dash	6th	7.28
	Dezerea Bryant	200 Dash	7th	23.36
	Jasmine Brunson	Triple Jump	8th	41-1.75
	Jasmine Edgerson (2nd)	60 Dash	12th	7.41
	Stormy Kendrick (2nd)	60 Dash	13th	7.42
	Keni Harrison (2nd)	60 Hurdles	14th	8.26
2013	Brianna Rollins	60 Hurdles	1st	7.79
	Dezerea Bryant	60 Dash	4th	7.24
	Dezerea Bryant	200 Dash	5th	23.00
	Stormy Kendrick	60 Dash	6th	7.40
	Brittney Waller	Weight Throw	3rd	70-10
	Marlena Wesh (2nd)	400 Dash	11th	52.96
	Keni Harrison (2nd)	60 Hurdles	13th	8.29
	Jasmine Brunson (2nd)	Triple Jump	15th	40-6.25
2014	Mimi Land	High Jump	T-5th	6-0.5
	Mimi Land (2nd)	Triple Jump	13th	41-4.5
2015	Natoya Goule	800 Meters	1st	2:01.64
	James, Fluker, Parrish, Goule	4x400 Relay	4th	3:30.88
	Samantha Elliott (2nd)	60 Hurdles	11th	8.22
	Iana Amsterdam (2nd)	Triple Jump	16th	38-11
2016	Ciluffo, Parrish, Farrow, Barnett	DMR	8th	11:12.68
	Myasia Jacobs (2nd)	60 Dash	9th	7.27
	Grace Barnett (2nd)	Mile	10th	4:48.55
	Anasterasia Terrell (2nd)	Triple Jump	16th	41-3

OUTDOOR TRACK AND FIELD ALL-AMERICANS

Year	Name	Event	PL	Mark
1981	Cindy Duarte	3000 (AIAW)	N/A	N/A
1982	Stephanie Weikert	3000 Meters	5th	9:33.93
1983	Tina Krebs	800 Meters	2nd	2:03.01
	Judith Shephard	3000 Meters	5th	9:14.5
1985	Tina Krebs	1500 Meters	4th	4:15.74
1986	Tina Krebs	1500 Meters	3rd	4:19.18
	Ute Jamrozy	10,000	4th	33:14.83
1990	Lisa Dillard	100 Dash	4th	11.48
	Lisa Dillard	200 Dash	7th	23.74
	Angela Dolby	Shot Put	11th	48-1.75
1991	Dillard, Fleetwood, Graham, Henderson	4x100 Relay	5th	44.39
	Kim Graham	200 Dash	4th	23.13
	Mareike Ressing	3000 Meters	4th	9:10.32
	Ane Skak	800 Meters	6th	2:06.98
1992	Kim Graham	200 Dash	2nd	23.24
	Karen Hartmann	1500 Meters	6th	4:22.72
	Angel Fleetwood	400 Dash	9th	52.78
	Angela Dolby	Shot Put	8th	50-1.75
	Nanette Holloway	Triple Jump	6th	42-8
1993	Kim Graham	200 Dash	4th	23.07
	Mareike Ressing	3000 Meters	6th	9:27.35
	Tonya McKelvey	Long Jump	11th	19-10.75
1996	Treshell Mayo	200 Dash	6th	23.12
1997	Nikki Sims	Shot Put	11th	50-10
	Wilson, Norsworthy, Watt, Weston	4x400 Relay	4th	3:32.18
1999	Nikkie Bouyer	400 Hurdles	6th	57.74
	Shekera Weston	200 Dash	7th	23.23
	Brown, Weston, Cutchin, Bouyer	4x100 Relay	7th	44.03
2001	Burgher, Mothersill, Smith, Weston, Cutchin*	4x400 Relay	1st	3:29.97
	Shekera Weston	200 Dash	4th	23.19
	Shekera Weston	400 Dash	10th	52.92
	Jamine Moton	Shot Put	2nd	56-4.75
	Murray, Burgher, Weston, Mothersill	4x100 Relay	4th	44.19
2002	Jamine Moton	Hammer	1st	220-6
	Gisele Oliveira	Triple Jump	7th	43-0.5
	Sheri Smith	Triple Jump	9th	42-7
2003	Gisele Oliveira	Triple Jump	3rd	44-6
	Gisele Oliveira	Long Jump	8th	20-5.75
2004	Gisele Oliveira	Triple Jump	3rd	44-10.75
2005	Gisele Oliveira	Triple Jump	2nd	45-0.5
2010	Patricia Mamona	Triple Jump	1st	45-11.75
	Golladay, Kendrick Scott, Edgerson	4x100 Relay	4th	44.12
	April Sinkler	Long Jump	10th	20-4.25
	April Sinkler	Triple Jump	15th	41-9.75
2011	Patricia Mamona	Triple Jump	1st	46-1.25
	Michaylin Golladay	100 Hurdles	7th	13.07
	Alyssa Kulik	Steeplechase	4th	9:57.51
	Golladay, Gracia, Morris, Edgerson	4x100 Relay	7th	44.51
	April Sinkler	Long Jump	8th	21-2.75
	Liane Weber	Heptathlon	2nd	5,857
	Bridgette Owens (2nd)	100 Hurdles	12th	13.21
	April Sinkler (2nd)	High Jump	15th	5-9.25
	April Sinkler (2nd)	Triple Jump	14th	41-6.5
	Jasmine Brunson (2nd)	Long Jump	15th	20-3.75
2012	Marlena Wesh	400 Dash	6th	52.13
	Alyssa Kulik	Steeplechase	7th	10:07.54
	Brianna Rollins	100 Hurdles	2nd	12.91
	Bridgette Owens	100 Hurdles	3rd	13.10
	Kendrick, Wesh, Bryant, Edgerson	4x100 Relay	3rd	43.52
	April Sinkler	Triple Jump	6th	44-4
	Dezerea Bryant (2nd)	200 Dash	12th	23.08
	Monique Gracia (2nd)	100 Hurdles	9th	13.07
	Keni Harrison (2nd)	100 Hurdles	11th	13.12
	Keni Harrison (2nd)	400 Hurdles	13th	58.03
2013	Brianna Rollins	100 Hurdles	1st	13.39
	Dezerea Bryant	200 Dash	5th	22.54
	Keni Harrison	100 Hurdles	5th	12.87
	Keni Harrison	400 Hurdles	4th	55.75
	Harrison, Rollins, Kendrick, Bryant	4x100 Relay	3rd	43.76
	Dezerea Bryant (2nd)	100 Dash	9th	11.27
2014	Whitney Fountain (2nd)	Long Jump	12th	20-3
2015	Natoya Goule	800 Meters	6th	2:05.19
	Fountain, Parrish, Hadley, Jacobs (2nd)	4x100 Relay	11th	44.45
	Samantha Elliott (2nd)	100 Hurdles	14th	13.16(w)
	Iana Amsterdam (2nd)	Triple Jump	9th	43-1(w)
2016	Mimi Land (2nd)	Long Jump	14th	20-2.25

Note: * denotes alternate for the event.

COACHES

1978-85 Sam Colson
1986-97 Wayne Coffman
1998-99 Ron Garner
2000 Ralph White
2001-08 Marcia Noad
2009-12 Lawrence Johnson
2013-Present Mark Elliott

WOMEN'S
Volleyball

ACC PLAYER OF THE YEAR

1999 Cindy Stern
2008 Danielle Hepburn

ACC DEFENSIVE PLAYER OF THE YEAR

2009 Didem Ege

CLEMSON VOLLEYBALL ALL-AMERICA PLAYERS

1999 Cindy Stern (2nd)
2004 Leslie Finn (HM)
2006 Jeannette Abbott (HM)
2006 Danielle Hepburn (HM)
2007 Didem Ege (HM)
2007 Danielle Hepburn (HM)
2007 Kelsey Murphy (HM)
2007 Meghan Steiner (HM)
2008 Danielle Hepburn (3rd)
2008 Kelsey Murphy (HM)

2008 Lia Proctor (HM)
2009 Sandra Adeleye (HM)
2009 Didem Ege (HM)
2009 Kelsey Murphy (HM)
2009 Lia Proctor (HM)
2010 Sandra Adeleye (HM)
2011 Sandra Adeleye (HM)

CLEMSON VOLLEYBALL COACHES

1977 Grace Lyles
1978-1979 Dennis McNelis
1980-1981 Linda Copeland
1982-1983 Margie Wessel
1984-1985 Wayne Norris
1986-1991 Linda White
1992 Ernie Arill
1993-2014 Jolene Hoover
2015-2016 Hugh Hernesman
2017-Present Michaela Franklin

CLEMSON
Wrestling

ALL-AMERICA WRESTLERS

1980 Noel Loban, 190
1986 Joey McKenna, 150
1989 Donnie Heckel, 118
1991 Donnie Heckel, 118
1991 Kurt Howell, 126
1993 Sam Henson, 118
1994 Sam Henson, 118
1994 Tim Morrisey, 190

ACC TOURNAMENT MVP

1982 Todd Sterr
1986 Joey McKenna
1991 Donnie Heckel

ACC WRESTLER OF THE YEAR

1994 Sam Henson

ACC CHAMPIONS

1978, Larry Cohen, 118
    Rick Drury 177
1979, Noel Loban, 177
    Alan Tanner HWT
1980, Noel Loban, 190
    Bob Isola HWT

1982, Todd Sterr, 118
1983, Joey McKenna, 150
    Gary Nivens, 177
1984, Jody Taylor, 134
1985, Mark Litts, 158
    Joey McKenna, 142
1986, Joey McKenna, 150
1987, Brian Stalnaker, 190
1988, Donnie Heckel, 118
    Jim Meetze, 167
1990, Kurt Howell, 126
    Bill Domasky, 142
1991, Donnie Heckel, 118
1992, Mike Miller, 158
    Scott Williams, 190
1993, Sam Henson, 118
    Troy Bouzakis, 126
    Tim Morrissey, 177
1994, Sam Henson, 118
    Mike Mammon, 150
    Tim Morrissey, 190

WRESTLING COACHES

Hewett Adams 1976-77
Wade Schalles 1978-83
Eddie Griffin 1984-92
Gil Sanchez 1993-95

CLEMSON
Olympic Champions

Name	Sports	Country	Event/Position	Medal	Yrs. at Clemson
1984					
Noel Loban	Wrestling	Great Britain	190 Pounds	Bronze	1978-1980
Michele Richardson	Swimming	United States	800 Free	Silver	1988-1991
Desai Williams	Track	Canada	Relay	Bronze	1979-1980
Tony Sharpe	Track	Canada	Relay	Bronze	
1988					
*Mike Milchin	Baseball	United States	Pitcher	Gold	1987-1989
*Mitzi Kremer	Swimming	United States	400 Free Relay	Bronze	1987-1989
1992					
Mark McKoy	Track	Canada	110 Hurdles	Gold	1980
Gigi Fernandez	Tennis	United States	Doubles	Gold	1983
1996					
Kim Graham	Track	United States	4x100 Relay	Gold	1991-1993
*Carlton Chambers	Track	Canada	4x100 Relay	Gold	1995-1998
Gigi Fernandez	Tennis	United States	Doubles	Gold	1983
*Kris Benson	Baseball	United States	Pitcher	Bronze	1994-1996
*Billy Koch	Baseball	United States	Pitcher	Bronze	1994-1996
*Matt LeCroy	Baseball	United States	Catcher/DH	Bronze	1995-1997
2000					
Sam Henson	Wrestling	United States	54 kg	Silver	1992-1994
2004					
Shawn Crawford	Track	United States	200 Meters	Gold	1997-2000
Shawn Crawford	Track	United States	4x100 Relay	Silver	
Michelle Burgher	Track	Jamaica	4x400 Relay	Bronze	2001
2008					
Shawn Crawford	Track	United States	200 Meters	Silver	1997-2000
Dwight Thomas	Track	Jamaica	4x100 Relay	Gold	2002
2016					
Brianna Rollins	Track	United States	100 Hurdles	Gold	2009-2013

*indicates athlete won the medal in a year they were a Clemson student
**John Wofford was the first Clemson participant in the Olympics.   Wofford was on the United States Show Jumping team.
Since no country finished the difficult course no medals were awarded that year. Wofford attended Clemson in 1914-18.